REVIVAL'S CHILDREN

A Religious History of Virginia's Eastern Shore

VIRGINIA'S EASTERN SHORE TODAY

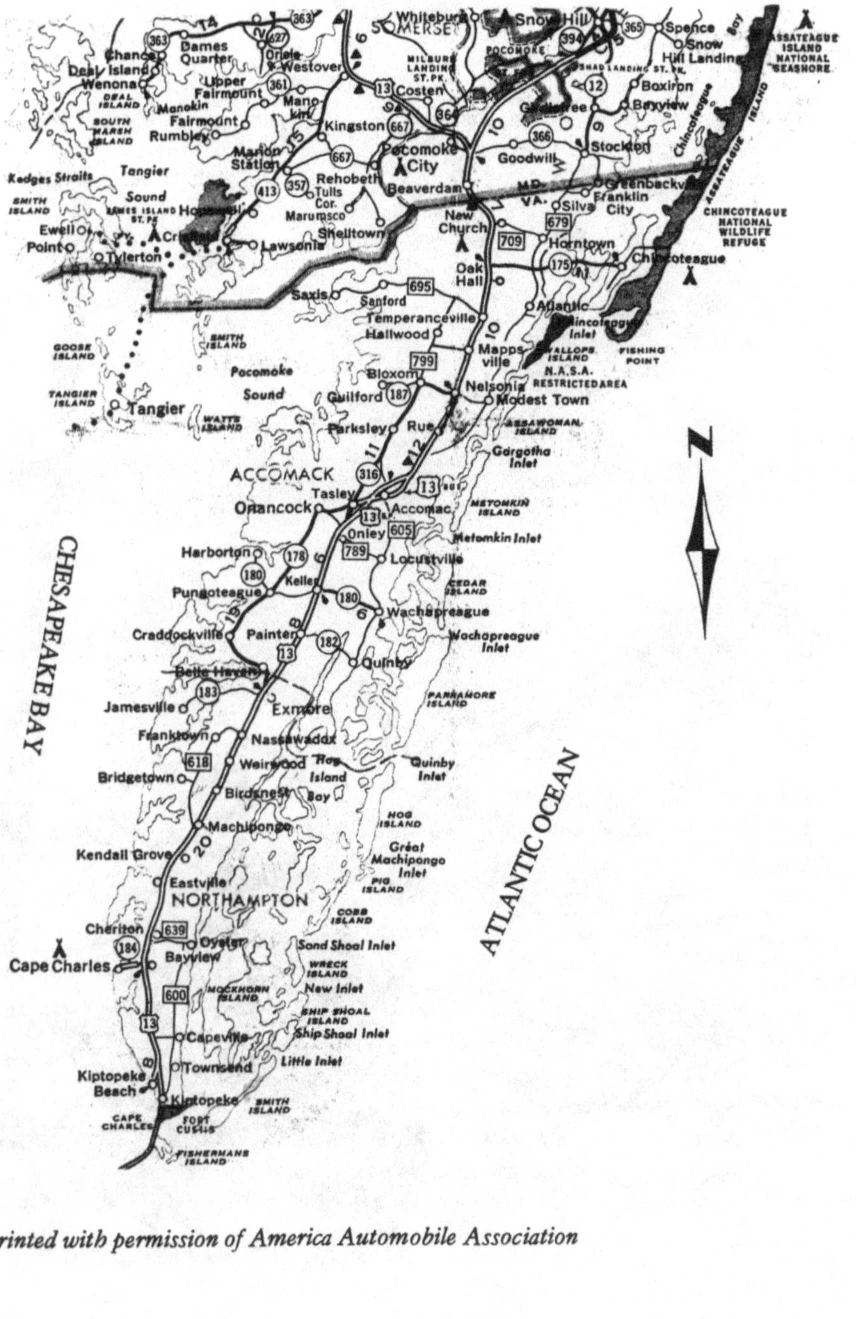

Map printed with permission of America Automobile Association

REVIVAL'S CHILDREN

A Religious History of Virginia's Eastern Shore

by Kirk Mariner

Designed and Illustrated by
Ronald Harman

A Limited Edition

PENINSULA PRESS
Salisbury, Maryland
1979

For information write:
Miona Publications
P.O. Box 517
Onancock, Virginia 23417

Second edition is a joint publication of Miona Publications and Secant Publishing, LLC, P.O. Box 4059, Salisbury, Maryland 21803
ISBN: 978-1-7359957-0-0 (paperback)

Foreword

Kirk Mariner's *Revival's Children: A Religious History of Virginia's Eastern Shore* is essential to an understanding of the Eastern Shore's past. In *Revival's Children*, Mariner traced the religious experience of the people of Accomack and Northampton counties from English colonization around 1615 to the time of the book's publication in 1979. Mariner was the first historian to emphasize the importance of the Methodist revivals of the late eighteenth century to the cultural development on the peninsula.He was also among the first to give the black experience on the Eastern Shore the attention that it deserves. In addition to a comprehensive narrative, Mariner also included an alphabetized list of brief histories of every church or synagogue, denominational or independent, whose existence on the peninsula he was able to verify. These histories have proved invaluable to those engaged in the study of individual churches. *Revival's Children* is well researched, clearly referenced, and written with Mariner's characteristic charm.

Kirk Chapman Mariner was a native of New Church in upper Accomack County. He attended Atlantic High School and Randolph-Macon College, where he was inducted into Phi Beta Kappa. He received advanced training at Yale Divinity School and at Wesley Theological Seminary. Called to the ministry, he served for thirty-seven years as pastor of five successive United Methodist churches in Virginia. After a career marked by ever-increasing responsibility, he retired in 2005 to Onancock on the Eastern Shore, where he resided until his death in 2017.

Throughout his adult life, Mariner devoted much of his time to the study of the history of his native peninsula. He published eleven books (of which *Revival's Children* was the second) and dozens of articles for local newspapers. To promote the distribution and sale of his books, he founded his own press, Miona Publications. His beloved friend Gail Harding, a newspaper publisher, oversaw design and production while Mariner, always sociable and ingratiating, distributed stock to bookstores and gift shops up and down the peninsula.

Mariner had a broad range of interests, which he pursued with disciplined zest. From childhood, he collected postage stamps, which he arranged meticulously. He sang and played piano, even recording on compact disk an album entitled *Church Basement Songs: The Rev. Mariner Performs Songs Not Quite Reverent Enough for Upstairs*. He decorated his home with maps, photographs, paintings, and modern furniture. He frequented yard sales and antique shops searching for Eastern Shore memorabilia of every type and description. He scanned dealer catalogs for old books, prints, newspapers, and manuscripts pertaining to the peninsula. He displayed some of his finds in his private museum and art gallery in New Church. He loved his daily routine—coffee, newspaper, and conversation at the Book Bin in

Onley in the morning; yardwork, artifact hunting, and book deliveries in the afternoon; arranging his collections and researching and writing history in the evening. Every Sunday he worshiped at the Market Street United Methodist Church in Onancock. He enjoyed sharing his knowledge of the Eastern Shore with family, friends, and strangers. His generosity extends to posterity. To the Eastern Shore of Virginia Heritage Center of the Eastern Shore Public Library, he bequeathed his large collection of materials relating to local history and culture. To the Eastern Shore Public Library Foundation, he left his home, to help fund an archival position in the Heritage Center.

Kirk Mariner's passions were the church and Eastern Shore of Virginia history. Those passions met most happily in *Revival's Children*. On several occasions, Mariner considered but rejected reprinting the book. He maintained that he must bring it up to date and that he did not want to take time away from new projects to revise the old. His meticulousness blinded him to *Revival's Children*'s status as a local classic without need of addendum. This reissue will introduce to new readers a book long out of print, while serving as a memorial to a dedicated historian and talented writer.

Brooks Miles Barnes
Onancock, Virginia
Ides of March 2021

to my parents

Preface

There are not a great many areas in this country that are predominantly Methodist, but the Eastern Shore of Virginia is one of them.

That is why I have dared to call this book a "religious history." From start to finish it is primarily a Methodist work. It began as a paper written for a course in Methodist history, and only later grew to include the other denominations. It treats in detail only the Methodists, not the other denominations, and systematically examines only the progress of the Methodists across the years. As might be expected, its author is a Methodist. And yet, because its subject is the Eastern Shore of Virginia, this book is more than simply a "Methodist history." For on this one little corner of the globe to tell the story of the Methodists is almost, if not quite, to tell the whole story of the Christian people.

I begin, then, not with an apology for, but with a confession of my Methodist focus. I have been aware from the first that one cannot tell the story of the Methodists without also speaking of the non-Methodist denominations, and I think this book will prove, as a result, to be an adequate general "religious history" that not only includes all the Christian denominations, but also does them justice.

This book divides naturally into two parts. The first half is a narrative history of the progress and development of Methodism on the Eastern Shore of Virginia, set against the background of the other faiths that also found a home there, or tried to. The second half is a catalogue of churches, a brief historical sketch of every known religious congregation, Methodist or otherwise, that has functioned on the Shore since it was settled by English-speaking people. Baptists, Pentecostals, Episcopalians, Presbyterians, Roman Catholics and many others are likely to find more of their own history here in this "Methodist" work, particularly in the second half, than in some other works devoted exclusively to their own denominations.

A number of people have left their imprint on this work, and to them all I express my thanks and appreciation:

To Maury Enright and L. Floyd Nock III, historians of the Eastern Shore in their own right, who were a constant source of information and encouragement.

To the staffs at the Clerk's Offices in Accomac and Eastville and at the Eastern Shore of Virginia Historical Society in Onancock, and especially to W. Robert Keeney and B. Miles Barnes and their excellent staff at the Eastern Shore Public Library in Accomac, who were outstanding in their helpfulness.

To the several persons who read the manuscript at various stages and made useful comments and suggestions: B. Miles Barnes, Shirley Nelms, James D. Righter, Nora Miller Turman.

To Patti B. Russell, proofreader and friend indeed.

To the several friends who lent their photographic skills: Carl H. Bundick, Ray Underwood, Scott Walker, Jr., Stephen Woodzell.

To Ron Harman, whose stamp is on every page, not only because he designed the book but also because he pointed the way in showing that it *could* be done.

Last but hardly least: To the people of Centreville United Methodist Church, who put up with a pastor who too often went to church functions with visions of Eastern Shore history dancing in his head.

All of these, and many others, have taught me a great deal. My hope is that others, on the Shore and off, Methodist and otherwise, will also find something to learn in what I have written.

Kirk Mariner
Centreville, Virginia
November 1, 1978

Contents

BOOK I

	The Surprising Work of God: An Introduction	xxi
I.	The Setting (1623-1776)	1
II.	Riders from the North (1772-1799)	18
III.	The Great Revival (1800-1814)	34
IV.	The Early Fathers (1813-1828)	53
V.	The Second Generation (1816-1844)	71
VI.	The Time of Troubles (1844-1860)	95
VII.	Brothers at War (1860-1866)	115
VIII.	The Great Division (1865-1884)	135
IX.	New Horizons (1884-1925)	154
X.	A Not-So-Plain and Simple People (1892-1945)	185
XI.	Full Circle (1925-1977)	210
	Going Forward: An Autobiographical Postscript	230

BOOK II

A Catalogue of The Churches of Virginia's Eastern Shore 241

BOOK ONE

Introduction

The Surprising Work of God

John Wesley carried a book with him as he set out from Epworth that October morning. For Wesley, time spent in travel was never time wasted, and whenever possible he read while on the road. In coaches, on horseback, even afoot when the weather was clear he had mastered the art of reading *en route.* And that Monday morning in 1738 was no exception.

The book he had with him was a new one, a small pamphlet lately published in the American colonies by one Jonathan Edwards, a Congregational minister in a place called Northampton in Massachusetts. Though a small book, it carried a long title: *A Faithful Narrative of the Surprising Work of God in the Conversion of Many Hundred Souls in Northampton.* And the little book soon had Wesley thoroughly absorbed.

The people of the church in Northampton, Wesley read, were not cold and lifeless Christians, though neither were they given to any excess in the display of noise or emotion in their religion. The people of his parish were, wrote Edwards, "in general, I suppose, as sober, orderly, and good sort of people as in any part of New England."

But "then it was," continued the *Narrative,* "in the latter part of December [1734], that the Spirit of God began extraordinarily to set in, and wonderfully to work amongst us; and there were very suddenly, one after another, five or six persons who were to all appearances savingly converted, and some of them wrought upon in a very remarkable manner." The sermons of the scholarly Edwards turned out somehow to be" a word spoken in season" that touched the hearts of his people as never before. As concern over their sinful condition swept across the congregation, the Northampton church began to be filled with remarkable sights and sounds. Worshipers began to mourn and cry and wail aloud during the services, only to experience a tremendous wave of relief as they received the overwhelming conviction of the saving grace of Jesus. Conversion followed conversion until soon the entire congregation, and with it almost the entire community, was transformed. "God made a glorious alteration in the town," Edwards reported. "It was never so full of love, nor so full of joy, and yet so full of distress as it was then. There were remarkable tokens of God's presence in almost every house. It was a time of joy in families on account of salvation being brought into them; parents rejoicing over their children as new born, and husbands over their wives and wives over their husbands." [1]

Three thousand miles away and four years later John Wesley was thrilled. "Surely this is the Lord's doing," the young clergyman exclaimed in his journal that day, "and it is marvellous in our eyes!" [2]

It is not surprising that Wesley was excited by Jonathan Edwards' account of a religious revival in New England, for Wesley himself was one of the foremost figures in a similar revival that was stirring in Europe. In the 1730's a great religious excitement swept across the English-speaking world on both sides of the Atlantic. What Jonathan Edwards was experiencing in New England was but one facet of a much larger phenomenon that has come to be known as the Great Awakening, an emotion-charged upsurge of interest in and experience of religion that erupted up and down the East Coast of America. In England, John Wesley had experienced his own personal awakening just a few months before at Aldersgate, proof that deep, heart-felt religion was not confined to the American colonies.

This great revival was to have profound consequences for both Englishmen and Americans, and before it would run its course it would see the birth of a new nation and a new church. In October 1739, George Whitefield, a friend of Wesley and like him a convert to this new religion of the heart, landed in Lewes, Delaware, and began the first of several great preaching tours that carried him the length of the American colonies. Whitefield had an almost hypnotic influence over an audience, and from Massachusetts to Georgia untold thousands flocked to hear him. In his wake what had been scattered pockets of revival flared into a great pan-colonial experience of religious excitement. For perhaps the first time the American colonies were joined in a common experience. In the Great Awakening lay some of the seeds of the American Revolution; it is not without reason that Whitefield has sometimes been called the "first American."

While in America religion was helping to mold separate colonies into a unified people, Wesley was nurturing his Methodist movement. A few months after reading Edwards' *Faithful Narrative,* Wesley took the bold step of preaching outdoors in fields and streets to the common and unchurched sections of English society, and in so doing he unleashed a spiritual and social revolution in his own country. It was not Wesley's intention to form a new church, but rather to reinvigorate the Church of England from within. Even so, on both sides of the Atlantic the movement that he founded ultimately became a new church. The burgeoning Methodist movement had converts and missionaries in the American colonies within just a few years of its formation. In 1784, a year after the cessation of hostilities between England and the rebel troops in America, the Methodists of America, with John Wesley's reluctant blessing, set themselves apart as a separate and new denomination, The Methodist Episcopal Church.

Far removed from either Wesley or Edwards, unknown to either of them as well as unaware of them both, lay a little peninsula known as the Eastern Shore of Virginia, an old and isolated and not particularly strategic corner of England's oldest colony in America. The tremendous excitement of the Great Awakening bypassed the people of this peninsula, who went their time-honored ways virtually unaware of the events that unfolded beyond their borders. If George Whitefield had turned south when he landed at Lewes in 1739, the Eastern Shore of Virginia might have been among the first places in America to hear his infectious preaching; instead Whitefield turned north for the great metropolis of Philadelphia and left the two Virginia counties untouched. In 1765 a small band of Presbyterians, fired by the excitement of the revival in Delaware, erected a church on the Virginia peninsula in Drummondtown, but the local inhabitants, they found, were indifferent to the new faith, and the new church soon died out. It was an old and conservative area, this Eastern Shore of Virginia, settled longer than any other portion of English-speaking America except Jamestown and its environs. Its churchgoers, as many as there were, were Anglicans, proud members of the state-supported Church of England who worshiped in handsome churches, some of which were elegantly appointed. Around them the Great Awakening shook the colonies. On the Eastern Shore of Virginia it created hardly a ripple.

Who could have foreseen that this little sliver of land would fall heir to the revival of Wesley and Edwards, of Whitefield and the Great Awakening, in a unique way? Who could have foreseen that on the Eastern Shore of Virginia the revival religion would ultimately take root and grow undisturbed as almost nowhere else? The Eastern Shore of Virginia became, in time, one of the most Methodist places in the world, one of those very few regions where Methodism predominates, and to this day it preserves some of the features of primitive Methodism, of the period of Wesley himself, that have long since vanished in most other places.

The Eastern Shore of Virginia had been Christian for almost a century and a half before the new revival faith crossed its borders. But in a real sense it is a land whose religious history begins not in the colonial Anglican churches that still stand there but in the revival of the eighteenth century. What Jonathan Edwards witnessed in Massachusetts and John Wesley felt in England would find its way to this Shore as well. This Shore, too, would be transformed.

The Setting 1623-1776

I.

On the highest and holiest day of the Church, in a year revered by the nation, on Easter Sunday 1776, a new age began for Virginia's Eastern Shore.

At Magothy, an Anglican church on Old Plantation Creek in Northampton County, the people were waiting for the rector to arrive. Outside the menfolk gathered in little clusters and talked, as they still do on warm Eastern Shore Sundays, about the weather, crops, politics. Inside waited the women and children, most of them already in their pews, also talking.

Waiting for the preacher to arrive was an old custom at Magothy. Although the faithful had been attending church in this neighborhood since the 1640's, the rector had always lived somewhere else, and Magothy churchgoers were used to waiting for him. There were times when he would not show up as expected, when weather or sickness or unforeseen events kept him from his rounds. On those days the people would simply disperse and go their way home after an appropriate visit with each other.

Easter Sunday 1776 began to look like one of those days. The Reverend Samuel McCroskey was apparently not going to show that day, and the people were on the point of leaving for home when two men arrived to join them, two men who expected to find the service already in progress and themselves late. One of the men was a stranger. The other the people recognized as Thomas Elliott, a man from their neighborhood who had recently moved across the bay to Gloucester. There was an exchange of greetings and introductions. And then, just as the people were starting to leave, Elliott's companion spoke up:

"If you will go with me down the road a little way," he said, "I will preach the gospel according to the light which the Lord has given me."

Such a proposal had never been heard at Magothy. Elliott's companion was obviously not a clergyman. He was rough and ordinary and obviously no more educated than any of the rest of them. The ministers they were accustomed to were gentlemen, cultured and refined. And why preach out-of-doors? Wasn't church supposed to happen in church?

With some misgivings the people agreed to hear this man, so they followed him down the road a bit, away from the churchyard, and there he mounted a tree stump and preached to them. His name was Elijah Baker. He was a minister, but one such as the Eastern Shore had never seen—a Baptist minister. He came to Magothy from Lunenburg County, where a great revival was raging strong. He preached loudly and excitedly. He was overflowing with spirit. And when he was finished preaching, that was enough for most of his listeners. Ministers, after all, were not rough, uneducated men who preached outdoors on tree stumps. Most of the congregation dispersed for home.

But a few were strangely affected by this man and his excited religion. He was invited into their homes, where he stayed for several days and obliged them with further preaching. Within the week he and Elliott left for Gloucester, but they promised to return on Pentecost and continue their ministry to these few interested folk.

It did not take the Reverend McCroskey long to learn what had happened at Magothy in his absence. No sooner had he heard that Baker would return on Pentecost than he appointed that as the day when he would preach against the heresies of the Baptists and prove them in error.

And so on Pentecost 1776, Samuel McCroskey stood waiting as, true to their word, Baker and Elliott returned to the church, accompanied this time by Leonard Baker, brother of Elijah and a licensed Baptist exhorter in his own right. The rector mounted his pulpit and preached against the Baptists as he had promised, and for most of the people present the issue was settled for good. McCroskey was the rector, the Church of England was the church, and they had heard enough of Elijah Baker. But again the same few invited Baker home, and Baptist preaching continued in that neighborhood from that date. The few interested Anglicans became the nucleus of a separate congregation, and in early spring of 1778, after two years of hard work, Elijah Baker organized five newly-baptized persons into Lower Northampton Baptist Church.[1]

Lower Northampton is the first permanent, non-Anglican church on the Eastern Shore of Virginia whose origins can be substantiated by the written record.* Quietly and with little fanfare, the great revival that was sweeping Europe and America had gained a foothold on Virginia's Eastern Shore.

When Elijah Baker began singlehandedly to wage battle against the Church of England on the Eastern Shore of Virginia in 1776, he took on no easy adversary. The Shore had been settled now for a century and a half, and the Church of England had been a part of that scene from the very first. It stood alone, the only church its people knew, established by law, and supported by the strong arm of the state.

But Baker's arrival was timely, for the Shore was ripe for spiritual change. Years of uncontested supremacy had made the Church of England lax and indifferent to the spiritual needs of the greater mass of people on the Shore, and 1776 was the beginning of its end.

In its earliest years the Church of England, like everything else on the Shore, was a very struggling affair. The first rector arrived some time between 1621 and 1623. His name was Francis Bolton, and very little is known of his work, probably because very little work was done in religious spheres while the settlers were literally carving their homes out of the wilderness.[2]

*Downing's Methodist Church in Oak Hall is perhaps earlier than Lower Northampton by as much as six years, but it is not found in the written record prior to 1783.

By 1634 the Eastern Shore had its first church building at "The Towne," a settlement on King's Creek west of what is now Cheriton, which was at that time the chief community on the peninsula. The first church was undoubtedly a rough and primitive building, enclosed with other public buildings by a protective stockade, and the first record of its existence shows that it was already in need of repair. A local inhabitant convicted of a misdemeanor was sentenced to fix its roof. The Towne was abandoned in 1677, its church with it, and for a generation or more churches sprang up and disappeared up and down the Shore depending upon the movement of population and the county court as settlement spread out over the peninsula. The second church was erected at Fishing Point on Old Plantation Creek in Northampton in 1641, only to be abandoned in 1669. At Cedar View Wharf in Accomack, Nandua Church stood by 1652, and Occohannock Church near Belle Haven by 1655. Both were abandoned after about a decade. By 1692 the church had followed the court and the people to a new town named Port Scarburgh, known today as Onancock, but this church in turn was abandoned by 1708. In all there were nine churches established on the Shore by the end of the 1600's—The Towne (1634), Fishing Point (1641), Hungars (1646), Nandua (1652), Occohannock (1665), St. George's (1676), Assawoman (1680), Magothy (1691), and Port Scarburgh (1692). Most of them were insubstantial, little frame buildings that passed quickly from the scene. Only two, Assawoman and Magothy, were brick buildings. Only two, Hungars and St. George's, are still in existence, but neither congregation worships today in the original building. And only St. George's of all churches on the Shore today occupies the original site it occupied in the 1600's.[3]

As settlement spread gradually over the Shore and plantations and communities became more fixed, the Church of England divided the two counties into parishes and erected churches in even spaces to cover the area completely. The Shore was divided into two parishes, Lower and Hungars, in 1643, and a third, Accomack, (roughly contingent with the present county), was formed in 1663.[4]

As the established church of the colony, the Church of England enjoyed the support of the arm of the law, and it is not inconceivable that it could not have survived these difficult first years without it. The local inhabitants were required by law to attend the parish church or be able to defend in court why they did not. They were required by law to pay their "tithe" of support for the rector and the church, whether or not they considered themselves Anglicans. The earliest court record now in existence on the Eastern Shore of Virginia indicates the form such requirements might take:

> *It is ordered by this court that the new Churchwardens shall have the power to distrayne {seize} upon the goods and chattels of all such of the inhabitants of Achawmack that have not yet fully paid their duties of corne and tobacco unto the minister.*[5]

Even with laws like this the rectors had difficulty collecting their salaries and supporting their families. It was just one more reason why, in the distant frontier edge of the colony, ministers were hard to come by, and the church a precariously-founded institution.

In support of the established church, the court could levy punishments for sins, and did so. In 1638, when the rector complained that one of his parishioners, a man named John, was guilty of fornication, the court ordered the offender to establish a ferry for public use on Old Plantation Creek. Others, for the same offense, were "set up by the heels in the stock" by court order. In 1664, John Major was hauled before the court for not attending Nandua, the parish church, but he was "cleared...in Respect hee uses Occohannock Church." The court could punish parishioners who criticized the pastor, as Henry Carleton found out in 1634. Carleton was overheard calling the rector "a black cotted Rascoll" and boasting that "if he had had Mr. Cotton [the rector] without the church yeard, he would have kicked him over the Pallyzados [stockade]." Cotton complained of this indignity to the authorities, and Carleton was ordered "to buyld a pair of stocks and sett in them three Sabouth days in the tyme of Dyvine Servis, and then aske Mr. Cotton forgiveness."[6]

Punishments for non-churchly offenses were often meted out by the court at the parish church. In 1647 one Richard Buckland was convicted of slander, and for his crime was ordered that "for the next sermon that is preached at Nuswattocks [Hungars] Church," he was to "stand at the Church doore." In 1652, Joan Pettyjohn was convicted of malicious gossip, for which offense she was ordered to Occohannock Church to "stand att the Church dore (during the tyme the psalme is singeinge) with a gagge in her mouth." Less fortunate was Genefra Jones, who for the same crime was "towed over the Creek at Nandue" from behind a boat.

And sometimes the church was the beneficiary of the labors of those being punished by the court, as in 1634 when a convicted parishioner had to repair the church roof at The Towne. Or in 1641, when all those who had disobeyed a certain law about carrying arms were required to "meet at the parish church of AcKowmack [Fishing Point] upon Satterday next and cutt up all the weeds about the Church." Even the foremost pillars of the church were subject to such actions: in 1635 one of the vestrymen was fined 20 shillings for missing a meeting.[7]

Anglicanism may have been the official, but it was not the only, religion on the Eastern Shore of Virginia, and for the better part of a century the established faith spent a good deal of its time combatting "dissenters." The England which sent colonists to the coast of America in the 1600's was supposedly a nation united under the Church of England, but actually there were many religious stripes in England. And three of them very quickly found their way to the Eastern Shore.

The first challenge to the established church came from Puritan New England and was found in a most unlikely corner, the Anglican clergy itself. There was considerable commerce and trade between New England and the Eastern Shore in the 1600's, due perhaps to the Shore's maritime location. And since it was hard to obtain proper Anglican rectors for the distant Shore, a succession of local ministers came from the ranks of the Puritan dissenters, much to the dismay of the Anglican authorities in Jamestown. It began in the 1630's with William Cotton, the first known successor to the original rector, Francis Bolton. Cotton conformed outwardly to the beliefs and practices of the established church, but his was the character "of a stern Puritan" and the "career...[that] smacks of New England." Upon his death in 1640 he was succeeded by Nathaniel Eaton, who arrived on the Shore after having been expelled as headmaster of the Massachusets school that later became Harvard. Eaton was succeeded in 1644 by John Rozier, a nonconformist of Puritan stamp. And last, after Rozier, came Francis Doughty.*

Francis Doughty was a non-conformist pure and simple, a man who had left England in the first place because he refused to recognize the divine right of the king to rule, a cardinal concept jealously guarded by the state church. He settled first in New England, but even that strict Puritan society was too lax for his tastes, so he moved on to New York and ultimately to Virginia. Once established in the rectory in Northampton, he soon ran afoul of the locals for his non-Anglican stance and shortly thereafter left for Essex County, where the locals brought suit against him for, among other things, denying the "supremacy of the King."

This Puritan infiltration of Northampton's churches was brought to a halt by Governor William Berkeley in 1676. When he sought refuge on the Shore during Bacon's Rebellion, Berkeley found to his horror that recent rectors had been Puritans and that Daniel Richardson, Doughty's successor, was not properly ordained. Berkeley quickly handpicked Isaac Key, a staunch Anglican, for the rectorship in Northampton. Since only in the lower county had the Puritans held sway, and Accomack Parish had long been under the influence of the able and thoroughly Anglican rector, Thomas Teackle, Puritan influence on the Shore was at last effectively ended. Yet a century later the outbreak of the American Revolution found Northampton County, where local rectors had questioned the right of the king to rule, inclined toward the side of independence, and Accomack County, where Anglican influence had escaped the Puritan taint, inclined toward the side of the royalists. After the Revolution the Accomack rector, John Lyon, was courtmartialed and jailed for "having given aid and comfort to the enemy in the late Invasion," while Northampton rector Samuel McCroskey enjoyed local esteem for having served as a county lieutenant on the American side.[8]

The second threat to the established church began during the pastorate of Francis Doughty. In 1657 the first Quakers debarked at Jamestown, where they were immediately arrested and deported. Most of them went to Maryland, and within a short time Quakers made their first appearance on the Eastern Shore of Virginia.

To the Anglican authorities, Quakers were an unprecedented cause for alarm, quite another thing from the ordinary nonconformist. The Society of Friends, as it called itself, was on the radical edge of the spectrum of religious groups and sects imported from England, a sect more determined than all others to continue the reformation of the church. Although they were plain and unpretentious people, generally above all personal reproach, Quakers were nonetheless radical reformers who believed that a new age was impending, and other Christians, Anglicans especially, saw them as a real threat. Quakers were quick to

---

*Cotton, Eaton, and Doughty had one thing more than their Puritanism in common: they all married the same woman. Ann Graves of Northampton, a respectable lady of good family, married each of them in turn, was widowed by each of them in turn, and lived out the remainder of her days on the Shore.

express their disapproval of established states and established religions. They rejected virtually everything about the Church of England, even its form of worship; their own worship was almost without form, for they gathered not to sing or read the psalm or hear a sermon, but simply to sit in silence until one of their number was led by the Spirit to speak.

By 1654 there were Quakers on the Eastern Shore of Virginia who were refusing to pay their tithes to support the state church. Four years later the Quaker missionary, William Robinson, came down to the peninsula, preaching and visiting the Quaker families. Robinson was hauled before the authorities, accused of being "a seducer of the people" and of denying the humanity of Christ. He was convicted and sent across the bay for punishment, and local Quakers who had given him lodging were imprisoned on the Shore. Such attempted suppressions did not deter the fervent Quakers. They continued to proselytize among the Anglicans, to criticize their clergy openly, and to import leaders from other areas. One Quaker named Henry White accused Thomas Teackle of preaching false doctrine, and declared that the Anglican clergy were little more than "ravening wolves and hungry dogs" who preached only when they were fed.

The number of Quakers on the Shore increased rapidly, and in 1660 the General Assembly at Jamestown passed a strict law to rid the colony of these troublemakers. The law had its desired effect almost immediately: most of the Shore's Quakers moved north into Maryland, where they were guaranteed religious freedom. But a significant number remained in Virginia, where, after some initial clashes with local authorities, they settled down to a quiet pursuit of their faith and were, when they complied with the laws regulating dissenting groups, left alone. Within a short time many of them had become prosperous and respectable citizens. John Custis IV, a faithful Anglican, declared that he had always been "a friend to that perswasion," and that he considered Quakers to be a "quiet, zealous, intelligent, good-natured, proper" sect.[9]

On the Eastern Shore the Quakers erected two meetinghouses: one in Franktown, which stood prior to the anti-Quaker acts of 1660, the other in Guilford, which they erected in 1683. In 1672 they were visited by George Fox, the foremost Quaker in his day and a famous preacher. By 1692 they were duly registered, dissenting congregations assembling peaceably according to law, and the Guilford congregation published this declaration to the public:

> *Wee the people comonly caled quaker do hereby Informe all persons conserned that we doe constantly meet on the first day of the weeke called Sunaday at our meeting house built for that use neare Gilford in this county and on the fifth day of the week called Thursday either at the house of Sara Coe widow or at the house of George Johnson.....*

When the Guilford meetinghouse burned in 1694, the congregation met in a home in Onancock until it was replaced in 1697. Apparently that community had also a number of Quaker inhabitants.

Left to themselves, the Quaker congregations ultimately died out. By 1720 both congregations were dwindling and all but extinct. Neither meetinghouse was used after 1729. The last public act of corporate Quaker worship on the Shore was a wedding that occurred in 1753 in what is now Captain's Cove near Greenbackville.[10] At least in part because the Church of England was allied with the powerful arm of the state it survived the threat of Quakerism with little or no trouble.

The third challenge came from the Presbyterians, or from one single Presbyterian who was one of the most famous and remarkable men ever to call the Eastern Shore his home: Francis Makemie.

It was in 1680 that the Presbyterians of Scotland received an appeal from one William Stevens of Worcester County, Maryland (himself an Anglican), to send a Presbyterian minister to them. The call inspired Francis Makemie, then a young man in his early twenties, to enter the ministry. He was ordained in 1682, booked passage to America in 1683, and spent the next several years of his life in the region of Norfolk and the Carolinas.

In 1687 Makemie settled in Accomack County, but he did not as yet do a great deal of work as a minister. Instead he chose Onancock as his home, married Naomi Anderson of that town, and with the backing of her wealthy father became a successful tradesman and landowner. He is known to have conducted services at Rehobeth, Maryland, at the church that called him to the ministry in 1680. And in 1692 he published *An Answer to George Keith's Libel Against a Catechism,* a theological treatise written after George Keith, a traveling schismatic Quaker, had dared to engage him in debate. Keith visited Makemie in Onancock in 1692, and this pamphlet was written in that town, perhaps the most famous theological work ever written on the Shore. But apart from these activities, Makemie was not so much minister as businessman.

From 1692 to 1698, Makemie lived in Barbados in the West Indies, where he looked after his business interests, and it was only on his return in 1698 that he took up the active ministry to which he had been called by the Presbyterians of Rehobeth some eighteen years earlier. On April 29, 1699, he registered as a dissenting minister, the second preacher in Virginia to do so, and secured permission to hold services at his two residences, one in Onancock, the other on Holden's Creek near Grotons. He built no church, but became the pastor of Rehobeth in Maryland, just across the line. Even so, it is likely that the local Anglicans viewed his now-vigorous activity with some alarm.

But although he lived and labored on the Eastern Shore of Virginia, Francis Makemie proved to be more of a national than a local figure, and he made but a slight impact upon the local scene. In 1706, acting in part in response to an increasingly aggressive Anglicanism that was from London trying to bring the dissenting movements in the colonies into line, he organized the first presbytery in America and served as its moderator at its first meeting in Philadelphia. Shortly thereafter he began a preaching tour, not in Virginia but in the North, where he hoped to promote the new denomination.

He was catapulted into national prominence in New York, where in 1707 he was arrested for preaching without a license, even though he was properly licensed in Virginia. The charge against him was for the most part groundless, but the case became a famous one because the dissenters viewed it as part of Anglicanism's new attempt to become the established church throughout all the colonies. Makemie was acquitted, and the case to this day is seen as a landmark decision in favor of religious liberty in America. After his victory in New York, Makemie journeyed on to Boston, where he was warmly received by such dissenting divines as Increase and Cotton Mather.[11]

FRANCIS MAKEMIE

as depicted by the Makemie Monument (1908) near Grotons, Accomack County. No contemporary likenesses of Makemie are known.

Within a short time bad health forced Makemie to return home, and there in 1708 he died, still a young man. He left Prebyterianism stronger in the colonies, but with him died all active Presbyterianism on the Eastern Shore of Virginia. The neighboring churches in Maryland remained active and were regularly attended by some Virginians, but Presbyterian worship in the two Virginia counties ceased. In 1765, during a revival, a comeback was attempted, and a Presbyterian meetinghouse was raised in Accomac, but this attempt was short-lived.[12] Not for 130 years after his death would there be a permanentPresbyterian congregation on the Shore.

Francis Makemie was too great a figure to be contained by the little Eastern Shore. He painted with such a large brush that the local Anglicans soon discovered that he was not that much of a threat to them after all.

By the beginning of the 1700's the Church of England was entering a new period on Virginia's Eastern Shore. The Shore itself was now more settled and shaped, its population more evenly spread out across the two counties. Challenges from Puritan, Quaker, and Presbyterian circles had been, or soon would be, effectively met. On a larger scale the Church of England was more actively at work to become the principal faith in America, and in 1701 it founded the Society for the Propagation of the Gospel, designed to send out missionaries to the colonies.[13] With the coming of the eighteenth century came the only real time in which the Church of England reigned in uncontested supremacy across the Eastern Shore. For the Church of England it was the golden period, and it was to last three-quarters of a century.

It was the eighteenth century that gave us the elegant colonial church buildings so admired in our day. After the short-lived church in Port Scarburgh closed, there were only four Anglican churches in the two counties: Magothy, Hungars, St. George's, and Assawoman. Hungars was by now in its second building on its second site. In 1709 William Byrd of Westover worshiped there and noted in his diary that the congregation was very much in attendance that day. The oldest church building now standing on the Shore, St. George's in Pungoteague, was erected in 1738. Four years later the present Hungars building, third for that congregation and second on the same site, was erected.[14]

ST. GEORGE'S EPISCOPAL CHURCH

As drawn by the Reverend James Wallace Eastburn, 1819.

Meanwhile newer churches sprang up in newer neighborhoods. The citizens of central Accomack County petitioned for a church, and by 1728 Middle Church stood on the central county road (present U.S. Route 13) opposite Accomack Wayside. Accomack Parish was divided in 1761 into Accomack and St. George's Parishes, and a new church was erected in each. New Church was erected in what is now the village of that same name soon after 1762, and the new church for St. George's Parish, now known as St. James', was erected south of Accomac* in 1767. Thus Elijah Baker would find seven Anglican churches evenly spread across the two counties: Magothy, Hungars, St. George's, St. James', Middle, Assawoman, and New Church.

It was during the eighteenth century that large glebes came into being, parish farmlands which were used to house and to support the rectors. The first glebe on the Shore was erected for William Cotton in 1635 and stood facing the bay south of the present town of Cape Charles. In 1654 Hungars Parish was bequeathed an estate in Church Neck west of Hungars Church, but it was not until well into the next century that the parish was able to take possession. When it did, Cotton's old glebe was sold and the proceeds used to purchase "slaves to be used on the {new} Glebe." This Hungars Glebehouse is still standing, an admired example of colonial architecture.

Accomack Parish acquired a glebe in 1713; it stood just south of the present town of Bloxom. And the new St. George's Parish purchased a glebe on Occohannock Creek in 1767. The Anglican clergymen did not always choose to live on their glebes; many of them had finer estates of their own. William Black, rector of Accomack Parish in 1724, declared that his glebe was unlivable: "Glebe and house good for nothing, rented for one pound. I do not live in it." Nonetheless, the days when the state had to twist the arm of the people to pay the clergy were past, and the life of the clergyman in this century was a good deal more desirable than in the previous century.

One of the responsibilities assigned to the established church by the state was the care of the poor. Both Hungars and St. George's Parish voted to erect almshouses for the homeless in the 1760's, but only Hungars Parish actually completed an almshouse, and that was after the Revolution when the church was no longer given that responsibility by law. After 1763 St. George's Parish would not support the poor and indigent unless they wore across their shirts the letters "SGP" (St. George's Parish) in red or blue letters. [15]

There seems to be every reason to believe that in the early part of this golden era the faithful of the Shore filled their churches at regular attendance on worship. So suggests the diary of William Byrd in 1709. So suggests a notation made by the Accomack Parish rector in 1724. Said he, "God be praised" there were only a few dissenters within the bounds of his parish. Persons came regularly from as far away as ten miles to attend worship, and the Anglican chapels could not hold them all. [16] Indeed, after the two Quaker meetinghouses closed in 1729, there were no other church buildings in use in the two counties for a full half century.

The rectors who served these churches during this time typified the state church and all that it aspired to be. For the most part they were men of breeding

---

* A word at the start about names and spellings. The present seat of Accomack County was known as Drummondtown until 1893, when its name was changed to Accomac, spelled without the final "k." This work follows correct usage: "Accomac" for the town, "Accomack" for the county.

and ability compared to whom the evangelistic preachers of the revival would appear to be upstarts. From the very first, the Anglican rectors on the Shore were well educated. Bolton was a graduate of Oxford, Eaton the headmaster of Harvard, and Teackle, who lived in a day when even Bibles were rare, had a personal library of over 300 books in English, Latin, Greek, and several other languages.[17]

The eighteenth century rectors, too, were educated, perhaps more so than their predecessors, as one story will indicate. When William Byrd of Westover visited Hungars Parish in 1709, the rector was named Dunn (history has not given us his first name). Byrd records his impressions of Dunn: "He is a man of no polite conversation, notwithstanding he be a good Latin scholar," and he describes an incident that suggests what this country parson was like: "We found some of the women...out of humor, and particularly my wife quarreled with Mr. Dunn and me for talking Latin....."[18] In a day when there was little education on the Shore, the local parson could still be counted on to be a man of erudition and knowledge.

But there is another side to the clergy and their church which may be illustrated by the career of William Black. Black was the rector of Accomack Parish, and he lived not on his glebe but on his own considerable estate east of Locustville. A former missionary sent out by the Society for the Propagation of the Gospel, he was a staunch Anglican who became a parish priest in 1712, and he set about his work with vigor and industry. He had a long pastorate that deteriorated as the years went by, and apparently the faithful young pastor became increasingly lazy, hard to get along with, and sloppy in his work. In 1730 the Grand Jury presented him for "Getting Drunk on the Sabbath Day," and the following year he acknowledged himself guilty of "swearing two prophane Oathes" and was fined. He was frequently in such trouble with the authorities. In 1731 he and his wife were fined fifty shillings for assault against Margaret Whale, and a record from 1734 reads: "The Reverend William Black, having misbehaved himself to this Court, it is ordered that the Sheriff take the said Black into his Custody and him safe keep till he enter into Bond...for his good Behavior." Still later there was another charge against him for "not preaching on the fifth day of November."

Black died in 1738, and was succeeded by the much more reputable Arthur Emmerson.[19]

Such was just one of the rectors who served the Church of England on the Eastern Shore during the 1700's. It is, of course, unfair to generalize from his particular case that there were more like him. On the other hand, it seems safe to assume that what the historians say happened in the rest of Virginia also happened on the Eastern Shore: that as the church became increasingly prosperous, limiting itself more and more to the polite circles of the landed gentry, it also became increasingly lax and out of touch with the majority of people. It is generally conceded that, as a spiritual factor, the established church in Virginia during the eighteenth century was a pronounced failure. An historian's portrayal of a typical Virginia Sunday was not meant to describe the Shore in particular, but it probably fits: "The planter and his family came in their coach and the parson read his homily; and then all went back to their week-day pursuits but slightly edified. It was very much of a Drowsyland, and a trumpet blast was necessary to arouse the sleepers." By the last half of the century, religion had for a great many become mere form. What was said and done on Sunday had little meaning or relevance to living in the world the rest of the week, even among those who faithfully crossed the threshold of the church each Sabbath.[20]

As for the common folk, increasingly the church had no influence over their lives at all, for they remained on the whole unchurched. The established church was by now part of the life of the gentry, the landowner, the planter, the parson who spoke Latin, but the average man rarely ever darkened the door of the church or had any association with it. The common people were basically unchurched, and the state church seemed satisfied to leave them that way. By the end of the century (the first census was taken in 1790) there were 20,000 inhabitants in the two counties.[21] In 1776 when Elijah Baker landed on the Shore, the Church of England had seven church buildings to minister to that number, and was apparently convinced that it was doing its duty. Small wonder that when the Methodists found their way to the Shore they more than once discovered that the average working man had not even the most rudimentary knowledge of the Christian faith, and had in some cases not even heard of Jesus Christ.[22]

It was during the eighteenth century, while men of breeding and knowledge pastored the parishes of Virginia's Eastern Shore and the Church of England grew more and more lax, content with its uncontested supremacy, that events of tremendous spiritual and social impact swept across the religious scene in Europe and America. It was while planters and their families rode contentedly to their chapels in fine coaches and working people in the backwoods lived in ignorance of Jesus and his Gospel that spiritual revival swept across New England and the Middle Colonies and into Virginia, and that John Wesley felt his heart "strangely warmed" at Aldersgate and began forming Methodist societies within the state church in England.

For half a century these great religious events swirled around the Eastern Shore of Virginia, and the Shore remained ignorant of them. Safe and secure on its isolated peninsula, Eastern Shore society knew little or nothing of Jonathan Edwards, John Wesley, or a host of other religious leaders who were changing the world. George Whitefield landed a few miles north of Virginia at Lewes, Delaware, and turned north to Philadelphia to begin his great preaching tour. The Anglican rector, Devereux Jarratt, embraced the revival in southside Virginia. And a revival among Presbyterians in Somerset County, Maryland, brought the Great Awakening to the very borders of the Virginia Shore. And Eastern Shore Christians knew very little or nothing about any of these happenings.

It was Elijah Baker who first planted them permanently there.

Elijah Baker was a thoroughgoing son of the Great Awakening. Born in Lunenburg County, Virginia, in 1742, he was baptized in 1769 "after a frivilous early life," and he began at once to travel and to preach the Word. Churches sprang up wherever he went. He founded several in Lunenburg, moved on to

ELIJAH BAKER

Chesterfield, and then headed east towards the bay through Charles City, James City, Henrico, York, and Gloucester Counties. It was in Gloucester, while he was in the process of organizing yet another congregation, that he met the Eastern Shoreman, Thomas Elliott, and accepted his invitation to cross the bay to Northampton.

Baker's followers described their pioneer as "a man of low parentage, small learning, and confined abilities. But with one talent he did more than many did with five." Baker began his work on the Shore shortly before the signing of the Declaration of Independence and labored there throughout the American Revolution. These were troublesome years for the peninsula. The British occupied Hog Island and made frequent raids upon the mainland for provisions. British warships roamed the bay, seriously restricting vital shipping and commerce. And neighbor watched neighbor to determine who, if any, were loyal to British or American sides.[23]

The times were also difficult for Elijah Baker. It took two years of hard work to organize Lower Northampton Baptist Church, and then that congregation, founded in 1778, had only five members. Opposition to Baker was frequent, and he was on occasion required to dodge apples and stones that were hurled at him by hostile crowds when he tried to preach.

But no sooner was Lower Northampton Church a reality than he moved off again, this time north to Accomack, ever eager to spread the Word. Almost immediately, on May 27, 1778, the churchwardens of Accomack charged him with vagrancy. The court required a hundred pounds' bail to be put up for him, "upon the express condition that the said Elijah Baker do depart this county as soon as convenient, and that he do not presume to preach therein until he produce proper credentials to the Court." Baker himself put up half his bail, and William Gibb, a sympathizer, put up the other half. But shortly thereafter Gibb asked to be discharged from his obligation, and on July 1, 1778, Elijah Baker was imprisoned in the debtors' prison in Drummondtown (Accomac).

Imprisonment was no deterrent to Baker. As the hot days of summer passed he preached to the people who gathered outside the window of his cell. Thomas Batson of Delaware heard him there and invited him to journey north to Sussex County to preach there should he ever get out of jail.

Baker spent a total of 56 days in jail, from July 1 to August 25, 1778. On the day of his trial the churchwardens failed to appear, and his case was dismissed.

Evidently some of the citizens of Accomack took it upon themselves to do outside the law what the law itself could not do: silence Elijah Baker. Apparently soon after his trial, perhaps immediately after it, he was seized by a gang of ruffians and forcibly put aboard a vessel about to depart for overseas. An arrangement had been made with the captain that he was to be worked for his passage and left somewhere, anywhere, in Europe. He was, so the captain was told, "a disturber of the peace."

There are two accounts of Baker's delivery from this fate. The simpler and more likely is that he was spirited aboard the ship on Saturday night and put to work immediately. The next day, Sunday, he obtained the captain's permission to sing and pray among the crew, and so impressed the captain that he without delay put him ashore, vowing then and there to have nothing more to do with any attempt to deport him. Baker's friends, meanwhile, had been working at informing the authorities of his kidnapping, and he was set free.

The more colorful account tells us that Baker was put immediately to work aboard the ship, "and for his praying and preaching and singing was ill used. The privateer being detained long in the harbor by contrary wind, the crew suspected that the cause was that preaching fellow, and therefore put him aboard another vessel. But the wind continuing contrary, that vessel began to be of the same mind with the privateer, and therefore shifted him to a third, and the third put him ashore."[24]

Delivered by whatever means from deportation, Baker shook the dust of Accomack County from his feet and headed north to Delaware to find Thomas Batson, and for the next several years he labored extensively in all three states of the peninsula. In all he organized no fewer than fifteen Baptist churches on the Shore, four in Delaware, five in Maryland, and six in Virginia. The Virginia churches, in addition to Lower Northampton, were Messongo (1779), Hungars or Red Bank (1783), Metompkin (1785), Chincoteague in New Church (1786), and Pungoteague or Hollies (1790). This seemingly indefatiguable man was aided in this work by George Layfield, his first ordained colleague. Their usual procedure was for Baker to "plant" the church and move on, and for Layfield to follow and "water" it with more settled ministry.

In the midst of his work, on November 5, 1787, Baker found time to marry Ann Widgeon of Northampton, his second marriage and her third. The Bakers made their home near the present village of Oyster in Northampton, not far from Lower Northampton Church, where he remained the pastor until his death. By his later years Baker was, despite the earlier persecutions, a respected man on the Shore. The Salisbury Baptist Association, founded in 1782, looked to him as father, and his son, Leonard (by the first marriage), was later elected to the state legislature from Northampton in 1811-1812. Baker addressed the Salisbury Association in October 1798, preaching "in a manner as if heaven and earth were come together," and died shortly thereafter. He was buried in Salisbury, and the gravesite has long since been forgotten.[25]

While Elijah Baker was laboring so vigorously to establish his church on the Shore, the established Church of England almost passed from the scene. During the War for Independence, even royalist Accomack County could not support a church so heavily identified with the enemy. Early in the war, Virginia withdrew all support from the church, crippling its financial operations and throwing the local parishes back on their glebes for support, ultimately stripping them of even their glebes. Quite suddenly Eastern Shoremen deserted the one church they had ever known, and it fell into what looked like almost total ruin.

Of the seven Anglican churches on the Shore in 1776, three disappeared altogether with the disestablishment, never again to be the site of Anglican or Episcopal activity: Magothy, Middle Church, and New Church. Hungars, too, was abandoned and fell into disrepair, lost to the denomination for some forty years. Only St. George's, St. James', and Assawoman remained open, and Assawoman Church was closed within a few years. In October 1784, the church was officially disestablished, upon the petition of its own clergy, and in May 1785 the remaining Anglican churches in the former colony were organized into the Diocese of Virginia of the Protestant Episcopal Church.[26] There were in that year two Episcopal churches and four Baptist churches on the Eastern Shore.

From all appearances, Elijah Baker seemed almost singlehandedly to have achieved a revolution. The Shore was open territory for a complete Baptist takeover. With the Episcopalians struggling for their very survival, the rector in

Accomack still the same James Lyons who had been imprisoned for aiding the British during the late war, the Baptists could have swept all challengers from the field, or so it must have seemed.

But it was not to happen. The Eastern Shore of Virginia never became a Baptist area, for another new faith had slipped into the region from the opposite direction. "For many years the Methodists have been a very increasing people on the Eastern Shore," writes a Baptist historian, explaining the hesitation of his denomination.[27]

The church that was to win the Eastern Shore was not the Baptist church, but the new Methodist faith founded by John Wesley, heir to the great revival on both sides of the Atlantic.

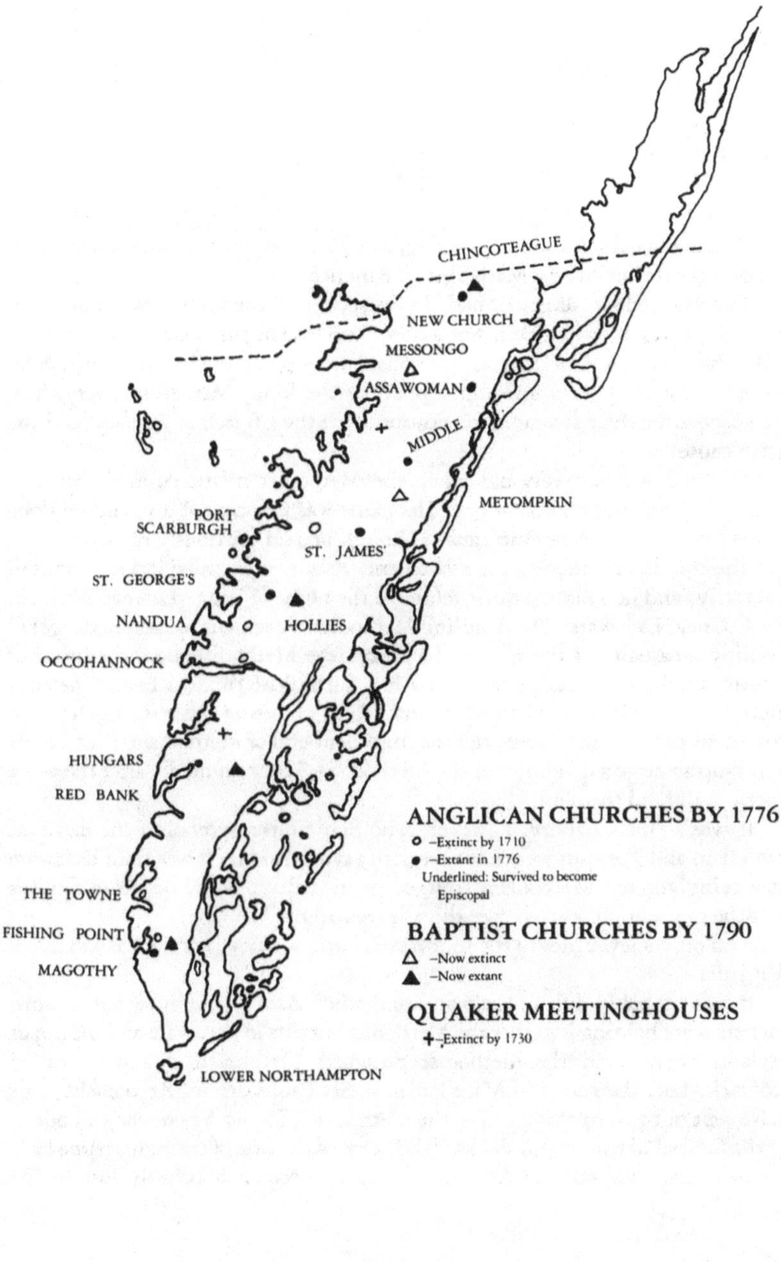
CHINCOTEAGUE
NEW CHURCH
MESSONGO
ASSAWOMAN
MIDDLE
METOMPKIN
PORT SCARBURGH
ST. JAMES'
ST. GEORGE'S
NANDUA
HOLLIES
OCCOHANNOCK
HUNGARS
RED BANK
THE TOWNE
FISHING POINT
MAGOTHY
LOWER NORTHAMPTON
ANGLICAN CHURCHES BY 1776
–Extinct by 1710
–Extant in 1776
Underlined: Survived to become Episcopal
BAPTIST CHURCHES BY 1790
–Now extinct
–Now extant
QUAKER MEETINGHOUSES
–Extinct by 1730

Riders from the North 1772-1799

II.

When the colonies went to war against England for their independence, it was not a good time to be a Methodist in America.

The Methodists, after all, had always spoken of themselves as a movement within the Church of England, not a new church. The missionaries whom John Wesley had sent to America did not constitute a separate church. When John Wesley was writing pamphlets in support of the king, Methodists everywhere were suspect for their strong identification with the Church of England and the British cause.

The war was not very old when the Methodist missionaries in America returned to England, all except one. His name was Francis Asbury, and he alone cast his lot with the American cause. Though he had previously ranged up and down the colonies promoting the movement, Asbury now found it wise to curtail his activity, and he sought a quiet refuge at the home of Judge Thomas White in Kent County, Delaware. The fledgling Methodist movement seemed in danger of becoming a casualty of the war, and at times the Methodists bore the brunt of patriotic wrath. Near Judge White's a few faithful Methodists began the construction of a brick church named Barratt's Chapel during the war, much to the amusement of locals who predicted the imminent end of Methodism. "It's no use putting up so large a dwelling for the Methodists," they taunted; "after the war a corncrib will hold them all."

It was Francis Asbury, however, who became the symbol of the fact that Methodism and Toryism were not necessarily synonymous. It was from Delaware that a reinvigorated Methodism, purged of its British taint, began to fan out across the new nation, even before the war was over.

And only a few miles to the south, ready and waiting, lay the Eastern Shore of Virginia.

It was probably during the war years, when Asbury and a few native-born preachers were holding together the Methodist circuits in Delaware and the upper Maryland Shore, that the Methodist preachers first heard of a place called Accomack. Like the nameless Macedonian in St. Paul's dream, Accomack seems to have sent out a compelling call to the Methodists, for one by one they set out to take the Gospel to this not-so-distant land. One of the first of them, his name long since forgotten, set out for Accomack only to become hopelessly lost in the swamps of the upper Pocomoke River below Delaware. After a period of aimless wandering he came by chance upon a farmhouse, the home of Jethro Bowen, not in Accomack and not even near it but no further south than Newark, Maryland. There he lodged and preached, and a new Methodist congregation sprang up, the first in Worcester County. No less a man than Freeborn Garrettson (1752-1827), who was imprisoned in Cambridge during the strongly anti-Methodist war years, also found himself lost in these same cypress swamps. It is said that once he came across a man in this region and, as he was wont to do, asked the man if he were acquainted with Jesus Christ.

"Sir," replied the man, "I don't know that man, and can't tell you where he lives." [1]

It was, in fact, a mysterious dream that brought Freeborn Garrettson as far south as Somerset County, one of the two Maryland counties that border Accomack on the north. Garrettson was a preacher on the "Delaware Lower Circuit" when, in 1778,

> *One night the state of the people of Somerset County seemed to be shown me. In my dream I thought I had a large circuit formed and the people were gathering to the banner of the Lord. On Friday, October 22nd, I set out to form a circuit in these counties. On Sunday 24th I arrived and had an opportunity of preaching in a forest, both morning and afternoon, to hundreds who gathered to hear the new doctrine. There was weeping on every side. I suppose that more than thirty were powerfully wrought upon, all of whom not longer after joined the society.*[2]

FREEBORN GARRETTSON

probably the first Methodist to preach on the Eastern Shore of Virginia, 1778.

Having worked his way this far south, Freeborn Garrettson did not then confine his work to Maryland, and no doubt the distinction of being the first Methodist preacher to cross into the Eastern Shore of Virginia belongs to him. "I travelled through and preached in every county on the Eastern Shore," reads his journal, "[including] three of Virginia." Garrettson seems to have mistaken the three Anglican parishes of the Virginia Shore for counties, perhaps because his visit to Accomack and Northampton was a brief whirlwind tour. By 1779, Garrettson was at work at a new post across the bay, but Asbury had heard by then his report of the work on the "Lower Circuit." "I am informed," wrote Asbury on January 2, 1779, "that there is a gracious work going on in Sussex in Delaware, and in Accomack and Northampton counties in Virginia." [3]

For two years Methodist activity on the Eastern Shore of Virginia continued to be such occasional work as the Maryland preachers could fit in, until late in 1780 when Asbury picked one of his preachers to be sent specifically to the Virginia Shore. Samuel Roe (1756-1791) was preaching in Sussex County when Asbury sent him down to Virginia. "I believe God has a work for us to do there," said Asbury, and he assigned Charles Twyford "to take Samuel Roe's place while he [Roe] goes down to the eastern Shore of Virginia." Although he was the first Methodist preacher assigned to the Virginia Shore, Roe labored there "only a few weeks time." He was soon back in Delaware, and four years later he left the Methodist ranks altogether and was ordained an Episcopalian. [4]

It was apparently Henry Willis (?-1808) who picked up where Roe left off. Willis, "whose services...were among the most extensive and distinguished in American Methodism," was the first person ordained by Francis Asbury. Just when he began to preach on the Virginia Shore is not known, but the first persistent presence of Methodism in Accomack County was probably his work. "We preached here some time before any regular circuit was formed," wrote Asbury about the Shore in 1784; "now brother Willis is stationed here and there are one hundred in society." Christiana Newton of Accomack was "awakened" to religion in 1782 when she overheard a Methodist preacher, probably Willis, leading worship in a neighbor's house. [5]

According to tradition, the first Methodist society on the Eastern Shore of Virginia was established in 1783, and in that same year Francis Asbury, having no doubt heard for years of the infant work in the area, visited the Virginia Shore for the first time. Asbury was making the rounds of the preaching places near Newtown (Pocomoke City), Maryland, in November 1783 when he wrote in his journal the almost nonchalant remark that lifts the curtain on the history of Methodism on the Shore:

There were few at Captain Downing's when I began to speak, but before I had done preaching we had a considerable company. [6]

It was their first entrance into the pages of recorded history, and the Methodists of the Eastern Shore were late to church!

Methodist work on the Virginia portion of the Shore began in earnest in 1784, when Asbury made an extended visit to the area:

FRANCIS ASBURY

1745-1816

Sunday (October 31, 1783), we rose early and rode twenty miles to Downing's. I lectured at Burton's in the evening.

Monday, after riding twenty miles to Col Paramore's, I preached with liberty. The family is kind; the father, mother, son and niece have tender impressions. The people hereabout are gay, blind in spiritual matters, well-featured, and hospitable, and good livers.

Tuesday after preaching at Garrettson chapel, I rode to Col. Burton's, and was kindly received.

Friday, I came back to Col. Burton's. Since I went from this house, I have ridden about one hundred miles, spent five hours in delivering five public discourses and ten hours in family and public prayer, and read two hundred pages in Young's Works. I have enjoyed great peace, and hope to see a great and glorious work.[7]

On his previous visit Asbury had only touched upon the Shore. This time he ventured halfway down it, visiting the places that Garrettson or Roe or Willis had opened up before him. Downing's was the home of Captain William Downing of Oak Hall. Paramore's was "Belle Vue," the home of Col. William Paramore on Finney Creek south of Locustville. Burton's was the home of Captain Thomas Burton, on Seaside Road north of Wachapreague. Jonathan Garrison (which Asbury always spelled Garrettson) lived on Seaside Road in Mappsburg, east of what is now Painter. As their titles suggest, all four of Asbury's hosts were leading citizens. Methodism had already made substantial inroads into the local gentry, a class only recently adhering to the Church of England. [8]

To the record of his visit in 1784, Asbury added a description of the Shore and a bit of its religious history:

> *The land here is low and level, and is refreshed with fine breezes from the sea; there is an abundance in the productions of the earth and of the waters; the people generous, social, and polished in their manners......*
>
> *The Presbyterians came down here about thirty years ago; many were moved, and some advances were made towards a reformation. A house was built for public worship. About six years past the Baptists visited these parts, and there was some stir among the people. I think the Methodists are most likely to have permanent success, because the inhabitants are generally Episcopalians.*[9]

Asbury ended his Eastern Shore tour at Downing's on November 6, 1784, and rode from there to Snow Hill and on to Barratt's Chapel. There he met Thomas Coke [1747-1814], recently arrived from England with instructions from John Wesley for organizing a separate church. Asbury and Coke dispatched Freeborn Garrettson, who was, in Coke's phrase, sent "like an arrow" to call the preachers of the south to a general conference in Baltimore at Christmas. [10]

THOMAS COKE

Coke, meanwhile, toured the Virginia Shore for himself. In November 1784, before crossing the bay to attend the conference, Thomas Coke made the rounds of the peninsula accompanied by "Black Harry" Hosier, a Methodist preacher. Like Asbury before him, Coke preached in the homes of Downing, Paramore, Burton, and Garrison, as well as in the courthouse at Drummondtown. To the learned English doctor, this part of the country must have seemed very primitive. "In this part of the country we have no preaching-houses,"* he wrote, "the work being of very short standing... But they talk of building, and I encouraged them... The [Anglican] clergy in general in these parts never stir out

* Coke says there were no Methodist preaching-houses in Virginia in 1784, while Asbury specifically mentions Garrison's Chapel. The likelihood is that the "chapel" at Garrison's was, in 1784, a separate building where preaching was held, but not one erected specifically for that purpose.

to church even on a Sunday if it rains. The people, I am told, expected me to be one of those lazy fellows." [11]

The following month Coke and Asbury and the Methodist preachers gathered in Baltimore for the "Christmas Conference." There they organized a separate denomination, the Methodist Episcopal Church, with Bishops Coke and Asbury at its head. There they created, for the first time, an "Accomack Circuit" and assigned James White to be its pastor.

Eastern Shore Methodism and the denomination of which it was a part were established officially in the same year.

Eastern Shore Methodists have preserved some traditions of their own about the coming of the faith to their area, and their stories differ substantially from the written records. Freeborn Garrettson, remembered the locals, was not the first, but the second, person to preach Methodism on the Shore. Years before he appeared on the scene the faith had already been planted by a mysterious "missionary" who came and went so quickly that no one could remember his name.

Could it be that the local traditions preserve some facts not contained in the records? From two separate communities come two separate traditions, completely absent from the written record, that may in fact be two chapters of the same story. From Oak Hall, a few miles below the Maryland border, comes the story that Captain William Downing, the first Methodist there, was converted in 1772 when he heard the preaching of a Methodist missionary who was traveling south down the peninsula to Norfolk. Downing's Church in that community has always measured its history from 1772, the traditional date of the conversion of Downing, and in 1972 unabashedly celebrated its bicentennial anniversary.

From the Seaside region below Melfa comes the local story, also unsupported by written records of the period, that William Elliott of Bradford's Neck was converted later in 1772 by the same missionary, this time traveling back up the peninsula from Norfolk accompanied by another Methodist who was talented as a singer. Some time later, so the story goes, Elliott was moved to establish a school in his home on Sundays to teach children to read the Bible, and thus he founded the oldest continuous Sunday school in America.

It is entirely possible, of course, that Methodist missionaries labored on the Shore prior to Garrettson's brief visit in 1778. If so, their work is absent altogether from the written record and retained only hazily in the traditions of the local people. Wessie Nock Eason, a local historian writing in 1909, tentatively identified the two missionaries who traveled up the Shore as William Watters and Robert Williams, two early Methodist preachers of considerable fame. [12] Her guess was not a good one, for neither man's journal will support her theory. Yet the identification stuck, and although it is erroneous it is still repeated on the Shore.

It is intriguing to note, however, that in regard to communities the local traditions seem to be on firmer ground. When the curtain does rise on the recorded history of Methodism in the area, there is already a flourishing society in Oak Hall in the home of William Downing, and in the region of William Elliott's home a society, Burton's, that ultimately inherited his Sunday school. Of the four places visited by Asbury in his first journey down the Shore in 1784, two are singled out by local tradition as sites of very early Methodist activity. Just how much of the tradition is factual will probably never be known.

Bishop Asbury made a total of fifteen visits to the Eastern Shore of Virginia, and his journal is the best record we have of the first years of the faith in Accomack County. Growth at first was painfully slow, although each time the bishop returned he found the work a little stronger, the enthusiasm of the people a little greater. In 1786 Asbury found the people at Burton's "panting after the perfect love of God," and he preached to a crowd of 100, half black, that filled Garrison's Chapel to hear him. In 1787 he found that a revival had taken place all around the circuit, and he noted with approval the "love and power among the people in the sacrament and the love feast" that he conducted. "The Lord has greatly blessed the labors of Brother [Robert] Sparks," the preacher assigned to the circuit that year, he wrote.[13]

In 1787 the new faith was carried into Northampton County by one of the most memorable of the early Methodist preachers, Joseph Everett (1732-1809). Everett was officially assigned to the Annemessex Circuit in Maryland when he first ventured down the Virginia Shore. He was a veteran of the Revolution, a rough-and-ready old campaigner, fearless and upright, and he blazed a Methodist trail into a county that had not heard Methodist preaching since Freeborn Garrettson's quick departure almost a decade before. In Belle Haven on the Northampton border Everett encountered some young toughs who informed him that they would resist any attempt he might make to hold preaching services. Everett was undaunted. "Gentlemen," said he, "I have been fighting the battle of the country for liberty and freedom. I shall now claim the enjoyment of both. Henceforth I am enlisted in a new warfare between virtue and vice, and call upon all good citizens to join me in the struggle." And he passed through their number unmolested.

A little later, deep into Northampton, he announced a time and a place to preach and arrived only to find a hostile crowd ready to make trouble. Everett retired to the woods and prayed at length before returning to the scene to preach. He began his sermon by taking off his coat, rolling up his sleeves, and flexing his muscles before the crowd. "Men of Virginia," said he, "this is old Everett. Look at him. He has large arms and willing muscles, and always feels ready to stand up for the cause in which, by the grace of God, he is now enlisted." He then rolled down his sleeves, put on his coat, and preached as usual, with no interruptions.[14]

Everett continued unopposed to the very tip of the peninsula, but found conditions in Northampton not to his liking. Cape Charles he found to be "a place poisoned by filthy Antinomian [extreme Calvinistic] principles," and when he openly preached in favor of the abolition of slavery he was "almost obliged to run the gauntlet."[15] Impatient with the Baptists and the slaveowners of Northampton, Everett put Virginia behind him and was content thereafter to stick to his work in Annemessex. But within two years the less fiery regular preachers were building upon the trail he had blazed.

When Asbury returned to the Shore in 1788, he was accompanied by another man who was himself to be, in 1800, elected bishop, Richard Whatcoat (1736-1806).

RICHARD WHATCOAT

Like Asbury, Whatcoat kept a journal, and what we know of the circuit in that year comes from two parallel, first-hand accounts written by bishops. Whatcoat and Asbury visited two communities that were thereafter added to the regular Methodist rounds: Onancock and Drummundtown. In Onancock the two men were entertained by William Seymour, who quickly became the guiding light of the new society formed there. In Drummondtown, where Coke had preached in 1784, a society was organized which five years later purchased a lot and began to erect a chapel. It was, however, in 1788 that Asbury visited the home of Thomas Burton for the last time. Some rift must have developed between the two men; Asbury only says cryptically in his journal that "the former inhabitants [of Burton's] have gone to the dust."[16]

By 1789 when Asbury returned with both Whatcoat and Joseph Everett, the Methodist rounds included Downing's, Paramore's, Garrison's Chapel, Drummondtown, and a new place called Johnson's. Asbury visited the home of Johannes Johnson south of Bridgetown in Northampton, and the following year Johnson gave to the church the land on which Johnson's Church stands today, a site which has been occupied by a Methodist church building longer than any other spot on the Eastern Shore of Virginia. It was not until 1789 that Asbury traveled for the first and only time clear to the tip of the peninsula. Here, like Everett before him, he left discouraged by the presence of Elijah Baker and his Baptists. "The Antinomians please them and gain them, alas for us," he wrote. "O that the Lord would send an earthquake of his power among them!"[17]

The bishop visited the Shore once a year every year between 1790 and 1793, and his usual rounds included Garrison's, Drummondtown, and Downing's. The Downing's society erected a new chapel in 1791, and here in 1793 Asbury himself conducted the Quarterly Meeting of the circuit. "Had a comfortable quarterly meeting at Downing's," wrote the Bishop. "I met the...official members, and we had sweet fellowship together."[18]

That was ten years from his first visit to this first Eastern Shore society. The number of Methodists on the Virginia Shore had, in that time, increased more than eight-fold, to 865.

Despite his frequent visits to the Shore, Asbury was not the pastor of the Eastern Shore Methodists. The task fell to the regularly appointed "traveling preachers" sent by the Annual Conference in Philadelphia, at least one and usually two men each year. Twenty such preachers served the circuit between 1784 and 1900, traveling up and down the peninsula independently of each other, meeting together occasionally for a Quarterly Meeting or at the home of some hospitable Methodist.

For the most part the men appointed to the Shore during these first years are shadowy figures about whom little or nothing is known. Three, however, deserve special mention. One was Christopher Spry, a local Shoreman who was ordained by Asbury at Garrison's Chapel in 1789. (It is Whatcoat's, not Asbury's, journal that records this ordination.) In 1789 Spry was, with Jeremiah Cosden, appointed to serve the Eastern Shore churches.[19]

A second man of note was Griffin Callahan (1759-1833), appointed to the circuit in 1791. Callahan entered the ministry in 1787 and is said to have been the first Methodist preacher in the territory northeast of the Ohio River, where he preached that year. It was on the Eastern Shore, however, that he found and married Susan Luker, thus becoming probably the first Methodist preacher on the Shore to marry. As was often the case in that day, his ministerial salary was too meager to support a growing family, so about 1820 Callahan was forced to "locate" and find other employment. He retired to Locust Mount in Accomack County, but continued to serve in the capacity of local preacher for many years. He died a beloved man in 1833, and a monument to him stands today in front of the Oak Grove Church.[20]

The third man from this period was probably typical of the rest, and indeed there were perhaps others who were more noteworthy then. One thing, however, makes him stand out from the others: he alone kept a journal that has survived to this day. His name was William Colbert (1765-1833). In 1795, at the age of thirty, he was appointed with Joseph Rowen to the Eastern Shore of Virginia, and thanks to the daily notations he made in his journal it is still possible to catch a glimpse of the life of the Methodist preachers of the peninsula in the late eighteenth century.

Colbert's pastorate—and undoubtedly those of his contemporaries were similar—was an almost endless round of traveling alone from appointment to appointment, with no home and little time to call his own. In the first two months of 1795, for instance, Colbert rode the length of the Shore on horseback two and a half times. During that period he visited or lodged at almost thirty different homes, preaching at almost every one of them at least once and some of them more than once. The circuit pastor, in that same time, conducted three funerals (usually held in the home of the deceased), two communion services, two class meetings (a task which was not strictly his responsibility), and one Quarterly Meeting. He met his colleague, Joseph Rowen, the other circuit preacher, only five times in two months. And once, quite by accident on the road outside Onancock, he encountered and rode along with another preacher, George Layfield, the assistant to the Baptist Elijah Baker. "He appeared very friendly," commented Colbert of Layfield. Meanwhile Colbert managed to work in a total of three days in reading and study—his reading material included *Address to the Deists* and *Paradise Lost* as well as the Bible—and he spent one day confined to his sickbed.

By 1795 the Methodist rounds included places not visited by Asbury, areas opened up by Colbert or his immediate predecessors. One of them was at Concord Wharf in Occohannock Neck, where Thomas Paramore, Colonel William's brother, lived. At first a regular stop for Colbert, Paramore's home had by September 1795 been termed "that disputing place" and dropped from the preacher's appointments. Even so, the society there prospered and a decade later erected a building known as Bethel Chapel.

There was by now a society of nineteen persons on Hog Island, and a new society in Ames Ridge between the modern towns of Keller and Painter. Colbert also repeatedly visited the Guilford area, where the society met in the homes of such people as William Onions, Scarburgh Bloxom, and Thomas Evans. In 1799 the Guilford society began the erection of its new meetinghouse.

In Belle Haven, where Joseph Everett had once been accosted by young toughs, Colbert found a friend in Captain James Powell. Here he preached a number of times, always outdoors for want of a meetinghouse. Captain Powell lived in sight of a tavern, and in May while Colbert was preaching in the captain's yard, the sounds of a heated card game wafted out over his congregation from the direction of the tavern. "I was so enabled to swell my voice as to attract the attention of some," wrote Colbert, "and draw them from their sinful amusements to hear the word of the Lord." Nonetheless, neither Colbert nor his successors were able to establish a Methodist society in Belle Haven for almost another century, and the community went down in Methodist annals of the time as perhaps the most ungodly place on the Shore.

It was a different story further south in Hadlock. Here the highly respected widower Benjamin Floyd was by now the local preacher and overseer of a Methodist society that bore his name. At times it met in Floyd's home, at times in the parlor of the mansion, "Fruitlands," in Hare Valley. Floyd's Meetinghouse, forerunner of the present Franktown Church, was erected in Hare Valley very early in the nineteenth century, or perhaps even earlier.

There was till no Methodist activity at all in Northampton County below Johnson's Chapel when Colbert began preaching and lodging in the home of Coventon Simpkins in Eastville. Simpkins, whose fine home, "Coventon," still stands in the village, was a trustee of Garrison's Chapel, but, like Belle Haven, Eastville was not receptive to Methodism. Colbert announced to the village that he would preach in the courthouse on January 10, 1795, but he left discouraged when not a soul showed up to hear him. By April he was drawing a small crowd, but they were merely "well-behaved," and far from excited about his preaching.

Colbert had better luck when Simpkins took him south to Cape Charles to visit his Simpkin's stepmother. Here in the Capeville area, in the vicinity of Lower Northampton Baptist Church, Colbert preached in a schoolhouse. It is apparent that Colbert himself founded the new society that sprang up here, and the Capeville congregation joined the list of Methodist preaching places, the southernmost on the Shore.

Finally, Colbert and Rowen opened up one more field of endeavor by accident. They set out together by boat from Hog Island to attend the Annual Conference in Philadelphia in September 1795, but fierce winds forced them ashore in the region of Wallops Island. Having made the decision to return to Northampton for their horses and finish the trip overland, they knocked at the first door to which they came to ask to borrow a horse for the journey to Northampton. The door at which they knocked was that of David Watt in the little settlement of Wattsville. Watt, they found, was a most congenial host who received them kindly. Soon his home, too, like so many others up and down the Shore, was being visited regularly by the circuit preachers, and from it grew the Wattsville congregation. [21]

On the Eastern Shore of Virginia the political revolution brought about by the War of Independence was followed swiftly by a religious revolution as two vigorous new faiths swept into the peninsula, the Baptists from the South and the Methodists from the North. To a degree never achieved by the Church of England, the two new churches made religion a vital force among the common people of the Shore, black and white. It is possible, in fact, that the quality and direction of life on the Shore was influenced more by this religious revolution than by the political one.

For two decades the Baptists and the Methodists fanned out across the peninsula, staking their claims to the area so lately ruled by the Church of England, and it is remarkable how little they came into contact with each other prior to 1800. Asbury's mention of the Baptists in the Capeville area and Colbert's chance meeting with George Layfield are almost the only indications we have that either knew the other existed. The Shore was ripe for harvest, and there was more than enough work to be done. For a time the two new faiths, similar in a number of ways, labored on almost oblivious to each other.

They were about equal in size and strength. The Baptists had more members—995 to the Methodists' 848 in 1792—but the Methodists could boast more congregations in more communities—eleven to the Baptists' six in 1795. The Methodists seem to have made the better showing among the black population. As Freeborn Garrettson noted, "Among other blessed effects of the Methodist ministry was the conversion of many of the colored people in that part of the country, both among the slaves, and those that were free..... To them particular attention was paid by the Methodist preachers." [22] The two new faiths together suffered a slight decline in membership beginning in 1795. The Methodist decline was the more serious; by 1799 membership in the two counties had dropped from a high of 865 to only 510.

The new faiths were similar in that in both of them a handful of preachers had charge of all the congregations until 1789, when a third Baptist preacher, John Elliott, became pastor at Red Bank (Pungoteague), relieving them of responsibility for that one church. [23] Similarly, the Methodists had only one, at the most two, preachers for all their churches up and down the Shore. These Methodist preachers were changed almost yearly.

But it was not for long that the two new faiths were to remain on such equal terms. The rivalry to win the Virginia Shore, whether or not it was a conscious rivalry at that point, was to be won decisively by the Methodists, and won in a relatively short time. Three factors combined to give the Methodists the victory over their Baptist rivals: theology, polity, and revival.

Theologically the Baptists and the Methodists were quite dissimilar, a fact which soon became clear to the people of the Shore and worked in favor of the Methodists. Although the Baptists aimed their message at the common people and worked among the common classes, theirs was not a faith for everyone. Instead, taking a nod from John Calvin, they taught that only the "elect" are saved, those persons preordained by God from the beginning of time. "Election," the choice of who was to be saved, was of God and not of men, said the Baptists with great conviction, and the elect, bound together by the symbol of baptism that gave them their name, constituted a church which stood in some sense apart from the rest of the world, its separateness a status to be carefully defined and jealously guarded. Baptists on the Shore, like Baptists across the state, were uncompromising on this doctrine of election in the years after the Revolution, and the result was that the initial vigorous growth of the movement was soon blunted. [24]

Methodism, on the other hand, entered the Shore with a theology more likely to win adherents. Its doctrines were both simple and democratic. Salvation was not dependent upon assent to carefully defined theological points, but upon a personal religious experience which was available to everyone. God's grace was extended not just to the elect, but to all people, and all anyone had to do to receive it was to respond to it and live the proper Christian life. Many a Methodist sermon of the period rested on three main points: that God's grace is free to all; that man is free to accept or reject it; and that man, once he has accepted it, can in this life "go on to perfection" and reach that state wherein he will be free from willful sin. [25] The Methodists were not so likely as the Baptists to stand apart from society or other churches, and characteristically exhibited a much more open attitude toward differences of opinion and varieties of doctrine.

Another factor that worked in favor of the Methodists was their polity and organization, a gift from the founder, John Wesley. The Baptists constituted a congregational system; each separate congregation was independent, a little democracy with no one over it to govern or control it. When it came to finding and supporting a minister, then, each church was on its own. The little churches of the Shore faced many struggles in their early years to obtain ministers and to keep them, and suffered through a number of undesirable pastors because they received no help from elsewhere in getting good ones. [26]

The Methodists on the other hand, were part of a highly connectional system that led all the way back to John Wesley himself, until his death in 1791. Methodist congregations were far from independent; authority in their system proceeded from the top downward. But the authority that was there to direct proved a positive force when it came to obtaining and supporting a minister, and the local Methodist congregations on the Shore were rarely if ever without the ministry of their own clergymen.

Central to the Methodist system was the conference, an idea deeply embedded in the movement from the very first. As conferences came into being, the Eastern Shore became a part of the Philadelphia Annual Conference and from that northerly direction received its pastors. Above the annual conferences was the General Conference, a national assembly of the church's ministers which met every four years. Each local congregation paralleled these bodies with its own conference, in our own day called the Charge Conference but in those days known as the Quarterly Meeting. As its name suggests, it met four times a year, and it was the organizational backbone of the local church.

The Quarterly Meeting was a time of high spiritual and social excitement for the early Methodists of the Eastern Shore. On these occasions, which lasted for a day or more, the entire circuit descended upon one of the larger churches—usually Downing's or Garrison's—for business, preaching, love feast, sacrament, and general sharing. The first recorded Quarterly Meeting on the Virginia Shore was held at Garrison's in 1778, and Asbury was present. The next year the Quarterly Meeting was at Downing's, and it consisted of love feast followed by preaching and communion. Asbury was present on that occasion, too, and his journal describes the powerful scene: "The first day the Lord was powerfully present, and the people were greatly agitated. On the second day at the love feast and sacrament, there was a shout. And I believe two hundred souls praised God at one time. My soul was among them." [27]

The love feast practiced on these occasions was a form of worship that the early Methodists found readily adaptable to the local scene. Wesley adapted the love feast, or *agape,* from the Moravians, whom he greatly admired. It was a ritual meal not unlike the communion, usually using bread and water, but it was always understood to be different from and lesser than the sacrament of communion. It also included, as did most Methodist gatherings of the day, singing, exhortation, and testimonies, and it often ended with a collection for the poor. The love feast was used in the absence of the local circuit preacher, and it proved to be a powerful force in the local congregation. Gradually it evolved into a gathering of only the most faithful members, an intimate fellowship of the most fervent believers. Non-members and visitors were almost always excluded, and as time went on the Methodists began to issue tickets of admission to the love feast; only those who had attended worship and class meeting could be eligible for the love feast. The first recorded love feast on the Shore was at the home of William Paramore in 1787, and it was followed by the eucharist. [28]

Finally the local Methodist congregations benefited from an important institution now all but vanished from the church: the class meeting. No sooner was a Methodist society formed than the preacher divided it into "classes" of ten or twelve persons. Sometimes the society was so small that class and society were synonymous. The classes were empowered to meet weekly without the presence or direct oversight of the pastor, and weekly across the Shore, Methodists gathered in small groups for mutual sharing, testimony, and support. A Methodist society was understood to be "a company of men having the form and seeking the power of godliness, united in order to pray together, to receive the word of exhortation, and to watch over one another in love, that they may help each other to work out their own salvation." More often than not it was in the weekly class meeting, rather than in a regularly scheduled worship service conducted by the circuit preacher, that the Methodist of the Shore attacked the task of "working out his own salvation." Here, under the watchful and often stern eye of the "class leader," Methodists shared their daily joys and woes, victories and temptations, testifying to the goodness of the Lord when times were good, receiving the loving rebuke of their fellows when they strayed from the straight and narrow. The tone of the class meeting was as serious as its setting was informal, and the sharing so intimate that at least during the year 1791 the local class meetings were divided into all-male and all-female groups called "bands."[29]

In these three practices—the Quarterly Meeting for organization and business affairs, the love feast for worship, and the class meeting for spiritual development—Methodism found a good part of the strength that led it to supremacy on the Eastern Shore. That Asbury considered these "disciplines" almost heaven-sent is suggested from a notation in his journal, written in Drummondtown in 1790: "We must continue to observe the order of God and our own discipline: attend to preaching, prayer, class meeting, and love feast. And then if they will shout, why let them shout!"[30]

The third factor that delivered the Eastern Shore of Virginia to the Methodists instead of to the Baptists was a great revival that broke out in Accomack County in 1800.

By 1799 the Baptists and the Methodists were still in competition, but despite their more appealing doctrines and their good local organization and discipline, the Methodists were falling behind their rivals in actual membership. In May 1799, Bishop Asbury touched briefly again on the Shore, his first visit since 1793. This visit proved to be an unpleasant experience. As he was riding south from Salisbury to Annemessex, his horse began to sweat, then to swell, then to tremble, and finally it fell over dead in the middle of the road. In Annemessex the Bishop borrowed another horse and kept going. In Newtown someone slipped $45 into his hand, and although he was not one to worry or complain about money as a rule, he wrote dejectedly in his journal that night: "It would have been a wonder for me to have as much money by me, but one hundred [dollars] or more might be needful to purchase another horse."

The next day he arrived and spoke at Downing's Chapel, where he met up with William Hardesty, the circuit preacher of the now fewer than 600 Methodists in the two counties. Together the two men set out for Philadelphia and the Annual Conference. Asbury surrendered his borrowed horse in Newtown, and "the only alternative was to put brother Hardesty's horse in the sulky and wedge ourselves with all our baggage together." Thus the two men rode north. [31]

Francis Asbury would not return to the Eastern Shore of Virginia for three years. When next he would cross the boundary from Maryland, the Shore would be ablaze with revival, and Methodism would be without a doubt the dominant faith on the peninsula.

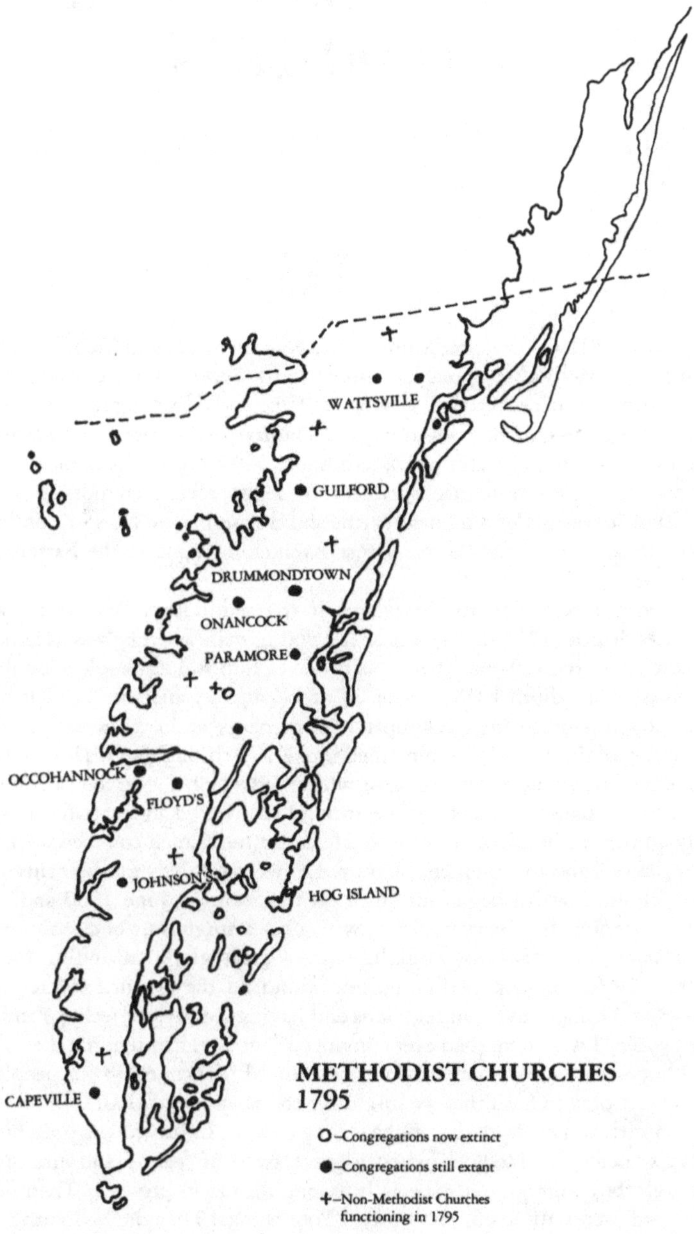
WATTSVILLE
GUILFORD
DRUMMONDTOWN
ONANCOCK
PARAMORE
OCCOHANNOCK
FLOYD'S
JOHNSON'S
HOG ISLAND
CAPEVILLE
METHODIST CHURCHES
1795
O –Congregations now extinct
● –Congregations still extant
+ –Non-Methodist Churches functioning in 1795

The Great Revival 1800-1814

III

In 1800 two new circuit preachers, Nathan Swain and Thomas Smith, were sent by the Methodist Episcopal Church to the Shore. Of the two, Nathan Swain faded into a quick obscurity, serving his time and departing for greener pastures and leaving little mark. His colleague, Thomas Smith, however, was to become one of the greatest figures of Eastern Shore Methodism, his name remembered with reverence for more than a century, his legacy alive even today.

For it was under Thomas Smith, and due in part to his spirit and abilities, that the revivals of the Second Great Awakening came to the Eastern Shore of Virginia.

Born in Kent County, Maryland, in the year independence was proclaimed, Thomas Smith (1776-1844) was still a young man when he was assigned to the Accomack Circuit. What there was to see of him was agreeable enough but not impressive: medium height, neat in dress, an easy manner. And if he lacked anything in stature, he made up for it in energy and enthusiasm. A thorough going son of the revival who remained unmarried throughout his life—"I have not the time," he would answer to those who asked why he never took a wife—he was a passionate man who had been spectacularly converted and who in turn spectacularly converted hundreds of others. He could move men to repentance from his own sickbed and in a moment be moved to weep publicly for their sins.

Thomas Smith began his work on the Shore in June 1800 and made the rounds among the several societies with only a single suit of clothes, a Bible, a hymnbook, and his horse. But he sense a great glory impending for his new charge. "After having performed one round on the circuit, and reviewed the classes and leaders and congregations and having learned the feelings and views of the people, I was more than ever convinced that God had sent me there, and that all I hoped for would sooner or later be realized. I encouraged our people to look for it, and pray in faith that we might see the salvation of God." [1]

Smith and his flock did not have long to wait. In July he was preaching to the Floyd's society in Hadlock when a great swell of feeling and emotion swept through the congregation, especially among the blacks present. "Their sable faces were bedewed with tears," he wrote. "Poor things! They did halloo and weep for their sins. Some found mercy."

Smith found Johnson's Chapel, the next church to the south, cold. Hungars Episcopal Church was still closed, and Smith blamed the lack of enthusiasm here on "the rich and the gay [who] assemble with us. Our Zion here is sickly; many are turned aside to worldly vanities," he wrote, and when his preaching fell on "unbroken ground," Smith "returned...to my chamber and wept, because I saw no fruit of my labor." Eastville, likewise, proved indifferent to Smith's excited preaching.

But gradually the northern half of the circuit began to stir. In September Smith's service at Floyd's ended in a great shout, and another meeting there a little later lasted "from 10 o'clock in the morning until 2 the next morning. During that day and night there were many souls born again and translated from the power of darkness into the kingdom of God's dear Son." In the homes on Ames Ridge, Smith's sermons began to have spectacular effect; eleven were converted there in one day, seven the next. "There was a great shout.... . Our societies are getting so large I know not how we are to meet them." At Thomas Ames' house "the crowd was so great we knew not where to put the people..... I preached, and the Lord worked for his own glory—truly it was one of the days of the Son of Man. The people fell to the floor in all directions, and cries for mercy went to heaven on every breath."

Within a short time the excitement had spread north to the Onancock society. By the time the circuit gathered for the Quarterly Meeting in March 1801, the crowds that were coming to hear Smith preach numbered as many as 3000. [2]

It was in Guilford that one of the most spectacular chapters of the revival unfolded. There, in the new meetinghouse only recently constructed, Smith and the presiding elder, Thomas Ware, began a meeting on April 1, 1801, and Smith's journal describes the events that happened there:

> *My appointment was at Guilford. I prevailed on brother Ware to go with me and preach. It was a time long to be remembered. The sky was clear, the sun was bright, and nature seemed smiling all around.*
>
> *When we arrived at Guilford the meetinghouse was already filled,* and hundreds were seated in the yard outside for want of room in the house. At ten o'clock brother Ware took the stand, and the meeting lasted six hours. Ministers and members were astonished at the power of Israel's God. The people were falling in all directions, indoors and without. The place was gloriously awful. Sudden and powerful were the awakenings, and sudden and powerful the conversions. Clouds of mercy overshadowed the place, and shower after shower descended. Parents were seen looking up their children and praying over them, and children were holding on to their parents crying, "O papa, come to Jesus! God will bless you!" and such crying for mercy and shouts of joy surely Virginia never heard before!*

At four in the afternoon 44 new members were received into the Guilford society, and the meeting was only getting started. Night was coming on, and

---

*According to local tradition, the old meetinghouse held about 100 people, with room for another fifty or so in the slaves' gallery.

THOMAS WARE

Presiding Elder during the Great Revival of 1800-1801; his preaching at Guilford initiated the revival there and resulted in 44 conversions in one day.

since there were no lights in the meetinghouse the congregation adjourned to the home of Thomas Evans and kept going until sunrise the next day.

"How many souls were converted that night," wrote Smith, "is a secret that we must leave until the resurrection morning reveals it!"

The excitement that Smith has unleashed at Guilford did not fade quickly. And when a second revival was held there the following year, in March 1802, the "sinners lay weeping on the floor until converted in large numbers." [3]

It was an excitement felt across the Shore, even by the non-churchly who were sometimes repelled by it. Ware's preaching offended four young men at the March 1801 Quarterly Meeting in Drummondtown, and they rudely stomped out of the church and stationed themselves at the door to have it out with the preacher after the service. When the meeting broke up, Smith passed out of the door between them, "brushing their clothes, and [seeing] their clubs," but no incident occurred.

A week later, however, Smith again ran into the four young men when he was riding away from the successful Guilford revival. Certain that they had "bound themselves under an oath that they would spill my blood that day for insulting them...at quarterly meeting," he approached them in fear and trembling. "On rising a hill I saw them in the road before me, with clubs in their hands, and seeing no way to escape, I said, 'Lord, what shall I do? I will put my trust in thee.' "

Smith set his horse to a full trot and rode straight at the men, who parted and let him pass between them at full steam. Once past them, he caught wind of their heated words with each other:

"Damn you, why didn't you knock him down?"

"Damn you, why didn't *you* knock him down?"

"Thus while they raved and swore at each other," wrote Smith, "I happily escaped as a bird out of the snare of the fowler." And he rode on to his next appointment, the revival all the while increasing.[4]

The most important phase of Thomas Smith's revival occurred even before the Guilford phase, in the center of the Shore in the region of Pungoteague and Burton's.

In the fall of 1800 Smith called a camp meeting in the Pungoteague area, a community where there was as yet no Methodist activity. Pungoteague, apparently, was a special concern to Smith, "a place so recently overrun with vice," he called it, " and where Satan's seat was." "Satan's seat" of opposition to the Methodist revival was what Smith called St. George's Episcopal Church, at the time the strongest Episcopal church on the Shore, under the able pastor, Cave Jones. It was hard going for Smith in this conservative, Episcopalian community, and the crowds that came to his camp meeting were small. He was determined to bring the revival to Pungoteague, however, and kept at it. By December, when he conducted a two-day meeting there, there were so many in attendance that it became necessary, for want of a church building, to rent a large warehouse for a night meeting. Here at last the revival broke out with excitement and several successful converions, and when the Methodists reconvened the next morning someone had tacked a note on the door of the building that read:

"I think that it is enough
To make the Devil stare
To see the warehouse
Become a house of prayer."

Rector Cave Jones was not one to take this Methodist invasion of his parish lightly. When some of the local Episcopalians became swept up in the revival excitement and joined the Methodists, he announced that on Christmas Day he would preach "the funeral sermon of the Methodists in Accomack County."

Thus far Smith's revival and Methodism throughout its course on the Virginia Shore had met with no real opposition from the Episcopal Church, and this show of resistance sent waves of alarm through the leading local Methodists. Cave Jones of St. George's was, after all, an opponent of no mean ability. William Paramore and others called upon Smith to invite the erudite Bishop Thomas Coke to appear in behalf of the Methodists, but Smith was confident and would have none of that. "We have a more powerful and eloquent advocate than Dr. Coke," he replied. "Be of good cheer! Our cause is in God's hands, and He will take care of it."

On Christmas Day 1800 the crowd at St. George's Episcopal Church was large and excited, and they were not disappointed. The rector delivered an eloquent address denouncing the Methodists, turning most of his sermon against

Wesley and his lack of authority to ordain ministers for the Methodist societies. The meeting closed without incident, although not until the rector poured "all the odium possible upon the Methodist Church, and especially upon the ministry."

Little did Jones realize, however, the extent to which his defense of Episcopalianism had backfired. One of the foremost of his parishioners who sat there that day was Captain Thomas Burton, the same Burton who had so warmly received Francis Asbury in his home between 1784 and 1788. What happened to create a rift between Burton and Asbury in 1788 is not known, but in the twelve succeeding years Burton had become not only a staunch Episcopalian, but an avid anti-Methodist as well. A well-to-do member of the gentry who fully enjoyed his worldly pleasures—Methodists often commented upon his love of fox-hunting—Burton had little patience with Methodist revivalism, refused to allow his servants to attend Methodist meetings, and had long since become "a Saul of Tarsus to the Methodists."

But Jones' Christmas sermon against the Methodists set at work something in Burton. He returned home from St. George's moody and depressed and remained so for three days. When Mrs. Burton asked him the cause of his distress, he announced his opinion of the Methodists changed altogether: it was they who had been right and he who had been wrong all along. He had persecuted them and maligned them unjustly. And he sent a servant off with a note to Thomas Smith, inviting him into his home for conversation.

Smith received the invitation with some apprehension; he, too, knew Burton as something less than a supporter of Methodism. When he consulted Paramore about whether to respond, Paramore exclaimed, "What can be the matter at Captain Burton's! Go, by all means! He is a gentleman, and his invitation insures you of a kind reception."

The next day Smith visited Burton, and the two talked at length. Burton plied Smith with questions about Methodism, and was relieved to receive Smith's assurances that the differences between the two faiths involved matters of polity more than matters of doctrine. Smith left Burton's home with an invitation to preach there on New Year's Day, and when Burton announced to the surrounding community that he had once again opened his home to Methodist preachers, the effect was electric.

On New Year's Day 1801 at 3:00 in the afternoon, Thomas Smith stood in the doorway of Burton's home and began his service by lining out the Wesleyan hymn, *"O For a Thousand Tongues to Sing."* He offered prayer, announced his text (Romans 16:20; "The peace of God will bruise Satan under your feet......"), and had hardly begun his sermon when the revival excitement and the conversions struck. "Before the sun rose the next day the enemy's flag was struck, and the banner of Jesus Christ was waving there." The revival at Burton's house continued uninterrupted for thirteen days. "In the house, in the yard, in the quarters, in groups in the fields, and along the roadside, the revival went on until it finally closed for lack of physical strength on the part of the participants."

On January 13, 1801, Thomas Smith formed a class of fifty new Methodists,

MEMORIAL WINDOW, OAK GROVE CHURCH (1871)

Oak Grove Church is the third building of the Burton's congregation. The main memorial window honors Thomas Smith, Thomas Burton, and William Elliott. The top part of the window reads from the outside of the building, the bottom portion from the inside.

and Captain and Mrs. Burton were at the head of the list. A second class of forty, mostly slaves on the Burton plantation, was formed shortly thereafter. Throughout the remainder of winter, weekly meetings continued in Burton's house. In the summer they moved to his barn, and in the fall the community united with him in the erection of a larger bower in the yard, under which an eleven-year-old named Jonathan Smith, later to become a beloved local preacher, was converted. Within a year the crowds had so outgrown the ability of Burton's home to handle them that he gave an acre of land across the road from his gate for a church. A building was erected there soon afterwards, and Burton proposed that the church be called New Friendship. The congregation voted him down; it became Burton's Chapel. His was the only dissenting vote. [6]

What happened at Guilford and Burton's was felt in virtually every community in Accomack County where there was a Methodist society. The home of William Paramore near Locustville had been a preaching point since Asbury's initial visits to the Shore, but by 1801 as many as 500 people were gathering there to hear Thomas Smith. Like the Burton's society, Paramore's also moved out into the yard under a bower during the summer. [7]

Even the outlying islands felt the revival. One member of the Hog Island society, Stephen Fletcher, happened to be on the mainland during the time of the excitement, and he insisted that Thomas Smith accompany him home to the island. There, too, Smith's preaching had great effect, and within a short time the whole community was brimming with religious enthusiasm. Among the austere islanders the revival seemed to have the same effect that Jonathan Edwards had noticed among the people of Northampton in Massachusetts years earlier; it completely transformed the community. What had been a rollicking sea town became a strict, Sabbath-abiding village. And the Methodist society there grew. While he was circuit preacher Thomas Smith nurtured the Hog Island congregation well, but apparently his successors found it too remote to give it much of their time. The island produced its own leadership, however, in the person of Isma Fletcher, who reached the status of exhorter and remained the principal pillar of the church for decades. [8]

Meanwhile up and down the Shore the picture was much the same. At Downing's Chapel "God's spirit passed sweetly over." At Garrison's Chapel "divine grace [was] powerfully manifested." "Heavenly fire ran from heart to heart when services were held at Brother David Watts'," and "God's banner waved triumphantly over Onancock." It is not unlikely that the society at Horntown in northern Accomack was founded during the revival. [9]

It was only on the opposite end of the Shore, in Northampton County below Floyd's Meetinghouse, that the revival did not occur. Johnson's and Eastville remained "unimpressed," and there is no mention at all that the revival was felt at the southernmost society, Capeville.

But in the two short years that Thomas Smith was the minister on the Eastern Shore of Virginia, a revival erupting in community after community brought thousands, black and white, into a direct religious experience. Before the revival, Methodists had numbered their crowds by the hundreds and their members by the score. Smith's two years on the Shore changed that. In 1801 he preached to a crowd of 4000 at Garrison's Chapel, and in the two years of his ministry a total of 1090 persons joined the Methodist Episcopal Church on the Eastern Shore of Virginia. The entire population of the Shore at that time was less than 23,000, [10] and because of the strict requirements for membership in the church at that time the membership figure is far lower than the actual number of people who worshiped with the Methodists and considered themselves a part of the church.

Just across the line in Maryland the picture was much the same. "The peninsula was a garden of God," and in the general revival that was sweeping the entire Shore over 1600 people joined the church in Sussex County, Delaware, 1000 in Talbot, and 1000 in Somerset County. The Annemessex preacher in 1801 was William Colbert, a familiar figure to Virginians, and his report for that year was almost ecstatic:

> *Good news from Pocomoke! The kingdom of Hell is falling, the borders of Zion are enlarging, and glory to God the prospect of a greater work than we had last year lies before us.... I believe the Peninsula has never known such a time as heaven now favors us with. Glory to Jesus on high! We have what is the most inviting among us, namely the Lord in power converting sinners, and the saints feel as if they were sunning in the beams of redeeming love, overwhelmed with glorious billows. Some fall motionless, and lie for some minutes, others for hours, and some for a great part of the night without the use of their limbs or speech, and then they spring up with heaven in their eyes and music on their tongues, overwhelmed with love divine. O glory to God! This work makes Pocomoke swamps like a blooming paradise to my soul....*
> *To God be all the praise!"*

While Thomas Smith was fanning the fires of revival on the Eastern Shore in 1800 and 1801, Francis Asbury was absent from the scene, molding the Methodist movement into a national church. In the spring of 1802, Asbury again touched the northern end of the Shore, his first visit since 1799. He preached at Downing's, Drummondtown, and Wattsville, and found the congregations much larger than before. "We have a most pleasing prospect in Accomack," he wrote; "a general revival is going through the country. [12]

The Methodist Episcopal Church was by now so large that a new office, that of presiding elder, had been created to help the bishops by overseeing "districts" within the annual conferences. In 1803, Dr. William P. Chandler was appointed presiding elder of the Delaware and Eastern Shore District, and on the shoulders of this renowned evangelist fell the revival mantle of Thomas Smith.

William Chandler (1764-1822), called "Doctor" because he had studied with the famous physician, Dr. Benjamin Rush, before giving up all else for the ministry in 1797, was an eloquent preacher and an effective revivalist. During the first Great Awakening in Jonathan Edwards' day, revival had been "the surprising work of God," something that happened to a completely surprised and unsuspecting people. Chandler was one of those who now, in the Second Great Awakening, advocated the use of human "means" to initiate and promote revival, confident that the event of revival feeling carried the surviving grace of God no matter how it was induced. To Chandler belongs, it is said, the distinction of having been the first to employ the "altar call," at a revival on the Eastern Shore of Maryland in 1799. Prior to that time worshipers struck by the conviction of sin during a service prayed aloud for forgiveness from wherever they happened to be seated. The altar call eliminated that kind of confusion and was quickly adopted as a standard revival practice. By 1801 the innovation had reached Philadelphia, by 1806, New York. And when its originator took up his work on the Virginia Shore in 1803, Methodists of the two counties took eagerly to the practice of "going forward" during the altar call at the end of the meeting. [13]

As presiding elder, Chandler had, however, an even more potent new "means" to introduce, the camp meeting. The camp meeting was still an innovation when Chandler brought it to the Shore. Though there had been outdoor preaching ever since the Great Awakening, it was not until 1799 that the churches tried an outdoor encampment of several days. Introduced with success at Cane Ridge in Kentucky in that year, the camp meeting idea spread rapidly in all directions. Thomas Smith is said to have conducted a camp meeting in Pungoteague in the fall of 1800. If his campaign there involved an actual camp meeting, not just a series of outdoor services, Smith was a pioneer in his own right. But the real father of the camp meeting on the peninsula was William Chandler, who announced that the first one for the Virginia section of his district was to be held in the woods near Pungoteague in the summer of 1805.

The Pungoteague camp meeting was only one of several held on the Delmarva Peninsula in that year, and it created even more excitement than Thomas Smith's revival of a few years before. From as far away as Maryland, from Somerset and Annemessex, the people came in great numbers, faithful Methodists and the merely curious. In a clearing near the center of the woods near Pungoteague, the exact site long since forgotten (although it was apparently just a short walking distance from navigable water), they pitched their tents, forming a circle around a preaching platform large enough to accommodate half a dozen preachers. And on Thursday, August 29, 1805, the camp meeting began.

It was a great moment, and our chief account of it is from the pen of Henry Boehm, pastor of the Annemessex Circuit, who sat on the platform that day. "A great multitude attended this camp meeting," wrote Boehm, "and the ministers preached with the Holy Ghost sent down from heaven, and the arrows were very sharp in the hearts of the King's enemies." [14] But though Boehm sat there that day with Chandler and the other pastors, including James Aikens, the circuit preacher, he was almost certainly overshadowed by another preacher who, by chance, happened also to be present. The most memorable figure on the platform that day was Lorenzo Dow, a man they tell tales about on the Eastern Shore.

HENRY BOEHM

Lorenzo Dow (1777-1834) was a Methodist preacher so remarkable and unusual that his contemporaries thought him "certainly eccentric, probably a crank, and possibly insane." "Crazy Dow" he was sometimes called, and his Methodist superiors and colleagues were among those apt to give him that name, because he was something of a continuing embarrassment to Asbury and the presiding elders. A native of Vermont, Dow simply would not stick to the circuit assigned him by the bishop, but preferred instead to take sudden missionary journeys to far-off fields. His first ministerial appointment was in his native New England, and he left it suddenly and without the bishop's approval or knowledge to journey to England to preach the Word. When he returned to America, the Methodists assigned him another circuit, only to have him leave a second time, this time for a preaching tour of the South. It was while he was traveling south, preaching on the way, that he found himself in Accomack County just as, in 1805, Chandler and his ministers were completing plans for the Pungoteague camp meeting. [15]

In a day known for its exciting preaching, Dow was among the most remarkable and eccentric of preachers. The most famous story about him is said to have happened near Newtown (Pocomoke City), Maryland, although many other localities also lay claim to the incident. On his way to a preaching engagement, he ran into a little black boy named Gabriel, who happened to be carrying a tin horn. A Gabriel with a horn was too much to pass up, so Dow gave the boy a dollar and promised him another if he would hide in the limbs of a tree in front of the meetinghouse and sit there without a sound until Dow shouted out, "Blow, Gabriel!"

"When I say, 'Blow, Gabriel!' ", Dow told him, "then you blow!"

As Dow had hoped, the meeting took place in the yard in front of the church, and he preached vigorously on the Day of Judgment. Working up to his climax, he had the congregation in the palm of his hand as he described that day when Gabriel, one foot on land and one on sea, would raise the silver trumpet to his lips. "Blow, Gabriel!" Dow shouted. And little Gabriel in the tree blew.

The effect on the congregation was immense. They fell to the ground and wept and wailed for their sins until someone discovered the little black boy up in the tree, and everyone turned to scowl at the preacher.

Dow was undaunted. "If a little boy can strike such terror into your hearts," he shouted, "what will you do when the great day really comes?" [16]

Even if that story is only a tale, as seems likely, Lorenzo Dow was a memorable preacher. He himself records how he surprised a Delaware congregation just a few days before his arrival on the Virginia Shore. He preached his sermon, ended it, turned quickly, and leapt out the pulpit window onto the back of his horse and rode off to meet his next engagement. [17]

His fame went before him, and there was no way Chandler could avoid inviting him to speak at the first camp meeting on the Eastern Shore of Virginia. Dow records the moment in his own journal:

LORENZO DOW

> *I stood up to speak on sanctification. About 3000 rose up in covenant, sundry of whom came up to be prayed for, and among them three young women, two of whom were prayerless three days before..... One of them found pardon in a few minutes, and shouted praise of God. The other was delivered shortly, and the third, who owned the campground, found deliverance that night. Thus the work went on, so that there could be no preaching until ten the next day, though [the] meeting had been appointed for eight at night and morning. When I left the place, the rain impeded the meeting, yet it continued until Monday. And on a moderate calculation, there was reason to believe that about 500 were hopefully converted.*[18]

Dow's "moderate calculation"—3000 in attendance, 500 converted—is substantiated by other writers. Three accounts of the 1805 camp meeting have survived, and all give substantially the same figures. Boehm of Annemessex states, "it was the opinion of the preachers and others who took pains to ascertain that four hundred whites and over one hundred and fifty blacks were converted. The work went on day and night without intermission from Thursday till Monday." [19]

One man who heard Dow speak that day was soon to be profoundly influenced by the revival experience, and was himself in his turn profoundly to influence the course of revival on his native Eastern Shore. Joshua Thomas, a boatman from Tangier Island in the Chesapeake, was present at the camp meeting, not because he was interested in the event himself, but because some Marylanders had hired him to ferry them across to Pungoteague. Joshua Thomas described the same scene as it looked, not from the preachers' platform, but from the congregation's rough benches:

> *There were a great many tents in a circle round, and seats made for people to sit on. There was a place built up with boards for the preacher to stand when he preached, and a great crowd of people moving about and talking together, while some were sitting in tents singing like the people on board the vessels.*
>
> *Everyone appeared glad to see us, and shook hands with us, inviting us to stay with them during the meeting. Pretty soon they had preaching, and the most singular looking man I ever saw was the preacher that time. His name was Lorenzo Dow, and it was while he was preaching...[that] a woman became happy and shouted aloud, when he said 'The Lord is here! He is with that sister!' I jumped up to see him if he was there, but could not see anything extraordinary except the woman clapping her hands and saying 'Glory! Glory!' A great many people commenced crying and some fell to the ground, others were talking to them, and telling them to look to Jesus, and it was very soon a time of great confusion.*[20]

Within a year the skeptical Joshua Thomas was himself converted at just such a camp meeting, and launched on his career as the greatest local preacher the Eastern Shore ever produced.

Bishop Asbury had a way of being absent from the Eastern Shore of Virginia during the big events, and he missed the excitement of the Pungoteague camp meeting just as he had missed Thomas Smith's revival. But early the next year he was back on his twelfth visit to the Shore, preaching at Downing's Chapel, Wattsville, and Drummondtown. In the cool of early spring it must have seemed as if the great camp meeting they were telling him about had passed with little effect. "I preached in the court house, Accomac," the bishop wrote. " It was an alarming season. The cold was great; and the winds are high. No rain—it is judgment weather—O Lord, arise!" [21]

But four months later, in the heat of summer, the Methodists opened their second Pungoteague camp meeting, and the excitement again broke loose.

Henry Boehm of Annemessex was again on hand to record the event:

> *On the 31st of July, I left home for a camp meeting in Virginia.... . On Thursday morning our camp meeting commenced, and the work of God broke out in several tents before a single sermon was preached. In the evening Alward White preached from Psalm 43, 'My tears have been my meat day and night.' The work went on all night..... On Tuesday morning [five days later] the Lord's Supper was administered after which we had our Christian parting..... The number of conversions reported in the [whole] course of the meeting was over nine hundred.* [22]

But on Friday, the second day, a violent incident marred the progress of the camp meeting. As Boehm put it, "the sons of Belial made a great stir and for a time somewhat hindered the progress of the work." While one of the several ministers was preaching on the lecture stand, his colleagues seated behind him and the congregation before him attentive to his words, a crowd, many of them merely curious, milled around the edge of the congregation. One man in the crowd, a man named Mr. Oliver, lit up a smoke. Camp rules explicitly forbade smoking, and so the preachers on the platform dispatched one of their number, John Chambers, a visiting preacher from Baltimore, to deal directly with the smoker. The speaker continued his sermon from the pulpit while Chambers walked over to Oliver and asked him to cease from this flagrant violation of the rules. Soon harsh words from Oliver's friends drifted out over the congregation, and as heads began to turn in that direction an unidentified fist flew out and struck Chambers to the ground.

Within a matter of seconds the Methodists from the congregation had closed in around Chambers' assailants, and a fist fight appeared to be in the making. Chambers, blood streaming down his face, stood up and shouted out "a powerful sermon" to restrain the congregation, but several scuffles began and the whole meeting disintegrated into a brawl. The Methodists succeeded in subduing young James Kellam, Chambers' alleged assailant, and tied him hand and foot. His friends, greatly outnumbered, mustered their forces around the edge of the camp and continued to threaten the crowd with a general attack if Kellam were not soon released. And under these tense conditions, preaching from the platform resumed.

Kellam spent the night bound and heavily guarded, and it was not until morning of the third day that things quieted down and the Methodists regained control of the situation. Early that morning Kellam was brought before the injured Chambers to be identified, and it was then that Chambers informed the horrified Methodists that he was not the culprit. Kellam was quickly released, but the Methodists found to their regret that he was a young man with connections. Later that morning the local sheriff arrived at the campgrounds with a posse and placed William Chandler, William Seymour of Onancock, and several other Methodist leaders under arrest for breach of peace and false arrest. They paid a fine and were quickly released, and the meeting was allowed to continue. [23]

Even these events did not long hinder the progress of revival. "There were two hundred and sixty-three conversions and one hundred and twenty-three reported to have been sanctified during the day and night," reported Boehm. [24]

Wrote Francis Asbury in Pennsylvania when he heard the news: "All earth and hell is roused against field {camp} meetings, but we will endure fines, imprisonment, and death sooner than we will give them up. We have $25 to pay on the Eastern Shore of Virginia—no law, no justice for Methodists!" [25]

Not long after he had heard Lorenzo Dow at Pungoteague in 1805, Joshua Thomas decided to attend another camp meeting, this one in Annemessex. Although all he had seen at Pungoteague did not convince him, he was intrigued by what he had seen, by how the Marylanders in his boat had sung songs of joy all the way, by the atmosphere of joy and friendliness that pervaded the entire camp.

His revered old uncle advised him to stay away from any more camp meetings. "If you go there," he told Joshua, "they will have you down to worship them. They are nothing but a parcel of Irishmen who have run away from their own country to keep from being hanged. They have great *larning,* and they know no other way to get a living but going about raising the devil by their preaching and carrying on."

"No, uncle," Joshua replied, "they will not get me down to worship them!"

And off he went to Annemessex.

On Saturday night at the campgrounds Joshua's companion, John Parks, who, like Joshua, had been skeptical of everything he had seen and heard so far, was converted. Joshua, too, began to be moved. "I then began to feel very uneasy," he recalled, "and much concerned about being changed in heart."

> *I felt so bad on Saturday night that I concluded I would go and kneel down with them at the mourners' seat and try it once, determined that I would not fall nor cry out as I had heard and seen others do. When praying persons came to talk with me, I would not let them, but rudely elbowed them off. I staid their some time, trying to pray secretly, until I became discouraged and concluded there was no reality in being converted, and so I arose and went*

away.

On Sunday morning there was a great meeting, and many professed to be born from above. They shouted all over the ground, and many fell and lay as dead on the earth. When they recovered, they began to praise God wonderfully. I watched all this, and thought much upon the scenes I had witnessed.

Having observed the strange occurrences that seemed to accompany conversion, Joshua decided to put them to the test:

I went away into the woods again, a great way from the camp, the crowd, and noise, and tried harder than ever to pray and get the blessing of a new heart there alone. After struggling a long time in prayer, and receiving no answer, I concluded I would try what virtue there was in falling*! So I looked me out a smooth place that was free from roots and sticks that I might not hurt myself in the fall, and kept my eye a little over one shoulder to see how to fall and not hurt myself: I then came down full length on the earth. I lay about ten minutes, praying to God to convert me there; and receiving no answer, I arose completely discouraged, and very impatient besides.*

It was only during the last sermon of the camp meeting that something happened to Joshua Thomas:

I obtained faith that I should be converted.... . I felt something drawing me right to the feet of Jesus. Immediately on the invitation being given, I went to the altar, and kneeled down and began to lift up my voice in earnest prayer.

And so in 1805, at the age of 29, Joshua Thomas was converted:

I was so filled with the spirit of life and love I could not help shouting to the glory of God with all my might.... . I went all over the campground in this way, telling everybody what a happy change I had experienced, and urging them to pray for it immediately. The whole night I spent in this manner, and sinners fell in heaps in different parts of the camp, crying to God for deliverance. A great many were converted that night.[26]

Joshua Thomas was to become the first great preacher the Eastern Shore of Virginia produced, and he began his ministry immediately after his conversion. He returned home to Tangier and immediately, with the help of his wife and John Crockett, arranged for a prayer meeting in Crockett's home. John Parks opened the meeting with the first extemporaneous public prayer ever offered on the island. At this first meeting two were converted, and from Crockett's house revival spread across the island. The converts set aside a different house to meet in each week, and regular worship services were held on Sundays. The little society grew and prospered quite apart from the regular circuit ministers on the mainland. Joshua himself, completely without learning or authority from the denomination, exhorted at the meetings. It was not until he returned from the mainland one day with a single hymnbook that the little group learned to sing. [27]

For three years the Tangier society met in this fashion. Then in 1808 two local preachers from Onancock, William Seymour and William Lee, crossed over to the island, pitched a tent in a grove of trees near Thomas Crockett's house on the south end of the island, and sent out the news up and down the bay and especially over to Smith Island to the north that a camp meeting was about to open on Tangier Island.

According to Joshua Thomas, the day of that camp meeting was "the most glorious day the island people had ever seen. Indeed, it was like a paradise below—a heaven on earth." Eight or nine people were converted, and a general religious awakening, much greater than the little Methodist society of Joshua and his neighbors had yet been able to produce, swept across the island, changing Tangier as it had changed Northampton and Hog Island. Then and there Joshua Thomas decided that the Tangier camp meeting would be an annual affair.

And he saw to it that it was. Every summer with but one exception from 1808 to 1857 boats from all over Chesapeake Bay descended upon Tangier's south beach, and the faithful scrambled ashore for preaching. Within a few years' time the number of persons attending the Tangier camp meeting was far greater than that of the Pungoteague meetings. In one season's camp meeting as many as 10,000 people are said to have heard preaching on Tangier. [28]

Meanwhile Joshua Thomas had carried the gospel message north into the creeks and inlets and islands of the Maryland Shore, and was well on his way to becoming the beloved "Parson of the Islands."

It was only during the War of 1812 that the annual Tangier camp meeting was not held, and with good reason. In 1813 a British fleet under the command of Admiral George Cockburn sailed into Chesapeake Bay, debarked at Tangier, and began construction of two forts on the site of the campground. Cockburn declared the citizens of Tangier prisoners of war, and used their island as his base for sallying forth against American targets. It was from Tangier that his forces set out for Washington and captured it, forcing President Madison to flee from his burning capital. At another time Cockburn's ships sailed east to Accomack County, where they engaged in battle with Captain Finney and his local militia on Pungoteague Creek. One of the men in the militia that day was Garrison Burton, son of the Methodist Thomas Burton. [29]

In the summer of 1814 the news spread across the island that the British troops were preparing an expedition against Baltimore, and Joshua Thomas, the parson of the island, received an order from the admiral to preach to the forces on the campground before they left. The parson was not unknown to the admiral. Earlier that year the intrepid islander had boarded the flagship of the fleet and petitioned its commander, successfully, to restrain the troops from cutting down the trees that shaded the campground.

Joshua Thomas accepted his invitation to preach to the Redcoats with some trepidation:

> *I did not refuse, and yet I was very unwilling to perform this duty. I thought and prayed over the matter, and it came to me that I must stand up for Jesus as a good soldier in the fight of faith; and as some of these men might be killed in battle and never have another opportunity of worship, that it was my duty and privilege to obey their order and hold the meeting.*
>
> *At the hour appointed the soldiers were all drawn up in solid columns, about twelve thousand men, under the pines of the old campground, which form the open space in the center of their tents. I stood on a little platform erected at the end of the camp nearest the shore, all the men facing me with their hats off and held by the right hand under the left arm. An officer stood on my right and one on my left and sentries were stationed a little distance to the rear. As I looked around my congregation I never had such feelings in my life; but I felt determined to give them a faithful warning, even if those officers with those keen glittering swords would cut me in pieces for speaking the truth.*

JOSHUA THOMAS PREACHING TO THE BRITISH TROOPS, TANGIER ISLAND, 1814

So Joshua gave them a faithful warning, as he had given many an island audience a faithful warning. Many of them would not return to Tangier but would die in battle, he told them. They should all be prepared to meet their maker in judgment, he told them. And—it is said as if by a bolt from the blue it came to him—he told them as well that they would not succeed in taking Baltimore, but would be repulsed by the Americans and meet defeat. And although he had begun his sermon in fear and trembling, his fear left him as he preached. "I proceeded in my exhortation as freely as I ever did in any place or before any people."

But this congregation was different, as different to him as he was to them. Here was no cultured and educated minister, they must have thought; here was a simple, unlettered man exploding with ungrammatical excitement. And they were no multitude of heavy souls groaning under the conviction of sin, Joshua noticed, not ready to rise up and shout the praises of God. They stood at strict attention, unmoving and unmoved.

When the sermon was over there were no shouts, no tremblings, no groans, and no conversions. A few soldiers stepped forward to thank the parson, or to say that they hoped he was wrong about their Baltimore campaign. As Joshua turned his face toward home, they set sail for Baltimore.[30]

It was during the unsuccessful British attempt to take Baltimore that Francis Scott Key sat in one of the ships, watching the bombs explode harmlessly over Fort McHenry, and penned the words of the song that became the national anthem. It may be that Admiral Cockburn, watching his mission fail, remembered the fervent prophecy of the simple parson of the island. When dawn broke, Cockburn turned his fleet around, sailed out of Baltimore Harbor into Chesapeake Bay, back to Tangier Island, and ultimately away.

Joshua Thomas' part in the war had been small indeed, but it was a substantial feather in his cap, and within a short time the fame of the parson of the islands was spreading far and wide.

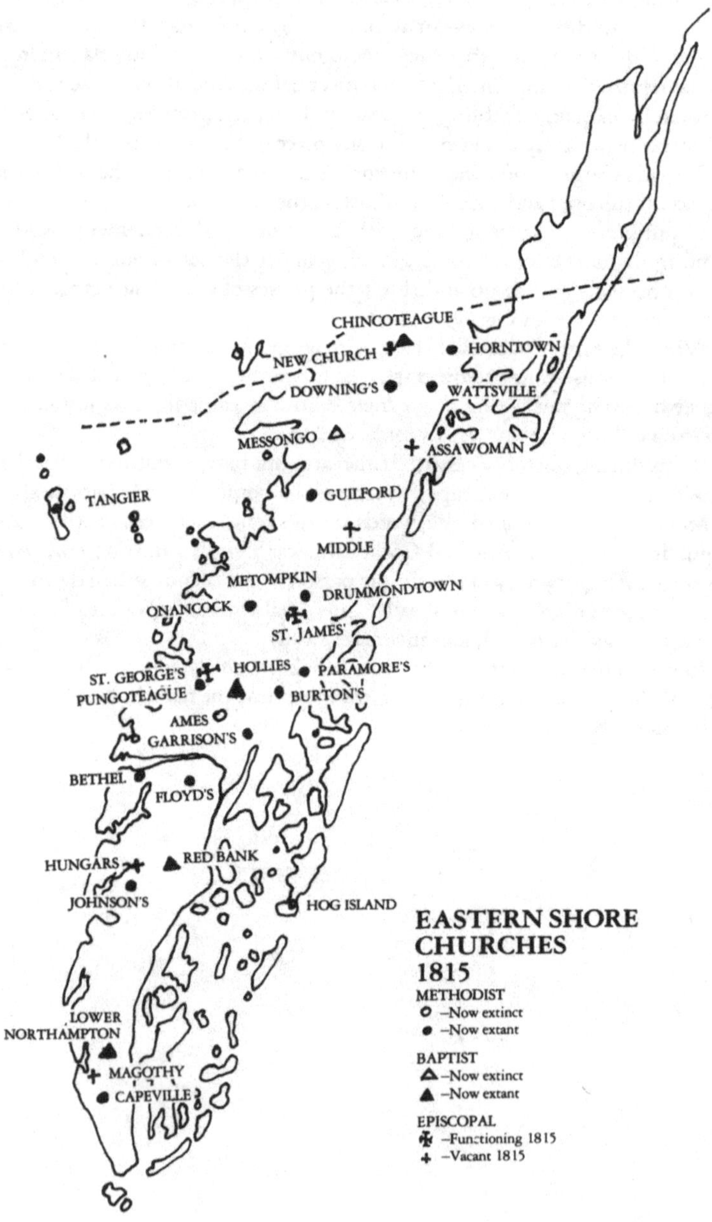
CHINCOTEAGUE
NEW CHURCH
HORNTOWN
DOWNING'S
WATTSVILLE
MESSONGO
ASSAWOMAN
TANGIER
GUILFORD
MIDDLE
METOMPKIN
DRUMMONDTOWN
ONANCOCK
ST. JAMES'
ST. GEORGE'S
HOLLIES
PARAMORE'S
PUNGOTEAGUE
BURTON'S
AMES
GARRISON'S
BETHEL
FLOYD'S
HUNGARS
RED BANK
JOHNSON'S
HOG ISLAND
LOWER NORTHAMPTON
MAGOTHY
CAPEVILLE
EASTERN SHORE CHURCHES 1815
METHODIST
–Now extinct
–Now extant
BAPTIST
–Now extinct
–Now extant
EPISCOPAL
–Functioning 1815
–Vacant 1815

The Early Fathers
1813-1828

IV

In the early years, the two counties of Virginia's Eastern Shore were visited by several first-magnitude Methodist personalities. No fewer than four persons who were or would become bishops preached on the Shore—Francis Asbury, Thomas Coke, William McKendree, and Richard Whatcoat—as well as two other Methodists of national reputation—Thomas Ware and Lorenzo Dow. As a rule, however, the Philadelphia Conference appointed only one or two pastors a year to serve the Shore. Since by 1805 the Methodists on the peninsula numbered over 1000 and the number of societies was sixteen, an Eastern Shore Methodist rarely saw his pastor. Only Downing's, Burton's, Garrison's, and Johnson's Chapels could count on preaching by the circuit pastor on Sundays, twice a month at each place. The rest of the time the preachers traveled up and down the Shore, visiting each society whenever they could, marrying, baptizing, administering the sacrament whenever a crowd would gather. The visit of the circuit pastor was a special event at each society, and at Tangier his arrival was announced by running a flag up a pole near the church. [1]

The absence of the regular minister during most of the week meant that the local congregations had to produce their own leaders to carry on the work of the church. And in virtually every corner of the Shore, able men and women stepped forward to fill the gap. For the most part they were not clergymen, but landowners or watermen or farmers or merchants. But they were called "preachers" or "Reverend" by their flocks, even though by the church's modern standards they would not be called either. By their service, however, and by the large imprint they left on the churches up and down the peninsula, they earned their title.

Generally the local fathers fell into one of two categories: those who came to their position of leadership and influence by their high standing in the secular community (a landowner, an important farmer, a captain in the militia), and those who became local leaders through outstanding lay work in the church itself. And for those in the second group, the path to a position of influence began with "exhorting."

"Exhorting," now completely lapsed in the Methodist churches, was in its day a practice of great importance. By the time of the great revival, it was quite common for the sermons of a regular preacher to be followed by an "exhortation," in which either another minister or an unordained person rose to interpret or explain or elaborate upon what was said to the congregation. As often as not it was the exhortation, and not the sermon, that struck home to the congregation, couched as it often was in the simpler language of the local exhorter, and many an exhortation ended with the congregation in a powerful shout of emotion. The Methodist Episcopal Church licensed many local men to exhort only. Beyond that first step lay the office of local preacher, then elder (full minister).

As early as 1795 a number of Eastern Shoremen were already exhorting, among them William Onions and Argoll Bloxom of Guilford; Stephen Drummond of Drummondtown; Shadrack Johnson of Johnson's; and James and William Melvin, who lived in upper Accomack near Maryland. In addition, it was not unusual for a non-native exhorter to make the rounds with the preachers. Abraham Thompson, a Negro, was one such who exhorted at Garrison's Chapel in 1795,[2] and there are records as late as the 1840's of other Negro exhorters who accompanied the circuit preachers.

William Colbert recorded a Methodist meeting on the Shore during which no fewer than four persons exhorted after his sermon: "After me, brother Willliam Melvin gave a beautiful discourse...after him Griffith Callahan...after him brother Rowen...and after him Argoll Bloxom gave an exhortation that concluded the meeting.... . I was fearful this morning that there were so many speakers among us that we should be in each other's way." [3]

In almost every case the man who exhorted when the pastor was present was the same man who was, for all practical purposes, the local preacher when the pastor was absent. They were a picturesque and varied lot, but their effect was everywhere much the same. They gave the Methodist Episcopal Church the stamp of the average, everyday people who composed it.

On the northern end of the peninsula lived the Shore's earliest Methodist, William Downing of Oak Hall. Appropriately, his was the first name that appears in the surviving records of local Methodism on the Shore, and he is almost without exception always listed first in the records of attendance at meetings and worship. Asbury, who lodged with Downing probably more often than with any other person on the Shore, never describes him personally in his journal. Colbert, however, paid him tribute with a short description: "Brother Downing holds an office in three Departments: he is a Justice of the Peace, a Captain in the Militia, a deacon in the church, and what is still the best, I believe, a good man." [4]

Even in these early years of the faith, Downing was recognized as the original father. In 1807, only two years after the first great camp meeting, the Methodists of the Shore passed "a vote of general thanks to William Downing for his Services in the capacity of steward for 15 or 20 years." Downing stepped down from active service at that time, and was succeeded as steward by his son, Samuel, who became an exhorter in 1813. Downing continued to be present at most Methodist functions on the circuit until shortly before his death in 1824, but increasingly in the capacity of elder statesman. [5]

A few miles to the east of Downing lived Drummond Welbourn, chief pillar of the Methodist society that sprang up in Horntown after 1800. Welbourn was quite unlike the venerable Downing; he was an ambitious man of many interests and varied pursuits. Already possessed of a good deal of land with prosperous acreage, in 1805 he applied for and obtained court permission to keep a tavern in his house in Horntown. That a local Methodist preacher was thus a tavern-keeper was not so scandalous to members of the faith as that he was also the village postmaster. That position, to which Welbourn was appointed in 1799, was, after all, a political appointment, and the Methodists at this period were adamant that members of society not become embroiled in any affairs of state or politics. Asbury passed through Horntown in 1810 and apparently met Welbourn. He wrote secretly in his journal that night, "Methodist preachers politicians—what a curse!" [6]

Welbourn was finally undone by his great ambitions. In 1811 he undertook the construction of a fine mansion in the village, and in a few years he had overextended himself into bankruptcy. His fine home was only half-finished when, in 1818, he hanged himself inside it. They carved upon his tomb what are said to have been his last spoken sentences, among which was his testimony that "The Scriptures are truer," and "Methodism is God's doctrine." [7]

Just to the south of Horntown lived David Watt, whose home became a Methodist preaching point after 1795. In 1802 Watt played host to Bishop Asbury himself, and in time the society that grew up in Wattsville around him was known as Friendship, perhaps because of the congeniality and hospitality of Watt himself. Watt became an exhorter in 1806 and was licensed as a local preacher in 1811. For more than forty years he permitted his home to be used by the Methodists for their meetings.[8]

The Onancock society had two strong pillars, William Seymour and William Lee. Both were residents of the town and members of the society there. Both became preachers. Seymour was licensed to exhort in 1805 and ordained a deacon in 1811, and Lee was licensed to preach in 1808 and ordained an elder in 1833. Both were widely known up and down the Shore, and so beloved that dozens of Methodist families named their sons after them. Joshua Thomas of Tangier named one of his sons William Seymour Thomas, and among the many Shoremen named for Lee was the Methodist preacher, William Lee Dalby of Northampton.

For a generation or more the Onancock society had no chapel and met either in homes or outdoors or in such public buildings as the schoolhouse. It was visited by the circuit preachers only once a week, and then not on Sundays, so Seymour and Lee took turns conducting the Sunday service for a number of years. Their parish, however, extended well beyond Onancock. Together they traveled the creeks and necks and islands of the bayside, preaching to whomever they met, marrying and burying and performing the pastoral functions to isolated families in isolated places. They were the ones who conducted the first camp meeting on Tangier Island in 1808. Home for Seymour was a beautiful house on Onancock Creek that he called "Wesley." Lee, a man of prodigious strength, was known as the "marrying and burying parson." It is said that at his death his estate included a wooden barrel full of nothing but marriage licenses. [9]

Another father of this same stock was William Elliott (1754-1836), said to have been, with William Downing, one of the two original Methodists on the

Virginia Shore. Elliott's contribution to the life of the early Methodist Church on the Shore was unique: he neither exhorted nor preached nor built a chapel, but instead founded a Sunday school. Because of it he is still at the center of a minor historical controversy.

William Elliott lived in Bradford's Neck near the modern town of Quinby and was a member of the Burton's society after the chapel was built in 1801. Like many another Methodist of his day, he was a firm hater of slavery. He had been a prisoner of war for a time during the Revolution, and politically was a Whig. He used slaves to work his sizable plantation, but always purchased them with the distinct understanding that, after the slave had worked out his purchase price at a fair wage, he would be free. He also employed local white workers and had "poor white boys bound to him until they became of age."

In 1785, just five years after a man named Robert Raikes in England founded the first Sunday school anywhere in the world, William Elliott established a school on Sundays in his home in Accomack County. Its purpose was simple: to teach reading and writing to members of his own family, as well as to those bondsmen and slaves on the plantation who wanted learning, in hopes that all would be able to study the scriptures on their own. Elliott set aside a regular hour on Sunday afternoons when his own children and the white bondsmen would be taught reading. Slaves and black servants and their children were also taught once a week, but on a different day and in another part of the plantation away from the main house.

The fame of the teaching available in Elliott's home soon spread throughout the surrounding countryside, and in that day before public education was generally available, other citizens in the area began to send their children to his school. Gradually, as some of the students became proficient in reading, other subjects were introduced, including catechism and direct readings from the Bible. Elliott remained the chief teacher of the school, and the school remained in his home, until 1818. In that year the Burton's congregation invited him to locate the school in their church. The school was transferred there, and after that date Elliott tended more and more to be the general superintendent of the several teachers in a growing Sunday school. He directed the school until his death in 1836, and the Sunday school he began in 1785 is still meeting each week almost two hundred years later. [10]

Elliott's school is without question the oldest Sunday school on the Eastern Shore of Virginia. No other contender even comes close, for Sunday schools did not begin to arise in other churches until the 1830's. For half a century Burton's Chapel could boast the only regular program of Christian instruction available in any denomination in the two countries, and one of the few schools of any sort, religious or secular. Undoubtedly the Elliott school was an important factor in making Burton's the strong and vital congregation that it was in the nineteenth century.

But a continuing question about Elliott's school is whether or not it is, as is often claimed, the oldest continuous school in the United States. At least one other Virginia Sunday school makes the same claim: that of St. Peter's Methodist

REV. THOMAS ANDROS ELLIOTT

1782-1815
a silhouette from life

Church in Montpelier in Hanover County. This Sunday school, also still in existence, is said to have been founded at about the same time by no less a person than Francis Asbury, who began it in the home of Thomas Crenshaw.

The question of which is the earlier of the two schools is complicated by several factors. The date of the origin of the Crenshaw school, for instance, is variously given as 1783, 1785, and 1786. If it was founded in 1783, it is indeed older than Elliott's school. But 1786 is the most frequently cited date, and there is no evidence that Asbury visited Thomas Crenshaw in that year. And much of the strength of the Crenshaw claim, which is usually favored by historians, is the presence of Asbury.

To complicate matters, the original documents on which each claim is based have been lost. Thomas Crenshaw's journal, which described the origins of his school, was destroyed when Richmond was burned in 1865. The original Elliott records and documents, including William Elliott's own Bible, were handed down in his family for generations, but the particular document involving the Sunday school was lost. Wessie Nock Eason, Elliott's great-great-granddaughter, studied the available documents and the family tradition in 1901, and it was she who first made the claim for priority of the Eastern Shore school.

Probably the controversy will never be satisfactorily decided, and the Eastern Shore's claim to have produced "the Father of the American Sunday School" will never go uncontested. Nevertheless, William Elliott was a pioneer of the Sunday school idea, and he made a lasting impact on the life of the Shore. It is highly unlikely that he had ever heard of Robert Raikes and the Sunday school movement in England. (On the other hand, the Crenshaw school in Hanover, thanks to Francis Asbury, was said to have been designed on the Raikes model.) On his isolated and distant Eastern Shore, simultaneously with some of the best minds of his day, he caught the vision of his duty, and by his response became one of the most honored of the local church fathers. [11]

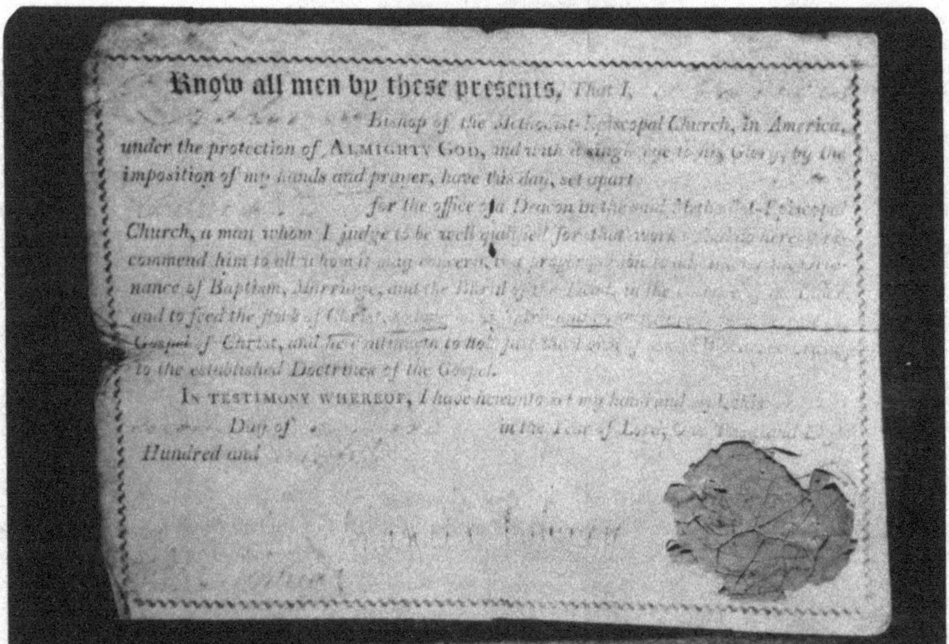
Know all men by these presents, That I, [illegible] Bishop of the Methodist-Episcopal Church, in America, under the protection of ALMIGHTY GOD, and with a single eye to his Glory, by the imposition of my hands and prayer, have this day, set apart [illegible] for the office of a Deacon in the said Methodist-Episcopal Church, a man whom I judge to be well qualified for that work [illegible] commend him to all whom it may concern [illegible] nance of Baptism, Marriage, and the Burial of the Dead, [illegible] and to feed the flock of Christ [illegible] Gospel of Christ, and he continues to hold [illegible] to the established Doctrines of the Gospel.

IN TESTIMONY WHEREOF, I have hereunto set my hand and seal this [illegible] Day of [illegible] in the Year of Lord, [illegible] Hundred and [illegible]

. . . his ordination certificate, signed by Francis Asbury, Philadelphia, March 22, 1808

Elliott was the founder of a line of Methodist leaders that spanned a century. His son, Thomas Andros Elliott (1782-1815), a product of the Sunday school, was converted at the age of nineteen and prepared for the ministry. The Philadelphia Conference received him on probation in 1806, and he was ordained an elder by Asbury in 1808. The greater part of his ministry was spent off the Shore and was cut short by his death while still a young man. [12]

John Wesley Andros Elliott (1813-1896), son of Thomas and grandson of William, was converted in 1833, licensed to preach in 1835, and ordained a deacon in 1845. Unlike his father, however, he never became a "traveling" minister, but served as a local preacher up and down the Shore for the rest of his life. In 1887 he estimated that he had in the course of 52 years preached 2500 sermons, conducted 1000 funerals, married 400 couples, baptized 75 persons, and offered public prayer 20,000 times. Not the least of his service to the church, however, were his historical writings and reminiscences, some of which were published locally under his pseudonym, "Septuagenarian." All are a valuable source of early Methodist history on the Eastern Shore. [13]

One of the most colorful of early church fathers of the Eastern Shore was Captain Thomas Burton.

Even after the Methodist society moved out of his home after Thomas Smith's great revival there in 1801, the Burton's society continued to revolve around Captain Thomas Burton, so recently converted from his careless, fox-hunting days. The new meetinghouse erected that year stood directly across the road from his gate, and despite his dissenting vote, the building was named Burton's Chapel.

Burton was neither a preacher nor an exhorter, but his local power was undisputed. They placed an armchair near the pulpit of the new chapel for the old man, at a point where he could both hear the sermon and keep an eye on the congregation. From here he kept watch over both preacher and parishioner. Any disorder in the congregation was sure to bring the stern tap of his cane on the wooden floor. Burton never tapped at the preacher, but the congregation knew when he was dissatisfied with the sermon. The old man had a habit of patting his foot continuously when he was contented, "keeping the spinning-wheel moving," the parishioners called it. Should the minister touch upon anything that did not sit right with the captain, the spinning wheel would stop abruptly until he passed on to some other topic, then the wheel would move on again. Generally any anti-slavery comments would stop the wheel, for Burton had little patience with his church's views on that subject.

It was Thomas Burton's feeling that no good church meeting was complete without a shout, and sometimes the services at Burton's Chapel were prolonged at his insistence until the shouting began. But at one of the meetings at Burton's, Captain William LeCato was present, well into his cups as usual. When the shouting began, LeCato joined in lustily, elbowing his way to the front of the building and quickly eclipsing all others in volume and enthusiasm. A few knowing glances in Burton's direction from some of the worthy sisters brought the old patriarch to LeCato's side. The visitor was led firmly but politely to the door, and before departing he apologized to Burton for his behavior. [14]

Thomas Burton, who before his conversion was never happier than when indulging in the chase with the other gentlemen of the community, was after his conversion never happier than when the circuit preacher rode into view. On these occasions he would often get his words twisted in his excitement. It is said that once he told his servant Samuel to attend to the arriving preacher with these words: "Sam, take this horse and hang it up in the porch. Take the saddle to the stable and feed it. Feed it well, Sam!" And the old man took seriously the Bible's instructions to pray secretly in one closet; it little mattered to him that, when he knelt down in his closet, that his feet stuck out, and that the servants noticed and snickered behind his back. [15]

From the revival of 1801 until his death twenty years later Thomas Burton wielded a power that must have been all but absolute at Burton's Chapel. When he died he left two sons, Joshua and Garrison Burton, to carry on his stead. Joshua Burton eventually became a local preacher and succeeded William Elliott as superintendent of the Sunday school at Burton's Chapel.

It was no easy thing to be a Methodist in those days, and fathers and mothers of the faith in this first generation willingly submitted to rules of conduct and lifestyle that were taken with utmost seriousness and jealously guarded from impurity.

Before the coming of the Methodist revival, when only the Anglican Church had kept in touch with the people of the Shore and that only by the slenderest thread, the Virginia Shore was a rough-and-tumble place, full of rustic country people, unrefined by a great deal of culture or breeding. When the Methodist preachers first came to the area, they had literally to fight their way in, sometimes with their fists. Thomas Smith, Joseph Everett, the Baptist Elijah Baker, and even Asbury himself had seen mobs and ambushes or been threatened or stoned. The evangelization of the Shore had been a rugged endeavor. As late as 1806, a full twenty years after Asbury's arrival, the yearly camp meeting had been brought to a halt by a fistfight.

In 1810, however, while he was spending the night in Newtown, Maryland, Bishop Asbury was able to observe in his journal that things had improved on the Shore: "There is a great change for the better in the morals and manners of all ranks of people in this end of the peninsula, and none pretend to deny the Methodists have wrought it." [16] This "change for the better" was accomplished only because those who joined in the new church took seriously its insistence that the godly were supposed to conduct themselves differently from the ungodly.

With the coming of Methodism came a long list of things that Methodists did and did not do as a result of their faith.

One taboo was fancy clothes and jewelry. Christiana Newton, a young lady who lived near Drummondtown, was converted to Methodism as early as 1782, but being a person of gay persuasions, she soon afterwards returned enough to her old manner of life to attend a ball. That night after she returned from this gala affair, pangs of conscience and a sense of remorse overcame her, and upon entering the house she ripped off her jewelry and fine accessories and cast them into the fireplace. Ballroom finery went up in flames, and Christiana Newton never again had anything to do with either of them. Shortly thereafter she married Isaiah Bagwell, a faithful Methodist who lived near what is now Greenbush, and lived thereafter a life of model Methodist simplicity. When she died at age 81 in 1838, she was said to be the last of the five original Methodists on the Shore, and it had long since been assumed, perhaps in part because of her example, that Methodist women wore the plain and simple clothing that befits the gospel. [17]

Dancing was, of course, another taboo. Joshua Thomas himself was an agile dancer before his conversion, and he became an agile *leaper* during ecstatic moments afterwards. [17] The playing of musical instruments was considered worldly and taboo. Although Methodists were known for their singing, it was inevitably unaccompanied. John and Charles Parks of Tangier were excellent fiddlers when they converted to Methodism, and they experienced "a severe struggle to give up the sweet strains of their catgut." In the end, however, Methodist lifestyle won out over this "unfruitful work of darkness," and the Parks brothers hung up their fiddles for good. There are records throughout the nineteenth century of other practices not permitted by Methodist (and Baptist) congregations: cooking on Sunday, ice-skating, shooting at a target, and, of course, non-attendance at worship. [18]

Such rules of conduct did not go unenforced, and many was the Methodist who was forced to defend his lifestyle before the other members of the society. Ezekiah Pitt of Jamesville was put on trial by the Bethel society for the unchristian practice of gossip, or "backbiting," as they called it, in 1808. "After hearing the charges against Mr. Pitt," the Quarterly Meeting recorded, "we respectfully heard him remonstrate on the case, acquitted him of the charge, and received him into full membership." Unfortunately, Ezekiah Pitt had other shortcomings, for "on discovering an unchristian spirit in Mr. Pitt, it was voted that Mr. Pitt should go back on probation for six months." [19]

Even those who held office in the church were not exempt from being called into account. Thomas Bradford, an exhorter, was summoned to hear charges of immoral conduct in 1806. He was apparently expelled from the society, for his name does not appear after that date anywhere in the annals of local Methodism. What his sin was is not recorded. Scarburgh Bloxom of Guilford, who had housed William Colbert on his rounds in 1795, was removed from the Methodist society there in 1807. His sin, likewise, is not recorded. William R. Finney was a local preacher of the Onancock society when, in 1810, he was charged with immoral conduct. His sin: he went to see a show. He was found guilty of the charge, but instead of expelling him, the Quarterly Meeting voted that he "remain silent in the congregation until he regain the confidence of his brothers." [20]

Although many church trials are known to have taken place in these early years of Methodism on the Shore, only one was recorded in detail. It gives a clear indication of how zealously the early Methodists guarded the purity and lifestyle of their ranks.

The only recorded trial is that of William Melvin in 1804. Melvin was certainly of reputable Methodist standing to begin with. He lived near Newtown in Maryland, which was part of the Accomack Circuit during the early decades of the 1800's, and he was a veteran of the Revolution. As early as 1780 he had opened his home to Methodist preachers, and Asbury himself had lodged and preached there. By the turn of the century Melvin's Chapel stood in Maryland not far from the Virginia boundary. In addition, Melvin conducted a school in his home and was generally considered one of the leading Methodist figures of his area.

In 1804, however, four of Melvin's students appeared before the Quarterly Meeting of the Accomack Circuit to accuse him of immoral conduct, namely drunkenness and improper advances toward members of the opposite sex. John Long, age 19, said that he had seen Melvin "frequently drink spirituous liquors in his school and behave very indecently to the female sex." The charge of immodesty and indecency was echoed by Tabitha Dormas, Betsy Mitchell, and Sally Mitchell, all teenagers, who gave their testimony "solemnly" and "seriously" and "if she was about to Dye," respectively. Littleton Long and Thomas Dixon, both adults, echoed the charge of drunkenness.

It did little good for Melvin to call to his defense the testimony of two others that he was an upstanding man who had never been seen to do such things. Nor did it matter much in his favor that he had been an upstanding Methodist for almost a quarter of a century. Members of Methodist societies must be above any reproach, and the committee appointed by the circuit to hear the case—William Downing was its chairman—declared themselves "of the Oppinion that he is Guilty of the Crimes against him." Melvin was expelled from the church. [21]

Two years later Melvin applied for license to preach, but the circuit rejected him. He apparently remained *persona non grata* with the circuit for the rest of his life, yet on the local scene in the vicinity of Melvin's Chapel he still managed to cling to both his Methodist standing and his leadership. His son, Avra Melvin (1780-1853), was licensed to exhort in 1805, became a preacher in 1806, and was one of the foremost Methodists on the Shore in his time. When William Melvin died in 1807 he was, although officially expelled from the church, a pillar of the Newtown congregation, an "officer of the church," and his son Avra preached his funeral. [22]

Far and away the most revered of the local patriarchs of early Eastern Shore Methodism was Joshua Thomas, the "Parson of the Islands." His life and activity span the first and second generation of Methodists on the Shore, and it is safe to say that this colorful personality is the most important native figure of church history on the Eastern Shore.

If you would know Joshua Thomas, it is not necessary that you search him out in dark libraries, turning the musty pages of forgotten denominational records. Instead, ask some of the watermen who ply the Chesapeake in their boats and spin their yarns of past adventures, real and imagined. Or ask even the schoolchildren of the bayside towns and islands. For Joshua Thomas is well remembered on the Eastern Shore to this day. He has, in fact, long since stepped across that line that separates history from folklore and become a genuine legend in his native peninsula.

JOSHUA THOMAS

If you ask about Joshua Thomas along the shores of the Chesapeake today, you might well gain the impression from what you are told that he was a man endowed with powers beyond those of most mortals, an almost Christ-like figure with the ability to perform miracles not unlike those in the Bible.

There was, for example, the time when he went to the home of a man who had been bedridden for years and asked the man to take him somewhere in his boat the next day.

"You must be crazy," the sick man said. "I haven't been out of this bed for years."

But Joshua replied, "If you could get up, would you take me?"

The man thought a minute and answered with a laugh, "Yes, if I could get up, I would take you."

Joshua instructed the man to meet him at the dock at nine the next morning, and went home to pray about it. The next day the sick man kept his appointment with the parson, his first venture away from his sickbed in years.

Or there was the time in Maryland when Joshua performed what looked like one of Christ's miracles in reverse. The people of Deal Island had a special "fishing hole" where anyone could catch fish at almost any time, even through the winter ice. When one day the people fell to quarreling with each other over the fishing grounds, Joshua in great disgust prayed that no more fish would ever be caught there. And, the story goes, none has to this day.

Yet another story of this larger-than-life man comes from Deal Island. It seems that a native of the island was ill and craved a piece of fish, the only food that his doctor would allow him to eat. But no fish could be caught, because there were no crabs to be had for bait.

Hearing the news, Joshua Thomas told the sick man's brother to go down under a stump on Little Island, look into the hollow of a root in a certain place, and there he would find a crab. If he would take that crab and use it as bait off the south end of Little Deal Island, he would get one bite on the line, and that would be a rockfish.

The man did as he was instructed by the parson. And sure enough, that night his brother dined on rockfish.

And one of the stories about Parson Thomas, if not so lofty, is at least of the fabric of which legends are made. It is said that one day the parson lost his false teeth overboard, and the people gathered around to help him recover them. Young men by diving overboard and grown men with tongs could not retrieve them and they were about to be given up for lost when there appeared on the scene one of the good ladies of the island with something concealed in the folds of her apron. Quickly, before anyone could see what it was, she threw it overboard, holding on tightly to the string which she had tied around it. A short wait, and soon she pulled the false teeth up out of the water at the end of her string.

"How did you do that?" everyone asked, amazed.

"There's only one way to catch a Methodist's teeth," she beamed triumphantly. "With a piece of fried chicken." [23]

The man behind the legend was perhaps a good deal more real than the stories make him out to be, a down-to-earth human being with feet of clay. Even so, he was a powerful force for good for almost half a century in the region of the Eastern Shore, a living remnant of the Methodist faith in its earliest period there. And the modern folk tales are contemporary equivalents of the love and respect that surrounded him in his own time.

Joshua Thomas was born, not on the Eastern Shore of Virginia, but in Somerset County, Maryland, in 1776, that important year in which, among other events, Elijah Baker first preached on the Virginia Shore. His father, John Thomas, was a waterman. One day when John was away on one of his frequent trips across the waters, his foot, where he had been bitten by a dog, became infected, and he stopped in at Tangier Island to be treated for it by relatives there. He died there a few days later, and not long afterwards Martha Hall Thomas brought her brood of children, Joshua among them, to Tangier to live. There Joshua was raised, like many another island boy a hardworking, God-fearing young man who fished the bay waters and raised a crop on the then still considerable acreage available on the island. Although he could dance a jig as well as anyone on the bay, he was more serious-minded than most, and when he found time attended Episcopal services on the mainland in his native Somerset. The rector of the church there, aware that a strange revival was brewing around his little parish, had at one point tried prayer meetings Methodist-style in his church, but he gave the idea up willingly when he found out that his parishioners, perhaps Joshua among them, did not like them. [24]

In 1799, at the age of 23, Joshua Thomas bought seventy acres of land on Tangier Island and settled down with his new wife, Rachel Evans, and began to raise a family. It was six years later, and almost by chance, that he encountered the event that was to transform his life. Hired to ferry a group of Marylanders to the Pungoteague camp meeting in 1805, there he heard the celebrated Lorenzo Dow preach, and became fascinated by the religious excitement stirred up by the Methodists and their camp meetings. A few weeks later at a second camp meeting in Somerset County he was himself converted.

It was only a matter of a few days from his conversion that Joshua Thomas began, with the help of Rachel and his friend, John Crockett, to bring the gospel to Tangier. The effort was successful from the start—two persons were converted at the very first meeting—and Joshua became the chief pillar of a budding society and the chief force behind a spreading revival on Tangier Island. Twelve years later he became a local preacher. [25]

The Methodist society on Tangier was virtually without contact with the rest of Eastern Shore Methodism, and Joshua was its sole ruler, until 1808, when William Seymour and William Lee of Onancock crossed over to the island and held the first camp meeting there. The idea of a yearly camp meeting on his own island fired Joshua's imagination, and he alone became the guiding force behind making it an annual event. With ready acquiescence the circuit and its preachers turned it over to him, and by the next year it was considered his own bailiwick.

The Tangier Campmeeting quickly became the great annual gathering place for thousands of people from all parts of the Chesapeake Bay region. And Joshua Thomas was always there, officially or unofficially overseeing it. Early in the history of the camp meeting the circuit decided in Quarterly Meeting not to continue the camp meeting. Already the Methodists could see commercialism increasing with each year's event, and a number of customs and practices peripheral to it that they considered undesirable. Joshua was not present when the decision was made to cancel the camp meeting, and he heard the news of the decision with great distress. Unable to get the decision changed, unable to persuade the presiding elder or the circuit preachers to preach at it or even to attend it, he finally decided to hold the camp meeting anyway and to preach it himself if necessary. (That idea filled him with dread; despite his license to preach, he always considered himself first and foremost an exhorter.)

In due time, under his direction the camp meeting opened as usual, and Joshua was about to undertake to preach without any other preachers present, when as if by divine intervention the presiding elder appeared on the campgrounds. He had been journeying up the bay and had put into Tangier when the boat was delayed by a calm. Unable to escape, he opened the camp meeting and carried it through to a successful conclusion, and the event remained an annual one.[26]

This incident suggests what was probably to some extent the true state of Joshua Thomas' relation with the Methodist Episcopal Church that he loved so well: he was more or less an unofficial character, a colorful figure who wielded his influence more by strength of character than by official authority. In fact, it is almost certain that at times the regular clergy of the circuit considered him something of an embarrassment, and as time went on he represented increasingly the simpler day of the founding patriarchs in an age when the church was becoming more sophisticated.

He was, by his own admission, an uneducated and even ignorant man. "I could not read," he said of himself in later life, "having gone to school in my life but two weeks." He had some rudimentary knowledge of reading, but stood in great contrast to the regular clergy who made their rounds with books in their saddlebags and attended dutifully, as Asbury and Wesley insisted, to study and education.

He was not an eloquent preacher and preferred not to think of himself as a preacher at all. When he was nervous he stammered, and at times appeared to be a country bumbler. But he was an exceedingly colorful figure before a congregation, and many a sermon preached by the more qualified and educated ministers was more memorable chiefly because Joshua Thomas exhorted after it was over.

A typical story of his manner in exhorting recalls the day when he was called upon to exhort in Dorchester County, Maryland. He had by now no small reputation, and all eyes were on him as he made his way to the pulpit. The congregation was silent and expectant as he first removed his hat, then his coat, and laid them carefully aside. He turned to the crowd as if to begin, but said first, "It comes to me, I must first *shout!*" Immediately he began to jump around on the platform, clapping his hands and shouting "Glory! Glory!" at the top of his voice. The effect on the congregation was almost immediate, and soon they were shouting with him in a great swell of emotion.

His contemporaries recall that the phrase he most often used in public speaking was "It comes to me...." And there were times when the regular clergy, their sermons finished, must have dreaded to hear him say it, wondering what had come to him this time. He was more than once taken to task by the circuit preachers for his actions, but he remained resolute in his belief that he was duty-bound to shout, and that shouting, far from being an unacceptable form of worship, was even a means of grace. Similarly, he was unrestrained by the disciplines of proper hymnody. Although he knew by heart as many hymns as most pastors and people of that day, he hesitated not a bit to rewrite and rearrange the texts to suit his purposes at any given moment.

The most strained relation with the denomination, and one of the most embarrassing episodes in his career, occurred during the early days of his work on Tangier, sometime between 1808 and 1814. The Baptist preacher, George Layfield, passed over to Tangier at about this time and did some preaching there, apparently with the hope of extending the Baptist faith to the island. Little came of Layfield's work, except the sudden fashion among some of the more devout Methodists there that baptism in the Baptist style, by immersion, was necessary for salvation. A number of Joshua's friends consented to be baptized in this manner by Layfield, and soon they were pressuring Joshua to submit to it as well.

JOSHUA THOMAS IN "THE METHODIST"

Joshua was alone in his boat—a place where he often thought things over, a place where he had been known to shout, to the sudden surprise of other watermen near him at the time—when he began to ponder the question of immersion. He reached the conclusion then and there that it was a desirable thing, so he prayed about it and thereupon dived overboard, in full belief that that was how immersion was accomplished. He learned from his friends later, of course, that his own immersion of himself was not valid, that he had to be immersed by someone who had himself been immersed. So he consented finally to be baptized properly by Layfield. The baptism, which Joshua received eagerly and joyfully, occurred on the shore at Tangier before a few of his friends. So excited was he on that day that he neglected to remove his trusty hymnbook and testament from his pocket before the ceremony and found them much the worse for wear after they, like him, had been immersed.

Imagine Joshua's distress when he learned that the Methodist brethren considered his baptism by Layfield to be a virtual withdrawal from their ranks, a repudiation of his own baptism as an infant (apparently in an Episcopalian sacrament), and an insult to the Methodist beliefs about baptism! Although he was not to be swayed from his Methodism, the unschooled parson no doubt learned some of the finer points about the Christian sacraments as practiced by the Methodists from this event.

Layfield, meanwhile, gave up his work on Tangier Island with little to show for it except the distinction of having given a Baptist baptism to the foremost of the local Methodist preachers of the Shore. [27]

Such was the very human man who established, nurtured, oversaw, and defined Methodism on Tangier Island and the region of the upper bayside Eastern Shore in the early years. His life and work span the first half of the nineteenth century and in the fifty years that he plied the bay in faithful canoe *The Methodist*, he earned the respect and love of thousands of people.

Ironically, his presence in the Methodist society of Tangier was so powerful that he kept it from falling under the direct influence of the regular preachers from the mainland circuit, and it was only as Joshua Thomas relinquished control of it over the years that the society there grew and prospered. In 1825 he and his second wife, Lotty, (Rachel had died in 1814) moved away from Tangier to Deal Island, and only after that did the Tangier society erect its first meetinghouse. Most of his work after that year was done in Maryland, although he was still the sole director of the annual Tangier camp meeting.

In 1835 Joshua Thomas was ordained by an elder by the Philadelphia Annual Conference. He was something of a celebrity at this gathering, and his presence created quite a stir. When his name was recommended for ordination, the only credentials presented in his favor were that this was the man who had preached to the British army at Tangier, and all the eyes of the conference strained to see him. When called to answer before the bishop the traditionbal questions about doctrine and discipline, he created a memorable scene very characteristic of himself. "He appeared for the moment to be under considerable embarrassment, but put the brethren in great good humor by his simple and emphatic answer: 'I don't understand as much about these matters as my beloved brother ministers here, but *as far as I know*, to the best of my ability I will conform to all the rules of the Methodist Church; *you may depend on it!*'"[28]

By 1844 the Tangier camp meeting was in decline for two reasons. One was that the Methodist Episcopal Church was now divided into two denominations over the slavery issue. The second was that Joshua Thomas was now an old man unable to oversee the event as he had almost singlehandedly for two decades. Yet as the camp meeting declined, the local Methodist church on the island took on new life. James Hargis and Valentine Smith, the Accomack Circuit preachers that year, became the first paid preachers from the mainland to supply the island with regular preaching.[29]

Joshua Thomas last visited the Tangier camp meeting in 1846. He was seventy years old, an old man who could hardly walk or even stand without the support of the many people who flocked around him to assist. He had arranged a kind of formal farewell program for himself at the camp meeting, aware that this would be his last visit. "I want Brother [James] Brindle to give out a certain hymn and sing," he told the presiding elder, "after which I want Brother [John] Laws to pray. I will then give an exhortation to the people, and you will have me carried by two of the largest men you have on the ground to my canoe, when I will pronounce the benediction." They carried out his wish in every respect. His oldest son, John, was one of the strong men who carried him to the boat for that last leave of the island, and his biographer tells us that "there were many tears shed that morning... and hopes exchanged that we might all meet to part no more at last."[30]

The last Tangier camp meeting was held in 1857. It did not assemble again because, it is said, the denomination was now seriously divided and the gathering had become increasingly worldly across the years, to the distaste of its leaders. Perhaps another reason it did not assemble again was that it could not long survive the man who was its lifeblood, Joshua Thomas. He died on Deal Island in 1853.

When Joshua Thomas died, the people of Deal Island and other places where he was known and loved anxiously sought pieces of his boat *The Methodist* as mementoes of him, and these relics of the venerable parson were treasured and displayed in private homes for generations. A gavel fashioned from the lumber of his house was presented to Bishop Newman in solemn ceremony half a century later in 1898.[31] His boat survived sufficiently intact to be destined for display at the Jamestown Exposition in 1907, but it was lost in being towed to the exhibit.[32]

He himself was buried near the church that he had founded on Deal Island. The inscription placed on his tomb was one that he selected:

> *Come all my friends, as you pass by,*
> *Behold the place where I do lie;*
> *As you are now, so once was I;*
> *Remember you are born to die.*[33]

Eight years after his death a Methodist preacher named Adam Wallace gathered reminiscences and sketches of him into a biography entitled "The Parson of the Islands." Much of the material for this book was drawn from a now-vanished manuscript prepared by the Reverend Levin Prettyman after conversations with the parson himself in 1815. Wallace's biography, the first published book describing Eastern Shore Methodism, did much to keep Joshua Thomas' name alive among people on and off the Shore.

But even before it was published, in the short eight years following his death, Joshua Thomas' name had already become a legend. The people of the Chesapeake had begun already to spin their tales and teach their children about the old parson. And one of the tales they still tell today—the story of the miraculous closing of the fishing hole at Deal Island by Parson Thomas—was already current, for it appears in the biography of 1861.[34]

There is a real sense in which this greatest of the early Methodist patriarchs of the Shore never really left the scene of his labors. As long as his memory is kept alive, the age of the early fathers of Methodism on Virginia's Eastern Shore will never fully be forgotten.

The Second Generation 1816-1844

V.

In the second decade of the nineteenth century, death began to claim, one by one, the patriarchs of Eastern Shore Methodism. And as a new generation of sons and daughters arose to take the reins from them, Methodism began to experience some very fundamental changes.

In 1816, six years after his last visit to the Virginia Shore, Francis Asbury died near Fredericksburg, Virginia. When they laid his worn-out body to rest in a simple grave, American Methodism lost the primary vestige of its connection with England. In that same year William Paramore of Accomack died. Johannes Johnson of Northampton had been dead four years. Drummond Welbourn of Horntown hanged himself two years later, in 1818. In 1821, two of the patriarchs of the Shore passed away: Thomas Burton of Burton's Chapel, and William Seymour of Onancock. And in 1824 the Shore's original Methodist, William Downing of Oak Hall, went to his reward. Important Methodists like Jonathan Garrison and Benjamin Floyd had been dead for years. Only three of the great fathers lived on: William Elliott of Burton's until 1836, David Watt of Wattsville until 1853, and Joshua Thomas—who was a young man at his coversion and whose life really spans two periods—until 1853.

The passing of the original generation meant one major change to Methodism that was almost immediate: it meant that in several places Methodism ceased to be a "society" meeting in the home of a friendly patriarch and became a "congregation" meeting within the walls of a chapel built especially for that purpose.

This is exactly what happened at Locustville, where the society had always met in Belle Vue, Paramore's fine home. After his death in 1816, the Methodists vacated those premises, moved their services to the local schoolhouse, and shortly thereafter erected their first meetinghouse, which they named Wesley Chapel.

It was the same in other places as well. In Onancock the Methodists had met in Seymour's home, "Wesley." But Seymour died heavily in debt in 1821, and "Wesley" was sold. Faced with the problem of no place to assemble, the Methodists purchased an old mill, where grain was ground by a horse who continuously circled a grindstone. With renovations and improvements, this building was ready for use by 1824, and ever since Onancock Methodists have occupied the site, where Cokesbury Church now stands.

In Tangier, the society was forced to move out of Joshua Thomas' house, not because he died but because he moved away to Deal Island in 1825. For another decade the island Methodists continued to meet in private homes, but finally in 1835 "Lee's Bethel," their first chapel, was erected on the site of the present church.

And at Franktown, where Matthew Floyd had inherited the mantle of leadership from his father, Benjamin, the patriarch also moved away. The Floyd's meetinghouse, which stood on his estate, was abandoned forthwith, and in 1843 the congregation erected a building on the present church lot in the village of Franktown.[1]

In each case, the erection of a meetinghouse was just one part of a more fundamental change: the local societies were becoming congregations, the open-air movement was becoming a denomination. As separate buildings were erected to house the faithful at worship, Eastern Shore Methodism settled down as never before. No longer were villages evangelized by outdoor revivals; now evangelism took place within church walls. No longer were religious experiences of converts free of ties to denomination and location; now people were converted within a certain building where forever after most of their religious activity was located according to the laws and standards and desires of the people who maintained it.

There were still a few societies that had not erected meetinghouses, but gradually the chapels appeared. Capeville Chapel and Pungoteague Chapel both stood by 1812, probably replacing private homes as gathering-places for the societies in those places. Horntown's society erected its first building in 1827, a quarter century after the formation of the society in that town. The Ames Ridge society built Ames Chapel in 1829, a full 34 years, at least, after the formation of that group. Last to be erected was Wattsville Chapel, where the patriarch was still living; this building did not make its appearance until the 1830's. The Hog Island society never erected a building, and in fact was by 1835 all but extinct.[2]

Gradually a new pattern began to emerge. As the church spread to new communities, the formation of the society and the erection of the church building occurred simultaneously. This happened in Craddockville by 1821, in Modest Town (Ebenezer Chapel) by 1827, and in Chesapeake in Northampton, where Salem Chapel was erected soon after 1828.[3] In these new communities Methodism was never really a "society" in the old sense. And all up and down the Shore the old society idea began gradually to be replaced by the new conception of the church as a group of people meeting together in a specific building. The movement that in 1801 was virtually uncommitted to property and location had by the 1830's entrenched itself behind wooden walls.

Inside the wooden walls what had begun as a movement was fast becoming an organization, and the passing of the years reveal the increasing institutionalization of the Methodist Episcopal Church. The new chapels and meetinghouses required trustees, and by 1812 as many as eight or nine persons per chapel were assigned that function. The office of steward, which first appears on the local records in 1806, was expanded to three persons in 1814, and by the 1830's a movement was afoot to increase the number to four. To the stewards fell the task of raising the money necessary to pay the preachers, as well as the task of setting the salary, and the methods of doing both became increasingly complex as the years passed. That venerable Methodist institution, the committee, became more and more common, with an increasing tendency to become permanent once it was created. By 1835 the format of the Quarterly Meeting itself had become fixed into a standard set of questions and answers.[4]

That something was happening to Methodism was obvious by 1834, when the circuit resolved unanimously that "one or more of our Bishops be respectfully invited to pay our Circuit a visit as soon as it may be practicable." Asbury, the first bishop, had been a regular fixture on the local scene for years, but now the church was so large that the several bishops had no time to deal directly with the tiny Eastern Shore of Virginia. The circuit repeated the invitation in 1845, changing "respectfully" to "affectionately," but to no avail.[5] There is no record of the visit of a Methodist bishop to the Virginia Shore between 1810 and 1854. In those years the distance between the local and the national levels of the church widened even further.

By the 1830's what might have been just a simple local question of administration became a heated issue, possibly because it revealed so clearly just how much Methodism was changing: it was the question of the division of the circuit.

By 1831 there were nineteen Methodist societies on the Eastern Shore of Virginia, and all of them had always been part of one circuit. It was becoming increasingly obvious that the circuit was too large and had to be divided, but the decision was not an easy one to make. Always the Eastern Shore had been one Methodist entity. When the congregations met for quarterly meetings, the people saw and greeted old friends from Capeville to Downing's (and even Newtown, Maryland), as they always had from the beginning. To divide the circuit might indeed reduce the workload of the preachers, but there was considerable local reluctance to admit that progress had necessitated this change in the beloved old church.

The first proposal to divide Accomack Circuit was approved in 1832 and promptly forgotten. Two years later the issue, by now a controversial one, was revived and debated at quarterly meetings for more than a year. Finally on June 6, 1835, the Quarterly Conference sent out the word that this hot topic would be the main order of business at the next gathering.

When the Quarterly Conference met in Drummondtown on August 22, 1835, the potential explosiveness of the issue was defused by careful attention to groundrules and procedures. It was first resolved that "no person shall be allowed to speak on the same subject more than twice," and secondly that "all persons in addressing the president rise from their seats." After considerable discussion, the question was put to a vote and it was decided, peacefully, to divide Eastern Shore Methodism into two circuits, Accomack and Northampton. The new "lower" circuit was to include Pungoteague, Ames Chapel, Garrison's, and all societies south of them.[6] There followed a flurry of institutional necessities—the election of stewards for the new circuit, the adjustment of funds collected. And by 1836 Eastern Shore Methodism as a single administrative unit was a thing of the past.

With the coming of the second generation came changes in the emphasis Methodists placed upon rules of conduct and lifestyle, a shift in focus that buried some old taboos and brought some new ones to life.

There arose an increased concern for Sabbath-keeping, a virtue presupposed among the mothers and fathers of the first generation. Now that there were more churches and twice as many ministers (for the new circuit had its own separate preachers), church services were more likely to occur on Sundays, and efforts to get people to observe the Sabbath became more concerted.

The keeping of the Sabbath became a much-talked-about issue near Belle Haven, that ungodly area where the Methodists had not yet succeeded in planting a church. In 1825 a non-churchman named Bigelow, an avowed disciple of Thomas Paine and anti-church rationalism, settled near Willis Wharf, then known as Downing's Wharf, and opened a considerable commercial establishment that hired a great many local people. Bigelow was an aggressive freethinker, and soon the neighborhood was flooded with what the Methodists called his "infidel" literature. Worse than that, Bigelow required his employees to work on Sundays. "The noise of saw and hammer rudely broke the Sabbath quiet, while smoke from his furnace fires defiantly curled upward."

JAMES A. MASSEY

In the background: meeting day on Tangier Island

After a short while, Bigelow's establishment was hit by a disastrous fire and reduced to ruin. The local Methodists were convinced that it was divine retribution for his violation of the Sabbath, and Bigelow entered their sermons and stories as an example of the need for proper conduct on that day.[7]

A new taboo arose: tobacco. The foremost attack on this sin was launched by the Reverend James A. Massey (1807–1871), who served as Presiding Elder in 1840–1842. It was Massey's intention to secure a total prohibition of "drams, pipes, and tobacco," but he met with only partial success. "He succeeded to a good degree in raising the standard of temperance in the church... But in the tobacco department he was less successful. He did what he could in the way of preaching and ridicule to break up the fraternity of smokers, snuffers, and those who chew."[8]

Alcoholic beverages received a new emphasis. What was to become Methodism's most ardent crusade had not seemed of any special concern to the first generation on the Shore. Drummond Welbourn had kept a tavern in Horntown where, presumably, guests could find something to drink. And William Seymour of Onancock, part owner of a mercantile house with John Ker, another Methodist, had had no scruples about dealing in the sale of rum. There is in existence a bill from the firm signed by Seymour and dated October 9, 1806, for 32 gallons of West India rum, and to it Seymour attached a note in his own hand:

> *Dear Sir:*
> *I have attended particularly to the despatch of your Boy & the measuring of the Rum, which I hope you will find on Tryal to be equal to expectation.*
> *I am very Sincerely your friend*
>
> *Wm Seymour*[9]

But now that the patriarchs were dead and the second generation in control, the use of alcohol reared its head as a problem deserving the attention of the people called Methodists.

The first temperance resolution by Methodists on the Virginia Shore is, to be sure, from 1805, when the early fathers resolved "that this Conference Oppose by Presept and example the daily Use of spirituous Liquors." But there is no further mention of "spirituous liquors" in the local records until the 1830's, and only then does the temperance cause begin to gain momentum. An 1831 resolution prohibited local Methodists from voting for political candidates who "treat with ardent Spirits directly or indirectly," and authorized the printing of a circular on the subject for general distribution. In 1836 the circuit recommended a return to the general rules "of Mr. Wesley in regard to the use of Spirituous liquors;" Wesley had been an ardent foe of alcohol. And finally in 1842 the Accomack Circuit made it more or less a rule:

> *Resolved that those members of the M.E. Church who are in the habit of drinking or using spirituous or malt liquors in any way unless in cases of necessity as a medicine are highly censurable & we earnestly advise them either to desist therefrom or to withdraw immediately from the church.*

Resolved that the above resolution be read publicly at each of the appointments on the circuit by the preacher in charge.....

These resolutions passed "nearly unanimously."[10]

The Methodists of Annemessex Circuit in Somerset County, Maryland, just across the line, also became concerned about alcoholic beverages at about the same time, and in 1831 they passed a resolution that survives:

That we will not drink spirituous liquor ourselves, nor give it to our families, or laborers, except we are convinced it is absolutely necessary as a medicine.

That we will neither make or sell it...

That we will deal with those merchants who will not sell it in preference to others.

That our preachers be requested to give a copy of these resolutions to each class leader, desiring him to use his influence to obtain the signatures of his members.....

The most memorable result of the Annemessex resolutions occurred shortly thereafter when Thomas Barbon, a local merchant who sold rum, rolled his casks of liquor out of the store into the yard and smashed them righteously with an ax. Local tradition has it that his turkeys, chickens, and geese flocked around and lapped up the flowing liquors, the last things ever to get drunk because of Barbon.[11]

Not everyone took the anti-alcohol campaign quite so seriously. The brilliant young lawyer, Henry A. Wise, an Episcopalian, happened upon a Baptist revival when he visited Chincoteague Island with some friends for the annual pony penning in the 1830's. Wise and his friends were in "convivial spirits," and some of them had been "imbibing freely." As they seated themselves on the rough campground benches, however, Wise himself cut a serious and dignified figure, and the preacher in charge assumed he was a visiting minister and called upon him to exhort. Never known to be at a loss for words, Wise walked to the front of the assembly and announced his text from Proverbs: "Wine is a mocker, strong drink is raging; and whosoever is deceived thereby is not *Wise*." It is said that his eloquence was so great that a number of persons were converted, and that the old preacher ever afterwards referred to Wise as a fellow-worker in the vineyard. His friends, however, were hardly able to contain themselves with suppressed laughter.[12] Not until a later generation would Eastern Shoremen cease to laugh at Methodism's temperance crusade, and endorse it wholeheartedly.

Meanwhile, as these new rules of conduct were being heralded by local Methodists, some of the older campaigns were being quietly laid aside. Instrumental music, once considered ungodly among the Methodists, was now more acceptable, and in the 1850's the congregation at Burton's Chapel became the first on record among Methodists of the Shore to install an organ in the church to accompany congregational singing.[13]

Baptists were no less zealous than Methodists in defining the Christian life, as the records of the Modest Town area prove. The Reverend William Laws, pastor of Modest Town Baptist Church (founded 1829), oversaw a congregation whose members were "censured" for such offenses as circulating unfavorable reports, "treating his wife in a disrespectful manner," and "going on the beach and saving wrecked goods and performing manual labor on Sunday for wages, when there were men enough of the world there present to do all the necessary work." Modest Town Baptists were subject to a fine of 25¢ for "chewing tobacco and spitting in church," and one member was expelled from the congregation for "being an abettor in burning a house."

Pastor Laws himself had an aversion to the worldly game of baseball, particularly when it was played on the Sabbath. Whenever the neighborhood youths were ready for a game, they sought an out-of-the-way place to play it lest the pastor catch them, but Laws was almost always able to sniff out a game in progress. One Sunday while out in his carriage he heard the distant shouts of a game and sped to the scene only to find that the culprits had fled at his approach. Since they had in their haste, however, left behind a motley collection of coats, hats, and shoes removed for the game, Laws calmly collected these articles of clothing and carried them back home with him. Those who later came to call for them were thus identified as the Sabbath-breakers and, no doubt, given a stern rebuke from the preacher.[14]

Unfortunately Methodism's intensified effort to weed out the card-player, the Sabbath-breaker, and the secret tippler was accomplished only at the expense of another old concern that was now being forgotten. Methodism entered the Shore afire with John Wesley's hatred of slavery, and the first generation shared some of his concern to eradicate that evil from American society. During the earliest years of the faith on the Shore being a Methodist meant freeing one's slaves and at least arguing for emancipation. Over the years that particular concern faded, with disastrous consequences for the future of the country and the church. By the 1830's the old rules against the owning of slaves were gone and all but forgotten, and Eastern Shore Methodists were no longer required to exercise their faith on that issue. Slavery and slave-owning were not something that the second-generation Eastern Shore Methodist had to concern himself with.

But Methodists of the third generation were not to be so lucky.

If the people called Methodists were changing with the turn of the generation, no less so were their preachers.

In Asbury's day, the "traveling preacher" was just that: a true traveling pioneer who gave up all hope of home, possessions, marriage, and family for his calling to the ministry. On the Shore as virtually everywhere else in the country the earliest Methodist ministers possessed only what they could carry with them in their saddlebags. Their home was where they found lodging with the people of the circuit. Needless to say they were, in overwhelming numbers, unmarried. To the end of his life Asbury was horrified by the possibility of a married Methodist clergy, and did what he could to persuade his preachers not to take that step.

In 1818, two years after Asbury's death, the Accomack circuit expressed itself unwilling to receive married preachers, and yet within a short time married preachers were as much the rule as the exception. With preachers who were married came the necessity of housing them and their wives and families. There was talk of a parsonage for the circuit preachers as early as 1823, but not until 1834 was the first parsonage built, in Onancock next door to Cokesbury Church. The deed for the land expressly stated that the new home was for married preachers only; when the preacher was unmarried, the house was to be rented out (a stipulation which was violated within a few short years). Two years later the new Northampton Circuit parsonage was built at Eastville. [15]

Preachers were still appointed to each circuit in pairs, but no longer were they equal as in the early days. There was now a "preacher-in-charge" and a "colleague" or "junior preacher" who was understood to be his assistant, and who was lucky if he made a third of what the older man collected in salary.

Clerical dress, too, was changing. As early as 1810 some of the more progressive ministers on the peninsula had begun to abandon the Asburian dress code: low-crowned and broad-rimmed hat, black frock coat, straight collar buttoned up to the neck, and breeches and leggings. Before 1820 pants had made their first appearance at Annual Conference sessions, much to the consternation of Bishop Asbury. [16]

The changes that were occurring in the style and substance of Methodist ministers are illustrated in the Eastern Shore careers of two preachers who labored on the scene in the late 1830's. One, Jefferson Lewis, was of the new school, and the other, John Hersey, was a colorful example of the old school.

In 1835 the conference sent Jefferson Lewis to be preacher-in-charge of the Accomack Circuit, with Joseph Carlisle, a young married man, as his "junior preacher." Lewis was of the new school of ministers, his modernity and forceful, businesslike manner altogether unlike anything the local Methodists had ever encountered in a preacher. He quickly set about whipping his rural circuit into shape, reinstituting some old neglected rules, abolishing some old local customs, and ushering in what would be remembered as a "new epoch" in the life of the church on the Shore. It was during his pastorate and thanks to his abilities that the explosive issue of dividing the circuit was defused and decided, and the question-and-answer format of the Quarterly Conference was introduced.

Lewis arrived on the scene to discover that his circuit, despite its large membership and prosperity, was notorious for being tight with money. For years now local Methodists had paid the pastor's salary by apportioning a "quarterage" among the members, a payment of 25¢ at each Quarterly Meeting. The salary provided from the quarterage was small (some members did not even bother to pay it), and yet even this levy was unpopular on the circuit. "I thought the gospel was free!" exclaimed one old member when the idea had first been introduced; "if I'm to be taxed for hearing preaching, you can take my name off." Another brother boasted with pride that in thirty years of being a Methodist his church had cost him only $30. When Lewis arrived, the stewards told him privately what they had told every incoming preacher for years: that money was not a popular subject on this circuit, and one to be avoided as much as possible.

Lewis would have none of this. The old days of the traveling minister in Asbury's style were, as far as he was concerned, gone for good, and he demanded a decent living and decent wage. When he pointed out that the new parsonage was not yet furnished, he was told that his predecessor had occupied the house without complaint and that he should do likewise. He pushed through the Quarterly Conference a proposal to increase the salary by providing an allowance for food and for the cost of keeping his horse, and when it appeared that both increased salary and parsonage furnishings might meet with heavy opposition, he took the unprecedented tack of pleading his cause in each of the local churches as he made his pulpit rounds. Lewis was an able preacher, and the opposition melted as his circuit came to know him. A round of revivals occurred on the circuit, and the people responded enthusiastically. The parsonage was duly furnished, and when the committee to set the food allowance recommended a yearly sum of $50, the Quarterly Conference overruled it and gave Lewis $100 instead. The junior preacher, Carlisle, fared less well; the Quarterly Conference voted only to reimburse him for "whatever he may have to pay for his and his wife's board."

Lewis made sweeping changes in the worship life of his circuit. Though a revivalist in the best Methodist tradition—Sally Ashby of Burton's Chapel, long remembered as one of the best "shouting" members on the Shore, was converted under his ministry—Lewis nonetheless created a new standard of order and decorum at all worship services. Several of the hymns used at camp meetings and revivals were proscribed. All "ranting and excessive excitement" were to be carefully controlled. "God, as an intelligent Being, demands an intelligent worship," he insisted, and to back that up he kept an eagle eye on the congregation during the prayers after revival sermons to make certain that the aisles remained clear and that penitents were not unduly jostled by well-wishers and those praying with them at the rail. He decreed an end to the several local camp meetings around the circuit, and the first "protracted meeting" on record on the Shore, an orderly indoor revival that gradually came to be the general custom in place of the camp meeting, dates from his pastorate.

AN EASTERN SHORE METHODIST WORSHIP SERVICE

c. 1840
The Reverend E. E. Kemp preaching in the church on Smith Island

He even dared tamper with the annual camp meeting at Tangier. "Hitherto," he announced to the assembled campers, "you have carried your services [on] into the night, and in consequence slept the next day during the sermon." Believing that "sleep and rest are just as essential at a camp meeting as anywhere else," Lewis instituted an eleven o'clock trumpet each night. At the sound of the trumpet, all services were to cease, the people to retire to their tents, and those without accommodations to leave the campgrounds. Lewis and his campground police strictly enforced this new rule, which met with much grumbling at first. In this as in his other innovations, however, the able Lewis ultimately carried the day, and after his one year on the Shore he left behind him a Methodism noticeably modernized.[17]

As representative of the old school as Lewis was of the new was a remarkable preacher who first put in an appearance on the Eastern Shore of Virginia in 1839, John Hersey. The Reverend John Hersey (1786-1862), a native of Wilmington, Delaware, was ordained an elder in 1829, by which time he had already embarked upon the career of peddling his own theological works up and down the East Coast. Though he lived in the time of the second generation, Hersey was very definitely of the old school, reminiscent of the time of the patriarchs. His lifestyle was as austere as that of the early circuit riders—up at dawn, preach by five o'clock (if there was anyone to listen), abstain from anything other than simple food and drink, scorn everything luxurious, from table sugar to featherbeds. It is said that he was never known to laugh. Yet he was a famous and forceful preacher and the crowds flocked to hear him, perhaps because he was now considered a colorful oddity out of the past.

John Hersey made three recorded visits to the Eastern Shore of Virginia—in 1839, 1845 (or 1846), and 1853—and did much of his work on the Maryland Shore. En route to the Tangier camp meeting on one of these occasions, he left Baltimore by steamer with a number of other passengers who did not measure up to his standard of behavior. "Two young females who wished to pass for ladies continued to play backgammon," his journal records, "though I admonished them most pointedly... After supper I preached a plain, pointed sermon—all were respectful and attentive."

During the 1840's Hersey preached at the Tangier camp meeting to a full and fascinated congregation who had gathered to witness this strange man. His text that day was Psalm 109:26: "Help me, O Lord my God," and Hersey waxed eloquent on the sin of pride and the ruin wrought thereby. One preacher on the stand behind him had the misfortune to be wearing a fine satin vest. In the midst of his sermon, Hersey turned suddenly and pointed to him with a long, crooked finger: "And pride has its roots right here in this pulpit," he shouted. Dashing from the pulpit to the side of the poor thunderstruck preacher, he ran his long, bony hand over the vest, stroking it in derision. Soon his well-dressed colleague, to the immense emotion of the crowd, was bathed in tears.

It is said that the next day when Hersey left the island, "the audience followed the man of God to the shore, weeping as did the elders of Ephesus when Paul took his leave of them to return to Jerusalem."

JOHN HERSEY

Despite his eloquence, Hersey was fighting a losing battle, and his enemy was the growing prosperity of the Methodists, as one final incident from his life will tell. Invited to the home of one of the Methodists in Virginia, he entered it only to find it was a veritable mansion, well furnished with glass and tapestries and elegant furniture. Hersey was aghast; he "raised his hands in holy horror," and stepping back to his hostess exclaimed, "Sister, Sister! Do you expect to take these things to heaven?"

The Methodist lady was ready with her reply: "Why Brother Hersey, you surprise me! I take such stuff as this as mean to heaven. Golden paved streets, jasper walls, and pearly gates would so outshine such trash as this that I would be ashamed to have it about. No indeed, I never thought of taking it to heaven!"[18]

For once the old man had nothing to say. And just as well, for although few persons in his beloved Methodist Episcopal Church lived in mansions, fewer and fewer every year could remember the simple rusticity which he represented and cherished. And on the Eastern Shore in 1841, two years after his first visit there, the local Quarterly Conference continued the work that Jefferson Lewis had begun with a resolution that would have horrified John Hersey:"...the great Head of the Church has ordained that they which preach the gospel should...receive a *comfortable support.*" And they laid down new rules about collecting the apportionment for the pastor's salary from each member.[19]

The second generation of Methodism on the Eastern Shore of Virginia saw an innovation, an institution that would in time become a profoundly influential and integral part of the local church life, the Sunday school.

The "Sabbath school," as it was originally called, was not at all a part of the early church scene on the Shore, even though in the school begun by William Elliott in 1785 the Shore had what was possibly the oldest Sabbath school in the country. For more than thirty years Elliott's school had no connection with a church; it was not until 1818 that he moved it out of his home into Burton's Chapel. For the most part, Eastern Shore Methodists went about the work of the church for a half a century or more before the Sunday school made the scene. And even then the Sunday school faced an uphill struggle to survive for some years to come.

The important year for Sunday schools on the Shore is 1834, for from that date comes the earliest mention of the new institution among both Methodists and Baptists of the peninsula, apart from the Elliott school. Modest Town Baptist Church, a strong new church founded in 1829, established a Sunday school in 1834, the second oldest continuous Sunday school on the Shore. By 1835 the Methodists could boast of four schools—Burton's, Downing's, Cokesbury, and Atlantic—with over 135 "scholars." By 1841 the number had grown to six schools with over 300 scholars, and among the Baptists there were two new schools, one at Lower Northampton, another at Metompkin operated by Modest Town Baptist Church. By then the preachers were actively promoting the Sunday school idea, and the Quarterly Conference agenda had a regular place for the "Sabbath school report." The Accomack Circuit resolved in that year that "each member of our church be requested to use their utmost influence to promote the Sabbath schools."

For a number of years the Sunday school would remain principally a warm-weather affair, operated only during the spring and summer months. Even the strongest schools would be discontinued with the coming of winter. The school operated by the Methodist congregation at Newtown managed to stay open throughout the winter of 1844-1845; it was apparently the first to do so, and such a record was seldom equaled during the first two decades of the Sunday school on the Shore.[20]

Two things about this new institution were noticeable right from the start. One was that it was an entirely new area for lay participation and control in the local church, an area where the preachers seldom had opportunity to work or interfere. Women were among those lay persons who rose to positions of leadership in the Sunday school, more so among the Methodists than the Baptists and Presbyterians. At least two Sunday schools—at Tangier and at Horntown—were founded by women, and these are the first real examples of female leadership in the local Methodist records.[21] Conversely, one of the original bastions of lay control in the local church, the love feast, began to decline when the Sunday school was born. The last mention of a love feast as a circuit function is from 1833, and thereafter the practice began its long decline.[22] The Methodist laity, their ministers more numerous now and more readily at hand, had a new part of the church in which to carve their niche.

The Sunday school, secondly, proved very early to be an effective new way in which to spread the church to new, unevangelized communities. A Sunday school could very easily blossom into a full-fledged church and congregation, as the Methodists proved in the village of Atlantic in the 1830's. But again it was Modest Town Baptist Church that set the pattern: by 1838 this active congregation was operating not one but three Sunday schools, one at Modest Town at their own church, one at Metompkin, and one near what is now Bloxom. By 1852 the Metompkin school had become Zion Baptist Church, and the Bloxom school, Bethel Baptist Church.[23]

By 1850 the Sunday school was on firm footing among both Baptists and Methodists on the Shore, and would soon appear among the Presbyterians as well. Virtually every congregation founded on the Shore in any denomination after that date was either first a Sunday school, or else created simultaneously with its own Sunday school. As the years went on the Sunday school became so firmly established that Eastern Shore churchgoers could not remember a period when there was no such institution, or conceive of a church without one.

Methodism established itself so strongly on the Eastern Shore of Virginia in the first three decades of the nineteenth century that other denominations faced a struggle just to get a foothold there, or else, as with the Baptists, once established found themselves affected by this overwhelmingly predominant faith. In the 1830's and 1840's new faiths found their way to the Shore, but the story of their origins there must be seen against the background of the strength of the Methodist Episcopal Church.

Episcopalianism, for all intents and purposes, was a small and struggling faith in the two counties at this point. There were only two functioning churches: St. James' near Accomac and St. George's in Pungoteague. Occasional Episcopal services were held in Eastville by 1813, but in that year there were as many vacant as there were functioning chapels among the Episcopalians on the Shore.[24]

In 1819 Episcopalianism was re-established in Northampton County with the repairing and reopening of Hungars Church, closed since the Revolution. An attempt was made at the same time to restore Magothy, but the old building there was beyond repair. It was sold and dismantled in 1824, and four years later its successor, Christ Church, arose in Eastville.[25]

St. James' Church in Accomack County, in particular, felt the full impact of the presence of Methodists. The village of Drummondtown did not exist when this old church was erected in 1767, and so it was built on the side of a country road. By the 1830's it found itself a mile outside of town, where the Methodists (and after 1837 the Presbyterians) had flourishing congregations. By 1838 the congregation at St. James' had so dwindled that the decision was made to move to town, and so the old building was dismantled, the bricks carted to the county seat, and there, just a block away from the Methodist meetinghouse, was erected the church building so admired today.[26]

Meanwhile, the abandoned Anglican chapels passed from view: the New Church burned in 1820, Assawoman Church fell into a final ruin around 1837.[27]

Though the Episcoplians could count among their ranks some of the more wealthy and influential citizens of the Shore, they were but a small denomination compared to the Methodists and Baptists.

It was in the 1830's that Presbyterianism at last succeeded in planting a permanent church on the Virginia Shore. It is said that its coming had a political context. For in 1830 Henry A. Wise moved back to the Shore with his wife, Anne Jennings Wise, and in 1833 was elected to Congress. Mrs. Wise was the daughter of a Presbyterian minister from Philadelphia, and it is he who suggested to the East Hanover Presbytery that the work of that church in the region of Francis Makemie's old home should be revived. In 1836 the Presbytery dispatched the Reverend Leonidas L. Smith to the Shore, and in 1837 Makemie Presbyterian Church was organized in Drummondtown. Anne Jennings Wise, for whom it was intended, died that year.

Presbyterian energies were consumed just in keeping their little congregations alive. By 1840 Makemie Church had only eight members, and in 1846 three of them were dismissed to form a second congregation, Holmes Church in Northampton. Holmes grew more rapidly than the original church. By 1854 it had 24 members, but all of its members were women. When the church wanted a Sunday school formed, the ladies felt required to recruit a male superintendent from nearby Salem Methodist Episcopal Church. And when the Presbytery met with Holmes in 1857, the ladies had to line up gentlemen chauffeurs to drive the visitors the several miles from the wharf to the church. Not until 1859 did Holmes have a regular pastor (and then only briefly), and not until 1867 did the menfolk of the neighborhood begin to infiltrate the membership.[28]

Another denomination made a spectacular, if short-lived, appearance on the Shore at this time. In 1840 a Reverend Mr. Chase, a Boston divine of the Universalist persuasion, came to the Shore to conduct the funeral of a lady of Cobb's Island, a place recently settled from New England. To him the Shore seemed fertile ground for his faith, and he sought in Eastville and Capeville for a place to erect a Universalist church. He met with no success in either place, but by 1841 he succeeded in erecting a chapel about a mile north of Belle Haven.

Universalism was a northern transplant on the Shore, a liberal New England doctrine of the period that later merged with the Unitarian Church. Its principal tenet was that "it is the purpose of God, through the grace revealed in our Lord Jesus Christ, to save *every* member of the human race from sin," a tenet which at the time grated against Methodist insistence that individuals had to respond to God's grace in order to receive it. Across the door of the Belle Haven church was inscribed this message: "We believe in the living God, the Savior of all men."

The sudden appearance of this new faith from outside did not escape the notice of the Methodists. They were quick to point out that only in Belle Haven, that unchurched community where Methodism had never been welcome, was Chase able to make any headway. Chase was succeeded in 1841 by an even more aggressive pastor, G.L. Lumsden, who upon arriving on the scene quickly issued a challenge to the other churches to a public debate on the doctrines of salvation. The challenge was accepted by Thomas J. Quigley (1805-1870), pastor of the

Northampton Circuit, and old Marshapungo Baptist Church, an abandoned meetinghouse just south of Belle Haven, was agreed upon as the scene for the debate. Lumsden invited a Dr. Dodd of Boston, his first name now unknown, to argue the Universalist cause, and Quigley, despite the misgivings of many Methodists who tried to dissuade him, agreed to meet him.

It was a day when public speaking and debates were a prime form of entertainment, and when the two opponents met in the old meetinghouse they found the building filled to overflowing with hundreds of eager spectators. For three days, morning and afternoon, the crowd sat in rapt attention as Dodd and Quigley debated the question, "Do the Holy Scriptures teach the unconditional Salvation of all mankind?" When it was over the judges awarded Quigley the honor of having presented the better argument, although Dodd was also cited as having "acquitted himself with distinguished honor."

Dodd left the Shore shortly after the debate, and perhaps because of Quigley's success against him, Univeralism on the Eastern Shore of Virginia never ventured beyond the Belle Haven area.[29] The church there lasted only about ten years. It was functioning when the census of 1850 was taken, but by the Civil War the Universalist building stood vacant and unused.[30]

Even the Baptists, second largest denomination on the Shore, lost ground to the Methodists in the first quarter of the nineteenth century. And events in their quarter illustrate the extent to which the Methodist predominance of the penisula could and did affect not only the growth but also the thought and practice of other faiths.

In 1809 when the seven Baptist churches of the Eastern Shore of Virginia banded together to form a loose confederation known as the Accomack Baptist Association, there were 890 members in the seven churches. Twenty-two years later in 1831 there was only one new Baptist congregation on the Shore—Modest Town, founded in 1829 (although one other, Marshapungo, had been founded, only to fade quickly)—and membership in the Association had dropped to only 526, a decline of 40% in one generation. The reason for the decline was a theological dispute that raged among the Baptists; as their own historian put it, "Antinomianism seems to have been the cause.[31]

Antinomianism—from a word meaning "against the law" or "without law"—was the word the Baptists themselves used to identify the theology of some of their own number who gave added, almost extreme, emphasis to the Baptist doctrine of election. In opposition to the Methodists, all the local Baptists taught the doctrine of election, that salvation depended not upon man's action or choice, but upon God's action in choosing or "electing" whom He would for salvation. Some Baptists, however, were eager to carry the doctrine even further: so completely was salvation God's work, they insisted, that men could not in any way effect their salvation. No human action or choice or response could alter God's actions; by God's eternal predestination each person's fate was already sealed.

When put into practice this "ultra-high Calvinism," as some called it, or "Antinomianism," as most knew it (for its primary tenet was that it was without "law" or human action that salvation occurred), had very decided effects upon the life of the church. Since everyone was predestined either to be saved or to be damned, and there was nothing anyone could do about it, the church should not waste its energies on evangelism. Missionary efforts were a waste of time, church schools a futile exercise for misguided "Arminians" like the Methodists. The busy activities that filled the life of the church in this period of increasing institutionalization were useless. All that was necessary was for the elect to attend to the Word of God, and preachers in proclaiming it should not even prepare their sermons by deliberation or planning but speak what flowed forth from the spirit when they stood up to preach. Needless to say, there was a real danger that congregations where Antinomianism was in control would shut themselves off from the world, live to themselves, and even die off.

Joseph Everett noted the presence of Antinomianism in the Magothy area as early as 1787, Francis Asbury in 1791. "There is a great work of God in the lower counties of Virginia," wrote the bishop after his first and only visit to Cape Charles, "but the Antinomian doctrines so liberally set forth by some greatly hinder."[32] The Antinomian tendency smouldered in the local Baptist churches for a decade or more, and then was fanned into prominence in 1815, when several of the local churches were visited by Luther Rice. Rice, a famous Baptist preacher known as the "pioneer of missions among Baptists of the United States," came to the Shore to further the cause of foreign missions, but his visit only opened up controversy as Antinomians responded by calling into question the very idea of missions. The battle raged with new intensity after his visit, and "Antinomian" and "Arminian" labels were thrown around by both sides in considerable heat. By 1823 the Reverend Noah Davis (who later founded the American Baptist Publication Society) was laboring on the Shore, and he observed that the local churches were "cold and barren under the withering influences of Antinomianism."[33]

In 1831 the issue flared into open conflict. The yearly associational meeting was held at Messongo Church in upper Accomack that year. Each party counted influential ministers and laymen in its ranks, and the lines between the "antimission" (Antinomian) and "mission" (regular) Baptists were obvious from the first. On the first day of the meeting a dispute arose over a procedural question, and before the day was out the Antinomians had withdrawn to form a separate association of their own. The Antinomians may well have been in the majority among all the Baptists on the Shore at that time. They were very strong in Lower Northampton, Chincoteague, Messongo, Pungoteague, and Metompkin churches. Only Red Bank and Modest Town were completely free of that faction.

For a full year the division continued, with tensions high on both sides. In 1832, when the Baptists gathered for the annual meeting at Metompkin Church, they found the Antinomians in a majority in that congregation and thus in possession of the meetinghouse, and were forced to assemble in a private home nearby. Later that year—the regular Baptists must have thought it was by divine intervention—a tornado completely destroyed the Metompkin meetinghouse, and the church was never rebuilt.

In 1833 the Accomack Baptist Association officially repudiated the Antinomians in their midst and urged its congregations to exclude from their ranks all persons of that persuasion. Gradually after that date the regular Baptists regained control of the local congregations, except for Messongo, which remained separate and became known in time as Messongo Primitive Baptist Church. Reduced to this one church, the Antinomian cause ultimately faded out; by 1876 the Accomack Baptist Association had grown to ten churches with over a thousand members, Antinomian Messongo was a small, declining congregation.

In two important ways the Antinomian dispute shaped the religious history of the whole Shore. First, it effectively eliminated the Baptists as real competition for the Methodists in the quest for new adherents during an important and crucial point in their history. Even though the Baptists were the second largest church on the Shore, they could mount no real threat to the Methodists, divided as they were into two camps, and Methodist growth proceeded apace.

Secondly, the dispute forced the regular Baptists, in repudiating Antinomianism, a step closer to the "Arminian" theology of the Methodists than they might otherwise have taken. At the very time when Methodists were becoming greatly exercised about cardplaying, dancing, theatre-going, smoking, and like issues, the Baptists were forced to decide whether how you lived and conducted yourself in these regards had any bearing on salvation. Most of them decided it had a great bearing. And because of that decision, their denomination went on to become as methodical as the Methodists in their attitudes towards social conduct and lifestyle. By the end of the 1830's the churches of the Accomack Baptist Association were approving, sanctioning, and promoting "Arminian" programs worthy of any Methodist: camp meetings (1832), home missions (1835), temperence societies (1836), Sunday schools (1834), and foreign mission societies (1836).[34]

The Baptists were not alone in experiencing division during the 1830's. Methodists, too, found themselves seriously divided, but the cause of division was not doctrine. Rather the controversy arose as Methodists encountered and reacted to some of the important political issues of the day, and it illustrates how the Methodist Episcopal Church was changing with the changing times.

The Methodist issue was one of church government. John Wesley had never been a democrat when it came to governing the church. In matters of polity he followed the Church of England which followed the Church of Rome in believing that the clergy were ultimately responsible for the governing of the church. Methodism was ruled from the top by its bishops and, as the office developed in the United States, its presiding elders, and on the local scene the power of the preacher held sway. Although there was a significant democratic streak in Methodism—perhaps more than Wesley would have chosen to admit—the last word in the church was nevertheless held by its ministers and their superiors, who were also ministers.

It was perhaps inevitable that so strongly non-democratic a concept of church government should find rough going in the United States. By as early as 1792 James O'Kelly, a Methodist preacher in southside Virginia, had made democracy in the church an issue and led his followers out of the denomination because it would not yield to his demand for more democratic representation for the laity.

By the 1820's, the period of Jacksonian democracy when the common man was asserting his rights and new state constitutions were being written to extend the franchise to greater numbers of people, the quest for democracy in the Methodist Episcopal Church gained new adherents and took the form of a movement. It was called the Reform Movement, and it came at last to stand for three specific measures: (1) the election of presiding elders by the Annual Conference (presiding elders were then as now appointed by the bishop); (2) representation of lay members in the Annual Conference (which had always been an annual gathering of ministers only); and (3) the representation of local preachers in the Annual Conferences.[35] The passage of these three measures would have made Methodism far more democratic, although not completely so. It was still presupposed, for instance, that bishops and not congregations would place pastors in churches. In later years the second measure, lay representation in the Annual Conference, would become church law. But the absence of all three of these measures from the practice of the church in the 1820's and 1830's created a crisis.

After 1824 and several attempts to have its platform approved by the church, it became obvious to the "reformers" that they had no hope of getting the church at large to accept their democratizing views. And so almost at once, as if by previous design, Methodists of Reformist persuasion began all over the country to withdraw from the Methodist Episcopal Church into their own congregations. In 1830 delegates of the Reformist congregations banded together in Baltimore and founded a new denomination, the Methodist Protestant Church. It was not a large denomination—its main sources of strength at first were Virginia and Maryland—but it was completely separate from the Methodist Episcopal Church. In doctrine and belief the two churches were almost identical. But Methodist Protestant polity was decidedly different: the church had no bishops and no presiding elders, but instead conference presidents, elected annually, who visited each charge once a year. And Annual Conferences were composed of equal numbers of ministers and laymen, all of whom could vote.[36]

The man who probably had more to do with the growth of the Reform movement in Eastern Shore Methodism than anyone else was the Reverend Avra Melvin (1780-1853). Though not strictly a Virginian—Melvin lived across the state line near Newtown, Maryland—he had strong connections with the Virginia Shore. It was there that he met and married Katy Bayley of Onancock in 1813, and it was there that he had assisted James Aikens, the circuit preacher, in 1805, one year before his own ordination. Although his father had been expelled from the Methodist society by a church trial in 1804, Avra Melvin was himself a highly respected Methodist preacher on the Shore. By the 1820's many Shoremen could identify him as the somewhat sanctimonious man who could quote more Bible verses than any other preacher they had known. "He preached more funerals, performed more marriage ceremonies, and baptized more persons than any other man in this section...in his day, and always had plenty to say on short notice," wrote one of his contemporaries. A less glowing remembrance was that he was a stiff and serious man, his bearing so dignified that he seemed to be a contemporary of Noah.

Not long after he was ordained a "traveling preacher," Avra Melvin decided, for reasons not now known, to "locate," and he accordingly settled down on the family lands near Newtown, left the regular pastorate, and supported his wife and family by other means. It was as "local preacher," not as traveling circuit preacher, that he did most of the work for which he was remembered on the Shore.[37] He often crossed the boundary into Virginia to perform his pastoral functions, and apparently one of his friends there was David Watt of Wattsville, who lived not so far away from Melvin's own home.

The decision to "locate" is probably what made Avra Melvin, years later, into a reformer. As an ordained traveling preacher he had full-fledged status, complete with the right to vote at Annual Conference. As a local preacher he had little or no status and no place at the Conference. Although there is no direct evidence of it, it is not unlikely that as the years went by this energetic and busy preacher, who was hardly less active than the traveling clergy though he ministered in his own spare time, chafed under the powerlessness of his local status. And so in 1827, when a large Reformer meeting was held in the Newtown church—the first one on the Shore—Avra Melvin was there, and with him was David Watt.[38] These two alone, apparently, represented the Reformist cause among the Methodists of the Eastern Shore of Virginia.

In 1832 Melvin and Watt led in the formation of the first two Methodist Protestant congregations on the lower Shore. In Newtown nineteen people met together in a schoolhouse to organize the Methodist Protestant Church of Newtown, and Avra Melvin's name was the first on the membership list. This congregation, forerunner of the present Bethany Church in downtown Pocomoke City, met for a while in Melvin's home and under his pastorate.[39]

At about the same time David Watt notified the Quarterly Conference of the Accomack Circuit that he was resigning from the Methodist Episcopal Church,[40] and with him the society at Wattsville passed into the Methodist Protestant Church. The Wattsville congregation was probably still meeting in Watt's home at the time, but shortly thereafter a meetinghouse, the last to be erected by one of the original Shore societies, was built nearby. In 1840 Watt deeded the property to the new denomination "for the prosperity of religion in the neighborhood of Wattsville, for the Protestant Methodist and other religious denominations to worship in." And although it is said that other denominations did indeed for a while use the meetinghouse, in a short time the church that stood at Wattsville was completely and exclusively Methodist Protestant.[41]

In 1837 the new denomination created its own Northampton Circuit and appointed Stephen Taylor to be its pastor. A new congregation was organized in Lee Mont and a chapel erected there by 1839. Within a year the circuit could boast 123 white and five black members. It was, and remained for many years, a small and struggling denomination in Accomack County, but already the two centers of activity were set: "Friendship" at Wattsville, and "Harmony," as the new church in Lee Mont was often called.

The Methodist Protestant schism did not seriously harm the main body of the church and on the Eastern Shore was hardly even noticed. The loss of Wattsville and the founding of Lee Mont attracted no more notice than the loss of Ames Chapel and the Hog Island society, both of which faded out at about that time. To offset Wattsville, a new congregation named Oak Grove arose in the village of Atlantic in 1832, and by 1835 a new society was functioning in Cashville in an old Baptist meetinghouse called Boggs Chapel.[42]

The older Methodist Episcopal congregations, meanwhile, prospered apace. By 1842 Tangier's first church, only seven years old, was already outgrown and replaced by a larger one. The people of Burton's Chapel spent the grand sum of $50 to make their building twenty feet longer in 1834. And in 1837 when the Accomack Circuit held a camp meeting near the new Oak Grove Chapel in Atlantic, it organized with great fanfare the Conference Missionary Society of Accomack Circuit. Members of the new society agreed to pay dues of fifty cents a year, which was to aid missionary causes. Despite the fanfare, the new Missionary Society proved no more important than the short-lived Tract Society founded in 1828, and by 1837 forgotten.[43]

The church had divided, but the division was so unequal that the main stream of the denomination was not appreciably weakened.

AN EASTERN SHORE CAMP MEETING

Deal Island, Maryland; the Tangier Campmeeting undoubtedly looked much like this

Throughout the years of change in the first half of the nineteenth century, the Methodists of Virginia's Eastern Shore gathered every summer on Tangier Island for the great camp meeting. And great it was. Every year from 1808 to 1857, the only exception being 1814 when Tangier was under British occupation, the yearly camp meeting of Joshua Thomas rode higher and higher. There was hardly a minister or member in Eastern Virginia who did not at some time or another visit the great Tangier camp meeting. John Hersey was there in 1839, in 1845, and in 1853, the year of Joshua Thomas' death.[44]

And this most exciting and colorful event of many a summer night might well have been lost to us completely had not Henry A. Wise, an Episcopalian, written down his description of it.

Wise, a native of Drummondtown was a young attorney in 1828 when he passed by Tangier Island on his way to meet his bride in Tennessee. A brilliant career lay before him. By 1830 he would be living again on the Shore, in Drummondtown. By 1833 he would be elected to Congress, and in 1844 appointed minister to Brazil. Finally, in 1855, he would be elected governor, the only native of the Eastern Shore of Virginia ever to attain that office.[45]

But he was also a writer, and his description of the Tangier Island camp meeting in its prime in 1828 is the longest and the best that we have today:

"There upon the bald sands of the beach every year have the tents of worship, wooden and sailcloth, been pitched by piety...to watch and pray and preach for weeks at a time, in humiliation and homage towards God, in the open air of heaven, by the bright waters of the grandest, loveliest bay of old ocean's salt seas.

"...It is a yearly feast of fruits and fish as well as of 'love,' and revivals of health as well as of spirit. There collect the great campaigners of the pulpit, some of the greatest divines and elders; there are fathers and mothers and sons and daughters of the Church; there collect people of the world of every degree and dignity; there are hucksters and caterers for the 'multitude come not to be taught;' there whole families with household utensils and every appliance which tent can afford to table. Some come in steamers from Baltimore, Annapolis, and Cambridge, Maryland, and from Norfolk and Fredericksburg and other towns in Virginia, and from both sides of the bay. And from every creek come vessels of all sizes, schooners, sloops, pungies, cats, canoes, and skiffs, loaded with people and provisions, until the island harbors are studded with shipping and a forest of masts, which gives the wharves and island the appearance of some considerable mart of commerce.

"The camp is regularly laid out in large squares, with wide streets. Bowers are erected on the pulpit-stands, and for the anxious benches and broad planks are nailed horizontally across the tops of posts for sand whereon to kindle light-wood flambeaux to illumine the scenes at night.

"A police is carefully detailed of saintly watchmen, of pious pith and discretion, to keep order and to guard the camp, and the exercises are conducted under orders duly proclaimed by authority.

"No Salisbury Fair ever exceeded it in variety of stranger scenes, grotesque and grave, ludicrous and sad, sacred and sinful, affected and real. Here a powerful learned man of God pouring out the word of truth in great volume of lungs and labor and love; there his contrast of a little exhorter. Here prayer and inward groaning of spirit struggling openly with conviction; there a loud-mouth braying of hymns sung by nasal Stentors of psalmody. Here a trance of mute adoration, and there a cotillion of *chasseing* shouters, cutting in and out and grasping of hands in a mazy dance of praise. Here one down under weight of sin, and there another leaping for joy and crying out for glory. Here a calm and solemn invocation to prayer, and there a stirring of anxious mourners. Here a crowd of whites worshiping without noise, decently, and there a mass of blacks and whites preaching, praying, exhorting, singing, shouting, bawling, yelling, up and down, whirling around in perfect Bedlam time of confusion worse confounded. Here the ministers of the Church winning souls away from Satan, and there the sons and daughters of vanity sipping the siren draught of sensual pleasure in all the ways of wanton delight. Here at night the camp at rest, and all its suburbs drinking, fiddling, dancing, and doing worse, uproarious in shameful frolic until morning light.

"The night is far spent, and at early dawn the horn is blown. The tents rise again to repeat the last day's scenes and exercises, and the sinners sink away to sleep until the curtain of night falls again. Whilst goodness is dealing out grace at the table of the lovefeast, huckster and vender are selling chicken pies, and barbecued, broiled, fried, and boiled fish, peaches and melons and cantelopes, cider, crabs, and gingercakes, June apples, lemonade and ice cream. And if you cannot find religion, you may—and if not always on guard you will—lose your purse, for campmeeting time is always a time for stripping orchards and robbing henroosts, wherewith to make a penny for expenses whilst on the lookout for the main chance of picking and stealing in the midst of the crowded camp and its concomitants.

"The camp of 1828 was most numerously attended. We had started in a sailvessel from a beautiful creek late in the evening and when within about two miles of the beach the breeze died away, and we were helplessly becalmed. The sun set clear over the bay, smooth, rippleless like a mirror... In a few moments, the island was not to be seen, until the moon effulgent rose over the eastern land and lighted up the glassy waters, and she had not risen high when suddenly the light-wood flambeaux of the camp shot forth their beams, and the rows and avenues of hundreds of broad and high blazes were like supernatural lamps of the heavens. Soon the hymns of the multitude came softly stealing by moonlight over the mirrored bay, mellowed by distance.....

"O, it was sweet beyond fancy's dreams!"[46]

This beautiful scene was not to last, for the controversial issues left at home threatened it, as the life of the lawyer who so vividly described it illustrates. Some thirty years later a man named John Brown was hanged for his raid on Harpers Ferry, and the governor of Virginia at that time was Henry A. Wise of Accomack. Wise went down in history as the "Governor who hanged John Brown." The nation was poised on the brink of war by then, and as the soldiers marched off to fight, the southern boys sang, "We'll hang John Brown on the sour apple tree." To which the Virginia boys would add:

Old Henry A. Wise
Put his specs upon his eyes
And sent him to the happy land of Canaan.[47]

Division would strike the Methodist movement even before it wracked the nation. And well before the nation had ever heard of John Brown and Harpers Ferry, the Tangier camp meeting was a thing of the past.

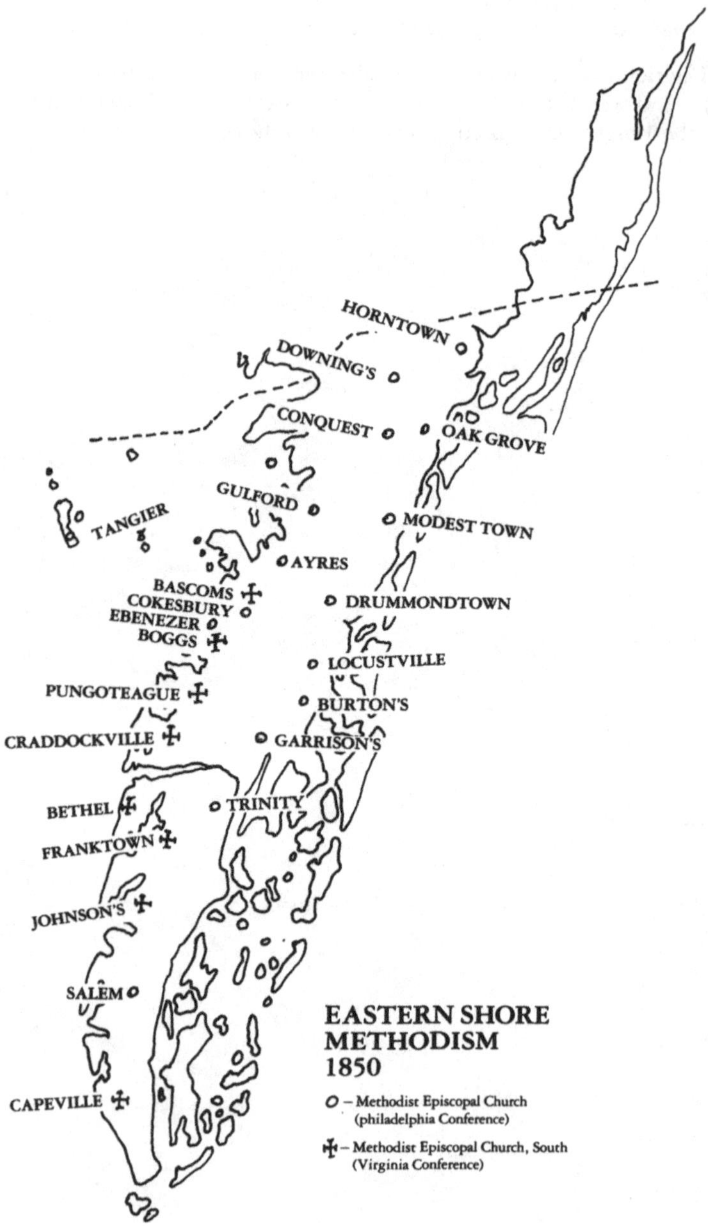
HORNTOWN
DOWNING'S
CONQUEST
OAK GROVE
TANGIER
GULFORD
MODEST TOWN
AYRES
BASCOMS
COKESBURY
EBENEZER
BOGGS
DRUMMONDTOWN
LOCUSTVILLE
PUNGOTEAGUE
BURTON'S
CRADDOCKVILLE
GARRISON'S
BETHEL
TRINITY
FRANKTOWN
JOHNSON'S
SALÊM
CAPEVILLE
EASTERN SHORE
METHODISM
1850
O – Methodist Episcopal Church
(philadelphia Conference)
✠ – Methodist Episcopal Church, South
(Virginia Conference)

The Time of Troubles
1844-1860

VI.

It was the issue of slavery that was to divide Methodism as it divided the nation. And it is the issue of slavery that best illustrates how Methodism on the Eastern Shore of Virginia changed as the years passed.

Methodism inherited from its founder a strong anti-slavery bias. John Wesley hated slavery and passed that hatred on to his preachers, so that as early as 1780, even before the Methodist Episcopal denomination was formed, the American Methodist preachers, meeting in Baltimore, put their anti-slavery feelings on the record:

> *Ought not this conference to require those traveling preachers who hold slaves to give promises to set them free?*
>
> *Does this conference acknowledge that slavery is contrary to the laws of God, man, and nature, and hurtful to society: contrary to the dictates of conscience and pure religion, and doing that which we would not others should do to us and ours? Do we pass our disapprobation on all our friends who keep slaves, and advise their freedom?*

The answer to both questions was a resounding "Yes!"

And so in 1784 when the Methodist Episcopal Church was formed, its founders wrote into the *Discipline* a rule that every slaveholding member must within a year agree to free his slaves. Failure to do so could result in suspension of membership, and all incoming members had first to agree to free their slaves before membership was granted. [1]

On the Eastern Shore of Virginia, as elsewhere in the nation, this rule was taken with seriousness at first. Asbury's preachers were loud in calling for emancipation of the slaves, as the bishop noted when he visited the Shore in 1788. [2] The rule was not always popular, but it usually worked. More than one slaveowner on the Shore freed his slaves when he became a Methodist.

One notable example was William Paramore. In the 1780's he went to the county courthouse to record:

> *Know all men by these presents that I William Paramore of Accomack in Virginia, being fully convinced of the just and equal Right that all Human Nature have to the happy enjoyment of Personal Liberty, as well*

> *as that Slavery of our fellow Creatures is Repugnant to and a Violation of our blessed Christian Religion, have and hereby do Manumitt, set free, and discharge my severall negro Slaves, To-wit, Jacob Bemane, Issac Wan, Phillis Roan, Phillis Anthony, Stephen Moses, Caleb Brister, Abel Daniel, Tabitha Christopher, Ezebella Joshua, Ester Roan.....*[3]

William Elliott allowed his slaves to purchase their freedom by their labors, and presumably a number of other Shoremen were similarly moved by their Methodist faith to end slavery. There is even a record that Thomas Burton, who grew upset when the question of slavery was mentioned from the pulpit at Burton's Chapel, granted freedom to his slaves when they reached the age of 35.[4]

With the passing of the years, however, anti-slavery zeal among the Methodists of the Shore began to wane, and before long they had begun to make excuses for the continued existence of slavery. In 1804, the very year that the Quarterly Conference passed a resolution condemning slavery, the circuit preacher, Richard Lyon, created a great deal of excitement and commotion by his vehement preaching against slavery. Such strong anti-slavery preaching as his had apparently not been heard on the Shore for some time by 1804. In most places on the circuit the Methodist congregations took Lyon's sermons in stride, but in Drummondtown trouble was only narrowly averted. Once while Lyon was preaching there, a prominent citizen, incensed by his denunciations of slavery, arose from his pew and advanced up the aisle with a bullwhip, obviously intent upon ending such preaching by force. James Ashby, another member of the congregation, rushed up to defend the preacher, but was pushed back by a blow on the head from the butt of the whip. Lyon really needed no assistance. He calmly stepped out of his pulpit, tripped his assailant, and threw him bodily to the floor. The service then proceeded as usual, and Lyon continued out his year undisturbed, but some members of the circuit took it upon themselves to observe and report all Lyon's statements on the subject to see if any were objectionable.[5]

Even in a climate of growing resentment against the anti-slavery rules, the early Methodists continued to express their concern about slavery during the first decade of the nineteenth century. The circuit was still anxious to "do all they can for the colored people," and the records contain many instances of members who produced a certificate of emancipation, duly registered with the court, within the space of three months from the purchase of the slave or their admission into membership.

By the early 1800's, however, the Methodists had ceased to free their slaves immediately, as William Paramore had done. Instead the emancipations, guaranteed by law and required by the church, were placed several years in the future. William Downing purchased a slave named Sarah in 1804 and in good Methodist form produced a certificate of emancipation for her, but she was not to be emancipated until age 35, after eleven years of service. Griffin Callahan's newly-purchased slave, Bathsheba, a girl of eleven, was required to serve eleven years. David Watt produced a certificate of emancipation for a slave named Stephen in 1806, but Stephen, age 35, was not to be freed until 1826, after a further twenty years of service. Such were the emancipations now practiced by these Methodists and others, such as William Melvin, James Poulson, Thomas Bagwell, and Major Colonna. And in all these cases the church that had in 1784 required virtual immediate emancipation acquiesced.

The record of slave emancipations by Methodists on the Shore stops suddenly in 1806, and it does not resume until 1814, and then only because the General Conference guidelines on the subject have filtered down. Certificates of emancipation, the Shore Methodists are reminded once again in Quarterly Conference, must be produced, freeing women not later than age 21 and men not later than age 25. Furthermore the preachers are still advised to "use their lawful and prudential influence to promote the freedom of slaves," and they are specifically instructed not to license exhorters who own slaves nor to appoint class leaders "who are unfriendly to the freedom of slaves."

After these reminders there begins the final period of emancipating slaves among the Methodists of the Shore, but by now the period of servitude required of the slave before emancipation has grown even longer. George Wescott of Northampton bought a slave woman named Bridget in 1816, freed her in 1817, but required her son, George, to serve until 1840, 24 years. The circuit accepted this arrangement, and thereupon licensed Wescott to exhort. Isaiah and William Bagwell in 1820 agreed to emancipate slaves Rose and Anthony, her son, in 1834 and 1849, respectively, an arrangement (and the church agreed to it) that required 29 years of service from Anthony. Frederick Conner bought a slave girl Nicey in 1822 and agreed to free her after fourteen years of service. And in 1823 Joshua Burton, Jr., bought a male slave 22 years old and produced a certificate of emancipation freeing him after 21 years of service, in 1844.

The last recorded freeing of a slave by an Eastern Shore Methodist is from 1836, when William D. Seymour, son of the venerable Onancock preacher, obtained permission from the circuit to sell a woman and her family owned by him. This sale, at least, was marked with compassion worthy of the earlier Methodists, for Seymour sold the woman to her own husband, thus making the entire family free.[6]

The rejection of the slavery rules by the Methodists of the Shore only parallels what happened nationally in the Methodist Episcopal Church. The rules became less and less rigid as time went by, and each succeeding General Conference brought only a newer form of accommodation to the institution of slavery. In 1796 the General Conference pronounced itself "more than ever convinced of the great evil of African slavery." Yet in 1804 it urged preachers to "exhort all slaves to render...due...obedience to their masters" and printed a special edition of the *Discipline* with no mention of slavery for use in the South. The Conference of 1808 left any rulings about the sale and purchase of slaves up to the several annual conferences, which meant that Methodists in slaveholding areas could do as they pleased. By the 1830's northern and southern Methodists were firmly entrenched behind their respective anti-slavery and pro-slavery positions. The issue caused a great deal of controversy at the General Conference in 1836, but the denomination finally announced that it had no intention to "interfere in the civil and political relation between master and slave as it exists in the slaveholding states of this Union." Two years later the Georgia Annual Conference passed this resolution:

> *It is the sense of the Georgia Annual Conference that slavery as it exists in the United States is not a moral evil... That we view slavery as a civil and domestic institution and one with which, as ministers of Christ, we have nothing to do further than to ameliorate...to impart...and aiding both on their way to heaven.*

Such was the fate of what had once been the most characteristic rule of American Methodism. Throughout the nation, the church had learned to adjust to the social and political views of the people. Only the Methodist clergy kept free of traffic in slaves, even in the South.[7] As for the Methodist people at large, they unabashedly owned slaves where it was legal and convenient to do so, no less on the Eastern Shore of Virginia than anywhere else.

In 1844 the inevitable division occurred. No sooner had the General Conference assembled in that year than the delegates fell into a procedural dispute over whether Bishop James Andrew of Georgia, who owned several slaves, should be allowed to continue as a bishop. Andrew had inherited slaves from the estate of his wife, and the laws of Georgia prohibited him from setting them free. Through perhaps no fault of his own he became the central issue around which the whole church took sides. After several days of angry dispute and discussion about him, the two camps finally decided to part ways. A Plan of Separation was drawn up, voted on, and passed, and shortly thereafter northern and southern ministers adjourned to hold separate conferences, in effect splitting the denomination into two almost equal churches. Within a few months the Methodist Episcopal Church, South, was formed in Petersburg, Virginia, identical to its northern counterpart in virtually every respect except that its *Discipline* contained no references to slavery.[8]

And for the Eastern Shore of Virginia, which lay on the border between North and South, a period of great turmoil began.

In 1844 when the Methodist Episcopal Church divided into northern and southern camps, few could have guessed that that division would lay more heavily upon the Eastern Shore of Virginia than upon almost any other area in the country. And yet perhaps because the area was so heavily Methodist, nowhere in the country was the schism accompanied by more violence or controversy.

In 1844 the two counties of the Virginia Shore could boast twenty Methodist Episcopal societies, plus two small Methodist Protestant congregations. The two Methodist Epsicopal circuits were a part of the Philadelphia Conference and together claimed about ten percent of the Shore's 25,000 inhabitants as active members.[9] Without question Methodism was the predominant faith on the Shore. All other denominations combined could muster only thirteen churches in the two counties. And more than a third of the Shore's Methodists were black.

The Plan of Separation was supposed to bring about an orderly and peaceful division of the denomination, but along the border the division quickly became an explosive issue. According to the Plan, the border between Church North and Church South was to be determined by three factors: (1) the starting point was the boundary between slaveholding and non-slaveholding conferences (since the Philadelphia Conference included both slaveholding and non-slaveholding areas, the southern tip of the peninsula was one such border); (2) congregations on this border could vote to choose which denomination to adhere to—which meant, according to some, at least, that the churches of the Virginia Shore were free to put the question to a vote; (3) only churches on the border were free thus to choose, and once the border was fixed all churches above it would be northern and all below it would be southern. The intention was that the boundary would be quickly decided, and that thereafter each denomination would attend to its own affairs within its own jurisdiction without interference from the other. [10]

Unfortunately it did not work out quite so simply.

In early 1845 the Methodists of Johnson's Chapel, interpreting the Plan of Separation as giving them the right to do so, put the question of allegiance to a vote and chose, 34 to seven, to leave the northern church and join the Virginia Conference of the southern church, across Chesapeake Bay. Within a matter of weeks another Northampton congregation, Capeville Chapel, followed suit with the same result, "with a few voting North." The Virginia Conference of the new southern church promptly sent Samuel T. Moorman to these two churches, which comprised a new circuit named Eastville. [11]

For a full year after these defections any further question of Methodist division lay dormant. Then, early in 1846, two local events began to arouse the general, non-Methodist public's interest. Dr. John Early of the Virginia Conference issued a warning about "abolitionist" ministers to the remaining Northampton Circuit members. And in August, George P. Scarburgh, a local judge and non-Methodist, took the Methodists to task in a public address in Drummondtown, "...impressing upon them the dangers which [might] result to the safety of the people, calling upon them...to sever their connections with the [Philadelphia] Conference. [12]

It was a difficult time for the Methodist Episcopal Church on the Shore. Back in February 1846 the Accomack Quarterly Conference had debated at length a series of resolutions "relative to the right of the world to intervene with our Church Polity," and ended up by tabling the motion. Then, shortly after Scarburgh's address in Drummondtown in August, a Portsmouth, Virginia, newspaper carried an anonymous article also criticizing the church in Accomack County. The Quarterly Conference promptly fired off a letter correcting the "misrepresentations" and demanded—unsuccessfully—the name of the anonymous author. [13]

Salem Chapel became the third church on the Shore to vote on the Plan of Separation, and by the time the vote was taken, in the spring of 1846, the interest of the general public was so aroused that the issue could no longer be considered a Methodist issue.

With the exception of Capeville, Salem Chapel in the village of Chesapeake was the southernmost Methodist congregation on the Shore. And yet when the vote was counted there, it was ten to six in favor of remaining in the Philadelphia Conference. For some reason not now known, the southern sympathizers in the congregation considered themselves cheated and demanded another vote. One of them canvassed the community and soon claimed to have changed enough minds to sway the vote in the opposite direction. But no second vote was taken, and there the issue stood undecided, to the great interest of the surrounding community. [14]

In May the congregation submitted the issue to the court at Eastville, which passed "resolutions prohibitory of the Philadelphia Conference preachers coming among them." [15] Still the Salem majority clung to the Conference, but by now the local community was as strong in its insistence that northern preachers were to be kept out as Salem was that they were allowed to be in. And so it was that on Saturday, July 11, 1846, on the day before the circuit preacher was to preach at Salem, one of the members rode north to warn him that trouble was brewing there.

The Reverend Valentine Gray arrived at Salem to find an unusually large crowd milling around the church. Some of the more familiar faces in the group greeted him and whispered warnings of trouble, but Gray set to his usual duties. No sooner had he mounted his pulpit to begin the service, however, than the crowd swarmed into the building and rushed up to surround him.

Gray later described the scene to the *Christian Advocate and Journal* in New York:

> *One of them came into the pulpit and took hold of my arm, while some cried, "Pull him over the top of the pulpit." Several of them reached over the pulpit, but could not get hold of me. While the one in the pulpit had me by the arm, another got upon the bench and reaching over caught me by the coat collar and cravat and choked me considerably, also pulled my hair. Two or three others came into the pulpit and forced me out of it.*

Gray refused to leave the church voluntarily, so "they seized hold of me again and forced me out of the church. During this struggle they tore my coat." [16]

Bright and early the next day Gray was in Eastville to file a complaint against his assailants, who showed up in full force to confront him a second time. He found no public or legal support at the county seat, "so I have been driven away without redress or protection," he wrote. Across the North thousands of Methodist readers were enraged by his account of the incident, and the editor of the *Christian Advocate and Journal* began coverage of the events on the Shore, complete with criticisms of Early, Judge Scarburgh, and local southern Methodists in general. [17]

Late in the summer the troubles spread to Accomack County. James Hargis, the other circuit preacher, was preaching to his congregation at Guilford Chapel when a large, noisy crowd appeared on the scene. People began "shooting around the church, throwing missiles against it, and hallooing to such a degree" that some of the members left the service. Hargis quit his sermon and went outside to invite the crowd in to talk, but his offer was refused. The crowd kept Hargis from resuming the service, and when he left warned him that "if he came there any more they would put him in the millpond which is near by."

Hargis, like Gray before him, sought redress and protection from the county authorities, and like Gray before him was refused. The Guilford congregation, however, mustered a defense of its pastor. Despite threats against his person, Hargis remained at his post, and when it next came time for him to preach at Guilford, fifteen or twenty of his members there armed themselves with pistols "and other deadly weapons" and personally escorted him to his pulpit. This particular Sunday was Communion Sunday, and although apparently no mob appeared to harass the preacher, his members knelt at the rail and received the sacrament with weapons strapped to their sides. "This greatly excited the community," reported the southern *Richmond Christian Advocate* of the event.[18]

Still later in the summer Accomack County Methodists held their own against another assault, this one on the preachers at the annual camp meeting on Tangier Island in August. By some means the campers got wind that a Guilford mob had formed again and was headed for the campgrounds. The islanders still tell the story of how the mob landed on the beach and marched unimpeded to the campgrounds, where they kicked over the firestands and took over the pulpit until, by prearranged signal, one of the camp leaders rallied the Methodists with a charge that sent the invaders scrambling "into mudholes and creeks to escape."[19]

The rest of 1846 passed without incident, but the spring brough fresh trouble. In March a large public meeting was held in Drummondtown in response to the *Christian Advocate and Journal*'s criticism of local events and persons. Out of this meeting came several "committees of safety," determined to keep watch on the local Methodist churches and "to communicate to each other all necessary information....."[20] Soon large, hostile crowds were again appearing at the churches on Sunday.

James Brindle found one such group at Burton's Chapel when he arrived there for his usual appointment. By quick work the church members ushered the new preacher into the building, and from there he conducted the service without interruption. The baffled crowd drifted away, planning better strategy for next Sunday when he was to preach at Garrison's Chapel. The intervening week was tense and hot, but when Sunday came the Methodists had packed the building, and the hecklers, far outnumbered, drifted away. However, by autumn local opposition had grown so strong that Brindle's own members were reluctantly advising him to leave for his own safety.[21]

The heated non-Methodist interference in church affairs began to discredit itself in the eyes of most locals after an event that occurred in Drummondtown in late summer of 1847. There again a mob of southern persuasion gathered and began shouting threats against any public official who might vote in favor of the northern church in any matter concerning division. So tense was the air in the village that, as Judge Thomas H. Bailey walked home from his chambers, the crowd accosted him and began to argue with him. In a heated exchange of words, Judge Bailey was struck to the ground, and no sooner was he down than he drew a pistol and shot one of the crowd's leaders—a man named William B. Finney—in the thigh. Finney was not badly wounded, but for the crime of shooting him the judge spent the night in jail. In the morning all charges against him were dismissed, and with his dismissal began the dissipation of such mobs and "committees of safety" as had harassed northern Methodist preachers for over a year. Judge Bailey was not himself a Methodist, nor had he in any significant way done anything to aid the northern Methodist cause. Public sentiment was entirely with him in this incident, and after it much of the Shore seemed to lose interest in the Methodist question altogether.[22]

It was during these two explosive years that the Methodist churches on the southern half of the Shore voted, one after another, on whether to remain in the northern church or secede to the southern church. In some congregations the decision was easily made: Bethel in Jamesville voted unanimously to secede to the Virginia Conference. Pungoteague and Craddockville followed suit in 1847, the first Accomack churches to secede.[23] By the end of 1847, Moorman's Eastville Circuit had a total of 257 white and 182 black members in the two counties.

In other churches the vote divided congregations seriously. When the Franktown congregation took its vote, perhaps as early as 1846, certainly by 1847, a great many inactive members showed up and threw the church into the southern column by a majority of one. The significant pro-northern minority was sufficiently angered to withdraw from the church and establish their own, and shortly thereafter Trinity Methodist Episcopal Church arose in Hadlock. There were similar events in Cashville in 1848. The people of Boggs Chapel there politely informed the Accomack Circuit that "it is the wish of a Majority of the members worshiping at that place to be united with the Virginia Conference & that they have resolved to place themselves under the pastoral care of that Conference." But there was a significant northern minority in Cashville as in Franktown, and the circuit determined that they "should have preaching and be attended to as heretofore by the preachers who may be sent to this circuit by the Philadelphia Conference." Thus was born Ebenezer, a new northern rival to Boggs, less than a mile away.[24]

The opposite situation prevailed at Cokesbury and Garrison's. Both of these congregations chose to remain in the Philadelphia Conference, and it was the southern minority that had to separate. Garrison's southern sympathizers withdrew and went to Franktown Chapel. Cokesbury's minority founded a new church in Onancock called Bascom's Chapel, erected in 1850 on King Street less than sixty yards from Cokesbury. Drummondtown and Burton's Chapel also voted to remain in the northern church, and there were no serious defections from these churches.[25] By 1850 the voting was over, and the Shore was seriously divided. Northern Accomack County was still firmly in the hands of the Philadelphia Conference. Northampton County, with the exception of Salem Chapel and Trinity, was Virginia Conference territory. Southern Accomack County, the central portion of the Shore, had both northern and southern Methodists in about equal numbers, their churches sometimes almost literally side by side.

This was the state of affairs that was to reign for another decade, and the two sides began to consolidate their positions. In repudiation of the violence that had erupted on the Shore, the southern Eastville Circuit assured the readers of the *Richmond Christian Advocate* that

> *neither the ministers nor the members of the Methodist Episcopal Church South have participated in any way in those violent proceedings against the preachers of the Philadelphia Conference. Neither of the pulpits from which the preachers of the Philadelphia Conference have been forcibly ejected has been or is now occupied by ministers from the Methodist Episcopal Church, South.*

And the southern churches were all "firmly and immovably attached to the Conference of our choice."[26]

The same, for now, was true of the northern churches as well, and apparently Methodist lines reflected the general attitude of the entire Shore. A decade later, when the state elected delegates to the convention that was to consider secession, the same situation still held: Northampton sent a secessionist, and Accomack a Unionist.[27]

In March 1847 the bishops of the northern Methodist Episcopal Church met in Philadelphia to discuss the violent incidents that had been reported from the Eastern Shore of Virginia and elsewhere. They issued a series of resolutions which they thought would settle the issue once and for all. It was their contention that the Plan of Separation had been misinterpreted by many on the Shore, that it provided for "taking the votes by conferences, stations, and societies, and not by circuits in fixing their church relations," and that the time for taking such votes had already run out anyway. The bishops insisted that when a congregation north of the line of separation received a preacher from the northern church without objection from the Methodist Episcopal Church, South, it could be assumed that that congregation was affixed for good to the northern church. Anyway, to be specific, the Chesapeake Bay boundary to the south meant that the Eastern Shore of Virginia and Maryland could not, within the meaning of the plan adopted in 1844, be considered border territory in the first place.[28]

The bishops spoke too late. On the Eastern Shore of Virginia the people were themselves already deciding. Already, by March 1847, much of Northampton County had seceded to the southern church, and there were more congregations yet to follow.

The violence of 1846 and 1847 seems to have been chiefly the work of non-Methodists attempting to influence the decisions of the local churches, and once the Methodists regained control of the situation the northern and southern branches of the church settled down to a decade or more of peaceful coexistence. Each of the denominations conducted revivals and camp meetings, erected new meetinghouses, founded new congregations, and proceeded as if it alone were the sole survivor of John Wesley's movement. From all appearances peace reigned within them and between them, and between the initial separation and the time when slavery was to plunge the nation into war there occurred a period of remarkable growth and prosperity.

The churches of the southern Eastville Circuit no sooner left the Methodist Episcopal Church than they plunged into a feverish period of revivals, camp meetings, protracted meetings, and growth. At the circuit campgrounds near Johnson's Chapel, fifty persons were converted in July 1847, and a September camp meeting netted another ninety converts. A meeting at Bethel produced another sixteen conversions, and a camp meeting in Accomack in 1848 gained 922 converts, more than the first camp meeting at Pungoteague in 1805.[29] In 1852 Salem Chapel, scene of the original violence against the northern preachers, moved at last into the southern fold. For six years this congregation, led by such stalwarts as Hezekiah Dalby, Thomas Brickhouse, and Luther Nottingham, held out against the secessionist attitude of the community and carried on Sunday school and worship under local pastors. However, in 1852 William Lee Dalby, son of Hezekiah and a popular minister from this congregation, joined the southern Virginia Conference. So great was his influence in the community that Salem in that year followed him and became a part of the Eastville Circuit.[30]

All was growth and prosperity in the southern church. The Craddockville congregation built a new meetinghouse in 1855, and Johnson's in 1857. A new preaching-point was opened in the Hack's Neck area west of Pungoteague—"Seatick Chapel" it was called—although it never became a separate congregation. And in 1848 a Northampton County campmeeting raised $7 for a new cause among Eastern Shore Methodists: Randolph-Macon College, a school of the Virginia Conference.[31]

The Methodist Protestants were the smallest of the three Methodist denominations on the Shore in the 1850's, and they alone declined in membership during that period. When the local Methodist Protestant circuit was formed in 1838 it had 268 members. That number dropped almost immediately, and not until 1874 was Methodist Protestant membership on the Shore that great again. Even so, both of the Methodist Protestant congregations gave birth to a new church during this period. From Wattsville was born Bethel Church in Chincoteague in 1853. From Lee Mont was founded Reese Chapel in Bayside in 1855, named for the prominent Methodist Protestant family of preachers.

The Methodist Episcopal Church was still, despite its losses, the largest of the three churches on the Shore, and its growth and prosperity during the 1850's were proportionately large. The old Tangier camp meeting continued unabated until 1857, now a northern affair. Revival swept Tangier Island in 1849 and significantly increased the size of the congregation there. The vigorous Downing's congregation gave birth to two new churches: Conquest Chapel at Temperanceville in 1845 and Pocomoke Chapel at Grotons in 1855. And a new church named Ayres Chapel was erected in 1845 in Bayside below Lee Mont.[32] The Indiantown Mission, however, established in or near Eastville in 1839, was abandoned after 1845 and the division, the last attempt ever to erect a white Methodist church in that vicinity.

In 1851 the northern church opened up a completely new community, one of the most distant and isolated sections of the Shore, when it conducted a camp meeting on Saxis, or Sykes Island, as it was then called. Within a year a new church named Conner's Chapel stood there. In 1857 E.W. Stickney, a retired preacher from New England who had moved to the Shore, was hired as a third circuit preacher to open up "Saxes Island...and other places below the mouth of Pocomoke River on the bay side, where there are no regular preaching appointments at present filled by the travelling preachers of this Circuit." The following year work in northern Accomack County had so increased that it was necessary once more to divide the circuit, and a new circuit named Atlantic, with a parsonage in Temperanceville, came into being.[33]

It was a period of great building in the northern Methodist church on the Shore, an age that left us the oldest Methodist buildings still used there. In addition to the buildings erected by the new churches—Saxis, Pocomoke, Conquest, Trinity—at least five older churches erected grander buildings, including Burton's Chapel (1848), Drummondtown (1852), and Horntown (1859). The original Downing's Chapel was replaced with a new building in 1854, and later that year a new building was begun by the Onancock congregation. Garrison's Chapel built a new sanctuary in 1855. When it was dedicated a revival swept across the congregation, and the first person converted in the new building was a little girl, Georgie Richardson (Quinby) (1845-1896), who years later became secretary of the Women's Foreign Missionary Society on the Eastern Shore.[34] Some of these buildings, with the new Johnson's Chapel erected in 1857 by the southern church, are the oldest standing Methodist edifices on the Shore today: Downing's (1854), Cokesbury (1854-55), Garrison's (1855), Johnson's (1857), Pocomoke (1858), Temperanceville (Conquest Chapel, 1858), and Horntown (1859). Most of them have been altered almost beyond recognition with the passing of the years; only Horntown Chapel still looks very much as it did when it was first erected.

Baptists, too, made a strong showing during the 1840's and 1850's. Four of their strongest congregations date from these two decades: Union in Chincoteague (1841), Bethel near Bloxom (1852), Zion north of Drummondtown (1852), and Onancock (1856).[35] And during the lull before the storm of war, Episcopalians founded two new congregations. St. Michael's was erected in Belle Haven in 1849, but in 1868 it was discovered that the denomination did not really own the land on which it stood, and the church was closed. More lasting was Emmanuel Episcopal Church erected in Temperanceville in 1860, successor to the now-vanished Assawoman Church. Emmanuel has been open continuously since 1860, although in 1887 it was moved from its original site in Temperanceville to its present site near Jenkins Bridge, four miles away. The stained glass windows in Emmanuel are said to have been the first in any church on the Virginia Shore, and perhaps date from the original construction in 1860.[36]

a - Downings, Oak Hall (1854)

b - Cokesbury, Onancock (1854)

THE TWO OLDEST METHODIST BUILDINGS ON VIRGINIA'S EASTERN SHORE

Even in this late period after the slavery issue had divided Methodism into two large branches, each of the Methodist denominations on the Eastern Shore had Negro members, and blacks and whites worshiped together in the same buildings at the same services.

Of the northern Methodists on the Shore in 1850, slightly less than a third—442 out of 1291—were black. There were only six black members among the 211 Methodist Protestants in the two counties. But in the Methodist Episcopal Church, South, was the greatest proportion of blacks to whites: 254 blacks to 331 whites in 1850. (During these same years the membership of the Newtown, Maryland, circuit just across the line was consistently more than half black.) Blacks and whites attended worship services together, as they had since the days of Asbury, although across the years the blacks had been relegated more and more to the rear of the churches, or to balconies which were being erected in the newer buildings specifically to contain them. At camp meetings, partitions separated blacks from whites, the blacks usually being placed behind the speaker's platform.[37]

By the 1840's, a native black leadership had begun to arise in the Methodist churches of the Shore, a small but devoted core of people who against impossible odds took their place at the Quarterly Meeting. Between 1839 and 1845, no fewer than nine persons are listed on the rolls of the Accomack Circuit as active "colored exhorters"—Stephen Waters, George Merrill, Herod Scott, Solomon Dixon, Levin Dennis, Levin Waters, Handy Long, Isaac Johnson, and Stephen Ward. Little or nothing is known of these men. One of them, Herod Scott, apparently had his license to exhort revoked for some charge not spelled out in the record; his name does not appear after 1843. Another of them, George Merrill, moved up the ladder from exhorter and in 1844 was licensed to preach.[38] There are no local negro leaders listed in the local records after 1845, one year after the schism. How long these local exhorters served their church, or in which local congregations, is not known today, but their presence on the record books indicates that even before emancipation the blacks of the Eastern Shore, though enslaved, were producing their own church leaders.

In 1856 a local preacher, a free black from Maryland named Frost Pollett, crossed into Accomack County to preach to anyone who would listen, black or white. He was promptly arrested by white authorities; the slave code did not allow free Negroes of one state to go into another. When the day of his hearing arrived, the court released Pollett without a fine, giving him a certain number of hours to leave the county. At their clemency, Pollett is said to have removed his hat, bowed politely, and assured them, "Thank you, gentlemen. You may see Frost down here some time this winter, but sure as you're born you're not going to see Pollett in these diggings any more."

Frost Pollett, six feet tall and a powerful preacher, one of whose sermons, in Negro dialect, has been preserved by contemporary accounts, became an influential church leader after the Civil War. He was one of the original members of the Delaware Conference, a black conference founded by the northern church in 1867, and served a term as presiding elder.[39] It is reasonable to suppose, although it cannot be authenticated, that others like him on the Eastern Shore of Virginia, influential local leaders in postwar black denominations, were already at work in the Methodist Epsicopal Church and the Methodist Episcopal Church, South, during the 1840's and 1850's.

It was in the Methodist Episcopal Church that hostilities smouldered beneath the peaceful surface. The congregations of the southern church, despite the greater proportion of blacks among their members, assumed that slavery was no longer an issue; it was, in short, a slave-holding church. On the Eastern Shore of Virginia, however, the northern church's continuing anti-slavery stance still made waves, and the best example of smouldering fires is the pastorate of the Reverend Adam Wallace.

Adam Wallace is best known today as the biographer of Joshua Thomas and the author of *The Parson of the Islands*. In his own day, however, he was one of the most controversial ministers ever to serve the Methodists of the Shore, and a vigorous proponent of Methodism's anti-slavery stance, much to the chagrin of many of his parishioners. In 1854 Wallace was appointed by the Philadelphia Conference to the Eastern Shore of Virginia (the northern circuit in that year was officially named Northampton, although only one church, Trinity, was in Northampton County). Wallace no sooner arrived than he promptly began to infuriate parts of his parish by reading to the Quarterly Conference, as his predecessors had calmly neglected to do, every last word of the *Discipline* on slavery. At one of his churches he invited the Negro members in attendance to communion at the same table with their masters, a practice which horrified the whites, half of whom rudely stomped out of church. Outside after the service some of his own congregation warned him to desist from such "incendiary practices" or be prepared to leave the state. Wallace continued his invitations in each of the churches in the circuit, but most often the Negroes declined for fear of reprisal from the whites.

LEVI SCOTT

The fortunate appearance on the scene of the bishop probably saved Wallace's pastorate. Bishop Levi Scott (1802-1882) happened by the circuit during the communion controversy, the first Methodist bishop to visit the two counties since Asbury in 1810, and leading members of the circuit gathered at the parsonage in Onancock to greet him. While the bishop was being introduced around, Wallace put the question to him abruptly: Should the pastor yield to pressure? Should he send the elements to the galleries, instead of inviting the blacks forward to the table with their masters?

The swarm of people at the parsonage grew suddenly quiet. The bishop mused a moment, and then upheld his pastor with a quiet pronouncement: "I would not do it."

Among the blacks of the Shore the new preacher quickly gained a reputation for courage, and they frequently consulted with him behind the backs of their masters. He is said to have met with a band of forty or fifty slaves one night in a thicket, and dissuaded them from trying to escape to the North. Though a firm detester of slavery, Wallace was, the blacks soon found out, not one to countenance violence or unlawful attempts at freedom. "Expect deliverance from the God of Moses and Israel" and "patiently pray and wait" was his advice.

The most spectacular event in Wallace's short pastorate on the Shore occurred in the neighborhood of Garrison's Chapel not long after the visit of Bishop Scott had settled the communion controversy. The young preacher and his new wife were riding in their carriage when they came upon a struggle in the middle of the road: two young white men in the process of subduing and binding an older black man. Wallace leapt from his carriage, thrust the two younger men aside angrily, and lifted up the older man, brushing the dust from his clothes and hair. An angry exchange followed: the two white men claimed the Negro as property on the estate of one of their wives, and were merely binding him to be sold, as they claimed legal right to do, to a slave trader. Wallace coolly informed them that he doubted the legality of their claim, and detested their violence against the unresisting older man, and that he himself would follow them to make sure that the man was not being illegally kidnapped.

All of this took place in front of a country store, and a gathering crowd of curious bystanders, among whom was Mrs. Wallace, "pale and trembling with apprehension" in her carriage. After the two men had departed with their alleged slave, Wallace learned from the onlookers that the man was indeed a freedman, a venerable member of Garrison's Chapel, and that not one of them was about to lift a finger to help him see that he got justice. One of the local preachers on the circuit advised Wallace to leave "on a visit" somewhere "until the storm he had in all probability raised should blow over," but Wallace would hear none of it. Leaving his wife off at the parsonage, he took off in pursuit of the ruffians, and arrived at the county seat on time to learn that the old man, whose name was Sam, had indeed been sold for $300, and was being held in the county jail where a gang of slaves was being made up to start in a few days for Richmond.

In a flurry of frenzied activity—for almost no one would help him—Wallace managed to obtain a writ enjoining Sam's removal, and a date was set for a magistrate to hear the case. The intervening days were anxious ones. Frightened Methodists called at the parsonage to express their dread of anticipated troubles; the pastor preached a sermon that Sunday "tinged with brimstone." And when the court convened, all at first seemed lost, for the chief magistrate turned out to be a wealthy slaveowner, "among the foremost in good society." Nonetheless, on hearing the details of the case, the magistrate shared the preacher's indignation, turned Sam free, and issued a warrant for the arrest of his would-be kidnappers, who promptly fled the scene.

The next Sunday, "Uncle" Sam was back in the gallery at the rear of Garrison's Chapel, where the young pastor had won yet another admirer among the black, if not the white, portion of his congregation.

On yet one more occasion Wallace dared to meet violence against the enslaved blacks head on. During a protracted meeting at Garrison's Chapel one night, the blacks assembled outside while the whites remained inside, built a campfire, and began their own, more spirited songfest. A band of mischievous young men, all white, collected around the black assembly and began to tease the blacks by hurling lighted sticks and branches into their midst. Wallace happened out of the church at about that time, the white part of the meeting over, and caught them in the act. When the white boys would not listen to his warnings to stop, he unceremoniously swung out and knocked two of the ringleaders to the ground, scattering their band with them. By now he had a reputation of courage, and this time both black and white Methodists rallied behind him to get rid of the troublemakers.[40]

Adam Wallace served two years on the Eastern Shore of Virginia, from 1854 to 1856. Shortly thereafter another incident of violence was only narrowly averted. The Reverend Andrew Manship traveled the peninsula between 1856 and 1862 as Tract Agent of the Philadelphia Conference, and at times did his work on the Virginia Shore. It was probably about 1857, the place now unknown, that Manship preached in this capacity to "an immense audience both of white and colored," only to be accosted after the sermon by an angry and threatening "slave-holding gentleman." "You ought to be tarred and feathered and rode on a rail," his critic fumed, convinced that the tracts that Manship was pushing were designed to incite slaves to rebellion. But Manship calmed the man down, met with him later in his own home, prayed with him, and won him over. The man's slaves gathered around to witness the strange sight of their master on his knees, and they shouted "Old Master's down!" while Manship and his new convert sang:

> We'll wait till Jesus comes
> And we'll be gathered home.

When Manship rose to go, the man (whose identity is not known today) gave him $5 for the tract cause and asked the preacher's forgiveness for having threatened him.[41]

Under capable leaders like Wallace and Manship, the tensions that seethed just beneath the seemingly calm surface of the northern Methodist churches were held in check. At least for a while.

The lull before the storm ended in 1860.

The General Conference of the northern church was meeting in Buffalo in that year when word arrived that Abraham Lincoln had received the Republican nomination for the presidency. Momentous political events followed rapidly, and within a matter of months South Carolina seceded from the Union, and there was talk of secession in Virginia. Even before that, Eastern Shore Methodists, most of whom were still in the northern church, were up in arms over the work of th e Buffalo Conference itself. The controversy was over the new rule passed there on slavery, the first new ruling on that subject since the separation of 1844. The new rule declared quite simply that "the buying, selling, or holding of human beings as chattels" was "contrary to the laws of God." In itself, the wording was not noticeably stronger than before, but this time the atmosphere in the nation and the church was different, and the resolution went on to call preachers and laymen alike to rid themselves for good of the evil of slavery. To persons on the border, to Eastern Shoremen, too, the implication seemed to be that slaveholders were about to be expelled from the church. From across the country, and especially from the border areas, the objections swelled.[42]

ANDREW MANSHIP

The congregation at Burton's Chapel reacted to all this furor quite simply and decisively by ejecting Alexander Wiggins of the Philadelphia Conference from his pulpit there on the last Sunday of the conference year. By previous invitation, the Virginia Conference pastor, Major S. Colonna, was installed. It is apparent that both pastors understood this action to be the decision of the whole Accomack Circuit, not just Burton's Chapel.[43]

The same kind of wholesale exodus to the southern church seems to have occurred in the Atlantic Circuit as well, although there are no details available.

The northern church was later to claim that the southerners of the Shore excluded northern ministers from their rightful pulpits "at the point of the bayonet," but there is no conclusive evidence that this was so. At any rate, feelings ran high against the northern church across the entire Shore. In the early summer a mass meeting was held at Pungoteague, and a vigilante Committee of Nineteen was appointed, charged with the duty of driving northern Methodist preachers from the Virginia Shore "by any means they might find necessary."[44]

Into this setting rode the two new northern Conference appointees, James Massey and George Cummins, and the events of fifteen years before seemed to be happening all over again.

On his first Sunday on the circuit, Cummins was interrupted during his service at Garrison's Chapel as the Committee of Nineteen (some sources say Nine) stormed into the building. But "so manifest was the Divine Presence," we are told, that the service continued without further difficulties. The committee satisfied themselves to warn Cummins and his congregation that no preaching would be allowed at Trinity that afternoon, and that should he attempt to preach there, he would be mobbed.

Cummins rode undaunted to his afternoon appointment at Trinity, and found there not only the committee but a noisy and angry mob. His congregation was not much in evidence. The crowd swarmed around him on every side as he dismounted and hitched his horse, but split and allowed him to pass into the building. There old Joshua Humphreys, the good local preacher, and a small çongregation were waiting for him. Cummins mounted his pulpit, and the crowd swarmed in after him (hats on, cigars in mouth, breaths reeking with whiskey, insist the northern accounts). No one took a seat; instead, everyone pressed around the preacher, jostling him left and right. There was talk of tar and feathers. A spokesman insisted that Cummins warn his colleague Massey not to preach at Garrison's next Sunday.

Cummins stood his ground. "Gentlemen," he said in a cool voice, "I shall decline to do any part of your dirty work for you. As to leaving the church and departing from the state, it is not my habit to allow anything to interfere with the attempt to perform my duty. Nor do I usually dismiss a service, under any circumstances, without at least offering a prayer."

Mr. Cummins," shouted someone in the crowd, "we are not exactly in a spirit to profit by your prayers!"

"Phew, I do believe that Methodist preacher would fight!" shouted another.

Cummins took stock of the situation, decided it was hopeless, and left, apparently without a parting prayer.

A week passed, and the next round fell to his colleague, James Massey. Massey, the same man who as presiding elder twenty years earlier had declared war unsuccessfully on tobacco, was a tall, angular, ungainly man with a vacant, almost absent-minded stare, "as honest a soul as ever trod the soil of the peninsula," but serious and stubborn to a fault. It was said that he was so absent-minded that he once tipped his hat and said "Good morning" to a cow, never stopping to notice that it was not some good village lady that he was meeting.

Like Cummins the week before, Massey found a faithful congregation waiting at Garrison's, but beyond that he was not to be so lucky. Soon after the service began, the committee again appeared on the scene, this time led by a giant of a man named Dick Ayres, who weighed over 250 pounds. Ayres led the crowd into the building and jumped up to the pulpit beside the preacher and began addressing the crowd. Massey was shoved out of his pulpit by those around him.

At this point a member of the congregation, an old lady of some seventy years, jumped up from her pew, climbed over the altar rail, collared Ayres, and before anyone could realize what was happening jerked him to the floor, grabbed his hair, and began to pound his head to the floor.

It was apparently a pre-arranged signal. Husbands sat stunned and motionless as all over the church ladies sprang to their feet ready to jump into the fray. Further fisticuffs were not necessary, for Massey regained his pulpit, calmed everyone down, and suspended the service.

The tradition lingered for a good many years that, given a few more minutes, the women of the church would have had the building completely cleared.

Cummins and Massey encountered the commitee once again about two weeks later, in the crowded courtyard at Drummondtown. Again the two preachers were surrounded by a hostile mob, and again they were ordered not to preach in Virginia. Again they held their ground, a stalemate resulted, and they left the scene in peace. Within a few weeks Cummins had been transferred to Salisbury. Massey continued his rounds, but with what success is not now clear.[45]

The nation stood on the brink of war, and violence had already erupted within the walls of Eastern Shore Methodism. The future of the faith seemed very cloudy and uncertain.

MAJOR SAMUEL COLONNA

The Methodist Protestant Church

♱ = Extant
✝ = Extinct

By Date of Organization:

1 - Wattsville (1795) 1832
2 - Lee Mont 1839
3 - Bethel 1853
4 - Reese Chapel 1855
5 - Berea 1874
6 - Union 1877
7 - Conquest Chapel 1887
8 - Signpost 1887
9 - Calvary 1888
10 - Grace 1892
11 - Atlantic 1893
12 - Grant 1893
13 - Hallwood 1903
14 - Greenbush 1911

Brothers at War 1860-1866

VII

The year 1860 may be the most confused year on the books for Eastern Shore Methodism, but it is probably no more confused to us now than it was to the Methodists of the Shore then. The Methodist Episcopal Church still claimed two-thirds of the local churches, and three of its ministers were still in the area: James Massey on the Accomack Circuit, and William Merrill and Charles Shepherd on the Atlantic Circuit. Yet at least one church of the Accomack Circuit, Burton's Chapel, had already gone over to the southern Virginia Conference, and possibly others as well. It is apparent that as the northern preachers made their rounds on the Shore the churches, one after the other, were closed to them. To make matters worse, self-appointed vigilante groups and "committees" were again in action, ready to "greet" any northern preacher who might show up to preach in a community where he was not welcome. All in all, just who was preaching where in 1860 is not at all clear now, and it was probably not very clear then.

On June 8, 1860, a meeting of "official and other members" of the Accomack Circuit convened, apparently just after the Quarterly Conference on that day, in Onancock and passed a series of resolutions reflecting the anger felt by the Methodists of the Shore against the Methodist Episcopal Church and its new rules on slavery:

> *Resolved 1st: that we find ourselves under the necessity of dissolving our connection with the M.E. Church...as soon as we conveniently can.*
>
> *Resolved 2nd: that we invite...the Border Conferences to take measures to hold a convention as soon as practicable...for the purpose of organizing a Central M.E. Church.*

Not only James Massey but also Henry Colclazer, the presiding elder, were present on July 28, the next Quarterly Conference, when these resolutions were presented and adopted, and it was moved to send a copy of the resolutions to the *Baltimore Christian Advocate.*[1] Such was the mood of the Methodists — angry at the northern church but still unwilling to secede to the southern — but no further action was taken. Despite the growing dissatisfaction, Massey remained at his post through January 1861.

When the Accomack Quarterly Conference met at Drummondtown on January 19, 1861, the situation had changed. By now Virginians had a new legislature which was about to consider the proposed Ordinance of Secession. Accomack had elected a pro-Union delegate, Northampton a Secessionist. Presiding Elder Colclazer gaveled the meeting to order, and when it was over the Methodists of the Accomack Circuit had committed themselves to an unusual course of action. "Believing that it represents the feelings and wishes of the membership on the Circuit," the Quarterly Conference voted to inform the presiding elder that "we decline receiving any preacher or preachers from the Philadelphia Conference for the next Conference year or while that Conference remains connected with the General Conference of the M.E. Church." "Unless the General Conference shall rescind its action on the subject of Slavery at its late session, a separation therefrom on the part of [these] Churches is a necessity," asserted the local Methodists. They went on to assert that the new rules on slavery were "unscriptural and inapplicable to our circumstances," and to propose that the Philadelphia Conference itself be divided into northern and southern portions.[2]

They had not seceded, but neither were they any longer part of the Methodist Episcopal Church. And since they had no pastor, having declined to receive a northern preacher, some further action was necessary. And so on January 29, 1861, at Onancock, Joshua Garrison gaveled to order a specially-called meeting of delegates from each of the circuit churches. A week later the proceedings of this meeting were published in *The National Recorder,* the local Drummondtown newspaper, and the Methodists of the central part of the Virginia Shore proclaimed to the world their bold course of action.

The first part of the account of the meeting was a defense of the circuit's middle-road position during the disruption of the past two decades:

> *We of Accomack, with but a minority exception, did not see cause for withdrawal from the main body of the Church...Being immediately on the border line between the two sections, we were necessarily placed in juxtaposition with those who differed from us in this relation, and consequently a strife arose which engendered bitterness. That we, during all this angry and protracted warfare, should have maintained our forces and kept our places should not have been thought probable, if indeed possible. Some churches have been violently wrested from us, some members coaxed away, while others have been influenced by motives unexplained to us.*

In return for such loyalty, the Methodist Episcopal Church had shown them "absolute contempt expressed in denunciating abuse and defiance!" (So distasteful were the new rules on slavery!) "Now is there anything in the Christian creed...that calls for our longer adhering to such a body?"

There followed four angry resolutions:

> *Resolved: that we of Accomack Circuit, Snow Hill District,*

Philadelphia Conference, in convention assembled, do now and from henceforth declare and hold ourselves as disunited from said general conference, and all other conferences, circuits, and stations thereto adhering, as said conference is now constituted.

Resolved: that we will gladly unite with the peninsula [of Maryland and Delaware] whenever it shall take a like stand with ourselves on this important question...

Resolved: that until we can form an agreeable and harmonious reunion [with some proposed Central Methodist denomination or conference], we shall stand detached and alone...

Resolved: that in the event of our not getting preachers...from abroad, then we will employ the Rev. Joshua Humphreys [a local preacher] as our preacher in charge.

The article carried six signatures — James Garrison, William Rew, Joshua Humphreys, Thomas Richardson, George Tyler, and Thomas Ayres — and the newspaper published it as the proceedings of the "Onancock Convention, Methodist Episcopal Church."[3]

Neither northern nor southern, the Accomack Methodists were determined to stand "detached and alone," even if it meant creating their own local denomination to do so.

Joshua Humphreys (1801-1879) assumed the pastorate of the circuit and served until the April Quarterly Conference, even though James Massey remained in the county until his appointment ended in March. In April the circuit met at Garrison's, and there they tackled the problem of forming the polity of the new church. First there was the need for a new book of rule. The *Discipline* of 1856, with certain changes, was adopted as official, but all sections that even mentioned slavery were simply omitted. It was agreed that membership of the convention was to consist of one delegate to every twenty white members of the church, provided that each church had at least one delegate and that all delegates were white, male, and at least 21 years of age. Lastly, the convention appointed a committee to select a pastor.[4]

It was a most un-Methodist task, finding and calling a pastor. Every pastor the Methodists had ever known had been appointed by a bishop. Now the circuit not only did not have a bishop, it also had to go out like the Baptists and find its own pastor. But the search was rewarded, for the committee found the Reverend William Gwynn Coe and invited him to take charge of the churches. Coe, fortunately, happened to be between jobs; he had been a member of the Baltimore Conference until March, when he withdrew to protest what he considered an unworthy appointment. Coe accepted the Accomack pastorate, and shortly after the outbreak of hostilities in South Carolina he and his family disembarked at Onancock and occupied the parsonage next door to Cokesbury Chapel.

WILLIAM
GWYNN COE

William Gwynn Coe (1832-1877), a native of Baltimore baptized in infancy by Father John Hersey, was a man of southern persuasions and an able pastor. It was he who was to give to the Accomack Circuit during the next several years the stamp of his own energy and personality, and even its name. He addressed his pastoral reports to "The Independent Church, Convention of Accomack County," and steadfastly maintained that it was independent of all other denominations. Except for the brief pastorate of Joshua Humphreys preceding his own, Coe was the only pastor his convention was to know during its brief lifetime. His domain consisted of only six churches — Cokesbury in Onancock, Garrison's, Drummondtown, Ayres Chapel, Trinity in Hadlock, and Ebenezer in Sluitkill Neck.[5] He was the most dynamic Methodist pastor on the Eastern Shore of Virginia throughout the Civil War, serving a strong and tightly-knit "denomination." His sermon-book, in which he listed what he preached, where and when, and part of his journal have survived, giving us a glimpse into the daily life of the Methodist minister during this trying time. It was not an easy time to be a Methodist on the Eastern Shore of Virginia, and especially difficult to be one who was neither northern nor southern.

By the beginning of the war, however, the course was set: the Methodists in the central part of the Shore would see it through independently, and Coe was at their head.

Four months after the Accomack Circuit withdrew from the northern church, eleven days before William Gwynn Coe arrived and preached his first sermon at Cokesbury, on April 17, 1861, Virginia seceded from the United States. With the exception of Chincoteague, the entire Eastern Shore voted unanimously to join the rest of the state in secession.

Now there was military and political, as well as ecclesiastical, confusion. No sooner was secession ratified in Virginia than the Union navy established effective control of Chesapeake Bay and blockaded the ports of the Eastern Shore of Virginia. Even before the first shot was fired, the Shore was cut off from the rest of the Confederacy. Blockade running became a way of life for the water-oriented Shoremen. There were two minor naval skirmishes between local and Union boats in late summer of 1861, one in Pocomoke River, one in Chincoteague Bay. And in August the first and only land battle of the war on the Eastern Shore of Virginia occurred at Pitts Wharf on Pocomoke River west of New Church. It, too, was a minor skirmish between about 300 Federal troops and local townsmen; one Yankee was wounded.[6]

Methodism was in a bind. Except for Coe's independent convention churches and the two Methodist Protestant circuits, all the Methodist churches on the Shore were now effectively a part of the Methodist Episcopal Church, South. But after the blockade, the southern church could do little more than list its Shore churches beyond its reach as "Miscellaneous Appointments within Federal lines." Fortunately for the southern churches, one preacher was able to make it through the blockade to serve the cut-off congregations. He was Benjamin T. Ames (1821-1881), a native of Locustville in Accomack County. Ames was preaching in York County when hostilities broke out. He returned home to the Shore immediately,

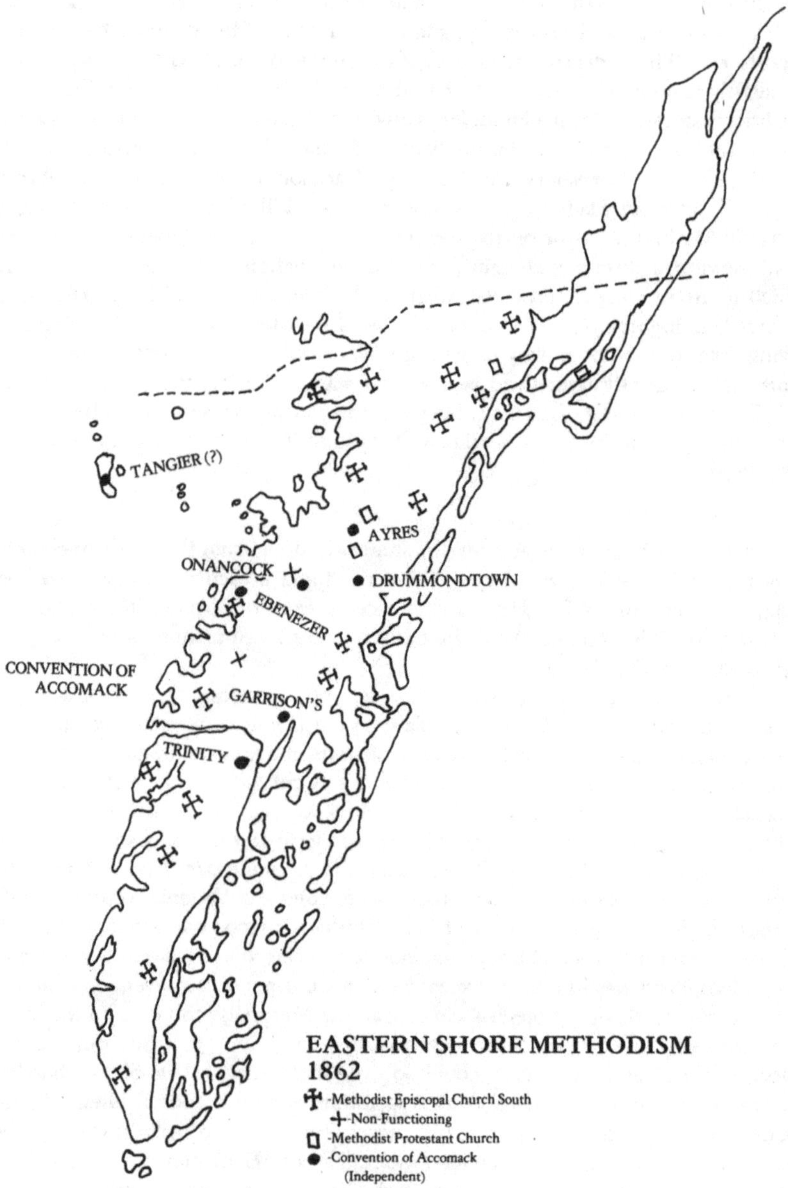
TANGIER (?)
AYRES
ONANCOCK
DRUMMONDTOWN
EBENEZER
CONVENTION OF
ACCOMACK
GARRISON'S
TRINITY
EASTERN SHORE METHODISM
1862
-Methodist Episcopal Church South
-Non-Functioning
-Methodist Protestant Church
-Convention of Accomack
(Independent)

slipping safely through the blockade. Once he was on the Shore, the Virginia Conference, meeting in Norfolk, elected him to elder's orders, ordained him *in absentia,* created the Atlantic District embracing the Shore, and named him presiding elder. There were seventeen congregations under his care, from Downing's to Capeville.

Ames bore this load alone, ably assisted by the local pastors who labored extensively on the Shore during the war, until 1863, when another Shore native named Lloyd Moore (1828-1877) arrived on the Shore to share the work. Thereafter Ames took the Atlantic Circuit in northern Accomack, and Moore pastored the Eastville Circuit in his native Northampton.[7]

The two small Methodist Protestant circuits were part of the Maryland Conference, and thus were not cut off from their affiliations. Their pulpits were regularly supplied each year throughout the war from the Conference. There were, then, four Methodist preachers on the Virginia Shore during the Civil War.

The war itself entered the Shore on November 17, 1861. A force of 4500 soldiers under the command of General Henry H. Lockwood of Delaware assembled in Newtown, Maryland, issued a proclamation stating that they wanted to enter the Shore peacefully, and then proceeded to march slowly down the peninsula. The local Confederate militia rushed up the Shore and encamped just north of Oak Hall on the main road to meet them, but fled before they arrived. The Union army occupied the Shore and returned it to the Union fold without a shot fired. The army settled into occupation, its soldiers stationed at Oak Hall, Drummondtown, Pungoteague, and Eastville.[8]

In Oak Hall, Drummondtown, and Pungoteague, the army commandeered local church buildings for its own use, and several churches were used as barracks, storerooms, or stables. In Drummondtown, the Methodist and Presbyterian buildings were used as stables, and their interiors ruined. Dr. Edward J. Young of the Presbyterian church rescued the pulpit of his congregation, but the interior of the Methodist church — walls, windows, pews, and chancel — was a total loss, and the Methodists did not reclaim and restore their building until 1871. St. James' Episcopal Church in Drummondtown was saved only through the intervention of Miss Kitty Bayly, who through northern friends secured the removal of the Negro troops who were quartered there for a short time.[9]

Downing's Church in Oak Hall was not so seriously damaged; it was back in use by 1861. But in Pungoteague the destruction was most rampant. The Methodist church, a frame building, was a total loss, and methodist services in the village ceased altogether until a new one was erected in 1868. Most unfortunate of all was the damage done to St. George's Episcopal Church in Pungoteague. The building was already more than a century old, an elegant colonial building with two wings and a circular apse that gave it the shape of the "ace of clubs" by which locals called it. The army used this building to stable its horses. Floors, galleries, and all interior woodwork disappeared, probably burned for firewood. One wing was virtually dismantled when the soldiers needed bricks to build a cookhouse. When the army left in 1870, only the shell of the building was standing. The church was not restored and services resumed until about 1880, and the building that is there today is only a portion of the larger church used by the army.[10]

Church buildings, however, are not people, and the Shore was fortunate to escape the widespread destruction and bloodshed of the long war. Two months after its victorious march down the Shore, on January 25, 1862, elections were held, and pro-Union candidates received an overwhelming majority of votes in both counties.[11]

Although war had been safely averted, life under the Union army was far from normal for the people of the Eastern Shore and for their churches. The population of the Shore was, to quote a Methodist of that day, "as near *man*less as a call to the defense of the State could make it," and the presence of the army grated at many points. The ports were blockaded, so most commerce was restricted. Trade with the army itself was rigidly controlled: anyone who offered food for sale to soldiers had to prove that it was safe by eating a portion of it himself in front of an officer. Many horses were confiscated for the army's use. And most of all, anyone who engaged in a profession, operated a business, shipped produce, or tried to leave the two counties was required to take the Oath of Allegiance to the United States.[12] That above all grated.

The people of the Shore were only nominally Unionists; most of the people in both counties still had decidely southern sympathies. And very often it was the churches that became the rallying points for their feelings and their frustrations. The two Episcopalian rectors on the Shore were non-political men "prudent in their conduct and zealous for the spiritual welfare of their flocks." The Presbyterian churches were without pastors, and they presented no difficulties for the army. Baptists, however, seem to have been a continual thorn in the side of the occupying forces. Baptist ministers of the Shore were, it was asserted, with one exception "raging secessionists, busy-bodies going from place to place, and supplying and propagating all kinds of sermons adverse to our country's cause." Patrick Warren of Onancock Baptist Church seems in particular to have been unpopular with the authorities, and Onancock was singled out as the place that had "concocted more mischief...in the way of blockade running and special disloyalty than... any other place of equal dimensions within this region."[13]

William Gwynn Coe was not long on the Eastern Shore before his southern sympathies began to show. One June 13, 1861, he conducted at Garrison's a service called a "Day of Fasting and Prayer for the Southern Confederacy." Though staunchly insisting that he was an independent Methodist, he nonetheless accepted invitations to preach at Bascom's Chapel in Onancock, Pungoteague Chapel, and Downing's Chapel, all southern churches. In October, as the militia was gathering at "Camp Wise" south of Drummondtown, Coe preached to them. And he became a close friend of his Baptist colleague, Patrick Warren, and preached for him in Onancock Baptist Church a number of times.[14]

Coe was not above running the blockade himself, especially to journey to Baltimore. The Reverend Henry Slicer Coe, his son who was just a small boy during the war, wrote about these illegal journeys years later:

> *I can remember trips made up the Bay with the captain and a small crew of a fishing smack who dared to "run the blockade" for small*

> *consideration; and I was able to share in my mother's uneasiness until the sloop slipped into port, bring us rich supplies of flour, sugar, butter, etc. I can remember also how a small Federal force sat down on the town, made barracks or stables of the churches, and seemed to find pleasure in vexing all citizens who appeared on the streets.*

But it was his steadfast refusal to sign the Oath of Allegiance that most frequently embroiled Coe in controversy with the Union authorities. He could not in good conscience bring himself to sign the Oath, and undoubtedly his signature would have been a symbolic victory of some importance for the army. Two years from the month he arrived on the Shore, a full year and a half after the arrival of the occupying army, Coe was placed under house arrest. ''From April 30 to May 19 [1863],'' he wrote, ''I was held a prisoner by Military powers in which time I passed 3 Sabbaths, on which I was not permitted to preach, the first of them was appointed for our first quarterly meeting.'' According to Henry Slicer Coe, this was not the only time his father was placed under arrest, and his confinement was for failure to sign the Oath:

> *The officer in charge frequently put my father under arrest, always on a trivial charge. Finding him steadfast in his refusal to take the ''oath of allegiance'' to the United States government, he would confine him to his own premises for weeks at a time, and even threatened to send him to a U.S. prison.*

For two years this uneasy coexistence continued, generally peaceful if not amiable. Methodists in Drummondtown and Oak Hall held their worship services out-of-doors or in other buildings, for the army controlled their churches. In Pungoteague both Methodist and Episcopal services were discontinued altogether because of the presence of the army. Services on Tangier Island, which was northern church territory, were occasional at best. Neither Methodist nor Baptist preachers were sufficiently loyal to the Union to please the commanding officer of the occupying army, but there was a truce of sorts.

Shortly after the Shore was returned to the Union fold there was a movement afoot to reunite the various Methodist denominations. The Convention invited delegates from all the churches to a meeting at Garrison's in February 1862 to consider merger. But opposition was strong from the southern Methodists, and the meeting adjourned in ''splendid spirits.'' The Convention churches, at least, adopted enough of a fraternal attitude towards the other two denominations to promote the exchange of delegates at conferences. Methodist Protestant visitors were present at the Convention's Quarterly Conference in August 1862, and the conference expressed the hope ''that the fraternal relations between that Church and ours may be perpetuated.''[16]

Attempts at unity and fraternal spirit failed, however. And the real problems that Methodists of the Shore were to face during the Civil War were less from the occupying army than from internal strife.

By 1864 a military victory for the Union forces seemed only a matter of time, but the ecclesiastical battle of the Methodists was about to enter a new phase. Now that large parts of the South were under Union control, a movement emerged in the Methodist Episcopal Church to expand into the South, and to use the advancing Union forces as an opportunity to re-establish the Methodist Episcopal claim to the entire nation.

The idea was at first that of the bishops of the northern church, whose address to the General Conference in 1864 directed attention to the "large and inviting fields of Christian enterprise and labor" that lay in the territory of the southern church now under Union control. The Methodist Episcopal Church had once held sway in this southern area, the bishops noted, and ought never to have consented to being excluded from it. "Now that the providence of God has opened her way, she should not be disobedient to her heavenly calling, but should return at the earliest practicable period." The General Conference responded enthusiastically by endorsing and funding a "mission to the South" designed to establish northern churches in the wake of the Union army's conquests.

This new aggressive policy on the part of the northern church created many bitter scenes across the nation, as northern Methodist missionaries swept in behind the army to occupy churches abandoned by fleeing southern preachers. Lengthy and involved property disputes, as both denominations fought for control of church buildings, erupted in many communities. But the Methodist Episcopal Church, South, was powerless to stop the advance of the northern church into its own territory. In 1865 the northern church organized the Holston Conference, the first of several northern conferences in the South.[17]

It was this new mood in the northern church and its attempts to enlist the support of the army occupying the Eastern Shore that brought about the end of the uneasy truce between Methodists and Federal forces and opened a new chapter of greater strife.

The Philadelphia Conference, along with the others, had visions of reclaiming its southern territories, Accomack and Northampton. One of its preachers named Vaughn Smith, who had served in Virginia in the 1840's, is said to have spearheaded the northern movement to reclaim the Virginia Shore "at the head of a detachment of Federal soldiers." But the two most energetic persons behind the move were not Smith, but Thomas L. Poulson, a Philadelphia Conference pastor serving as a chaplain in the Union army, and Adam Wallace, the former circuit preacher who was now the presiding elder of the Salisbury District of the Philadelphia Conference.

Late in 1863 Wallace and Poulson began the battle with a letter to General Lockwood, commander of the occupying forces, informing him of the Methodist Episcopal Church's intention of asserting its claim to the pulpits of the churches on the Shore. Lockwood's response, on November 24, 1863, was positive but generally non-committal:

> *...inasmuch as there exists a clear legal right in the Philadelphia Conference of the M.E. Church to the M.E. churches in Northampton and Accomack counties, I shall feel myself bound to protect the duly accredited ministers of the Conference in and to the exclusive occupancy and use of said churches, and shall certainly do so when asked so to do.*[18]

The next month Lockwood was transferred, and the command of the Shore fell to General B. F. Butler, head of the military department in Fort Monroe. Col. Frank J. White, a young New York lawyer who had distinguished himself in battle in Missouri, replaced Lockwood on the Shore. Poulson, therefore, wrote a second letter, pleading his cause before Butler, reminding Butler that most of the Methodist ministers on the Virginia Shore were "secessionists" who had not taken the Oath of Allegiance.[19]

In Butler the northern preachers found a more ready ally. "I have the honor to say," he wrote them in January 1864, "that no man will preach in Drummondtown or elsewhere in this Department unless he has taken the Oath of Allegiance. Call the attention of the Provost Marshal to this...If the present clergymen do not take the Oath of Allegiance, send them to me."

Butler promptly issued Special Order No. 49, which instructed Eastern Shore pastors to take the Oath. It was not long before Benjamin T. Ames, Patrick Warren, and William Coe, among others, received their instructions to take the hated Oath:

> *I do solemnly swear, in the present of Almighty God, that I will henceforth faithfully support, protect, and defend the Constitution of the United States and the Union of States thereunder; and that I will in like manner abide by and faithfully support all acts of Congress passed during the existing rebellion with reference to slaves...and that I will, in like manner, abide by and faithfully support all proclamations of the President made during the existing rebellion...So help me God.*

Ames wrote back to Butler from Drummondtown on January 29 to protest "how heavily your 49th order bears on me." He was a preacher, not a politician, Ames insisted. He had never borne arms against the Union and had in fact refused a military commission in the Confederacy. Half of his family holdings were in the Confederacy and half in the Union. Should he lose his property in the Confederacy, as he would by taking the Oath, he had small hopes of being able to support his family.

Butler was unmoved. "Your case," he replied, "is a hard one. I wish you could have said your sympathies and wishes were not with the South; in that case I might have made an exception, but looking carefully through your letter I can find nothing which shows a spark of loyalty. I can then only say that you must take your case as you have made it."[20] Whether or not Ames took the Oath is not recorded. It is certain, however, that he continued to preach in the southern churches on the

Shore. How Coe and Warren responded to the order is not known; chances are they ignored it as Coe, at least, had ignored previous attempts to get him to take the Oath.

Simultaneous with the pressure from the military authorities came pressure from some of the laity for more accommodation with the occupying forces and a closer relationship with the Methodist Episcopal Church. The northern church's attempt to reclaim the Shore bore most fruit at Onancock, where a strong pro-northern faction had arisen. George C. Tyler, a member of Cokesbury who had served as the original secretary of the Convention when it was formed in 1861, had by 1863 become the leader of the accommodationist position. He was now tax collector for the Union, and would soon be one of four civilian superintendents of labor on the Shore, overseeing such government programs as those that required all able-bodied Negroes over fourteen to obtain work. The move by Adam Wallace and Thomas Poulson to re-establish the Methodist Episcopal Church's supremacy on the Virginia Shore found a strong and able ally in Tyler.

By March 1864 Tyler and his pro-northern party were in the majority at Cokesbury in Onancock, and they were ready for an end to Coe's pastorate and the independent Convention. Coe's yearly appointment as pastor ended on March 1; he himself insisted that he held the job not by appointment of a bishop but by call from the lay Convention. When the Convention's quarterly meeting was held on March 16, the delegates, much as Coe had expected, did not recall him to his fifth year, but instead drew up a "plan of separation" of their own. It was agreed to allow the individual churches in the Convention to withdraw "to avoid strife and promote, as far as possible under the circumstances, harmony of feeling." The agreement was that each church in the Convention would by simple majority determine whether their preacher would be supplied by the Philadelphia Conference or by the Convention.[21]

Cokesbury put the matter to a vote almost immediately and by an overwhelming majority, 104 to seventeen, decided to return to the northern fold. Ayres Chapel followed suit shortly thereafter, and the Philadelphia Conference was duly informed that there was once again an Onancock Circuit that desired a pastor from its ranks. Wrote Coe in his journal: "So the old Circuit is dissolved — the minority are so bent on having a Philadelphia Conference appointee that to accomplish their end they scruple not to tear the Circuit asunder. What the result will be I cannot divine. O Lord, bless all the members of my old charge!"

A month later a layman from the circuit, John Tyler, wrote to Coe urging him to join the Philadelphia Conference himself "and thus be the means of uniting the Circuit." Coe was unmoved.[22]

Hostilities ran high at this division of the Convention. When he learned that the seventeen remaining Convention Methodists in Onancock were going to try to lay claim to the church building before the new Philadelphia preacher arrived, George Washington Mason, one of the pro-northern majority, left his home in Savageville, drove the several miles to Onancock, locked the church door, put the only key in his pocket, and returned home. The building remained firmly in the hands of the Methodist Episcopal Church. Later that year northern Methodist services resumed there, and Adam Wallace himself returned to the building to lead worship and the Quarterly Conference.[23]

It was George Tyler's intention that Cokesbury and Ayres Chapel be only the beginning; the northern church must reclaim the entire Shore. On March 25, 1864, a week after the division of the Convention, Tyler wrote to Colonel White to appraise him of the situation, and to ask his support. "We have seen an order from your Department requiring churches in Norfolk and Portsmouth to be occupied only by ministers of known loyalty to the Government. We approve of such an order very much, and would like to have the same...in the counties of Accomack and Northampton." After a detailed history of the division of the Methodist denomination on the Shore from 1844 to 1864, Tyler then made his appeal:

> *...as long as Secession preachers are allowed to occupy churches of any denomination, our [loyal M.E. church] will have but small congregations. We think if they are not allowed to occupy churches of any denomination, a great opportunity to mislead the ignorant and keep up the strife would be taken away and the people would have time to reflect more for themselves, and thus a great step would be taken towards restoring the church to her proper status, and benefiting the State at the same time...*[24]

No written reply from White to Tyler is known. But the next few months would prove that the appeal had not fallen on deaf ears.

The division of the circuit, coupled with the resurgence of pro-northern sentiment in several of the congregations, seemed almost to deal the deathblow to the independent Convention and to William Coe's pastorate. It was not until the new northern preacher arrived to take possession of the Onancock pulpit and parsonage that the other churches in the Convention began to rally. the new minister, T. L. Tomkinson, arrived in Onancock on April 1, 1864. "Well, well," wrote Coe, "the Philadelphia preacher is come. Long looked for, come at last! He has come on [April] Fools day, and I am thinking his errand is no better than the day — and so the result will prove unless I am mistaken."[25] Still jobless, Coe preached for his friend, Patrick Warren, in the Baptist church that Sunday and returned home to begin vacating the premises.

But the rest of the Convention began to rally. On April 9 Coe received word that the remaining Convention churches wanted him to preach to them at Garrison's the next Sunday. He poured himself into the task joyfully and preached a rousing revival sermon. Soon Coe and his family were relocated, first in a house near Belle Haven, next on Ames Ridge ("not a neighbor in sight," his son remembered), and by May a revitalized Convention was taking shape.

No sooner had the Convention rallied, however, that it suffered another defection. By the end of April, Garrison's Chapel had second thoughts and joined Cokesbury and Ayres Chapel on the northern circuit. George P. Cutler, a prominent

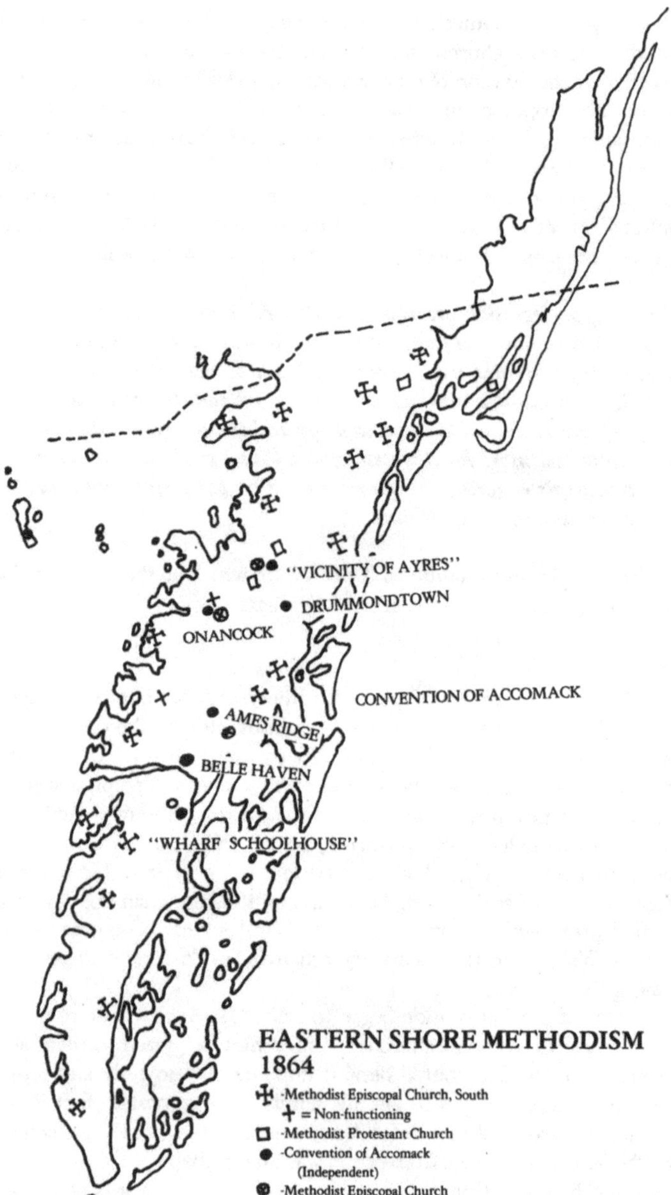
"VICINITY OF AYRES"
DRUMMONDTOWN
ONANCOCK
CONVENTION OF ACCOMACK
AMES RIDGE
BELLE HAVEN
"WHARF SCHOOLHOUSE"
EASTERN SHORE METHODISM
1864
-Methodist Episcopal Church, South
= Non-functioning
-Methodist Protestant Church
-Convention of Accomack
(Independent)
-Methodist Episcopal Church
= Non-Functioning

layman there, was responsible for that decision. "He was the author of our trouble at Garrison's Chapel," commented Coe. "If he had gove with us, the Philadelphia preacher could not have occupied that church."[26] With the loss of Garrison's, the Convention was left without a single church building. To that extent at least the northern church had made good its claim to the church property of the Shore. The Convention's principal seat now was not Onancock, but Ames Ridge, where Coe preached in a schoolhouse. Services were resumed in the Hadlock area during the summer, but not in Trinity Chapel there; Coe's Convention Methodists acceded to the northern claim to that building, which was not reopened. By August the Convention had resumed services in Onancock "in the school house of our worthy sister Elizabeth Fosque." In Drummondtown the Convention resumed services in October, after a lull of one year; they met in the schoolhouse, for the army still had possession of the church building there.

Before the year was out there was a Convention congregation meeting in the old Universalist church in Belle Haven, and a congregation in the vicinity of Ayres Chapel for the non-northern remnant there. The Onancock congregation had moved out of Fosque schoolhouse into Temperance Hall, and Coe had preached several times at Holmes Presbyterian Church in Bayview, further south than the Convention had ever before ventured, by invitation of that congregation who were without a pastor.[27]

But no sooner was the Convention on its feet again than it felt more pressure from the army, now allied with the Methodist Episcopal Church. On May 13, 1864, Coe received a letter from the Assistant Provost Marshal of the Federal Army in Onancock with instructions concerning Order No. 49. Patrick Warren and Benjamin T. Ames received similar instructions at the same time. For all three of them the letter presented a dilemma, for none of them could in good conscience follow the orders it contained:

> *Enclosed please find a copy of the President's proclamation. I would respectfully ask you to read the same to your congregation on your next regular day of worship and offer up a prayer to Almighty God for the President of the United States and those in authority, which is only carrying out the sacred obligation of those who have sworn to support all proclamations the President made during the existing rebellion.*[28]

Coe was off to Eastville shortly afterwards to protest personally to White. With a letter of introduction he was ushered into the presence of the Colonel (whom he mistakenly referred to as Major), and found him "very polite." "My visit to him," he wrote, "was on the subject of our Church difficulties. From what he says (and he is now the supreme power here, although I doubt if he is 25 years old), I think our Church will get along without any trouble." Coe fasted that night, apparently convinced that the independent Convention, at least, would be spared further interference from the military.[29]

Colonel White, despite Coe's thinking to the contrary, was not convinced of the loyalty of the Methodists, and may well have tired of the whole issue. Why he did what he did is not known. Perhaps Tyler's letter had raised doubts in his mind, or maybe there were further developments not now known. At any rate White took the matter in his own hands and on July 12, 1864, he ordered the Methodist churches of the Shore closed.

His explanation for doing so illustrates how closely allied were the army and the Methodist Episcopal Church:

> *At the request of various loyal members of the Methodist Episcopal Church on the Eastern Shore of Virginia, an investigation has been made into certain charges of disloyalty...made against elders and congregations belonging to that church in their religious capacity.*
>
> *It is not the desire or the intention of the military authorities to claim jurisdiction over matters solely pertaining to religious belief or the exercise of any form of worship, but by the introduction of political questions or by affiliation with organizations avowedly disloyal, both ministers and congregations bring themselves properly within such jurisdiction.*
>
> *A majority of the congregations of the Methodist Episcopal Church on this Shore at the outbreak of this rebellion committed various acts of mob violence, driving away from their pulpits at the point of the bayonet ministers against whom no charge could be preferred other than that of loyalty to their country. They held... public meetings in which disloyal sentiments were expressed... They passed resolutions dissolving all connection with the General Conference of the Methodist Episcopal Church because of its loyalty and giving their adhesion to the Methodist Episcopal Church South, an organization now and then avowedly disloyal...*
>
> *These acts have never been repudiated publicly as they were committed, and hence these congregations, until absolved from the responsibility attaching to them, cannot be permitted to continue their present organization.*
>
> *It is therefore ordered that no public assemblies or congregations belonging to the Methodist Church upon this Shore, except such as are under the Jurisdiction of the Philadelphia Conference, shall be permitted until at a public meeting, called for that purpose, a majority of the members of each congregation shall, by published resolutions, declare themselves loyal, and repudiate any and all connection with the Methodist Episcopal Church South, or other disloyal organization.*

Upon proper proof that the above conditions have been complied with, permission to resume worship will be given from this office.

It was exactly what Wallace and Poulson had hoped for: complete loyalty to the Union was to be guaranteed by the army, and accompanied by a return to the Methodist Episcopal Church. The order was clearly a slap in the face of the Methodist Episcopal Church, South, and Coe's independent Convention of Accomack. The Baptists were more vehemently secessionist than the southern Methodists, at least in Onancock, but their churches were not closed. The Methodist Protestants, though not a part of the Philadelphia Conference, were not (as it turned out later) included in the order. White's argument that he was closing down disloyal organizations, not meddling in church politics, did not ring true with the southern and independent Methodists. They saw in the order the deliberate attempt by the Methodist Episcopal Church to reassert its claim to the churches of the Eastern Shore. How else could you account for the fact that the only churches, according to the order, that were to be allowed to stay functioning were Cokesbury, Ayres Chapel, Garrison's, and (possibly) Tangier, which, when supplied with a preacher at all, were supplied from the northern circuit?

To the independent Convention the order read like military intervention and it was simply ignored. Coe met his regular preaching assignments at Holmes Presbyterian, Belle Haven, and at the Fosque schoolhouse in Onancock as if there were no ban on his congregations' assembling, and the crowds that greeted him were as large as before. The Convention gathered in Quarterly Conference and calmly appointed Coe and James Garrison to visit White, "present him with our journal, and request a hearing before him in the presence of our accusers, and obtain a trial that a correct and true account of our position may be manifest, and that we have justice done us in the premises." The order, insisted the Convention, was obviously founded on false information.[31]

Presumably the reaction among the southern Methodists was much the same: the order was ignored. There is no record that any church voluntarily complied with the order, and no record that the army showed up anywhere to force compliance. Neither Coe, Ames, nor Lloyd Moore were arrested or jailed for holding services in disobedience to the order, and since it is known that Coe continued to meet his appointments, it is likely that the others did, too.

In fact, what happened next is not altogether clear today. It could be that the Methodists submitted to the order as required and satisfied White as to their loyalty, but it is certain that they did not repudiate the Methodist Episcopal Church, South, as the order required. The most likely explanation is that the Methodists were able to convince White that they could be loyal without being members of the Methodist Episcopal Church. Perhaps, too, they were able to convince him that he had been given false information, that the churches had not turned away preachers "at the point of the bayonet," that the notorious, violent incidents of which he had heard had occurred twenty years ago at the division of the denomination in the 1840's, and then at the hands of non-Methodists.

It is clear that some sort of compromise was reached, that the Methodists succeeded in convincing White of their loyalty to the United States and he in turn was satisfied not to require them to repudiate the Methodist Episcopal Church, South. Apparently over the next several weeks White received in turn each of the three Methodist ministers, and peace was made, for over the next several weeks the order was rescinded in stages.

On August 25, 1864, White's Special Order No. 43 was issued:

> *The Independent Methodist congregations at Belle Haven, Onancock, Hadlocktown, Drummondtown and in the vicinity of Ayres Chapel and on Ames Ridge, under the charge of the Reverend W. G. Coe, having passed resolutions prescribed by Circular from this office and having acknowledged themselves loyal, will be permitted to assemble at such times or places as they may desire for public worship.*

The independent Convention was the first to convince White that they were loyal.

On October 15, 1864, the restrictions were removed from the churches of the Eastville Circuit: "Methodist congregations at Capeville, Salem, Johnson's, Franktown, Bethel, Craddock[ville], Locustville, Burton's and Andrew Chapel." These were Lloyd Moore's churches. The members may well have sworn allegiance to the United States, but it is clear that they never repudiated the southern church, as White had originally demanded.

Finally on November 4, 1864, White lifted the restrictions from the churches of the Atlantic Circuit: "Downing's, Conquest Chapel, Horntown Chapel, Pocomoke Chapel, Saxe's Chapel, Modestown Chapel, Guilford Chapel and Oak Grove Chapel."[32] These were the churches under the care of Benjamin Ames. Like those of the Eastville Circuit, it is doubtful that they were ever actually closed by force; they remained southern churches.

It may be that Colonel White began his course of action in these events by playing into the hands of the Methodist Episcopal Church and its new aggressive policy of moving into the South. His closing of the churches, however, and their subsequent reopening finally established to the army's satisfaction that the Methodists of the Eastern Shore of Virginia were loyal and posed no threat to the United States of America, regardless of their denominational leanings or their ecclesiastical politics. Once the churches of the Atlantic Circuit were reopened in November 1864, friction between the Methodists and the occupying forces ceased, and the Methodists were left to go their own way.

There was at least one more attempt by the northern church to reassert its claim to the Shore. On July 24, 1866, John Taft, the new circuit preacher of the northern churches, reopened the whole issue in a letter to George H. French, assistant superintendent of the Freedmen's Bureau, asking his help against the southern churches who "still hold unlawful possession of our church property." French passed the letter on to his superiors and nothing ever came of it, possibly because, as Taft had lamented in it, "every lawyer at the bar in these two counties has, upon the supposition that it is our intention to bring suit at law, signed a paper circulated by one of the Southern Methodist ministers pledging himself that without remuneration he will do all he can to defeat us.''[33] That is the extent to which, two years later, the whole issue was settled in the minds of the people of the Shore, as well as of the army.

In January 1866, Garrison's left the northern church for the second time and rejoined the Convention, leaving to the Methodist Episcopal Church on the Eastern Shore of Virginia only Cokesbury, Ayres Chapel, Tangier, and two practically vacant buildings, Trinity and Ebenezer Chapel in Modest Town. The once greatest denomination on the Virginia Shore finished the Civil War as only a shadow of its former self.

Despite all the troubles that brewed around it and the division that almost wrecked it in 1864, the independent Convention of Accomack remained remarkably vigorous and active throughout the war years, a tribute to the leadership of William Gwynn Coe. A protracted meeting began at the Ames Ridge schoolhouse in September 1864, only six months after the disastrous schism, and it lasted for three weeks. (During this time the southern churches were still officially, if not actually, closed by army order.) Coe preached a total of sixteen times to the crowds that came, in addition to meeting his regular preaching assignments elsewhere. More than 130 persons made a profession of faith, ''a number exceeding the capacity of the house,'' and the converts joined Baptist and Methodist churches across the Shore. Coe is said to have converted and baptized hundreds of persons during his five-year pastorate on the Shore.[34]

And even in the midst of a time of political turmoil, purely spiritual matters were still a concern of the congregations. Coe addressed one of his last reports to the Convention from his home on Ames Ridge on February 17, 1865, and expressed great concern about ''an evil that prevails among us: I allude to indiscriminate visiting on the Sabbath, a sin in which some engage who would consider their souls almost burned if they partook of a meal cooked on that holy day. I suggest...if this be not verily straining at a gnat and swallowing a camel — albeit let it be distinctly borne in mind that we dare not countenance the practice of Sunday cooking...''[35]

The Convention met for the last time in Drummondtown on April 18, 1866, and passed one final resolution: ''In view of having united with the Baltimore Conference of the Methodist Episcopal Church, South, and there being no further necessity for an Independent Church, we do now dissolve.''[36] And so the five-year-old denomination came to an end. In the fall of 1865 the Convention had petitioned the Baltimore Conference (South) for a preacher. Garrison's had returned to the ranks in January, and in March, the start of the new conference year, Adam B. Dolly arrived to assume the pastorate. The remaining Convention congregation in Onancock moved out of Temperance Hall into the abandoned and defunct Bascom's Chapel Methodist Episcopal Church, South, reviving that prewar church just a stone's throw from northern Cokesbury. In May the southern church transferred the Accomack Circuit, as the Convention had once more become, to the Virginia Conference, and the war of alignments was over.

Militarily the Civil War passed lightly over the Eastern Shore of Virginia. There were no significant battles, only one minor land skirmish, and it is said that only one person was wounded in fighting on the Shore. But religion languished during the war years, no church more so than the Methodist church. The Baptists, each of them an independent unit, managed to keep up their congregations and Sunday schools without much lapse or interference. "The depressing influence generated by the contest were only temporary...A few even enjoyed refreshing seasons to a limited extent, during the period of strife."[37]

Not so the Methodists. In 1860 the Methodist Episcopal Church was still the strongest, most central and active denomination on the Eastern Shore of Virginia; by 1866 it was only three churches and two empty buildings. When the 1860's began, all the Methodist churches on the Eastern Shore were racially mixed: black slave, free black, and white master worshiped together in the same churches. By the end of the sixties there were almost no blacks left in the Methodist churches of any stamp, North, South, or Protestant. To a man they had left for their own churches. The 1860's brought to Eastern Shore Methodism a legacy of ill-will and distrust that has never been fully overcome. To this day the town of Onancock has two Methodist churches, still known as the "northern" and the "southern" church. To this day, hardly a single Methodist church in the two counties has both black and white members.

Further, the war years left Methodism on the Shore weakened because it was divided into more streams than ever before, with more churches duplicating more efforts and expanding more energies and hiding behind more misunderstandings and barriers than ever before.

The Methodist churches survived the time of troubles that broke a nation. But to a great extent the problems that face a great many Methodist churches on the Eastern Shore of Virginia today are those that have not yet been solved from the 1860's.

The Great Division
1865-1884

VIII

The new missionary landed on Cherrystone Creek in Northampton County in the year 1865.

He was a missionary in the truest sense of the term, like Paul to Macedonia or Wesley to Georgia, driven by nothing so much as his own inner calling to preach the Gospel. But of all missionaries, he was most like Elijah Baker. He landed near that spot where the Baptist had landed almost a century before. He came and went quickly, planting churches that others would water and nourish, as Baker had done. And like Baker he was to leave behind him a new faith, and an indelible imprint on the religious life of the Eastern Shore of Virginia.

His name was James Johnson, and he was black.

In the autumn of 1865 the bishop of the Baltimore Conference, a different Baltimore Conference than that to which the independent Convention of Accomack was petitioning for a minister, Bishop Daniel Payne of the African Methodist

DANIEL PAYNE

Episcopal Church, dispatched one of his preachers to the Eastern Shore of Virginia to evangelize the black people and to establish new churches there. James H. A. Johnson, his choice for the job, was the first fully ordained black Methodist to preach on the Virginia Shore. On December 20, 1865, he landed on Cherrystone Creek, and his whirlwind mission to the Shore began.

Johnson held his first service that first day outdoors half a mile from Eastville, where a mixed crowd of blacks and whites gathered to hear him. He preached on the text "God is a Spirit, and they that worship him must worship in spirit and in truth," and although forty persons put their names down for membership in a new church, Johnson was off instead to Drummondtown. There a few days later he organized the First African Methodist Episcopal Church of Drummondtown, later renamed Macedonia. There were eighteen charter members, and the first Quarterly Conference was held on January 2, 1866.

No sooner was the Drummondtown congregation formed than Johnson returned to Eastville, where his second church was organized in a schoolhouse on January 7, 1866.[1] It was originally named Eastville African Methodist Episcopal Church, but since that time it has borne two other names: Wayman's Chapel, and Bethel. On the day it was organized, William Coe was preaching to his independent congregation in another schoolhouse on Ames Ridge.[2]

For his third field of labor Johnson chose Modest Town in Accomack County, where he preached for four months before a congregation was formed. On April 9, 1866, eight members constituted the new Christian Union African Methodist Episcopal Church in Modest Town, and no sooner was it organized than Johnson left the Shore to report to Bishop Payne.

Payne received with great joy Johnson's tidings of the budding work on the Virginia Eastern Shore, and he dispatched another energetic preacher, John Henry Offer, to pastor these new churches, which he designated the Eastville Circuit.[3]

In less than half a year an entirely new denomination had made a firm foothold on the Shore. And John Henry Offer was to be, if anything, even more energetic than his predecessor in the years that followed, years that were perhaps the greatest period for the founding of new congregations on the Eastern Shore of Virginia.

The sudden and virtually total defection of black members from the churches is one of the most significant events in the religious history of the Eastern Shore, but one whose story has been obscured by a lack of written records and the passage of more than a century. What is true of the nation in general is also true of the Virginia Shore: even before the Civil War was over, there began a mass exodus of black Christians from the established churches in which they had always worshiped, and new black congregations and new black denominations were formed. Nowhere did this event constitute a more complete reversal of the status quo than on the Eastern Shore of Virginia, where half the population was black, where blacks and whites had always worshiped together, and where almost half the members of the two largest denominations, Methodist and Baptist, were black.

On the Eastern Shore it happened first in Northampton County. In at least two communities, Eastville and Capeville, blacks were gathering outdoors and in private homes for their own worship services before the end of the Civil War. The inevitable discussion of the possibility of a completely black church arose in both communities, but the blacks of Eastville were the first to act upon the idea. In 1863, in a private home near Townfields, the new congregation was organized. Samuel and Matilda Bibbins of Eastville gave a piece of land for the erection of the building, and on July 2, 1865, the Eastern Shore's first Negro church, Union Baptist Church, was dedicated there.[4]

Negro churchmen at the other end of the Shore were only a few steps behind. Black members of, presumably, Downing's Chapel and Wattsville Methodist Protestant Church effected their own organization and by October 1865 had purchased a lot in Wattsville. Shortly thereafter arose Friendship Methodist Episcopal Church, the Shore's second black church. The building that stands there now was erected in 1868, one of the two oldest Negro church buildings on the Virginia Shore.

Thus even before James Johnson brought the African Methodist Episcopal Church to the peninsula, the defection of the blacks from the local churches had begun. In 1865 the Eastville Circuit of the Methodist Episcopal Church still carried 114 Negro members on its rolls, but in a few years they were all gone. In 1866 there were still 266 black members in the churches of the Accomack Baptist Association. By 1867 more than half of them had withdrawn; by 1868 there were only twelve. The Association encouraged its black members to form their own churches in 1866. Four years later there were only six blacks remaining in the Association, five at Onancock and one at Union in Chincoteague.[5]

It is not without significance that Johnson's first African Methodist Episcopal service on the Shore at Eastville was attended by whites as well as blacks, and by Federal army officers in particular. The Shore was still occupied by the Federal army in 1865, and so jealously was the army guarding the question of loyalty to the government that it had only in the previous year shut down almost every Methodist church on the peninsula until their loyalties were proven. Now that war was over and the southern cause lost, now that former black slaves were free, the feeling of the whites against the blacks seemed to be running higher, not lower. As a few months' time would tell, the army was needed to protect the very lives of the black citizens of the Shore.

On April 12, 1866, just two days after James Johnson returned to Washington, the most serious racial incident in the history of the Eastern Shore occurred in Pungoteague. There John Holden, a black man accused of killing two persons, was hunted down by a white vigilante group and lynched, hanged from a tree near the entrance to St. George's Episcopal Church. This is the only lynching known to have ever occurred on the Shore. It was not, however, the end of the violent racial strife that gripped the Shore after the Civil War.

A few weeks later the possibility of another lynching arose in the area of Lee Mont when 300 white men at a public meeting swore vengeance on a black man who had attempted to murder a white. So high was feeling against the blacks that the mob vowed "to drive all colored people out of that county, and those who were in the U.S. army shall not remain on the Shore." It took military intervention to control this situation. Troops were sent in from Fort Monroe, and after their arrival on July 27, 1866, the community calmed down.

It was George H. French, assistant superintendent to the Freedmen's Bureau on the Shore at the time, who reported this incident to the authorities. His report suggests the tense air that hung over the peninsula:

> *This feeling is mostly confined to Accomack County, where there is an organized band for the avowed purpose of driving all colored people from the Shore. Some of them already have been compelled to leave their houses and crops to save themselves. This band is again about nightly disarming all colored people and they not only take arms but money, when found, and valuables of any kind. If resistance is made, they are shot at or cruelly beaten.*

By late August the Shore lay quiet again, but only "owing to the prompt interference of the military." In upper Accomack County there had been groups of up to fifty persons who terrorized the blacks. One such vigilante whom the army arrested turned out to be the local constable. Northampton County was apparently free of such activity.[6]

It was in this atmosphere that the black Christians of the Eastern Shore first built their churches, and with the creation of the black churches the single greatest schism in the religious history of the Shore occurred. The division of the churches sealed the virtually total separation of the two races for a century to come. Cut adrift from one another, the black churches and the white churches developed along different lines, evolved different styles, and ministered to completely different worlds. On the Shore, as elsewhere in the nation, the black church became the real center for the hopes and dreams and aspirations of the black people, one of the few places the black citizen had to go to voice his feelings about anything. It was in the church that his social, economic, and political as well as his spiritual life was discussed and molded.

In some places the whites feared the results of allowing the blacks to gather in their own churches, sensing perhaps the strength of identity and power that might emerge there. Such was the fear behind the last incident of organized racial persecution of the period. It occurred in Modest Town in 1868. There a gang of whites gathered and set the torch to Christian Union African Methodist Episcopal Church, burning it completely "to prevent the colored people from holding a contemplated public meeting" that may not have been entirely religious in nature.[7] After that incident, such events disappeared from the Shore. The blacks of Modest Town faithfully re-erected their church, although the congregation there never grew to any size and within a few years had disappeared from the scene.

After 1868, the whites seemed more than willing to let the blacks go their own way in their own churches, and even assisted in setting them up as separate congregations. The blacks were "rarely opposed, but [even] aided by their white brethren, especially when they sought their advice and counsel."[8] But the aid sometimes afforded by the whites was less brotherly than segregative, as subsequent years were to prove. Once the parent churches had set up the new black congregations, the aid was ended, and communication between the two races ceased.

A great tragedy had been in the making on the Shore since that first moment when the new Methodist movement had accommodated its anti-slavery beliefs to the prevailing pro-slavery attitudes of the people. Now the breach was complete. The division of the people of the Shore into two separate racial groups had received the sanction of the Christian churches. It would take more than a century to heal the breach.

Left alone to pursue their own life in their own way, the black congregations of the Eastern Shore grew phenomenally. There had never been a period in the life of the Shore that saw the birth of so many new churches.

Three denominations contended for the allegiance of the black Christians on the Shore. The oldest of them was the African Methodist Episcopal Church (A.M.E.), founded in Philadelphia in 1816 by black leaders of St. George's Church who refused to be excluded from the main floor and relegated to the gallery during worship. (Another black Methodist denomination, the African Methodist Episcopal Zion Church [A.M.E.Z.] arose out of a similar event in New York City in 1820, but never found its way to the Eastern Shore of Virginia.) The second was the Methodist Episcopal Church, which separated its black members into segregated conferences, beginning in 1864. These black conferences of the northern church, forerunner of the Central Jurisdiction of the twentieth century, formed for all intents and purposes a separate denomination, and one of them, the Delaware Conference, found a home on the Shore. (In 1870 the southern church dismissed its black members to form a separate denomination called the Colored Methodist Episcopal Church, later changed to Christian Methodist Episcopal [C.M.E.],[9] but this church founded no congregations on the Shore either.) The third black denomination was Baptist. Like all other Baptist churches, the new black congregations formed on the Shore beginning in 1865 were congregational in polity, independent churches who joined themselves into free and voluntary associations with no ruler above them to group them together. The several black Baptist congregations on the Shore remained separate and independent until 1884, when at Cherrystone Wharf in Northampton they organized the Northampton Baptist Association with the Reverend Leonard Treherne as moderator. Years later when a congregation in Maryland applied for membership, the name of the group was changed to the Eastern Shore of Virginia-Maryland Baptist Association.[10]

In the late 1860's these three denominations set out to win the allegiance of the Negro Christians of the Eastern Shore of Virginia. Together they met with remarkable success, and changed the religious scene completely within a short time.

When the second A.M.E. pastor arrived on the Shore in 1866, he found three functioning congregations left by his predecessor, James Johnson: Macedonia in Drummondtown, Bethel in Eastville, and Christian Union in Modest Town. The new pastor, John Henry Offer (1825-1902), set to work with great vigor, and his achievements on the Shore soon eclipsed that of the pioneer Johnson. Within two years Offer had organized two new congregations: Bethel in Onancock (1868) and Ebenezer in Capeville (1868), in the latter place annexing the Methodist half of the interdenominational community group that had been gathering outdoors for worship for several years. When Offer left his pastorate in 1870 there were five more congregations: Allen Memorial (Franktown), St. Paul's (Pungoteague), St. Joseph (Belle Haven), Shorter Chapel (Bridgetown), and Mt. Zion (Jamesville), so many that the original circuit had to be divided. Two years later St. Luke's A.M.E. Church was established in Daugherty, and in 1873 Gaskin's Chapel A.M.E. in Savageville.[11]

Thus by 1873, just eight years after the arrival of the first A.M.E. pastor on the Shore, the two counties could boast twelve African Methodist Episcopal congregations. The only denomination on the Shore with more churches than that was the Methodist Episcopal Church, South. Although it was a phenomenal record, the congregations were only as powerful as the persons who composed them, and the A.M.E. members were poor Negroes only recently freed from slavery. Their new churches were erected either in rural areas well outside the existing towns (as in Belle Haven, Franktown, and Capeville), or on the edge of town (as in Eastville, Drummondtown, and Onancock). Not a single A.M.E. church building arose in the middle of an established community; the mainstream of Eastern Shore life was still too much in the hands of the whites to permit that.

So rapid was the growth of this denomination on the Shore that on April 26, 1883, Bishop Payne convened the seventeenth session of the Virginia Annual Conference of the African Methodist Episcopal Church in Bethel Church in Eastville. Although Eastern Shore Methodism was by then a century old, never before had an annual conference ever convened there. It was a proud moment for the African Methodists of the Shore. Bishop Payne and Bishop A. W. Wayman were both present, and both preached. Long before the appointed hour for the beginning of the conference the church was crowded "to its utmost capacity," and the swell of people overtaxed the insubstantial frame structure. Beneath the crowd the floor gave way, "and the wildest excitement followed" in which fatalities were only narrowly averted. The A.M.E. Church, however, if not its building, was now vital and strong on the Shore, and the conference proceeded despite the inconvenience.[12]

The Delaware Conference of the Methodist Episcopal Church established itself in that portion of the Shore, namely the northern half, where the A.M.E.'s did not take root. Friendship Church in Wattsville was its earliest congregation, but within a few short years there were three separate areas of Accomack County where the work of this denomination was growing fast.

In northern Accomack, Friendship Church expanded in every direction. In 1876 St. John's Church was founded from it in Messongo, in 1877 Deas Chapel north of Horntown. In 1879 Freewill was erected on Chincoteague Island, a small congregation of only eleven members. In that year these four congregations comprised the Horntown Circuit, a strong circuit which in 1881 reported great "outpourings of spirit" and began the erection of a parsonage. By 1890 another congregation, Mt. Zion in Withams, had been formed, and the circuit was split.

Still another church, another St. John's in Atlantic, was founded in the twentieth century.

An entirely new area of work opened up for the Delaware Conference farther down the county in 1870. In that year, Burton's Chapel, the venerable old church of Thomas Burton, was struck by lightning and burned to the ground one Sunday afternoon shortly after the worshipers had dispersed. The congregation decided not to rebuild on the old site, but moved instead to a new location about a mile to the west. There they erected Oak Grove Methodist Episcopal Church, South, at the time one of the grandest church buildings on the Shore, which they dedicated in 1871.

a - Bethel A.M.E., Onancock (1868)

b - Friendship Methodist, Wattsville (1868)

THE TWO OLDEST BLACK CHURCH BUILDINGS ON VIRGINIA'S EASTERN SHORE

The fire provided the Burton's congregation with the perfect opportunity to separate their Negro members off into a church of their own. And so the congregation purchased a lot nearby from Richard Ames so that the remaining blacks might build "a house of worship for the use of the colored members of the Methodist Church residing in the neighborhood of said church...but for the use or benefit of no other person or persons whatsoever other than such religious congregation" (like many other such deeds on the Shore, this one testifies to the fear of the whites that the blacks might use their building for more than religious purposes).[13] By 1875 a chapel was standing on this lot close to the original Burton's site. The new church took the name Burton's Methodist Episcopal Church; fifty years after the death of the old patriarch who had no truck with anti-slavery talk the whites abandoned his name, and the grandchildren of his former slaves carried it on.

By 1881 Burton's had, like Friendship, expanded in several directions. There was a large Sunday school in operation "on the border of Northampton County," and another at a place called "Big Woods." Soon each of these places had a church of its own: "Big Woods" had become Grace Church near Wachapreague, and near Northampton stood Snead's Church, named after G. E. Snead, the pastor who was responsible for much of this work.

And a third work burst forth in another part of the county. In 1870 a new church named Metropolitan Methodist Episcopal Church was founded on the Bayside Road north of Onancock, a little below Reese Chapel M.P. Church. This church, too, grew quickly, and in 1878 it gave birth to Adams Church in Whitesville, south of Parksley, named for J. K. Adams, the founding pastor. Adams began his Whitesville congregation in a tent, and it was not until the 1880's that a frame building was erected there.

Between them the Methodists, A.M.E. and Delaware Conference (M.E.), divided the Shore almost equally, the southern portion falling to the A.M.E. Church, the northern portion to the Delaware Conference. With the exception of the Eastville area, where Union Baptist Church was the earliest of all black churches on the Shore, the Baptists were generally a few years behind the Methodists in the establishment of new churches, and when Baptist churches were founded they tended not to be gathered into circuits but scattered about without pattern in response to local need and action.

Within relatively short order, Union gave birth to two other churches: African Baptist in what is now Cheriton (1869) and First Baptist in Capeville (1877), formed from the Baptist portion of the earlier community congregation there. African and Union joined together in 1879 to establish a third church, Cherrystone, near the wharf where James Johnson landed in 1865. Much of the first public education for Negroes in Northampton County was due to members of these churches. Eugenia Davis Burrows, wife of Union's first pastor, taught school in the new church at Eastville. In 1910 the local Baptists crowned this endeavor with the founding of Tidewater Institute in Chesapeake, a public school which continued in operation until 1936, a vital force for education in the county throughout its existence.[14]

Elsewhere Baptist churches sprang up in random pattern. In 1875 black members of Hollies Baptist Church founded Shiloh in Boston, and First Baptist Church

EASTERN SHORE METHODISM
(WHITE)
1866
-Methodist Episcopal Church
= Non-Functioning
-Methodist Episcopal Church, South
= Non-Functioning
-Methodist Protestant Church

in Mappsville was founded, probably by black members of Modest Town Baptist Church. The year 1876 saw two more: Christ's Union Baptist in Chincoteague, formed from Union Baptist Church there, and Mt. Sinai Baptist north of New Church, erected so close to the Maryland line that undoubtedly many of its original members came from Maryland. Already by that year there were almost a thousand members of black Baptist churches in the two counties. New churches continued to appear: Metompkin, founded from Zion Baptist (1877); Jerusalem Baptist in Temperanceville (1878); Mt. Zion Baptist south of Painter, founded from Shiloh (1881); and Bethel Baptist Church in Franktown (1882). In 1884 these congregations banded together to form their own association; two years later they reported a combined membership of over 2500.[15]

In the short period of less than two decades a revolution had been accomplished in the Eastern Shore churches. In 1883 when Bishop Payne convened his Annual Conference in Eastville, just eighteen years from the landing of James Johnson at Cherrystone, 34 new congregations had been founded in the two counties, all of them black. One third of the Shore's churches were erected, owned, and operated by blacks. And in them lived a Christianity that was increasingly different from that left behind in the white churches.

The separation of the blacks into churches of their own, although willingly aided and abetted by the whites of the Shore, brought about a difficult period of decline and stagnation in the older churches.

It could hardly by otherwise, judging from numbers alone. As many as half the members, in some places more than half the members, were gone, and the work and life of many of the churches declined accordingly. Lower Northampton Baptist Church numbered 220 members in 1860 at the start of the war, and well over half — 122 — were black. Thirteen years later, after the separation, the membership was completely white, but there were only 91 members. Hollies Baptist suffered even more: there were 216 members of both races in 1867, but by the next year when the black exodus began membership was cut by more than half, to 105. Five years later the white congregation had dwindled to only 32 members.[16]

Economically, too, it was a difficult period for many Eastern Shore whites. Although both Civil War and Reconstruction passed lightly over the Shore, in comparison to many other parts of the South, still many a fortune had been lost, and many a family was struggling through hard times. It was a time of "extreme poverty which took years to overcome,"[17] and the strain showed in the churches as in other dimensions of life.

The result was a dormant period for most of the white denominations and congregations on the Shore. A few congregations, such as the Methodist churches in Craddockville and Horntown, experienced revivals and prosperity soon after the war, but for the most part the two decades following the Civil War were, for the white Christians of the Eastern Shore of Virginia, a period of struggle, retrenchment, and standstill.

Methodist expansion came to a halt, at least among the whites. During the period that saw the founding of 22 new black Methodist congregations, the Methodist Episcopal Church, South, largest denomination on the Shore, founded not a single new church. There were, in fact, some losses in that camp. Oak Grove Chapel in Atlantic apparently closed its doors for good soon after or even during the war; the last mention of activity there dates from the year 1864. Two other churches, Trinity in Hadlock and Ebenezer in Modest Town, were barely alive, Ebenezer with half a dozen members and Trinity with even fewer than that. The southern church did not even bother to dispute the northern church's claim to Ebenezer when it was reopened by them in 1869. Trinity was never reopened.

The end of the war found Methodist Protestantism still a small presence on the Shore, only four small congregations. The Wattsville church managed to give birth to a fifth congregation, the present Berea Church, which began in 1874 in a schoolhouse in the region of Miona west of New Church.

The war years had been for the Baptists of the Shore "a time that tried men's faith, of what sort it was," and yet they emerged more united and less scathed than the Methodists. There was accordingly a degree of growth and expansion among the Baptists. In that period when eleven new black congregations arose, the white Baptists founded only five: Drummondtown (1870), Atlantic (1877), Eastville (1877), Beulah in Chincoteague (1878), and Lee Mont (1880), which later moved to Parksley.[18] Four of these new congregations grew, with the passing of the years, into strong churches; only Beulah does not survive to this day.

The Presbyterians, exception to the rule, struggled through the war with their two churches, Makemie and Holmes, virtually non-functioning, only to blossom into a period of renewed strength after the war. In five years four new churches were formed: Belle Haven (1879), Powelton (1881), Naomi Makemie in Onancock (1883), and Second Presbyterian in Cedar Grove (1884). Although Second Presbyterian proved short-lived, the strength of that denomination virtually doubled during the generally dormant period after the Civil War. They were threatening now, for the first time, to close the distance between them and the Episcopalians on the Shore, who were content during this period to restore and reopen the devastated St. George's Church in 1880, and to begin a Sunday school in Onancock in 1878, from which a new church would ultimately be formed.[19]

Most devastated of all was the Methodist Episcopal Church, once the strongest denomination on the Shore. Although the black Delaware Conference was making rapid strides, the white Wilmington Conference, which was completely separate from it and rarely if ever had any dealings with it, was a mere shadow of its former self. When the northern church created the Wilmington Conference in 1869, and that Conference took over the jurisdiction of the Virginia Shore from the old Philadelphia Conference, there were only three white congregations left functioning in its Virginia territory: Cokesbury, Ayres Chapel, and Tangier, who together mustered only 259 members. The new conference also laid claim to Ebenezer Chapel in Modest Town, which had fluctuated between north and south during the war, but it was virtually extinct, with but a handful of members.

From all appearances the days of this denomination were over on the Virginia Shore. And yet this denomination alone of the white Methodist churches experienced growth, small though it was, following the war. In 1869 it began to put back the pieces, and it laid a claim to two new areas which were to be sources of its strength for years to come: Chincoteague Island and the rural Bayside area north of Onancock.

Although there were two churches on Chincoteague Island in 1869, Union Baptist and Bethel Methodist Protestant, the island was isolated and both congregations were at a low ebb when two Methodist Episcopal preachers, J. M. McCarter and J. L. Kenney of Federalsburg, Maryland, happened to visit the town. Here was a chance, they agreed, for the Methodist Episcopal Church to make a foothold for itself, and the two men seized the opportunity. They obtained permission to hold services in Bethel M.P., and there fifty people were converted who became the nucleus of a new congregation. By fall the island's third church building stood between Main Street and the water.[20] The church grew and prospered, often at the expense of the Methodist Protestant congregation in town. In 1884, the pastor received seventy members by transfer from Bethel M.P., and Christ Methodist Episcopal Church of Chincoteague became one of the larger northern Methodist congregations on the Shore.

Methodist Episcopal work in the Chesconnessex area began more slowly, but there, too, the denomination found new strength. In 1872 Perry Leatherbury, a local preacher from Onancock, began to hold services outdoors, assisted by his daughter, Edith, who played the organ and led in the singing. Two years later this budding congregation erected a building, with $200 aid from the denomination, and Leatherbury Methodist Episcopal Church was formed. Through the efforts of the Cokesbury congregation, the northern church effectively staked its claim to this area. A second church, Riverview, would be founded in later years, and the area from Ayres Chapel south to Cokesbury would be northern Methodist territory.

PERRY LEATHERBURY

In all, between 1865 and 1883, when so many new black churches were erected, the white Christians of the Shore founded only eleven. And the largest denomination of all, the Methodist Episcopal Church, South, founded none.

It was not a period of growth for the whites, but the southern church was far from dead. The old fires of Methodism still burned despite economic depression and hard family struggle. Revival and experiential religion lived on, and soon the camp meeting was revived, a new camp meeting in a new setting. It was the new camp meeting that was to see the main body of the church through this difficult period, and when prosperous times resumed there could be no doubt: the Eastern Shore of Virginia was still very much the bailiwick of the Methodist Episcopal Church, South.

In 1871, after a lapse of fourteen years, the camp meeting resumed. This time it was sponsored by the Eastern Shore District of the Methodist Episcopal Church, South, the largest and strongest denomination on the Shore. The old Tangier Island site was abandoned (Tangier was northern church territory, and the campground there was increasingly under the encroaching waters of the Chesapeake anyway), and a new site secured. James Turlington, who lived just south of what is now Melfa, let the Methodists use a wooded part of his farm for the campground with one stipulation (his wife's): that no tent be put up opposite hers so as to obscure her view of who entered by the main gate. A bush bower, a stage of rough-hewn lumber with a thatch and log roof, was erected in the center of the lot, and in August the people began to gather and set up family tents, encircling it one and a half times. The Pungoteague Circuit, official hosts of the event, built their pastor a tent, torches were set up on posts throughout the camp for the night sessions, and late on an August day in 1871 the preaching began.[21]

By now, however, it is not only religion that brings the people to camp meeting at Turlington Campgrounds. The scene now is rather a curious mixture of sacred and secular, a tableau of increasingly prosperous rural life. It is not without significance that the Accomack County Fair is also held at the campground in 1871 and 1872, for the line between secular fair and sacred gathering is, at this point, thin indeed.

And so they come, their crops laid by or not yet ready for harvest, their wagons loaded with frying chickens and a potpourri of vegetables and fruits, figs, grapes, family dishes, cantaloupes, watermelons. There are trunks in which young girls have packed what they will need for a full week of camping and religious services and socializing. There are carpets and mattresses, dishes and bed linens, lamps and clocks and rocking chairs stacked high on wagons as entire families arrive for what is undoubtedly the high point of the secular and sacred year. The grounds have been cleared in the week preceding the camp meeting, and the first sight of the family tents being put up, the freshly lighted fires in the cookstoves, the color and activity against the brown and green of the pine forest is a thrill to everyone in the family, young and old.

The camp janitor rings the big bell and the families take their seats on the benches before the bower. The preachers in their long frock coats line up in solemn assembly on the stage and the Pungoteague pastor announces one of the grand old Methodist hymns. The camp meeting begins again!

It lasts a week, and everyone jumps into it with full devotion and enthusiasm. Each morning at seven the big bell rings and families rise to eat breakfast and get to prayers by 7:45. From eight until ten in the morning nothing is scheduled, and this is the time that the children love most. At ten the love feast begins, a time set aside for testimony. At eleven there is the first sermon, followed by the midday meal. There is preaching at 3:00 and 7:30 in the evening, all with singing and revival excitement. At night the smallest children, dutifully in bed by eight, sit up on their mattresses and peek through the cracks of the shed-tents or pull aside the curtains to take in the spectacle of the older folk moving past to the final preaching service, and the distant swelling sound of *Blessed Assurance* or *What a Friend We Have in Jesus!*

But it is not all religion by any means. It is the common meeting ground of every walk of life, every occupation, every working man and landed gentleman on the Shore. The warm August moonlight finds eligible young men and women "promenading" around the principal thoroughfares while women trade recipes and farmers stretch their leisurely conversations into the wee small hours.

The Turlington Campmeeting convened every August without interruption from 1871 to 1899, and in those three decades the Methodist Episcopal Church, South, which sponsored it (there were some Methodist Protestants who attended, and some northern Methodists, and some blacks, but it was principally a southern Methodist affair) oversaw what was probably the largest and most eagerly anticipated annual gathering of people on the Shore at any time in its history. With each succeeding year the camp meeting became grander, finer, larger, more organized, more institutionalized, and further removed from the early camp meetings. By 1876 the bush bower had been replaced by a wooden tabernacle, and soon organs and pianos began to appear inside the pavilion to assist the singing. In 1891 the tabernacle was rebuilt and enlarged at a cost of $500, and a choir loft added for the visiting and local choirs who practiced for months before their appearance. And always on the fringe there was a whole host of secular traditions and establishments in the process of becoming institutions: the ice cream and candy stand where the children spent their allowance, the corral where the kindly black man stabled your horse and, for an extra tip, had your riding whip ready at hand when you needed it, the ever-present promenade after each night's sermon, when young people marched arm in arm six abreast, and a pretty girl would never think of being seen making the same round twice with the same beau. In 1885 as many as 8000 people attended some phase of the camp meeting. In 1889, 1500 people were in attendance on a single night.[22]

It is hard to say where the sacred ended and the secular began, for the two are now hopelessly intertwined in this one happy week of the year when all is right with the world. The Reverend Ray, rising to preach one evening, squelches the whispering and giggling from the back row where the "dates" sit with a quick quip: "Any young lady here tonight who cannot wait to hear her fate until the service is over has my permission to talk and whisper with the young man with her." And for that service socializing languishes and religion prevails.

But one morning when the testimonies come in very slowly at the love feast and the pastor in charge keeps pleading, "Another testimony, another testimony..." a small boy, perhaps eager for the service to be over so he can chase frogs in the woods, rises up in his seat and shouts, "Another testimony!" And because of the gales of laughter, religion languishes at that service, and a small boy's leisure pastime prevails. On another day one venerable old pillar of Oak Grove Church gets muddled in the middle of his testimony and rambles on endlessly until his wife, bored and embarassed like everyone else, tugs at his sleeve and whispers in an audible stage whisper, "Sit down, sit down!"

YOUNG LADIES AT THE TURLINGTON CAMPMEETING, 1882

The last Methodist camp meeting on the Eastern Shore of Virginia became increasingly prosperous and worldly with the passing of the years, as the fine dresses of these girls would indicate.

The world had a way of intruding upon the minds of those at worship at Turlington Campgrounds. A very pretty young lady in black satin marches down the center aisle and takes her place up front for the afternoon meeting, unaware that a corset string hangs carelessly from the placket in the back of her dress. Not until one member of her family can slip across the aisle and tell her during a prayer does she slip back to the tent, leaving religion unencumbered by her presence. And at night service a sedate and dignified visiting preacher literally drops his false teeth while preaching. "Let us pray," he mouths quickly, and falls to his knees in a mad scramble for his dentures which every bowed head sees.

And the plain and simple clothes that the Methodist women wear, no trimming and no jewelry, gradually give way to more and more finery. Soon the simply dressed women sitting near the mourner's bench are the very ones who, back home in the churches, are the well-dressed and stylish leaders of the local Foreign Missionary Society. And soon the plain dresses are left at home altogether, and young ladies bring black satin dresses for the afternoon meeting.

The cause is still spiritual, and if "worldly" things have crept in, it is still a time of great religious excitement. In 1881 a young man on his way to college at Randolph-Macon stopped by the camp meeting with his father. He was put up for the duration in one of the several large "boarding tents," where "good meals and a clean mattress on hard boards could be gotten at a moderate price." And years later in his memoirs this young man recalled some of the more spiritual aspects of the meeting:

> *The substance of the preaching was the same as...we had in our home church. There was somewhat more pressure brought to bear upon the church members to bestir themselves to hunt out the sinners, and stronger more impassioned appeals to the sinner to forsake their ways and turn to God...*
>
> *As the meeting progressed the interest steadily increased. The atmosphere was laden with cries of penitents and prayers. That there was some excitement I will not deny. Some mothers and fathers sometimes shouted praises to God at the conversion of their children. Sometimes there was a sweeping outburst of hallelujahs, followed by prayer and song, when some well-known sinner made profession of faith, but I never saw...anything not entirely warranted by the Scriptural idea of joy over the repentance and salvation of sinners.*
>
> *Yes, there was nothing dull in a Sunday night camp meeting service. There was intense earnestness, a real unconcealed effort to stir the emotions of the hearers to compel men to think of "righteousness, temperance, and judgment to come," to arouse fear at the consequences of open and hidden sins, and to picture the blessedness of forgiveness and peace with God after a full confession and renunciation of sin.*

The young man who made these observations was James Cannon, Jr. (1864-1944), a native of Salisbury, Maryland, who later rose to fame in the southern church as president of Blackstone College, bishop, and the foremost spokesman for the temperance cause in the South. The people of the Shore had their own remembrances of Cannon's visit, for they tell the story of the time he entered the tent of several young ladies of the Blackstone school. The girls were having a good laugh when he entered, making fun of an old lady in the next tent who sat in a rocker smoking a pipe, unaware that her shadow, alternately large and small as she rocked back and forth, was cast in great detail upon the wall of her tent. Even as a young man Cannon was a serious crusader, and he used the occasion to deliver a brief lecture on the evils of smoking to his young contemporaries.

It is a long way from that first camp meeting in Pungoteague in 1805, or even from the Tangier camp meetings of Joshua Thomas, and a look at the relations between the blacks and whites at Turlington Campgrounds gives us a clue as to how Methodism has changed in the interval. Although the blacks have their own camp meetings from time to time on the Shore, local ones at Nock's Branch near Oak Grove or Moore's Woods near Belle Haven or Chinchtown near Wattsville, they are present as well at Turlington Campgrounds. It is, however, a white man's week. An old Negro near the corral holds the reins as the white Methodist dismounts. A beloved cook works in the cooking sheds and wins renown for her recipes. Each year one black man is hired to tend the torches and to shine the preachers' shoes. The tents of the blacks are invariably a portion of the circle to the rear of the preacher's stand. And during every sermon they sit and stand around the pulpit, their heads bowed reverently, joining in with those older whites who occasionally shout "Amen."

But when the services are over the blacks gather in their own portion of the campground and begin their own services, much as the old exhorters used to extend the early meetings. And here, without benefit of clergy (for their own black pastors seem not to be much in evidence), the great revival of old lives again. Here there is shouting and weeping, here Methodists jump for joy and fall to the ground in repentance. Here the singing reaches an earnestness and intensity beyond that of the regular preaching services. Here Thomas Smith and Joshua Thomas would, no doubt, feel very much at home.

At times the whites come around to observe, interrupting the conversation or the promenade to watch them jump and shout or to hear the singing. A strange thing this black religion is to them, a remarkable kind of Methodism!

And after a week, trunkfuls of memories and wagonloads of paraphernalia are again carted up and carried back to the homes where the good life goes on. Each year the week spent at Turlington Campgrounds makes life a little brighter and a little happier, and each year there slips a bit the expectation that it is supposed to make anyone a little bit different.

Meanwhile the waters of the Chesapeake Bay lap up and finally over the spit of land on Tangier where Joshua Thomas, long dead, lit the campfires of an earlier and different kind of revival.

The Turlington Campmeeting did not, of course, escape the notice of the northern Methodist church, and at first pastors and congregations of these churches participated in it wholeheartedly. In his yearly report of 1874 the northern presiding elder called it "our" camp meeting and noted that it had given "us" "an increase of 32 tents from the line of our heretofore unfraternizing friends, with a congregation of over 2000 people from Accomack and Northampton to preach to." "So great is the change in spirit and conduct of the people there that it seems...like a pleasant dream," he wrote. And the next year he added a hopeful report: "Our campmeeting...has become a popular fixture."

A great many animosities, however, still smouldered beneath the surface. By 1877, the sixth year of the camp meeting, serious questions had arisen in the northern Methodist churches about the new camp meeting and some of its practices, and their Quarterly Conference passed a resolution condemning camp meeting abuses which were clearly aimed at the Turlington Campmeeting. Chief among the objections were the practice of camping on Sundays, when northern Methodists with their smaller churches thought Christians should be in church, and the growing commercialism of the camp itself. In the presiding elder's report of 1885 the issue still lingers on, and the abuses are called the "campmeeting ulcer".

The year 1885 is the last year in which the northern Methodists participated in the Turlington Campmeeting. The camp meeting itself was a raging success that year. More than 8000 people attended, as many as 500 of whom came from as far away as Norfolk. C. A. Grice of Cokesbury, the local northern preacher, was in attendance part of the time, but this is the last record of a northern Methodist presence. Shortly thereafter Methodists of the northern church began to hold their own camp meetings, which were usually smaller and more localized. The first on record was at Parksley in 1888, followed by two very successful camp meetings at Parksley and New Church in 1889 which did "much in breaking down the old animosities..." Other northern camp meetings were held at Hallwood and Red Hills (on Chincoteague Bay near Signpost) during the 1880's and 1890's.

The Methodist Episcopal Church, in abandoning the great camp meeting to the southern church, had not abandoned the Eastern Shore in general, as events in the extreme northeastern corner of the Shore were to tell. In 1876 the first railroad reached down through Maryland to the Virginia Shore, touching Accomack County near the village of Greenbackville on Chincoteague Bay. To this point the Frankfort & Worcester Railroad laid tracks in that year, erected a wharf on the bay, and by a system of barges and trains opened up Chincoteague Island, seven miles across the open water, to railroad commerce for the first time. The new railroad was a great boon to that end of the county, and around the tracks a prosperous little village called Franklin City sprang up almost overnight. A new community meant a new church, and by 1877 the Methodist Protestants had established Greenbackville Chapel in the older village.

In 1876 the northern presiding elder noted the coming of the railroad to this end of the Shore and commented hopefully: "If in other years with limited means of communication [in] our work Methodism grew...how rapid and permanent must be her future growth!"

It was a prophetic statement. In 1884 the Wilmington Conference had a new church facing the railroad at Franklin City.[24] And in that year another railroad made its way down the Shore to Cape Charles. The coming of the railroad in 1884 was a momentous event to the Shore as a whole. After 1884 the Eastern Shore, and the many churches that served it, would never again be the same.

New Horizons 1884-1918

IX

The Eastern Shore as we know it today began with the coming of the railroad.

By 1883, one year before the railroad, the Eastern Shore of Virginia had been settled for 260 years, yet in many ways life there was more like it was in 1783 than in, say, 1903 or 1913. Farmers planted crops which were consumed locally. Fishermen harvested seafood for local consumption. You could buy almost anything you needed in towns like Horntown and Pungoteague, villages that today sell only the bare necessities, and most of what you could buy there was made locally — clothes, shoes, buggies, or any other of a number of now abandoned crafts. Travel was still slow by land, and most commerce was waterborne. It took twelve hours to go from Eastville to Horntown by stage on a good day. There were no large towns, and entire communities of importance today — Cape Charles, Cheriton, Exmore, Onley, Parksley — as well as a dozen smaller ones did not even exist.

Down the backbone of this isolated peninsula, settled since the 1600's and in many ways unchanged since then, the New York, Philadelphia, and Norfolk Railroad laid tracks in 1884. Almost overnight the Shore was changed. The focus of the peninsula shifted immediately from the coastlines to the interior. The railroad passed through only two previously existing towns, New Church and Eastville. There were few other towns in the interior. But within a matter of a few years the interior was dotted with new communities that had sprung up around the tracks, towns like Hallwood, Melfa, Painter, Exmore. An entirely new kind of community, placced and built from scratch with a regular grid of streets and houses in neat rows, appeared in Cape Charles and Parksley and to a lesser extent in Keller. Farmers and fishermen could now ship their harvests to distant markets, and the economy of the Shore changed rapidly when they began to do so. Shoremen who could before travel by steamer from Pitt's Wharf to Baltimore in twenty hours could now hop a train in Cape Charles at 8:00 one morning and be in New York City the next day.[1]

So complete was the shift in focus that in each county there was talk of moving the county seat. In 1885 Accomack voted on a referendum to move the court house from Drummondtown to the new town of Parksley on the railroad, and in 1890 Northampton on whether to move it to Cape Charles. Both moves were defeated. But when a monument to the Confederate war dead was to be erected in Accomack County in 1899, it was given not to Drummondtown but to Parksley as a consolation prize for having been denied the county seat.[2]

For the denominations of the Shore the railroad ushered in an era of unprecedented prosperity. Here, after a lapse of half a century, was new and untouched ground, unchurched communities ready for evangelism. And the churches set to work.

What happened to the Shore can be glimpsed by looking at two towns on opposite ends of the peninsula, Cape Charles and New Church. Each owed its life to the railroad, and each became the site of frenzied church building and activity.

By the time the railroad tracks reached their southern terminus on Chesapeake Bay on October 25, 1884, the new town of Cape Charles was already in the making there. A northern entrepreneur, William L. Scott of Pennsylvania, had laid out a town just a few months before on land purchased for the staggering sum of $55,000. The town was a perfect square, with avenues named for famous Virginians and streets named for trees, a space for a park, a school, and 644 building lots. By 1886 the town was incorporated and contained a tavern, two hotels, a post office, a livery stable, several stores, a number of homes, and many businesses. A new harbor had been dredged south of town, and to it was plying the two-wheeler *Cape Charles,* a steamer with railroad tracks on either side to carry sleeping cars to Norfolk.[3]

Never had Eastern Shore Christians seen such a fertile field for church-building, and the several denominations flocked to the little town in haste. The first to arrive were the northern Methodists. In May 1885, John A. B. Wilson, presiding elder of the northern churches, preached the town's first sermon in the office of the superintendent of the railroad, a room which, he noticed, was "connected with a saloon." A congregation was formed immediately and a building erected. Within a year or two the building was outgrown, and by 1890 a new $3000 Gothic structure, Bethany Methodist Episcopal Church, stood on the corner of Peach and Randolph.

Not to be outdone, the southern Methodists dispatched the Reverend George Rives of the Capeville Circuit to organize a congregation in the new town in 1887, and by May 1888 Cape Charles Chapel stood on the north side of Tazewell Avenue. Like their northern Methodist rivals, the southern Methodists outgrew their first building in a short period, and in 1895 a new brick building was erected down the street (in the same block as Bethany) and named Centenary Methodist Episcopal Church, South.[4]

The other denominations were swift on their heels. First Baptist, a black congregation known at first as Hollywood, was organized in 1885. A year later the black Delaware Conference purchased the first Bethany building and established a mission on the corner of Monroe and Plum. Cape Charles Baptist Church, a white congregation, erected its first house of worship in 1887. Emmanuel Episcopal Church was begun in 1888, and two years later First Presbyterian Church was organized.[5]

It was in Cape Charles that Roman Catholicism established its first permanent foothold on the Virginia Shore. Since colonial times there had never been more than a few scattered Catholic families on the Shore, and never had there been a Catholic congregation until 1889, when Father Edward Mickle of Baltimore arrived to begin

EDWARD MICKLE

the work of building a church. No denomination has a more honorable pioneer on the Virginia Shore than Mickle. When he arrived in the new town, his congregation (what there was of it) was a few German railroad workers, all quite poor. He himself carried the bricks and mortar from which the new church, named St. Charles Borromeo, was erected. The Shore's first priest struggled for years to form a parish in a land that had hardly ever seen Roman Catholics. It took him eight years to open a school, and then he had only four pupils. It is said that more than once he conducted Mass for a congregation of only one. Yet not only did he establish his church on a firm footing, he also won for himself a revered place in the hearts of the townsfolk, Catholic and Protestant alike. Within a few years the pupils at his school numbered 100, of whom fully 85 were Protestant. By 1905 the local newspapers were citing Mickle as a promotor of "a better understanding and a spirit of charity among people of all denominations." The 25th anniversary of his ordination in 1914 was a community-wide event. In 1927, three years before his death, Mickle was made Domestic Prelate and given the title Monsignor by Pope Pius XI, "an honor the Holy Father rarely confers upon the pastor of so small and scattered a congregation." On that occasion the people of the town, Protestant and Catholic alike, chipped in to buy him an automobile and to build him a garage.[6]

Last but not least was a congregation of Jews founded in the new town. William Brown, a Jewish immigrant from Russia, arrived in Cape Charles in 1894, and shortly thereafter was instrumental in aiding three other brothers in settling there. The Brown families banded together to continue the customs and observances of

Orthodox Judaism that they had known in the old country. Although never a large congregation, Temple Ohel Rooven, as it was called, continued in operation until 1945.

Such was Cape Charles, the first planned community of size to spring up after the coming of the railroad. It was the least Shore-like of towns on the peninsula, and had a distinctive northern orientation, with a greater variety of churches than any other community around. In fact, so oriented to the North was the town that its most famous resident in the 1890's was a minister who lived there during the week and preached on Sundays in New York City. His name was Thomas Dixon.

THOMAS DIXON, JR.

Thomas Dixon, Jr., of North Carolina — Baptist minister, novelist, playwright, actor, and lawyer — was already one of the most famous preachers in the country when he made Cape Charles his home. Still a young man barely thirty years old, Dixon was pastor of Twenty-Third Street Baptist Church in New York City, where each week he filled the house to overflowing with crowds eager to hear his sermons, or, as some called them, his inflammatory lectures. Beset with ill-health, Dixon sought a home on the water within commuting distance of New York, and late in 1894 moved his family into a new home on Tazewell Avenue in Cape Charles.

Dixon lived on the Eastern Shore less than three years, but during that time he was no less busy or successful than he was at any other time in his career. He preached to capacity crowds at Cobb's Island, Onancock Baptist Church, and Wardtown, served on the Town Council of Cape Charles, amassed a great deal of property, and in 1896 became part owner of the Cape Charles newspaper, *The Headlight*. All of this was in addition to his duties as pastor. He would work on his sermons and lectures in Cape Charles during the week, board the train on Friday morning for New York, and return home on Mondays. After he left the Shore, Dixon became even more famous. He embarked on a career as a writer, electrified the nation with such novels as *The Leopard's Spots* (1902) and *The Clansman* (1905), which glorified the Ku Klux Klan and the racial attitudes of whites in the deep South. In 1915 D. W. Griffith made his epoch-making motion picture, "The Birth of a Nation," from *The Clansman* with Dixon's help.[7] Although by then Dixon's brief residence on the Shore was a thing of the past, Shoremen still followed his career with interest and often claimed him as one of their own. And thanks to the railroad which carried him back and forth to New York each week, Cape Charles and the Eastern Shore were more than ever in contact with the outside world.

At the other end of the Shore lay a town much smaller and much more native, but it, too, was changed by the coming of the railroad. New Church was a small collection of houses and a store a quarter mile from the new railroad station in 1884. To the east sat old Chincoteague Baptist Church, two miles to the west in Miona a new Methodist Protestant congregation that met in a schoolhouse. Within a matter of a few years this village had grown to almost a mile long, and the churches had descended upon New Church almost as upon Cape Charles. The Methodist Protestants picked up and moved to town from Miona in 1885, taking the name Berea Church. By 1888, Graham's Chapel Methodist Episcopal Church stood on the northern edge of town. By 1895 the Episcopalians were holding services in the village, but without a permanent result. By 1896 the Delaware Conference had a Sunday school there from which St. Mark's Methodist Episcopal Church ultimately derived. Finally, in 1909, after years of talk about moving the old church to town, Chincoteague Baptist Church divided, and First Baptist Church was founded in the heart of the village. Not all of these churches were to last a great many years, but within two decades after the railroad there were four churches in this village which never counted more than 200 inhabitants.[8]

And what happened in Cape Charles and New Church happened to some degree at almost every railroad station in between, up and down the Shore, in every denomination. Within a few years the face of the peninsula was changed, and with it changed the religious complexion of the two counties.

The first and most concerted effort to evangelize the new railroad towns was conducted by the white Methodist Episcopal Church, which staged a remarkable comeback in 1886. The previous year the district's report was full of hope and expectation: "Now the opportunities open and beckon to us with many hands to come to new centres, where we will collide with no rival, nor build on another's foundations." And within a year the northern Methodists, rising to the challenge, were busy building churches for these new railroad communities.

In November 1886, by special invitation from the local presiding elder, Bishop Willard F. Mallalieu (1828-1911) of New Orleans, the northern Methodists' special envoy for the building of new churches across the South, landed at Pitt's Wharf west of New Church and began a seven-day tour of the Shore. Mallalieu was the first white bishop to visit the Shore in over thirty years (Bishops Payne and Wayman of the A.M.E. Church had been in Eastville only three years before), and his visit made a great impression. In one week he preached at Pitt's Wharf, Crowsontown

(Justiceville), Hallwood, at old Ebenezer Chapel in Modest Town, and finally in Parksley, the budding new community on the railroad. In Parksley he dedicated a new Methodist Episcopal church which was named in his honor, and in all the other places he visited with the exception of Ebenezer a new northern Methodist congregation was formed.[9] The four new northern churches in Accomack County — Crowsontown, Pittsville, Hallwood, and Parksley — were small and struggling (Parksley had only thirty members in 1887), but they were part of a remarkable resurgence.

Nor did Mallalieu visit all the new northern Methodist churches that were established in 1886; there were three he did not see. Graham's Chapel in New Church was there, sharing its pastor with Pittsville, and he passed it up. On Chincoteague Island a new church named Goodwill came into the Methodist fold in 1886 when the denomination annexed what had been an interdenominational chapel on the northern end of the island. Melson's Church at Morley's Wharf in Northampton was begun in 1886, but when Mallalieu was on the Shore it was a southern Methodist church. When the southern church was unable to complete the erection of the building, the northern church purchased it and carried it through to completion in 1888. By 1894 Melson's had given birth to a second church, Harmony, which stood in Jamesville. This new northern circuit also secured a lot for yet another church in Exmore, but that congregation was not formed.

Meanwhile, after Mallalieu departed from the scene, the ever energetic Presiding Elder A. D. Davis journeyed across upper Accomack County holding revival services in a tent called Bishop Mallalieu's Tent in 1887. In February of that year he preached in the village of Assawoman, the first religious service in that community since old Assawoman Episcopal Church closed a century before. From there the tent moved on to Horntown, then to Chincoteague, where it housed a two-week revival. According to the local newspapers, the tent held about 400 people and was crowded daily on Chincoteague, "notwithstanding the revival services held in other parts of our island."[10] The Wilmington Conference voted funds to erect new church buildings in Assawoman and Horntown, but no lasting congregations materialized in the wake of the tent revivals, and the money was applied to Graham's Chapel and Christ Church in Chincoteague.

A decade later the Onancock Circuit bought an old schoolhouse in south Chesconnessex and in 1897 began holding services there. This neighborhood was already northern Methodist territory, and in 1910 Riverview Church was erected by this new congregation.

By the end of the century the Methodist Episcopal Church, which had numbered only six white congregations when the railroad came, could claim seventeen. Once in disfavor among the people of the Shore, it could by 1898 boast over 1100 members. "The ministers do not receive us cordially," reads the report from 1887, "but the people...with true Virginia hospitality receive us kindly and see that we have fair play and a hearing. They begin to find that we are Southern people like themselves, and love our sunny South in common with them." The Eastern Shore was still decidely pro-southern, and at least one northern preacher, J. A. Connelley, a local preacher assigned to Hallwood and Pittsville in 1887, was pelted with eggs by unfriendly natives of the Pittsville area. But hard work and the coming of the railroad made the Methodist Episcopal Church once again a force to be reckoned with on the peninsula.

Most of the new northern Methodist congregations proved to be short-lived and after about ten years began to fade away. Pittsville closed in 1897, and Graham's Chapel, the other half of that circuit, was attached to Melson's and Harmony in Northampton, some forty miles distant. All three churches on this New Church-Exmore Circuit were closed the next year. Parksley and Hallwood struggled on until 1901, and when they both closed in that year old Ebenezer in Modest Town finally died with them. Three of the new churches remained open and strong for the time being: Crowsontown, Riverview, and Goodwill. Crowsontown in particular prospered, for it fell heir to some of the congregation of the abandoned Parksley church. Those that failed remained small, poor, and struggling congregations throughout their brief history. Hallwood Circuit, for instance, when it consisted of Hallwood and Ebenezer never mustered more than 34 members total between them, and in the last decade of its existence was served by only one pastor who was fully accredited, not just a supply pastor.

By 1900 the white churches of the Methodist Episcopal Church, stronger than had seemed possible at the close of the Civil War yet weaker than had seemed likely in 1886, were much as they would be until the Depression: strong churches in Onancock, Tangier, Cape Charles, and Chincoteague (Christ and Goodwill); four smaller, but vital, rural churches founded from Cokesbury: Ayres, Crowsontown, Leatherbury, and Riverview; and Grace Church in Franklin City, which was usually served by ministers from Maryland and had little communication with the rest.

Only a few years behind the white colleagues were the black members of the Methodist Episcopal Church, who also made an attempt to evangelize the new railroad towns with the establishment of new churches.

In seven years, the Delaware Conference established four new congregations in the two counties, all in communities along the railroad. The work began in Cape Charles in 1889, after the white northern congregation abandoned the new church building that they had dedicated only two years previously. "We have bought a church at Cape Charles...for $600, in which we have organized a church and Sunday School," read the proud report for that year. And a small black congregation gathered in the town's oldest church building.

The new black congregation in Exmore was not so fortunate as to find a ready-made building. "We have a Sunday school numbering 50 and upwards," read the report from Exmore in 1889. "By permission we held preaching services and Sunday school in a potato house from July to November, at which time the potatoes took their place and we had to close..." Against almost impossible odds this new congregation, which numbered only nine, had by 1894 purchased a lot on the southern edge of town and erected a building on it at a cost of $1100.

In 1892 the church moved into Eastville. Here sixteen members raised a meetinghouse just east of Eastville Station for only $450 in 1894. In 1896 the church moved into the New Church area, where a Sunday school with thirty scholars was established. "This is a growing town on the NYP&NRR, and ought to be looked after," read the report for that year.

Despite the concerted effort to evangelize these towns, the new black churches met with only limited success. The Eastville mission, beset with financial difficulties, was closed and the property ordered sold by the conference in 1896, only two years after the church was built. The Exmore church, which was named John Wesley, managed to hang on until the 1920's, reporting "critical financial conditions" almost every year. "We are in a territory already pre-empted by the Baptists and the African Methodists," lamented the church's report in 1907. The congregation had already dwindled seriously when the church burned in 1924.

Only the new churches at the opposite ends of the Shore, Cape Charles and New Church, survived. It is not certain that the Delaware Conference work in New Church was continuous from the founding of the Sunday school there in 1896, but a revival there in 1912 fell heir to the earlier work, and in 1917 St. Mark's Church was dedicated just north of town.

The Cape Charles church survived only because it was rescued by another denomination. Once established in its new building in 1889, the congregation there drops from the records of the Delaware Conference and apparently almost ceased to function. In 1896, however, William J. Beckett, an African Methodist Episcopal minister, stepped in, assumed the pastorate, and restored the church to life. From that year the congregation became an A.M.E. church, which ultimately moved the building to a new location and took the name St. Stephen's.[11]

The black Methodist Episcopals were finally even less successful than the white Methodist Episcopals in bringing churches to the railroad communities. Their strength, in the end, remained in those rural areas where the original circuits had sprung to life.

The other denominations of the Shore shared in the prosperity that the railroad brought, and established many new churches. Their growth, however, was due to the strength of older congregations in the older areas, and not to new programs to evangelize the railroad communities.

The Methodist Protestant Church, for instance, entered the period of its greatest growth and established six new congregations between 1887 and 1903. Although three were in new railroad towns, all were outgrowths of one or the other of the original foci of Methodist Protestant strength, Lee Mont or Wattsville. From Wattsville was established Jester's Chapel in Signpost in 1888 and Atlantic in 1893. From Lee Mont came several churches in quick succession: Conquest Chapel M.P. south of Temperanceville in 1887 (occupying an old site abandoned by the southern Methodists when they moved their Conquest Chapel to Temperanceville the previous year), Calvary in Hopkins in 1888, Grace Church in Parksley in 1892, and Grant Memorial, established near Deep Creek Mill in 1893 and moved to Tasley in 1910. Finally, in 1903, two years after the northern Methodists abandoned Hallwood, Methodist Protestants from Conquest Chapel established Hallwood M.P. Church there. By far the strongest of these new churches was in Parksley. Grace Church quickly outdistanced not only the older mother church in Lee Mont and the other Methodist Protestant churches on the Shore, but the northern Methodist church in Parksley as well. The building burned in 1909, and when a new brick structure was erected in 1911 at a cost of $17,000, Grace was Parksley's most prosperous church and claimed the only pipe organ on the Eastern Shore of Virginia.[12]

When the railroad came in 1884, there were six Methodist Protestant churches on the Shore, one of which (Reese Chapel) was virtually defunct and one of which (Berea) had not yet erected a building. By 1903 the Methodist Protestants could boast twelve congregations and 1042 members.

African Methodist Episcopal growth during this same period was not so spectacular. After the railroad five new A.M.E. churches were established: Weirwood (1889), Keller Mission (1893), Mt. Olive in Hack's Neck (1897), Ward's Chapel near Chesconnessex (1898), and Mt. Zion in Treherneville (1904).[13] Of the five, only Mt. Zion still functions. Keller Mission passed quickly from the scene without even erecting a building. Weirwood was closed by 1920. Mt. Olive closed in 1919 and in 1926 was reopened as a Baptist church. Ward's never grew to great size and closed finally in 1959. Even the church buildings at Weirwood and Chesconnessex have disappeared.

The white Baptists of the Accomack Association numbered fourteen congregations in 1884, and by 1900 numbered 23. Nine new congregations were formed up and down the peninsula: Cape Charles (1887), Hall's Chapel near Messongo (1888), Mappsville (1888), Harborton (1896), Wardtown (1896), Horntown (1897), and Saxis (1897). Virtually all were outgrowths of earlier congregations, and only the new Cape Charles church stood in a railroad community. There was little attempt by the Accomack Association to place new churches along the railroad. Zion Baptist Church conducted a mission in Hopeton on the railroad in 1891, but the work was short-lived, and no church was established. In 1897, however, the Lee Mont Baptist congregation moved to Parksley, erected a new building, and took the name Parksley Baptist Church, only a block away from the railroad.[14]

Black Baptists increased the number of their congregations by fifty percent from 1884 to 1900, but not because of any campaign to establish churches in railroad communities. With the exception of First Baptist Church in Cape Charles, founded in 1885, all of their new churches were in older communities or rural areas: St. John's in Onancock (1884), Mt. Olive near Jenkins Bridge (1887), Mt. Nebo south of Savageville (1891), Horntown Tabernacle (1896), and Ebenezer in Wardtown (1898).

Presbyterians established two new congregations, First Presbyterian in Cape Charles (1890) and Clarke Presbyterian in Daugherty (1894), only to lose Second Presbyterian in Cedar Grove by the end of the century. Thus there were seven Presbyterian churches on the Virginia Shore by 1900, all of which function today. Episcopalians spent the period consolidating old strengths rather than establishing new congregations. Two new churches were founded — Emmanuel in Cape Charles (1888) and Christ Church in Bloxom (1896), both a conscious attempt to evangelize new railroad towns. Holy Trinity in Onancock, begun as a Sunday school in the 1870's, was erected in 1886. And Emmanuel Church, erected in Temperanceville in 1860, was dismantled, moved, and re-erected in Jenkins Bridge in 1887, just after the southern Methodists moved their church to a site in Temperanceville just across from the church.[15]

That leaves one other denomination, the Methodist Episcopal Church, South. As the prosperity ushered in by the railroad was to prove, this church was the heir to the greatest part of Methodist heritage on the Shore. With the coming of the railroad it established itself beyond the shadow of a doubt as the predominant faith on the Eastern Shore of Virginia.

Between 1866 (the dissolution of the independent Convention of Accomack) and 1882, the Methodist Episcopal Church, South, established no new congregations on the Eastern Shore of Virginia. For sixteen years, while the other denominations were staking out claims to new areas, the largest body of Methodism stayed within its own walls, content with its own territory. In 1882, however, only two years before the coming of the railroad, it burst forth into an unprecedented spurt of prosperity and began to spread to new communities. There were eighteen functioning southern Methodist congregations on the Shore when the railroad came through. By 1900, sixteen new congregations had been added. By 1908 there were thirty congregations, most of which survive to this day. With the exception of outlying Tangier and Chincoteague Islands, there is no area of the Shore to which the southern church did not ultimately extend itself. No other denomination on the Shore could match this success or this strength, and no other denomination on the Shore was so successful in planting new churches in the new towns of the future that sprang up along the railroad.

The march began in 1882, two years before the finishing of the railroad. In that year the Reverend Thomas G. Pullen was appointed to start a mission on Cobbs Island, an oceanside island in Northampton that had been settled since the 1830's.

THOMAS G. PULLEN

Within two years a lot had been secured there on the beach, and by 1887 there was a chapel with a congregation of twenty members. Also in 1882 Woodbury Methodist Episcopal Church, South, was built near Rue north of Drummondtown, and a new church erected in ''Powelton'' (Wachapreague) for a congregation there that grew out of Oak Grove.[16]

In 1883 the Methodists returned to Hog Island. After his successful mission next door on Cobbs Island, Pullen was appointed to found a mission in the village of Broadwater on Hog Island, where there had been no Methodism now for fifty years. By the end of 1883 a new church building stood there, even before the donors of the land could register the transfer of the property at the court house. The new church was known as Pullen's Chapel, after its founder, and was part of the Capeville Circuit. Also in 1883, Sanford Church was established in northern Accomack, outgrowth of a Sunday school established by the older Pocomoke Church there.

In 1885 the Pungoteague congregation divided. Part of the congregation stayed in Pungoteague and erected a new building there (the present church), while the other half moved the old building further down into Hack's Neck and established Evergreen Methodist Episcopal Church, South.[17]

The year 1886, when Bishop Mallalieu visited the northern churches, saw the establishment of four southern Methodist churches. In Belle Haven, where a century earlier Methodist preachers had met with scorn, the Methodists at last succeeded in planting a church; a lot was purchased in 1886, and by 1888 a new church stood on it. At Sunnyside (Cheriton) on the railroad a new Sunday school was established by Salem, and within a year a new church building stood there, its congregation fifty members strong.[18] Amiss Chapel, a new church on the Drummondtown Circuit named for Joseph Amiss, the presiding elder, was erected north of Greenbush in 1886. And at Morley's Wharf in Northampton construction was begun on a church which, two years later, was sold to the northern Methodists and became known as Melson's.

In 1887 the Capeville Circuit pastor, George Rives, established Cape Charles Chapel in the bustling new town, and the first church building there was dedicated on Tazewell Avenue in 1888.

We are not yet halfway through the list. The year 1891 saw two new churches: Broadwater Chapel between Willis Wharf and Exmore, established to serve the increasing numbers of people moving into this neighborhood because of the railroad and because nearby Hog Island was washing away into the sea; and Onley Church (McMath Chapel), an outgrowth of the Locustville congregation, erected near the railroad in the new town of Onley.

In 1893 a new congregation out of Guilford Chapel secured a lot south of Guilford and began the erection of St. Thomas Church.

In 1894 Evergreen Church in Hack's Neck, only nine years old, divided, and Harborton Methodist Episcopal Church, South was founded from it.

In 1896 the Reverend G. E. Booker Smith, pastor of the Wachapreague church, led in the construction of a new church in Quinby. The church, completed the following year, was named Smith's Chapel in his honor.

In 1897 a second church was born from Guilford in the course of four years:

Bloxom Methodist Episcopal Church, South, erected in the new railroad town of that name.[19]

Of these sixteen new congregations, only four proved short-lived. Melson's had been purchased by the northern Methodists by as early as 1888, and Amiss Chapel was discontinued in 1901. The other two fell victim to the encroaching Atlantic. The erosion of Cobb's Island became severe after 1891, and in 1896 Nathan and Sally Cobb, the final inhabitants of the community there, abandoned the island and moved to the mainland. The Cobbs Island Mission passed from the records with the community. Hog Island ultimately met the same fate, but not until well into the twentieth century. In 1904 the little church was prospering; the lighthouse-keeper reported that the island had 250 inhabitants, "all intensely religious, orthodox to a painful degree." The church prospered until heavy erosion set in around 1930. By 1937 the island was all but evacuated. Most of the inhabitants moved to the Willis Wharf area, where Broadwater Chapel (its name was changed to Epworth in 1931) received them.[20] Pullen's Chapel was officially discontinued in 1940. The congregation in Oyster purchased the old building, floated it over to the mainland, and attached it to their sanctuary, where it is still in use.

The march of new churches swept past 1900 into the twentieth century. In 1901 two new churches were established: Townsend in Northampton, founded from Capeville; and Assawoman in Accomack, a southern church where the northern Methodist church had failed to plant one some years previously. In 1905 there were new churches in two railroad towns: Painter Church was founded from Garrison's, after years of indecision about whether or not to move the old church; and construction was begun on Mears Memorial Church in Keller, dedicated in 1908, an outgrowth of the Oak Grove congregation. In 1908 there were two new churches established in Northampton County: Travis Chapel in Oyster, founded from Salem; and Nassawadox in the new town of that name on the railroad, founded from the Franktown church. In northern Accomack, Pittsville Methodist Episcopal Church, South, was established in 1910, within sight of the old northern Methodist church of the same name abandoned in 1897. Finally in 1913 Melfa Church was founded from Oak Grove in the new railroad town of Melfa.[21]

The southern Methodists, more than any other denomination, illustrate the gradual shift of the Eastern Shore's people towards the center of the Shore. They had no concerted campaign, like that of the Methodist Episcopal Church in 1886, to evangelize the new communities, but more so than any other church they followed the people to these new communities as the years went by. Again and again up and down the Shore an older country church would establish a daughter mission in the new railroad town, only to be surpassed in time by its own creation. This happened to Salem Chapel, which gave birth to Cheriton Church in 1886, dwindled in size, and closed in 1911. Locustville gave birth to Onley, and subsequently dwindled in size while Onley grew at its expense. Venerable Oak Grove was the mother of two new churches, Melfa and Mears Memorial in Keller. In time it, too, was surpassed by one of them, Melfa. The same fate might well have happened to Garrison's, from which Painter Church was born in 1905, had not later the Garrison's congregation merged with Painter and carried their building to town with them. It happened to non-Methodist churches as well, most notably to Wardtown Baptist Church. Founded in Occohannock Neck west of the railroad in 1896, it dismissed a number of members to found Exmore Baptist Church in the heart of that town in 1907. Ten years later, while the Exmore church was prospering, Wardtown closed its doors, a victim of the shift in population.[22]

All of the denominations grew during the prosperous period following the coming of the railroad; the Methodist Protestant Church doubled in size. But the greatest beneficiary of the prosperous times was the Methodist Episcopal Church, South, perhaps because more than any other church it cast its lot with the new communities created by the railroad. It was a fortunate move, for the shift towards the center of the Shore was a permanent one. By the early part of the twentieth century many of the older communities of the Bayside and the Seaside were literally fading away, victims of the railroad and later of the automobile. By then the center portion of the Shore paralleling the railroad was the main artery of the Shore's life, and the Methodist Episcopal Church, South, without question the church most in touch with it.

In 1900, sixteen years after the coming of the railroad, there were 143 churches in the two counties of the Eastern Shore of Virginia. There was hardly a back country road, hardly a tiny settlement without a church of some persuasion, black or white. Since the population of the Shore was 46,000, there was a church for every 324 persons of all ages. The Eastern Shore of Virginia was a heavily churched area. And it was heavily Methodist. About sixty percent of its churches were of one of the Methodist denominations. Accomack and Northampton Counties, taken with the Maryland and Delaware portions of the Delmarva Peninsula, formed one of the few portions of the United States, even of the world, where Methodism predominated. Nor had the growth ceased; some of the most important Methodist churches on the Shore today had not yet been founded in 1900.

It was a far cry from that day when, before the arrival of the Methodists and the Baptists, the Church of England had ministered to perhaps as many as 20,000 inhabitants with no more than seven churches. A great crusade shared by all the denominations, to evangelize the entire Eastern Shore of Virginia, had met with remarkable success. No longer were there portions of the Shore where people had not heard the Gospel of Jesus Christ and could not attend one of his churches.

It was now time for the Eastern Shore Christian to turn his attention to other things, to lift his eyes to further horizons. With the railroad came increased contact and communication with the world beyond, and new projects in the minds and hearts of the churchgoers of the Eastern Shore. There were new crusades in which to do battle, crusades intent upon changing not just the Shore, but the world. Whether or not Christians from the Shore succeeded in affecting the course of the world with their new projects can be debated. What is certain is that they left an indelible imprint on the life of the Eastern Shore churches themselves.

The first new crusade to engage the life of the churches was in reality two crusades. The ostensible cause was foreign missions. But a second and not-very-hidden issue behind it was the place of women in the church.

In the early part of the nineteenth century, "missions" for Methodists meant both home missions and foreign missions, and it was not until the task of home missions was complete — the planting of a church in every community — that the church turned its full attention to foreign missions. Although in 1837 the Accomack Circuit created a Missionary Society whose members agreed to support foreign missions, and although there was continual talk about the importance of missions, it was not until the last quarter of the century, when on the home front the church stood at last in virtually every community, that Eastern Shore Methodists began really to look beyond their own shores.

The earliest foreign missions work on the Shore belongs chiefly to the Baptists, who were perhaps forced into some interest in the subject by the anti-missions controversy of the 1830's. The Baptists were the first on the Shore to set what would become the prevailing pattern: missions was women's work. In 1836 Red Bank Baptist Church reported a "female benevolent society," and two years later there were similar groups at Lower Northampton and Modest Town. None of these societies was long-lasting, and such groups came and went among the churches of the Accomack Baptist Association for about twenty years before the Civil War. By 1843 Lower Northampton was boasting a Ladies Sewing Society (a sewing society raised money which it was free to give anywhere it chose; a mission society's fund went entirely to missions). And for two decades there were sewing societies or mission societies for women and youth at Lower Northampton, Pungoteague (Hollies), Zion, Onancock, and Modest Town, none of them permanent. By 1874, when Virginia Baptists asked women across the state to support a mission school in Tengchow, China, run by two Virginia Baptist women, the only Eastern Shore church to make a contribution was Red Bank, and the "mite society" that raised the money for the cause in that year had been only recently formed.[23]

In 1878 the Methodist Episcopal Church, South, resolved that "in view of the fact that in most heathen countries women are only accessible to teachers of their own sex, the women of the M.E. Church, South, are hereby authorized to organize special missionary agencies." And in that same year, apparently under his own local initiative, the Reverend C. C. Wertenbaker of the new Oak Grove Church organized the Woman's Foreign Missionary Society at his church. Later that year Eliza Scott organized seven women into a similar society at Capeville. (Mrs. Scott was a member of Johnson's and married to a staunch Baptist; she later belonged as well to the Baptist mission society at Red Bank.) These early Methodist groups did little other than pay dues which went to mission causes. In four years there were sixteen members of the society at Oak Grove, and they sent the grand total of $10.80 to the Conference for mission work.

When the Woman's Missionary Society was organized on the conference level in 1879, Eliza Scott was made district secretary for the Eastern Shore. In that capacity she traveled up and down the Shore for eleven years, speaking at church after church, organizing the women of the churches to support the cause of foreign and domestic missions. Under her leadership new societies were founded at Johnson's (1880), Franktown (1880), Pungoteague (1882), Market Street in Onancock (1886), and Andrew Chapel (1886). In her last year as district secretary, Mrs.

ELIZA O. SCOTT

Scott brought to the Shore the president of the society for the whole denomination, Lucille Hayes, wife of the President of the United States, the famous "Lemonade Lucy" who refused to serve alcoholic beverages in the White House, and who like many another upstanding Methodist woman of her time espoused both the cause of missions and the cause of temperance.

Two other women contributed significantly to the formation of the Woman's Missionary Society among the southern churches of the Shore. In 1894, Ella Rue Coffey, a young missionary about to set sail for China, made a whirlwind tour of the Shore's churches, and in her wake no fewer than ten new societies were formed from Cheriton to Temperanceville. And three years later the tireless Bettie A. Rue of Willis Wharf became district secretary of the missions work, where she served continuously for 25 years. By the time she retired in 1922, there were 35 societies among the southern Methodist churches on the Shore.[24]

The records of such work in the local churches of the other Methodist denominations on the Shore are skimpier, but it is safe to assume that the work itself did not lag far behind. In Parksley, 34 women banded together in 1894 to form the Ladies Aid Society of the Methodist Protestant church there. The last record of Hallwood Methodist Episcopal Church on the books of the denomination is a list of individuals who donated to missions in 1901, and a similar list for Grace Church in Locust Mount indicates that missions work was also a concern among the black churches of the Delaware Conference. African Methodist Episcopal women interested in missions held a "mass meeting" at Bethel Church in Eastville on December 8, 1906. There were at that time at least four local societies in that denomination on the Shore — Bethel (Eastville), Shorter Chapel, Ebenezer (Capeville), and Mt. Zion (Trehernville) — and about 800 women were present for the mass meeting.[25]

Among the non-Methodists the story was much the same. The Woman's Missionary Union was organized by the Southern Baptist Convention in 1888, Mrs. J. W. M. Williams, a native of Northampton, having been one of its chief advocates and pioneers. Already by that time there was a vice-president for woman's work for the Accomack Baptist Association, and a mission society at Drummondtown (1887). Under district workers new societies sprang up at Zion (1890); Lower Northampton (1890); Cape Charles (1892); Eastville (1892); Red Bank (1892), where Eliza Scott was the only Methodist member; Hollies (1893); and Mappsville (1895). By 1900 there were fourteen societies among the twenty churches of the Association, and such groups as "Sunbeams" or "Young People's Missionary Societies" for young Baptists at Modest Town and Mappsville. Two years later women in these societies gave one-third of the total amount of money given by the local Baptist churches to general denominational causes. By 1910 the number of contributing societies had grown to 29.[26]

The earliest female missionary society among the Presbyterians was at Holmes in 1878. Naomi Makemie's society of fourteen included three men in 1891. Powelton had a Sewing Circle by 1899, but little Clarke Presbyterian Church in Daugherty had perhaps the most successful group. In 1897 Maude Harding of that church organized a Missionary Society there that had a membership of almost 100 persons, men, women, and children. The group met monthly with dues of 1¢ a month, and in its first year of existence sent $50 to the Presbytery for foreign missions.[27]

The results of such local efforts were often spectacular and far-flung. By sewing and quilting, cooking and serving, pledging and saving, women across the Shore helped to raise schools and churches in other parts of the state and nation and around the world. The southern Methodist church, between 1878 and 1900, sent out 96 women missionaries to China, Mexico, Brazil, Korea, and Cuba, and built a school, Scarritt College in Tennessee, to train the missionaries who were supported by the women back home in the local churches. Baptist women gave to mission work in Mexico and China, and Methodist Protestant funds ended up in Japan, India, and China. The giving was spirited and generous. The Eastern Shore District women were the first in the southern Virginia Conference to raise $1000 in one year for missions, in 1898. When this was announced during the reports at the Annual Conference session in Portsmouth, "there was a burst of praise and the whole Assembly arose and sang 'Praise God from Whom All Blessings Flow'." Southern Methodist women and their pledges sent Ella Rue Coffey and Sallie Smith

Estes to China, where in Huchow they raised a school and began to teach. Before the Virginia School was closed in the subsequent political upheavals there, women from Accomack and Northampton had paid for the furnishing of two rooms in it, and named them after Eliza Scott of Capeville and Georgie Quinby of Belle Haven.

GEORGIE RICHARDSON QUINBY

In 1910 local Methodist women saw some of the results of their labor firsthand when Woo Kia Noo, a Chinese Methodist known as Peter Davis Woo, visited the Shore, lectured at Johnson's and Salem, and spoke at the District Meeting.[28]

In time the societies began to contribute not just their money but also their members to the cause of missions. Three women of the Shore became missionaries in their own right. The first was Beulah Nock Allen of Chincoteague Baptist Church in New Church. She accompanied her husband, the Reverend Walter Allen, to his mission field in India in 1921. After his death in 1925, she served another mission in Burma. The lone Methodist missionary to go out from the Shore was Fannie Harmon of Wachapreague. She sailed for China in August 1923, and served

FANNIE HARMON

there until her failing health and political conditions forced her to return four years later. Frances Carter Jones, though not a native of the Shore, was the daughter of the pastor of Red Bank Baptist Church when she entered the mission field. Trained as a medical missionary, she sailed for Nigeria in 1936, and died there of yellow fever in 1937 at the age of 35.[29]

If the missions crusade reaped results in such a short time in other places, it also changed things just as spectacularly in just as brief a time at home, for behind the missions facade lay another whole issue: the place of women in the church. The dry statistics of the formation of female mission societies do not do justice to the revolution that was occurring in the local churches because of them. For the first time, women — presumably half the membership of the average church on the Shore — demanded and received positions of leadership and responsibility in the local congregations. Up until this time leadership had been overwhelmingly, almost exclusively, male. Ladies like Edith Leatherbury were allowed to play the piano or cook the church suppers or, in some instances, teach in Sunday school, but until Eliza Scott and Bettie Rue took to the stump in behalf of missions, Methodists and Baptists and Presbyterians on the Shore little expected to see a woman rise up in the church to speak about anything.

It was not all smooth sailing for the women in this new cause of missions, principally because they demanded the right to direct the movement themselves. The Accomack Baptist Association, for instance, tacked two qualifiers to its recommendation of 1887 that local congregations form women's missionary groups: that the women must work not only for missions but also for the whole program of the local church, and that their money must be channeled, not through separate female treasuries, but through the regular channels. Behind such provisos lay a storm of opposition to women's work in the church and the feeling upon the part of a great many Shoremen that it should not be allowed.

The Virginia Conference was meeting in Petersburg in 1878 when the issue of creating a Woman's Board of Foreign Missions was raised. It, too, met with a storm of opposition. "The movement met with great opposition from the Chairman of the Board of Stewards," goes the report. "While the organization was being effected, this much agitated chairman was restlessly pacing up and down in front of the Church, rubbing his hands together, and saying to all who would come near and listen, 'It should not be allowed. Women cannot run such a movement themselves. It will not succeed!"

The same kind of opposition had to be overcome at the local level. Presbyterian women on the Shore found that they had to have two men added to a woman's group before it could organize. Baptist women struggled for years to get on the agenda at the Association's annual meeting. Required instead to meet before the official gathering, they found their still-unfinished meeting gaveled out of existence by the male moderator of the regular session in 1895, and chose thereafter to meet on another day and in another place. In both Methodist and Baptist churches, it was not uncommon for the women to make the pastor the president of their society, in order to get approval from the male pillars of the church.[30]

The women, however, carried the day at home as they had abroad. By 1901 the chairman of the Accomack Baptist Association was praising the women on the Shore in his address to the Association, just three years after the Virginia Conference had risen to sing the Doxology in appreciation of the Methodist women's efforts.[31] In a relatively short time the churches of the Eastern Shore had joined one liberal bandwagon, the cause of foreign missions, and found in so doing that they had changed things irrevocably on the home turf. Since not all of the work of the "ladies aids" and "women's societies" dealt with missions — they also concerned themselves with the local church, particularly improvements of the properties — women were often now a very powerful group in the local church, as one incident from Christ Methodist Episcopal Church in Chincoteague will illustrate. During a succession of unmarried pastors, a ladies' group was formed at that church. In 1895 the report from the church showed that the church women were tired of unmarried pastors: "The ladies have provided [furnished] a parsonage and desire a married man next year [as pastor]." They got him.

By 1920 Eastern Shore Methodist women had found their way to the floor of the Annual Conference as delegates. In that year Mrs. C. A. Milbourne of Bethany Church in Cape Charles became the Shore's first female lay delegate to the Wilmington Conference, and Mrs. C. R. Waters of Onley the first to the Virginia Conference. Female conference delegates were still, at that time, something of a rarity; Mrs. Waters was one of only six from the entire Conference that year. The first female delegate to the Maryland Conference of the Methodist Protestant Church was Miss Addie W. Bevans of the Greenbackville church in 1925. Gradually as the years passed women found their way into virtually every church office in the local churches.

Such strides by the local women left only the pastorate itself an all but exclusively male enterprise. Methodists at this time had no laws prohibiting female pastors, but women in the ministry were rare. On the Eastern Shore of Virginia the first female ministers were found not among the Methodists, but in the new Holiness churches, where there was a strong tradition of women pastors. The first among the Methodists was Mrs. J. H. B. Hubbard of Grace Methodist Episcopal Church in Locust Mount. When her husband, who was the pastor, fell ill in 1911, she assumed the pastorate and served successfully for three years. Not until a generation later, when the Reverend Mrs. G. V. Bell began her three-year pastorate on the Withams Charge of the Delaware Conference, was there a second. Not until another generation later, in the 1970's, was there a white female pastor among the Methodists, or did women in the ministry become more common.

Much of the path trod by these pioneer female ministers had been carved out by the local mission societies. Thanks in great part to the cause of foreign missions, the churches of the Eastern Shore could no longer pretend to be an exclusively male enterprise.

A second great crusade to engage the energies of the Eastern Shore churches began just a few years after the formation of the first female missionary societies, and ran its course simultaneously with the campaign for missions. It, too, illustrates the broadened horizons of Eastern Shore churchgoers, for it came to have as its goal the creation of national legislation to achieve Christian ends. It was the temperance movement, and as if to signify that it was no longer an isolated or unimportant peninsula, the Eastern Shore contributed to it some very prominent state and national figures.

Although Eastern Shore Methodists had been condemning the use of "ardent spirits" for generations, it was not until the late nineteenth century, when the Shore was fully churched and Christians could turn their attention to new issues, that the full force of the churchgoer's concern with alcohol was felt. By then, many of the older crusades of behavior and lifestyle were being given up for lost or neglected: theatre-going, dancing, smoking, Sabbath-breaking. All the enthusiasm and passion of the past insistence upon these things were poured finally into the temperance movement.

When the railroad came to the Eastern Shore, there were 26 barrooms in Accomack County and 25 in Northampton, and already there were local organizations bent on closing them. The Onancock Council of the Friends of Temperance, formed by 1881, had already sent the Reverend L. E. Barrett to Charlottesville for a statewide Local Option Convention. The Independent Order of Temperance was at work in Locust Mount by 1882, and in 1884 the Independent Order of Rechabites was organized in Saxis. Each of these groups had as its goal the initiation of local option referenda on the sale of alcoholic beverages. In 1885 the Prohibition Party, remnant of one of the earlier stages of the temperance movement, fielded a slate of candidates against the Democrats on the Shore: Rev. J. W. A. Elliott, the local preacher from Oak Grove for State Senate; George Washington Mason of Cokesbury for Delegate; and E. L. East for floater delegate from the two counties. All were roundly defeated; Elliott received less than six percent of the vote. But their defeat was not due to public distaste for their platform. Mason was defeated by T. T. Wescott, an avowed temperance advocate in his own right.[32] John Neely, the commonwealth's attorney of Accomack at the time, was an avowed prohibitionist. As yet, however, temperance was not able to replace other political issues or elect its own one-issue candidates.

In 1886 a strong grass roots interest in temperance and prohibition surfaced throughout the Shore, and to the earlier societies in Onancock, Locust Mount, and Saxis were added lodges of the Independent Order of Good Templars at Tangier and Evergreen, and enthusiastic local option rallies in Drummondtown, Locustville, Cashville, and Eastville. In April 1886, L. E. Barrett of the Onancock Council of the Friends of Temperance denounced alcohol and called for local option in forceful speeches around the area, and meetings were soon held in both Accomack and Northampton to choose delegates for a Lynchburg convention on the subject. Chosen to represent the Shore were Dr. George W. LeCato, at that time a member of the State Senate, T. T. Wescott, the re-elected member of the House of Delegates from Accomack, and John E. Nottingham, a member of Red Bank Baptist Church and one of the wealthiest citizens of the Shore.

So strong was this upsurge of interest that within one year the Shore's communities had voted on local option throughout the two counties. In Accomack County the sale of alcoholic beverages was defeated by a decided majority, except in Pungoteague District, where supporters of licensing its sale defeated the "dries" 653-511. The reason for that defeat, so went the logic of the times, was that the greater number of Negroes in that district had thrown it into the "wet" camp. Local option decisions were not, however, by law final; any vote could be reversed by the next election two years later. Neither side treated any election result as final, and so most districts voted on local option every other year. From the viewpoint of most Methodists and Baptists on the Shore, something a good deal more final had to be done.

Where the Independent Order of Rechabites had only limited success, the Good Templars, which began to spring forth on the Shore in 1886, achieved a great deal in influencing public opinion in favor of prohibition. Founded in England in 1851, the Good Templars were a lodge in the full sense of the term, complete with passwords, rituals, and regalia. But the vow of the lodge was to total abstinence

JOHN WESLEY
ANDROS ELLIOTT

from alcohol, and both men and women could be and were members. In 1886 Good Templar lodges were formed in Tangier and Harborton (Evergreen Church), and by the next year a lodge at Craddockville boasted over 100 members and a new hall.

By 1888 the Good Templars were busy up and down the Shore. They held a rally at Turlington Campgrounds in September and organized lodges in Drummondtown (at the Methodist church), Onancock, and Belle Haven. In October they filled the Onancock Town Hall for a rally and listened to Captain W. C. Dutton, Grand Lecturer of the I.O.G.T. of Virginia; Presiding Elder A. D. Davis of the Methodist Episcopal Church; and Miss Edith Leatherbury at the organ accompanying the singing of the Good Templar Choir. Over the next two years they continued to expand, with an annual rally at the campgrounds and new lodges in Locustville, Marionville, Hack's Neck, Guilford, Modest Town, Mappsville, and Johnsontown.

In 1895 the Good Templars engaged an Eastern Shoreman to lecture for their cause up and down the Shore, and their choice fell on John W. Guy, a Baptist minister who lived in Bridgetown. Guy attacked his lecture circuit with great vigor. In one year he preached or lectured at twenty places from Cape Charles to Greenbackville, including four lectures in one day at Chincoteague. "He held his audiences spellbound. He was very highly complimented on every occasion...[He] has created a Temperance sentiment which has done a great deal of good," lauded his District Chief Templar at the end of Guy's year.

From his lecture tour on the Shore, Guy was catapulted into a position of statewide influence in the order. Before he tendered his resignation to the order in 1899, he had preached in many places throughout the state and across the South and had served as Grand Chief Templar (1897-98) in Virginia. By that time there was at least one more lodge on the Shore (Atlantic), and the order's periodical, *Good Templar News,* was being read by Eastern Shore boys sent to fight the Spanish in Cuba.

Almost as suddenly as they had gained prominence, the Good Templars lost momentum and were supplanted on the Shore by other groups. Even before his speaking career was ended, Guy was eclipsed by another Shoreman named William T. Bundick (1847-1908). In 1894, the year before Guy began his lecturing, Bundick, an Onancock merchant, was converted and joined Onancock Baptist Church, where his friends urged him to take to the speaking circuit. Bundick had a flare for public speaking. Though not well educated, he had entertained his playmates as a child by "preaching" at them from a treestump, and through extensive personal study and wide reading had developed a forceful and ornate style.

Bundick gave up his store in Onancock and took to the circuit, his local fame already considerable. Within a few years he was widely known. He became state chairman of the Prohibition Party, and in 1901 was the party's unsuccessful nominee for lieutenant-governor. In 1904 he published a book containing six of his most popular lectures — with titles like "Belshazzar's Feast" and "A Blot on Our Civilization" — and was soon on the lyceum circuit in several states with a speech known as "Git, Grit, and Gumption," which was known for its "wit, humor, and pathos."

By the time of his death in 1908, Bundick had toured throughout the East,

WILLIAM T.
BUNDICK

"16 states and the District of Columbia, lectured in over 2700 churches, had been endorsed by 1450 prominent clergymen, and received more than 500 complimentary press notices in different parts of the country." His press notices were from papers from Boston to Georgia, from Washington to Memphis, and he was widely regarded as the South's finest temperance orator.

Needless to say, the Shore followed his career with great interest. Here as a businessman he had developed his reputation for speaking against alcohol. Here his style had been developed at many local gatherings. Here the citizens counted each year on his presence and addresses at the Turlington Campgrounds.[33]

It was a time when public speaking was held in high regard, on the Eastern Shore as elsewhere in the nation. Debates and lectures were a form of public entertainment, and traveling lecturers could count on halls crowded with spectators. Preaching had power and prestige, as Thomas Dixon illustrated by filling Association Hall in New York City on Sundays, only to return to Cape Charles on Mondays, his ministerial tasks finished for another week.[34] And it is safe to assume that lecturers like Guy and Bundick were not without influence wherever they were heard, and that they helped to make the Eastern Shore of Virginia the "dry" place that it was.

Two influential movements appeared late on the scene and carried the temperance movement through to its completion on the Eastern Shore of Virginia: the Woman's Christian Temperance Union (WCTU), and the Anti-Saloon League. Together they effectively ended the work of the local barrooms, as well as that of the earlier temperance lodges.

The WCTU was twenty years old when it reached the Eastern Shore. Organized in Cleveland in 1874 by Frances E. Willard, a devout Methodist laywoman of great organizational skill, it contained, like the missions movement, two causes in one, temperance and women's rights.

It was in 1894, the year William T. Bundick was converted and Ella Rue Coffey visited the local Methodist churches, that Mrs. J. W. Castles of Cape Charles organized a WCTU chapter or "union" in her home. Mrs. Castles was the state union Superintendent of Work Among Soldiers and Sailors. A member of Bethany Methodist Episcopal Church, she was not a native of the Shore but had come to Cape Charles from Pennsylvania with her husband, a railroadman. Though in a few years the Castleses would move away, leaving no Eastern Shore connections, Mrs. Castles was the pioneer of WCTU work on the peninsula. By 1896 her Cape Charles union reported 21 members who had made thirty visits to the sick, three visits to the alms house and jail, and distributed almost 15,000 pages of free temperance literature.

The real work of the WCTU on the Shore began in 1896 when Mrs. J. W. Newton, State Organizer, arrived to begin local unions. She organized groups at Belle Haven, Chincoteague, and Drummondtown. Within the year another organizer had added unions at Parksley and Onancock and made the indefatiguable Bettie A. Rue district chairman.

In the eight years that Bettie Rue oversaw the WCTU on the Shore, new chapters were organized at Onley (1898), Wachapreague (1900), Oak Grove (1901), and Tangier (1902). She also reorganized Chincoteague's chapter after a lapse, and established Loyal Temperance Leagues, a youth auxiliary, at Belle Haven, Craddockville, Chincoteague, and Stockley's Gate.[35]

Although interdenominational, the Woman's Christian Temperance Union was also decidely churchly, the most church-oriented of all the temperance groups formed on the Shore. Methodist, Baptist, and Presbyterian women were as happily joined in the temperance cause as they were separated in the missions cause, and composed a powerful phalanx in the local churches. Although not affiliated with any denomination, the WCTU maintained cordial relations with all of the churches, who willingly loaned their buildings for meetings and their members for work. And the example of Bettie Rue, advocate of missions and temperance, was duplicated by hundreds of women up and down the Shore.

Like the Good Templars whose thunder they were stealing, the WCTU held a rally at Turlington Campgrounds in 1900 and 1903. The first one was well attended in spite of great rains, but the second was phenomenally successful. There were hundreds in attendance, most of them women, throughout a three-day event. The renowned evangelist, Sam Jones, had been invited to appear, but the crowds were satisfied instead by Miss Belle Kearney of Mississippi as speaker. There were 230 WCTU members across the Shore in that year, and it is worth noting that the

BETTIE A. RUE

great camp meeting, which last assembled in 1899, was superseded not only by a secular county fair, but also by a large rally on the same spot to hear temperance lectures. The cause had become the one, great, final religious crusade of the churches of the Shore.

In 1902 the Anti-Saloon League, last of the great temperance organizations on the Shore, made the scene. It was organized in 1893, in Cleveland as was the WCTU, and it had but one aim, to fight alcohol politically in any way possible. William T. Bundick and William L. Elzey of Exmore were already state officers in the League when the Eastern Shore branch was organized at Onley in 1902. Spencer Finney Rogers, another Onancock Baptist, was elected its first president.

It is the Anti-Saloon League, with its avowedly political ends, that is generally credited with carrying the temperance crusade through to the triumph of Prohibition nationally. Religious conviction, however, had already shaped the politics of the predominantly Methodist Eastern Shore by the time the League was organized there, and on the Shore the League had little to do other than chime in with what everyone else was already saying. No local politicians needed convincing; for the past decade and for the next to come every candidate for election to significant office in both counties espoused only a hard "dry" line. Most of the Shore had managed to stay "dry" despite the constant local option referenda. Henry R. Bennett, the Episcopalian who laid out and sold the town of Parksley in 1885, had decreed even then that intoxicating beverages and gambling would be forever banned in his new town. And most other civic leaders on the Shore at the time, given the same opportunity, would probably have made a similar decision.

Still the Anti-Saloon League comprised a formidable fraternity of power and influence, almost as if the churches had created an ecumenical interlocking directorate. Spencer Finney Rogers, the first president, owned a store, a fleet of schooners, had served on the Accomack Board of Supervisors, was president of a bank in Onancock, and would in a few years buy the *Accomack News.* A. H. Gordon Mears, another influential charter member and a Wachapreague Methodist, made a comfortable living for himself through farming and fishing, then built the successful Hotel Wachapreague in 1902. William L. Elzey, the state officer, a member of Epworth Methodist near Exmore, was a highly successful farmer who organized the Eastern Shore of Virginia Produce Exchange in 1899. John E. Nottingham of Red Bank Baptist Church was another member. In addition to serving as clerk of the Accomack Baptist Association for eighteen years, he sat in the House of Delegates (1899-1904), owned a mercantile business and several farms, and was one of the wealthiest men on the Shore.

Add to this influence and power the fact that many a man of equal stature and means in the League was married to an active WCTU member: Lloyd and Sadie Savage of Onley Baptist Church, he a merchant and leading pillar of the church, she Accomack WCTU president for 28 years; William James and Bettie Rue of Belle Haven Methodist, he the owner of a fleet of schooners and builder of Rue's Wharf, she president of the WCTU and district missions secretary; William and Bertie Townsend of Bethany Methodist in Cape Charles, he a prominent merchant, she a local WCTU president and active in the movement for over a quarter of a century.[36]

It was in the temperance movement, and in the Anti-Saloon League in particular, that Eastern Shore churchmen and politicians joined hands for joint effort as never before or since. What had begun as a purely religious issue, particularly among the Methodists, ended as an alliance between religious and political forces, an indication of how completely the thought and teachings of the churches had entered and influenced the life of the Shore. The first person to address the Anti-Saloon League upon its formation in Onley in 1902 was Benjamin T. Gunter, an example of the political and religious alliance that was taking place. Gunter, the State Senator from the Shore, was an influential member of Drummondtown Baptist Church, and a former moderator of the Accomack Baptist Association (1888-1895).[37] Even more representative of the forces of religion and politics combined were two other Shoremen, one of them a rival of Gunter, G. Walter Mapp and James Cannon, Jr.

G. WALTER MAPP

G. Walter Mapp (1873-1941) was the product of an "orthodox Methodist environment," raised in a home where ministers were frequent visitors, and to the end of his life he could boast that he had never taken a drink. A member of Drummondtown Methodist Church, Mapp was in 1912 elected to the State Senate, succeeding Gunter, and he quickly established himself as one of the foremost political figures in the state. He was a man of progressive outlook whose legislative program included, among other things, woman's suffrage, the abolition of the death penalty, Negro rights, and controls on gambling and false advertising, but it was for his strong support of temperance legislation that he was most widely known. Mapp was, in short, the foremost "dry" political figure in the state, a natural consequence of his belief in "a militant church" and his "humane ideals."[38]

Sharing the "dry" spotlight with Mapp was another Shoreman even more

JAMES CANNON, JR.

widely known, James Cannon, Jr. A native of Salisbury, a minister of the Methodist Episcopal Church, South, Cannon unabashedly joined pulpit, political lobby, and press to plead the temperance cause. In 1901 he began a forty-year term on the executive committee of the Anti-Saloon League of America. In 1910 he founded a daily newspaper, *The Richmond Virginian,* to espouse the cause of temperance, and became superintendent of the Virginia Anti-Saloon League. He served, meanwhile, as pastor and college president, and after 1910 was listed annually in ''Who's Who.''

Mapp and Cannon first met while still young men on the Eastern Shore; it is known that the Cannons once visited the Mapp family tent at the Turlington Campgrounds. The two men first worked together politically in 1912, but their real alliance began in earnest in 1914. In that year a statewide referendum was held on the question of the prohibition of alcoholic beverages. With Cannon at their head the "dry" forces won a resounding victory; the vote in Mapp's district (the Eastern Shore and Princess Anne County) was, for instance, 3526 to 712 in favor of some form of prohibition. With the need for state temperance legislation now established, Cannon and Mapp joined forces, and in their vigorous and powerful alliance Eastern Shore Methodism attained its moment of greatest influence.

Mapp shared the authorship of the legislation with others, but the Prohibition Act of 1916 was widely known as the "Mapp Act," or the "Quart-a-Month Act." It prohibited the sale, manufacture, serving, and shipment of alcoholic beverages, and established heavy fines and jail terms for violation. There was one exemption: each household in the state could import from "wet" areas as much as one quart of whiskey, or one gallon of wine, or three gallons of beer in a month. The "quart-a-month" exemption was written into the legislation by its pro-temperance authors simply as a safety valve to insure the passage of the bill.[39]

When the "Mapp Act" came to the floor of the Senate for approval early in 1916, Cannon and Mapp were arrayed in its favor literally side by side. Mapp, who had arisen from his sickbed to defend his bill, had secured for Cannon a desk next to his on the floor of the Senate. Although his official capacity in the room was that of press representative, for the *Richmond Virginian,* Cannon, thanks to Mapp, exercized a presence and a power in the Senate that was not only remarkable but also, said his critics, clearly illegal. "Seated next to Senator Mapp, Cannon was able to confer with him at any time concerning legislation," and the minister was also said to have prompted Senators in their speeches with impunity.[40]

With such vigorous backing the "Mapp Act" passed, and Cannon exulted by praising his colleague in the *Richmond Virginian*: "Large, indeed, is the debt which the temperance people of Virginia will owe Walter Mapp for insuring the enforcement of prohibition in Virginia." Eight months later, on November 1, 1916, when the measure took effect, the Eastern Shore celebrated. A joyous company of people paraded through Accomac, "every section of the county...represented," their automobiles and wagons "decorated with tree branches, flowers, and flgs." When the parade gathered at the speaker's platform for triumphant oratory, some of the speakers noted with regret that Mapp was not there to celebrate with them. When Sadie Savage of Onley, president of the WCTU of Accomack County, rose to speak, she was greeted with an ovation.[41]

Mapp and Cannon, however, were busy at work on the next stage of the battle, a constitutional amendment to secure nationwide prohibition. Congress submitted the proposed Eighteenth Amendment to the states in 1917, and Cannon rallied the Virginia legislature to pass it. The amendment was approved by both houses in Richmond in January 1918, but Cannon's hope that Virginia might be the first state to ratify it were quashed when Mississippi foiled his plans by approving it three days earlier.[42]

On the crest of his prohibition victory, Cannon was elected to the episcopacy of the southern Methodist church in 1918. In that same year Mapp, backed by the dominant party machine, sought the Democratic nomination for Congress from the First District, but lost it; the First District was a strong anti-machine stronghold. In 1921 the Democratic nomination for governor seemed his for the asking, but he turned it down for personal reasons based on health and finances. He served in the State Senate until 1922, and sought the gubernatorial nomination in vain in 1925 and 1929.[43]

On the Eastern Shore of Virginia, which claimed both men even if Cannon was a Marylander by birth, the question of prohibition had been decided by religious conviction long before it became a political issue. (In Accomack and Northampton the 1914 vote was 84 percent for prohibition.)[44] A generation of Christians had heard it proclaimed from the pulpit, sung about, prayed about, and promoted from almost every conceivable rostrum. The temperance movement was the last great ecumenical Protestant endeavor on the Shore, an effort that involved both the simple churchgoer and the cream of Eastern Shore society. The events of 1916 and 1918 represented the high point of the influence of the Church on the life of the Shore and the nation, the people who molded those events the most famous religious leaders the Shore had produced.

Who could help but rejoice at the Church so triumphant?

A Not-So-Plain and Simple People 1892-1945

X

During the last two decades of the nineteenth century a new phenomenon appeared in the churches across the Eastern Shore: the fund-raising social. There is hardly a weekly newspaper of the period that does not invite the people of the Shore to some such function somewhere in the two counties.

In 1893, Freewill, the black Methodist church on Chincoteague Island, planned one such event: "They have engaged a brass band," advertised the county papers, "and will have many match games of baseball, croquet, etc., for the entertainment of those in attendance." In 1896 the southern Methodists of Smith's Chapel in Quinby advertised "an interesting drama entitled 'The Flower of the Family'...perfect stage management, talented dramatists, a thorough entertainment, and a variety of refreshments served at usual prices." The Methodist Protestants of Parksley announced a fair in 1895: "Among the many interesting features will be a donkey party and fish pond. There will be a bicycle race each afternoon beginning at 3 o'clock. A handsome prize will be awarded to the successful contestant."[1] And there were hundreds more: festivals, cakebakes, balloon ascensions, picnics, ice cream socials, even parades. By the end of the century the announcements alone fill entire columns in the county papers.

From Wachapreague in 1885 came another announcement in the papers suggesting that the Shore and its churches were becoming more modern:

> *That fascinating amusement called "Dancing" is now the rage among our country denizens...We hear that even the quaint old Methodists have in some instances become contaminated with the fascination to such an extent that their feet have become unruly, and ceased to listen to that discipline by which they promised to be governed. Our good old Brother [J. W. A.] Elliott gave our Methodist brethren some sound advice upon the subject a few days ago from the pulpit...We would suggest that a wholesome dose of the Methodist church discipline be administered, and we doubt not but it would have a salutary effect upon those whose feet have become troubled with lightness.*[2]

In 1899, Thomas E. Martindale, presiding elder of the northern Methodist churches, lamented that class meetings were being neglected:

> *I believe that a deliberate return to the former well-nigh universal attendance on this means of grace would result in a great spiritual awakening. Let our people once begin to come together in private meetings before God and break the long silence with contrite confession and downright repentance in the presence of their Church associates, and there will follow a mighty upheaval of the tides which are now so low and sluggish in much of our church life.*

The plain fact was that the Methodists were changing, and their churches were changing with them. Once the automatic center of village life, the churches were now forced to compete with the many other things that an increasingly prosperous and up-to-date constituency could do. As if to signify that fact, the final general camp meeting was held at the Turlington Campgrounds in 1899, replaced for all practical purposes by the very secular Keller Fair, held almost next door to it.[3]

To many persons inside the church, Methodism was simply becoming more worldly. The people who had once placed their colleagues on trial for attending shows were now putting on shows. The old campaigns against cardplaying, dancing, Sabbath-breaking, theatregoing were no longer being waged so vigorously; instead Methodists were fighting for national legislation, for social and not individual change. The church's old concern for "signs of salvation" was fast diminishing. And to a great many Methodists, even national legislation on temperance, however great an achievement that might be, could not hide the simple fact that religion was supposed to change individual people and the way they lived.

Against a background of increasing modernity and worldliness, and in specific reaction to it, a new movement reared its head in Methodist churches across the country and on the Eastern Shore. It was called the Holiness movement. It, too, was connected in an unbroken line of descent to the early days of the Methodist movement, but the connecting link was far more individual than social. And its force was to change the course of Methodism, on the Shore as on the national scene, and to illustrate just how much the denomination had changed over the years.

The origins of the Holiness movement lay in two things decidedly Methodist: the teachings of John Wesley on perfection, and the evolution of his church into a modern denomination in America.

In the early days of Methodism, no teaching was considered more characteristically "Methodist" than the doctrine of "perfection," a venerable teaching of the Church to which Wesley gave a new emphasis. "Going on to perfection," a Wesleyan catchphrase, meant not that persons could become sinless, but that they could enter a state of grace in which the "perfect love of Jesus" became the ruling passion of their lives. There were, taught Wesley, two distinct steps to salvation, both of which were available to all people. The first was "justification," the step taken when one repented of his sins and was converted. Beyond justification lay "sanctification," a "second blessing" in which the Christian could enter yet an-

AN EASTERN SHORE WORSHIP SERVICE, 1907

Rev. Ervin Thomas Liddell preaching in Union Baptist Church, Chincoteague; on the platform behind him are the deacons of the church, one of whom is a woman.

other state of grace and experience "perfect love." For Wesley and his followers this "second blessing" was considered altogether possible and desirable within the present human life.[4]

The second blessing idea remained firmly embedded in Methodism as the movement spread across America and to the Eastern Shore. The report from the Pungoteague camp meeting of 1806, for example, states that "there were two hundred and sixty three *conversions* [justifications], and one hundred and twenty-three reported to have been *sanctified* [perfected] during the day and night."[5] And for a century or more the idea was contained peacefully in the teaching and practice of the Methodist churches.

By the end of the Civil War it was becoming increasingly obvious that two separate strands of thought and action had evolved from Wesley. The great body of Methodists were content now to see the Christian life after conversion as a process of growth in grace. The old emphases upon personal behavior and lifestyle as a response to the gospel were, among these people, increasingly addressed as "social concerns." For a smaller but increasingly vocal group of Methodists, the Christian life still meant the pursuit of individual holiness, even a second sanctifying experience. The social dimension of religion, for these people, was not nearly so important as the individual dimension; the way to save the world was by the sanctifying of individuals. To the people of this latter point of view, Methodism had simply fallen away from the very thrust that once made it effective, the pursuit of personal holiness. The "plain and simple people called Methodists," as Wesley had described them, were gathering in larger and more elaborate churches, worshiping in more formal and less spontaneous ways, and fast becoming a cold and sedate middle-class church.[6]

By the 1890's the parting of the ways had been reached. In 1894 the bishops of the southern church denounced the Holiness wing of the church as disruptive and exclusivist. With other such rulings and increasing tensions within the church came the widespread withdrawal of the Holiness people from the ranks of Methodism. Unlike the Methodist Protestants half a century earlier the schismatics in this case did not form one distinct new church. Instead, dozens of small independent new groups sprang up around the country. For decades the new Holiness groups merged, divided, and merged again, until finally a number of Holiness denominations arose. Two of the larger ones, the Pilgrim Holiness Church and the Church of God (Anderson, Indiana), found their way to the Eastern Shore of Virginia.

But by the time they arrived, one Eastern Shore church had already been wracked with a Holiness schism, and given birth to its own new sect. That story is one of the most remarkable chapters in the religious history of the Shore, or of Virginia.

It was on Chincoteague Island, in a now-vanished church named Goodwill, that the Holiness movement first appeared on the Eastern Shore of Virginia.

Goodwill Church was founded as early as 1876 by the residents of the northern end of Chincoteague Island, and it was conceived and erected as a community church for persons of all religious persuasions in that neighborhood. The northern end of the island constituted a distinct and growing community at that time; a recent influx of people, many of whom were members of Goodwill, had recently arrived from Maryland and Delaware. The church's official name was Goodwill Independent Church, and the pastors of the three other white churches on the island, Baptist, Methodist Protestant, and Methodist Episcopal, took turns preaching there. Such ecumenicity apparently produced a good deal of theological ferment. The first mention of Goodwill in the local papers is from 1884, when each of the island's pastors is mentioned by name as having preached there recently with the result that "the congregation at Goodwill Independent Church are very much divided... and they are not likely soon to be of one mind."[7]

Goodwill Church did not stay independent for long, for by August 1884, J. M. Reese, the Methodist Episcopal pastor on the island, persuaded the congregation to become Methodists and annexed them to his charge as the Goodwill Class. In 1886 when the downtown congregation abandoned their old building for a newer one, it was given to the "upper" church of Goodwill, who moved it north to their end of the island, outfitted it for use, and moved out of their older building.[8]

The Methodist Episcopal Church had gained a vital new congregation, but with it came the seeds of controversy.

The controversy began with Joseph B. Lynch (1840-1900), a native of Sussex County, Delaware. Lynch had moved his family to Chincoteague by as early as

1869, was a member first of the downtown Methodist church, then of independent Goodwill, and finally of Goodwill when it became a Methodist church. In 1887, Joseph Lynch became "deeply convinced that he could not be saved without holiness." Though a stalwart and influential member of the church, he longed for the second blessing about which he read in scripture and which the older Methodists still spoke of. And so "he sought and obtained the blessing of sanctification by the power of the Holy Ghost...and immediately commenced preaching and teaching to all whom he had the opportunity."

JOSEPH B. LYNCH

Lynch had plenty of opportunity to make his views on sanctification known, for he was leader of the class meeting at Goodwill. As in so many other places on the Shore, this once small and intimate institution had swollen in size to more than 100 persons at Goodwill, and resembled more a large Sunday school class than the old time of mutual sharing and quest. Lynch testified to his experience of sanctification frequently as class leader, and soon a cluster of other sanctified Methodists grew up around him, chief among them Sarah Collins, a dynamic woman who obtained sanctification in 1889. By 1892 the group had grown in size and enthusiasm so much that "their zeal was more than their minister could endure." When George P. Jones, the young Methodist Episcopal pastor of Chincoteague, proved that he had little patience with them, they petitioned Bishop Edward G. Andrews of the Wilmington Conference to send "a holy man of God to preach to them."

The request was not unlike any number of other requests received by other Methodist bishops across the country from Holiness groups, but it was unbearable to Pastor Jones. Its clear implication was that he was not "a holy man of God," and he rose to this challenge by dismissing Lynch from his position as class leader and forbidding any of the 51 persons who had signed the petition to conduct classes or hold meetings at Goodwill. At the next Quarterly Conference of the congregation, all officers of the church who had signed the petition were deprived of their positions by the rest of the congregation, most of whom were not in the sanctified group. And so, "the sanctified people, feeling that the entire Methodist Episcopal Church was in opposition to them, organized themselves into a body on February 14, 1892," and began to hold classes and services in a nearby "workshop." They chose a completely new name for themselves: Christ's Sanctified Holy Church.

On the next Sunday a committee of ten waited upon Jones to present him with a second petition that asked his formal consent to the withdrawal of members "who had already joined Christ's Sanctified Holy Church." Sarah Collins handed Jones the list of names before the service opened, but Jones ignored it and began the service as usual. After a hymn and a prayer, Joseph Lynch arose to ask publicly that the pastor attend to the request. Jones refused, and the ten sanctified people present left the building. On the following Tuesday the regular Methodists brought the committee of ten before a magistrate on a charge of interrupting public worship, but the charge was dismissed. The nineteen members of Christ's Sanctified Holy Church dated their new organization from that day before the magistrate, February 16, 1892. Heading the list of the names of the new congregation were Joseph Lynch and Sarah Collins.[9]

The new Holiness church took to the field in a big way. By summer they had erected their own church building, and it was the largest one on the island. (It stood next door to Goodwill.) By October the group had spread to Franklin City on the mainland and were holding services there. By the next summer they held a revival on the island, and the bower erected to house it was "the largest and most expensive ever put up on the island," and the large crowds that attended came from as far away as Delaware. Before long the faith had been carried north into Worcester County, Maryland, where services were held in an abandoned Methodist church near Boxiron.[10] The Maryland effort was short-lived, but even farther north in

Sussex County, Delaware, where the sanctified people had many relatives and friends, a second new church was ultimately established.

The Methodists of Goodwill, meanwhile, went their way, glad to be rid of the dissidents. The 1892 report for the Chincoteague congregation reads: "Chincoteague Island has given us a striking illustration of the baneful results of zeal without knowledge, but Brother Jones the pastor has brought victory out of seeming defeat. With the disturbing element out of the church, the sailing is plain for the future."

Thus did the Methodists dismiss, in a casual way, the first appearance of Holiness doctrine on the Shore. Little did they know that this was just the first of a new wave of churches, and that the future into which they sailed was to be far from smooth.

Never before had an Eastern Shore congregation separated itself so completely from the Methodist mainstream as did Christ's Sanctified Holy Church in 1892. The churches formed by schism in the 1830's and 1840's were still called Methodist; even Coe's independent Convention of Accomack was avowedly Methodist. These earlier defections had involved differences in polity or practical affairs. The new Chincoteague dissidents differed at a more fundamental point, that of belief.

Lynch and his new congregation set about drawing up a rule of order, and by 1893 he and Sarah Collins had produced *The Doctrines and Disciplines of Christ's Sanctified Holy Church.* This remarkable little book (referred to from the beginning as the "Dis-CIP-line") is one of the few theological works ever published on the Shore. It is still republished and updated quadrennially as the definitive statement of rule and order for the church.

The doctrines in it, often stated in question-and-answer form, illustrate how the Holiness people drew their inspiration from Wesley, but in an entirely different manner from the main body of Methodism:

> *Are you a sanctified holy person?*
> *I am.*
>
> *Are you a witness that [sanctification] is not a growth in grace, but received instantaneous after justification?*
> *I am.*
>
> *Were you ever saved before you were sanctified?*
> *No.*

In some ways the new church reflected its Methodist origins, for there were created annual conferences, deacons and deaconesses, a Board of Church Extension, and even the term "Discipline." In some ways the new sect reflected social attitudes of the Methodists at that time, as when the *Discipline* directed that "There shall be no person received into full membership that votes to give license to any person to sell intoxicating liquors, nor uses or sells tobacco, but only to join on probation." But in other ways the new sect saw itself as the Church purified and made holy, as Methodism in its view was not. The *Discipline* is critical of salaried and learned ministers, and states uncategorically what must have seemed to be a non-issue to most Methodist churchgoers on the Shore at that time: "Christ's Sanctified Holy Church shall not hold any festival, nor anything that will not promote and honor God."[11]

Chincoteague's new sanctified church might well have lived in peaceful coexistence with the rest of the island, once the initial hard feeling of its formation was over, had not new doctrines arisen within its ranks, further extensions of the Holiness understanding and experience of Christian life that drove even further the wedge between the sanctified people and rest of the community. At first the new church went about its way without interference from the islanders. Its ministers, Joseph Lynch, James Workman, and Sarah Collins, the first female minister on record on the Eastern Shore of Virginia, married and buried and preached as did the other ministers of the island. Membership increased rapidly, from nineteen in 1892 to as many as 120 in 1894, swelled perhaps by converts among family connections still moving to the island from Delaware and Maryland.[12]

Soon, however, the island community learned of two of the church's teachings that brought peaceful coexistence to an end. The first was a teaching concerning marriage between sanctified and unsanctified persons. The *Discipline* forbade such mixed marriages:

> *Any minister of Christ's Sanctified Holy Church joining unequal persons together, holy and unholy, white and black, the minister shall be expelled, also the matrimony shall be void.*[13]

Yet the experience of sanctification had split many a marriage and family, as husband or wife or child obtained it alone of the household. There was only one thing to do: those marriages contracted before the experience of sanctification must be dissolved, if either partner were unsanctified. Married sanctified persons must separate from unsanctified spouses and come out from among even unsanctified children, where practical.

The islanders were horrified by this development, which seemed to them to be "indecencies totally at variance with the moral law!" The county papers carried indignant reports of the strange goings-on of this new sect: "A Mrs. [Charlotte] Gray has deserted her husband and four little children. She left the children alone while asleep one night last week while her husband, who was a surfman at Green Run Life Saving Station, was from home, and who has since been compelled to resign his position to take care of them." Another person singled out for such reprehensible actions was John W. Johns, one of the original nineteen founders, a "worthy and thrifty man...until he joined the [sanctified] band." Johns, it seems, had also left unsanctified wife and children for the sake of his religious convictions.[14]

As if this were not enough, the island soon got wind of a second practice among the sanctified band, something they called "two-plus-two." At heart it was a simple and innocent idea: basing their belief on the Biblical observation that Jesus always sent his disciples out two by two, not singly, the sanctified people insisted that scripture was to be studied and proclaimed by pairs of believers. This belief came about in part because of the sect's reaction to the "unholy" ministers who held sway in Methodism. The *Discipline* explained:

> *Are the professing ministers out today according to God's Word? No. The Scriptures teach us all Christ's disciples were sent out two and two and those that are out single today preaching...are not sent by God.*[15]

The islanders were more than ready to believe that what happened when the sanctified people gathered two-by-two was more scandalous than the study of scripture. Gradually a few eagle eyes announced what so many were more than willing to believe: some of the sanctified people, Joseph B. Lynch among them, had done more than repudiate their old marriages to unsanctified spouses; they had also taken new husbands and wives from among the band of the faithful.

Had the Eastern Shore not been so isolated, reaction to this development might not have been so heated. Chincoteague's sanctified people were hardly unique among Holiness sects of the time in repudiating old marriages and contracting new ones, with or without benefit of law. As it was, few if any saw any saving grace in the deep religious conviction of the sanctified people, and soon the county papers were alive with reports of "orgies" and "free love" on Chincoteague Island.[16] Not only the island but also the entire county was soon buzzing with moral indignation, made all the worse no doubt by the standards that decreed that Christian men and women of that day did not even speak of such possibilities.

By the fall of 1894 the sanctified congregation was held in hostile contempt by most of the rest of the island. Even apart from their doctrines were their meetings, which in good Holiness fashion were much noisier than most Methodist and Baptist services of that day. "Wild frantics," the islanders called them, and they were increasingly convinced that they had to go.

On September 1, 1894, the island's antipathy erupted into violence.

It was Saturday night on the island, and eleven young men of the village, apparently out for fun, determined to exact some punishment from the sanctified people for their "immoralities." They mounted their horses and rode noisily up Main Street towards the church looking for James Workman, "to get a move on him." Workman was nowhere to be found, so the gang turned around to go home when one of them produced a gun. This time their ride down the street was punctuated by whooping and shouting and shots fired into the air.

One of the shots went aside into the Main Street residence of Aaron T. Bowden. Bowden was asleep in his second-floor bedroom when a bullet went through the side of the house and struck him. He died a few hours later.

The incident sent shock waves across the island community. The eleven young men were arrested and jailed, but the island rose to their defense. "The young men," read the county paper, "made the mistake...[of] taking the law in their own hands, but there is no doubt that so great is the indignation of people on the Island generally against [Workman] and others of the Sanctified Band that they reflected by their action the sentiment of the best people of the Island..." The community was all but unanimous in their opinion that "the young men implicated in the affair are among the best of the Island," and that, as for the Sanctified people, "the wonder is that the lewd and lascivious habits of the Sanctified crowd practiced by them under the guise of religion has not lead to bloodshed before."[17]

Aaron T. Bowden, the victim, was said to have been a completely innocent bystander, in no way connected with either group. Yet Bowden was one of the original nineteen founders of Christ's Sanctified Holy Church, and had left it in August 1894, only shortly before his death. Though his death was termed accidental, at least one of the men charged with it had been fined previously for assaulting Joseph Lynch, and was known for his strong dislike of the Sanctified people.[18]

Convinced that they knew who the real villains were, and that the wrong people were in jail, a group of islanders brought charges against four the Sanctified band within the week. Joseph Lynch, Sarah Collins, John Collins, and William Chandler were arraigned before a justice of the peace and charged with four misdemeanors:

> *(1)...that they did...conspire with one another to commit acts of indecency*
> *(2) That they did cause Mary E. Burton to leave her husband Woolsey Burton*
> *(3) That the said persons did conspire together and promulgate "free love," teaching married women to disregard their marriage vows*
> *(4) That said persons did conspire to appoint a male and female member as fellow-watchers, to sit up at night and watch.*[19]

When the four refused to put up bail, they were jailed in Accomac.

On the island the air was hot and heavy for action against the Sanctified people. While Lynch and his comrades sat in the county jail, a petition circulated to get the court to revoke the license of Sanctified preachers to marry, and locals vowed that "if the grand jury and courts do nothing, the aid of the Governor will be invoked — and if neither act, then means will be found in some way perhaps to rid us of them." "This fool craze has got to stop, say our citizens, by peaceable means if possible — by forcible means if necessary."[20]

In October 1894, the four Sanctified leaders were tried before a crowded courtroom. John Collins was acquitted. The other three were found guilty and given different sentences: Joseph Lynch was fined $250 and given eight months in jail; William Chandler was fined $150 and given six months; and Sarah Collins, $100 and four months. All put up bail and were released pending an appeal.[21]

It was obvious to Lynch and his people that the time for decision had come, and the community breathed a sign of relief when the word spread that the Sanctified people were preparing to leave the island altogether. Joseph Lynch left first, heading for Baltimore to find a place where his people could live in peace. In his absence, Sarah Collins and the others prepared themselves for departure, and the trustees announced that the church was to be put up for sale. "The Sanctified band has about disbanded," reported the newspapers. "Private meetings continue to be held occasionally, but will not continue to be held long, it is believed."[22]

By the end of 1894 there had begun one of the strangest chapters in the history of the Eastern Shore: a religious migration, not unlike that of the Mormons under Brigham Young fifty years before. Thirteen members of Christ's Sanctified Holy Church sailed by schooner from Chincoteague Island, rounded Cape Charles into Chesapeake Bay, and joined up with their leader near Baltimore. The rest of the band stood ready and waiting to leave at a moment's notice, as soon as word reached the island that a new home had been found. Lynch led the vanguard southward to Montross, Virginia, on the Northern Neck, where they were very obviously made to understand that they were not welcome. Southward down the Bay sailed the community, and within a few weeks they sent word to their brethren in Chincoteague that a refuge had been found in northeastern North Carolina, near Elizabeth City.

In May 1895 the bulk of the congregation said goodbye to the island. "The sanctified band sold at public auction on last Saturday all their real estate and personal property, and will leave for North Carolina as soon as possible. They expect to take all with them that cannot afford to pay their way by sail boats — and among them will be husbands deserting their wives and wives deserting their husbands."

In all, there were three waves in which the Sanctified people left Chincoteague Island. The first was over by the summer of 1895, when most of them left to settle in North Carolina. The remnant left on the island were led by Parker Bowden, under whom the church there was virtually dormant.[23]

The second wave occurred the following summer, when "seventeen more of the sanctified band, and the last of them, left here to join the band in North Carolina last week. They sold their oyster boats, houses, etc., at a sacrifice." In the fall of that year the church building, erected only four years before for $2000, was auctioned off for $100.

In December 1896, after the second migration, some of the band returned to Chincoteague, having found that North Carolinians were no less hostile to them than Chincoteague Islanders. By early 1897 there were enough on the island to resume worship services, the islanders keeping a close watch. Meanwhile from across the Bay came news that Lynch, quitting North Carolina, had once again taken his "floating ark" into Chesapeake Bay. Again an attempt was made to settle on Northern Neck, and again the attempt was repulsed.[24]

The third and final movement from the island began on May 15, 1897, and lasted throughout the summer. A party of 18 left in May, after selling all their property, and sailed away in a schooner. "Their departure is due to the fact that they would not be permitted by our citizens to indulge in their 'frantic meetings' here any longer," wrote the Chincoteague correspondent to the county paper.[25] By August when another small band left, the old church building had been purchased again, this time by none other than the congregation of Goodwill Methodist Episcopal Church, who were busy painting it and putting in new pews for their own use. Methodist Episcopal records of that year read: "Perhaps this will rid the island of that old heresy."

For the six years following 1897, when the Methodists occupied the building in which the Sanctified people had worshiped, there is, for all practical purposes, no history of Christ's Sanctified Holy Church on either Chincoteague Island or the Virginia Eastern Shore. Apparently a few Sanctified persons remained on the island but there was no church and apparently no organization or worship or gathering. The real story of the sect during this period is found off the Shore, as the band moved from place to place looking for a place to settle. Joseph Lynch died in 1900, and the group moved on. Gradually parts of the Sanctified band found homes in various places until the sect was dispersed across the South, from Norfolk to Oklahoma. In 1939 a headquarters was established in Perry, Georgia, when a camp meeting ground and a cemetery were purchased. By then Christ's Sanctified Holy Church was one of many similar, independent Holiness sects scattered across the country, and Eastern Shore names could be found in places far distant from the Shore.

It was in 1903 that the Chincoteague remnant resurfaced, reorganized, and reestablished the faith on the island. A. J. Dolbow of Wilmington and T. F. Tabler of Philadelphia began a revival[26] that resulted in the establishment of a permanent Sanctified congregation and the erection of a new church building not far from the old site. Here the congregation began again the same old-fashioned, noisy services that had previously been dubbed "wild frantics," but this time they encountered no opposition from the community. The Sanctified persons whose marital practices had offended the community were now gone, and the new congregation was blameless with regards to what had been the chief bone of contention a decade earlier. Freed from what the community considered the one unforgivable taint, the new Chincoteague congregation of Christ's Sanctified Holy Church grew unmolested. With the passing of the years, the individual Sanctified members moved from ostracized persons to acceptable stalwart citizens to prosperous and respected people. By 1920 there were some sixty Sanctified persons in the congregation, and social ostracism was so much a thing of the past that one of the persons who conducted services in the church that year was Ervin Thomas Liddell, a Baptist evangelist who only a few years before had been pastor of Union Baptist Church in Chincoteague. By then both church and community had, by a kind of unspoken consensus, drawn a veil of silence over their former differences, a veil which in large part remains to this day.

There are several interesting footnotes to the story of Christ's Sanctified Holy Church. One of them involves the absence of Mormons on the Eastern Shore of Virginia. In September 1894, the month in which Lynch and his comrades were jailed, two Mormon elders named Taylor and Nibley entered Accomack County from the south and worked their way up the peninsula "distributing tracts upon their faith among the people." By late September they were in Accomac, by November in Parksley. It was their misfortune to arrive in Chincoteague in early December, just as the Sanctified people were preparing to quit the island. It had been only four years previous to their arrival, in 1890, that the Mormon Church,

CHRIST'S SANCTIFIED HOLY CHURCH

The congregation sat for this picture in front of their church in 1920, dressed in the plain and simple clothes that were characteristic of them. Ninth from the left in the second row (holding a Bible) is the Reverend Ervin Thomas Liddell, former pastor at Union Baptist Church who later preached at this church

after many delays and under great pressure from the United States government, had revised its laws and ended its long-standing practice of plural marriage. Chincoteague, of course, wanted nothing to do with them and dismissed them with obvious contempt. "Our people, still sore over the two-by-two arrangements, are not prepared to listen with much patience to the teachers of strange doctrines," wrote the local correspondence to the county newspaper.[27] Taylor and Nibley apparently passed quickly on to Maryland, and Mormonism never gained a foothold on the Eastern Shore of Virginia.

A second event worthy of footnoting took place in Louisiana. It was at the same time that Sanctified services were resuming on Chincoteague Island that the black people of Calcasieu County received a strange set of visitors. Three "saints" from Virginia came into their midst preaching a new doctrine called "Holiness," which the black people received with enthusiasm. "Many of them believed their doctrines and began reading their Bibles and praying, and sought and obtained the blessings of sanctification." The first of the new converts was C. E. Rigmaiden, a black woman who began preaching in her own right.

On April 16, 1904, the "white saints" from Virginia organized some of the former members of the Colored Methodist Episcopal Church of West Lake, Louisiana, into a new church named Christ's Sanctified Holy Church Colored. One of the founding "saints" was Mrs. Charlotte Gray, formerly of Chincoteague Island, who ten years earlier had left husband and children to find a new home with her spiritual family.[28]

In time Christ's Sanctified Holy Church Colored was set apart from the parent sect as an independent church. Today it boasts some 600 members in thirty separate congregations. The white members of Christ's Sanctified Holy Church now number about a thousand in 21 communities from Delaware to Louisiana. Both of them stand as a monument to the life and experience of Joseph B. Lynch, the first person on the Eastern Shore of Virginia to recover something of what John Wesley had taught about "going on to perfection."

No sooner had Chincoteague Island weathered this turmoil than a Holiness storm began to brew for the entire Eastern Shore of Virginia.

It was in Wachapreague that the Eastern Shore's second Holiness congregation appeared, founded by Cole Hope (1873-1954), a preacher of the denomination known then as the International Apostolic Holiness Union and Churches. Hope, a Marylander who was converted and later sanctified in the woods of his father's farm, was living in Wachapreague when he invited three Holiness preachers, Mr. and Mrs. Harvey Adams and Miss Etta Gibson (later Mrs. Hoffman), to conduct a tent meeting in the village.

Like Chincoteague a decade before, Wachapreague did not at first look kindly on this noisy and aggressive new religion, and it was not long before a delegation of townspeople appeared at Hope's door with orders for the three visiting evangelists to leave town. The Holiness people calmly ignored the order. Etta Gibson, an accomplished singer and harpist, even stood on the front porch of the Hope residence and sang, throughout the tense incident, "The Judgment Day Is Coming."

Local disfavor was not enough to dampen Holiness spirits, and the Wachapreague tentmeeting was such a success that by 1907 a small congregation had been formed and a church erected on Lee Street. Chief pillars of this congregation were Cole Hope, who later moved on to establish another church in Shelltown, Maryland, and Levin Badger (1871-1936), who actually owned the church building. Once the church was established, townsfolk tended to leave the Holiness people alone. Mrs. Badger, however, once had to dodge the eggs thrown at her one night as she walked home from the worship services. And some of the people who lived next door to the new church were known to insist for years that Holiness worship services were so loud because the devil himself was present.

In 1909 Annie Bradford Pearson, a Methodist of Johnson's Church, first heard Holiness preaching from T. Lewis Adams and Etta Gibson at the Wachapreague church, and she became the founder of the Shore's third Holiness church. Returning to her home in Birdsnest, she began a prayer meeting group that ultimately evolved into the present Community Church of God, which is affiliated with the Church of God of Anderson, Indiana.

All of this was mere prelude to the advent of the man who was to be for the next thirty years the foremost advocate of Holiness doctrine on the Eastern Shore of Virginia, the Reverend William Vickers.

William Vickers (1882-1945) was a minister in the same church as Cole Hope, a church that in 1922 changed its name to the Pilgrim Holiness Church.[29] Born on Taylor's Island, Maryland, Vickers was in his early life a waterman and a Metho-

COLE HOPE (standing)
LEVIN BADGER
(seated)

dist until he was turned around by Holiness preaching. After obtaining the experience of Holiness for himself, he became an active minister and evangelist. "He carried a burden for souls," they said of him, and his aggressive preaching was to make him simultaneously the most revered and the most reviled preacher on the Shore.

It was as a young man — stout, almost corpulent, and a prodigious eater — that Vickers began his ministry on the Shore. In the summer of 1916 he arrived in Grotons in upper Accomack County, pitched a large tent, and announced a series of services. For the next four weeks the community resounded to his spirited preaching, once a day and once a night and all day on Sundays. When he moved on he left behind him a small group that met for prayer meetings in private homes. He returned to Grotons in 1917, pitched his tent in a different spot, and by the end of the year a new congregation had been organized and had erected a church building on the site. After Grotons, Vickers repeated his performance in Chincoteague,

WILLIAM VICKERS

and then in Saxis, where a church stood by 1918. In Chincoteague large crowds flocked to the Holiness Tabernacle which he constructed, but he was unable there to establish a lasting congregation.

In each of these communities Vickers conducted a hard-sell, well-advertised campaign that generated either enthusiasm or hostility. His message was an outright criticism of the worldliness of the churches and of Christianity gone bad. Had not the great camp meeting become a worldly county fair? Were not Baptists and Methodists alike more concerned about fine clothes and fine buildings with stained glass windows than about the pursuit of the holy life? Should not Christians turn from their worldly pursuits and seek the holy life? Vickers made no bones about it: he called to repentance sinners who were within the churches, as well as the unsaved outside the churches.

Vickers' message and his medium created a sensation in upper Accomack, and as the devout and the merely curious filled his tent to overflowing the established churches, the Methodists in particular, began to feel the heat. The Methodists were now, for the first time in their life on the Shore, in the defensive role, and many a pastor and congregation must have breathed a sigh of relief to be still intact when Vickers pulled up his stakes, literally, and moved on to another town.

In 1920 Vickers ventured into Bloxom. When the locals there burned his tent, he erected a more substantial tabernacle and announced not a tent meeting but a camp meeting. It was a fortunate move. Not since the last Turlington Campmeeting in 1899 had the whites of the Shore had a general and not just a local encampment, and the Bloxom Campmeeting was a huge success. A small Bloxom congregation was on the record books by 1925 because of it. In 1929 Vickers with the help of two other evangelists, Mayme Parker and Winifred Mears, conducted an even more successful camp meeting in Bloxom. Over $7000 was received in offerings, and with it the denomination was able to purchase the campground and put its Accomack work on a sound footing. By the end of the year a new parsonage stood on the edge of the campground, and a full-time pastor, F. C. Walls, was firmly established there. "His address is Bloxom," reads the report of that year, "but Accomack County is his parish. His preaching places are so many, his schedules so complicated, that his wife is often at sea to know where he goes next."

In the early 1920's Vickers was elected to the district superintendency and he set out to do all across the Shore what he did best of all: pioneer the faith in new regions. Heading south, he took his tent to town after town in a concerted effort to preach Holiness to the entire Eastern Shore of Virginia. He arrived in Wachapreague to find Cole Hope's earlier church there "practically gone down" after Hope had moved to Maryland. It was reorganized and set up under a new pastor, Merrick Lowry. Vickers himself bypassed Wachapreague and concentrated his efforts on nearby Quinby, where by 1925 he had set up his tent, held his spectacular meetings, and left behind him a small band of Holiness people meeting in private homes. Soon there were tent meetings in Oakland Park, just south of Exmore, with the same result. The tent made its appearance in Chesconnessex, in Mearsville, and in Oyster. By 1933 the tent had been raised in Cape Charles and a congregation formed there. Meanwhile Levin Badger had held similar tent meetings in Poulson, west of Hallwood, and near Greta, west of Atlantic. Though not every community had hosted a Holiness tent, Holiness doctrine was at last becoming something to be reckoned with throughout the two counties.

Vickers did not march down the Shore; he became a part of the scenery. Each year the tent would appear again, the curious and the faithful would flock to it, the inevitable criticisms of the worldliness of the churches would echo across the community, the Methodists and the Baptists would steel themselves for the duration, and then in time the tent would move on again. His appearance upon the horizon was especially dreaded by the Methodists. In 1931 the pastor at Smith's Chapel in Quinby reported to his superiors that few menfolk were attending Methodist services there because they were drawn away to Holiness meetings.[30] In Riverview and Leatherbury, the northern Methodist churches of Chesconnessex, the people were "torn apart" after Vickers and his tent appeared there. The Methodist cause was not aided when T. S. Dixon (1881-1953), pastor of Ayres Chapel Methodist Episcopal Church, surrendered his Methodist credentials and joined the Holiness people shortly after the first Bloxom camp meeting. Dixon was ordained in the Pilgrim Holiness Church in 1927 and assigned to Mardela Springs, Maryland, where he founded and built a new church. He preached a great many times on the Virginia Shore after that date, but in Holiness, not Methodist, churches.

Vickers, meanwhile, was ever-present and ever-vigorous. In a typical year (1926) he preached 390 sermons, more than one a day, a practice that had not been

WILLIAM VICKERS AND HIS HOLINESS TENT

Vickers is standing third from the left, hat in hand

common among the Methodists for almost a hundred years. He established seventeen new congregations in Maryland and Virginia and "endured many types of opposition to open work in new fields and to establish churches." Although there is no record that it happened in Virginia, it is known that he was on at least one occasion pelted with eggs by an angry crowd.

Two possible courses of action lay open to the Methodists: either fight the Holiness movement on its own ground, or ignore it and go a different way. There was some attempt made to take the former path, to recover the Methodist claim to some of the Holiness message. Instead of their usual annual revival, the Methodists of Belle Haven imported a special guest evangelist in the summer of 1922 and widely advertised the Reverend Victor Lightbourne and his "Big Gospel Tent." And the southern Methodists resurrected the old Turlington Campmeeting in 1923 in hopes of combatting the growing Holiness defection. The camp was a great success, but despite continued talk about keeping it open it was not repeated.[31]

In fact, most Methodists were finally content to ignore Vickers and to separate themselves from everything he represented. The result was that while Vickers railed against the growing worldliness of the churches, Eastern Shore Christians, Methodists chief among them, rushed headlong into what was perhaps their most prosperous, worldly, and acculturated period.

The prosperous period that began with the coming of the railroad, the prosperous period that ushered in the comfort and prosperity against which the Holiness people reacted, continued unabated from the 1880's into the 1920's. The first quarter of the twentieth century was indeed a "golden age" for the Eastern Shore. Population increased and villages grew. Farms prospered and bountiful crops brought a high degree of comfort, even wealth to a great many. Communication and transportation were modernized, and the Shore became less and less isolated, and more and more in touch with and concerned about the world beyond its shores.

With the 1920's came the full-scale advent of the automobile, that invention which would in the next decades end the railroad's domination of Shore life. Automobiles were still a rarity in 1910, but by 1920 they were plentiful in the two counties, and such modern amenities as paved roads, parking spaces, gas stations, and traffic accidents were becoming commonplace. The state began the paving of Route 13, the Shore's main artery, in 1923, starting at opposite ends in Cape Charles and New Church and working towards the center. Not until 1931 was the "stone ribbon" complete, but by then even the outlying communities off the main track were hard at work to get smooth, paved roads.[32]

The twenties themselves were a period of unprecedented progress and change. In 1922, Chincoteague, the largest town, was connected to the mainland by a causeway. In 1927 electricity, previously available only in a few of the larger towns, was made available throughout the peninsula. In 1928 the railroad put into service the "Virginia Lee," a handsome steamer that plied the mouth of the Chesapeake Bay between Cape Charles and Norfolk. It could ferry eighty automobiles, and it made Route 13 a major north-south road for East Coast traffic. Northampton-Accomack Memorial Hospital was opened in Nassawadox in 1928, and two years later a second ferry line was in competition with the railroad at Cape Charles.[33]

The churches, like the rest of life on the Shore, prospered. Membership increased, and many a congregation entered into the brightest period of its history.

One measure of the prosperity of the churches is their buildings, and church buildings in the first part of the twentieth century became increasingly elegant and expensive on the Shore. Between the erection of St. James' Episcopal Church in Drummondtown in 1838 and the end of the century, there were only two brick church buildings erected on the entire Shore, both in Cape Charles: Centenary Methodist and St. Charles Catholic. Brick has always been an expensive commodity on the Shore, but by the second decade of the twentieth century local congregations began to build brick buildings as never before. The first was Grace Methodist Protestant Church in Parksley, which replaced its burned frame building with a $17,000 brick structure in 1911. Onley Methodist, Lower Northampton Baptist, and Drummondtown Baptist erected brick churches in 1913. There followed a whole series of new, expensive, and often ornate brick buildings at the rate of almost one a year, among them: Zion Baptist (1917), Drummondtown Methodist (1918), Atlantic Baptist (1919), Atlantic Methodist (1922), Modest Town Baptist (1921), Allen Memorial A.M.E. (1924), and Woodbury Methodist (1926). In 1920 both the Baptists and the Methodists began new buildings in Cheriton, vying with each other in grandeur from opposite corners of the street. If cost is the deciding factor, the Baptists won; they spent $65,000 to the mere $45,000 spent by the Methodists. The stone for the new Gothic-style building erected by Christ Methodist Episcopal Church in Chincoteague had to be shipped from the North by railroad to Franklin City, then by barge seven miles across Chincoteague Bay to the island, since the new highway causeway was not yet complete. So large and grand was this building that in 1921 the Wilmington Conference voted to convene there in

1922; the causeway to the island was not, however, completed in time and the Eastern Shore narrowly missed playing host to a second Annual Conference session. Last was the stone building erected by Cape Charles Presbyterians in 1925. It cost over $70,000, more money than had ever before been spent on a church building on the Eastern Shore of Virginia.[34]

And for every new brick church erected during this period, there was a host of smaller congregations who somehow renovated, repainted, improved, enlarged, or otherwise "rebuilt" their more modest structures. Some buildings were moved distances of several miles to more desirable locations (Grant Methodist Protestant Church from the Chesconnessex area to Tasley in 1910, Garrison's Methodist Episcopal Church, South, from Mappsburg to Painter in 1928). And among the other improvements made on church buildings were such diverse things as the $1250 spent by the Negro Burton's congregation to repair their little frame building in 1923, the $5200 brick veneer that the Episcopalians added to their frame building in Cape Charles in 1928, and the careful and expensive restoration of the unique *trompe l'oeil* fresco painted on the wall behind the altar of St. James' Episcopal Church in Accomac, which was accomplished in 1929.[35]

FIRST PRESBYTERIAN CHURCH, CAPE CHARLES

Erected 1925; in its time the most expensive church building on the Shore

In their new buildings, the local congregations experienced increased contact with the outside world, stronger ties to their individual denominations, and added formality and solemnity in worship. Pipe organs appeared in some of the larger churches, and stained glass windows began to replace the plain windows of earlier periods. A "split chancel" similar to those of large urban churches was built into the new Christ Methodist Episcopal Church in Chincoteague. And even rural church structures began to reflect affluence, prosperity, and the outside world. Locustville Methodist Episcopal Church, South, for instance, built a new building in 1923. Although the building was small, it was designed in an elegant classical revival style from plans suggested by the denomination in Nashville.[36]

One story from Makemie Park Baptist Church will speak for the growing formality and sophistication of worship. The preacher there was J. A. Willoughby, who one day quizzed a parishioner as to why the man had ceased to attend church. The man replied that he did not have clothes fine enough to wear to church, and so the next Sunday Willoughby showed up to preach dressed in overalls, to illustrate the apparently forgotten point that finery in dress was not necessary for church attendance. A number of newspapers picked up the story, and Willoughby was forced to defend himself against the charge of lowering the dignity of the pulpit.[37] Nonetheless the incident, which occurred just after World War I, illustrates what had been happening in even the rural churches for years: increased finery of dress, more formality, more dignified preaching, the old plainness and simplicity of former years — the Holiness reaction notwithstanding — shoved aside and forgotten.

With the prosperity of the churches, and widely used as a measure of it, came increased contact with the several denominations at their national levels. The old Methodist "class" disappeared altogether except in such isolated places as Saxis, Harborton, and Tangier, but the Sunday school was by now complete with denominational curricula and standardized quarterlies sent from Nashville. Epworth Leagues (for Methodist youth), Rosebud Societies (for Methodist children), and Sunbeam Societies (for Baptist children) sprang up and flourished all over the Shore, as did other similar programs sponsored and defined by the denominations. In 1914 the Accomack Baptist Association adopted an eleven-point plan for measuring the vitality of its congregations. Among those things that each up-to-date church was supposed to have were a year-round Sunday school, monthly contributions to denominational boards and agencies, weekly prayer meetings, Baptist Young People's Union once a week, a quota of subscriptions to Baptist journals and magazines, and regular contributions to foreign missions. W. C. Royal, pastor of the New Church Baptist field, was proud to report that First Baptist Church in New Church was only one point from reaching that goal in 1915, and that Chincoteague Baptist had attained 75 percent.[38]

Circuits by now were small enough and ministers numerous enough that even rural congregations could expect regular preaching services, as often as not every Sunday. Although most churches still shared their pastor with other churches, by 1911 there were 25 Methodist preachers for the white congregations alone in the two counties. Most communities by now had a parsonage of some sort, and most of them a minister who was a year-round resident.

From this golden era come the first records of interdenominational cooperation among the churches of the Shore. Larger towns like Cape Charles and Parksley seem to have led in this new spirit of ecumenicity that began gradually to replace the old rivalries. In 1917 the Gerge Sisters, traveling evangelists, were imported by the Cape Charles churches for a series of interdenominational meetings, and that fall the Baptist and Methodist churches in Parksley sponsored a joint tent meeting. Three years later when Bethany Methodist Episcopal Church in Cape Charles held its annual revival, the Reverend J. L. Carrick of Lower Northampton Baptist Church was one of the preachers on hand to help conduct it. In 1925 Billy Sunday, one of the most famous evangelists in America, happened through Cape Charles, and a crowd of about 4000 from all over the Shore gathered to hear him speak from a platform near the railroad. Seizing upon the new mood of cooperation among the churches, twelve Northampton congregations pledged $9000 to bring Sunday to the Shore for a full-fledged crusade the following year, but when a mutually satisfactory time could not be arranged with Sunday the idea was abandoned. Even so, Protestant ministers formed the Eastern Shore Ministerial Association at Accomac in the fall of 1926, and proclaimed as one of their first joint projects a ''Go-to-Church-Sunday'' for May 1927.[39] The finest example of ecumenicity on the Shore was undoubtedly Macon Union Chapel, an interdenominational Sunday school in Wilsonia Neck in Northampton founded by William Bullitt Fitzhugh in 1904. Although the declining population of that community foreshadowed the closing of the chapel in the late 1920's, for two decades the people of Wilsonia Neck attended services in their chapel without feeling compelled to choose among the Methodist, Baptist, Episcopalian, and Presbyterian preachers who took turns preaching there.

World War I may have done much to foster this spirit of cooperation among the churches, for local communities and local churches invested that struggle with an almost religious significance. Shore preachers were, almost without exception, forceful in their support of the Allied cause for the duration of the war, and Methodist, Baptist, Presbyterian, Episcopalian, and even Roman Catholic chapels resounded to patriotic sermons and services. At the end of the war, as community after community celebrated the victory and the homecoming of the local servicemen, preachers found themselves sharing platforms with each other for perhaps the first time. At the homecoming celebration at Eastville, for instance, on April 28, 1919, four clergymen took part: J. B. Ferebee (Baptist), J. R. McAllister (Episcopalian), Edward Mickle (Roman Catholic), and P. M. Hank (Methodist).[40] No doubt such examples of ecumenicity were not lost on either laymen or clergy up and down the Shore.

The founding of new churches proceeded apace clear up into the 1920's, even though the larger denominations had already spread to virtually every corner of the Shore. The Methodist Protestants did not stop their spread until they had laid a claim to Greenbush with a church established there in 1911. The last southern Methodist church to be organized was Melfa in 1913. Among the northern Methodists, Riverview in Chesconnessex (1910) was the last white and St. John's in Atlantic and Mt. Hope in Keller (1915) the last black churches to be established. St. Paul's in Fairview was the last A.M.E. congregation of the period, organized 1914. By 1915, Methodist expansion to new communities was over.

Non-Methodists, however, were still founding new churches. Between 1900 and 1923, the white Baptists of the Accomack Association established no fewer than eleven new congregations. The mortality rate, however, was high, and only five — Cheriton (1900), Hallwood (1901), Exmore (1908), Onley (1908), and First in New Church (1909) — survive today. Black Baptists founded nine new churches during that same period, of which fully seven are still functioning, and in 1926 the old Mt. Olive A.M.E. Church in Hack's Neck was reorganized and reopened as a Baptist Church. St. Michael's, the last Episcopal church to be founded on the Virginia Shore and the second of that same name in Belle Haven, was organized in 1906. And there were two new Presbyterian churches organized in the twentieth century: Eastville (1904) and Greenview, south of Wachapreague (1919).

By the middle of the 1920's it appeared, in short, as if Christianity had triumphed on the Eastern Shore of Virginia. The law of the land prohibited the manufacture and sale of alcoholic beverages, thanks to the energies of the people in the churches. Two Eastern Shore women were spreading the gospel in overseas missions. Eastern Shore churchgoers were sending money all around the world for Christian causes, and worshiping at home in finer buildings and finer clothes than ever before. Among them, the denominations could claim 164 congregations in the two counties, one church for every 321 persons.

Small wonder that the *Accomack News* could make this boast:

> *Strangers coming to Accomack County are struck with the appearance of the churches in general. They all show that the people are generous and painstaking along that line. In almost every town there are two or more churches, and the rural districts are also taken care of. There is truly no reason for any one in Accomack County staying from church on account of distance.*[41]

The same could be said of Northampton as well. Let the Holiness people rail, in the minds of most people in this most Methodist of areas, the churches had never been in finer form.

By the early 1930's, by which time William Vickers had preached virtually everywhere on the Shore, it was obvious that Methodism would have no difficulty surviving the Holiness challenge, and that on the Eastern Shore of Virginia the Holiness people were destined to remain a small minority.

The 1930's found the Pilgrim Holiness presence on the Shore limited to a few communities. In northern Accomack were the three original congregations: Bloxom (by now the largest on the Shore), Grotons, and Saxis. In the central part of the Shore were two more recent congregations. Quinby and Oakland Park, which were still meeting in private homes. In Cape Charles was an even newer congregation whose first house of worship would not be erected until 1940. The church in Chincoteague had been abandoned, that in Wachapreague was about to be abandoned, and Holiness preaching in Chesconnessex had not yet issued into a separate congregation (when it did, in 1951, the Holiness people of Chesconnessex would leave the Pilgrim Holiness Church for another denomination).

The 1930's found Christ's Sanctified Holy Church in Chincoteague on the verge of an outburst of energy and growth. Never having fully abandoned its hope of evangelizing that portion of Maryland that lay between Chincoteague and Delaware, the Sanctified congregation spent the next two decades crisscrossing Worcester County with a portable tabernacle that saw service in Stockton, Girdletree, and Ironshire in Maryland, and Greenbackville and Signpost in Virginia. By 1943 the Chincoteague congregation had grown so large that it purchased the old Methodist Protestant property downtown and held services there, in a much more spacious building. Such growth was, however, short-lived. By the 1950's the

Sanctified congregation was declining in numbers, and was back in its smaller building on the northern end of the island.

Despite the consternation that it caused on the Shore, despite the heated discussions and the tireless efforts of men like William Vickers, the Holiness movement approached its half-century mark still a minority movement on the Shore. By 1944, the Pilgrim Holiness congregations could together muster only 115 members, and it is doubtful that there were ever more than 200 white Holiness people on the Shore at any one time. The strength and importance of the movement were, of course, greater than the small number of adherents would indicate. For one thing, Holiness churches had a rigorous standard of membership. Members, after all, were only those who were specifically called out from the world to the experience, or at least to the pursuit, of sanctification. Unlike the Methodists and the Baptists of the time, Holiness people could boast that the number of persons who attended their services and participated in the life of their churches was usually greater than the actual membership, often as much as twice as great. In sheer numbers, then, there were probably as many white Holiness Christians on the Shore by the mid-1940's as there were Episcopalians.*

For the most part, the Holiness movement made its way most strongly among the poorer people of the Shore, and the Depression intervened in the life of many of the budding congregations just in time to keep them poor and small and struggling. The Holiness people made up for this fact, however, by spirited discipleship. In 1940 the 115 Pilgrim Holiness members on the Shore had a per capita giving rate more than twice that of the Shore's 10,000 Methodists. The comparison illustrates how much Methodism had become like the established church it had once challenged.

The real impact of the Holiness movement was not, finally, in numbers, which only in a small way altered the religious complexion of the Shore. The real legacy of Joseph Lynch and William Vickers and Annie Pearson was not that they had founded new churches, but that they also altered the course of the Methodist church from which they withdrew. Methodism survived the theological challenge from within its own tradition, but it was changed irrevocably in the struggle. Although by 1940 it was obvious that the great host of Methodists on the Shore would remain comfortably Methodist, the lines were now clearly drawn. Something that had always before been present in the Methodist churches — some old teaching, no matter now weak or neglected, that perfection was attainable in this life, and that the simple holy life was the way to attain it — that old belief was now the property of someone else. Methodism might remain large and strong, but as it put the struggle behind itself, it was very obviously never going to be quite the same again.

In May 1945, William Vickers arrived in Cape Charles to preach a two-week revival. Sister Mary Garrett was in the fifth year of her sixteen-year pastorate at the Pilgrim Holiness church there, and as they talked together during the week Vickers confided to her that he had preached over 10,000 sermons in his lifetime, and that he wanted nothing more than to continue his evangelistic career in full force until he should "die in the pulpit." He was 63 years old and not feeling

*Holiness membership is difficult to measure since many of the churches, chief among them the Church of God (Anderson, Indiana), do not maintain formal membership rolls. Though many black congregations of the Eastern Shore bear the name "Holiness," they are without exception not "Holiness," but "Pentecostal," in doctrine (see Chapter XI).

especially well. Perhaps he was indulging in some reflections upon the accomplishments of his life.

On the evening of May 16, services began in the little frame building on the corner of Madison and Strawberry, and Vickers seemed strangely subdued during the opening song service. When he rose to preach, he chose as his text that favorite of Holiness preachers, "Ye must be born again." He preached no less spiritedly than usual, although he did cut his sermon unusually short. Then, as always, he gave an altar call, repeating the text and adding, "Now what are you going to do about that?"

Those were his last words, he clasped his hands suddenly to his chest and collapsed, dead in his pulpit.[42]

Vickers was by then a man revered by his people. His body was taken to Cambridge, where four days later he was buried before 2000 people who attended the funeral. The mound of flowers sent by loved ones and admirers was said to have been nothing less than immense. Twenty-nine Pilgrim Holiness preachers served as honorary pallbearers. The funeral sermon was preached by his old friend, the former Methodist, T. S. Dixon.

Few men had ever labored as hard as he had on the Eastern Shore or hoped so much to change the people of the peninsula. Yet he died with his work incomplete. The Eastern Shore of Virginia was still, by and large, a Methodist area. Had every Holiness person on the Shore gathered in one place to do him homage at his death, they would not have been able to fill Metropolitan Methodist Church, one of many black churches that dotted the rural countryside. With him passed the fear of the local Methodists that the Holiness people would claim their Shore.

Little did they foresee, however, that William Vickers was but one of many, that new forces were arising to challenge Methodism on the Shore, and that Methodism's vast numerical advantage in Accomack and Northampton Counties was no guarantee that the church could yet rest from its labors.

Full Circle
1930 to the Present

XI

The great Depression of the 1930's brought to a swift end more than a century of almost continuous growth among the churches of the Eastern Shore of Virginia, and in a real sense the modern period of the history of the churches begins with that great turning point. And yet even before the dark decade of the thirties had rolled around there were signs that at least some of the Shore's churches, so long growing and so long prosperous, were headed for trouble.

In recent years, it has been pointed out that Americans experienced not one but two "depressions" during the first half of the twentieth century. The Great Depression of the 1930's was the second; the first was a religious depression that hit the churches of Protestantism during the 1920's. A new mood of disillusionment beset many of the country's churches after the first World War. Interest in foreign missions and evangelism began to wane, and the prevailing theologies of the major seminaries fell into decline. Well before economic depression hit the nation in the 1930's, church after church across the American countryside had already begun to experience a noticeable decline in contributions and attendance.[1]

On their isolated and rural peninsula, the little churches of the Eastern Shore of Virginia were hardly at the forefront of this new religious depression. Future decades would look back to the twenties as the high point and the thirties as the low point in the history of the Shore's churches. And yet even before the end of the twenties there were signs that here, too, some sort of decline was already in motion, a decline which would be hastened and intensified by the economic Depression to follow. The Methodist Protestants of the Shore must have noticed it after 1928, for their collections dropped sharply after that date to hardly more than half what they had been before. Among all the Methodist denominations of the Shore, 1927 was the year when giving was at its highest. In the 1930's contributions to the local churches would plummet, but by the 1920's the decline had already begun.

On the Shore two local factors helped to set the decline in motion even amid the prosperity of the 1920's. One was the simple fact that the Eastern Shore was over-churched, its population unable to support the many congregations that had sprung up throughout the two counties. A second factor was the migration of its Negro citizens out of the area to the cities of the North, the impact of which began to be felt in the 1920's.

During the decade of the 1920's, well before the Depression itself, no fewer than eight congregations ceased to function on the Shore. With one exception, all were white congregations, and most of them owed their existence to the last attempt of one of the denominations to stake a claim to a new community. The first to close was Eastville Presbyterian Church, which ceased to function in 1920. This congregation, founded in 1904, had never mustered more than ten members and never succeeded in erecting a building. Throughout its brief life its members worshiped in the YMCA building that stood on the present site of the firehouse in Eastville.

A string of closings followed: Goodwill M.E. (founded 1876, merged 1922); Mt. Zion Baptist near Parksley, the lone black congregation among them (founded 1920, mortgaged 1924, and closed soon afterwards); Nassawadox M.E., South (founded 1908, closed after 1924); Greenview Presbyterian (founded 1919, closed 1926); Painter M.E., South (founded 1905, merged 1927); Macon Union Chapel (founded 1904, closed about 1927); and Christ Episcopal Church in Bloxom (founded 1896, closed 1929). Most of these churches were young; Greenview Presbyterian, for instance, had been in existence only seven years when it was abandoned. Most of them were small; Christ Episcopal never had a membership of more than eighteen, and only Goodwill among them all had ever had a sizeable membership. Four of the congregations simply merged back into the churches from which they had been so hopefully created: Goodwill with Christ M.E., Painter with Garrison's, Nassawadox with Franktown, and Greenview with Powelton.

Meanwhile from the black communities of the Shore a small trickle of people seeking better opportunities in the North soon widened into a steady stream. Young black citizens of the shore, and in some cases older ones or even entire families, packed up their belongings and sought their fortunes elsewhere. Philadelphia and its environs, and to a lesser extent New York and Baltimore, absorbed most of the exodus. The 1920 census showed that the population of Accomack County was already declining. The Oak Hall Charge of the Delaware Conference, St. John's and Mt. Zion churches, was seriously depleted in membership by as early as 1917 because of these migrations. By the mid-twenties Freewill in Chincoteague and Deas Chapel in Horntown, the latter one of the strongest black churches on the Shore, had felt the loss of significant numbers of members. For many a black congregation on the Shore, the 1920's were not a period of prosperity, but a time when the churches felt the loss of many of their most valuable and energetic members.

When the Great Depression came, it came gradually. The stock market crash of 1929 was not generally felt across the Shore at first. It took a year or two of economic distress and bad crops to plunge the whole populace into the Depression, but by 1934 the full impact was felt.[2] In the difficult years that followed no part of Shore life suffered more than church life. And no part of Shore life was to emerge from that period more changed.

It was not for lack of members that the churches suffered on the Shore during the Depression, at least not among the Methodists. Northern Methodist membership actually increased during the 1930's, bolstered by a strong influx of new members at Tangier, whose congregation swelled to 730 by 1938. Southern Methodist membership rose steadily, if not spectacularly, throughout the decade, and only the Methodist Protestants suffered an actual loss.

The churches suffered for lack of contributions, not members. In the two years after 1930 the missionary giving of the white Baptists in the two counties dropped by over $3000. By 1936 Methodists on the Shore were giving less than 50 percent of what they had been putting in the collection plate in 1927. In 1934 the southern church, largest and strongest denomination on the Shore, received from its members only a little more than a third of what they had contributed in 1931. It was not until 1945 that Eastern Shore Methodists were again giving to their churches as much per member per year as they had in 1927.

And statistics do little to convey the struggle that each of the local churches faced. In 1933 the Tangier minister received only two-thirds of his salary, even though a hundred new members had joined the church there two years earlier. The money was simply not there to be paid him. The members of Hallwood Methodist Protestant Church, determined to meet their obligations despite the general lack of money, cut down trees on their farms, carted them to the sawmill where they were cut into lumber, and gave the proceeds to their struggling church. The blacks faced the hardest struggle of all. A. F. Winder, pastor of Burton's Methodist Episcopal Church during the Depression, often passed the offering plate and saw it return to its place on the table with only 35¢ or 50¢ on it.[3]

Up and down the Shore the Depression forced the closing of church doors on what had been strong and venerable churches. Six churches closed early in the decade: Bethel M.P. in Chincoteague, Conquest Chapel M.P., Ayres Chapel M.E., Crowsontown M.E., Townsend M.E., South, and the Pilgrim Holiness Tabernacle in Chincoteague. Within a year or two St. Michael's Episcopal Church in Belle Haven was virtually defunct. Harborton Baptist, having dwindled to a small number by the late 1920's, last reported to the Accomack Association in 1932. The on-again, off-again Pilgrim Holiness church in Wachapreague was finally abandoned in 1935. Two churches of the Delaware Conference, Freewill in Chincoteague and John Wesley in Exmore, closed in 1937. In 1938 an entire Methodist Protestant circuit vanished when old Lee Mont church burned and Grant Memorial in Tasley was destroyed by a storm. Although both fell to natural and not economic forces, the local members had neither the funds nor the energy to build them back, and 120 persons were lost to the Methodist Protestant rolls. By 1939 the Accomack Baptist Association had lost three more churches: Saxis, Makemie Park, and Taylor Memorial. And by the end of the decade Messongo Primitive Baptist Church stood empty and abandoned, pulpit and Bible still in place and no longer used by the handful of surviving members.

In all, one-fifth of the white Baptist churches on the Shore in 1920 were gone by 1940, one-fifth of the Episcopalian churches, one-third of the Methodist Protestant churches. Those congregations that managed to survive struggled through the most difficult period of their lives. Adams and Metropolitan, the two churches of the Wiseville Circuit that had for years been the pride of the Delaware Conference were by 1935 "considerably reduced." Deas Chapel by 1937 had sunk "seemingly...to the very lowest possible for maintenance." Burton's M.E. was, its presiding elder reported in 1935, very nearly "dead." Five black congregations had their church buildings sold out from under them for want of funds to pay off the mortgages: St. Joseph's A.M.E. (1933), St. John's Baptist (1934), Snead's M.E. (1936), Mt. Hope M.E. (1936), and Bethel A.M.E. in Eastville. Though each of the five managed to survive the decade and ultimately to reclaim its building, the struggle to do so was immense. Bethel in Eastville, for instance, owed $9000 on its building, a debt incurred during the most prosperous 1920's when a great many improvements had been made and a new parsonage erected. The Depression intervened to make it impossible for the congregation to raise so great a sum, and during the early 1940's the church withdrew from the Virginia Conference (A.M.E.) while its members worked "diligently and faithfully" to buy back their church.[4]

BETHEL A.M.E. CHURCH (Eastville)

Three Annual Conferences have convened on this spot, in 1883 in an earlier building, and in this building in 1913 and 1950.

Never had the churches of the Shore experienced such a sapping of energy and enthusiasm as during the Depression. Previous periods of trial had been known to bring about religious revival; this one did not. As families struggled simply to survive, churches took a back seat. The Accomack Baptist Association did not even convene in 1933, the only time since at least 1831 that that body failed to gather.

As if to add insult to injury, the year 1933 brought the repeal of Prohibition, as the constitutional amendment for which so many men and women of the Shore had preached and prayed and worked for so long went down to defeat. Accomack voted to retain the amendment, Chincoteague, Accomac, Craddockville, and Harborton alone of its precincts voting "wet." Northampton's vote was overwhelmingly "wet," not a single community voting in favor of retaining Prohibition. In Eastville the vote was 119 to four in favor of repeal. On the Shore as elsewhere this defeat of a favorite cause was "the greatest blow to their pride and self-confidence that Protestants as a collective body had ever experienced."[5] To many a churchman of the two counties it must have seemed as if the banner of Christ were everywhere in retreat.

When finally the decade was over and some of the old prosperity began gradually to creep back into the churches, it was a different scene that Eastern Shore Christians faced. The modern period witnessed an entirely new religious landscape on the Shore. The great gulf of the Depression had been bridged, but with better times came momentous changes.

Methodism, the predominant faith on the Shore, was the first to recover from the dark decade of the Depression, and its people were aided by an important development on the national scene: Unification.

In April 1939 twelve thousand Methodists from all parts of the country gathered in Kansas City to effect the long-worked-for and long-awaited unification of American Methodism. They arrived as delegates of the Methodist Episcopal Church, the Methodist Episcopal Church, South, and the Methodist Protestant Church, and they stayed to vote their respective denominations out of existence. When they left, the three branches of Methodism had been united into The Methodist Church.[6]

With Unification, Methodism on the Eastern Shore of Virginia was itself reunited, or almost so. For the first time since 1832, when David Watt had led his congregation into the Methodist Protestant Church, the Eastern Shore of Virginia was once again a distinct Methodist entity: the Eastern Shore District of the Virginia Annual Conference of the Southeastern Jurisdiction of The Methodist Church. Judging from numbers alone, the southern church had surpassed its rivals during those old days of competition and duplication before Unification. The Methodist Protestants contributed ten congregations and 885 members to the new district. The Methodist Episcopal Church contributed fewer congregations, only seven churches, but considerably more people, 1467 members. By far the largest of the three denominations on the Shore at Unification was the southern church, whose 37 congregations contained an even 7900 members.* Altogether there were 9995 members in the new Eastern Shore District in 1940; about one-fifth of the inhabitants of the two counties were on these Methodist rolls.

It was not, however, a complete union. The African Methodist Episcopal Church remained a separate denomination. Even more noticeably absent from the fold were the black churches of the former Methodist Episcopal Church. Unification did not result in equality for black and white Methodists. All Negro congregations in the new church were placed in a separate unit, the Central Jurisdiction, with the result that local black churches were not related to the circuits, districts, and conferences in which they were located geographically. The twelve black Methodist congregations on the Shore in 1939 were not made a part of the new Eastern Shore District, but were placed in the Central Jurisdiction, where they remained a part of the Delaware Conference. Nationally, Unification was achieved at a high price on the race question; locally, communication between the white and black congre-

*The southern church had its own Eastern Shore District prior to 1939, extending all the way north to Cambridge, Maryland. Seventeen former southern churches with a membership of over 3100 in this area were included in the new Peninsula Conference, created in 1939, comprising Delaware and the Eastern Shore of Maryland.

gations of The Methodist Church on the Shore remained virtually nonexistent for another generation.

Nor was it a real union at the local level, for very few Shore communities witnessed the merger of local congregations. There were only two such local mergers, at opposite ends of the Shore. In 1939 Bethany (M.E.) and Centenary (M.E., South) in Cape Charles voted unanimously to merge and took the name Trinity. In 1941 Greenbackville (M.P.) merged with Grace (M.E.), whose building had been destroyed by fire; these two churches took the name Union.* Such mergers were, however, the exception and not the rule. In Onancock in particular two churches of the same denomination now stood on the same street within a few blocks of each other, yet Cokesbury (M.E.) and Market Street (M.E., South) remained steadfastly separate. Since, too, there was no attempt made to incorporate the Central Jurisdiction churches into the District, a number of communities now had both black and white Methodist churches that were, for the first time, in the same denomination: New Church (Berea and St. Mark's), Wattsville (Wattsville and Friendship), Horntown (Horntown and Deas Chapel), Atlantic (Atlantic and St. John's), Keller (Mears Memorial and Mt. Hope), Wachapreague (Ocean View and Grace), and, after 1948, Exmore (Epworth and Spence Memorial).

There were now new tasks and new opportunities to be faced because Eastern Shore Methodism was united. Circuits, now called "charges," had to be rearranged to make better geographical units where before the denominations had overlapped. Charge alignments shifted frequently for a decade or more after Unification until they became fixed by about the mid-1950's. The presiding elder, now called the "district superintendent," was provided with a "district parsonage" in Parksley in 1941. As the years passed, task gave way to opportunity and local Methodists tackled larger projects that had not been possible when they were divided among three denominations. In 1948 the District bought a home in Cheriton for the use of retired preachers. In 1959 a farm on Occohannock Creek west of Craddockville was purchased, and the District opened Camp Occohannock, a camping and retreat center equipped at a cost of over $100,000. Seven years later the Virginia Conference erected a modern retirement home called the Hermitage in Onancock, a two-million-dollar facility to which Eastern Shore Methodists subscribed about one-fourth the cost.

Statistically and materially, the churches prospered after Unification. By 1949, Methodit membership on the Virginia Shore had passed the 11,000 mark, an all-time high. In the fifteen years after 1949, no fewer than sixteen Methodist churches in the two counties erected educational buildings or made major new additions to their church plants, more than one each year. The ability of the local congregations to build and maintain facilities was perhaps best exemplified by Grace Methodist Church in Parksley. That congregation dedicated a large educational annex costing $87,000 in 1955. Just as the debt on the new building was being liquidated in 1958, the parsonage burned to the ground and had to be replaced. A new house was ready by 1959, and the congregation was still able in 1966 to spend $13,000 to rebuild its pipe organ. Ten years later they replaced their ailing brick church with a brand new structure that cost over $350,000.

*Prior to this merger, Grace, although located in Virginia, had been a part of the Peninsula Conference, and the Greenbackville Charge had included one church, Portersville, which was located in Maryland. With the creation of Union Church, Portersville was given to Peninsula, Grace's members to Virginia, and the state line became in fact the boundary between the two conferences.

But even amid such signs of progress, there were evidences of waning which statistical and material prosperity could not hide. After 1949, a slow but steady decline in membership set in among the Methodist churches of the Shore, a decline interrupted only briefly when the Central Jurisdiction churches were at last absorbed into the District in 1969. By 1975 membership in Methodist churches on the Shore, black and white combined, was only about equal to what it had been among the whites alone at Unification, some 10,300 members. Part of the decline can be explained by the Shore's declining population, but many a local congregation saw the number of its worshipers dwindle in fact. Some of the churches dwindled in size almost to the point of extinction; the average number of Sunday worshipers in 1975 showed a number of venerable congregations reduced to just a few persons: Horntown (ten), Mears Memorial (fifteen), Locustville (twelve), Wattsville (seventeen).

Nor did membership figures themselves mean what they once had. In the early days of Methodism on the Shore, the churches had a rigorous standard of membership. The half-hearted were not likely to find their way into actual membership, and were not likely to remain there if they did. The result was that many more people attended Methodist services and participated in the life of Methodist churches than the membership figures suggest. By the end of the Depression, however, the opposite condition prevailed, a trend that had been long years in the making. Membership was now easily had and seldom terminated, and an increasingly high percentage of the "members" of the local churches of the Shore were members in name only. In 1939 the white Methodist Episcopal churches in the two counties listed fourteen percent of their members as "inactive." A decade later fully 21 percent of the white Methodists of the Shore were officially "inactive." By 1969, a generation after Unification, only about 38 percent of the Methodists on the local rolls bothered to attend worship on any given Sunday.

The impulse for founding new churches ground almost completely to a halt among the Methodists after Unification. Only two new congregations were founded by The Methodist Church on the Shore after 1939 — Spence Memorial in Exmore, and Tasley, both established in 1948. Within twenty years both of them had disappeared from the scene. The only lasting Methodist congregation founded on the Shore after 1939 was Coles Chapel A.M.E., founded in Bayview in 1954.

The second half of the twentieth century found The Methodist Church strong and prosperous on the Eastern Shore of Virginia. But where it had once been growing, it was now only stable, and the church that had once seemed remarkably vital now seemed curiously static.

The non-Methodist churches of the Shore found the years after the Depression to be also a time of prosperity, if not of growth. Between 1949 and 1966, Southern Baptists of the Eastern Shore spent over $800,000 on new buildings and furnishings, including more than $100,000 each for completely new churches at Bethel (1949) and Exmore (1952). During the same period they founded no new congregations and lost one, Cedar Grove, to merger in 1956. The year 1974 found Southern Baptist membership on the Shore almost exactly what it had been in 1939: about 4500 persons, of whom fully 21 percent were "non-resident members."

Black Baptists, always less intent upon recording membership statistics, were no less enthusiastic about new facilities. They erected new church buildings at St. Mark's in Melfa (1946), Union in Eastville (1950), and Metompkin (1959), and founded an entirely new congregation named Gospel Temple in Keller in 1965. Among their many other churches that expanded or improved their facilities during the same period were African, Bethel, Cape Charles, Capeville, Jerusalem, and New Mt. Zion.

Only two denominations showed real and permanent growth on the Shore after the Depression: Episcopalians and Roman Catholics. By 1975, Episcopalian membership in the two counties had climbed to 626, the highest ever and an increase of more than 35 percent since 1940. Of the seven Episcopalian congregations on the Shore, only one did not build a new structure or a major addition between 1949 and 1966. Roman Catholic growth was even more rapid, reaching 523 in the two counties in 1972.[8] Two new Catholic congregations were founded: St. Peter's in Onley (1942) and St. Andrew's in Chincoteague (1949). Presbyterian membership on the Shore peaked in the mid-1950's, and twenty years later there were fewer than 600 Presbyterians in the two counties. Yet between 1955 and 1959 these seven small congregations added three new educational buildings to their churches and erected two new parsonages.* The only new denomination to succeed in establishing a permanent congregation on the Shore after 1940 was Lutheran (Missouri Synod); First Lutheran Mission of Cheriton was founded in 1975.

When once they put the Depression behind them, the denominational churches of the Shore entered a period not of growth, but of stability. The major denominations, Methodism chief among them, held their own, safe and secure with, at worst, some slight decline, their patterns fixed and comfortable. In these denominations, Eastern Shore Christians attended prosperous and successful churches, their buildings increasingly larger and better, their activities increasingly defined by the several denominational headquarters off the Shore. The evangelism of the Shore seemed to them complete, the two counties more than adequately carved up among the denominations. It was a godly area where the Church was still taken seriously by its people. Peace and prosperity reigned, and local churchmen were content to satisfy themselves with ecclesiastical housekeeping.

What so many churchgoers failed to notice was the tremendous swirl of religious activity around them outside the denominations. For the years after 1939 brought new movements, new doctrines, new religious issues and activities to the Eastern Shore. The excitement generated by these new movements was often found among the poorer and less privileged people of the peninsula, and the new churches that sprang up were often on back streets or in remote regions where the people of the mainline churches did not notice them. But while the Shore's denominations settled down into comfortable routines, completely new patterns of religious life began to emerge up and down the peninsula. And much of the religious history of the Shore since the Depression is the story of entirely new sects and movements, not of the older denominations.

Much as Methodism had once been a movement of simple people outside the walls of the Church of England, so now did much of the Shore's new religious

*Despite their long histories, these three denominations — Episcopalian, Presbyterian, and Roman Catholic — remain at best a small presence on the Eastern Shore of Virginia today. There are almost as many Methodists and Baptists on roll in the two churches of Chincoteague Island alone as in these three denominations combined.

activity take place outside the "established" denominations.

Eastern Shore Methodism had come full circle.

The years after the Depression brought to the Eastern Shore of Virginia an almost bewildering diversity of new churches and movements among all classes of society, black and white. But generally the religious activity outside the major denominations falls into one of four categories:

(1) the advent of Pentecostalism

(2) the emergence of conservative fundamentalism in specific reaction to the denominations

(3) the emergence of the indigenous, black, preacher-centered church, and

(4) the importation of new, often unusual sects from off the Shore.

Although these categories were not always separate and distinct — some of the movements weaved back and forth among them with confusing frequency, some churches representing not just one but two or even three of the categories — most of the seemingly confusing swirl of persons, issues, and movements outside the denominations can be made comprehensible with these categories.

First and foremost among them, both chronologically and in influence, was Pentecostalism.

Pentecostalism is Christianity rooted in an emphasis upon and the experience of the third person of the Trinity, the Holy Spirit. It takes its name from the events described in the second chapter of Acts, where on the day of Pentecost the disciples of Jesus received a remarkable infusion of the presence and power of the Holy Spirit. Such experiences of the Spirit are, Pentecostals insist, not only available to Christians today, but also central to the very meaning of salvation and the Christian life. The infusion of the Spirit is called the "baptism" in the Holy Spirit, the most important sign of which is usually understood to be the ability to speak "with other tongues as the Spirit gives utterance." Other "gifts of the Spirit" sought and practiced by Pentecostals include prophecy and healing.

Pentecostalism grew up alongside the Holiness movement and to a certain extent came out of it, stepping one step farther away from its Methodist antecedents than the Holiness people. The modern Pentecostal movement is usually traced to Charles F. Parham, a Methodist minister, and to the Bible college that he founded in Kansas in 1900. There on January 1, 1901, one of his students was visited with the experience of speaking in a tongue that she did not understand. A general baptism in the Spirit, manifested by such tongues, swept across the campus and out into the surrounding countryside. When it reached California in 1906, there occurred a remarkable revival at the Azusa Street Mission in Los Angeles that lasted day and night for almost three years. The Azusa Street revival became the impetus for the sudden spread of the movement across the nation and into other countries.

In a real sense the Pentecostal movement was a further extension of Holiness thought and practice. There were, said most Pentecostals, not two but three separate and distinct steps to salvation that God visits upon his people: justification, sanctification, and the baptism in the Holy Spirit. Much of the early movement made its headway among the Holiness groups, many of whom at first called themselves a

"Pentecost" people. By 1925, however, the two movements had separated, and "Pentecostal" came to describe the "third-blessing" or tongues-speaking churches. Like the Holiness movement, the early Pentecostal movement created a great many new church bodies that frequently shifted, merged, and divided. Like the Holiness movement, it grew rapidly, at first at cultural levels which the major denominations found easy to ignore. The movement began as an interracial movement, and the Azusa Street revival is remarkable for its interracial fellowship at a time of heightened racial tensions, but by the time it found its way to the Eastern Shore of Virginia, black and white Pentecostals had separated into segregated churches.[9]

Pentecostalism entered the Eastern Shore of Virginia via Cape Charles, when in 1929 a black preacher from Norfolk named Sister Kellam arrived and gathered a small congregation. Within a short time Sister Kellam's preaching had borne fruit, and blacks in Cape Charles were experiencing the baptism in the Holy Spirit. Like most Pentecostals of that day, the Cape Charles congregation was far from affluent, and Sister Kellam's congregation attracted little notice. They met for years in homes and various buildings around the town, their worship characterized by the public practice of speaking in tongues, congregational excitement, and a literal belief in the possibility of divine healing. Sister Kellam ultimately moved on to establish other congregations off the Shore, but not before the Cape Charles church produced a strong leader of its own in James Davis. In 1937 the congregation purchased its first building, the abandoned colored school property in Cape Charles, and established there the Philadelphia Church of Christ Disciples. By then there were several other congregations founded by Sister Kellam, and all of them looked to the Cape Charles church as the mother church of the sect.

Over the next several years four other churches of this sect were established on the Eastern Shore of Virginia: Mt. Olive in Accomac (1937), Mt. Olive in Exmore (1944), Weirwood Happy Mission (1945), and Pentecostal House of Prayer near Birdsnest (1956). But the sect remained a small and struggling enterprise. By 1960 the mother church in Cape Charles had dwindled to hardly more than a handful of people. Bishop James Davis, Jr., assumed the pastorate in 1969 and restored the church to its former vigor. With about thirty members, the Cape Charles congregation is the largest church of this sect on the Virginia Shore today.

White Pentecostalism entered the Shore from the opposite direction. In 1937, Clarence J. Abbott, a pastor in the Church of God (Cleveland, Tennessee) — one of the largest Pentecostal churches in the nation and one of dozens to bear the name Church of God — pitched a tent on the present site of Chincoteague High School and began a revival. By the end of the year 38 people had embraced the new faith, manifested the tongues-speaking experience, and organized the Church of God of Chincoteague. They held their meetings in William Vickers' abandoned Holiness Tabernacle until 1948, when they erected their own church next door. The Chincoteague church was the only white Pentecostal congregation on the Shore until 1950, and the only Church of God (Cleveland, Tennessee) congregation until a second was founded in Melfa in 1977.

A third Pentecostal church found its way to the Shore in 1941 when Lily

Pertilder came as a missionary and gathered a small congregation in Cheapside in Northampton. Pertilder represented the Mt. Sinai Holy Church of America, Inc., founded in a storefront building in Philadelphia in 1924 by Bishop Ida Robinson. By 1945 the Mt. Sinai Holy Church in Cheapside had erected a small house of worship there.

This Pentecostal import from Philadelphia met with greater success on the Shore than either of its predecessors, principally because of Estelle Dillard Smith, a preacher who rose from the local ranks. Smith was a member of the Cheapside congregation when in 1942 she began to preach in the Fairview area. Within a short time her services had overflowed into ever larger buildings, and Bishop Robinson had set her apart as pastor of the second Mt. Sinai congregation on the peninsula. Smith and her congregation bought the abandoned building of St. Paul's A.M.E. Church in Fairview, a structure dating from 1869, and refitted it for worship in 1943. In 1948 she founded her second church, Mt. Zion Holy Church, in the old Reese Chapel building in Bayside north of Onancock. Later she founded a third church in Norfolk.

Doctrinally the Mt. Sinai churches were fully Pentecostal: membership depended not only upon conversion and sanctification, but also some experience (usually speaking in tongues) of the baptism of the Holy Spirit. Membership, once obtained, could be abrogated for failure to continue in a holy life, and among the practices that Bishop Robinson condemned were divorce, finery in dress and appearance, and drinking intoxicants. The church was black and proud of it, and the founding bishop also frowned upon the widespread practice of straightening the hair artificially.[10]

Smith's Fairview Church grew steadily across the years and became the largest Pentecostal congregation on the Eastern Shore of Virginia. She herself designed the several additions and improvements that were made to the building there. In 1975 she was ordained a bishop.

By 1950 Pentecostalism on the Shore was beginning to reflect some of the growing diversity of doctrine within Pentecostal ranks nationally. In that year Paul Boyce, a pastor of the Assemblies of God, brought that new faith to Accomack County, where Faith Assembly of God was established in Lee Mont. In 1951 the Reverend Julian Goggin and his wife carried a portable tabernacle into Northampton and established the faith there as well. The Assemblies of God had a different understanding of Pentecostal doctrine from any yet seen on the Shore. Salvation, they taught, consists of only two steps, not three: sanctification and the baptism in the Holy Spirit are virtually the same thing. Even further removed from most other Pentecostals was the Church of the Lord Jesus Christ of the Apostolic Faith, a black congregation founded by S. C. Johnson in Cape Charles in 1953. This was the first "Oneness" or "Jesus Only" congregation on the Shore. Pentecostals of this persuasion baptized in the name of Jesus only and argued against Trinitarian understandings of the nature of God.

The 1970's brought a new wave of Pentecostals called "Charismatics" or "neo-Pentecostals" to the Shore. At first this Holy Spirit Christianity had left the major denominations untouched, but now affluent whites in the older churches began to experience the baptism in the Holy Spirit. Baptist laymen from Exmore were the first to experience the baptism, and they subsequently founded the Christian Love Center in Melfa and the Teaching the Way Center in Mappsburg, two short-lived endeavors. Rock Church of the Eastern Shore, a mission of an independent Charismatic congregation in Virginia Beach, was established in Onley in 1976, and inherited some of the members of these earlier movements.

In short, within half a century of its introduction to the Eastern Shore of Virginia, Pentecostalism became one of the major Christian faiths of the peninsula. Some thirty Pentecostal congregations were founded in the two countries between 1929 and 1977, of which about two-third were black. Since many of the local churches did not maintain strict records of membership, it is difficult to estimate the strength of Pentecostalism on the Shore, but by 1977 only Methodists and Baptists could claim more congregations in the two counties than Pentecostals, and there were more Pentecostal congregations than Episcopalian, Presbyterian, and Roman Catholic churches combined. From a handful of poor blacks in Cape Charles in 1929, this largely unrecognized phalanx of churches had grown into perhaps the third largest Christian group on the Shore.

A second frequently-occurring motif on the religious scene of the Shore since the Depression is what might well be called the "conservative reaction." In Methodist circles the old Holiness arguments against the growing modernity and liberalness of the church continued to find adherents. Gradually, however, the conservative reaction lost its Holiness moorings and became a fundamentalist thrust. Unlike Pentecostalism this movement emerged principally among the whites of the Shore, and chiefly among the Methodists and the Baptists.

And no community felt its impact more than Tangier.

Few persons would have referred to the Eastern Shore of Virginia, or to Tangier in particular, as a liberal or progressive place in the 1940's. It was a staunchly rural area, conservative and traditional in outlook. The Methodist churches in Saxis, Harborton, and Tangier could still boast the weekly "class meeting," an ancient institution that had long since withered away virtually everywhere else in Methodism. In 1940 municipal ordinances in Tangier still legislated a strict, Methodist-style Sabbath, and local authorities had been known to arrest citizens for such infractions as sitting on the front porch of the house when they should have been in church. Yet it was in Tangier that the conservative reaction was to take on new life and new forms.

In 1943 James C. Richardson became the pastor of the Methodist church in Tangier, and his pastorate there became for Richardson personally a time of great spiritual quest. The catalyst for Richardson's quest was Stella Thomas, an islander recently returned from several years as a missionary in Africa. Like Miss Thomas, Richardson became convinced that the modern church and its people were in need of a deeper commitment and a greater spirituality than they were currently practicing. His parishioners noticed a decided shift towards this direction in his preaching, and some of them joined him in a regular prayer and study group. In 1946 Richardson decided to hold daily morning services in the church, in addition to the usual weekly services. He found the church doors, however, locked against this endeavor, and the congregation sufficiently exercised that he was assigned to another church by the Conference shortly thereafter.

When Robert F. Bryan, his successor, arrived to assume the pastorate, Richardson elected to remain on the island. He withdrew from the Conference and, with a number of persons from the congregation, established a "House of Prayer" in a rented storehouse on Main Street not far from the Methodist church. The "schism" rocked the island, a community where religion had always been exclusively Methodist. Homes and families were divided by religious differences. In the fall of 1947 the tense situation erupted into violence when unidentified townsfolk broke into the new church, ripped away screens and doors, tossed furniture on the roof, scrawled graffiti on the walls, and threw the organ into the Chesapeake. Richardson himself endured harassment, although the Methodists insisted that such actions were not from any of their number.[11]

In this tense situation the New Testament Congregation, as Richardson's new church was called, took shape. Its principal tenets struck some of the old Holiness chords, although the language and style were different. The Congregation adopted an apostolic model of church government and life and, at Richardson's insistence, a shared "priesthood of all believers" instead of a professional clergy.

For ten years the New Testament Congregation met in private homes or rented buildings on the island. Then in 1956 a simple church building was erected on Main Street south of the Methodist church, by which time Richardson had formed a second Congregation in Deep Creek on the mainland. In 1958 the Methodists invited a "wise old patriarch of the Church," the Reverend Andrew Johnson, to conduct a revival. Johnson was a colorful and forceful speaker, at one time a candidate for Vice-President of the United States on the Prohibition Ticket, and he took as his theme the very "deeper life" issues that had divided the community. When he preached "the doctrines of the deeper life so clearly that it would have been difficult for anyone to misunderstand," a revival occurred that leapt across the lines of controversy, and members of both churches worshiped together fraternally for the first time in twelve years. After 1958 relations between the two Tangier churches became more cordial, but Christianity there remained divided into its liberal and conservative groups.[12]

As early as the 1950's there were signs that the Baptists, too, were vulnerable from the right. Edward Jones, former pastor of the New Church Baptist churches, established a short-lived, independent Bible Church in New Church in 1953. It was Jones' intention to provide a theologically conservative and Biblically literalistic alternative to the neighborhood churches, but Bible Church was remarkable as well for being interracial. The church closed in 1956 and proved to be little of a threat to the Accomack Baptist Association.

The full force of conservative Baptist dissatisfaction came later. In the fall of 1972 Hall's Chapel near Messongo severed its ties with the Association and the Southern Baptist Convention and became Hall's Chapel Church of Christ. Soon new independent Baptist churches began to appear up and down the Shore: Calvary Baptist in Cape Charles in 1969, Central Baptist in Onley in 1975, Baptist Bible Church in Accomac in 1976. All were independent of the Southern Baptist denomination, and avowedly more conservative and fundamentalist. Central Baptist styled itself "the old-fashioned church preaching the old-fashioned gospel." Baptist Bible Church published as a part of its agenda the establishment of a conservative Christian school in Accomack County.

That black Baptists were also not immune from the conservative challenge became obvious in 1974, when Keller Church of Christ was organized by a former Baptist minister. Yet there were fewer conservative inroads into black Baptist churches than white, perhaps because most of the blacks of the Eastern Shore were decidely fundamentalist anyway.

If in the conservative category are included all the churches on the Shore founded from or in reaction to the denominational churches, in opposition to the increasing modernity of the denominations, this remained a smaller movement than Pentecostalism. Counting even the Holiness churches that separated from Methodism as far back as 1892, there are only fifteen specifically "conservative" congregations on the Virginia Shore, all of them quite small. Yet the 1970's found the movement a growing force, particularly among the Baptists, and the coming years were perhaps to bring even more activity on the right.

No churches on the Eastern Shore defy classification more than those of the third category of post-Depression Christianity, the indigenous, black, preacher-centered churches. As often as not these churches were a fleeting part of the religious scene, and it is not improbable that many such churches came and went even before the Depression, leaving no trace behind them. After the Depression, at least, this very different, very black, and very undenominational kind of religion appeared in virtually every section of the Shore.

The most characteristic thing about the churches in this category is that they grew up and centered around dynamic local preachers. As such, they challenged the denominations on the very definition of "church" itself. To the Methodist or Baptist or Presbyterian, "church" almost inevitably meant not simply a building but also, and more important, a group of people, as often as not a group of people stretching from the local scene across the country and around the world. Preachers could come and go; what composed the church was the laity.

Among a significant segment of black society on the Eastern Shore, where the black pastor has always enjoyed a higher status in the community than his white counterpart, an entirely different conception of "church" held sway. For these Christians, the church was defined by the preacher, not by the laity. It was understood to be the preacher who called the church into being, built it, ran it, paid its bills, even owned it outright, and abandoned it when he was through with it. Wherever the preacher happened to be preaching, there was the church. There were no membership rolls and sometimes not even any "members" as such. There was no affiliation with any sect or denomination or any other congregation unless the preacher chose to have it, and then it could be ended at his discretion. Doctrine and teaching were shaped by the preacher, who was independent and accountable only to God. The times of worship as well as the place and manner of worship were set by the preacher. Even the seasons during which the church would be open might depend upon the preacher, who as often as not was also engaged in secular employment and might well be out of the area for extended times.

Many is the Eastern Shore community that has seen the church gathered under these conditions by local black preachers. In Whitesville below Parksley two old abandoned storehouses heard at one time or another the songs and prayers of public worship led by local black preachers. In Keller, Robert Edwards gathered a congregation of his own in a building which he owned and which he used for his own services until 1965, when he sold the building to the Baptists and it became Gospel Temple Baptist Church. Up until the 1950's Moses Simpkins of Accomac, an independent local preacher, had an unusually fine building in which to conduct services. It was the old Methodist church itself, replaced in 1918 by the present structure and used by Simpkins for his own services until it burned.

Typical of the black, preacher-centered church was Gospel Tabernacle, on the southern edge of New Church. Powhatan Barnes erected, established, and named this church in 1946, and there for years gathered his congregation. Barnes' work often carried him away from the Shore for months at a time, but in season Sundays would find him preaching in the Tabernacle. His was a Pentecostal ministry (the hand-lettered sign on the front door advertised Wednesday night healing services), and his congregation poured themselves into worship with a noisy enthusiasm that could be heard half a mile away. When Barnes left the area in 1969, he sold the Tabernacle to Levi Warrington, another local independent preacher. Warrington used the building until his death a short time later, and afterwards others carried on in his stead.

More widely known was Joseph Turner of Atlantic, also called "Papa Joe" by blacks and whites alike. In 1940, Turner established not one but two new churches, St. Joseph Holiness Church in Atlantic and Mt. Olive Holiness Church in Whitesville, Pentecostal churches which he pastored until his death. Turner was the mentor of a number of younger Pentecostal preachers who at various times worked with him or under him. One such protege was John Crippen, who began his ministry under Turner in the 1950's, established his own church near Bloxom in 1962, and in 1975 bought and restored a bigger and better building near Makemie Park which he named St. John's Faith Church. Another pastor who studied under Turner was his own son, M. C. Turner.

The most successful of all the local independent black preachers was, however, Jesse Handshaw. Another Turner protege, Handshaw, a native of Suffolk, began his work in Cape Charles, where with a handful of followers he established Gospel Tabernacle Apostolic Faith Church of God Live On in 1936. A carpenter by trade, Handshaw raised the building with his own hand, and from it slowly but surely his ministry radiated out to other communities. In 1944 he established Grace Mary Tabernacle of the Apostolic Faith Church of God Live On in Melfa, one of a growing number of churches established, erected, and owned by him. In time Handshaw could claim five churches on the Shore — Cape Charles (1936), Melfa (1944), Nassawadox (1960), Trehernville (1973), and Makemie Park (1962) — and the Church of God Live On, of which he was the founder and presiding bishop, numbered not fewer than 53 congregations in Virginia and North Carolina.

Not all of the preacher-centered churches were independent, for some of the other, more centralized sects gathered their congregations in much the same manner. The Firstborn Church of Christ Disciples, described among the Pentecostal churches, depended upon local preachers like Arthur Boggs, Southey Satchell,

A BLACK "PREACHER-CENTERED" CHURCH

Mt. Olive Pentecostal Church of Christ Disciples, located since 1976 in an abandoned store in Hopeton.

Isabelle Finney, and Madeline Beckett for the founding of churches and the spread of the faith. The denominational connection in such instances was sufficiently tenuous to leave the preacher virtually independent, and his congregation "preacher-centered." The Mt. Sinai congregations, though more strongly centralized, also illustrated some of the characteristics of this type of church.

That churches of this sort have come and gone without leaving a trace seems almost certain. Those that managed to enter the written records were usually the more successful ones, those where the preacher was able to purchase the building or advertise in the newspaper or even just paint a name on a sign in front of the building. Ironically, as such churches appeared and disappeared up and down the peninsula, it was most often the building that was remembered by local residents as the "church," when in actual fact the preacher was what made the church, and the building had little or nothing to do with it. It is regrettable that so much of the work of the local independent black preachers must go unsung. They were dynamic and charismatic men and women who worked against impossible odds, including in some cases their own illiteracy. Though their individual names may be forgotten, together they constituted one of the major thrusts of the religious history of the Shore after the Depression.

New faiths imported to the Shore from far-away places constituted a fourth category among the religious movements that emerged after the Depression. Not only were the imports new, most of them were also decidedly different, some of them bordering on what seemed to the Eastern Shoreman to be almost bizarre expressions of Christianity. Taken as a whole they represented the almost infinite variety of belief and practice that abounded in Christianity across America, a variety that did not begin to be felt on the Shore until after the Depression.

The Jehovah's Witnesses were the first of the new imports to find their way to the Shore. An unknown missionary first preached the new faith in the Belle Haven area in 1920, and a second congregation sprang up in Chincoteague in 1926. Both of these congregations remained small and struggling for a number of years. It was not until 1937, when Nathan Knorr, later the national president of the Watchtower Bible and Tract Society, spoke in Exmore that the Witnesses began to increase in number on the Shore. The 1940's found the Exmore congregation worshiping in a new building, and in 1952 when hundreds of Witnesses gathered at Keller Fairgrounds for a three-day assembly, there were more than fifty Eastern Shoremen in attendance.

The Witnesses proclaimed a radically adventist message: the world was already in its last age, and the final consummation of time was near. Door to door they "published" their urgent appeal to separate from the worldly and prepare for the end by study and proper living. Perhaps because they attacked false teaching in the churches as well as outside them, and questioned the very heart of orthodox Christian doctrine, the divinity of Christ and the Trinity, they made little headway among the people of the Shore. By the 1970's there were fewer than 200 Witnesses on the Shore, worshiping in one of the two centers, Exmore or Chincoteague.

In 1946 a Christian Science Society was founded in Parksley. This small group, founded from an earlier society in Pocomoke City, at first gathered private homes and in the local firehouse. In 1952 they erected a building on Adelaide Street, only to dwindle and fade out, their doctrines and practices having failed to take root among more than just a few on the Shore. The year 1975 brought to the Shore the faith most far removed from the doctrines and practices of the mainline churches, Baha'i. Baha'i was of Persian origins, incorporating elements of Judaism, Islam, and Christianity, and it proclaimed the unity of all religions. The small Baha'i group that gathered in Northampton in 1975 consisted of only four persons.

These churches were white, but the same decades brought new black faiths to the Shore, bringing distinctive teachings and practices with them. A faith called the International Brotherhood of Yahshuas Disciples for the Finishing Work Inc. was brought to the Whitesville area in 1968 by Joseph and Earl Vicks of Brooklyn, New York. This sect was strongly oriented to the Old Testament, worshiped on Saturdays instead of Sundays, and used the Hebrew word Yahshua to refer to God. Many of its members came to Whitesville directly from Brooklyn, and lived in a tightly-knit, almost communal existence. Their only theological ally on the Shore was the Smyrna Assembly of Yajshua Disciples in Makemie Park, whose leader Mary Artis, the "Barefoot Prophetess," also emphasized Old Testament practices and a strong community identity.

In 1967 Franklin Barber brought a new faith from Florida to Cape Charles, where the Alpha and Omega Church was established. The church, too, was strongly communal. Its members, not required to live together or to dress distinctively, nonetheless shared meals together at least once a day as a rule. Doctrinally this church was radically perfectionist. The Christian can, it taught, achieve a perfection in this life which will mean that he can live in this body and never die. When this teaching was proclaimed in Cape Charles, it caused considerable comment and theological discussion in the black community.

In one or more of these four categories — Pentecostalism; fundamentalism; the local black, preacher-centered churches; or new imported sects — can be found virtually all of the churches, movements, and issues that made up the religious scene outside the major denominations on the Shore after the Depression. The decades in which these movements were establishing themselves on the Shore were a period of considerable theological ferment and activity, among both whites and blacks, though the denominations themselves settled down to quiet internal housekeeping. The fact that, for the most part, the churchgoers in the major denominations went their way without noticing the mosaic of issues and ideas suggests how the larger churches, Methodism chief among them, had, like the Church of England of Elijah Baker's day, too exalted a view of how well they were ministering to the entire population of the Shore, black and white, rich and poor.

In 1968 in Dallas, Texas, The Methodist Church merged with the Evangelical United Brethren Church (E.U.B.) to form the United Methodist Church. Although with this merger every local Methodist congregation on the Shore, the A.M.E.'s excepted, received a new name, the merger itself seemed a remote issue to a peninsula that had never known an E.U.B. congregation. Far more important to the

Methodists of the Shore was a second impending merger: the assimiliation of the black Central Jurisdiction churches into the Eastern Shore District.

The Central Jurisdiction into which black Methodists were cast in 1939 was never popular among the black congregations of the Shore, to whom it represented enforced segregation and inequality. When the plan for Methodist union had come before the Delaware Conference in 1937, opposition to it was so strong in that body that it took parliamentary maneuvering even to get the measure presented on the floor. When counted, the vote against the proposed union and its proposed Central Jurisdiction was 116 to eighteen among the clergy, and 102 to one among the laity.[13] Even so, the blacks of the peninsula were swept up into The Methodist Church, where for another generation they remained so segregated that white Methodists in the same communities often did not know the name of the nearest black church, or were even unaware that the black church down the street might also be Methodist.

The civil rights movement of the 1960's passed lightly over the Eastern Shore of Virginia, where blacks and whites alike seemed, if not content with the prevailing pattern of segregation, at least unlikely or unwilling to change it. Atlantic Baptist Church was one of the congregations on the Shore who put the question of admitting Negroes to worship to a vote, and in April 1964 it was decided there that "any Negro attending should be seated without rejection or incident." Some weeks later when local Negroes showed up at the Sunday school hour, they were admitted as visitors. The day passed without incident, and the churches of Atlantic remained segregated.[14]

Part of the effect of civil rights on Methodism, however, was the gradual demise of the racially defined Central Jurisdiction. The white annual conferences voted, one after another, to assimilate the black congregations within their boundaries, and the Delaware Conference, which stretched from New York to Wachapreague, was dissolved in two stages beginning in 1964. On April 28, 1965, the Peninsula Conference and others north of it formally absorbed the black congregations within their boundaries, and the Conference was dissolved. The Virginia Conference was not yet ready, however, to absorb the four remaining charges in Accomack and Northampton, and these churches were temporarily transferred to the North Carolina-Virginia Annual Conference, a black conference across the bay to which they had never been related and were not attached geographically.

In 1968, almost three decades after Unification, the 1134 black Methodists of Accomack and Northampton Counties became a part of the Eastern Shore District. The event is remarkable not for its newsworthiness or drama. It was achieved without incident, the only resistance taking the form of the cancellation of some District events by white churches who feared the presence of Negro delegates. Nor was the event remarkable for having solved the racial problems that separated Eastern Shore Methodists; local congregations remained steadfastly segregated, with only clerical and district and conference functions integrated. The importance of the event seemed to be the promise that it held for the future. For the first time in over 100 years blacks and whites were together in the same denomination on an equal basis. Methodism, the strongest faith on the Shore, was now the only large church in the two counties where even administrative integration was a fact. In 1975, Albert Gingrich was appointed pastor of Adams and Metropolitan churches, the first white pastor to serve more than a handful of black Methodists since Reconstruction. His successful ministry there was well received by the parish, proving that old racial barriers could be bridged.

Could the churches of the Eastern Shore overcome that single greatest division that beset its people, the division of virtually all of life, including religion, into black and white? For now the answer seemed to be in the hands of the members of the United Methodist Church.

Going Forward: An Autobiographical Postscript

This story does not just end. But where, at last, does it take us? What are the most recent events, who the latest characters in the still-unfolding narrative?

Many an earlier Methodist might have expected the story to end on a personal note. The people on the preceding pages had a way of insisting that it was quite permissible for the historian to let some of his own life story intrude upon the narrative. Not for them our modern insistence upon a coldly objective, detached story; they were not at all above crossing back and forth over the line that separates history from autobiography. They preferred to write their history as personal memoir, or reminiscence, or in other forms equally as autobiographical. And some of them went so far as to spend thirty or forty pages telling their own life story before moving to the main body of their historical narratives, when they wrote in narrative form.

This autobiographical streak in the Methodist historians of the Shore did not stem from conceit, nor from sloppy writing. Its origins lay much deeper in their understanding of the faith. To them, to proclaim the faith was necessarily to become involved in the telling of one's own religious story. They could not hope, and they rarely tried, to tell the story of the Gospel of Jesus without also telling the story of what the Gospel had done in their lives. Many a sermon boiled down finally to what Jesus Christ had done for me. And many a historical narrative reflected that same autobiographical dimension, always just beneath the surface of the story.

And so it is that this story, too, ends on an autobiographical note. For our last episode we look to Greenbackville in Accomack County, in the mid-1950's, to events in the life of the author. The reason for ending in this manner is not that that place, that time, or that character have any special importance. The reason is, rather, to venture across that line that our ancestors in the faith crossed so boldly. By their lives and actions and ideas they set the stage on which we now live out our lives, faithfully or not. The narrative may draw to a close, but the story lives on and becomes our story.

Today there are thousands of Methodists living on the Eastern Shore of Virginia whose lives have been shaped by all that has been described thus far. What follows is an attempt by just one of them to translate that history into autobiography.

When it is time for me to claim my part in this unfolding narrative, I find myself seated at the church organ. It is not the moment of my own conversion that lingers most vividly in my memory, but my part in providing the music that accompanied conversion at the Annual Revival.

I was twelve years old when I began to play the organ for the worship services at Union Methodist Church in Greenbackville. By then we Methodists had long since evolved into a decorous, even dignified people. We no longer gathered for camp meetings nor shouted at worship, nor conducted worship services with quite so much abandon as our forefathers had done. Joshua Thomas, no doubt, would have found our Sunday mornings rather tame to his tastes.

But once each year when the Annual Revival rolled around, the heritage of our ancestors peeped through, and for two weeks we threw our modern dignities to the winds and poured ourselves with energy and enthusiasm into nightly services that would have made Joshua Thomas feel right at home.

From the organist's bench I was afforded an unusual view of this practice to which all the previous years had brought us. From time immemorial, since long before anyone could remember, revivals had always ended in Altar Calls, and our congregation was long since accustomed to expect them. The final hymn was the crucial moment. It was certain to be a moving hymn — "Just As I Am" or "I Am Coming to the Cross" — and everybody knew that the time between the verses was understood to be the preacher's last chance to save the sinners. From the pew it appeared to be the most natural thing in the world: a verse would end, and likely as not the preacher would issue a fervent "invitation." His appeal ended, the music would resume. It had the smoothness and naturalness of things that had always been.

I had not finished playing for my first Revival, however, when I learned to my shock that the Altar Call was neither natural nor smooth, that the divine power was not visited without human aid, and that my own part in the process of saving souls was crucial. It took the proper interplay of music and words to produce the conversions, the proper reading of cues by the preacher and the organist. The organist's problems were compounded by the fact that he sat with his back to the preacher and most of the congregation, unable to see the one in charge. And I very quickly learned to spend the hymns (and ultimately the entire service) in sheer dread of the end of the verse when the preacher might (but also might not!) speak.

By the beginning of each refrain the old terror would reassert itself: What do I do at the end of the verse? Shall I keep on playing, or pause long enough to give him a chance to speak? What if I pause and he doesn't give an invitation this time? What if I keep playing and he starts to speak at the same time?

Somehow, of course, it would all fall into place. The verse would end, and after a slight pause (not really the eternity that it seemed to the organist to be) the preacher would give an "invitation." With hymnbooks open the people would stand by patiently, with fingers poised over the keys the organist was ready to go at a moment's notice. The invitation would end and the music would resume, proof that the machinery was still in fine working order. And at the end of the next verse the same process, until at last from the back of the room someone would rise to make his way to the front of the church. Success: someone has "come forward!" The old magic still works, the faith lives on!

This is a reminiscence, not a caricature. And the point of the reminiscence is that now, after almost two centuries of Methodist on the Eastern Shore, it is not without considerable human input that people are persuaded to "come forward" and be converted. In Jonathan Edwards' day conversion seemed to come exclusively from God. When Edwards witnessed remarkable conversions in his congregation, he labeled them "The Surprising Work of God," and like others in his day understood such things to be something that God poured out upon his people when and where and how He saw fit. Conversion was not something that people could produce. All they could do was pray for it and wait for it; when and where and how people were to be converted lay hidden in the wisdom of God.

When the Methodists brought their new faith into the Eastern Shore of Virginia, conversion was still by and large "the surprising work of God." Thomas Smith had only to stand in the doorway of Thomas Burton's house on January 1, 1801, and begin to preach; almost immediately, without warning and with little or no human prodding, the "surprising work" struck and brought converted people to their knees. At the Pungoteague campmeeting of 1806, "the work of God broke out in the several tents before a single sermon was preached."[1] The kind of conversion that changed lives and made Methodists needed no help from mere humans.

But already by the time Methodism gained a foothold on the Shore the Great Awakening of Jonathan Edwards and his contemporaries had given way to the Second Great Awakening. And in this new phase of revival men and women felt free to supplement the "surprising work of God" with some of their own efforts, which they called "means." Unwilling or unable to wait patiently for God to pour out his surprising power to convert, Christians began now to add human measures to initiate conversion, or at least to initiate the feelings and actions that often accompanied conversion. Conversion, they were confident, was sure to accompany these signs, no matter how the signs were induced. By the first decade of the nineteenth century the "means" were in widespread use across the Shore: the anxious bench, the camp meeting, and, most lasting of them all, the Altar Call.

And as the years passed, conversion became more and more a matter of applying the proper human means, and less and less a wait upon the surprising work of God. By the time the curtain rises on my own life, the human means seem uppermost in the process.

A glimpse at three Eastern Shore camp meetings will suggest how the work of God became progressively the work of man. The first scene is one we have already visited, the camp meeting in Annemessex where Joshua Thomas was converted in 1805. We have Joshua's own account of how he tried to put into effect for himself some of the new "means" that he had seen being used around him:

> *After struggling for a long time in prayer and receiving no answer, I concluded I would try what virtue there was in falling! So I looked me out a smooth place that was free from roots and sticks, that I might not hurt myself in the fall, and kept my eye a little over one shoulder to see how to fall and not hurt myself; I*

> *then came down full length on the earth... Receiving no answer, I arose completely discouraged, and very impatient besides. I felt almost ready to declare, "I do not believe in their way of being converted, and I will try no more."*[2]

For Joshua Thomas in 1805 the fact that there was some degree of human action in conversion was undeniable. The "means" were already so well defined that one could put them to the test. What Joshua found, of course, was that there was a distinction between the way God used those means and the way humans used them. Men and women might be able to some extent to rely on some specific human "means," but they could not command the when and the where. The human means had not replaced the divine surprise.

Some thirty years later there was another camp meeting at which Joshua Thomas was again present, and by then the process of conversion had changed somewhat. One day at Deal Island camp meeting the Reverend John S. Taylor, a man "universally beloved in his day," arose to address the assembled throng. The crowd sat lifeless and dead before him. "Dearth and dullness seemed to have fallen upon the people, and the exercises of the camp were progressing without much apparent good being done." Taylor was not one to permit such indifference.

> *"I want every Christian here, in the stand and out of it," said he, "to join me in one short simple prayer, and when I utter it, to say AMEN."*
>
> *He then slowly and devoutly prayed, "Lord have mercy on careless sinners!"*
>
> *A few voices responded, "Amen."*
>
> *"Come," said he, "let us try it again. All who have a desire for salvation of souls will speak out and say AMEN!"*
>
> *Again he uttered the prayer, and the Amens were more emphatic and more numerous.*
>
> *"Once more," said he with increasing earnestness, "Lord have mercy on careless sinners!"*
>
> *"AMEN!" was thundered with startling eagerness by the suddenly aroused people. The next instant a cry arose from all parts of the camp, "Lord have mercy!" "Lord save or I perish" and sinners came rushing forward in scores to the place of prayer. The spell was broken, the enemy routed, and victory was gained on the side of Immanuel.*[3]

By this time man's participation in the process of conversion had increased markedly. By now it seems almost as if the clever preacher can through his own efforts initiate "the surprising work of God." One is tempted to wonder, of course, how much of the feeling that swept across the crowd that day at Deal Island was sent from God, and how much was manufactured by man.

About fifty years later, in 1881, James Cannon, Jr., visited the Turlington Campmeeting near Melfa, and he noted the "pressure brought to bear" on sinners in the congregation. By now it was taken for granted that humans would participate openly in the production of conversion, and Cannon describes how they did so:

> *As the meeting progressed, fathers and mothers arose from their seats and went out in search of their children, sometimes even as far as buggies parked on the edge of the row of tents. [Thus] the interest steadily increased [until] the atmosphere was laden with cries of penitents and prayers... Some mothers and fathers shouted praises to God at the conversion of their children, [and] sometimes there was a sweeping outburst of hallelujahs followed by prayer and song...*[4]

"Hunting out the sinners" is what Cannon calls his parental invitation to the altar. It was probably common practice on the Shore by the 1880's, for he does not seem surprised by it or critical of it. Human responsibility in the process of conversion has grown so much since the time of Joshua Thomas that now Christians are ready to lead down the aisle to the "place of prayer" even those who may not be ready or interested. By now, "going forward" has its own objective existence quite apart from being a "means" of conversion.

At the end of this progression stands my story and those of thousands of others on the Shore today. By the time the faith of our fathers was passed on to us, conversion in the manner that Methodists preached it, promoted it, heard it, expected it to happen, and experienced it had long since moved dangerously close to being not something that God poured out unexpectedly on his people, but something that men and women controlled and commanded as the occasion required. We found the old forms of conversion intact. But across the years a very basic underlying assumption, about whether the forms belonged to God or to man, had changed.

One did not have to view the scene from the organist's bench in order to observe another obvious fact about the Annual Revival on the Eastern Shore in the 1950's: only the converted people came. The very purpose of the Revival was, of course, to save the unconverted. But by the 1950's the unconverted found it easy to ignore the Annual Revival, and the pews were filled (when they were filled) not with the unsaved but with the most devout members of the church.

Not quite so obvious was another fact no less significant: though only the converted came to revivals, the revival message continued to be directed at the unconverted who were not there. Over the centuries the audiences who heard revival preaching had changed, but revival preaching had not.

The first of these facts, that only the converted came to revivals, was noted by no one more than the revival preachers themselves. No series of revival services was complete until at some point during the week the evangelist swept his arm out over the half-filled room or pointed to empty seats and asked the anxious question, "Why all these empty pews? Where are all the people who need to accept Jesus Christ? These are the people who need to hear what I have to say to them!"

The second of these facts, that now revival worshipers were hearing sermons intended for someone else, was hardly ever noted, or if noted never voiced. Some may have thought it (one twelve-year-old on the organist's bench among them), but no one ever said it, "Why preach to the empty pews instead of to the people before you? Why not preach to us?"

This reminiscence from my own life suggests something else about the progress of Methodism on the Shore: as the years went by, Methodist preaching became increasingly fixated on only one dimension of the faith, conversion. What began as a valid emphasis on the necessity of individual conversion became, with the passage of time, an over-emphasis that excluded other equally valid parts of the Christian message and life.

Methodism entered the Eastern Shore of Virginia with a two-pronged message: the necessity of individual conversion, and the importance of living out the new life in the world after conversion. There were two dimensions to the faith in the days of Wesley and Asbury. One was vertical; men and women were linked to God by a direct vertical experience that was profoundly individual. The second dimension was horizontal: how converted men and women live out their faith in the world is of crucial importance. One could not be a mature Methodist in those days and attend to only one of those two dimensions. The Christian life was not simply the question of one's own individual salvation, but an involvement in the redemption of society as well. Gradually, however, the emphasis upon the second dimension faded. The Methodists of the Shore became, as the years went by, less and less concerned to save society, and more and more concerned to stroke their own individual conversion experiences.[5]

The most obvious example of this tragic development is the changing attitudes towards slavery in Methodist circles. It is not without significance that the very early Methodists of the Eastern Shore freed their slaves when they joined the church. A staunch anti-slavery attitude was the most tangible sign in that day of Methodism's insistence that religion was not simply vertical, but also horizontal. The record of the waning of the anti-slavery impulse can be found, however, in the preceding pages. The people who in Francis Asbury's day freed their slaves because they thought the Christian life demanded it were, by the 1840's, convinced that theirs was a religion concerned with saving souls, not with freeing bodies in bondage. By the 1860's the religious life of the Shore, and with it virtually all of life, was split into black and white, and Christians of both races indulged in the pursuit of individual relationships with God without bothering about the relationship between brothers across racial lines. By the 1940's the message about the individual, vertical relationship to God was unblunted, while the message about the horizontal relationship to one's brother of another race was neglected or absent altogether.

Paralleling the waning emphasis upon the Christian life after conversion was a waxing over-emphasis upon conversion itself. The first step of the Christian life was all but elevated into the whole of the Christian life. Preaching centered on producing conversion to the exclusion of the nurture of Christian life after conversion. And ironically, as individual conversion became more and more the sole content of Methodist preaching, the Methodist churches of the Shore filled with the converted. The denomination spread successfully across the two counties, the number of the unsaved and the unevangelized dropped and all but disappeared in the two counties, and Sunday mornings found the pews filled with converted individuals, yet the intensity with which the Methodists preached conversion and only conversion increased.

By the year of my birth The Methodist Church alone could boast that one-fifth of the number of the inhabitants of the Shore were on its rolls. The church, Methodist and otherwise, was firmly established in every conceivable corner of the peninsula. There was hardly a person on the Shore who could grow up out of the sight of a church steeple or away from the proclamation of the Gospel. And yet rare was the Methodist sermon that addressed the congregation as anything other than unconverted sinners, and rarer still the sermon that attempted to come to grips with what it means to live the fullness of the Christian life after conversion. Sermons were like a broken record stuck in the groove on Step One of the faith. Before the preachers sat the converted churchgoers who needed to be nurtured in the adventure of taking Step Two and Step Three, but the message was stuck.

It should cause no surprise that my third reminiscence of the Annual Revival is that its main result was to "save" again those who were already saved. Since no revival service was thought to be complete until someone had "come forward," and since the only ones there to do it were those who had done it already, the converted went forward again and again. "Going forward" became a way of life for many Methodists during two weeks of the year. It had taken on a life of its own quite apart from any attendant conversion. I myself was thus "converted" twice, convinced at the time that my second experience (which like the first happened at a revival service) was the authentic one. Union Methodist Church had its small group of persons who could always be counted on to respond to the invitation, and even one or two persons who went forward at virtually every opportunity. And if the results were to be had no other way, sometimes the preacher would so extend his invitation that the whole congregation would come forward to kneel before the altar.

The Altar Call, as I saw from the organist's bench, was hard work. It took a lot of effort to get the conversions started. Part of the reason, perhaps, was that we were really only trying to heap conversion experience upon conversion experience.

And part of the reason, no doubt, was that in overemphasizing Step One to the neglect of all that was supposed to follow we had left out of our religion something that was exceedingly vital and life-giving.

In the end the narrative becomes biography, the history our story. Shaped by the persons and events and ideas of the past, we claim the story for our own and with our lives begin to carve out the next unwritten chapters.

Let there be no doubt about it: as we take our places upon the stage, we become the living testimony that the faith of those who went before us was real. It was authentic religion, vital faith, genuine piety that was experienced and practiced and that took deep root on this small corner of the globe. Our spiritual ancestors may not have lived perfectly (which human beings ever have?); their own living out of the faith may have been riddled with inconsistencies or shortcomings. But they passed on to us a living flame. If we criticize, it is from within the ranks of the believers that we make our critique. And as we take our place upon the stage, we prove that throughout it all it was a Divine presence that moved them, and redeemed them, and unites us to them.

Perhaps as we take our places on the stage we can learn from the story that has gone on before, and reach back into our spiritual heritage for some of the ideas that made them so alive.

Perhaps from the time of Jonathan Edwards and Francis Asbury and Thomas Smith we can recover a sense of the necessity of waiting upon the movement of God. They recognized fully that human actions can neither anticipate nor contain the fullness of all that God does when He acts. Concerned though they were that God act to redeem their time, they were faithful enough to wait and pray for the movement of the Spirit, and honest enough to call it, when it came, God's "surprise."

Perhaps from the time of John Wesley and Joseph Everett and William Paramore we can recover a sense of concern not just for the next world, where each individual will know and see God, but also for this one, where brothers do not yet live together in peace. They knew that true faith must manifest itself in concern for the condition of one's brother in this world. And though some of their descendants chose to forget or overlook that fact, let us claim it as our own.

Our age calls for faith and devotion no less spirited or profound than theirs. For today as the narrative is passed on to us, the whole of life on the Eastern Shore of Virginia is still divided into black and white. Social and economic strata separate potential brothers. Too many Christians who have known the converting power of God in their own individual lives have not yet begun to translate that power into a force to redeem the whole of society.

This being the case, not yet can the curtain ring down. Although in this land the faith has taken deep root, there is still much to be done.

BOOK TWO:

A Catalogue of the Churches of Virginia's Eastern Shore

Book Two is intended as a companion work to the narrative of Book One, and contains an historical sketch of the almost three hundred individual religious congregations mentioned in Book One. What follows is, in fact, a catalogue of every known religious congregation on the Eastern Shore of Virginia, from 1634 to the present.

The churches are listed alphabetically by their most recent name and denominational affiliation.

An asterisk (*) indicates a congregation that is no longer functioning.

Locations of church buildings, where known, are marked on maps of individual communities, which are listed alphabetically throughout the text. Under each community can be found a list of the churches that are or have been located there.

Since denominations differ from one another in the manner of dating the formation of their congregations, the first date assigned to each congregation in the bracket after its name is the earliest substantiated date of any sort of religious activity in that vicinity. The date given may thus refer to the erection of a building, the organization of a congregation, the founding of a Sunday school, the purchase of a church site, the beginning of preaching services, etc., and may in some cases differ from dates traditionally cited by the local churches.

The method of footnoting used in Book Two differs from that in Book One. Since individual footnotes would in many cases result in notations longer than the text, reference is made only to the sources employed in each individual historical sketch. These sources are given at the end of each sketch, and refer to the works listed and numbered in the Bibliography at the end of the entire work.

The reader should resist the inference that those churches with longer sketches are more "historic" or more important than those about which less is written here. These sketches reflect not the relative size or importance of the Shore's congregations but the amount of historical material available about each.

Likewise, since costs prohibit the inclusion of a photograph of every extant church building on the Eastern Shore, priority has been given to those photographs with historic value, such as those that depict buildings no longer in existence. The photographs on the following pages are not in any way representative of the church buildings now in use on the Eastern Shore of Virginia.

The maps in Book Two were printed by the U.S. Geological Survey, and the author expresses his gratitude for permission to use them.

The author acknowledges beforehand the inevitable fact that in a compilation of this sort there will be a number of inaccuracies. Should the reader fill the margins of his book with corrections, let him do so without criticism, aware that it was the author who prodded him to record his own more accurate historical information.

ABBREVIATIONS:

ABA - Accomack Baptist Association
[white churches of the Southern Baptist Convention]
AG-S - Assembly of God, Springfield, Missouri
AME - African Methodist Episcopal Church
CCD - Jerusalem General Assembly of Firstborn Church of Christ Disciples
CE - Church of England [became Protestant Episcopal Church 1789]
CGLO - Church of God Live On
[local Pentecostal sect of Bishop Jesse Handshaw]
ESBA - Eastern Shore of Virginia-Maryland Baptist Association
[black churches of the Baptist General Association of Virginia]
IAHC - International Apostolic Holiness Church [became Pilgrim Holiness Church 1922]
IAHUC - International Apostolic Holiness Union and Churches [Became IAHC 1913]
ICA - Independent Convention of Accomack
[local Methodist denomination 1861-1866]
M - The Methodist Church [became United Methodist Church 1968]
ME - Methodist Episcopal Church [became The Methodist Church 1939]
ME-S - Methodist Episcopal Church, South [became The Methodist Church 1939]
MP - Methodist Protestant Church [became The Methodist Church 1939]
PE - Protestant Episcopal Church
PH - Pilgrim Holiness Church [became Wesleyan Church 1968]
Pres - Presbyterian Church in the United States
RC - Roman Catholic Church
UMC - United Methodist Church
W - Wesleyan Church
WBTS - Watchtower Bible & Tract Society of Jehovah's Witnesses

ACCOMAC

see: *Baptist Bible Church*
Drummondtown Baptist Church
Drummondtown United Methodist Church
Macedonia African Methodist Episcopal Church
Makemie Presbyterian Church
**Presbyterian Meetinghouse*
St. James Episcopal Church

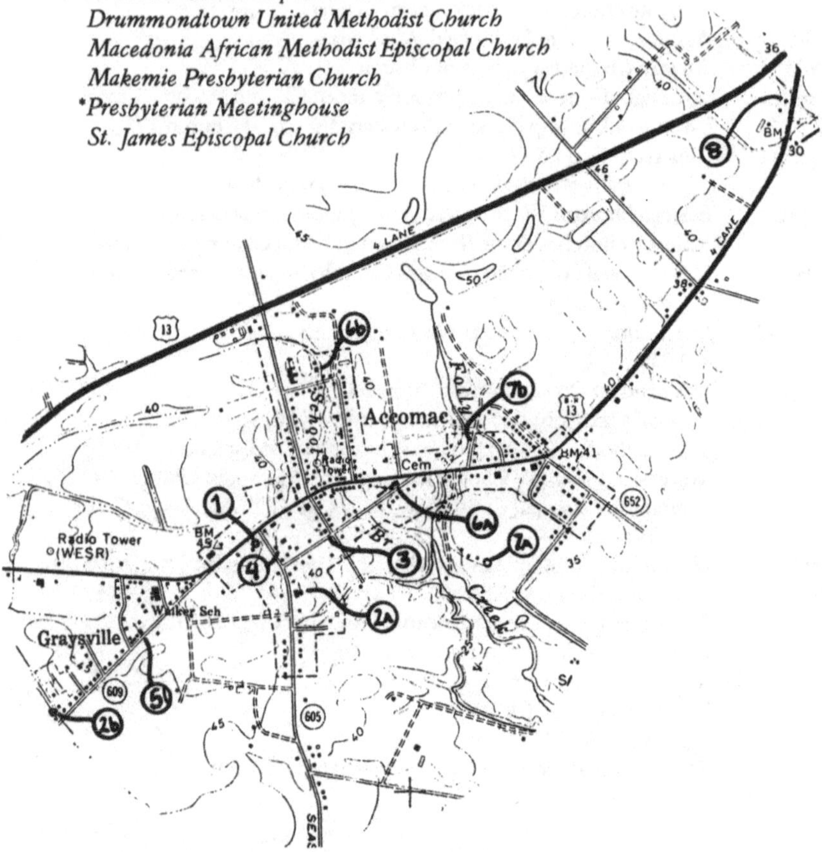

1 - Presbyterian Meetinghouse: site 1765-1790
2a - Drummondtown UMC: site since 1793
2b - Drummondtown UMC: building II moved to this site 1918-c1950
3 - Makemie Presbyterian
4 - St. James Episcopal: site since 1838 [for original site 1767-1838 see TASLEY]
5 - Macedonia AME
6a - Drummondtown Baptist: site since 1870
6b - Drummondtown Baptist: building I moved to this site 1913
7a - Mt. Olive Church of Christ Disciples: original site 1937-43
7b - Mt. Olive Church of Christ Disciples: site 1961-65 [for present site see HOPETON]
8 - Baptist Bible Church

ADAMS UNITED METHODIST CHURCH

("Morris Chapel")
[ME 1878, M 1939, UMC 1968]
Whitesville

Adams Church was founded from Metropolitan in 1878 and named for J. K. Adams, its first pastor. It took a number of years to build the church. In 1884 the congregation was meeting in a tent, and not until 1887 was the first building finished.

Together with Metropolitan, with which it has always shared its pastors, Adams formed the "Wiseville" or "Lee Mont" Circuit, which was a strong one in the Delaware Conference. Although in its early years Adams was always smaller than Metropolitan, it, too, participated in those progressive programs which were the pride of the presiding elder: ever-recurring revival (1899, 1903), church library (1903), the use of church offering envelopes (1924), vacation church school, and Epworth League (1933).

Adams improved its little building with the addition of a steeple and a new facade in 1914, and installed its first organ in 1910.

By the 1920's the congregation had outgrown its original building, and in 1923, under the Reverend E. E. Rogers, renovation began. An old store building, which was originally the first church of Calvary Methodist Protestant Church in Hopkins, had been moved to Whitesville to be outfitted as a school. When a different building was finally used as the school, the Adams congregation purchased the store, dismantled it, and used the lumber to rebuild and enlarge their own building. These renovations were completed in 1928. In 1945 the building was elevated and a basement built beneath it.

In 1975 Albert Gingrich became the pastor here, the first white man to serve a black Methodist congregation on the Virginia Shore. A new parsonage was erected during his pastorate.

With a membership of about 200, Adams is today the largest black United Methodist congregation on the Shore.

[Sources: 110, 113, 123, 176]

Location: see PARKSLEY

AFRICAN BAPTIST CHURCH

[ESBA 1868]
Cheriton

African Baptist is the second oldest black Baptist church on the Shore, and the oldest congregation in the town of Cheriton.

The church was founded from Union Baptist in Eastville under the leadership of the Reverend Alfred J. Spady, shortly before 1869. Tradition says that the congregation was organized ''under a big oak tree'' on the Seaside and met for some time in various places until a house of worship could be erected. Early in 1869 a lot was purchased and a building erected east of the present town. William H. Corbin, the second pastor, was serving at that time.

In its early years African shared its pastors with Union, and it joined with that church in 1879 to erect Cherrystone Baptist west of Cheriton. African, Union, and First Baptist in Capeville together erected a parsonage in Bayview in 1880.

It was lack of space for burial ground that forced the congregation to move from the original site, and in 1891 the present site in Cheriton was purchased. A new building was erected there in 1892, after which the older building was demolished and its space used for a cemetery. Once in the new building, the congregation called George E. Reid as its first full-time pastor. Reid served 22 years in all, the longest pastorate in the church's history, during which time the church building was enlarged, a parsonage was erected next door, and the congregation grew steadily.

Pastor during the 1920's was A. B. Lee, who conducted a great revival in which 113 persons were baptized in one service. He was succeeded by W. B. Carrington, who led his people in the remodeling of the church building even in the midst of the Depression. In all, only eleven pastors have served the church in its more than a century of existence. The present pastor, Charles F. Mapp, began his pastorate in 1961.

The building completed in 1892 is still in use, and it has been considerably enlarged and changed over the years. The stained glass windows were added after the church was in use, and more recent improvements include an annex with kitchen and a brick veneer around the entire building.

Booker T. Washington spoke at this church on May 6, 1913, during a tour of the Eastern Shore.

African is one of the largest congregations on the Shore, and boasted over 500 members as early as the 1940's.

[Sources: 26, 109, 124, 146, 165, 176]

Location: see CHERITON

ALPHA AND OMEGA CHURCH

[Independent 1967]
Cape Charles

The Alpha and Omega Church was founded by Oliver E. Netherton in Florida in the early 1960's. Franklin Barber planted the faith on the Eastern Shore at Cape Charles in 1967, where Virginia Evans was his first convert. The church has been in continuous existence in Cape Charles since that time, and today gathers in a storefront building on Jefferson Avenue.

Believing that the Old Testament was fulfilled by Jesus, the Alpha and Omega Church bases its beliefs and practices entirely upon the New Testament, which its followers interpret in a literal manner. The church's teachings are neither Pentecostal nor sanctificationist nor adventist, but perfectionist. Perfection, it is believed, is attainable in this present life, and the person who attains it can live "in this body and never die."

Perhaps the most distinctive characteristic of this church is that it is not simply a congregation, but also a community. Believers are not required to live or work together, yet most of them meet to share at least one meal daily. There is no distinctive form of dress, but the fifteen members of the Cape Charles congregation share an almost communal life. The church operates the "Alpha and Omega Restaurant" next door for its members and others.

The Alpha and Omega Church is unique on the Eastern Shore of Virginia. The nearest other church of this sect is located in Dorchester County, Maryland.

[Source: 176]

Location: see CAPE CHARLES

*AMES CHAPEL METHODIST EPISCOPAL CHURCH

[ME 1795-1837?]
Ames Ridge

Ames Ridge, between Painter and Keller, was Methodist territory by 1795, when the circuit preacher William Colbert was a frequent guest among the several Ames families of the neighborhood. One of them was Shadrach Ames; Colbert said of him and his wife, "they are a free hearted people who delight in making everything agreeable to their friends." Richard Ames was another, and a third was Thomas H. Ames, who was licensed to exhort in 1817.

For more than two decades the Ames Ridge society went its way without a meetinghouse. The great revival of 1800 burned strong here, but the society continued to meet in the various Ames homes. When the nearby Pungoteague congregation erected a building in 1812, Shadrach Ames of this society was named one of its trustees.

In 1829 the congregation secured the land for the erection of a church, and Ames Chapel at last came into existence. Of its seven original trustees, no fewer than four were Ameses: Jesse, Richard, Thomas, and Shadrach.

Almost as soon as the meetinghouse was erected the Ames Ridge congregation faded away. The last mention of it in any record is from 1837, when the Reverend George Wiltshire took his trustees to the courthouse to be examined and recorded. The congregation thereafter drops from the records, and the building apparently vanished in a short time.

In 1864, William G. Coe, pastor of the independent Methodist churches of the Shore, moved to Ames Ridge and directed his work from that neighborhood, but there is no mention of the presence of a chapel at that time. Coe, in fact, met with a Methodist congregation in this neighborhood, but it gathered in a schoolhouse, not in Ames Chapel, which apparently had long since disappeared.

The exact location of Ames Chapel is not known today, but it apparently stood west of Painter near the intersection of the Ames Ridge road with the road to Pungoteague. Certain late nineteenth century newspaper notices refer to Ames Chapel events during the 1880's and 1890's, but these are misprints for Amiss Chapel (M.E., South), and should not be confused with this early, obscure, and long since lost church.

[Sources: 15, 70, 100, 111, 123, 176]

Location: see PAINTER

•AMISS CHAPEL METHODIST EPISCOPAL CHURCH, SOUTH

("Coard's Branch")
[ME-S 1886-1901]
Greenbush

This church was founded by J. W. Carroll, pastor of the Drummondtown Circuit, who organized a Sunday school and erected a bower near Coard's Branch north of Greenbush in 1886. James and Harriet Hurst sold the land, and the church was erected in that same year. It was named for Joseph H. Amiss, presiding elder of the Eastern Shore District at the time, but it was often known among local residents as Coard's Branch Church.

In 1890 the congregation held a "fair and festival" to help pay off the debt on the church and to complete the building. The building was a small frame structure not unlike its contemporary in Drummondtown. It had no steeple and no stained glass windows.

Amiss Chapel always shared its pastors with Drummondtown, and after 1897 with Locustville and Onley as well. In 1901, during a reshuffling of circuit boundaries, Amiss Chapel was closed, and thereafter it drops from the records. In that same year the funeral of Dr. William H. Coard, a local physician and a prominent member, was held in the church, one of the last services there.

In 1912, Jesse Hurst moved the building half a mile north and across the road and remodeled it into a store. Hurst's store remained in operation for several decades, then stood abandoned for a number of years before it burned to the ground in the 1960's.

The church pews were purchased and taken to Cedar Island, where they were used on the front porch of a popular hotel then in use there, and according to a familiar story Warner Ames (1878-1938), a prominent local attorney, owed his life to one of them. Ames, then a young man, was swimming in the Atlantic surf in front of the hotel one day when he swam too far from shore and was in danger of drowning. His friends, seeing his distress, grabbed the nearest thing available to reach to him, an old Amiss Chapel pew from the front porch, and on it he pulled to safety. Thus was he "saved" years after the church was closed.

[Sources: 105, 109, 116, 123, 176]

Location: see GREENBUSH

ANDREW CHAPEL UNITED METHODIST CHURCH

("Boggs Chapel")
[ME 1835, ME-S 1848, M 1939, UMC 1968]
Cashville

The land on which this church is situated had a considerable history of religious importance even before it became Methodist land. In 1698 it was acquired by Francis Makemie, the Presbyterian minister, and his wife Naomi. Although the Makemies never lived on it, it remained in the hands of their families and heirs until 1802. In that year, it was acquired by Francis Boggs.

Just when Boggs built a meetinghouse on his land is not known, but by the 1830's Hollies Baptist Church was using the Boggs Meetinghouse that stood on this site. When the missions controversy split the Baptist churches, a rival congregation called Baptist Church of Christ of Pungoteague worshiped in this building from 1831 to 1835. The Methodists must have followed close upon the heels of the anti-mission Baptist congregation, for the society in Sluitkill Neck is first mentioned in the year 1835. It, too, met in the old meetinghouse and was known as Boggs.

In 1848 the membership of Boggs Chapel informed the Methodist Episcopal Church that "it is the wish of a Majority of the members worshipping at that place to be united with the Virginia Conference [M.E., South] & that they have resolved to place themselves under the pastoral care of that Conference." The northern church responded by creating a short-lived rival congregation of its own called Ebenezer to minister to the pro-northern minority at Boggs. By 1864, when the church was closed for a short time by the Union army, its name had been changed to Andrew Chapel, to honor James O. Andrew, the slave-owning bishop of Georgia over whom the denomination split in 1844.

The Boggs meetinghouse was used until 1877, when the congregation purchased the property from James Boggs for $1 (it had always been owned by the Boggs family until that time) and erected the present structure. The church was a strong one at that time, one of the leading Methodist appointments on the Shore. In 1909 the building was considerably enlarged and improved upon.

Andrew Chapel today has a membership of just over 100. In 1947 it was joined to two former northern Methodist churches, Leatherbury and Riverview, and the charge was given the name Cashville in 1949.

[Sources: 39, 116, 103, 123, 176]

Location: see CASHVILLE

ANTIOCH BAPTIST CHURCH

[ESBA 1902]
Treherneville

This church was founded by the Reverend Leonard Treherne of Treherneville. In 1902 he organized a Sunday school in the village and named it Antioch Mission. The Sunday school soon blossomed into worship services and a small congregation, which met in a nearby fraternal lodge.

In 1915 the present building was erected and occupied, the church officially constituted, and admitted into the Association. The cornerstone was laid in 1920, when the debt on the building was paid. The church was dedicated in honor of Treherne, "a great leader ever to be remembered, honored, and respected."

Treherne served as pastor of this church until he was advanced in age, and there have been eight other pastors since him. In recent years the church has shared its pastor with Herbert Baptist Church in Wachapreague.

[Sources: 26, 124]

Location: see TREHERNEVILLE

*ASSATEAGUE BAPTIST CHAPEL

[ABA 1919-1922]
Assateague Island

The now-vanished village of Assateague once clustered around the road leading from the water to the lighthouse on the western side of the island. At its apex it could boast of stores, a school, a factory, a number of homes, and as many as 35 families. For the convenience of these people, who sometimes found it difficult to cross the water to Chincoteague to go to church, Union Baptist Church began to hold services in the schoolhouse early in the twentieth century. Both Baptists and Methodists attended these services.

In 1919 Union Baptist erected a meetinghouse for church services in the village, but shortly thereafter the village was abandoned. The building was used only until 1922. In that year, like several of the village homes, the church was floated over to the east side of Chincoteague Island and there converted into a dwelling, which is still in use today.

[Source: 176]

Location: see CHINCOTEAGUE

(photo c. 1920)

ASSAWOMAN

see: **Assawoman Episcopal Church*
Assawoman United Methodist Church

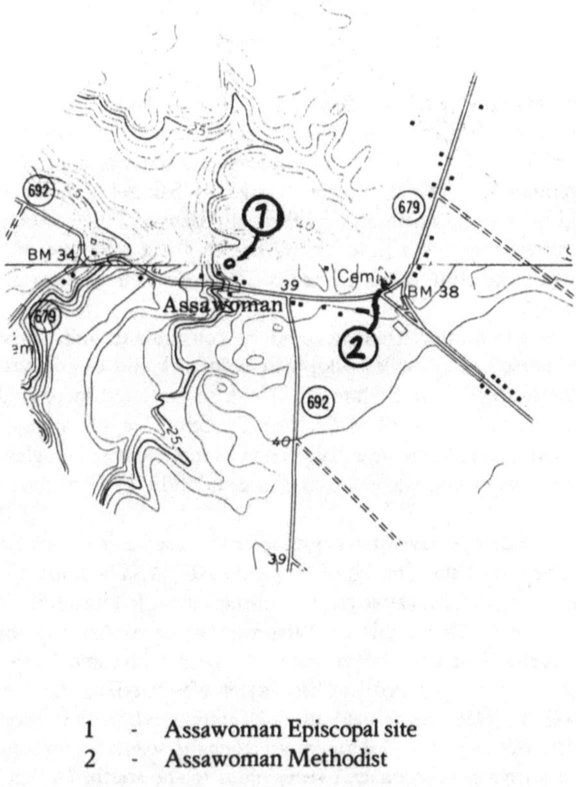

1 - Assawoman Episcopal site
2 - Assawoman Methodist

*ASSAWOMAN EPISCOPAL CHURCH

(''Occocomson Church,'' ''Upper Church'') [CE 1680, PE 1789]

Assawoman

The Accomack Parish built this church in or around 1680, just two years after St. George's was erected in Pungoteague. Two local residents gave two different tracts of land for the church, but the one chosen was a site in Assawoman offered by William Taylor. Had a site deeded by Samuel Tailer been used, the church would have stood north of the village of Atlantic. The new church building was brick, and it stood on a little hill overlooking the millpond on Assawoman Creek. Just when the church was erected is not known, but it is certain that it was standing by 1696.

In 1710 two local magistrates ordered the constable to find out who were the ''ill disposed person or persons [who] hath been so bould to enter the Church at Assawaman and carry in sundry household stuff severall and there abiding and doe many ereligious acts.'' In April of that year Timothy Coe was arrested for storing bricks in the sanctuary. Some years later one Colonel George Douglas left a legacy for the church, and from it was purchased in London in 1749 a silver communion chalice.

It is doubtful that Assawoman continued to be used as a place of worship after the disestablishment of the Church of England in 1784. The building was used as a school for a while, and then after years of abandonment fell into ruin around 1830. In a letter written in 1890, Edward Wharton Taylor of Assawoman stated that he had been baptized in the church, went to school there, and ''saw the Church fall down about sixty years ago.'' That Taylor was baptized there suggests that some services, at least, were held in the building after the disestablishment.

Years after the church had disappeared from the scene, a cup was found lying in a field on a farm near Accomac, twenty miles to the south, and on the cup was the inscription: ''For the use of the Parish Church of Accomack at Assuaman.'' It was the silver cup made in London in 1749 from the Douglas legacy, and it had apparently been used as a drinking cup by slaves. It was subsequently returned to the parish and is now owned by Emmanuel Episcopal Church in Jenkins Bridge, successor to this church.

The church stood just north of Seaside Road as that road begins to descend to the creek, in an open field. As late as the 1950's farmers' plows were still upturning there pieces of old colonial brick from the ruined structure. In 1977 the site was excavated by archeology students at the Eastern Shore Community College.

[Sources: 70, 90, 109, 176]

Location: see ASSAWOMAN

ASSAWOMAN UNITED METHODIST CHURCH

[ME-S 1894, M 1939, UMC 1968]
Assawoman

The tiny village of Assawoman had no church for almost a century after the old Anglican church there finally caved in around 1830. A. D. Davis, the northern Methodist presiding elder, preached in the village in 1887, and the Wilmington Conference voted funds to erect a church there, but no northern congregation was founded.

It fell to the ladies of the Atlantic Circuit of the southern church to stake out a claim to Assawoman. By as early as 1894 they had a Sunday school in operation in the village. In 1896 a festival was held to benefit the school; it included bicycle races, oratory, music, and refreshments.

From this effort was born the Assawoman Church. A lot was secured in 1901 and a building erected within a short time. In March it was dedicated with a sermon by Dr. W. E. Judkins. The building was remodeled and improved in 1906, but not enlarged; the congregation has always been small, and this is one of the smallest Methodist buildings on the Shore. A separate building next door was obtained by the congregation for use as a church hall.

The southern Atlantic Circuit which founded this church is still for the most part intact (Downing's, Temperanceville, and Assawoman), although the name was changed to the Oak Hall Charge in the 1950's. Today as always Assawoman, the youngest church on the charge, is still the smallest. The present membership is 82.

[Sources: 109, 110, 116, 117, 123]

Location: see ASSAWOMAN

ATLANTIC

see: *Atlantic Baptist Church*
Atlantic United Methodist Church
**Oak Grove Methodist Episcopal Church, South*
St. John's United Methodist Church
St. Joseph Holiness Church
Shiloh Baptist Church

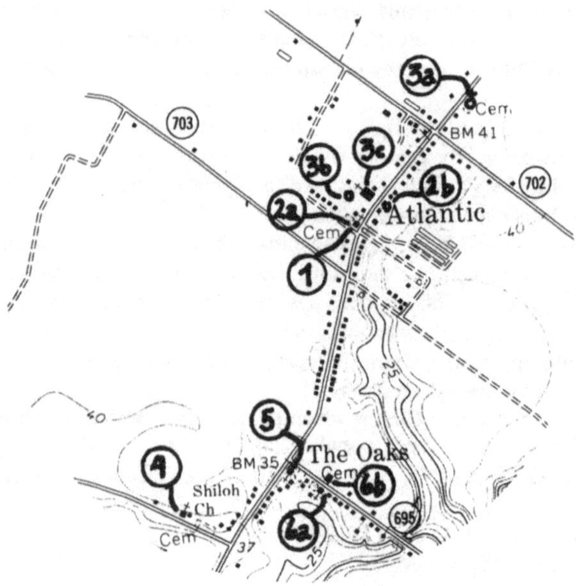

1 - Oak Grove ME site
2a - Atlantic Baptist: all buildings since 1877
2b - Atlantic Baptist: building I (Oak Grove ME bldg.) moved to this site 1919-1964
3a - Atlantic Methodist: original site 1893-1921
3b - Atlantic Methodist: building I moved to this site 1921
3c - Atlantic Methodist: since 1921
4 - Shiloh Baptist
5 - St. John's Methodist
6a - St. Joseph Holiness: building I 1940-1963
6b - St. Joseph Holiness: building II since 1963

ATLANTIC BAPTIST CHURCH

[ABA 1877]
Atlantic

(photo prior to 1916)

In 1877 Baptists of the Atlantic area, members of the churches at Modest Town and Bethel, began to meet for services in their village. They gathered in the abandoned building of Oak Grove Methodist Episcopal Church, South, and there on July 1, 1877, organized Atlantic Baptist Church. There were twelve charter members. John W. Hundley was the pastor.

The Atlantic Baptists purchased the old Oak Grove building and did some minor repairs to it. Within two years thirty new members had joined their ranks. Within ten years it was necessary to enlarge the building to accommodate the growing congregation. In 1888 the building was extended towards the front by twelve feet, and a steeple added.

In 1902 members of Atlantic joined in the formation of Makemie Park Baptist Church, and in 1918 the congregation became a station, even though its pastor continued to serve Makemie Park.

In 1919 the congregation moved the old building aside (to a site across from the present Atlantic Methodist building) and began construction of a new brick church. The building was dedicated in 1920 and cost $29,000. A twenty-room educational annex was added in 1957 during the pastorate of Paul Moore. The present parsonage, next door to the church, was purchased in 1968.

Atlantic is today a strong station church of 245 members. Since 1951 its pastors have also served Mappsville Baptist, although the two churches are independent of each other.

[Sources: 122, 123, 132]

Location: see ATLANTIC

ATLANTIC UNITED METHODIST CHURCH

[MP 1893, M 1939, UMC 1968]
Atlantic

Photo 1922

Atlantic Methodist Protestant Church was organized by 21 members from Wattsville and one from Berea in 1893. Captain Sam Davis provided a lot on the northern edge of the village east of Seaside Road, and a small frame building was erected in that year. This original building was improved and repaired in 1905, and slowly but surely the new Atlantic Church eclipsed the mother church in Wattsville to the north.

In 1921 the congregation began the construction of a much larger brick building on a different site. The old building was moved to the new church lot and placed behind the new structure, where it was used for church and community events until it was dismantled in the 1960's. The new building cost $40,000, and was dedicated free of debt on December 10, 1922, by Dr. (later Bishop) James H. Straughn.

After World War II, Atlantic prospered beyond the other churches on the charge due to its proximity to Chincoteague Naval Air Station, which later became Wallops Station of N.A.S.A. In 1954 it withdrew from the New Church Charge and became a station appointment. A parsonage was erected next door at a cost of $15,000, and in 1958 a new $28,000 educational unit was dedicated.

In 1970 Atlantic was again joined to Berea and Pittsville from the old charge, but this time the charge was named Atlantic-New Church. Atlantic is the largest and strongest church on the charge, and the pastor resides in the new Atlantic parsonage.

[Sources: 114, 123, 163, 176]

Location: see ATLANTIC

*AYRES CHAPEL METHODIST EPISCOPAL CHURCH

[ME 1845?, ICA 1861, ME 1864-1930]
Bayside

a - front view

b - back view
(photos 1970)

The name Ayres first appears on the Methodist records of the Shore in 1810, when Levin Ayres was licensed to exhort. This Ayres was the first of many. He became a licensed preacher in 1821, and it is possible that Methodist services in this area commenced at about that time. There may have been an early meeting-house here, but the first recorded mention of a church building is from 1845 when Francis Ayres, Edward Gunter, and William Copes were appointed a building committee for Ayres Chapel. The building was apparently erected soon afterwards. Gunter sold the land on which it was erected to the denomination for $1 in 1852.

In 1861 Ayres Chapel joined with five other churches to form the independent Convention of Accomack under William Coe, the northernmost church to do so. When the Convention itself split in 1864, Ayres cast its lot with Cokesbury and returned to the northern Methodist fold. At the end of the war, only Ayres and Cokesbury of the five Convention churches remained in the Methodist Episcopal Church, and up until its very last years Ayres was thereafter closely tied to Cokesbury.

Ayres Chapel was a prosperous church during the last half of the nineteenth century, when (as in 1894) as many as 1000 people were wont to attend the annual Sunday school picnic at Half Moon Island. The church building was improved in 1895. In 1919 the Ayres Chapel Charge was created, with Crowson's and Leatherbury.

By the 1920's, however, the church was in decline. One pastor, T. S. Dixon, left the Methodist Church altogether when the Pilgrim Holiness Church in Bloxom was founded, and by the end of the decade as often as not it was only two or three families who carried the work on. In 1930 the denomination ended the Ayres

Chapel Charge and closed the church. The pastor at that time was the venerable J. F. F. Ayres, who died four years later at the age of 79. The building was sold at public auction in February 1933, and thereafter stood unused.

The building remained intact until just a few years ago, but now it has fallen into a ruin of rotted planks and lumber. The parsonage still stands nearby and is used as a dwelling.

[Sources: 105, 109, 110, 117, 123, 174, 176]

Location: see BAYSIDE

BAHA'I GROUP OF NORTHAMPTON COUNTY

[1975]
Machipongo

Robyn Slater of Jamesville was the first, and for almost twenty years the only, follower of the Baha'i faith on the Eastern Shore of Virginia. When in the fall of 1975 three other Baha'i followers moved to Northampton, she joined with them to establish the Baha'i Group of Northampton County.

Baha'is follow the teachings of a Persian named Baha'u'llah, executed in 1850, whom they believe to be the latest in a series of prophets or "Manifestations" of God. Baha'i teaching proclaims the unity of all religions, and includes elements of Islam, Christianity, and Judaism.

The Northampton Group meets regularly in private homes in Eastville, Machipongo, and Jamesville, and its principal activities on the Shore have been programs of education about the faith, including a weekly radio program from Exmore. Baha'i teaching has long promoted racial equality, and Baha'i activities on the Shore have been racially mixed although the four members of the Group are white.

The number nine has special significance for Baha'is, and until there are nine adherents the Northampton "Group" will not become a full-fledged "Assembly." The nearest other Baha'i Assembly is in Virginia Beach.

[Sources: 109, 176]

*BAKER MEMORIAL BAPTIST CHURCH

[ABA 1898-1937]
Chancetown

In 1898 the Reverend T. S. Dunaway of Hollies and Drummondtown Baptist organized a Sunday school in a schoolhouse between Locustville and Wachapreague, and from his efforts this congregation grew. Four years later a frame building had been erected at a cost of $3000, and twenty members of Drummondtown Baptist withdrew to constitute the new congregation. The congregation took the name Baker Memorial, in honor of Elijah Baker, and was admitted to the Accomack Baptist Association in 1903.

Although Baker Memorial was founded from Drummondtown, it quickly became attached to Hollies Baptist, which was nearer. By 1911 it shared its pastor with Hollies and Harborton Baptist. In 1915 the congregation reported a membership of 81, the largest in its history.

By 1924 Baker Memorial, having dwindled in membership, left the Hollies field and called in other pastors to fill its pulpit on a part-time basis. The first supply pastor was the Onley Baptist pastor. The last pastor on record was from Zion. By the early 1930's the church was virtually extinct; in 1935 only the Girls' Auxiliary of the Woman's Missionary Union was still functioning, and it contributed $1.10 to missions in that year. In 1936 the Accomack Association appointed a committee to investigate the condition of Baker Memorial, and the next year the committee reported that Baker Memorial had ceased to exist.

Since the deed to the land contained a reversion clause, the original owners again took possession. The building was dismantled and the lumber used to erect a home in Wachapreague. The church furniture was given to Clarke Presbyterian Church in Daugherty, which is of about the same size and design as the Baker building.

The Chancetown area where the church is located is referred to in some county deeds as "Kidd's Chapel." Baker Memorial apparently also bore that name, after Rev. H. S. Kidd, pastor of Drummondtown when this church was dedicated.

[Sources: 69, 122, 123, 150, 176]

Location: see CHANCETOWN

BAPTIST BIBLE CHURCH

[Independent 1975]
Accomac

This congregation was founded in 1975 by the Reverend A. R. Madron, a former Southern Baptist pastor. The new church first gathered in Parksley, where services were held in a storefront building adjacent to the firehouse and occasionally in the firehouse itself.

The small congregation describes itself as "Fundamental and Bible-believing," preaching "salvation with no apologies for those who accept and believe on the Lord Jesus Christ."

In 1976 the congregation built and occupied its permanent church building north of Accomac. The congregation established a private Christian school at the church in 1978.

[Source: 109]

Location: see ACCOMAC, PARKSLEY

First building, Parksley

•BAPTIST CHURCH OF CHRIST OF PUNGOTEAGUE

("Boggs Meetinghouse")

[ABA 1831, Independent 1831-1836]

Cashville

James Boggs, a layman from Pungoteague (Hollies) Baptist Church, erected this building at his own expense on his own land. The new building seems to have been his contribution to an attempt by Pungoteague Baptist tc establish a new congregation in Sluitkill Neck, and on October 7, 1831, the "Pungoteague Church meeting in Sluitkill Neck" first assembled and called James Rounds to the pastorate.

The attempt to establish the new congregation was frustrated by the anti-missions controversy which erupted among the Baptists in 1831. When Pungoteague Baptist divided over that issue, the anti-missions party occupied the new meetinghouse, taking the name Baptist Church of Christ of Pungoteague. The earlier congregation was apparently forced out of the building by this development and ceased to function.

The Baptist Church of Christ of Pungoteague, though an anti-missions congregation, remained in contact with the pro-missions Accomack Baptist Association. Some of the names reported as members of this church were also claimed by Hollies, and relations between the two congregations were agreeable. In 1836, when Hollies offered this congregation the use of its own church building for meetings provided it would help bear the cost of repairing it, the anti-missions people politely refused the offer, and remained in Cashville.

There is no mention of the anti-missions congregation in any records after 1836. Apparently it faded away in relatively short fashion like most of the other anti-missions groups at that time. Record books of the congregation from 1831 to 1834 are preserved at Hollies.

Baptist activity ceased in the building after 1836, by which time a Methodist congregation calling itself Boggs Chapel was established there. The original building remained in use until 1877, when it was dismantled and the present building of Andrew Chapel erected on the same site.

[Sources: 69, 150]

Location: see CASHVILLE

*BARRETT'S METHODIST EPISCOPAL CHURCH

(see Harmony Methodist Episcopal Church)

*BASCOM'S CHAPEL METHODIST EPISCOPAL CHURCH, SOUTH

[ME-S 1850-1882]
Onancock

In 1850, after a majority of the members of Cokesbury Church in Onancock had voted to remain in the northern Philadelphia Conference, a minority withdrew to establish a southern church. Later that year Bascom's Chapel, named for Bishop Henry Bascom of the Methodist Episcopal Church, South, was erected on land provided by Thomas Copes. It was at that time the northernmost church of the southern Virginia Conference on the Eastern Shore of Virginia.

Bascom's Chapel stood on King Street facing the town square, a scant sixty yards from Cokesbury, and its proximity to the older church only served to increase the rancor in an already tense situation. During warmer months when the windows of the two buildings were raised, each congregation could hear the other at worship. Neither church would yield either its location or its time of worship, and the result was a "strife and feelings that were unhappy" for a number of years to come.

Bascom's Chapel was not a large congregation and did not grow for some years. William Coe, pastor of the independent Cokesbury, preached there by invitation in 1861 and in 1863, but it is apparent that some time after that date the southern church virtually abandoned its activity there. After Coe's Convention split in 1864 and northern Methodists reclaimed Cokesbury, the increasingly pro-southern Convention Methodists met not in Bascom's Chapel but in the Fosque residence and Temperance Hall. There was no congregation worshiping in the church when the Union army ordered the closing of all Methodist churches on the Shore in 1864. For some reason Bascom's Chapel remained closed and unused, even though after 1864 there was a Methodist congregation of southern persuasion in the village that had no building to meet in.

In 1866 the Convention dissolved and joined the Methodist Episcopal Church, South. It was in that year that the southern remnant of Coe's congregation occupied the Bascom's building. Once again the northern and southern Methodists worshiped within hearing distance of each other until in 1882 the revived congregation abandoned the site, erected a new building, and took the name Market Street Church, where it continues in existence today.

In 1883 the building was purchased by the Presbyterians of Onancock, who worshiped there until Naomi Makemie Presbyterian Church was erected in 1895. Abandoned a second time, the building was subsequently purchased by Captain J. P. L. Hopkins of Onancock, an Episcopalian, who in 1903 loaned it to Holy Trinity Episcopal Church to house a Sunday school. In 1906 the building was dismantled, "the lumber...all pine oak and cypress heart...as sound as the day it was built." The church's windows were incorporated intact into the new home that Hopkins built on Market Street, which still stands across the street from Cokesbury.

[Sources: 99, 105, 110, 123, 141, 176]

Location: see ONANCOCK

BAYSIDE (WHITE RABBIT)

see: **Ayres Chapel Methodist Episcopal Church*
Metropolitan United Methodist Church
Mount Zion Holy Church
**Reese Chapel Methodist Protestant Church*
**Wise Chapel Baptist Church*

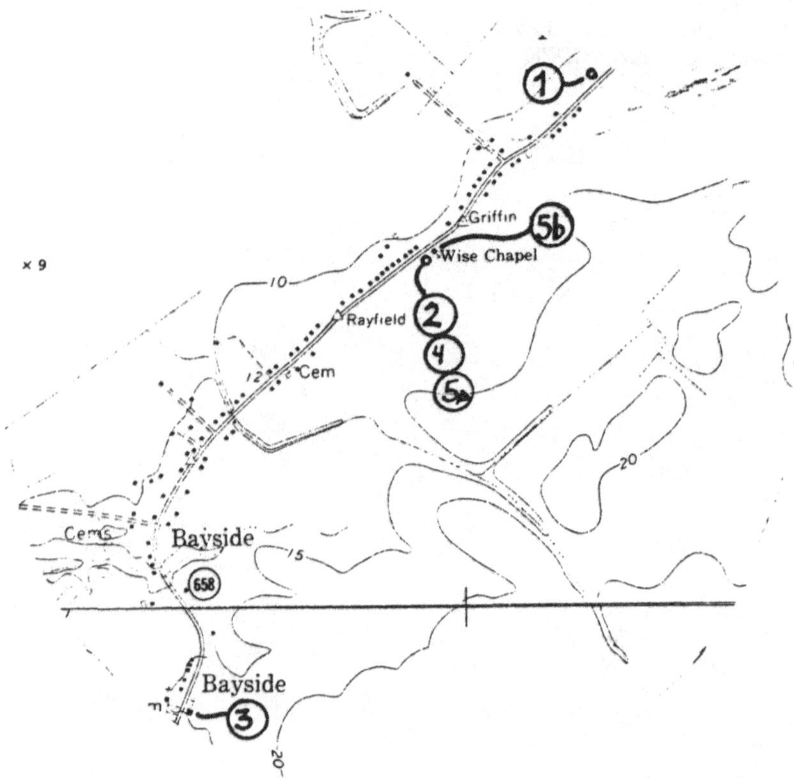

1 - Ayres Chapel
2 - Reese Chapel
3 - Metropolitan UMC
4 - Wise Chapel: used this building 1905-1925?
5a - Mt. Zion Holy Church: used this building 1948-1950
5b - Mt. Zion Holy Church: site since 1950

BAYVIEW

see: *Bethlehem Temple Mission*
Coles Chapel African Methodist Episcopal Church
Greater Mt. Sinai Gospel Tabernacle Church of Christ Deliverance
Holmes Presbyterian Church
**St. Paul's African Methodist Episcopal Church*

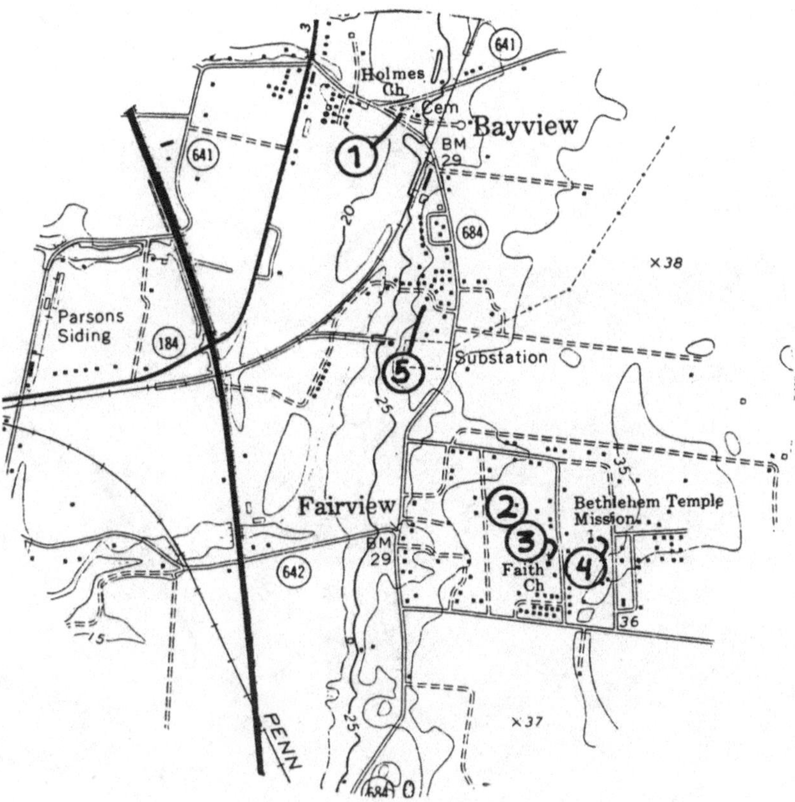

1 - Holmes Presbyterian
2 - St. Paul's AME: site 1914-1943
3 - Greater Mt. Sinai Tabernacle
4 - Bethlehem Temple Mission
5 - Coles Chapel AME: site since 1962 (for site of building prior to 1962 see CHERITON)

BELLE HAVEN

see: *Belle Haven Presbyterian Church*
Belle Haven United Methodist Church
**Belle Haven Universalist Church*
**Marshapungo Baptist Church*
**Occohannock Church [Church of England]*
St. Joseph African Methodist Episcopal Church
**St. Michael's Episcopal Church*

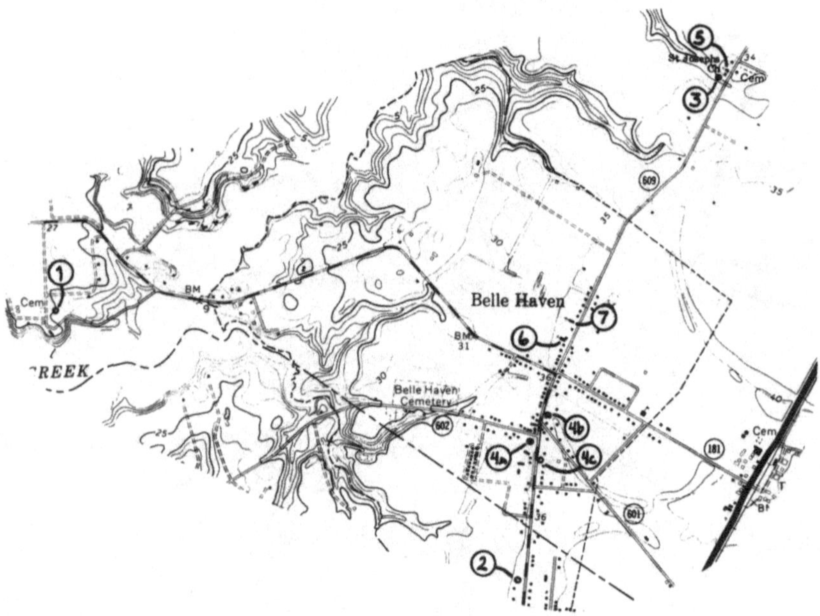

1 - Occohannock Church [approximate site]
2 - Marshapungo Baptist [approximate site]
3 - Belle Haven Universalist [approximate site]
4a - St. Michael's Episcopal I: original site 1849-1868
4b - St. Michael's Episcopal I: building moved to this site 1868-c1915
4c - St. Michael's Episcopal II: site 1906-1940
5 - St. Joseph AME
6 - Belle Haven Presbyterian
7 - Belle Haven Methodist

BELLE HAVEN PRESBYTERIAN CHURCH

[Pres 1879]
Belle Haven

The Presbyterians were the first to establish a permanent church in the town of Belle Haven. By the 1870's, by which time the Baptists, Episcopalians, Methodists, and Universalists had all tried and failed, Presbyterian preaching by the minister from Holmes was frequent in the village. Early in 1879 a series of revival services resulted in the conversion of twenty persons who petitioned the East Hanover Presbytery for the formation of a new church. The church was officially organized on May 4, 1879.

The church building was occupied by November 1879. It cost $1200 and was free of debt when dedicated. Preaching was at first held there every other Sunday and the pastor shared with Holmes. The church school, founded simultaneously with the congregation, was interdenominational in its earliest years, until Belle Haven Methodist Church was founded in 1886.

In 1897 a manse, immediately south of the church, was purchased for $1200, and in the same year a Missionary Society was formed. The Norfolk Presbytery met with this church in 1903 and 1909.

Belle Haven shared its pastor with Holmes until the 1940's, when it was first attached to Naomi Makemie in Onancock. In 1948 it was joined to Powelton in Wachapreague, and that arrangement is still in effect.

There have been two major additions to the church buildings. The first, now known as Fellowship Hall, was completed and dedicated in 1950. The second, an educational unit, was dedicated in 1964.

Belle Haven's membership has fluctuated up and down in this century. A maximum membership of 116 was reached in 1925 and again, after a slack period, in 1940. Membership again declined after 1940, but has built back up since then. Membership today is 80, and this is the third largest Presbyterian church on the Eastern Shore of Virginia.

[Sources: 119, 120]

Location: see BELLE HAVEN

BELLE HAVEN UNITED METHODIST CHURCH

[ME-S 1886, M 1939, UMC 1968]
Belle Haven

The village of Belle Haven had an unsavory reputation among the early Methodists of the Shore. Not only was there no church in that place, but also Methodist preachers were jeered at and insulted there. In 1806 James Herron was appointed the circuit preacher, and the Belle Haven wags, hearing the news, took wagers on whether he was really a shad.

By as early as 1795 Methodism was preached in the village, for William Colbert describes a sermon he delivered outdoors near a local tavern. From the tavern came the sounds of a heated cardgame, distracting his listeners. "I was so enabled to swell my voice as to attract the attention of some, and draw them from their sinful amusements to hear the word of God," he wrote. Even so, no permanent church of any denomination was established until 1879, when Belle Haven Presbyterian Church was founded. By then Baptists, Episcopalians, Methodists (under William Gwynn Coe), and Universalists had tried and failed.

Methodism was finally planted permanently in the village by Charles B. Crawley, the preacher who began to hold services in the local Grange Hall in 1886. In that same year the cornerstone for a church building was laid, and the new congregation met in the Presbyterian church while the building was being erected. The church was dedicated in 1887. Growth and prosperity proceeded apace, and the congregation added a steeple to the building in 1893.

By 1911 the old building was outgrown, so the congregation moved it back on the lot and erected a new sanctuary in front of it. The old building became the Sunday school annex, and for several decades the composite building retained the steeples of both structures. The steeple of the earlier building was later removed, and subsequent additions to the building, including an extensive annex added in 1956, have erased all exterior signs of the earlier structure.

Throughout most of its history Belle Haven has shared its pastor with the church in Craddockville, to which it was first joined in 1915. The church has today over 300 members, and the pastor lives in the parsonage in Belle Haven.

[Sources: 99, 100, 101, 109, 111, 116, 123]

Location: see BELLE HAVEN

*BELLE HAVEN UNIVERSALIST CHURCH

[1840-1850?]
Belle Haven

The Eastern Shore's only Universalist church was founded in 1840 by a Mr. Chase, a Boston divine who came to the Shore to conduct the funeral service of a Cobb's Island lady. Intent upon establishing the New England faith on the Shore, he sought out places in Eastville and Capeville to do so, but without success. Finally he managed to erect a church near Belle Haven, in the middle of what Methodists considered the most unrighteous and free-thinking area of the county. Above the door of the church was painted the basic tenet of the new faith: "We believe in the living God, the Savior of all men."

Chase, the founder, did not remain on the Shore to pastor the church, and the congregation's only pastor throughout its short history was G. L. Lumsden, who proved even more aggressive in his desire to evangelize the Shore than did Chase. In 1841 Lumsden issued a challenge to pastors of other denominations to debate the doctrines of salvation publicly, and T. J. Quigley of the Northampton Circuit accepted the challenge. For two days hundreds of excited spectators filled the old building of Marshapungo Baptist Church near Belle Haven to hear the opponents debate the topic, "Do the Holy Scriptures teach the unconditional Salvation of all mankind?" Quigley's opponent was not Lumsden but the more renowned Dr. Dodd, imported from Boston for the debate. When the debate was over, Quigley took the prize and Dodd left the Shore, leaving behind him memories of some of the most eloquent oratory that had ever been heard there.

Little is known of the life of the Universalist congregation in Belle Haven. In 1846 Lumsden was still the pastor, and he performed a marriage now recorded at the courthouse. The last mention of the church is from 1850, when it was listed in the census of that year. Apparently the church closed not long afterwards.

William Gwynn Coe, pastor of the independent Methodist churches of the Shore during the Civil War, held services in the abandoned Universalist building during the summer of 1864. This was one of the churches ordered closed by the Union army in that year, by virtue of the fact that Coe's congregation was meeting there.

The Methodists abandoned the building later in 1864, and thereafter it gradually went to decay and burned. By the 1880's a school stood on the site, adjacent to the present site of St. Joseph's African Methodist Episcopal Church, about a mile north of Belle Haven.

[Sources: 39, 99, 102]

Location: see BELLE HAVEN

BEREA UNITED METHODIST CHURCH

("Pittsville M.P.") [MP 1874, M 1939, UMC 1968] New Church

This church was born not in New Church, where it stands today, but several miles west in "Pittsville," now known as Miona. Land for the church was purchased there in 1874, but instead of a church the congregation erected a schoolhouse in which worship services were held. Until 1879 the Pittsville congregation was attached to Wattsville M.P., from whence it was founded, but after that year it was joined to the new Greenbackville church.

In 1884 the railroad came to the Shore, and this congregation moved to the nearest point on the railroad, the village of New Church. John and Esther Brittingham provided a lot and building commenced alongside the bush arbor where the congregation was worshiping. Rev. W. H. Stone of Greenbackville organized the congregation, which took the name Berea.

The building, dedicated March 28, 1886, was a one-room frame building with primitive furnishings. The windows were plain, and its seats were kitchen chairs nailed to a plank. In 1908 the building was substantially altered: a steeple entrance was added, the old entrance became a window, a pulpit alcove added to the side of the original room, and new pews installed at right angles to the length of the building. At this same time colored glass windows were installed and a large church school room added. The building has remained essentially unchanged since 1908, except for renovations in the steeple in 1948, and interior remodelings of both rooms.

Berea, like the village in which it sits, reached its maximum growth in 1930; there were 130 members of the church at that time. Since then church and village have declined together. After Unification in 1939, Berea was the principal church of the New Church Charge, which also contained Atlantic, Wattsville, and Pittsville. In 1954 the charge was reduced to three churches when Atlantic became a station. In 1970 Atlantic rejoined the charge (as Wattsville dropped out), but this time the charge was named Atlantic-New Church, and Berea was no longer the main church. The parsonage and main strength of the charge were now in Atlantic, and the Berea parsonage, erected next door in 1899, was put up for rent.

In the 1970's Berea was the recipient of two large bequests of money, and extensive interior renovations were completed in 1978.

[Sources: 36, 111, 114, 116, 123, 176]

Location: see MIONA, NEW CHURCH

*BETHANY METHODIST EPISCOPAL CHURCH

[ME 1885-1939]
Cape Charles

(photo c. 1910)

John A. B. Wilson, the presiding elder of the northern Methodist churches on the Virginia Shore, preached the first religious service in the new town of Cape Charles in 1885. The service was held in the office of the superintendent of the railroad, but Wilson observed only that the room in which he preached was "connected with a saloon."

From this beginning grew Bethany Methodist Episcopal Church, the first church in Cape Charles. The first building was erected on the south corner of Plum Street and Monroe Avenue in 1887, when there were only eight members. The first public school sessions in Cape Charles are said to have been held in this building.

In 1889, when other congregations were beginning to appear in the new community, Bethany began construction of a new and larger building on the corner of Peach and Randolph. The second structure was completed in 1890 at the cost of $3000. There were 26 members in that year. The older building was subsequently sold to a black Methodist congregation, who moved it to Jefferson Avenue where it is today St. Stephen's A.M.E. Church.

Although it was ultimately outdistanced in size by the southern Methodist church founded in Cape Charles in 1887, Bethany was a prosperous and vigorous church throughout most of its history. The Shore's first WCTU chapter was founded here in 1894, and a Brotherhood Society in 1909. By 1896 there were 96 members. By 1910 an annex had been added to the building. In 1921, when the membership had grown to 229, there was talk of a new building, but no new building was erected.

In 1939 when the three major Methodist denominations merged, Bethany and Centenary, the southern church on the same block, voted unanimously to merge as well. The new congregation took the name Trinity and occupied the southern Methodist property. The northern Methodist property, abandoned in 1939, was sold in 1943. The building was purchased by another congregation, who floated it in pieces across the bay and reerected it in Portsmouth, Virginia. There it stands to this day as West End United Methodist Church, its appearance much changed by subsequent additions.

[Sources: 110, 111, 113, 117, 124, 176]
Location: see CAPE CHARLES

BETHEL AFRICAN METHODIST EPISCOPAL CHURCH

("Wayman's Chapel," "Eastville")
[AME 1866]
Eastville

It was near Eastville that James H. A. Johnson preached the first A.M.E. service on the Eastern Shore of Virginia in December 1865. Three weeks later he returned to Eastville and on January 7, 1866, organized this church in a schoolhouse near the present site. Bethel is the oldest A.M.E. church in Northampton County, and the second oldest on the entire Shore, after Macedonia in Accomac.

It was under the second pastor, John Henry Offer (1866-1871), that the present site was purchased and the first building erected on it in 1868. The new church was a small frame building that stood between the present church and the parsonage, and it was known as Wayman's Chapel, after Bishop A. W. Wayman of the A.M.E. Church. By 1870 there was a parsonage adjacent to it, and no fewer than five congregations on the Eastville Circuit.

In 1879, under the fifth pastor, Robert Davis (1878-1882), the congregation replaced its original building with a new one that cost $1000. In this building occurred one of the church's proudest moments: the convening of the 17th Session of the Virginia Annual Conference of the African Methodist Episcopal Church, opened by Bishop Daniel Payne on April 26, 1883. So many persons were in attendance that the building was unable to hold them, and the floor gave way, creating "the wildest excitement...which came near resulting in the loss of many lives."

The present building, the third, was erected in 1901 during the pastorate of George Jimmerson (1898-1903), and its large size reflects the growth that the church experienced at the turn of the century. In 1906 almost 800 persons, most of them women, thronged the church for a mass meeting in support of missions at which conference officers spoke. The following year after a revival netted some sixty new members, the membership reached 700. In 1913 an even more successful revival resulted in 160 converts and 129 new members. Bishop Coffin convened the 47th Session of the Virginia Annual Conference in the church that same year.

The church building, while still quite new, was only narrowly saved from a fire believed set by an arsonist in 1907, and since that time it has received the almost constant attention of a congregation that has repeatedly repaired and improved it. The Depression of the 1930's hit the church hard, and when the 1940's began the congregation was deeply in debt and the building mortgaged. In 1942 the church building was sold at public auction and purchased by Mrs. Benjamin Mears. The congregation voted to leave the Virginia Conference until the building could be regained, and the church was served by local pastors for the three-year period during which "members worked faithfully and diligently" to raise the $9000 needed to buy it back.

On May 4, 1945, Bishop W. H. Davis preached the sermon at which the church was returned to the Conference and the mortgage note burned. Five years later the 84th Session of the Annual Conference convened here.

Bethel is one of the largest black churches on the Shore, a strong and vigorous congregation. The pastor lives next door to the church.

[Sources: 7, 110, 124, 129]

Location: see EASTVILLE

BETHEL AFRICAN METHODIST EPISCOPAL CHURCH

(''Onancock'') [AME 1868] Onancock

This congregation was founded in 1868 by the Reverend John Henry Offer, the active successor to James H. A. Johnson who pioneered A.M.E. work on the Shore. In 1868 the congregation bought a lot from Margaret Snead for $100 and erected their first building on it, north of town on what is today North Street extended, opposite the Hermitage.

The Onancock congregation first appears on the records of the denomination in 1870, when W. F. Williams was pastor here and at Drummondtown. By 1875 the Onancock church was a station church, although it did not always remain so in the early years of its history.

By the turn of the century most of the members of this church lived some distance to the east, in the black settlement where St. John's Baptist Church was erected in 1885. The decision was made to move the building to this neighborhood. A lot on Boundry Street was purchased in 1902 and the building moved to it in 1908. The cost of moving and rebuilding the church was $1900, and when the relocated building was finally dedicated in 1911, $300 was still owed on it.

When moved to its present site the church was still known as Onancock A.M.E. In this century its name was changed to Bethel. It has been a prosperous and vigorous church in recent years.

[Sources: 7, 105, 123, 169, 176]

Location: see ONANCOCK

BETHEL BAPTIST CHURCH

[ABA 1845]
Bloxom

(second building, photo 1931)

As early as 1782 Joshua Johnson gave a plot of land near Bloxom's Bridge to the Baptists, the very site where Elijah Baker is said to have preached. The site became known as "the Baptist acre near Muddy Creek," and it was from time to time used for various functions. By 1845 the Baptist acre was the site of a Sunday school operated by Modest Town Baptist Church, and in that year the Modest Town congregation resolved "that our brethren on the Bay Side take up a subscription to see what can be raised to build a meeting house on the Baptist acre near Muddy Creek." By 1846 the Muddy Creek meetinghouse, a mission of Modest Town, was standing there.

Modest Town granted letters of dismissal to several members to form a new church at Muddy Creek in 1846, but the organization was not effected until 1852. In that year twenty members constituted the new Bethel Baptist Church, and in

August the congregation was admitted into the Accomack Baptist Association. The church grew and prospered quickly; fourteen members joined during the first year.

During the last quarter of the nineteenth century Bethel was the founding force behind several new congregations in the area. It joined with Modest Town to found Atlantic Baptist in 1877. Later it was the mother church of Shiloh (1887), Mappsville (1888), and Hallwood (1901).

In 1887 the original Bethel building was dismantled; like so many other churches on the Shore it had a gallery for slaves across the back, and from it many a black Baptist had led the congregation in prayer. A new building was erected on the same site. This second building was rebuilt and enlarged in 1909 at a cost of $8300. The pastor at that time was R. S. Monds, who served from 1904 to 1920, the longest pastorate in the church's history.

On December 20, 1946, the second Bethel building burned to the ground, and the congregation assembled for worship in Bloxom School while their third building was being erected. The present brick building cost $100,000, and was dedicated in 1949. By 1953 it was free of debt.

Bethel has been a station church since 1913, the ninth year of Monds' pastorate. It is today the third largest Baptist church on the Eastern Shore of Virginia, after Union and Exmore, and has just over 300 members.

[Sources: 69, 70, 105, 127, 176]

Location: see BLOXOM

Bethel Baptist Church No. 3

BETHEL BAPTIST CHURCH

[ESBA 1882]
Franktown

This church was organized in 1882, "the result of the community prayer meeting that was held in different homes." The building was erected in that year under Tom Byrd, the first pastor, who also founded St. John's Baptist Church in Onancock.

Over the next fifty years six pastors served the church, which grew in membership from a tiny number to over 140. Under C. C. Weathers, the fourth pastor, whose term began in 1919, the congregation first began to gather for worship every Sunday. By the beginning of the 1930's the building had been improved by the addition of a baptismal pool and a social hall.

In 1934, L. Leon Ford, a native of Buckingham County who came to the Shore to teach in the public school system, was called to the pastorate. When he arrived "the spirit of the church was at a very low ebb." Ford served the church a total of 41 years, one of the longest pastorates on record in any church on the Shore, and to tell the history of the church since 1934 is almost to tell the story of its pastor.

In its years under Ford's capable leadership the church prospered. Membership more than doubled, and among the extensive improvements made to the building were a new exterior facade (1957) and an annex at the rear of the church (1969). In 1951 Ford was awarded the Doctor of Divinity degree by Virginia Seminary, his alma mater. At his death in 1975 the membership of the church was well over 300.

Since Ford lived in his own home throughout his long pastorate, it was not until after his death that this vigorous congregation acquired its first parsonage, even though it is one of the largest black congregations on the Shore.

[Sources: 26, 105, 109, 110, 124]

Location: see NASSAWADOX

*BETHEL METHODIST PROTESTANT CHURCH
[MP 1853-1930]
Chincoteague

(photo c. 1920)

This was the second church on Chincoteague Island, after Union Baptist, and the first of several Methodist churches. The earliest known preacher on the island is said to have been Avra Melvin of the Methodist Protestant Church, who preached to both Baptists and Methodists in a schoolhouse. This ecumenical endeavor ended in 1841 when Union Baptist was organized. Twelve years later in 1853 Evaline Sharpley sold the lot on Church Street on which the Methodist Protestants erected their building shortly thereafter.

During its early years this church struggled through some very lean times. At first attached to the Wattsville Church, it did not become a circuit in its own right until 1876, when I. T. Atkins was the pastor. Even having a pastor to itself did not ease the financial burden. In 1880 the church reported that it had lost five of its most influential and best-paying members, and petitioned to be attached to the Greenbackville church, which the Conference would not do. The next year the Conference reprimanded the congregation for selling the parsonage to pay the pastor's salary, and in 1885 the church lost perhaps as many as seventy members who transferred to the newer Methodist Episcopal church in town.

Toward the end of the century the congregation prospered a bit more, although it had already fallen behind Christ M.E. in size. In 1887 the original building was replaced by the present one; there were 83 members when it was dedicated in 1888. In 1899 the congregation purchased land for a parsonage, and in the following year the church was enlarged by the addition of a wing.

In the early years of the twentieth century the church once again declined, and in 1930 the denomination declared it "extinct." The property, which ultimately fell to the old rival Christ Methodist, was sold in 1943 to Christ's Sanctified Holy Church, which used it for a number of years for worship and meetings. When that church, too, declined in numbers, the building again sat vacant until in 1965 it was sold to the Roman Catholic Church. Since that time it has been St. Andrew's, founded from the Holy Name of Jesus Church in Pocomoke City.

When originally erected in 1887 the building had a steeple, which was removed at an early date.

[Sources: 105, 110, 114, 123, 143, 176]

Location: see CHINCOTEAGUE

BETHEL UNITED METHODIST CHURCH

(''Occohannock Neck'') [ME 1795, ME-S 1846, M 1939, UMC 1968] Jamesville

Bethel's origins lie in the society that first gathered at the Concord Wharf home of Thomas Paramore, brother of William Paramore of the Locustville society in Accomack. The circuit preacher, William Colbert, was meeting with this society as early as 1795, though he soon labeled it ''that disputing place, Occohannock Neck'' and dropped it from his rounds. Even so the society continued and prospered.

Just when the first building was erected here is not known, but it was standing by 1808 on the present church site. It was from the very first known as Bethel Chapel, and the records of 1812 list its five trustees.

Not much is known of life at Bethel until 1846, when the congregation seceded to the Methodist Episcopal Church, South. Once in the southern church, the congregation grew and flourished. A revival held in 1847 added sixteen converts to the church. Bethel was apparently not at all disrupted during the troubles that beset the Methodists during the division between north and south, and grew steadily.

It was not until 1883 that Hezekiah and Sarah James sold to the church for $1 the lot on which the building had stood for generations. In that same year the old building was moved away and the present one erected. The older building was moved to a nearby farm and saw service as a schoolhouse, then as a dwelling, and stood abandoned until well into the second half of the twentieth century. The newer building, when erected, was a simple, one-room building with plain windows and no steeple, typical of Methodist churches of that period.

By 1903 Bethel could boast almost 300 members, and it was necessary to improve the building. The sanctuary as it is today — steeple, colored windows, and chancel — was dedicated in 1905.

The building remained unchanged for another forty years until in 1948 the church school annex was added. Part of this addition was destroyed by fire in 1958, and was restored shortly thereafter.

Bethel is today on a charge with Garrison's in Painter, an arrangement that dates from 1965. The present membership is about 150.

[Sources: 100, 111, 116, 124, 149]

Location: see JAMESVILLE

BETHLEHEM TEMPLE MISSION HOLINESS CHURCH OF GOD IN CHRIST JESUS

[Independent 1955]
Fairview

May Ella Harmon was a member of Mt. Sinai Gospel Tabernacle in Fairview when she withdrew to establish this church. In 1955 she and her small congregation purchased a lot across the street from Mt. Sinai, and the present building was subsequently erected.

The Bethlehem Temple Mission has never been a large congregation, and in recent years has dwindled even more in size. Fewer than a dozen persons still meet regularly for worship here. Harmon has been pastor of the church since its formation; R. A. Car has served as bishop.

The separation of this congregation from Mt. Sinai was not attended with the usual bad feeling that often accompanies schism. Over the years this church has remained on amicable terms with the older neighborhood church, to which it is doctrinally similar.

[Sources: 124, 176]

Location: see BAYVIEW

*BEULAH BAPTIST CHURCH

[ABA 1879-1913?]
Chincoteague

Captain John W. Bunting of Chincoteague, a self-made man of considerable wealth, was the founding force and chief pillar of Beulah Baptist Church, the second white Baptist church on Chincoteague Island. The church was erected in 1879 at 501 South Main Street, and Captain Bunting was almost singlehandedly responsible for its existence.

Despite the influence of Bunting, Beulah Baptist had few other supporters among the island community where Union Baptist remained strong. By 1887 there were only fourteen members, and the church had already been closed for some time. In 1893 Bunting and his wife, Susan, provided new land for the church on Willow Street south of the main village, and the building was moved to that site, farther away from Union to a more unchurched end of the island. Even relocation did not forestall the church's decline. Bunting died in 1905, and the church fell into a quick decline. The parsonage was sold in 1909, and there is no record of the church's operation after 1913.

In 1929 Union Baptist Church fell heir to the abandoned property, and the deed noted that the church "...is not and has not for some years past been a self-sustaining house of worship." Union subsequently used the building as a meeting-house for worship and other purposes across the years. The last church activity in the building was a Sunday school conducted by Union in the early 1960's.

After even Union ceased to use the building, it stood alone and deserted for another decade. It burned completely to the ground in August 1973.

[Sources: 105, 110, 123, 176]

Location: see CHINCOTEAGUE

*BIBLE CHURCH

[Independent 1953-1956]
New Church

Edward Jones, former pastor of the New Church Baptist Field, founded this church in 1953. The congregation met in a rented store building in New Church.

Although doctrinally fundamentalist and conservative, Jones and his church were liberal on social issues. This congregation was composed of both whites and blacks, and much of Jones' ministry was done among the blacks of the area.

Although founded as a conservative alternative to the Baptist churches of the New Church area, Bible Church made little or no inroads into those congregations, and was discontinued in 1956.

[Sources: 36, 176]

Location: see NEW CHURCH

BIRDSNEST

see: *Community Church of God*
Pentecostal House of Prayer
**Taylor Memorial Baptist Church*

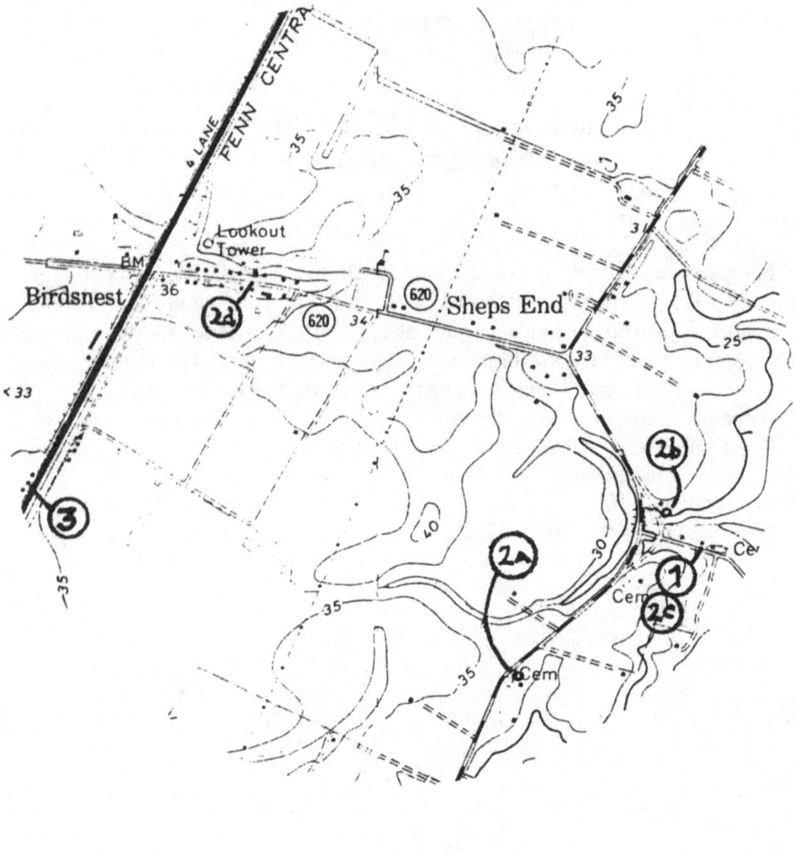

1 - Taylor Memorial Baptist
2a - Community Church of God: original site 1917-1933
2b - Community Church of God: building moved to this site 1933-1947
2c - Community Church of God: congregation worshiped here 1940?-1953
2d - Community Church of God: site since 1953
3 - Pentecostal House of Prayer

BLOXOM

see: *Bethel Baptist Church*
Bloxom United Methodist Church
Bloxom Wesleyan Church
**Christ Episcopal Church*
Macedonia Baptist Church

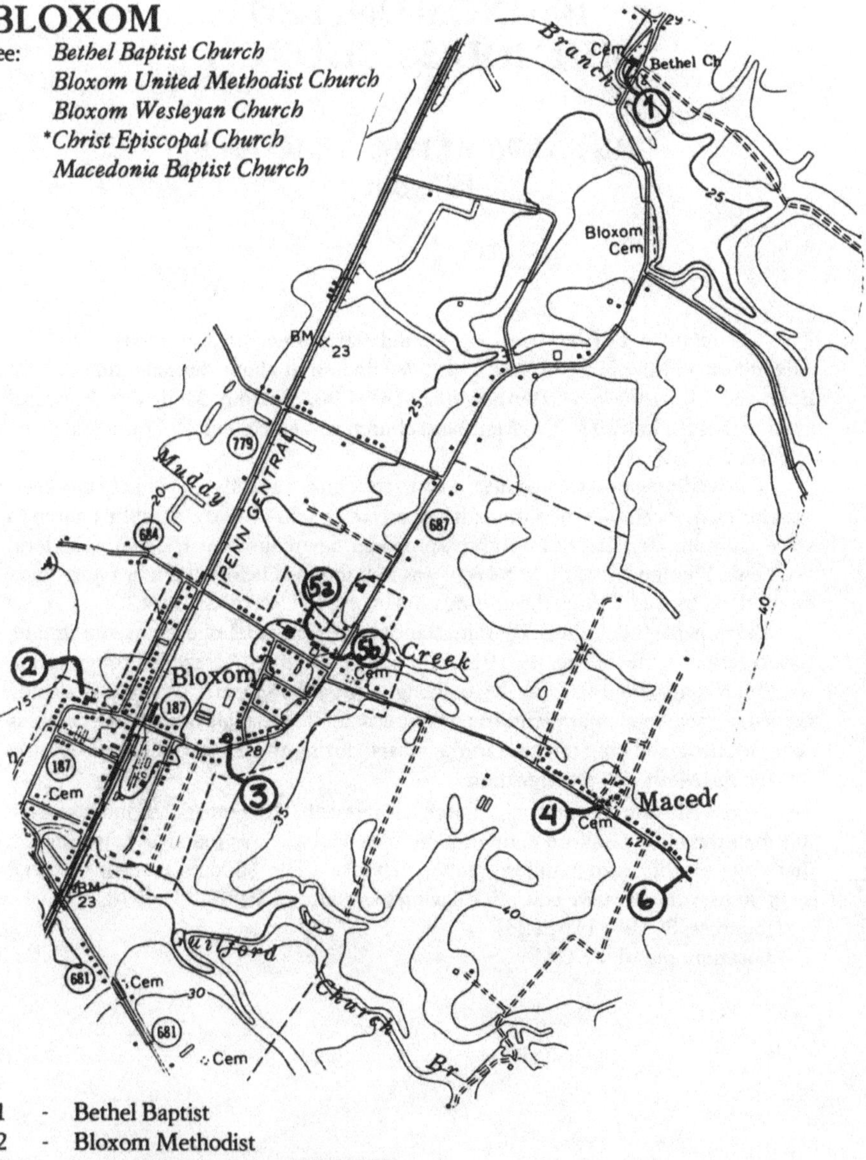

1 - Bethel Baptist
2 - Bloxom Methodist
3 - Christ Episcopal: site 1896-1946
4 - Macedonia Baptist
5a - Bloxom Wesleyan: tabernacle and campgrounds
5b - Bloxom Wesleyan: building since 1946
6 - St. John's Faith Church of God Live On: site 1962-1976 [for location since 1976 see MAKEMIE PARK]

BLOXOM UNITED METHODIST CHURCH

[ME-S 1896, M 1939, UMC 1968]
Bloxom

The town of Bloxom grew up around the railroad in the 1890's, and the Methodists and the Episcopalians descended upon it at about the same time. Christ Episcopal Church was established there in 1896, Bloxom Methodist Episcopal Church, South, in 1897. The Methodist church was erected in 1897 on land given by David W. Bloxom.

The Methodist parsonage next door to the church at Bloxom actually antedates the church and congregation there; it was erected a year or two before the church to serve Guilford, St. Thomas', and the proposed new church at Bloxom. The local Women's Foreign Missionary Society was also founded before the new church was established, by Ella Coffey, the visiting missionary, in December 1894.

Bloxom Methodist quickly outdistanced the Episcopal church as the leading congregation of the village. By 1917, when the prosperous Methodist congregation was improving and enlarging its building, Christ Episcopal Church had already peaked in membership at eighteen communicants. The establishment of a Holiness camp meeting and congregation in the village during the 1920's did not seriously weaken the Methodist congregation.

Today Bloxom is a strong church of about 170 members, slightly smaller still than the older Guilford congregation from which it was founded. It has always shared its pastors with Guilford and St. Thomas. The building erected in 1897 is still in use; an extensive educational wing was added in 1958.

[Sources: 8, 109, 116, 123]

Location: see BLOXOM

BLOXOM WESLEYAN CHURCH

[IAHC 1920, PH 1922, W 1968]
Bloxom

The Turlington Campmeeting had been abandoned for two decades when in 1920 William Vickers, the Holiness evangelist, conducted a camp meeting in the town of Bloxom. It was the first general, not local, camp meeting among the whites of the Shore for twenty years, and with its establishment the Holiness movement began to be a force to be reckoned with throughout the Shore.

The Bloxom congregation undoubtedly grew out of the camp meeting there and first made its appearance on the records of the denomination in 1925, when there were 44 members and Vickers himself was the pastor. Vickers was succeeded in 1928 by F. C. Walls, who was pastor a year later when the most successful camp meeting of all was held. The 1929 camp meeting, which Vickers conducted with the help of Mayme Parker and Winifred Mears "under the leadership of the Holy Ghost," was "blessed of God along both spiritual and financial lines." Over $7000 was raised at the camp meeting, and with it the local congregation was able to set itself up on a strong footing.

In 1929 the campground, a four-acre site, was purchased for $6000, and the congregation moved its services to the tabernacle there, boarding it up for the winter months, opening it to the fresh air during the warmer seasons. Of more urgent necessity than a permanent church building was a parsonage, which was soon erected near the tabernacle. Of Walls, the pastor, the 1929 report said: "His address is Bloxom, but Accomack County is his parish. His preaching places are so many, his schedules so complicated that his wife is often at sea to know where he goes next."

In 1932 a Woman's Foreign Missionary Society was organized at the church. Six years later, when there were 39 members and C. C. Elzey was pastor, the congregation surpassed the older Grotons congregation in size and became the largest Pilgrim Holiness church on the Shore. It has never relinquished that lead.

In 1941 P. F. Bean became the pastor, and under his able leadership the congregation began saving for a permanent church building. In 1946 the abandoned building of Christ Episcopal Church was purchased. The congregation moved it up the street to the edge of the campground, added a room to either side and veneered the exterior with brick. When Bean left the charge in the summer of 1947 these renovations were almost complete.

Though not the oldest, Bloxom is now the largest and strongest of the Wesleyan churches on the Eastern Shore of Virginia. Its present membership is about 45, its average attendance on Sunday almost twice that. The Bloxom camp meeting has long since become an annual affair.

[Sources: 110, 121, 123, 176]

Location: see BLOXOM

BOGGS CHAPEL METHODIST EPISCOPAL CHURCH, SOUTH

(see Andrew Chapel United Methodist Church)

*BOGGS MEETINGHOUSE

(see Baptist Church of Christ of Pungoteague)

BOSTON

see: *Holy Trinity Baptist Church*
**Nandua Church (Church of England)*
Shiloh Baptist Church

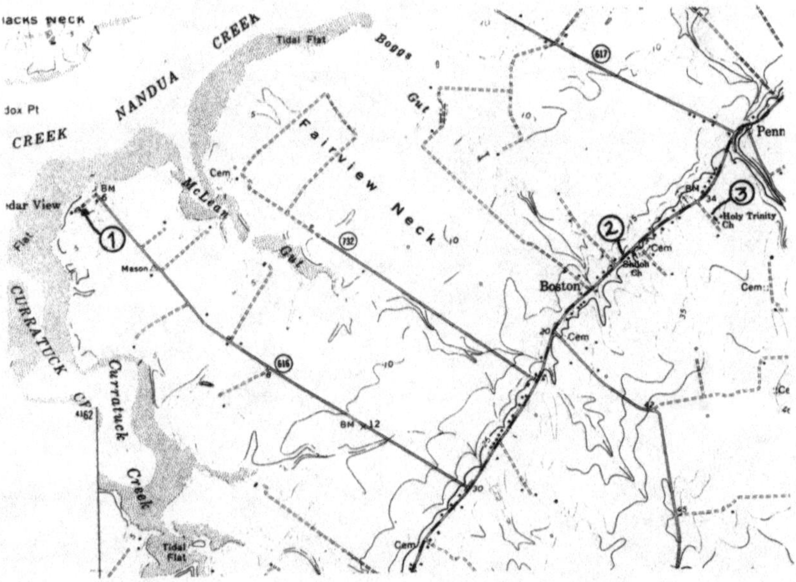

1 - Nandua Church: site c1652-1667 [approximate]
2 - Shiloh Baptist
3 - Holy Trinity Baptist

BRIDGETOWN

see: *Hungars Episcopal Church*
Shorter Chapel African Methodist Episcopal Church

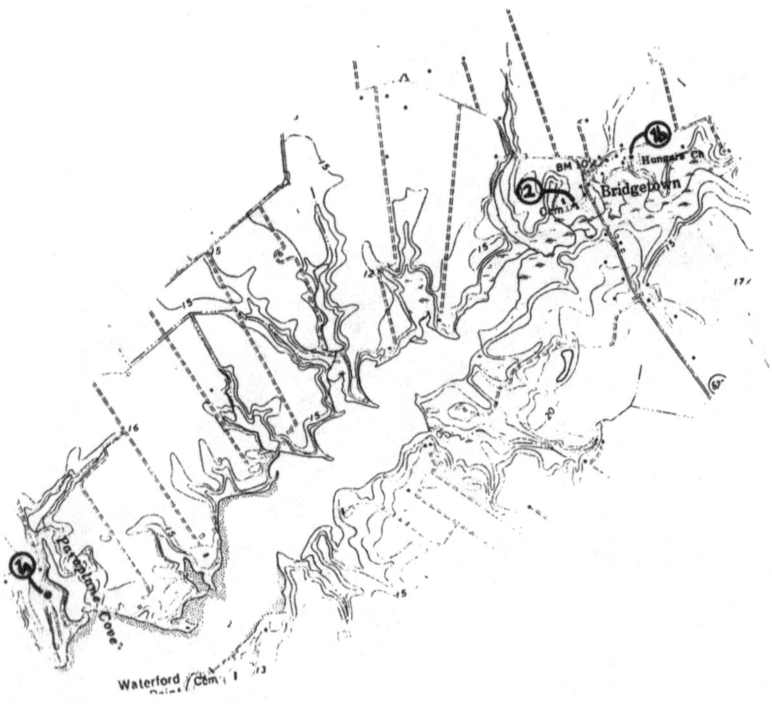

1a - Hungars Episcopal: original site 1646?-1680 [approximate]
1b - Hungars Episcopal: site since 1680
2 - Shorter Chapel AME

BROADWATER CHAPEL METHODIST EPISCOPAL CHURCH, SOUTH

(see Epworth United Methodist Church)

BROADWAY BAPTIST CHURCH

[ABA 1884]

Cashville

Mr. and Mrs. William Cobb were the only Baptists living in the Cashville area in 1883 when the Accomack Baptist Association employed H. N. Quisenberry as "colporteur." It was Quisenberry's task to visit among Baptist families in areas not served by churches, and at the Cobb home "he found comfort and aid." His work in Cashville began with prayer meetings in 1884. By 1886 a Sunday school had been organized, a church building erected, and Quisenberry had moved on to other fields. In commendation of him, the Association resolved: "His work at Sluitkill Neck [Broadway] is worth to us many times over what it has cost to maintain him."

On January 9, 1887, Broadway Baptist Church was organized with ten charter members, two of whom, William Cobb and his wife, were from Onancock Baptist Church. J. W. Hundley of Onancock was in charge of the new church.

The church was erected on land donated by B. T. Parker, owner of an Onancock hotel. It was dedicated in December 1885. The dedicatory sermon was delivered by Alfred E. Dickinson, editor of the *Religious Herald.* Prior to its dedication the infant congregation had held evangelistic services in Andrew Chapel Methodist Episcopal Church, South, the last Baptist activity on that venerable site of old Boggs Meetinghouse.

William Cobb remained a faithful member of Broadway until his death in 1931. The church in its earliest years most often shared its pastors with Onancock Baptist Church, but after the turn of the century it became a station church and purchased a parsonage of its own.

The original building is still in use and has not been substantially altered, except that an educational annex has been added. Since 1931 Broadway has shared its pastors with Onley Baptist Church, and the parsonage in Onley has been used. The present membership at Broadway is 68.

[Sources: 69, 122]

Location: see CASHVILLE

BURTON'S CHAPEL METHODIST EPISCOPAL CHURCH, SOUTH

(see Oak Grove United Methodist Church)

BURTON'S UNITED METHODIST CHURCH

[ME 1871, M 1939, UMC 1968]
Chancetown

The fire that destroyed venerable old Burton's Chapel in March 1870 resulted not only in the erection of Oak Grove Church but also in the creation of this congregation. The whites of Burton's Chapel released the black members of the congregation to form their own church, and in 1871 Richard Ames sold the land on which the church stands. The deed specifically states that the land was to be used "for the use and benefit of no other person or persons whatsoever other than such religious congregation." The blacks erected their new church not far from where Captain Thomas Burton had built his first chapel, and gave it his name at the very time that the white congregation abandoned it.

It was from Burton's that the black Methodist work in this area radiated. Grace Church in Locust Mount was founded from here in 1879, Snead's in 1881, and for a while even St. Luke's A.M.E. in Daugherty was under the care of this pastor. George E. Snead, the pastor for whom Snead's Church was named, served here and was buried here in 1885. The circuit of which this church was the center was known as "Locust Mount" and "Fair Oaks" before it became "Wachapreague" in this century.

By the turn of the century Burton's and the other churches on the circuit were prospering. The present Burton's building was erected in 1897, and in 1900 there were fifty conversions on the circuit. In 1903 the first parsonage was erected.

The building was remodeled in 1923 at a cost of $1250, but a decade later the Depression almost killed the church. A. F. Winder was pastor at that time, and it was not uncommon for him to find a total weekly collection of 35¢ or 50¢ in the offering plate on Sundays. In 1935 the presiding elder reported that Burton's was "dead," but the church never closed and managed to survive the Depression.

Although a small church today, with only 56 members, Burton's is one of the oldest black churches on the Shore. Measured from 1801, when the original Burton's Chapel was founded by blacks and whites alike, it is one of the oldest of all congregations on the Shore, and like nearby Oak Grove is a direct descendant of the Great Revival under Thomas Smith.

[Sources: 113, 116, 123, 129, 158]

Location: see CHANCETOWN

CALVARY ASSEMBLY OF GOD

[AG-S 1951]
Nassawadox

This was the first white Pentecostal congregation in Northampton County, and it was pioneered by the Reverend and Mrs. Julian B. Goggin in July 1951. The Goggins assembled their congregations in a portable tabernacle which was used up and down the county in several places, principally Exmore and Oyster.

Howard Ryan was the pastor when, in 1957, the growing congregation began the search for a permanent location. A lot in Exmore just behind the Pilgrim Holiness church was purchased in that year for $10, but was never used. Instead the congregation was able to obtain an abandoned store building in Nassawadox. This building was refitted for worship and as a parsonage in 1958, and has served both purposes ever since.

This congregation has grown slowly but steadily over the years and now numbers 24. There are, however, more than twice that number of "adherents" in active relationship with the congregation.

[Sources: 124, 176]

Location: see NASSAWADOX

*CALVARY BAPTIST CHURCH

("Milford")
[ABA 1902-1911]
Greenbackville

Short-lived Calvary Baptist Church was organized and admitted into the Accomack Association in 1902. In September of that year Lower Northampton Baptist Church, at the opposite end of the Shore, sent an offering of $21.50 to aid the struggling new congregation. The Greenbackville Baptists worshiped in the original building of the Methodist Protestant church, abandoned in 1895. Although the church property was not purchased until 1903, it was dedicated on November 9, 1902. C. L. Corbitt, pastor of Red Bank Baptist Church, preached the dedicatory sermon.

Little is known of the life of this church, possibly because there was little life to know. One of the pastors was Charles Clement, who also preached at Atlantic, Horntown, Chincoteague, and Makemie Park during the same period. Calvary was the weakest of this field of churches and dropped from the record in 1911.

The church building, erected in 1877, was later sold and dismantled; the lumber was used in the erection of a barrel factory in the village.

[Sources: 69, 110, 123, 139]

Location: see GREENBACKVILLE

CALVARY BIBLE CHURCH

("Calvary Baptist")
[Independent 1969]
Cape Charles

Robert Fornsberger, a layman in the Air Force, was the chief instrument in the founding of this congregation, which was organized in 1969. It was originally known as Calvary Baptist Church, and was the first of a new wave of independent fundamentalist Baptist congregations to be founded on the Virginia Shore.

The congregation first gathered in a rented building on Pine Street in Cape Charles. The present location on Randolph Avenue was occupied in 1971.

This is not a large congregation, although it is now two or three times its original size. There are about forty members, some of whom come from as far away as Machipongo. Although a conservative white congregation, Calvary is one of the few churches on the Shore that can claim to have been racially mixed.

In 1978 under the fifth pastor the name of the church was changed to Calvary Bible Church.

[Sources: 109, 176]

Location: see CAPE CHARLES

CALVARY UNITED METHODIST CHURCH

("Hunting Creek")
[MP 1888, M 1939, UMC 1968]
Hopkins

Hunting Creek Methodist Protestant Church was founded from Lee Mont in 1888, and its first building, a small frame structure, was erected in that same year. The cornerstone ceremonies were held on July 5, 1888, and featured a parade from Lee Mont to the site of the new church, and a large community feast.

Hunting Creek was a deliberate attempt by the Methodist Protestants to revive the work of Reese Chapel, which closed a few years before. According to a notice in the county newspapers announcing the erection of the church, the original plan was to call this church, too, Reese Chapel. That name was never used, but this church at least, unlike the earlier Reese Chapel, proved lasting and permanent.

By 1910 the congregation had grown sufficiently to need a larger building, so the old building was sold and moved and a new one erected in its place. The new building, when completed, became known as Calvary Church, and the name Hunting Creek was dropped. The old building was used for a number of years as a storehouse, then in 1923 it was purchased by Adams M.E. Church in Whitesville, who used its lumber in remodeling their own building there.

The tradition of a supper on the grounds of the church on or near the Fourth of July has been maintained by this congregation since its inception. By 1906 the church supper had become a public event. In 1929 a tabernacle was erected next to the church to house the supper, and in 1940 a kitchen was installed. Calvary's Fourth of July supper still goes on each year, a tradition now almost a century old.

Calvary has shared its pastors with Grace Church in Parksley since that church was founded in 1892. The parsonage is in Parksley. The present membership is 116.

[Sources: 110, 114, 116, 176]

Location: see LEE MONT

CAPE CHARLES

see: *Alpha and Omega Church*
**Bethany Methodist Episcopal Church*
Calvary Bible Church
Cape Charles Baptist Church
Cape Charles Wesleyan Church
Church of the Lord Jesus Christ of the Apostolic Faith
Emmanuel Episcopal Church
First Baptist Church
First Presbyterian Church
Gospel Tabernacle of the Apostolic Faith Church of God Live On
Philadelphia Church of Christ Disciples
St. Charles Roman Catholic Church
St. Stephen's African Methodist Episcopal Church
**Temple Ohel Rooven*
Trinity United Methodist Church

1a - Bethany ME: original site 1885-1889
1b - Bethany ME: site 1885-1943
2 - Cape Charles Baptist: site since 1887
3a - Trinity UMC: site 1888-1895
3b - Trinity UMC: site since 1895
4a - First Baptist: site 1888-1901
4b - First Baptist: site since 1901
5 - St. Charles Catholic: site since 1889
6a - St. Stephen's AME: site 1889-1912
6b - St. Stephen's AME: site since 1912
7 - Emmanuel Episcopal: site since 1893
8 - Temple Ohel Rooven: used this building
9a - First Presbyterian: site 1901-1926
9b - First Presbyterian: site since 1926
10 - Gospel Tabernacle: site since 1936
11 - Philadelphia Church of Christ: site since 1937
12 - Cape Charles Wesleyan: site since 1940
13 - Church of the Lord Jesus Christ
14 - Calvary Bible Church
15 - Alpha and Omega Church
16 - New Life Church [see Appendix I]
17 - Full Gospel Mission [see Appendix II]

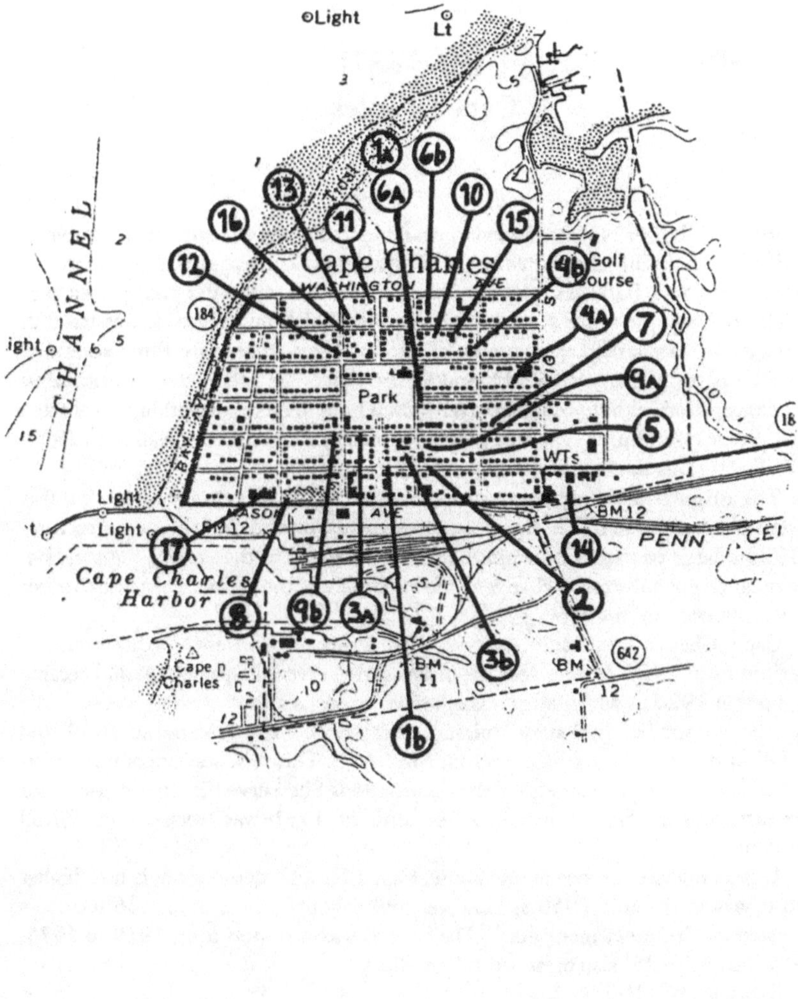
Light
Lt
CHANNEL
Cape Charles
WASHINGTON AVE
Golf Course
Park
WTs
BAY AVE
MASON AVE
BM12
PENN CE
Light
Light
Cape Charles Harbor
Cape Charles
BM 11
BM
184
642
1a
6b
6A
10
15
13
11
16
12
4b
4A
7
9A
5
17
14
2
8
9b
3A
3b
1b

CAPE CHARLES BAPTIST CHURCH

[ABA 1887]
Cape Charles

In 1887, Lower Northampton Baptist Church appointed seven men to serve as trustees and building committee for a "proposed Cape Charles Baptist Church." Eastville and Red Bank also contributed to this work, and later that year a new church building was erected on the corner of Randolph and Plum. It was the fifth church to be established in the town of Cape Charles, then only three years old.

Two pastors, James M. Hope and Henry Petty, are credited with organizing the congregation, although neither ever served here. The organization was effected in 1889, and the church admitted into the Accomack Baptist Association in 1890. J. W. Turner was the first pastor.

The original building was used until 1902, when the present structure was erected. As late as 1904 the congregation was still remodeling the new structure. In 1923 a large two-story educational annex was added to the back of the building. The most recent substantial change to the building was the addition of a brick veneer to the front portion in 1976.

Cape Charles shared its pastors with Eastville, Lower Northampton, or Cheriton until 1919. In that year the congregation erected a parsonage and became a station; in 1920 C. M. Billings was called to the pastorate.

The Woman's Missionary Union of this church was organized in 1909, and the following year one of its members, Mrs. A. S. Downes, was appointed superintendent of all such chapters in the Association. She served in that capacity for 21 years, and at the conclusion of her term in 1931 was elected state WMU president.

Unlike many churches on the Shore, Cape Charles' membership is now higher than it was in the mid-1950's. However, only about a third of its 236 members are listed as "resident members." The church was a station from 1919 to 1975, after which its pastor also preached at Eastville.

[Sources: 69, 108, 122, 124, 139]

Location: see CAPE CHARLES

CAPE CHARLES WESLEYAN CHURCH

[PH 1933, W 1968]
Cape Charles

By the 1930's William Vickers had carried the Holiness faith all the way to the southern tip of the Shore, and in 1933 ten persons were organized into a Pilgrim Holiness congregation at Cape Charles, the southernmost church of that faith on the Shore.

The congregation at first assembled in private homes, then rented a commercial building on the corner of Mason and Nectarine. In 1940 the church lot at Strawberry and Madison was purchased, and soon afterwards was erected there a small building, the first church. It was in this building that William Vickers preached his last sermon. On the evening of May 16, 1945, he completed a sermon on the text "Ye must be born again," extended an altar call, collapsed and died.

The Cape Charles congregation had 26 members when, on November 13, 1949, the present brick building was dedicated by H. D. Dukes, and a two-week revival was held under the Reverend L. R. Bowling. The new building cost $16,000, and was two-thirds paid for at dedication. The old building stood next door until 1958, when it was dismantled to make room for a parsonage.

Of the sixteen pastors who have served this church since its formation, five have been women, including the first pastors, Etta Mitchell and Etta Clough. The longest and most remembered pastorate was that of Miss Mary P. Garrett (1940-1956). In addition to pastoring this church during its most prosperous period, she also organized the Pilgrim Holiness congregations in Exmore and Quinby, and between 1948 and 1950 tried without success to found another in Oyster.

A slow but steady decline in membership set in by the mid-1950's. One pastor, Calvin Hudston (1964-1965), died while serving this church, and for three of the next five years there was no appointed pastor. The church began the 1970's with only ten members, and there have been no resident pastors during this decade. Although the church has shared its pastors with the Exmore congregation, other recent pastors have served while living as far away as Delaware and the Western Shore of Maryland.

The present membership is ten, and there is no official pastor. The congregation still meets faithfully every week under local leadership.

[Sources: 110, 121, 124, 176]

Location: see CAPE CHARLES

CAPEVILLE

see: *Capeville United Methodist Church*

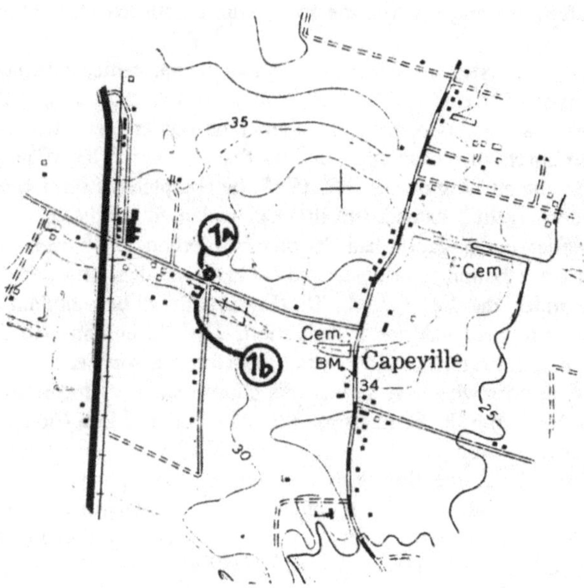

1a - Capeville Methodist: site 1847-1905
1b - Capeville Methodist: site since 1905

Location unknown:
Capeville Methodist site prior to 1847

CAPEVILLE UNITED METHODIST CHURCH

("Magothy Bay Chapel")
[ME 1795, ME-S 1845, M 1939, UMC 1968]
Capeville

Joseph Everett preached the Methodist faith in this area, where the Baptist Elijah Baker began his work on the Eastern Shore, in 1787, and Francis Asbury in 1789. Both of them found the area staunchly Baptist and resistant to Methodist preaching. "The Antinomians please them and gain them," wrote Asbury. "O that the Lord would send an earthquake of his power among them."

Despite what seemed like an unpromising area, the circuit preachers succeeded in forming a Methodist society here and by 1795 William Colbert was meeting regularly with a group that gathered in a schoolhouse. A lot for a meetinghouse was secured in 1812, and by 1814 a chapel, called "Magothy Bay Chapel," had been erected.

The Capeville society remained a part of the Accomack Circuit until the creation of the Northampton Circuit in 1838. In 1845 it seceded to the Methodist Episcopal Church, South, the second congregation on the Shore to do so. The church was ordered closed by the Union army for a brief period in 1864. By then the name "Capeville" had long since replaced "Magothy Bay."

It is apparent that the original chapel was abandoned when a second building was erected opposite the present church in 1847, and its original site cannot be determined today. Two church buildings were erected upon the second site between 1847 and 1905, when the present building across the road was erected during the pastorate of W. G. Bates. Both buildings were moved and demolished, and their site taken over completely by the surrounding cemetery.

Over the years the Capeville church grew into a strong congregation from which several others were formed. It was the mother church of Cobb's Island Mission (1882), Cape Charles (1887), and Townsend Mission (1901). As the old southern Eastville Circuit was subdivided, Capeville was placed on a circuit with Cheriton and Salem in 1891, but in 1896 it became a station. It has remained one ever since, except for the time during which its pastors preached also at the Townsend Mission.

The present building was renovated in 1930 and an educational annex added in 1960. The separate education building was dedicated by Bishop W. Kenneth Goodson in 1973. Capeville remains a vigorous station church today; its present membership is about 250.

[Sources: 3, 39, 100, 103, 109, 111, 112, 116, 124, 128, 176]

Location: see CAPEVILLE

CASHVILLE

see: *Andrew Chapel United Methodist Church*
**Baptist Church of Christ of Pungoteague*
Broadway Baptist Church
**Ebenezer Methodist Episcopal Church*

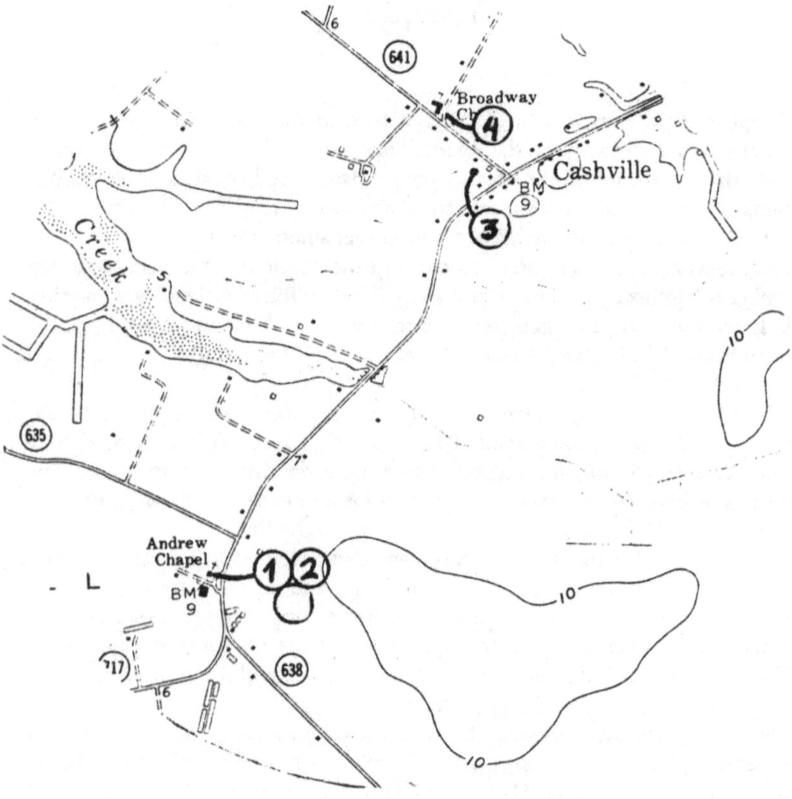

1 - Boggs Meetinghouse: housed Baptist Church of Christ of Pungoteague 1831-1836
2 - Andrew Chapel: all buildings since 1835
3 - Ebenezer ME [approximate]
4 - Broadway Baptist

CEDAR GROVE

see: **Cedar Grove Baptist Church*
**Second Presbyterian Church*

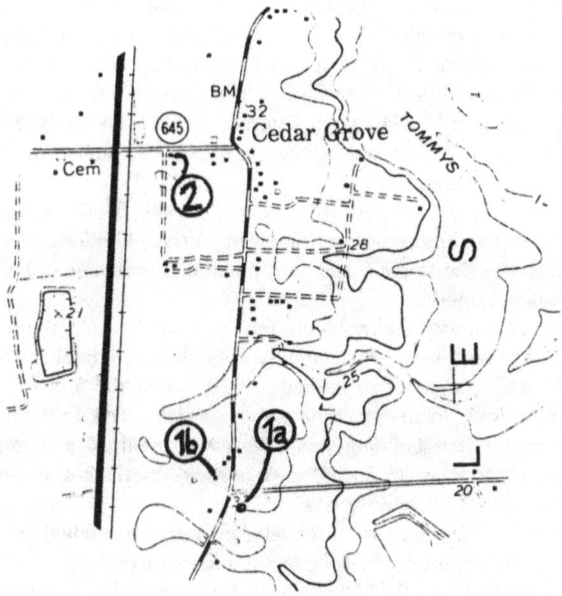

1a - Second Presbyterian: site 1884-c1891
1b - Second Presbyterian: present site of building [Hopewell School]
2 - Cedar Grove Baptist

*CEDAR GROVE BAPTIST CHURCH

("Hopewell")
[ABA 1898-1956]
Cedar Grove

In 1898 Lower Northampton Baptist Church appointed a committee to investigate the possibility of establishing a church farther down the tip of the Shore. And within a matter of months the Baptists had a thriving Sunday school in Cedar Grove, from which Cedar Grove Baptist Church was born. Services were held at first in the building of Second Presbyterian Church, by then known as Hopewell School. The State Mission Board sent a preacher from Richmond to conduct services every other Sunday afternoon.

Four years later, on January 19, 1902, Cedar Grove Baptist Church was constituted and the new building dedicated. Nineteen persons withdrew from Lower Northampton to organize the church, and Dr. William E. Hatcher of Richmond preached the dedicatory sermon.

Cedar Grove was a Sunday afternoon church, partially because it sometimes shared its pastors with older Lower Northampton. Both Sunday school and worship services were held on Sunday afternoons until 1918, when the worship service was moved to the morning and an evening worship service added. In 1930, when C. L. Corbett was pastor, the building was extensively enlarged and improved; rooms for the Sunday school were added, new heating installed, and electricity provided. The membership in that year was 143.

The founding of Cedar Grove ultimately proved detrimental to Lower Northampton. By 1945, when Cedar Grove reported a membership of 176, Lower Northampton had dwindled to only 55 members. In January 1956, when Lower Northampton was without a pastor, the older church initiated merger proceedings, ''believing that the interests of the Kingdom in Lower Northampton County would be served best by one Baptist church rather than two.'' Cedar Grove's congregation was invited to take over the property of Lower Northampton and merge the two congregations. The offer was accepted, and on Easter Sunday 1956 the merger was effected. The congregation took the older name, Lower Northampton, and Cedar Grove dropped from the records. At the time of the merger, there were 146 members from Cedar Grove and 29 from Lower Northampton.

Both the buildings used by this congregation are still standing in Cedar Grove. Second Presbyterian Church (the old Hopewell School) has been moved across the road from its original site and is now a dwelling. The Cedar Grove church is now being used as a storage barn for a farm.

[Sources: 69, 139, 176]

Location: see CEDAR GROVE

CENTENARY METHODIST EPISCOPAL CHURCH, SOUTH

(see Trinity United Methodist Church)

CENTRAL BAPTIST CHURCH

[Independent 1975]
Onley

The Central Baptist Mission was established in 1975, one of a growing number of independent, white Baptist congregations on the Virginia Shore. Doctrinally it styled itself "independent, fundamental, and pre-millenial," and at its organization advertised that it was "the old-fashioned country church preaching the old-fashioned gospel."

By the end of 1975 the small congregation was worshiping north of Tasley adjacent to Whispering Pines, in a building which had once served as a fruit-stand. Services were subsequently moved to a second building south of Onley. Construction of a permanent building at the Onley site began in 1978.

This congregation was founded from Central Baptist Church, an independent congregation in Hampton.

[Sources: 109, 123]

Location: see ONLEY, TASLEY

CHANCETOWN

see: **Baker Memorial Baptist Church*
Burton's United Methodist Church

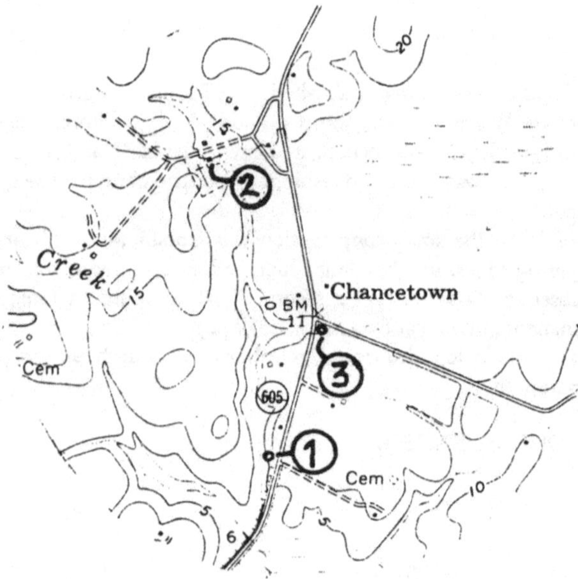

1 - Burton's Chapel ME: original site 1801-1870 (approximate) [for location since 1871 see Oak Grove UMC, MELFA]
2 - Burton's Methodist
3 - Baker Memorial Baptist: site 1902-1937

CHEAPSIDE

see: Ebenezer African Methodist Episcopal Church
Mt. Sinai Holy Church

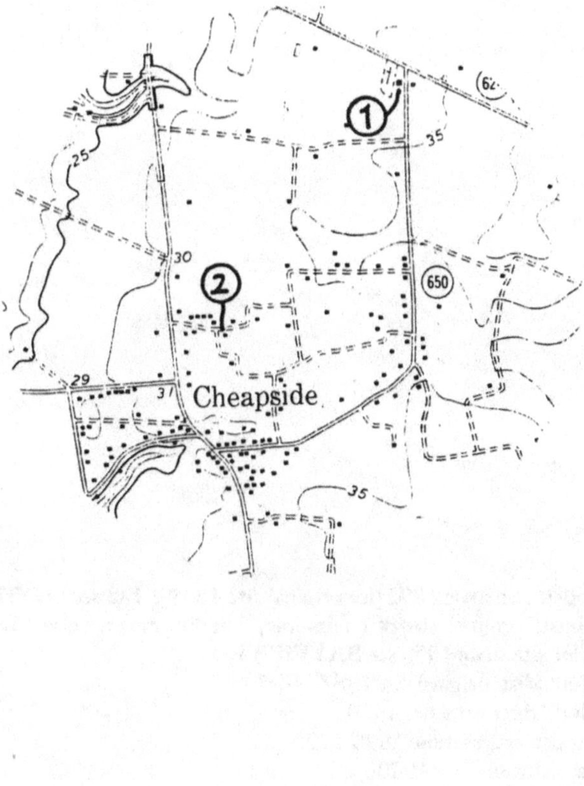

1 - Ebenezer AME
2 - Mt. Sinai Holy Church

CHERITON

see: *African Baptist Church*
Cheriton Baptist Church
Cheriton United Methodist Church
First Lutheran Mission
Gospel Mission House of Prayer
**St. Andrew's Episcopal Mission*

1a - African Baptist: site since 1892 [for original site 1869-1892 see OYSTER]
1b - African Baptist: original site of community building, now Coles Chapel AME [for site since 1954 see BAYVIEW]
2a - Cheriton Methodist: original site 1887-1920
2b - Cheriton Methodist: site since 1920
3a - Cheriton Baptist: original site 1898-1920
3b - Cheriton Baptist: site since 1920
4 - St. Andrew's Mission: site 1921-1925
5a - Gospel Mission House of Prayer
5b - Gospel Mission House of Prayer: Mission No. 1
6a - First Lutheran Mission: occupied this building 1975-1977
6b - First Lutheran Mission: since 1977
7 - Christ Church of Universal Love Inc. [see Appendix II]

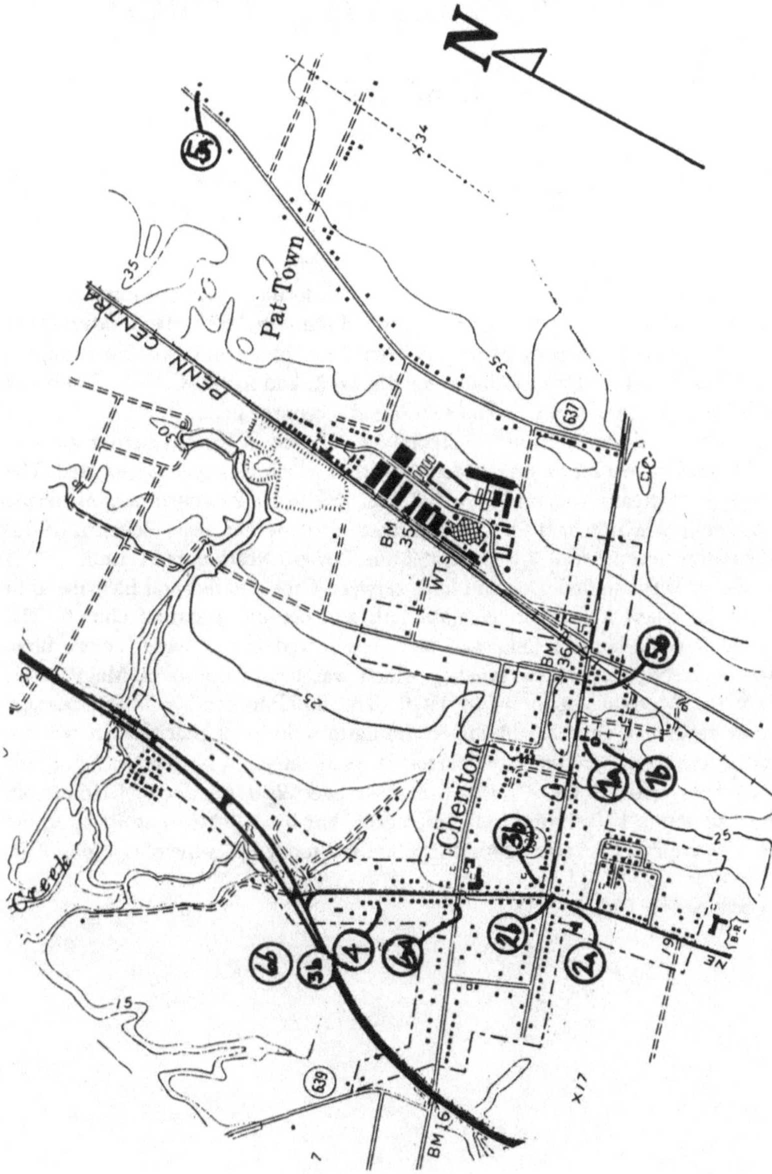
N
Pat Town
PENN CENTRAL
Cheriton
Creek
637
639
BM 35
BM 36
BM 16
WTs

CHERITON BAPTIST CHURCH

[ABA 1889]
Cheriton

When the Methodist church at Cheriton was formed from the interdenominational mission Sunday school that was operated there in 1887, the Sunday school fell by default to the care of the Baptists. Henry Petty, pastor of Lower Northampton and Red Bank, assumed responsibility for the work, and Miss Mary W. Smith was recruited as superintendent when no man would accept the job.

Soon from this work came the second new church in town, Cheriton Baptist. J. D. Thomas gave a lot on north Main Street on which a chapel was erected. The Reverend J. W. Reams organized the church in 1890 with 27 constituent members. The building was not paid for and dedicated until twelve years later, in 1902.

Cheriton was served by pastors from Lower Northampton until 1902. Thereafter it was shuffled back and forth between Cape Charles and Eastville until the 1920's, when it took on new strength and became a station church. The Reverend James Manning Dunaway, who also served Cape Charles at one time, led in the erection of a new building which was begun on south Main Street, opposite the Methodist church, in 1920. The building cost $65,000, perhaps the most expensive church building on the Eastern Shore at that time. It was not dedicated until it was completely paid for 24 years later, on November 12, 1944.

Cheriton entered the 1930's with well over 200 members. Membership declined to about 170 during the next decade, but by 1950 was again up to old levels. The church has remained a strong one and today has a membership of 232.

[Sources: 69, 124, 176]

Location: see CHERITON

CHERITON UNITED METHODIST CHURCH

("Sunnyside") [ME-S 1886, M 1939, UMC 1968] Cheriton

(first building, photo c. 1910)

This church in the new village of Sunnyside, as Cheriton was then known, is an outgrowth of a Sunday school founded there in 1886 by Lower Northampton Baptist, Holmes Presbyterian, and Salem Methodist churches. The Sunday school met in the local schoolhouse, and from it came, in order, the Methodist and the Baptist congregations in Cheriton.

The first Methodist church in the village was erected in 1887 on Main Street just north of the school, across from the present church. The congregation grew rapidly, and the simple frame building was crowded by the early twentieth century. The present brick building was erected in 1920 at a cost of $45,000. It was at that time a very expensive building, the cost of which on the Virginia Shore was exceeded only by Cheriton Baptist Church, begun in that same year across the street. At the completion of the new building, the old structure was dismantled. The name of the church was changed from Sunnyside to Cheriton in 1927.

During the pastorate of Carl Sanders (1936-1940), who in 1972 was elected a bishop, a large brick educational annex was dedicated, costing $15,000. Bishop W. W. Peele delivered the dedicatory address on November 26, 1939.

Cheriton has always shared its pastors with other churches. The circuit consisted of Salem, Capeville, Cheriton, and Cape Charles until 1896, when Capeville and Cape Charles became separate stations. Travis Chapel was added in 1908, and Salem dropped three years later. Cheriton and Travis Chapel have formed the Cheriton Charge since 1911. The pastor lives in the parsonage erected in 1902 just south of the church. The present membership at Cheriton is just under 300.

[Sources: 116, 124, 131, 176]

Location: see CHERITON

CHERRYSTONE

see: **Cherrystone Baptist Church*
**The Towne Church [Church of England]*

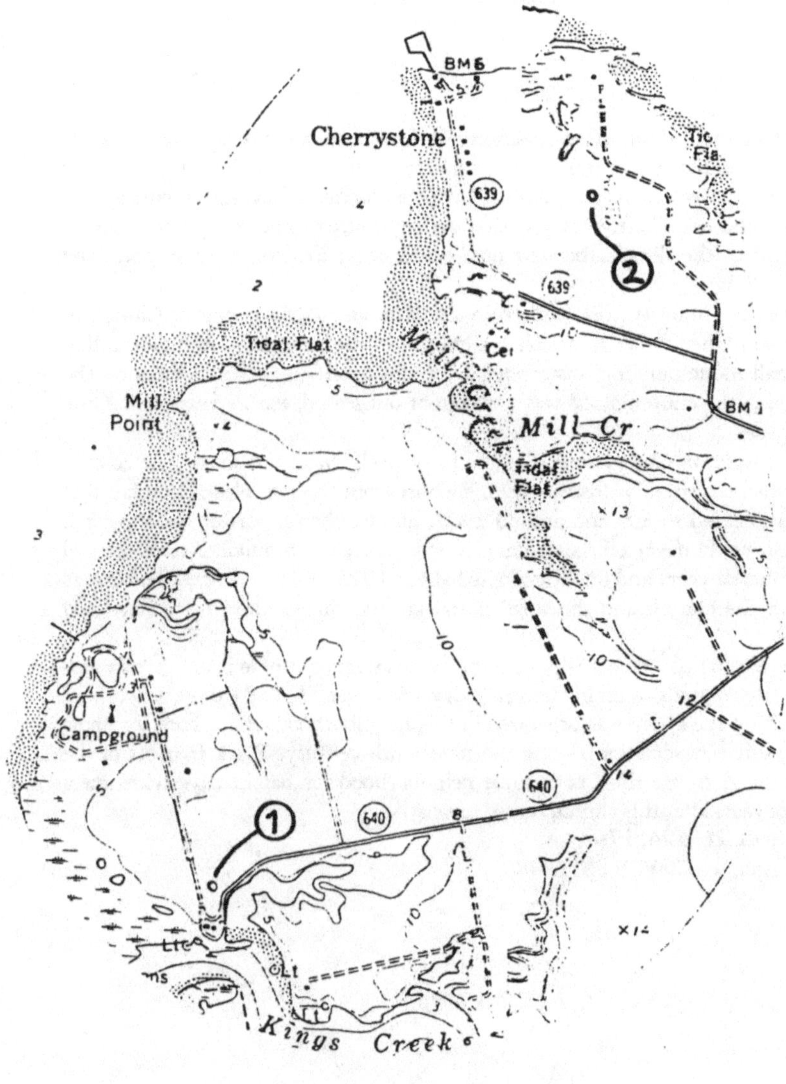

1 - The Towne Church: site c1634-c1677 [approximate]
2 - Cherrystone Baptist: 1879-c1920 [approximate]

*CHERRYSTONE BAPTIST CHURCH

[ESBA 1879-1907?]
Cherrystone

Cherrystone Wharf, west of Cheriton, had been an old landing place for waterborne commerce for more than a century when in the 1870's Leroy Taylor decided to develop a town there. Taylor hired a planner to lay out an entire community around the wharf, with regularly arranged streets and many building lots. By the end of the decade the new port could boast a hotel, a large store, and several dwellings.

In 1879, Union Baptist Church in Eastville and African Baptist Church in Cheriton combined forces to establish a church in the new town, and during that year a small frame building was erected. Like all the building sites in the town the lot on which the church stood was not bought but leased, for 99 years at the rate of $1 per year.

The church in Cherrystone, like the town itself, was short-lived. The congregation, which apparently drew its main support from the two black churches that founded it, ceased to function around 1907, and by then it was obvious that the town itself would never take shape as planned. The church building stood unused for a number of years and finally collapsed about 1920. Today an open field covers the site of the church and the small burial ground that is thought to have surrounded it.

Whether the church actually bore the name assigned it here is not certain, nor are there any records of its life known today. However, in 1884 the black Baptist association on the Shore was organized in this neighborhood, and it bore the name of Cherrystone Association during the nineteenth century. Black Baptists of the area continued to use the Cherrystone neighborhood for baptismal services for a number of years after this church ceased to exist.

[Sources: 26, 124, 176]

Location: see CHERRYSTONE

CHESCONNESSEX

see: **Holiness Christian Church*
Leatherbury United Methodist Church
New Testament Congregation
Riverview United Methodist Church
**Ward's Chapel African Methodist Episcopal Church*

1a - Leatherbury UMC: original site 1872-1913
1b - Leatherbury UMC: site since 1913
2 - Ward's Chapel AME
3 - Riverview UMC
4 - Holiness Christian
5 - New Testament Congregation

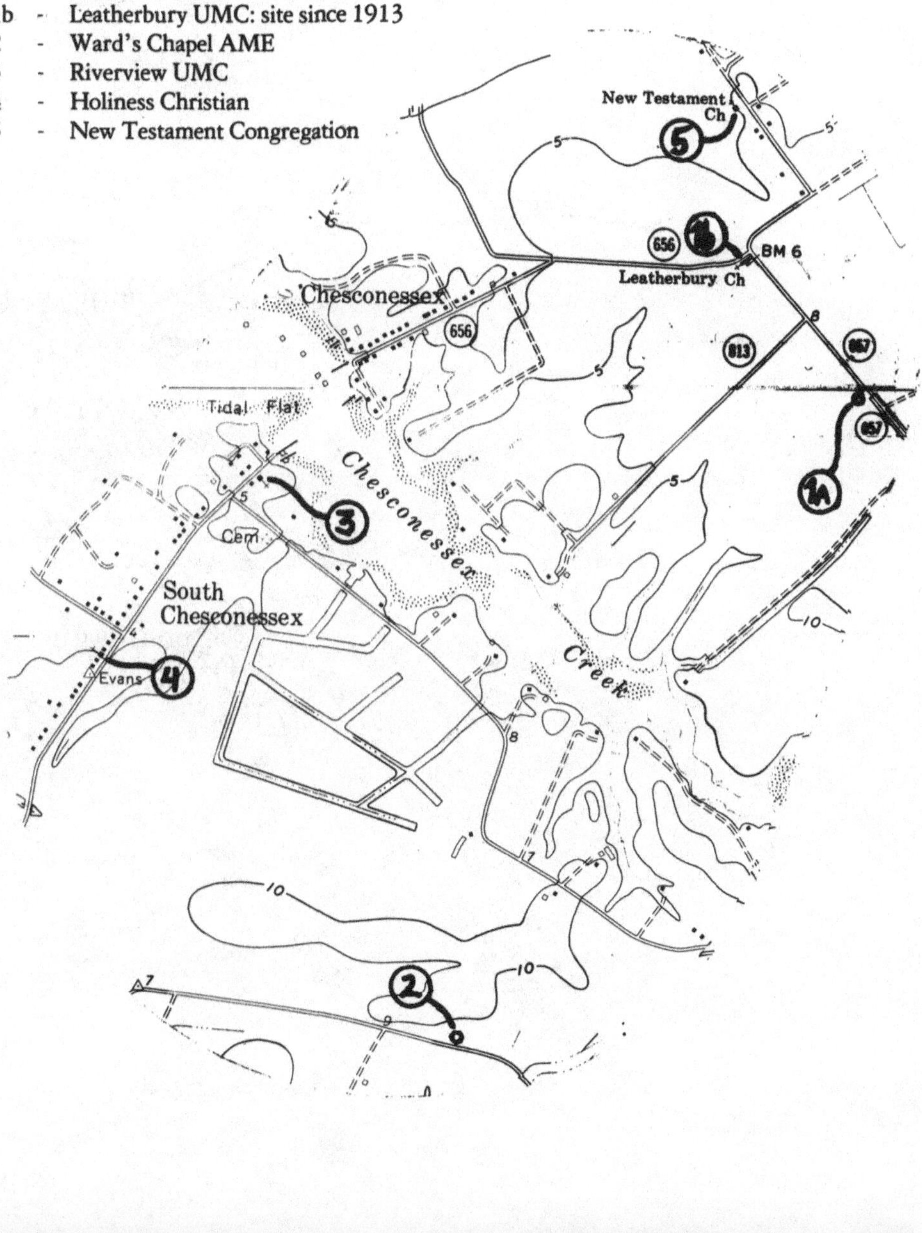

CHINCOTEAGUE

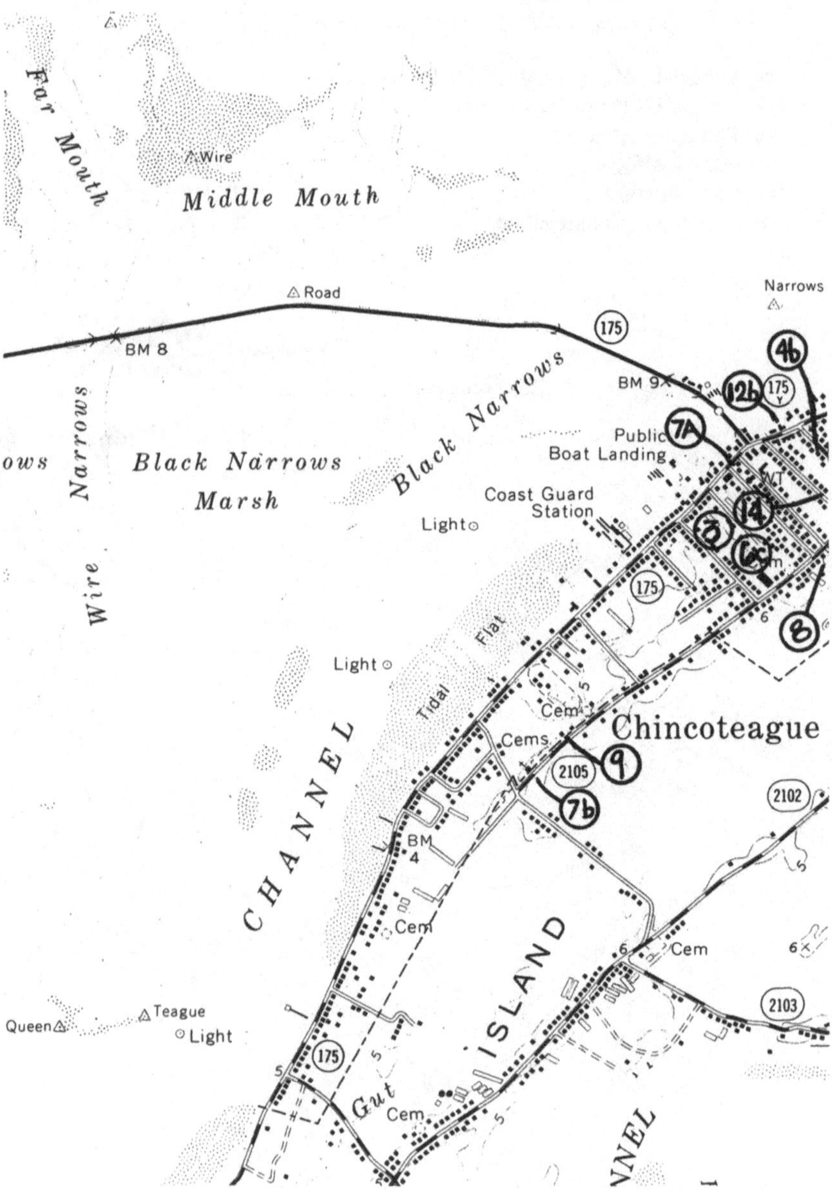

[see next page:]

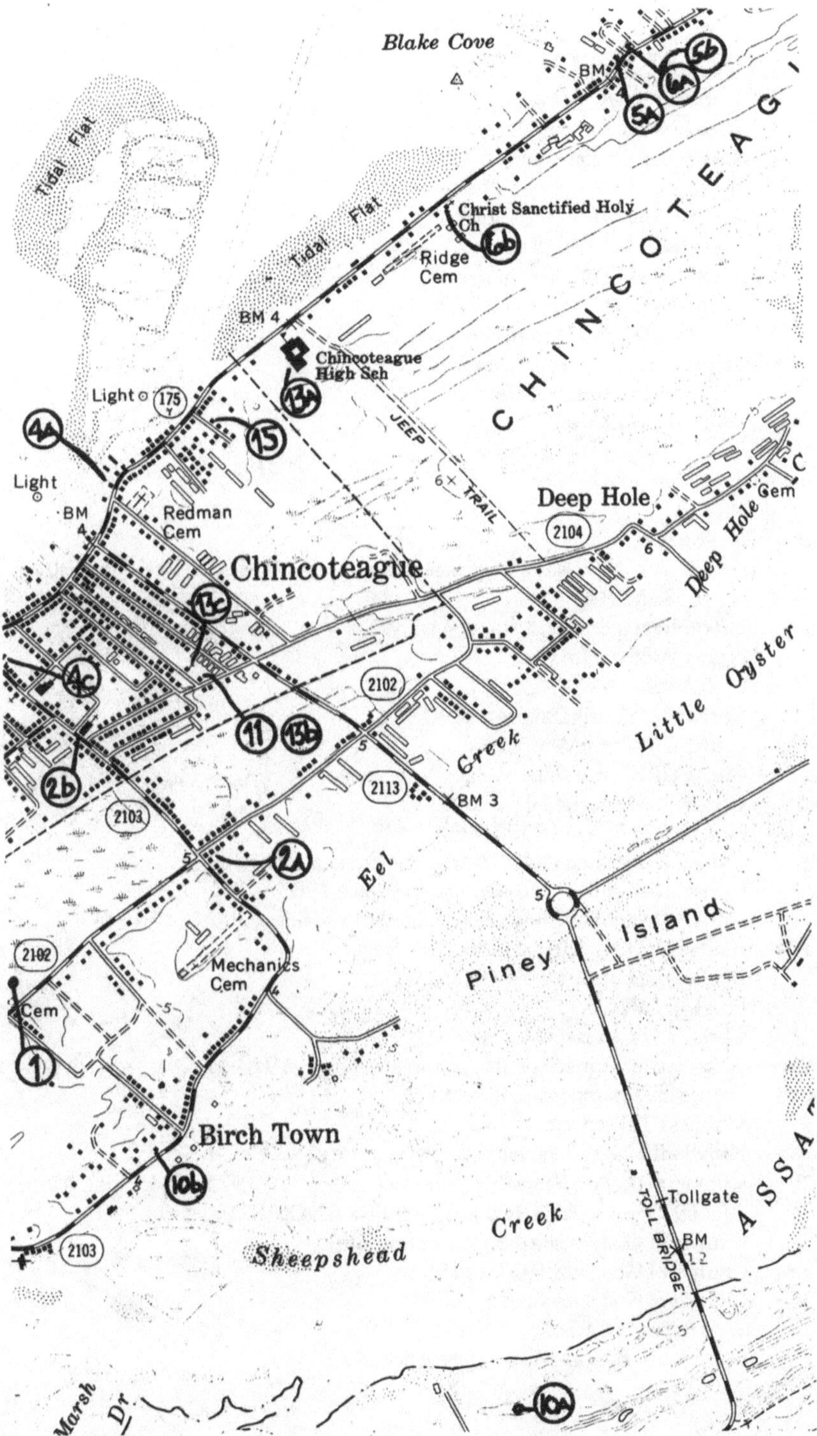
Blake Cove
Tidal Flat
Tidal Flat
BM
Christ Sanctified Holy Ch
Ridge Cem
CHINCOTEAG
BM 4
Chincoteague High Sch
Light
175
JEEP TRAIL
Light
BM 4
Redman Cem
Deep Hole
2104
Chincoteague
Deep Hole
Cem
Little Oyster
2102
Creek
2113
BM 3
2103
Eel
Piney Island
2102
Mechanics Cem
Cem
Birch Town
Tollgate
TOLL BRIDGE
BM 12
ASSA
Creek
Sheepshead
2103
Marsh
Dr

CHINCOTEAGUE

see: **Assateague Baptist Chapel*
**Bethel Methodist Protestant Church*
**Beulah Baptist Church*
Christ United Methodist Church
Christ's Sanctified Holy Church
**Christ's Union Baptist Church*
Church of God of Chincoteague
**Freewill Methodist Episcopal Church*
**Goodwill Methodist Episcopal Church*
**Holiness Tabernacle of Chincoteague*
St. Andrew's Roman Catholic Church
Union Baptist Church

(see map next page:)

1 - site of schoolhouse where first religious services were held on island c1830-1841
2a - Union Baptist: original site 1841-1896
2b - Union Baptist: site since 1896
3 - Bethel MP
4a - Christ UMC: original site 1869-1886
4b - Christ UMC: site 1886-1922
4c - Christ UMC: site since 1922
5a - Goodwill ME: original site 1886-1898
5b - Goodwill ME: site 1898-1933
6a - Christ's Sanctified Holy Church: original site 1893-1898
6b - Christ's Sanctified Holy Church: site since 1903
6c - Christ's Sanctified Holy Church: used this building also 1943-1964
7a - Beulah Baptist: original site 1879-1893
7b - Beulah Baptist: site 1893-1973
8 - Freewill ME
9 - Christ's Union Baptist
10a - Assateague Baptist: original site [approximate] 1919-1922
10b - Assateague Baptist: site since 1922
11 - Holiness Tabernacle
12a - Kingdom Hall of Jehovah's Witnesses: site c1927-1956
12b - Kingdom Hall of Jehovah's Witnesses: site 1956-1975 [for locations since 1975 see WATTSVILLE, TEMPERANCEVILLE]
13a - Church of God: original camp meeting site
13b - Church of God: site 1937-1948
13c - Church of God: site since 1948
14 - St. Andrew's Catholic
15 - Missionary Baptist Mission [see Appendix II]

CHINCOTEAGUE BAPTIST CHURCH

[ABA 1786]
New Church

Chincoteague Baptist Church was organized in 1786 by Elijah Baker. It was the fourth Baptist church on the Virginia Shore, and the third oldest of those still in existence. It was named Chincoteague, according to local tradition, because Chincoteague Islanders are said to have had to travel this far to come to church. A more likely explanation is that the name Chincoteague in the late 1700's referred to a wider area of the Shore than it does today.

Chincoteague quickly grew and prospered. Its first church, erected soon after 1786 on a nearby site, was replaced by a second one on the present site in 1809 or 1810. In that latter year the membership was 132, the largest in the church's history. When Thomas Waters became pastor in 1809, the church declined as quickly as it had grown. Waters was one of the foremost advocates of the anti-mission cause on the Shore, and during his 23-year pastorate Chincoteague's membership dwindled away almost to nothing. His "ultra-Calvinism put the church to sleep, and caused the do-nothing party to prevail."

When finally the mission controversy divided the Association in 1831, Chincoteague "wavered between the two camps." Waters' pastorate ended with his withdrawal from the Association in 1832, and for several years thereafter Chincoteague was without a pastor and sent no report to the Association. This period of dormancy continued until 1843, when William Wilkerson became pastor. "There are at present here indications that God is about to revive his work," read the report for that year. ''She [Chincoteague] has begun to repair her house of worship, and her prospects are more encouraging than formerly.''

In 1858 the congregation erected their third building, the present one. Three years later a Sunday school was formed, but its activity has not been continuous from that date. The church's greatest period of prosperity was the 1890's. A Woman's Missionary Society was organized in 1892, the same year in which the building was improved and enlarged and stained glass windows installed. The successful pastorate of Walter Rhodes began in 1897; during his six years at Chincoteague there were fifty baptisms.

Much of this strength was siphoned off by the founding of two new congregations: Horntown in 1897 and First in New Church in 1909. First Baptist, in particular, quickly outdistanced the older congregation and became the leading church of the field. The two earlier churches had built a parsonage in the village there in 1901.

In 1921 Beulah Nock Allen of this church became a missionary to India. In 1924 between 800 and 900 people thronged the church to hear Newton Hastings, a child evangelist.

In 1966 First Baptist left the two other churches on the field and became a station. Since that time Chincoteague and Horntown have supplied their pulpits with local preachers. In 1975 Chincoteague was bequeathed a parsonage in New Church; it stands next door to the older parsonage now owned by First Baptist. Despite its long and venerable history, Chincoteague is today one of the smallest Baptist churches still functioning on the Eastern Shore of Virginia. Its present membership is 67.

[Sources: 36, 69, 71, 122, 167]

Location: see NEW CHURCH

*CHRIST EPISCOPAL CHURCH

[PE 1896-1930]
Bloxom

Christ Church in Bloxom was founded from Emmanuel in Jenkins Bridge, and was a "monument to the zeal and Christian fortitude" of Flora Himel Bowdoin, who was instrumental in its formation. The congregation was established in 1896 and the building erected soon afterwards. In 1900 the diocese reported that the church consisted of ten communicants who worshiped in a wooden chapel valued at $1000, all under the care of the rector of Emmanuel. Bishop Tucker dedicated the building in 1909.

The small membership and lack of growth of Christ Church was due in part to the fact that many of its members lived not in Bloxom, but in Parksley. Bishop Tucker held services in the Baptist church in Parksley in the fall of 1911, and there were Episcopal services in private homes in that town as late as the 1920's, but Parksley Episcopalians had as a rule to travel to Bloxom for regular worship services. One who did so was the Sunday school superintendent at Christ Church, who faithfully walked the distance each week.

By 1918 membership at the church had climbed only to nineteen, and it never climbed higher. The church closed in that year, only to reopen for services early in the 1920's. By 1927 membership had dwindled to seven. Of these only the Bowdoin family lived near the church, and one of them was away at school; the four other members lived in Parksley, Modest Town, and Onley. The following year the church reported only five members. In 1930 regular services, which had not been held for over a year, were officially discontinued, and the church was listed as "Dormant." After that year the diocese received no report from the church.

The little frame chapel stood unused until 1946, when it was purchased by the Pilgrim Holiness congregation in Bloxom, moved to a new site, covered with a brick veneer, and once again put to use. It still stands today as Bloxom Wesleyan Church.

[Sources: 65, 118, 123, 176]
Location: see BLOXOM

CHRIST EPISCOPAL CHURCH

[PE 1813]
Eastville

For more than two decades after the disestablishment of the Anglican Church, Episcopalianism was dormant in Northampton County. Hungars and Magothy were vacant and falling into ruin, and it was not until the second decade of the nineteenth century that the denomination began to revive.

As early as 1813 Northampton Episcopalians were again at worship, this time in the courthouse at Eastville. In 1819 Hungars was reopened for worship, but Magothy proved to be beyond repair. Magothy was sold in 1824 and it was then, during the pastorate of Simon Wilmer, that plans were made to replace it with a new church in the county seat.

Christ Church, successor to Magothy, was erected on the northern edge of Eastville in 1828 at a cost of $2960. The land on which it was built did not belong to the denomination. In fact, it was not until 1858 that survivors of Severn Parker found an unwitnessed deed of gift of the land among his papers after his death. The paper was produced in court, witnesses testified that it was in the late donor's handwriting, and title thus passed to the church thirty years after the building had been opened for use.

The building of Christ Church is unquestionably one of the loveliest churches on the Virginia Shore. Fourth oldest church building in the two counties (after St. George's, Hungars, and Hollies Baptist), it has seen but minor changes since 1828. The west (altar) wall, originally flat, has since been extended. A steeple was added early in the twentieth century, only to be damaged by a hurricane in 1949 and replaced by another. The originally clear windows were, one by one, replaced by stained glass beginning in the late nineteenth century; these windows, all made in Germany, are the finest on the Virginia Shore and are valued in the hundreds of thousands of dollars. The interior of the church was carefully restored to its original appearance in 1906. A parish house was erected at the back of the church in the 1970's.

Additional land on either side of the church was deeded in 1890 and 1904 for a cemetery. Both deeds stipulate that only white persons are to be buried there, a condition not uncommon in deeds of that period.

In 1828 when Christ Church was established, Hungars had already been closed for further repairs, so at that early date this church became the larger of the two and ultimately the largest Episcopal congregation on the Virginia Shore. Only in

1971, when it was surpassed in size by Holy Trinity in Onancock, did it relinquish that lead.

The rectory of the church is in Eastville. The pastor serves Hungars and Emmanuel in Cape Charles in addition to Christ Church.

[Sources: 62, 70, 108, 118]

Location: see EASTVILLE

CHRIST UNITED METHODIST CHURCH

[ME 1869, M 1939, UMC 1968]
Chincoteague

(second building)

In 1869 the two churches on Chincoteague Island, Baptist and Methodist Protestant, were both at low ebb, a fact which did not escape the notice of two Methodist Episcopal preachers who chanced to be visiting the town in that year. J. M. McCarter of the M.E. church in Federalsburg, Maryland, and J. L. Kenney, a local preacher from the same place, seized the opportunity for the Methodist Episcopal Church. They secured permission to hold services in Bethel M.P. Church, and there in "a wonderful manifestation of God's saving power" some fifty people were converted. A class was formed which met in private homes on Main Street, sixteen people became charter members of the congregation in August, and by fall of 1869 the town's third church building stood on the west side of Main Street opposite Taylor Street.

There were fifty members of this church in 1871 when Adam Stengle was pastor and the Wilmington Conference first listed the congregation in its records. The church grew rapidly, often at the expense of Bethel M.P. and Union Baptist. The most spectacular accessions occurred in 1884, when pastor J. D. Reese added thirty probationers and seventy former Methodist Protestants to the roll, "a good showing for his first year," glowed the presiding elder. Most of these new members lived in the north end of the island, and Reese organized them into the Goodwill Class on August 24, 1884.

The little church building was by now both overcrowded and dilapidated, and its location no longer pleasing to the congregation. In 1886 the congregation, now 121 members strong, abandoned the building and gave it to the Goodwill contingent, who moved it up the island and repaired it. The congregation met in Temperance Hall, where the post office now stands, awaiting "a favorable opportunity to build in keeping with their requirements." In 1888 they purchased a lot on the south side of Church Street, erected a new building for $3500, and in the following year took the name Christ Church.

Christ Church, having long since outdistanced the Methodist Protestant church on the island in size, prospered and grew during the latter part of the nineteenth century. In 1893 the original lot was sold, and in the same year a cemetery purchased. In 1895 the church reported that its "ladies have provided a parsonage, and desire a married [preacher] next year" to fill it. A married preacher was appointed forthwith. In 1899 the new building was renovated and enlarged, and in 1900 land for a parsonage next door purchased.

In 1919 the congregation began the construction of its third building, the present structure. Stone for this building, purchased in Philadelphia, was shipped by rail to Franklin City, carried by boat to a wharf opposite Church Street, and then carried by hand to the site by local members. The Gothic-style building, which cost over $39,000, was occupied in 1922. The Wilmington Annual Conference was to have convened in it in April 1923, but the Conference was moved to Dover "owing to the condition of the new road from the mainland to the island, which route those attending will have to take." At the completion of the new building, Goodwill Church, founded from the class at the northern end of the island and long since defunct in fact, was officially merged back into the parent congregation. The Goodwill Men's Bible Class which functioned here for a number of years afterwards was the last remnant of the "upper" church.

Since 1922 Christ Church has been a station. There have been subsequent additions and renovations to the building, including the installation of a pipe organ in 1949. The building of 1888 still stands across the street and is used by the congregation for a number of activities.

Christ Church is today the third largest United Methodist church on the Eastern Shore of Virginia, with a membership of about 450.

[Sources: 105, 109, 110, 116, 117, 123, 154, 156, 176]

Location: see CHINCOTEAGUE

*CHRISTIAN LOVE CENTER

[Independent 1971-1976]
Melfa

This church was begun by a group of laypersons principally from the Exmore area, the first Charismatic congregation on the Eastern Shore of Virginia. The experience of baptism in the Holy Spirit, with concurrent evidences of divine healing, was first felt by the members of a Baptist prayer group in Exmore. Under the leadership of L. W. Wyatt, they opened the Christian Love Center in a rented building in Melfa in an attempt to minister to the youth of all churches in the area.

Although not begun as a separate church, the Christian Love Center became in fact a separate congregation when the anticipated support from other local churches failed to materialize. Although as many as seventy young people attended services there in the early years, the congregation ultimately leveled off to about 25 members of all ages. The congregation carried on its work without a professional clergy, exercising a priesthood of all believers.

After a few years the congregation declined, and the Center closed in 1976. Rock Church of the Eastern Shore, a Charismatic congregation, was founded in Onley at about that time, and some of the supporters of the Center moved to that congregation. In 1977 the Melfa Church of God, a Pentecostal congregation, occupied the building that had housed the Center.

[Source: 176]

Location: see MELFA

*CHRISTIAN SCIENCE SOCIETY OF PARKSLEY

[1946-1966]
Parksley

A Christian Science Society was founded in Pocomoke City, Maryland, in 1931, and from it in 1946 was born this congregation in Parksley, the only Christian Science society in the history of the Virginia Shore. The small congregation that withdrew from the Pocomoke society to establish this new group first met in the home of Clara Kernodle, but by July 1947 services had moved to the Parksley firehouse, where they were held at 11 a.m. every Sunday.

In 1948 the infant society made its first attempt to erect a building. A lot on Bennett Street was purchased in that year, but the society was unable to raise the building. In 1952 a second lot, on the north side of Adelaide Street at the railroad crossing, was purchased, and here within a short time a small building was erected. The Bennett Street site was sold in 1955.

The Parksley society was small in number and proved to be short-lived. The new building was used for less than two decades, for the group disbanded in 1966. In 1967 the building was sold and was later converted into a dwelling, which is still in use. The few remaining Christian Science adherents on the Shore have since had to travel great distances to attend worship services.

[Sources: 110, 123, 176]

Location: see PARKSLEY

*CHRISTIAN UNION AFRICAN METHODIST EPISCOPAL CHURCH

(''Modestown'')
[AME 1866-1887?]
Modest Town

This church was organized on April 9, 1866, by the Reverend James H. A. Johnson, founder of A.M.E. work on the Shore. ''This concluded the earnest, faithful and successful labors of our missionary, and April 10, 1866, he left [for] Washington.'' This was the third A.M.E. church on the Virginia Shore, and the most northerly. It had at its formation only eight members.

In 1868 a mob of angry whites burned down this new church ''to prevent the colored people holding a contemplated public meeting'' there. Apparently fear of white reprisal hindered further A.M.E. work and growth in this neighborhood. A second building was erected on land purchased in 1873, but it did not house a strong or growing congregation. In 1887 the Modest Town church was listed as a mission, and after that there are no further mentions to be found of it in the records of the denomination.

The second building was a very simple and primitive structure that fell gradually into ruin with the passing of the years. There was no steeple or ornamentation, and local residents recall its very rough-hewn benches inside. The land was sold in 1911, and the building was gone by then. The site can today be reached only by unpaved farm roads, across Gargathy Creek behind Modest Town Baptist Church.

[Sources: 7, 123, 176]

Location: see MODEST TOWN

CHRIST'S SANCTIFIED HOLY CHURCH

[1892]
Chincoteague

Not only is this the oldest Holiness congregation on the Eastern Shore of Virginia, it is also the mother church of an entire sect of more than 1000 members, spread from Delaware to Louisiana.

The Sanctified church on Chincoteague Island grew out of Goodwill M.E. on the north end of the island. In 1887, three years after that church was annexed by the Methodists, Joseph B. Lynch, a class leader there, obtained sanctification. With Sarah Collins he became the leader of a growing sanctified faction at Goodwill. In 1892 the group petitioned the bishop for a "holy man of God to preach the gospel to them," and they were subsequently removed from office by the Methodist congregation. Nineteen persons constituted Christ's Sanctified Holy Church as a separate congregation on February 14, 1892.

The first Sanctified church building was erected just north of Goodwill on Main Street during the summer of 1892, and was at that time the largest church building on the island. By the next year the new faith had adherents in Franklin City, and as far away as Maryland and Delaware. By the fall of 1893 the congregation had begun those religious practices that so incensed the rest of the island: the repudiation of marriages previously made with unsanctified persons, and the establishment of the practice of "two-plus-two" for the study and proclamation of the scriptures. Acrimony between the congregation and the rest of the island intensified sharply after that time. After A. T. Bowden was accidentally killed by a band of young men on their way to punish members of the congregation in September 1894, Lynch and Collins and two others were hauled into court, convicted of several misdemeanors, and found guilty.

It was at this point that the congregation, perhaps as many as 120 members strong, began to migrate from the island, following Lynch and a party of believers who were gone by December 1894. Over the next three years the congregation sold homes and businesses at great loss and left the island, leaving behind a small remnant that were not permitted by the community to hold services. Some of the group returned in 1897 only to leave a second time during the final phase of departure in the summer of that year. Off the island, the sect found its first home in eastern North Carolina and continued its gradual journey across the South. The church building was auctioned off and purchased by the Goodwill congregation in 1898, who remodeled it for their own use, thinking that the Sanctified congregation was at last gone from the island.

In 1903 the island remnant, long since purged of those whose actions the community found objectionable, resumed services, erected a new building, and became a permanent church. The ill will of the previous decade was now past, and the little congregation grew rapidly. By the 1940's it had outgrown the small church building, and in 1943 it purchased the abandoned Bethel M.P. Church on Church Street. Services were held here for a number of years until the congregation again dwindled in size. In 1964 the Church Street building was sold to St. Andrew's Roman Catholic Church. The original Sanctified building, abandoned by the Methodists, burned in 1933.

The doctrines for which the island congregation suffered so much harassment in the 1890's are still in force among the members of the sect, whose members are now held in respect throughout the community. Festivals and fund-raising events are still forbidden. Women members use no jewelry or makeup. Music is without accompanying instruments, and hymns are still "lined out" in old Wesleyan style. The sect has its own hymnbook, many selections of which were written by members from Chincoteague. Marriage with unsanctified persons is still forbidden and is not practiced, with the result that the sect, even at its national level, resembles and is often referred to as "one big, happy family."

The congregation at the mother church on Chincoteague Island is now reduced to only seven members, all women. Worship in the Chincoteague church is now only occasional, but the members maintain an active relationship with the rest of the sect, and travel regularly to Omar, Delaware, to meet with that larger congregation. Island members also regularly attend the annual camp meeting in Georgia, and it is still the usual practice for members of the Chincoteague congregation to be buried in the Sanctified burial grounds there.

On a national scale, Christ's Sanctified Holy Church and Christ's Sanctified Holy Church Colored (headquarters in Jennings, Louisiana) claim together a total of about 1700 members. Though a small sect nationally, it is the only national denomination of Eastern Shore of Virginia origins, and a direct link for the Eastern Shore to the theological issues of the last decade of the nineteenth century.

[Sources: 32, 109, 110, 117, 123, 176]

Location: see CHINCOTEAGUE

*CHRIST'S UNION BAPTIST CHURCH

[ESBA 1876-1961]
Chincoteague

There were still seven black members of white Union Baptist Church in Chincoteague when this church was founded in 1876. It had been ten years since the Accomack Baptist Association had released its black members to form their own congregations, and on the island the black Baptists still attended Union, climbing still to their separate gallery by the outside stairs. The new black congregation took the name Christ's Union Baptist Church and apparently erected their own building soon after the congregation was organized in 1876.

In 1902 the county paper reported that "Christ's Union Baptist Church...is nearing completion and will be a credit to the colored brethren." Apparently the building was improved at this time, probably by the addition of the steeple and (the following year when the repairs were finished) a cornerstone with both building dates, 1876 and 1903. The windows of this church are unlike any others on the Eastern Shore of Virginia, clear glass with delicate designs painted on them, and may date from the same period. It was not until two years after these repairs were completed that the congregation bought the land on which the church stands.

Christ's Union was never a large congregation, and like the black population of the island itself it dwindled away with the passing of the years. By the 1950's there were only a few families left, by 1961 only ten members. In that year the church ceased to function, and its members dispersed to other churches, among them Shiloh Baptist in Atlantic and Jerusalem Baptist in Temperanceville.

The church building still stands, abandoned and decaying, on Willow Street behind the local carnival grounds.

[Sources: 96, 105, 123, 176]

Location: see CHINCOTEAGUE

CHURCH OF GOD

[Independent 1976]
Withams

Elder Laurinetta Crippen, a local independent preacher, founded this church in 1976.

Although Crippen has been its pastor since that time, pastors of several other persuasions have preached there since its formation. During a series of services celebrating the church's first anniversary, visiting ministers were from a number of local black congregations, including Baptist and Church of Christ churches.

Elder Crippen's small congregation meets in a private home in Withams west of the United Methodist Church.

[Source: 109]

Location: see WITHAMS

*CHURCH OF GOD AND SAINTS OF CHRIST

[1920-1933?]
Exmore

This sect was founded by William S. Crowdy, a cook employed by the Santa Fe railroad, after a vision from God called him to lead the Negro people into true religion in 1896. Crowdy subsequently founded the Church of God and Saints of Christ and served as its prophet until his death.

By 1926 the sect had nineteen churches and almost 1300 members in Virginia, and one of the churches stood near Belle Haven Station north of Exmore. "Uncle" John F. Dickerson was the leader of the Exmore congregation, which bore the same name as the sect. The congregation bought a lot from George and Mary Annis in 1920 and erected there a very simple frame building.

Local people remember this congregation principally for its practice of foot-washing at the Lord's Supper, but actually there were a number of more distinctive beliefs and practices. Crowdy taught that the Negro race is descended from the ten lost tribes of Israel, and although his church was avowedly Christian it had also such a strong Jewish and Old Testament streak that it was often called "Black Jews." There was a strong emphasis on the Ten Commandments, the observance of the Jewish Sabbath, and use of the Jewish calendar. The church is strongly fundamentalist and its practices follow literally the Biblical instructions to greet members with a "holy kiss" and "bring tithes into the storehouse." Districts of the church still maintain "storehouses" from which groceries and other necessities are sold to members.

Little is known of the life of the Exmore congregation, which was never sizable and had a short life. There are no local records of its existence after 1923, and it is doubtful that the congregation survived the Depression of the following decade. The church building subsequently disappeared.

[Sources: 48, 124, 176]

Location: see EXMORE

CHURCH OF GOD AND TRUE HOLINESS

[Independent 1944]
Simpkins

The Church of God and True Holiness dates from 1944, when it was founded by an Elder Garris and erected on land purchased for $147 from Charles and Margaret McCune.

Although this has never been a large congregation, membership has declined in recent years. There are at present fewer than a dozen members, although attendance at worship is frequently greater than that.

Doctrinally this church is Pentecostal. The present pastor lives in Cheriton and has served since 1967.

[Sources: 124, 176]

Location: see SIMPKINS

CHURCH OF GOD OF CHINCOTEAGUE

[Church of God: Cleveland, Tennessee 1937]
Chincoteague

This congregation was born in 1937 when the Reverend Clarence J. Abbott pitched a tent on the island where the high school now stands and began a successful revival. By the end of the year, 38 persons had been organized into a new church, the first Pentecostal congregation in Accomack County.

For eleven years the Church of God worshiped in the abandoned building of Holiness Tabernacle, on Poplar Street at Deep Hole Road. In 1948 this building was converted into a dwelling and sold, and the congregation purchased a lot next door. Here they erected their own building in 1948, which was enlarged in 1959.

The Church of God of Chincoteague is affiliated with the General Assembly of the Church of God of Cleveland, Tennessee. Like the denomination of which it is a part, the Chincoteague congregation is fundamentalist, sanctificationist, and Pentecostal. Speaking in tongues is practiced, and footwashing is an ordinance of the church.

The Chincoteague congregation has been a small one throughout its history. The maximum size of the congregation occurred in the early years until 1945; thereafter membership declined. The present membership is 23. Most of the pastors of this church have lived off the island.

[Sources: 123, 176]

Location: see CHINCOTEAGUE

CHURCH OF GOD OF MELFA

[Church of God: Cleveland, Tennessee 1977]
Melfa

James Caldwell, district pastor of this denomination in Crisfield, opened this church on May 1, 1977, with an afternoon service. Shortly thereafter the Reverend Daniel Seyda assumed the pastorate. The congregation has met regularly on Sunday evenings since that time.

The church meets in the rented building which formerly housed the Christian Love Center and includes in its membership some of the former members of that earlier Charismatic congregation.

[Source: 109]

Location: see MELFA

CHURCH OF THE LORD JESUS CHRIST OF THE APOSTOLIC FAITH

[General Assembly of the Church of the Lord Jesus Christ of the Apostolic Faith Inc., 1953]
Cape Charles

Bishop S. C. Johnson was the founder of the churches of this name, the headquarters of which are located in Philadelphia. H. M. Shelton founded this Cape Charles congregation, which was established in 1953.

This congregation is the oldest of the "Oneness" or "Jesus Only" churches of the Shore. The church is Pentecostal in doctrine, but rejects Trinitarian formulas and baptizes only in the name of Jesus.

The Cape Charles congregation is part of Bishop Johnson's Philadelphia-based denomination, and not a part of the Church of Our Lord Jesus Christ of the Apostolic Faith, a denomination of similar persuasion and similar name founded in 1919 by R. C. Lawson and now based in New York.

[Sources: 124, 176]

Location: see CAPE CHARLES

CLARKE PRESBYTERIAN CHURCH

(''Clarke's Chapel'')
[Pres 1894]
Daugherty

Byron Clarke, pastor of Makemie Presbyterian Church in Accomac, began this church with the founding of a Sunday school in the schoolhouse at Daugherty in 1894. Before the year was out James Daugherty had given a lot and local citizens had erected a chapel, which became Clarke's Chapel in the pastor's honor. The congregation was for two decades an unorganized mission served by the pastors of Makemie.

In 1897, Maude Harding, a local member, organized a Missionary Society which could within a short time boast almost 100 members, men, women, and children. Although monthly dues were only 1¢ a member, the Society contributed $50 to missions in its first year. In 1902 a Ladies Aid group was split off from this Society. In 1922 the two groups were recombined into the Woman's Auxiliary, by which time the group had become for women only.

Clarke's Chapel progressed steadily, grew in membership, and on April 9, 1916, was organized by the Presbytery into a congregation in its own right. Marion S. Huske was pastor at that time.

In 1920 the congregation purchased the schoolhouse lot next door, where the Sunday school had been formed. Two years later the church building was moved aside to this lot and a new church, the present structure, erected on its site. Since 1922 the older building has been used as a church hall and is officially known as Fletcher Memorial Hall, after Judge James H. Fletcher, a prominent member. In the late 1930's the furnishings of the abandoned Baker Memorial Baptist Church were given to this church.

Clarke reached its maximum membership of 81 in the early 1920's. It has slowly and steadily declined since that time, and its membership today is 23. It has always shared its pastors with Makemie in Accomac and occasionally with other churches, but in recent years it has been served by a retired pastor.

[Sources: 119, 120, 123, 173, 176]

Location: see DAUGHERTY

*COARD'S BRANCH METHODIST EPISCOPAL CHURCH, SOUTH

(see Amiss Chapel Methodist Episcopal Church, South)

*COBB'S ISLAND MISSION, METHODIST EPISCOPAL CHURCH, SOUTH

[ME-S 1882-1897]
Cobb's Island

The organization of this church was due to the "suggestion and liberality of Mrs. Hamilton Easter," a "generous Christian lady" of Baltimore who was a frequent visitor to Cobb's Island. When she offered money for the establishment of a church there, the Virginia Conference accepted the offer and in 1882 sent Thomas G. Pullen to the island. Pullen, a young man, built the small, frame chapel with his own hands, completing it by the winter of 1882. Nathan and Sally Cobb, owners of the hotel and the island's chief citizens, deeded the land to the church in 1884 for $1.

Cobb's Island was a popular resort in that day, and Pullen's efforts were soon "crowned with happy results." There were twenty members in 1887. The church stood just south of the big hotel, and although it was very small it boasted a steeple complete with a bell. One guest at the hotel described the church in a letter to a friend: "It is a touching sight to see visitors from different parts of the earth, of various states and denominations, meet together for the first and perhaps the last time to engage in Christian worship." According to the same letter, there was a Sunday school library at the church, which the island children were encouraged to use.

One of the most famous persons to visit the island was the Reverend Thomas Dixon, renowned preacher from New York. He preached on the island in July 1893, though whether in the church is unknown. The island was even then beginning to erode into the sea, and some of its inhabitants had already moved to the mainland. The church dwindled with the community's population, and after 1895 was attached to the Wachapreague Circuit as a mission. The most severe erosion occurred in 1896, after which the Cobbs themselves abandoned their island. By 1897 the island was deserted, and after that year the church drops from the records of the denomination.

The abandoned island was a favorite haunt of curious visitors for a number of years thereafter. J. R. Sturgis, pastor of the Bloxom Circuit, visited the island in the winter of 1897 and described it, with its "wrecked and remaining buildings" for the local newspapers. Thomas Dixon returned to the island in 1898, not to preach but to hunt. Within a short time the church and the other buildings on the island were swept away by the tides, and the ocean divided the island with a channel at about where the village once stood. The pulpit furniture and the pulpit Bible were removed from the church before its destruction, and are today the property of Smith's Chapel in Quinby.

[Sources: 91, 109, 110, 116, 124, 176]

Location: now under water

COKESBURY UNITED METHODIST CHURCH

("Seymours")
[ME 1788, ICA 1861, ME 1864, M 1939, UMC 1968]
Onancock

Though a small congregation in our own time, Cokesbury has played an important part in the history of Methodism in Onancock and on the Shore. Its history is remarkably well-documented, and within its walls were made some of the most important decisions of Eastern Shore Methodism.

Methodism in Onancock began with the visit of Francis Asbury to the home of William Seymour in 1788. Asbury preached in a schoolhouse in the village on that visit, but the society that was formed met generally in Seymour's home. Onancock was a lesser society at this point (Asbury visited it only once more, in 1806), and the work of leading the small flock fell on Seymour, who was licensed to preach in 1805. Shortly thereafter Seymour built his beautiful mansion on Onancock Creek and called it "Wesley," and meetings were moved to this location. Seymour's business partner was Major John S. Kerr of Kerr Place, who was visited by the presiding elder, William Chandler, in 1805 on the eve of the first great Pungoteague camp meeting. As Chandler was about to leave Kerr's elegant mansion, he turned to his host and remarked, "Well, Major, this mansion is too beautiful to leave behind you, and yet you will soon have to leave it and go to that narrow house appointed for all living." The word struck home; Kerr was converted and became a Methodist. He died the next year.

In 1808 another townsman, William Lee, was licensed to preach, and in that year began the extensive co-ministry of Seymour and Lee. The two men preached to the society on alternate Sundays, the circuit preacher visiting only on weekdays. In 1808 they conducted the first camp meeting on Tangier Island, and for years ministered to the creeks and necks of the Bayside wherever they were needed. Seymour was ordained a deacon in 1811, and Lee an elder in 1833. Lorenzo Dow visited Onancock on his way to the camp meeting in 1805, and after he preached, he records, "we had a shout."

Seymour died heavily in debt in 1821, and "Wesley" was sold, and it was not until this time that the Onancock Methodists needed a meetinghouse. They had secured one by the following year, an abandoned mill forty feet square. This building was renovated, and in 1824 William D. Seymour, son of the society's late pillar, deeded to the church the lot on the town square on which the building stood. This is the present site of Cokesbury. In 1834 Seymour sold a parcel of land immediately west of the building to the denomination, and here the first Methodist parsonage on the Eastern Shore of Virginia was erected in 1836. This parsonage is no longer standing, but its erection in Onancock probably indicates that the Cokesbury society was gradually becoming a more important and larger congregation.

In 1854 the present Cokesbury building was erected, only a few months behind the second Downing's Chapel in Oak Hall. These two buildings are the oldest Methodist sanctuaries on the Virginia Shore. It was in this building in June 1860 that the congregation dissolved its affiliation with the Methodist Episcopal Church, and it was here on January 19, 1861, that the independent Convention of Accomack was formed. Cokesbury remained under the care of William Coe of the Convention until 1864, when by a vote of 104 to seventeen it returned to the Philadelphia Conference and the northern church. Shortly after that vote, George Washington Mason locked the church door and kept the key at home, thus securing the building for the northern majority of the congregation.

Only Cokesbury, Ayres Chapel, and Tangier were left to the Methodist Episcopal Church by 1866 and the end of the Civil War. Cokesbury, though quickly outnumbered by the southern congregation in Onancock, was the largest and most central church of this little circuit, and a parsonage was erected on King Street in 1869. It was from the Cokesbury congregation, thanks to the efforts of its local or appointed pastors, that other northern Methodist congregations were formed on the Shore: Leatherbury (1874), Crowsontown (1886), and Riverview (1910). In 1886 even the fledgling northern congregation in Cape Charles fell to the care of the Cokesbury pastor. Tangier was separated from the Onancock Circuit in 1883, Ayres, Crowsontown, and Leatherbury in 1919. Not until then did this church become a station. A third parsonage was erected in 1920 on Market Street.

The Cokesbury building was renovated in 1885 and a steeple added for the first time. The very next year lightning struck the new steeple and destroyed it, but it was quickly replaced. It was damaged a second time by Hurricane Hazel in 1954.

The building was extensively remodeled in 1894 and at this time the gallery was removed and stained glass windows were installed, as in so many other churches up and down the Shore.

By Unification in 1939 Cokesbury was by far the smaller of the two Methodist churches in Onancock. It remained a station until it was attached to Market Street in 1947, during which year the church's parsonage was sold. This arrangement lasted until 1960, when it again became a station. Since that time the church has been served by retired or supply pastors. Ironically, Market Street, the southern church founded from this congregation, is the largest Methodist church on the Eastern Shore today, and Cokesbury, the northern church, with about twenty members, is the smallest.

[Sources: 3, 4, 15, 16, 39, 99, 101, 103, 116, 117, 168, 174]

Location: see ONANCOCK

COLES CHAPEL AFRICAN METHODIST EPISCOPAL CHURCH

[AME 1954]
Bayview

Coles Chapel is named for its founder, Eli H. B. Coles, a layman from St. Stephen's A.M.E. Church in Cape Charles. It began in 1954 as a Sunday school for the children of the Bayview area. Gradually parents began to attend, and when membership had reached about a dozen adults a separate worshiping congregation was organized.

In 1962 the little congregation secured an old building from African Baptist Church, moved it to a lot in Bayview, and refitted it as Coles Chapel. The building had previously stood in Cheriton behind African, which used it for dinners and meetings.

Coles Chapel has always been a small congregation, ministering to a few families who reside in the Bayview and Cape Charles area. Coles himself served the church until his death in September 1966, and thereafter the church has been served by pastors from St. Stephen's.

[Sources: 109, 176]

Location: see BAYVIEW

COMMUNITY CHURCH OF GOD

("Locust Grove," "Community Chapel")
[Church of God: Anderson, Indiana 1907]
Birdsnest

Mrs. Annie Bradford Pearson of Birdsnest was a member of Johnson's Church when she first saw, in a Methodist magazine, an advertisement for Daniel Warner's Holiness periodical, *Gospel Trumpet.* She quickly subscribed, and became an eager seeker of the Holiness experience described in it. In 1909 she attended her first Holiness services at the Wachapreague church, and later that year with others of her family was baptized at a camp meeting in Maryland. The camp meeting was held under the auspices of Warner's Church of God (Anderson, Indiana), and the congregation that subsequently grew up in Birdsnest around Mrs. Pearson and her family became a part of that church.

For eight years the small congregation met in private homes in the area. Then in 1917 a building known as Locust Grove Church of God was erected on Seaside Road. In 1933 the congregation moved the building about a quarter mile north of its original site; it was known at that time as Community Chapel.

After Taylor Memorial Baptist Church closed, the Church of God was left the only congregation in Birdsnest, and beginning in the early 1940's the congregation occupied the old Baptist building, which was larger than their own. During their use of the Baptist building, they made a number of repairs and improvements on it. Their own original building was sold in 1947. It was jacked up and placed on a truck to be moved, but the building burned on the truck the night before it was to be moved.

In 1953 the congregation purchased its present site in Birdsnest. The present building was erected there subsequently, and the congregation abandoned Taylor Chapel when the new building was ready.

This congregation has never been a large one. Although at one time it had a pastor of its own and rented a parsonage for him, recent pastors have lived as far away as Salisbury, Maryland, and preaching here has been twice a month. Like other congregations of the Church of God, it does not have formal membership figures. However, at the present time about 25 persons are active participants, and there are about fifty Sunday school scholars.

This is the only church of its kind on the Eastern Shore of Virginia. Miss Pearl Pearson, daughter of the founder and one of the original members, is still an active churchgoer here, and still a faithful reader of *Vital Christianity,* which since 1966 has been the name of the periodical, *Gospel Trumpet.*

[Sources: 124, 176]
Location: see BIRDSNEST

CONNER'S CHAPEL METHODIST EPISCOPAL CHURCH, SOUTH

(see Saxis United Methodist Church)

CONQUEST CHAPEL METHODIST EPISCOPAL CHURCH, SOUTH

(see Temperanceville United Methodist Church)

*CONQUEST CHAPEL METHODIST PROTESTANT CHURCH

[MP 1887-1927]

Temperanceville

The Methodist Protestants founded Conquest Chapel in 1887, one year after the southern Methodist church of the same name was moved to Temperanceville from the south corner of the same intersection (Route 13 and Hallwood Road). The church was an outgrowth of the Methodist Protestant congregation in Lee Mont, but throughout most of its history was grouped to the Wattsville cluster of M.P. churches.

In November 1892 the building, only five years old, burned to the ground. The present building was dedicated on the same spot in 1893.

Hallwood M.P. was founded from this church in 1903, and in 1911 the two churches purchased a parsonage in the village of Hallwood. Conquest Chapel was ultimately eclipsed in size and importance by the younger church, and in 1927 the name of the charge was changed from Conquest to Hallwood. In that same year Conquest Chapel reported 27 conversions at a revival. That report is the last mention of the church in the records of the denomination.

By 1933, Conquest Chapel had begun its long history of being used for secular purposes. In that year it was already a service station. Since that time it has served as a dwelling, a store, a garage, and is at the present an antique shop. A large addition has been added to the building, but the original church design can still be plainly seen. When erected, the building had a steeple, but that was removed early in the 1930's and for a while sat on the lot off to itself.

[Sources: 105, 109, 110, 114, 124]

Location: see TEMPERANCEVILLE

CRADDOCKVILLE

see: Craddockville United Methodist Church

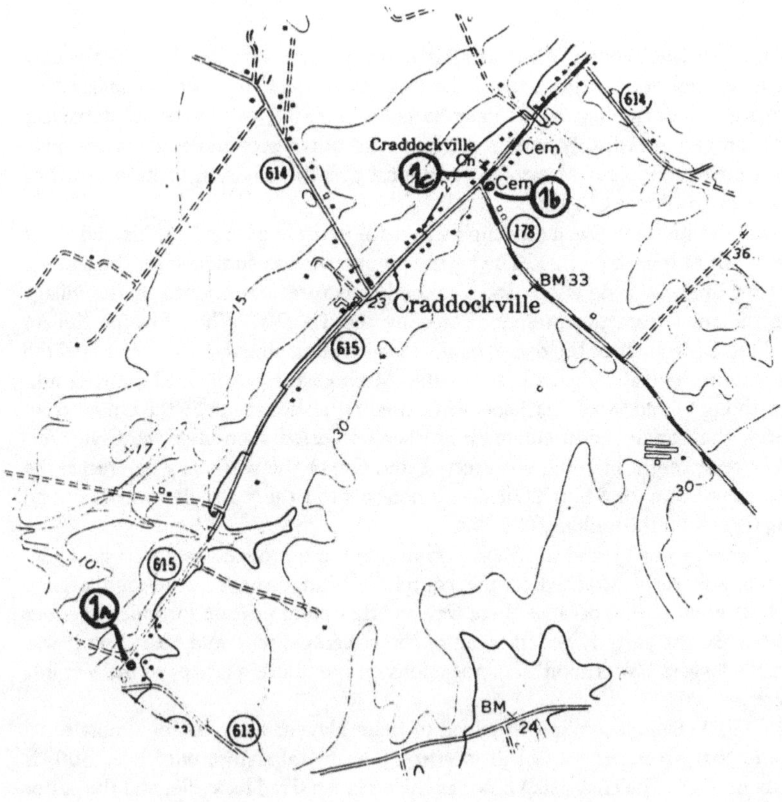

1a - Craddockville Methodist: original site c1821-c1850
1b - Craddockville Methodist: site c1850-1871
1c - Craddockville Methodist: site since 1871

CRADDOCKVILLE UNITED METHODIST CHURCH

[ME 1821?, ME-S 1847, M 1939, UMC 1968] Craddockville

Craddockville is one of the earlier Methodist churches on the Shore, but exactly when it was founded is uncertain. The local tradition that it was established by Lorenzo Dow, preaching in this neighborhood in 1806, cannot be substantiated. The congregation probably arose toward the end of the second decade of the nineteenth century. William Mears, an early local preacher, is said to have preached here and also at Ames Chapel.

The first building was a meetinghouse made entirely of logs, and it stood about a mile south of town by 1821. The log meetinghouse was sufficient for the congregation for about a generation, and a second structure was erected in the village across the road from the present church by the 1850's. When Erastus Kellam deeded the church lot to the denomination the building already stood on it, and the congregation had already seceded to the Methodist Episcopal Church, South.

Although Craddockville Chapel was closed for a short time by the Union army in 1864, the congregation entered a prosperous period soon after the Civil War. In 1871 the present building was erected, and one of the workers who erected the church salted away a $100 Confederate note behind the walls. It was discovered during repairs on the building in 1957.

As years went by and the Shore's churches were grouped into circuits, Craddockville was early attached to the church in Pungoteague. Although a rural church, it grew strong because there was no other congregation for miles in either direction. By the early twentieth century the congregation could boast that it was one of the largest "afternoon" congregations on the Shore, perhaps in the Virginia Conference.

In 1915, Craddockville was joined to Belle Haven, a church of almost equal size, and that arrangement is still in effect. The membership, once over 300, is now about 275. The charge is known as Belle Haven-Craddockville, and the pastor lives in Belle Haven.

In 1958 the Eastern Shore District purchased and opened Camp Occohannock, a camping and retreat center west of Craddockville. By virtue of their proximity to the camp and their interest in it, pastor and people of Craddockville Church have been active in its operation ever since.

[Sources: 39, 109, 111, 116, 123, 176]

Location: see CRADDOCKVILLE

*CROSSROADS MEETINGHOUSE

[ABA 1833-1836?]
Onley

By the 1830's the vigorous congregation of Pungoteague (Hollies) Baptist had constructed three extra chapels for meetings and worship: Boggs, Zoar, and Crossroads. Crossroads Meetinghouse stood in or near what is today Onley (known before the coming of the railroad as Crossroads), and it was used by pastors who served Hollies as well as by others for religious purposes.

Little is known of Crossroads Meetinghouse. It was definitely standing by 1833, and in 1836 it was moved from its original location to a site ''out on Locustville Road.'' Sometime before 1890 it was destroyed by fire, and subsequently a schoolhouse was built upon its site. It is not unlikely that the meetinghouse itself was used as a schoolhouse before it burned.

Neither of the building's locations, either in Crossroads or on the Locustville Road, can today be determined with any accuracy.

[Source: 150]

Location: Unknown

CROWSONTOWN

see: *Crowsontown Methodist Episcopal Church*

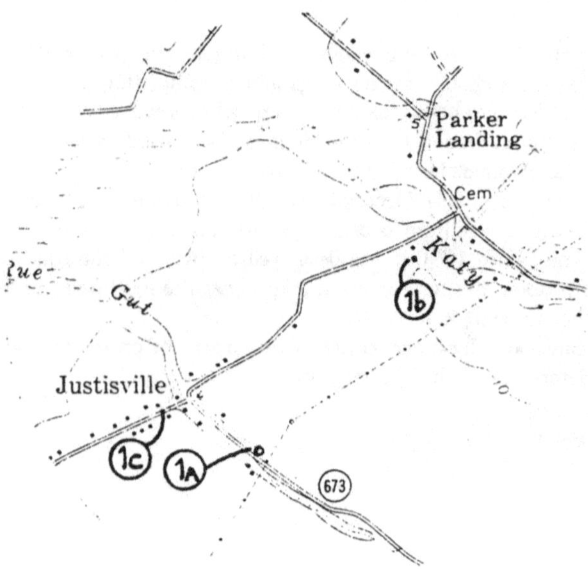

1a - Crowsontown ME: original site 1884-1934
1b - Crowsontown ME: present site of back half of building
1c - Crowsontown ME: present site of front half of building

*CROWSONTOWN METHODIST EPISCOPAL CHURCH

("Crowson's")
[ME 1884-1930]
Justisville

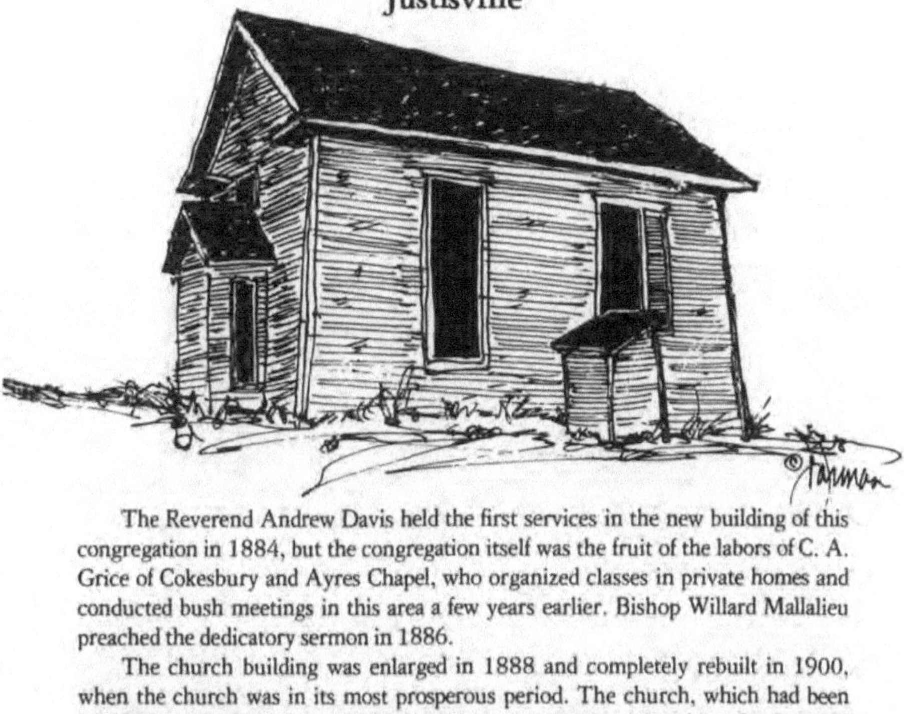

The Reverend Andrew Davis held the first services in the new building of this congregation in 1884, but the congregation itself was the fruit of the labors of C. A. Grice of Cokesbury and Ayres Chapel, who organized classes in private homes and conducted bush meetings in this area a few years earlier. Bishop Willard Mallalieu preached the dedicatory sermon in 1886.

The church building was enlarged in 1888 and completely rebuilt in 1900, when the church was in its most prosperous period. The church, which had been attached to the Parksley congregation, became a station church under Baynard Wheatley in 1900. A parsonage was secured in 1902, but in 1906 the church was attached to the Onancock Circuit. Its membership at that time was 71.

By the 1920's the Crowsontown church had declined seriously, and it closed altogether with the advent of the Depression. The last service held in the church was the funeral of Sally Dennis Rew Crowson, widow of the man who had erected the building.

Since the church lot had been given with the provision that regular services be held on it, it reverted to the owners. In 1934 the building was sold and split into two parts. The front half was incorporated into a dwelling nearby and is not today recognizable as a church building. The back half became a barn, and passersby can still glimpse the features of church architecture as it sits in the field about a mile north of Crowsontown at Parker's Landing.

[Sources: 105, 109, 110, 117, 157, 176]

Location: see CROWSONTOWN

DALBYS

see: *First Baptist Church (Capeville)*
**Fishing Point Church (Church of England)*
Lower Northampton Baptist Church
**Magothy Church (Church of England)*

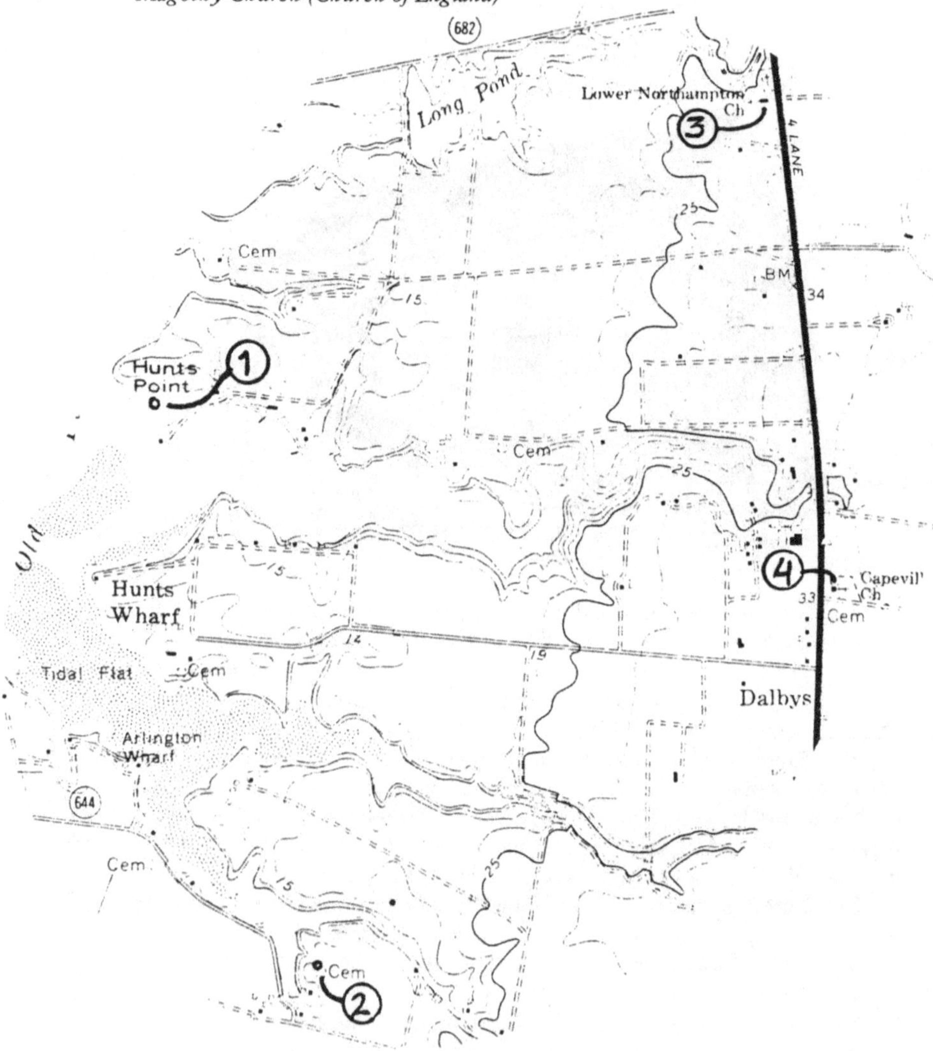

1 - Fishing Point Church: site c1641-c1669 (approximate)
2 - Magothy Church: site c1691-1826 (approximate)
3 - Lower Northampton Baptist: site since 1798
4 - First Baptist Church

Location unknown: Lower Northampton Baptist Church site 1785-1798

DAUGHERTY

see: *Clarke Presbyterian Church*
St. Luke's African Methodist Episcopal Church
**Zoar Baptist Meetinghouse*

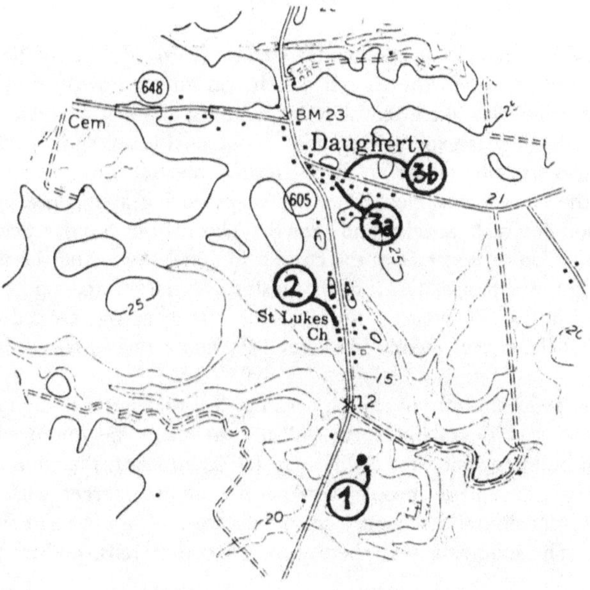

1 - Zoar Baptist: site 1833-1851? (approximate)
2 - St. Luke's AME
3a - Clarke Presbyterian: site since 1894
3b - Clarke Presbyterian: building I moved to this site 1922

DEAS CHAPEL UNITED METHODIST CHURCH

[ME 1877, M 1939, UMC 1968]
Horntown

Deas Chapel was erected in 1877 and named for R. M. H. Deas of New York, who gave the land on which the church sits. It was an outgrowth of Friendship Church in Wattsville, and like Friendship was a strong and vigorous church from the start. By 1881 it was experiencing great "outpourings of spirit." By 1884 the presiding elder was citing it for its "lively spiritual meetings."

In 1904 the church was closed for five weeks during a smallpox epidemic, but this did not diminish activity and growth. The district Sunday School and Epworth League Convention met at the church in June 1911, and the presiding elder, W. J. L. Hughes, praised Deas and Friendship as "the strongest circuit on the district, perhaps in the Conference." In 1915 the parsonage was erected near the church. In 1919 the circuit membership was 149, and a revival added 56 in the following year.

As early as 1922 this strong church began to feel the effects of the migration of its members to the cities of the North. Still the parsonage was improved (1927) and the church building renovated (1931). By 1932, however, the church was in dire economic straits, and its people were petitioning for merger with another circuit. By 1937 the church had sunk "seemingly...to the very lowest possible for maintenance." The following year there were 23 conversions, and an upswing began.

Except for a brief period beginning in 1913 when Friendship was made a station, Deas Chapel has always shared its pastor with that church. The pastor lives today in the new parsonage completed in 1974 near the church. There are today about 100 members.

[Sources: 113, 116, 123]

Location: see HORNTOWN

DEEP CREEK METHODIST EPISCOPAL CHURCH, SOUTH

(see Locustville United Methodist Church)

DISCIPLES CHURCH OF NEW YORK

[International Brotherhood of Yahshua's Disciples for the Finishing Work Inc. 1968]
Whitesville

This congregation was established by Joseph and Earl Vicks of Brooklyn, New York. In 1968 they purchased the old school property in Whitesville, which subsequently became a home for members of the congregation. Worship services are held in a rented building nearby.

The Disciples Church is part of a Brooklyn-based sect which is strongly oriented to the Old Testament. Members of the group use the Hebrew word Yahshua to refer to God, and following Mosaic law worship on Saturdays. There is a strong sense of community identity among the people of this small group, many of whom live on or around the property purchased in 1968.

This congregation maintains strong ties to the original community in Brooklyn through the Vickses, who continue to reside in New York City although they serve as trustees and leaders of the Whitesville group. The only other congregation of similar persuasion on the Eastern Shore is the Smyrna Assembly of Yajshua Disciples in Makemie Park, with which this congregation shares congenial relations.

[Sources: 123, 176]

Location: see PARKSLEY

DOUGLAS TABERNACLE BAPTIST CHURCH

(see Horntown Tabernacle Baptist Church)

DOWNING'S UNITED METHODIST CHURCH

[ME 1783, ME-S 1860, M 1939, UMC 1968]
Oak Hall

Downing's is without question the oldest Methodist church on the Eastern Shore of Virginia. It is named for Captain William Downing (17??-1824), in whose home the society first gathered. Downing is said to have been converted by Robert Williams in 1772, and although this tradition cannot be substantiated it has been retained by the congregation, who celebrated their bicentennial anniversary in 1972. The recorded history of the congregation begins with the first visit of Asbury in 1783. It seems likely that the society grew out of Methodist work in the region of Pocomoke City, Maryland, and thus became the first society to be formed as the new faith moved southward into Virginia.

Bishop Francis Asbury visited Downing's Chapel no fewer than thirteen times between 1783 and 1810, more than any other Virginia Shore church. At an early date Downing's became one of the foremost churches on the Shore, one of only four that could expect regular preaching by the circuit preachers on Sundays. Other Methodist notables who preached at Downing's Chapel in the early years were Richard Whatcoat (1788), William McKendree (1810), and Lorenzo Dow (1805 and 1813).

Asbury first indicates the existence of a meetinghouse at Downing's in 1791, and in 1794 Downing deeded to the denomination the land on which it was located. It stood just west of the present railroad and north of the road to Withams. This first building was used until 1854, when it burned to the ground.

In November 1853 a committee was appointed to attend to erecting a new church, and the building was completed by the close of summer 1854. Its erection caused some disagreement among the members of the congregation and the circuit regarding its location, for the old site was abandoned and a new one selected across the road. The building completed in 1854 is still in use, though much changed over the years, and is the oldest Methodist church building on the Eastern Shore of Virginia, as well as the eighth oldest church building among all denominations.

During the first half of the nineteenth century Downing's proved to be a strong and vigorous congregation, and three other churches derived from it: Oak Grove in Atlantic (1838), Temperanceville (1845), and Pocomoke (1855). The Pocomoke congregation was at first one of several classes at Downing's. Temperanceville began as a Sunday school conducted by this church, and the early members of Oak Grove came principally from Downing's.

Shortly before the outbreak of the Civil War, Downing's seceded to the southern church. The Union army occupied the village in 1861, and the church building was commandeered for use as a stable for the troops' horses. It is not clear how long the building was so used, but it was returned to the congregation a ruin: roof peppered with bullet-holes, pews chopped up for firewood. The congregation was again worshiping in it by 1864, and in that year it was closed for four months by order of the army. In 1915 Congress passed a bill awarding the congregation the sum of $235 for damages done to the building by the army in 1861.

In 1884 the railroad lines passed through the village to within a few feet of the church building, and it was not long before passing trains were disturbing worship. In 1888 the railroad agreed to move the building. The present site on Route 13 was obtained, and the building moved to it in that year. Since that time the structure has been extensively changed, with major improvements and additions in 1906, 1935, and 1953. As in so many other churches across the Shore, the steeple and stained glass windows are later additions, and the gallery that was once across the back has long since been removed, with the result that the building bears little resemblance to its original appearance.

According to local tradition, a little girl of this church helped to establish one of the agencies of the Virginia Conference. In 1866 D. P. Wills preached here on the need for an educated ministry in the Conference, and the lack of funds available to support prospective ministers through school. The tiny granddaughter of one of the members responded to the sermon by placing all of her savings in Wills' hands, and moved by her example, the people raised a significant sum. With it the Conference helped to establish the Preachers' Educational Society.

When the original Accomack Circuit was divided in 1858, Downing's became a part of the Atlantic Circuit, where it remained until after Unification. The church is today part of the Oak Hall Charge, with Temperanceville and Assawoman, and the parsonage is near the church in Oak Hall. The present membership is about 170.

After the original site of the old Downing's Chapel was abandoned in 1854, a dwelling was erected there. Here, generations later, a Methodist minister, Jack Beverley Taylor of the Virginia Conference, was born in 1910, just one more in a long line of those who have kept the faith alive from this oldest of Methodist churches on the Shore.

[Sources: 3, 4, 16, 39, 100, 103, 110, 116, 123, 176]

Location: see OAK HALL

DRUMMONDTOWN BAPTIST CHURCH

[ABA 1870]
Accomac

(first building, photo prior to 1912)

Drummondtown Baptist and Onancock Baptist churches were built with funds bequeathed by Anna C. Taylor at her death in 1850. Each church was left $1800 to be administered by Louis D. Drummond. Onancock Baptist was established within a few years of Mrs. Taylor's death, but not for another twenty years was there to rise a Baptist church in the county seat.

Drummond purchased the church lot for $500 as early as 1858, but it took the combined forces of the Virginia Baptist State Mission Board and Zion Baptist Church to establish the congregation. The Mission Board sent a pastor, Henry Petty, in 1870 to oversee the establishment of the church, and Zion dismissed eight members to constitute the congregation on December 30, 1871. The first building was erected and dedicated in 1870.

After the first pastor, Petty, Drummondtown shared its pastors with Onancock Baptist until 1890, then with Hollies until 1898. The Reverend T. S. Dunaway (1898-1901) began the Sunday school that issued in Baker Memorial Baptist Church in 1902. H. S. Kidd was pastor of Drummondtown when Baker Memorial was constituted, and the new church was often called Kidd's Chapel in his honor.

By the first decade of the twentieth century Drummondtown was a prosperous church about to outgrow its building. Construction of a new building began in 1912, and the old building was used until October 13, 1913. On November 2, 1913, the present brick building was dedicated. The Reverend F. W. Boatwright and R. H. Pitt spoke at that occasion. The older building was subsequently purchased by Mrs. E. M. B. Tiffany, moved to a new location near the public school, and presented to the school board for use as an auditorium. A front porch with Ionic columns was added to the old building at this time.

In 1926 the Accomack Baptist Association erected a memorial to Elijah Baker which stands in the yard of this church. The present brick building was later enlarged by a significant addition at the back.

Drummondtown has been a station church for virtually all the twentieth century. Its present membership is 189.

[Sources: 43, 69, 122]

Location: see ACCOMAC

DRUMMONDTOWN UNITED METHODIST CHURCH

[ME 1788, ICA 1861, ME-S 1866, M 1939, UMC 1968]
Accomac

It is said that Freeborn Garrettson labored in the vicinity of Drummondtown as early as 1778. It is known that Thomas Coke preached in the courthouse there in 1784. But the real impetus for the formation of the Methodist society in this county seat was the visit of Francis Asbury in 1788. Asbury was accompanied by Richard Whatcoat when he stopped in Drummondtown in November of that year. Both men preached in the village, and soon thereafter a Methodist society was formed. John and Esther Drummond sold the land on which the church now sits in 1793, and a chapel stood there by 1795.

photo prior to 1918

In the early years of this new town Methodist activities were not always confined to the meetinghouse. In 1801 Thomas Smith preached to a gathering of 3000 blacks who met outdoors while the whites conducted the Quarterly Meeting in the church nearby. Asbury preached in the courthouse in 1806. Lorenzo Dow spoke to "near three thousand in Drummingtown" in 1805, and observed good decorum in the crowd "except in a few." Later when the slavery issue divided the denomination in the 1840's, a good deal of anti-northern activity took place in the village, including public meetings and Judge Bailey's wounding of William Finney in 1847. This activity, too, occurred not in the Methodist church but on the village streets and greens. There is no evidence that the Methodist congregation itself was disturbed by the issue at this time.

In 1852 the Methodists at Drummondtown replaced their original building with a new one; nothing is known of what happened to the first structure. It was in the new church that William Gwynn Coe preached after the congregation became a part of the independent Convention of Accomack in 1861. The Union army occupied the village in the fall of that year and used the Methodist church building as barracks and stable. Forced out of their building, the congregation met in the courthouse. There were no Methodist services at all in the village from October 1863 to October 1864, by which time the Convention had been much weakened by schism.

While still in the hands of the army, the church building was used by the new African Methodist Episcopal congregation founded in Drummondtown in 1865. The building remained in the army's hands until 1870, and in 1871 the white congregation, then a part of the southern church, reclaimed it. John W. Edmunds described the church as it looked at that point:

> *The church was badly torn up... It was badly defaced on the inside... The walls badly broken; the window panes were out...pews badly damaged and my recollection is that many of them were gone. I know that the chancel rail was entirely destroyed because I bought another one and had it replaced myself.*

In 1915 the Congress of the United States voted $300 to the church "for the rental value with damages in excess of ordinary wear and tear."

Once restored, the building was used for another generation. The broken windows were replaced with colored panes arranged in random order; the members later grew to hate these windows and no one would claim responsibility for having chosen them. The slave gallery was removed during the restoration, as was a vestibule that had been added to the building after 1852. As late as the 1890's the two front doors and the two sides of the interior were understood to be reserved for the separate sexes, men on the right, women on the left, and it was considered scandalous for this pattern to be broken. In 1898 a pipe organ costing $250 was installed.

In 1918 the third and present building was erected on the same site, a brick structure with elaborate stained glass windows befitting a church in the county seat. The older building was purchased, moved, and remodeled into a home by Moses Simpkins, who also used it for occasional preaching services until it burned in the 1950's.

Drummondtown gave birth to Woodbury Church in 1882, Amiss Chapel in 1886, and Tasley Church in 1948. Today it shares its pastor with Woodbury, as it has every year since 1882. The present membership is about 120.

[Sources: 3, 15, 16, 39, 43, 70, 99, 100, 103, 109, 116, 168]

Location: see ACCOMAC

EASTVILLE

see: *Bethel African Methodist Episcopal Church*
Christ Episcopal Church
Eastville Baptist Church
**Eastville Methodist Episcopal Church*
**Eastville Presbyterian Church*
**Indiantown Mission, Methodist Episcopal Church*
**Macedonia Christian Church*
Mt. Sinai Church of God
Union Baptist Church

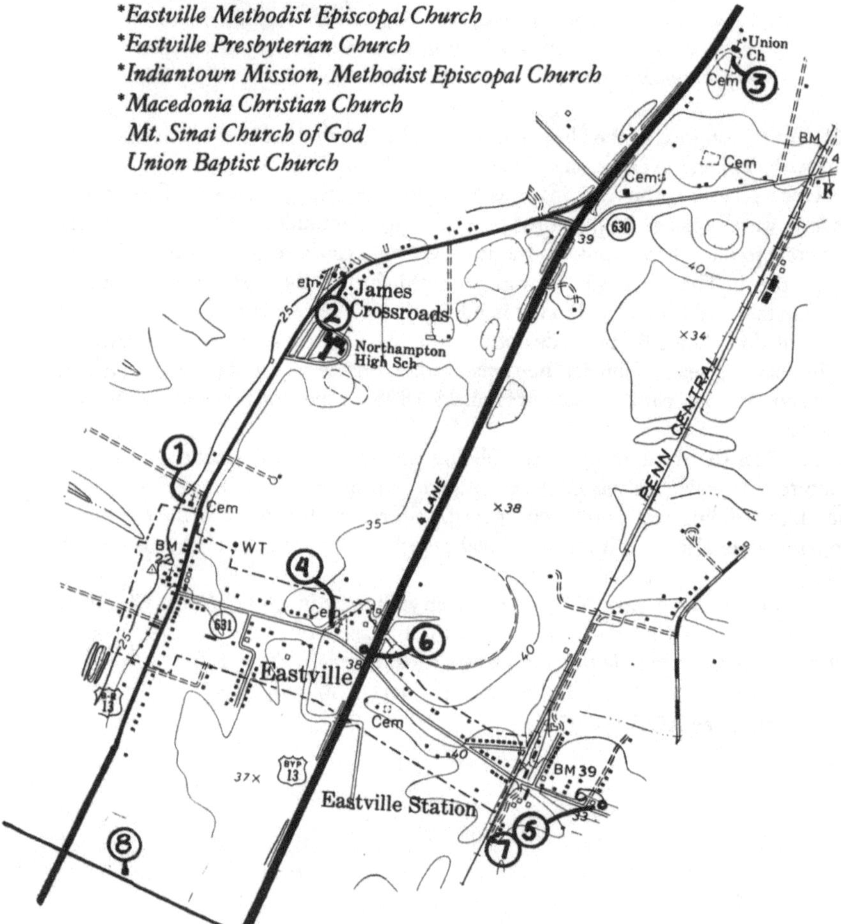

1 - Christ Episcopal
2 - Bethel AME
3 - Union Baptist
4 - Eastville Baptist
5 - Eastville ME
6 - Eastville Presbyterian: owned by the church but never used 1914-1926
7 - Macedonia Christian
8 - Mt. Sinai Church of God

Location Unknown: Indiantown Mission ME

EASTVILLE BAPTIST CHURCH

[ABA 1876]
Eastville

"Our Pastor has preached occasionally at Eastville, where we — Red Bank and us conjointly — hope to erect a suitable house of worship and organize a church." So reads the report of Lower Northampton Baptist Church to the Accomack Association in 1876, and the pastor who opened up this work was William T. Hundley, who served that church and Red Bank.

In October 1877, sixteen people, eight from Red Bank and eight from Lower Northampton, organized Eastville Baptist Church. John and Eliza Scott gave the land on which the church was erected, and the Reverend A. E. Dickinson preached the sermon when the new building was dedicated in 1878. Andrew Broaddus, Jr., was the first pastor.

For many years growth at Eastville Baptist Church was slow. The church shared its pastor with other congregations, and there was preaching only twice a month. By 1889 membership had increased by only three, to nineteen. Red Bank and Eastville together purchased a parsonage in the following year.

By the second decade of the twentieth century Eastville had entered more prosperous times. A second Sunday school was operated by the congregation in Savage's Neck until 1911. A new parsonage was erected in 1912, and shortly thereafter the church became a station. Membership in 1920 had increased to 121.

In 1904 the church building was extensively remodeled and altered. The roof was raised, stained glass windows installed throughout, and two small classrooms added to the back. A second renovation, with an extensive addition of several classrooms, two assembly halls, and a kitchen, was completed in 1952.

Eighteen pastors have served this church since it was founded, one of whom, Louis E. McKenney, served 25 years (1936-1961). When the church celebrated its centennial in 1977, there were 141 members. Since 1975 the congregation has shared its pastors with Cape Charles Baptist Church.

[Sources: 69, 122, 138]

Location: see EASTVILLE

*EASTVILLE MISSION, METHODIST EPISCOPAL CHURCH

[ME 1892-1896]
Eastville Station

In 1892 the black Methodists of the Delaware Conference succeeded in doing what the white Methodists had never done: placing a Methodist church in Eastville. In that year Thomas and Henrietta Scott sold an acre of land on the crossroads near the station, and two years later the presiding elder was at last able to report that "a Mission house has been built at Eastville, Virginia."

Unfortunately the Eastville church was short-lived. It cost $450 to build, and by the time it was finished only $125 had been raised from the sixteen members and probationers who worshiped there. The little congregation was not given much of a chance to pay for the rest, for in 1896 the denomination ordered the church "closed out, property sold and accounts adjusted."

The building stood unused for some years until it was purchased by Macedonia Christian Church in 1915 for $525. That congregation apparently used it for a while, but ultimately the property was abandoned, and the building disappeared.

[Sources: 113, 124, 176]

Location: see EASTVILLE

*EASTVILLE PRESBYTERIAN CHURCH

[Pres 1904-1919]
Eastville

A. S. Venable, the pastor at Holmes Presbyterian Church, organized this congregation in October 1904. Venable, who also founded the more lasting Presbyterian church in Cape Charles, met with his Eastville congregation on Sunday afternoons until 1907, when his successor, W. C. Flournoy, continued the effort.

The little Eastville congregation never had a building of its own. It worshiped in the YMCA building in Eastville, erected in 1890 on the present site of the firehouse. In 1914 the church obtained a lot in the village adjacent to the public school, but no building was ever erected.

The congregation, never larger than a "handful of people," numbered only ten in 1917. It was last listed in the records of the Presbytery in 1919, and thereafter the group disbanded. Most of the members went to Holmes, where two of them are still members today. The Holmes congregation sold the unused church lot in 1925, and the YMCA building in which the Eastville Presbyterians had gathered was dismantled in the 1920's.

[Sources: 12, 124, 176]

Location: see EASTVILLE

EBENEZER AFRICAN METHODIST EPISCOPAL CHURCH

("Capeville")
[AME 1868]
Capeville

Even before the end of the Civil War, the black residents of the Capeville area were gathering out-of-doors for religious services of their own. From this gathering came two churches: Ebenezer and First Baptist Church.

Local tradition has it that the Methodist portion of the interdenominational gathering had erected its first building and effected the organization of a church before 1865, when James Johnson, the African Methodist Episcopal pioneer, arrived on the Shore. Denominational records, however, do not list the Capeville church until 1868, when John Henry Offer, Johnson's successor, was pastor. It is indeed possible that Offer simply annexed to his A.M.E. circuit a previously existing building and congregation. Ebenezer is at any rate one of the oldest black churches on the Shore. In 1870 when the Eastville Circuit was divided, it was placed on a new circuit with Bethel and Shorter Chapel in Bridgetown.

The land on which the church is located was not purchased until 1875. The church became a station in 1892, although it has not been one continuously ever since. In 1917 the original frame building was replaced with a second one on the same site.

In January 1938 the second building was destroyed by fire, and the congregation worshiped in a nearby Masonic lodge while the present church was being erected. The building was completed and dedicated later that year.

Ebenezer is today a strong church that shares its pastor with Mt. Zion in Treherneville.

[Sources: 7, 105, 109, 124, 129]

Location: see CHEAPSIDE

EBENEZER BAPTIST CHURCH

[ESBA 1871]
Wardtown

Ebenezer was organized in 1871 by the Reverend Jasper Savage. Savage and his charter members were originally members of the new African Methodist Episcopal church in Occohannock Neck, Mt. Zion. What caused their withdrawal from that congregation is not known today, but in 1871 a large body of members withdrew and were baptized by the Reverend Caleb Burrows of African Baptist into a separate congregation.

It seems likely that a church building was erected soon after the formation of the congregation, but the land on which the present church stands was not deeded until 1898. The present building itself was erected in 1910. The location and fate of any previous buildings is not known.

Jasper Savage served the church until his death and was succeeded in 1909 by Leonard Treherne, who served until his death. During these years the church was strengthened by an influx of members from the area of Shiloh Baptist in Boston. Mt. Zion A.M.E., meanwhile, dwindled and ultimately closed.

In the more than 100 years of its existence, only seven pastors have served this church. The present pastor has served since 1953 and also preaches at First Baptist in Cape Charles. Ebenezer is a vigorous and prosperous congregation and boasts that it was the first black congregation on the Virginia Shore to worship in an air-conditioned building.

[Sources: 26, 124]

Location: see WARDTOWN

*EBENEZER METHODIST EPISCOPAL CHURCH

("Sluitkill Neck")
[ME 1848-1861]
Cashville

In 1848 when the members of Andrew Chapel in Sluitkill Neck informed the Accomack Circuit that they had withdrawn to the southern church, the circuit resolved not to abandon that neighborhood without a fight. There was a pro-northern minority at Andrew Chapel, and the Accomack Circuit determined that they "should have preaching and be attended to as heretofore by the preachers who may be sent to this circuit by the Philadelphia Conference."

Thus was born short-lived Ebenezer, the northern rival to Andrew Chapel. William Rodgers, one of its members, gave land for a church in 1849, a building was erected, and the northern church clung to its claim to the Cashville area. The society was regularly supplied with preaching by the circuit pastors. The records of 1856 indicate a flourishing Sunday school. In 1859 the society had 28 members under class leader William Rew.

In 1861 Ebenezer became one of the original members of the independent Convention of Accomack under William Gwynn Coe. Coe, however, preached there only through October of that year, and after that date the society drops from the records, apparently abandoned.

Some earlier writers confuse this Ebenezer with the church of the same name in Modest Town. Local Methodist records prove without a doubt that it was this Cashville church, not the one at Modest Town, that was a part of Coe's Convention.

It is not certain exactly where the church stood, but it was in the vicinity of the present Broadway Baptist Church. What happened to the building is not known.

[Sources: 39, 99, 103, 123]

Location: see CASHVILLE

*EBENEZER METHODIST EPISCOPAL CHURCH

[ME 1827, ME-S 1861, ME 1869-1901]
Modest Town

The first reference to Methodism in Modest Town is from 1823, when John Laws of that village was licensed to exhort. Laws apparently became the chief pillar of a society there, and in 1827 he deeded a quarter-acre lot for the building of a church. The church, which was probably erected soon afterwards, first appears in the records in 1834, and it was known as Ebenezer Chapel.

The Methodist society at Ebenezer revolved around the Laws family and prospered only as long as they were there to support it. In 1831 John Laws married Mary Henderson Welbourn, widow of Drummond Welbourn of Horntown. In 1833, John Laws, Jr., was licensed to preach. The elder Laws died in 1839, but the younger went on to become a deacon (1841) and an ordained elder (1848). There is little sign of activity at Ebenezer after John Laws, Jr., joined the traveling ministry.

Ebenezer seceded to the southern church with the rest of the Atlantic Circuit in 1860, and was closed by the Union army for a short while in 1864. Apparently activity there had virtually come to a halt by the end of the Civil War, for neither northern nor southern Methodists laid claim to the church until 1869, when the northern Wilmington Conference was organized and assumed control of the property. "Our brethren are contemplating the erection of...a church at Modest Town," reported the Conference in that year, but no new building was erected. The congregation was a small and struggling one; as late as 1885 there were only five members.

The last years of Ebenezer were spent grouped to the new churches founded by the Methodist Episcopal Church. Bishop Mallalieu preached there in 1886, and by 1889 Ebenezer shared its pastor with the new M.E. church in Hallwood. The last pastor on record was J. S. Bozman, who preached in Hallwood in the evenings and Ebenezer in the afternoons. Under him the church building was repaired in 1899, but the church closed soon afterwards. There are no records of it in the conference journals after 1901.

The building stood until 1912, when it was burned to the ground. It was being used for the storage of hay at the time, and local rumor always had it that an adjoining neighbor set the fire deliberately to prevent another citizen from buying the property and converting it into a dwelling. It was a small frame building of primitive design, without steeple or stained glass windows. There was one central front door and no front windows, and the slave gallery was never removed.

Today only two large trees that once stood in front of the building mark the site. Mary Welbourn Laws, widow of the founder, lies buried in the burial ground adjoining the site.

[Sources: 39, 103, 110, 117, 123, 176]

Location: see MODEST TOWN

EMMANUEL EPISCOPAL CHURCH

[PE 1888]
Cape Charles

Episcopalians in the new town of Cape Charles first assembled in 1888, when George Easter, rector of Hungars Parish, began to hold services every other Sunday. A Sunday school and a Woman's Guild were organized, and before a chapel could be erected the fledgling congregation met in Kellam's Hall (a store on the corner of Mason and Peach), Masonic Hall, and Centenary Methodist Episcopal Church, South.

The new church building was completed by 1893, and the cornerstone was laid during impressive ceremonies witnessed by visitors from as far away as New York. However, the layman in charge of the church's finances absconded with the funds, and it was not until 1899 that Bishop A. M. Randolph was able to consecrate the debt-free building.

In 1914 Emmanuel built a rectory and separated from Hungars Parish to become a parish in its own right. M. Colgate Daughtrey was the first rector to serve this church alone; he served two pastorates (1914-16 and 1923-28). In 1928 the original clapboard chapel was altered significantly by the addition of a brick veneer and a steeple, improvements that cost $5236.

Two missions were begun by Emmanuel; the second St. Michael's in Belle Haven, and the short-lived St. Andrew's Mission in Cheriton. Two other congregations have met in its chapel: the Seventh-Day Adventist congregation of Cape Charles in the 1960's, and First Lutheran Mission for a short period in 1975.

The communicant membership of this church hovered around seventy throughout the 1920's and the 1930's, but began a long decline after 1940. In 1975 Emmanuel was the smallest Episcopalian congregation on the Shore, with only eighteen members.

[Sources: 62, 109, 125]

Location: see CAPE CHARLES

EMMANUEL EPISCOPAL CHURCH

[PE 1860]
Jenkins Bridge

As early as the 1850's two Episcopalian pastors, John Crosdale of Pocomoke City and John Atkinson of Onancock, held occasional services in homes in and around the town of Temperanceville. But Emmanuel Church itself was founded by Crosdale with the help of a local couple, Mr. and Mrs. Spencer Fletcher. Emery White gave a lot for the church, and in 1860 the little frame building was erected. Union soldiers used the building for sleeping quarters during the Civil War, but no harm was done to it.

Not long after the Civil War a member of Emmanuel founded a Sunday school in a schoolhouse at Jenkins Bridge, west of Temperanceville. Eleanor Fletcher, the second wife of Spencer Fletcher, the founder, became superintendent, and it was probably through her influence (she was often called the "Bishop of Emmanuel") that the decision was made to move the church building. In 1887, the congregation dismantled its church, carried the lumber four miles to Jenkins Bridge, and re-erected it there facing Holden's Creek on land given by James Fletcher. They thus abandoned Temperanceville to the southern Methodists of Conquest Chapel, who had moved their own building to a site just across the street from Emmanuel only the year before.

In 1896 Christ Episcopal Church in Bloxom was added to the parish, and a rectory was built at Jenkins Bridge for both churches. The parish also held services in New Church (1895), Wishart's Point (1906), and Parksley (1920's), but no congregation was founded at any of those places. Christ Church later closed, and the rectory was sold. In 1946 Emmanuel came under the direction of the minister serving all three parishes in Accomack County.

Until relatively recent years Emmanuel was the smallest Episcopal church on the Virginia Shore. As late as 1940 it had only nine communicant members, as late as 1951 only seventeen. The church has grown substantially in recent years and in 1973 could boast 77 communicants, the highest in its history.

The building standing today at Jenkins Bridge is identical to that erected in Temperanceville over a century ago and is much admired for its quaintness and charm. This congregation still owns the communion cup given to Assawoman Church by Queen Anne in 1749, and the stained glass windows in the church are said to be the oldest on the Shore.

[Sources: 62, 64, 66, 118, 176]

Location: see JENKINS BRIDGE, TEMPERANCEVILLE

EPWORTH UNITED METHODIST CHURCH

("Broadwater Chapel")

[ME-S 1891, M 1939, UMC 1968]

Exmore

(first building, "Broadwater Chapel;" photo c. 1920)

This church was originally known as Broadwater Chapel, and it was erected in 1892 on land purchased the previous year for $1 from H. Clay Johnson. The building was dedicated in 1893, and during its early years the church shared its pastors with Bethel in Jamesville.

Exmore in 1892 was a completely new town and a growing one. Less than a mile to the south stood the abandoned Trinity Church, a northern Methodist structure. Trinity had not been used for years, and the need for a church for the new town occasioned some controversy as to whether Trinity should be reopened. Ultimately the few remaining Trinity Methodists agreed to affiliate with the southerners in the establishment of a new church on a new site. A cornerstone was prepared that said "Broadwater" on one side and "Trinity" on the other but, according to local tradition, when this was about to be set in place it fell out of the workers' wagon with "Broadwater" facing outward. The Trinity inscription was obscured by subsequent construction, and that old church passed finally out of existence.

The history of Broadwater Chapel was intimately tied to that of another southern Methodist church, Pullen's Chapel in the village of Broadwater on Hog Island. As Hog Island began to wash away in the early part of the twentieth century, many of the inhabitants moved to the mainland and settled in the Willis Wharf area near this church. This church inherited the strength and the members of that other Broadwater. By 1919 the failing Pullen's Chapel was placed under supply pastors and was called "Broadwater Mission."

Broadwater Chapel grew also because the town of Exmore grew, and in 1931 the congregation changed the name of the church to Epworth, after the home of the Wesleys in England. The parsonage next door to the church was purchased in 1916. It is still owned by the church, although a new parsonage next door to it is used by the minister at the present.

In the early 1930's the congregation determined to erect a new and larger building and not to go into debt doing so. The old building was moved aside (it is today a boathouse in Willis Wharf), and construction begun on the present brick building. For years the congregation worshiped in the Sunday school section of their uncompleted building, and not until 1940 was the finished building dedicated. In that same year, Pullen's Chapel on Hog Island was discontinued for good.

Epworth is today a station church of over 400 members, the fifth largest Methodist congregation on the Eastern Shore of Virginia.

[Sources: 50, 116, 124, 176]

Location: see EXMORE

EVERGREEN UNITED METHODIST CHURCH

[ME-S 1885, M 1939, UMC 1968]
Hack's Neck

As early as 1848 the Methodists of the Pungoteague congregation were active in the Hack's Neck area, and it was probably in that year that Seatick Chapel was erected near the present Evergreen Church and used for occasional services.

The first permanent Methodist church in Hack's Neck was, however, Evergreen, founded in 1885 when the Pungoteague congregation divided. The Hack's Neck portion of the congregation moved the Pungoteague building (erected in 1868) to the present site, renovated it, and opened Evergreen Church in 1885. In 1893, when Evergreen was only eight years old, it too divided, and Harborton Church was founded and erected less than a mile away.

The Evergreen building was extensively changed in 1900. It originally had two front doors and two aisles inside, with outside steps across the entire front of the building. This was changed to one central door, with one central aisle. A pulpit alcove was added, and the pitch of the roof was made steeper. The windows and shutters are original. Although it is much changed, Evergreen is one of the oldest Methodist church buildings still in use on the Eastern Shore of Virginia.

Evergreen has always shared its pastor with Pungoteague. The present charge alignment with Pungoteague and Harborton was created in 1911. The pastor lives in Pungoteague, and the present membership of Evergreen is about 150.

[Sources: 40, 116]

Location: see HARBORTON

EXMORE

see: **Church of God and Saints of Christ*
Epworth United Methodist Church
Exmore Baptist Church
Exmore Wesleyan Church
**John Wesley Methodist Episcopal Church*
Kingdom Hall of Jehovah's Witnesses
**Mt. Olive Church of Christ Disciples*
New Mount Calvary Baptist Church
**Spence Memorial Methodist Church*
**Trinity Methodist Episcopal Church*

1 - Trinity ME: site 1851-1900
2 - John Wesley ME: site 1889-1924
3a - Epworth UMC: site since 1892
3b - Epworth UMC: original building moved to this site c1935
4 - New Mt. Calvary Baptist
5 - Exmore Baptist
6 - Church of God: site 1920-c1935 (approximate)
7a - Exmore Wesleyan: met in this home 1942-1946
7b - Exmore Wesleyan: site since 1946
8 - Mt. Olive Disciples: site 1944-c1964
9 - Kingdom Hall
10 - Spence Methodist: site 1948-1975
11 - Pearly Gates Baptist (see Appendix II)

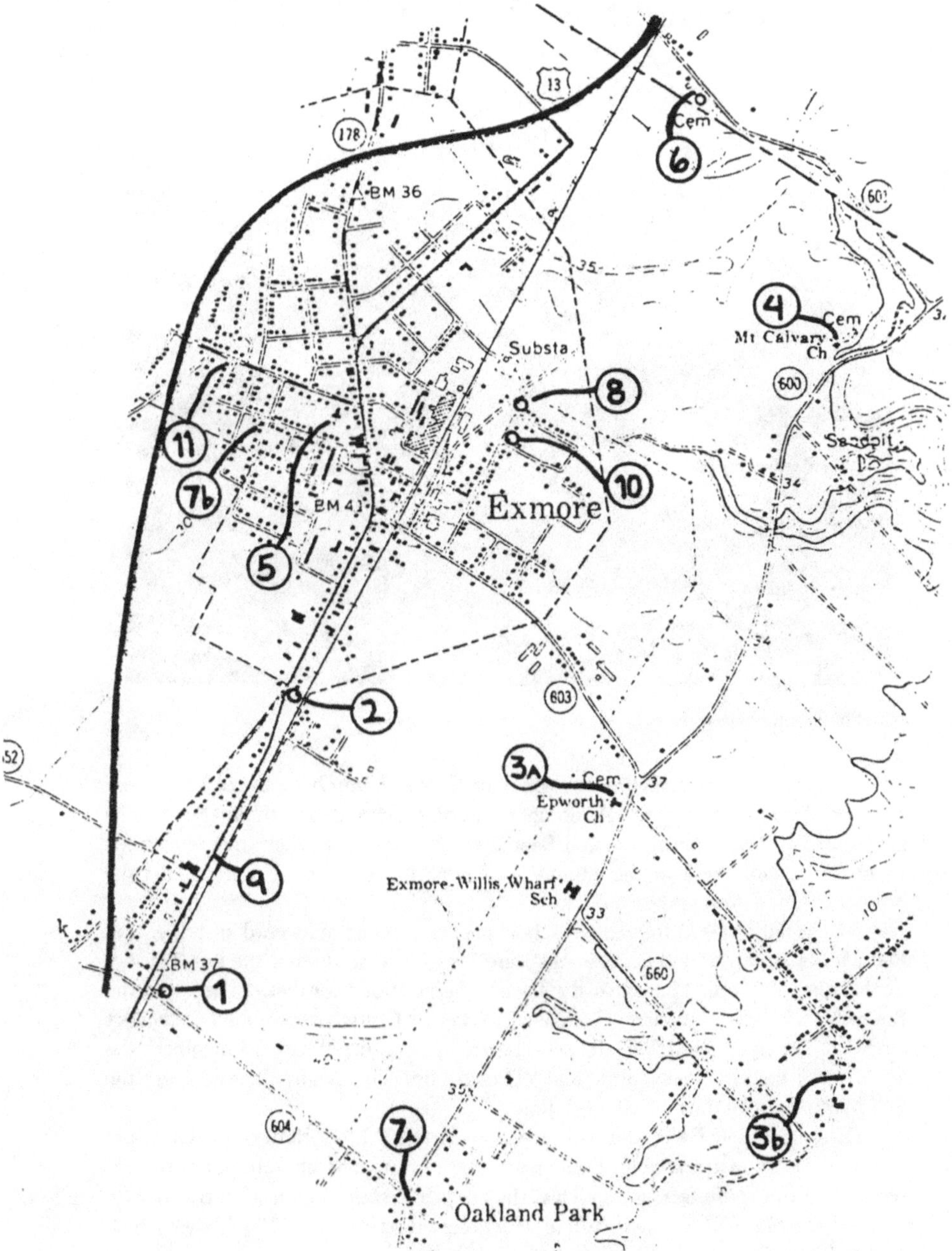
13
178
BM 36
Cem
6
603
35
4
Cem
Mt Calvary
Ch
Substa
600
8
Sandpit
11
7b
10
34
BM 41
Exmore
5
34
603
2
52
3A
Cem
37
Epworth
Ch
9
Exmore-Willis Wharf
Sch
33
BM 37
1
660
35
604
7A
3b
Oakland Park

EXMORE BAPTIST CHURCH

[ABA 1906]
Exmore

(first building, photo c. 1940)

Like the town in which it sits, Exmore Baptist Church is, by Eastern Shore standards, relatively young. A group of women who called themselves "The Christian Workers" began the first Baptist work in Exmore when they established a Sunday school there in the summer of 1906. It was from that work that the present congregation grew.

By the fall of 1906 the Sunday school had moved out of its outdoor bower into Red Men's Hall, and public meetings were being held to discuss the possibility of establishing a Baptist church in the town. The sum of $600 was raised, and the Reverend Charles Clement of Chincoteague Baptist Church summoned to conduct a revival. On April 11, 1907, the new church was organized with 29 members; the service was held in the evening, and "Crown Him with Many Crowns" was the first hymn sung by the new congregation.

Pastors of Red Bank and Wardtown, namely C. L. Corbitt, John Guy, and Will Guy, were instrumental in the organization of the new church, but none ever served at Exmore. In fact, so rapid was the growth of this congregation that it soon eclipsed the older Wardtown church, which closed its doors in 1917, after which many of its members moved to Exmore.

The first church building was erected in 1907 on the present site, which was donated by J. W. Chandler. It was used until 1952, when the present brick structure was completed and dedicated. The older building was subsequently dismantled; its cornerstone can still be seen in the newer building.

It was in this congregation that the modern Charismatic movement first appeared on the Eastern Shore of Virginia, in the late 1960's. The experience of Pentecostal gifts by several members of the congregation created a serious division that was not alleviated until a small number withdrew to form the short-lived Christian Love Center.

Exmore has been a station church throughout most of its history. It has grown steadily since its inception and is today the second largest congregation on the Eastern Shore of Virginia. Its 545 members are more in number than the combined membership of the seven Presbyterian churches of the Virginia Shore.

One of the most prominent members of this church was the Reverend Kenneth Lee Smith, ordained in the 1950's, who was teacher and friend of Martin Luther King, Jr., at Crozer Theological Seminary.

[Sources: 69, 109, 110, 122, 176]

Location: see EXMORE

EXMORE WESLEYAN CHURCH

(''Oaks,'' ''Oakland Park'')
[PH 1942, W 1968]
Exmore

In Exmore as in Quinby it took a number of years for the Holiness movement to issue into a full-fledged church. William Vickers held tent meetings in the Oakland Park area south of town during the 1930's, but all he left behind him was a small group that met for cottage meetings in private homes in that area. This group first appears on the records of the denomination in 1942, when Sister Mary Garrett of the Cape Charles congregation was pastor.

In 1944 Sister Garrett officially organized the work in this area by joining together the Quinby and Exmore groups into ''Quinby-Oakland Park,'' with ten members. ''Brother Vickers has faithfully sown the good seed of the Gospel in this section of the District for some years,'' reported the district superintendent, ''and now we are seeing some fruit.''

The expectation was that both Quinby and Oakland Park would erect new buildings and become separate congregations, and this was accomplished in 1946. On their new lot on the corner of Jackson and Westfield Streets in Exmore, the Oakland Park congregation conducted a six-weeks' tent meeting in the fall of 1946, and then began their building. In 1948 the completed structure was dedicated and the separate Exmore congregation officially organized. Etta Mitchell and Etta Clough, the pastors, conducted a revival in the new building in that year.

Despite the fact that membership was small (only nine in 1949), the new church prospered and established itself on a firm footing. In 1953 another tent meeting was held. By 1964 the debt on the building had been liquidated and the congregation was able to improve the parsonage. In 1966 additions were made to the church building. And during all this time the membership did not rise above fourteen.

Today Exmore is, after Bloxom, the second strongest Wesleyan congregation on the Virginia Shore. Although actual membership is only seventeen, that is larger than it has ever been at any other time in the church's history, and as with so many other Wesleyan churches, attendance at the church is significantly greater than actual membership.

[Sources: 121, 124, 176]

Location: see EXMORE

FAITH ASSEMBLY OF GOD

[AG-S 1950]
Lee Mont

The Assemblies of God faith was first established on the Shore at Lee Mont, where in 1950 a lot for a new building was purchased. The Reverend Paul Boyce was the pioneer pastor of the new church that was erected there soon afterward, and he remained pastor until 1954.

After a full decade of existence, the Lee Mont church could boast only seventeen members. Growth became more rapid after 1959, however, and today this church is the largest white Pentecostal congregation on the Virginia Shore. Though there are only 22 official members, the number of "adherents" who worship with this congregation is more than four times that number, only slightly less than 100.

The pastor of this congregation lives in the parsonage which stands behind the church in Lee Mont.

[Sources: 109, 123, 176]

Location: see LEE MONT

FAITH BAPTIST MISSION

[Independent 1978]
Hallwood

This church was born in a schism from Hallwood Baptist Church. In the spring of 1978 when a majority of that congregation voted to call a new minister, a significant minority withdrew. With Ralph Michael, the old minister, they formed this mission, and met for worship in a rented store building in Hallwood.

Although both pastor and people of this mission are of Southern Baptist persuasion, they do not at this writing have any official affiliation with the Accomack Baptist Association, and are for that reason listed here as independent.

The number of persons who worship at this mission is fewer than 25.

[Source: 176]

Location: see HALLWOOD

*FAITH TABERNACLE ASSEMBLY OF GOD

[AG-S 1976-1977]
Onley

This was the third Assembly of God congregation on the Virginia Shore, and it was founded by the Reverend Mrs. Lindy Hinman in 1976. The congregation first gathered in June of that year in the firehouse at Tasley, intent upon establishing a new Pentecostal church in the central area of the Shore between Faith in Lee Mont and Calvary in Nassawadox.

After a short while in Tasley, the congregation moved to new quarters in a building in Onley. Later Mrs. Hinman assumed the pastorate of Holiness Christian Church in Chesconnessex, and the two congregations, despite some differing beliefs, worshiped together.

By the end of 1977, Holiness Christian Church had ceased to function, and with it died the effort to establish the new Assembly of God congregation. The membership of this congregation, prior to merger with the Chesconnessex church, was about ten.

[Sources: 109, 176]

Location: see ONLEY

FAITH TABERNACLE HOLINESS CHURCH OF GOD LIVE ON

[CGLO 1960]
Nassawadox

This was the third Church of God Live On congregation established on the Eastern Shore of Virginia, and was founded in 1960 by Walter Trower.

Trower, a protege of Jesse Handshaw, began his ministry at Cape Charles in the early 1940's. Like Handshaw a carpenter by trade, he himself erected the Nassawadox church.

Trower, who lives in Cape Charles, has served as pastor of this small congregation since its formation. He was often assisted in the work by his wife, Charlotte, until in 1973 she established her own church in Treherneville.

[Source: 176]

Location: see NASSAWADOX

FIRST BAPTIST CHURCH

("Hollywood")
[ESBA 1885]
Cape Charles

Black Baptist activity in the new town of Cape Charles began with prayer meetings held in homes in 1885. By the end of the year a new congregation had been constituted there, and worship services were being held regularly under the Reverend J. B. Randolph in a rented building on Strawberry Street downtown. The new church was known as Hollywood Baptist Church.

The new congregation erected its first building in the 600 block of Monroe Avenue in 1888. Randolph served as pastor until 1893, when he was succeeded by W. M. Dixon. At the end of Dixon's pastorate in 1899, the congregation had grown to more than 65, and the name of the church had been changed to First Baptist.

In 1899 a new lot, the present one, was purchased on the corner of Madison and Nectarine, and in 1901, under the Reverend W. H. Davenport, the old building was moved to it. Here the original building became part of a new and larger structure, dedicated in 1901. This building was in turn extensively remodeled in 1914, by which time the membership had more than doubled.

G. C. Campbell, who became pastor in 1946, was the first to live in the parsonage, which was purchased during his pastorate.

Altogether ten pastors have served this church, one of them, P. W. Cook, twice (1914-26, 1939-46). An annex costing $10,000 was added to the back of the building during the term of the present pastor, which began in 1958.

Today the pastor of this church serves Ebenezer in Wardtown as well, and lives in the parsonage on Madison Street.

[Sources: 26, 124, 129]

Location: see CAPE CHARLES

FIRST BAPTIST CHURCH

[ESBA 1877]
Capeville

First Baptist Church, like Ebenezer A.M.E., had its origins in the inter-denominational gathering of blacks who first worshiped outdoors in Capeville during the Civil War. Prior to 1870 the Methodist half of this group was organized into an A.M.E. congregation. In 1877 the Reverend John Smith came from Union Baptist Church in Eastville and organized the other part of the group into First Baptist Church of Capeville.

The first building was erected in 1877 on the present site, which was purchased from John Henry Goffigon. The present building is the second, and was erected during the 22-year pastorate of the second pastor, T. W. Nettles.

During the early years of its history, First Baptist shared its pastors with Union and African. Together the three churches built a parsonage in 1880 near this church.

In 1920 J. A. Martin was called to the pastorate, and under him occurred the "greatest revival in the history of our church," resulting in 120 conversions. A parsonage for this church alone was secured during Martin's pastorate, which lasted until 1932.

D. J. Black succeeded Martin in 1932 and served for almost twenty years. During his pastorate the present parsonage was erected, and an anteroom was added to the church building. There have been a number of other improvements to the building since that time, including a large annex costing $20,000 added to the back of the church in 1970.

[Sources: 26, 109, 124, 129]

Location: see DALBYS

FIRST BAPTIST CHURCH

[ESBA 1875]
Mappsville

By as early as 1864 the black Christians of the Modest Town area were quitting the older churches there, and the white members of Modest Town Baptist Church felt called upon to let them know that "their presence on preaching and their church meeting will be required as formerly," and that "unless they attend to their church relations they will be excluded." Two black churches were subsequently founded in this neighborhood: the short-lived A.M.E. church in 1866 and the First Baptist Church of Mappsville in 1875. The A.M.E. church ultimately faded and died, but First Baptist prospered and became in time one of the strongest black churches on the Shore.

There is a local tradition that black Baptist work in northern Accomack County radiated out from a log chapel built by local residents soon after the Civil War, and it is a fact that in 1873 the Reverend Abel J. Satchell led in the purchase of a lot for a black Baptist congregation somewhere in this area. First Baptist was, however, officially organized in 1875 under Satchell, and it was only in that year that the present church site on Seaside Road east of Mappsville was purchased.

Satchell served here only a short time and soon moved on to establish Metompkin Baptist Church. The Reverend Collins, his successor, arrived in 1879 to find "a small building in which they were holding worship service." Considering the building inadequate and primitive, Collins led the congregation in the erection of a proper church, which was completed in 1879.

By the turn of the century First Baptist had grown into a strong and vigorous congregation. The building was completely remodeled in 1900, and the following year a lot was purchased near Bloxom on which a daughter congregation, Macedonia Baptist Church, was established in 1903.

In 1925 the church erected its first parsonage, and four years later called M. T. Boone as pastor. It was during the first years of Boone's pastorate that the church building was again completely remodeled. In 1939, having survived the difficult years of the Depression under Boone's capable leadership, the congregation was able to buy additional land adjacent to the church for a burial ground.

Boone served, in all, a 31-year pastorate, the longest in the church's history and one of the longest on record in any church on the Eastern Shore of Virginia. He resigned in 1960.

First Baptist, the oldest black Baptist church in northern Accomack County, is today one of the largest black congregations on the entire Shore.

[Sources: 26, 123, 129]

Location: see MAPPSVILLE

FIRST BAPTIST CHURCH

[ABA 1909]
New Church

In New Church as in other places up and down the Shore the coming of the railroad in 1884 shifted the local population and caused controversy about the location of the older churches. By the end of 1886 the congregation of old Chincoteague Baptist Church were debating whether to move their building to the growing railroad village of New Church, "at least the matter is being agitated and is meeting with favorable consideration," reads a newspaper report from that year.

It was not until 1909 that a decision about relocation was made. In that year 49 members were dismissed by Chincoteague Baptist for the purpose of founding a new congregation in New Church. The First Baptist Church of New Church was completed and dedicated on July 24, 1909; Charles Clement and R. H. Pitt preached on that occasion.

Like a number of other churches on the Shore, First Baptist prospered through the 1920's only to decline during the Depression. There were 77 members in 1932, but by 1940 the membership had fallen below the original figure of 49. Not until the 1960's was the church again as large as it had been at its formation.

New Church Baptist, as the church is often called, shared its pastors with Chincoteague and Horntown until 1965. In that year the church left the field and became a station, calling Robert Baker as its pastor. The church has prospered and grown steadily since that time, and now has a membership of over 100, the largest in its history. The pastor lives in the parsonage not far from the church, a home which was built in 1901 by Chincoteague and Horntown before this church was founded.

The building of 1909 is still in use. An annex was added to the back for classrooms in the 1960's, and there have been several interior renovations and changes, the latest of which were completed in 1976. In 1977 the congregation began the construction of a church hall located behind the church.

This is the youngest Southern Baptist congregation functioning on the Shore, and as late as the middle 1970's members could point with pride to the fact that two of its charter members were still living.

[Sources: 36, 69, 110, 122, 176]

Location: see NEW CHURCH

FIRST LUTHERAN MISSION OF THE EASTERN SHORE

[Missouri Synod 1975]
Cheriton

On January 26, 1975, fifteen people attended the first Lutheran worship service ever conducted on the Virginia Shore, which was led by Dr. Martin C. Poch at Cape Charles Air Force Base. It was resolved at that time to hold services twice a month for all Lutherans "residing on the lower half of the Delmarva Peninsula," and the First Lutheran Mission was born.

In April 1975 the new congregation moved its services to Emmanuel Episcopal Church in Cape Charles, and by the end of the year to a rented brick building on Main Street in Cheriton. Permanent quarters were obtained late in 1977 when the congregation occupied the original building of Cheriton Baptist Church.

This small congregation is a mission of Christ Lutheran Church in Norfolk, a Missouri Synod congregation of which Poch is the pastor.

[Source: 109]

Location: see CHERITON

FIRST PRESBYTERIAN CHURCH

[Pres 1890]
Cape Charles

This congregation was organized in the auditorium of Centenary Methodist Episcopal Church, South, on December 14, 1890. A. S. Venable, pastor of Holmes Presbyterian, was its first pastor, and most of its thirteen charter members came from Holmes.

For eleven years the people of First Presbyterian met on Sunday afternoons in the Methodist church. Then in 1901 they dedicated their first building, at Tazewell and Plum, across the street from Centenary.

In 1925 the congregation broke ground for a new building on the corner of Tazewell and Strawberry. At the laying of the cornerstone, the choir sang an original anthem, "Laying the Stone," written for the occasion by Dr. L. P. Bowen, Presbyterian pastor and historian. The new building ultimately cost over $70,000;

it was, at that time, the most expensive church building on the Shore. It was formally opened in September 1926, although it was not until December 23, 1928, that the congregation was able to worship in the auditorium of the completed building. The building was finally dedicated on October 26, 1930. The old building became the Northampton Public Library in Cape Charles.

For years First Presbyterian prospered along with the town of Cape Charles. It shared its pastors with Holmes until becoming a field to itself in the twentieth century. By 1960 the congregation numbered 156 communicants. Thereafter membership dropped sharply, and its present membership figure of 66 makes it fourth among the seven Presbyterian churches on the Shore.

[Sources: 119, 120, 124, 159]

Location: see CAPE CHARLES

*FISHING POINT CHURCH

[CE 1641?-1669?]
Dalbys

Fishing Point, on Old Plantation Creek west of Lower Northampton Baptist Church, was settled early in the seventeenth century as population moved slowly down the Shore from the principal settlement at the Towne, near Cheriton. As often occurred in these early years, court and church followed the center of population, and the church at Fishing Point, the second church ever erected on the Eastern Shore of Virginia, stood by 1641.

An early description of this church in a now-vanished document described it as being "of insignificant dimension, constructed of roughly riled [sic] logs, cemented loosely with wattle; the whole enclosed by Pallysadoes [stockade] for protection against the Indian tribes, an ever present menace to peace and safety." The authenticity of this description is now doubted by some historians. The Fishing Point Church was long thought to be the first ever erected on the Shore, but more recent research has proven it to be second to the church at the Towne.

The first record of the completed church is from 1641, when local citizens were ordered to "meet at the parish Church of Ackowmack upon Satterday next and cutt up all the weeds about the Church." There were a number of other such punishments inflicted near the church over the next several years, as was the custom of the time. By 1669, when Christopher Stribling's will read, "I bequeath my body to the earth to be buried before the Chappell of ease att the old Plantation Creeke," this church had once again become secondary to the older church at the Towne. It does not appear in records after 1669.

In later years "Fishing Point" became known as "Hunt's Point," and even later as "Baptizing Point." It was at Hunt's Point that Elijah Baker, the Baptist pioneer, landed on Easter Sunday 1776. By then this church had long since disappeared, and Baker's first Baptist sermon on the Shore was preached farther south at Magothy.

[Source: 70]

Location: see DALBYS

FLOYD'S METHODIST EPISCOPAL CHURCH

(see Franktown United Methodist Church)

FRANKTOWN UNITED METHODIST CHURCH

("Floyds")

[ME 1795, ME-S 1846?, M 1939, UMC 1968]

Franktown

The Franktown church is the direct descendant of the Floyd's society, which was meeting in private homes in the Hadlock-Hare Valley area by at least as early as 1795. Benjamin Floyd was the first leader of this society, which is said to have met at times in the parlor of the home "Fruitlands" in Hare Valley. It was at Floyd's that the first stirrings of Thomas Smith's revival occurred in 1800.

At an early but unknown date, presumably not long after the 1800 revival, this congregation erected a meetinghouse in Hare Valley, and named it Floyd's Meetinghouse. The mantle of leadership fell to Matthew Floyd, son of Benjamin, and when he moved to Accomack County, the old meetinghouse was abandoned. The congregation bought a lot in Franktown in 1843 (where the Quaker meetinghouse had once stood), and by 1846 a new building stood there. Years later the original meetinghouse was, after much discussion, sold, removed, and converted into a barn. Its site before or after the removal is not known today.

Franktown's decision to secede to the southern Methodist church in 1846 was carried by only one vote, and in consequence of the controversy that ensued a large pro-northern minority withdrew from the congregation and founded Trinity in nearby Hadlock. Franktown remained in the southern fold and became a part of the original Eastville Circuit of the Virginia Conference. It was one of those churches closed by order of the Union army from July to October 1864.

The year 1894 was important to this church for two reasons: the present building was erected then (the fate of the earlier one on that site is not known), and the church was first joined to Johnson's Chapel to form a circuit. The two churches built a parsonage in Franktown in that year and have shared their pastors ever since. The new Franktown church was only one year old when it was damaged by lightning in 1895.

Nassawadox Mission, begun in 1908, was an outgrowth of this church, which has remained a strong and vigorous congregation across the years. With more than 300 members, it is today one of the largest Methodist churches on the Eastern Shore of Virginia.

[Sources: 39, 70, 100, 101, 102, 110, 111, 116, 124]

Location: see NASSAWADOX

*FREEWILL METHODIST EPISCOPAL CHURCH

[ME 1874-1935]
Chincoteague

The black Methodist church on Chincoteague Island was erected on land purchased in 1874, and was first listed by the Delaware Conference in 1879 when J. W. Langford was pastor and there were eleven members. The building was standing by 1879 and was improved in 1881, when the tiny congregation spent the sum of $45 to add new seats and new shutters.

As early as 1884 the congregation was making plans to erect a parsonage, but apparently this was never done. The church was connected to mainland circuits throughout most of its history; in 1890 the pastor was E. T. Outen, who lived in Stockton, Maryland.

The church had grown to 42 members by the 1890's, and in 1897 the present frame building was erected next to the other, which then became a schoolhouse. The new building cost $525. The following year the church was joined to Deas Chapel and Friendship, an arrangement in which this church was "strictly a mission."

After 1909 Freewill was supplied with local pastors from Pocomoke City and was a dwindling congregation. By 1917 it was not supporting itself financially and asked to be attached to a mainland circuit, a request that the Conference did not honor. Its membership was even more seriously depleted by the wide-scale migration of blacks from the island to the North in the 1920's.

In 1935 the church was once again attached to Deas Chapel and Friendship, and this is the last mention of the congregation in the records of the denomination. The original building, which became the schoolhouse, stood until recent years. The building of 1897 is still standing on Willow Street.

[Sources: 113, 123, 176]

Location: see CHINCOTEAGUE

FREEWILL METHODIST EPISCOPAL CHURCH

FRIENDSHIP METHODIST PROTESTANT CHURCH

(see Wattsville United Methodist Church)

FRIENDSHIP UNITED METHODIST CHURCH

[ME 1865, M 1939, UMC 1968]
Wattsville

On October 4, 1865, George Wallop sold to the Methodist Episcopal Church the land on which this church stands. It was the earliest deed of land to a black congregation in Accomack County, second only to Union Baptist Church in Eastville on the entire Shore. The building that was erected on this lot in 1868 is one of the oldest, if not the oldest, black church building of any faith on the Eastern Shore of Virginia.

Friendship was founded apparently from the pre-war Methodist churches of this area, most likely Downing's and Wattsville. It was a strong and vigorous church from the start. Deas Chapel in Horntown was founded from it in 1877, as was probably Freewill in Chincoteague in 1874. By the turn of the century the congregation had rebuilt their building (1891), established an Epworth League, one of the earliest on record on the Shore (1894), and received 63 new members as the result of a revival in 1900.

The long and successful pastorate of J. S. Coulbourne began in 1902. In 1905 Coulbourne abolished the local yearly camp meeting, thereby achieving "a steady increase for good." By 1912 the Horntown Circuit (Friendship and Deas Chapel) was the strongest circuit on the district and, boasted the presiding elder, probably in the Delaware Conference. By 1908 Coulbourne was receiving the highest salary in the district. He served, in all, 23 years, from 1902 to 1925, the longest Methodist pastorate on record in the two counties.

In 1915 Friendship began the work of establishing St. John's Church in Atlantic, and in 1921 when that new church was dedicated, renovated its own building for $600. There were 67 conversions on the circuit that year. In 1927 the congregation voted to spend $1000 to improve the building yet again, and the rebuilding was completed in 1929.

Friendship entered a period of difficulty with the coming of the Depression, but in 1939 the church was reporting new life. In 1942, 34 new members were received on the circuit, and over the years the church's membership has grown to its present 135. The pastor lives in Horntown and serves Friendship, Deas Chapel, and St. Mark's.

The building erected in 1868 is still in use in Wattsville, although it has been altered so many times over the years that it bears little resemblance to its original appearance.

In recent years Friendship has been at the forefront of those congregations on the Shore that are involved in community development and social witness.

[Sources: 113, 123, 176]

Location: see WATTSVILLE

GARRISON'S UNITED METHODIST CHURCH

("Garrison's Chapel," "Garrettson Chapel")
[ME 1784, ICA 1861, ME 1864, ICA 1866, ME-S 1866, M 1939, UMC 1968]
Painter

Garrison's is not only one of the oldest Methodist congregations on the Eastern Shore of Virginia — only Downing's can claim a longer continuous recorded history — it has also the distinction of having erected the first and the second Methodist buildings in the two counties.

The home of Jonathan Garrison in Mappsburg was a stopping-place for the Methodist ministers as early as 1784, when Francis Asbury made his first trip down the Eastern Shore of Virginia. As early as that first visit Asbury records that he preached in a church — "Garrettson Chapel," he called it — and he mentions the chapel again on his second visit in 1786. This chapel is without question the first Methodist building on the Shore, although it is doubtful that it was erected primarily for religious purposes. More than likely it was an unused building on the Garrison estate that temporarily housed the Methodist preaching services.

Garrison apparently did not consider this building a sufficiently good "chapel," for in 1787 he deeded to the denomination an acre of land "for the Express purpose of Building a Preaching house on for the use of the Methodice [sic] Preachers." Thus the Garrison's congregation also built the second Methodist building on the Shore. It stood in a grove of trees just north of the intersection of Seaside Road with the Quinby Road, and was apparently completed in 1788, when Asbury preached in it on his third visit. There were no other Methodist buildings anywhere else on the Virginia Shore at that time; the next one, Johnson's Chapel, is not mentioned until 1790.

In all Asbury visited Garrison's Chapel six times, once in the company of Richard Whatcoat (1789), the last time in 1792. Garrison's quickly established itself as one of the primary congregations on the Shore, one of only four that could expect preaching services on Sundays. Lorenzo Dow preached at the church in

(at the old site in Mappsburg,
c. 1920)

1805, Christopher Spry and Conner Simpkins were ordained there in 1789, and the membership included such local Methodist notables as William and Thomas Paramore and Coventon Simpkins.

Garrison's did not escape the disturbances that beset the denomination after the schism of 1844. The circuit preacher, James Brindle, found a crowd of hecklers when he arrived to preach one Sunday in 1846, but the congregation had packed the building with a friendly crowd, and the hecklers, greatly outnumbered, drifted away without doing any harm.

In 1855 the congregation erected a third building on the same site. The fate of the earlier two buildings is not known. It was in this church in 1861 that the new independent Convention of Accomack drew up the polity and rule of their denomination, under the chairmanship of Joshua Garrison, grandson of Jonathan. Here, too, the Methodists from all the Shore's denominations met in February 1862 to consider merger, which was never effected.

William Coe of the independent Convention preached regularly at Garrison's until the Convention itself split in 1864. Then, under the influence of the local member, George P. Cutler, Garrison's cast its lot with Cokesbury and Ayres and returned to the Methodist Episcopal Church. It was not closed by the Union army in 1864 because it was at that time part of the northern church. However, in January 1866, Garrison's again joined the Convention, just in time to be absorbed into the southern church in April of that year. In the first four months of 1866, the congregation belonged to no fewer than three different denominations: Methodist Episcopal, independent Convention of Accomack, and Methodist Episcopal, South.

The railroad bypassed the village of Mappsburg where Garrison's was located, and a long controversy began as to whether to relocate nearer the tracks. In 1905, after a generation of discussion, the congregation divided amicably and part of them founded Painter Church nearer the railroad. The Garrison's congregation remodeled their building the next year, removing the gallery and installing stained glass windows throughout.

By 1927 the town of Painter had so outdistanced Mappsburg that it was decided to reunite the congregation and to move Garrison's Chapel to Painter. The two congregations merged, the old site was abandoned (it was sold in 1931), and the Garrison's building was moved to Painter and attached to the more recent building there. The church looks today much as it did then: two obviously different buildings set at right angles and joined at the back. The Garrison's building is used as a sanctuary, the Painter building as the church school hall. The congregation retained the name Garrison's even after moving to Painter, but the name Painter Church has been used with increasing frequency in recent years.

Garrison's has been on a number of different charges and circuits since the turn of the century. In 1965 it was joined with Bethel in Jamesville to form the Painter-Bethel Charge. The present membership is 227.

The Garrison's building of 1855 is still in use and is, after the buildings at Downing's and Cokesbury, the oldest Methodist sanctuary on the Shore. Both in the date of its building and in the date of the congregation Garrison's is second only to Downing's on the Virginia Eastern Shore, and in each case it is second only by one year.

[Sources: 3, 16, 39, 44, 70, 99, 116, 123, 176]

Location: see PAINTER

GASKIN'S CHAPEL AFRICAN METHODIST EPISCOPAL CHURCH

[AME 1873]
Savageville

This church was founded by John Henry Offer in 1873, and named for John Gaskin, a prominent member at that time. About a quarter of a mile west of the present church site, on land purchased from George Washington Mason, the black Methodists of Savageville raised their first church building, a simple log structure, which was not completed until 1879.

In its earliest years Gaskin's Chapel shared its pastors with Bethel A.M.E. in Onancock. In 1880 the Savageville Circuit was created, and at least as early as 1883 the A.M.E. churches were holding large camp meetings at Gaskin's Chapel. Offer served a second pastorate from 1891 to 1894.

In 1905 during the pastorate of John E. Cooke the log structure was remodelled into a much larger and more substantial building, which was again remodelled in 1913, when J. H. Thomas was pastor. Charity Elizabeth Parker, a faithful local member, made the first contribution of $5 to these improvements.

E. A. Easterling was pastor when, in 1947, the congregation decided to abandon the old site and purchased a new lot on Bayside Road in Savageville. In 1951 the old church building was moved to this site, where it became part of a much newer structure. These improvements cost $5000. Since that time the church has been improved and renovated a number of times. The most recent improvements, in 1977, included a major addition to the back of the building.

Gaskin's Chapel is today a vital and flourishing congregation of about 260 members. The old building is the tallest part of the present structure, and is located at the rear of the church.

[Sources: 7, 123, 160, 176]

Location: see SAVAGEVILLE

GLORIOUS CHURCH OF JESUS CHRIST OF THE APOSTOLIC FAITH

[Independent 1969]
Onancock

This is one of the several congregations of Bishop J. W. Bowser of Newport News. It was founded by Bowser, with the help of Fred Parker, in 1969, and meets in the former Negro school property on Boundry Street in Onancock.

Doctrinally this church is Pentecostal. In 1976 Bowser and members of his church met in formal public debate with pastor and people of the Keller Church of Christ to discuss Pentecostal doctrines.

Among Bowser's other churches are congregations in Newport News and Washington, D.C., all of which bear the same name as the Onancock church. [Source: 109]

Location: see ONANCOCK

*GOODWILL METHODIST EPISCOPAL CHURCH

("Salem," "Upper")
[Independent 1876, ME 1884-1922]
Chincoteague

Although completely vanished from the scene and all but forgotten today, Goodwill is an important church in the history of Methodism on the Shore, for it was here that the Holiness movement first made its appearance in the two counties.

Goodwill began not as a Methodist church, but as an interdenominational church for people on the northern end of Chincoteague Island. The church was already in existence in 1876, when the trustees bought additional land on all sides of the building. Apparently it was the practice at Goodwill for each of the white preachers of the island, Baptist, Methodist Protestant, and Methodist Episcopal, to preach there in turn. One of the first records of the church is from 1884, when a notice in the county paper cites the three community pastors by name, states that they have preached recently at Goodwill, and comments: "The congregation of

Good Will Independent Church are very much divided...and they are not likely soon to be of one mind.''

It is possible that the division at Goodwill was due to growing Methodist strength in the congregation, for the independent church did not stay independent for long. By August 1884, J. M. Reese, the Methodist Episcopal pastor on the island, had organized the congregation into the Goodwill Class, and annexed them to Methodism. Two years later the downtown M.E. congregation abandoned its church building, gave it to ''the people of Goodwill,'' and it was moved up the island and outfitted for worship there. From that time on the church was known as Goodwill Methodist Episcopal Church, and it was served by the M.E. pastor on the island.

The ''upper'' church prospered in its new Methodist affiliation. A woods meeting was held in an adjacent grove in 1888. The building, a small structure erected in 1869, was improved in 1889. The report to the conference in 1894 calls the church not Goodwill but ''Salem.''

Joseph B. Lynch, one of the original trustees of the congregation, was a class leader at Goodwill when in 1887 he obtained sanctification. Over the course of the next several years a sizable group of members followed Lynch in the pursuit of sanctification. A serious schism hit the church soon after the ''sanctificationists'' petitioned the bishop for ''a holy man of God to preach the gospel to them,'' and on February 16, 1892, fifty-eight members withdrew to form Christ's Sanctified Holy Church. The schism was attended with much bad feeling and strife, and by the end of 1892 the rival Sanctified church building, largest church on the island at that time, stood just north of Goodwill.

By 1898 most of the Sanctified congregation had left the island for other fields, and Goodwill purchased their larger building in that year for $1000. Goodwill, however, seems to have been seriously weakened by the sanctificationist schism, and by the early years of the twentieth century was in decline. It is possible that services ceased to be held regularly there by as early as 1913, but the church was not officially closed until 1922. In that year the new stone M.E. church building was erected on Church Street downtown, and Goodwill's congregation officially merged with the downtown church.

In 1928 A. J. Hill purchased the old Goodwill building for $400 and used it for the storage of fishnets until it burned in 1933. By then not only the old church but also the old Goodwill School, once located at the ''turntable'' at the northern end of the island, had been discontinued, and the name Goodwill was preserved only in the Goodwill Men's Bible Class at Christ Church downtown.

[Sources: 32, 105, 109, 110, 117, 123, 154, 176]

Location: see CHINCOTEAGUE

GOSPEL MISSION HOUSE OF PRAYER

[Independent 1970]
Cheriton

This small black congregation was established in 1970, when a lot northeast of Cheriton was purchased and the present frame building erected on it.

In 1974 the congregation purchased a second building, an abandoned storehouse, at Cheriton Crossing, and opened there the Number One Mission House of Prayer.

This church is a mission of St. Stephen's Holiness Church of Norfolk. Despite the word "Holiness" in its name, both St. Stephen's and this mission are what is referred to as Pentecostal in this work.

[Source: 124]

Location: see CHERITON

GOSPEL TABERNACLE

[Independent 1946]
New Church

Powhatan Barnes, an independent black local preacher, founded and erected this church in 1946. The land was purchased from Milton White in that year for $350.

For two decades Barnes conducted Pentecostal services in the building, often on a seasonal basis depending upon his own presence on the Shore.

In 1969 Barnes sold the property to the Reverend Levi Warrington of New Church and a number of trustees. Warrington, also a preacher without denominational affiliations, used the building until his death shortly thereafter, and the small congregation of which he was a part still holds occasional services there.

[Sources: 123, 176]

Location: see NEW CHURCH

GOSPEL TABERNACLE OF THE APOSTOLIC FAITH CHURCH OF GOD LIVE ON

[CGLO 1936]

Cape Charles

It was in Cape Charles that Jesse Handshaw began the Eastern Shore phase of his long and successful Pentecostal ministry. The lot on which this church stands was purchased by Handshaw and others in 1936, and shortly thereafter the simple frame building was erected by Handshaw himself, who was a carpenter by trade.

From his base in Cape Charles, Handshaw extended his own Church of God Live On to other parts of the Shore, beginning with the establishment of Grace Mary Tabernacle in Melfa in 1944. Handshaw was a close worker with Joseph Turner when the latter founded St. Joseph Holiness Church in Atlantic in 1940, but that church never came under the Handshaw aegis.

Today this church is the largest of the Handshaw churches on the Virginia Shore, and one of only two (Grace Mary Tabernacle is the other) that is visited by the bishop once a month for worship services. Handshaw himself lives in Suffolk, and to the community of Holland in that city preachers from his 53 churches repair for assemblies with each other and the venerable founder.

[Sources: 124, 176]

Location: see CAPE CHARLES

GOSPEL TEMPLE BAPTIST CHURCH

[ESBA 1965]

Keller

Gospel Temple is the most recent black Baptist church on the Eastern Shore of Virginia. It was founded in 1965 by J. M. Douglas, who was at that time moderator of the Eastern Shore Virginia-Maryland Baptist Association.

The church building was purchased from Robert Edwards in 1965. Edwards was himself a local preacher, and he had conducted services in the building for some years. The Baptists renovated and expanded the building in 1967. By 1970 there were 110 members.

J. M. Douglas, the founder, is still the pastor at Gospel Temple. The church does not have a parsonage.

[Sources: 26, 109]

Location: see KELLER

GRACE MARY TABERNACLE OF THE APOSTOLIC FAITH CHURCH OF GOD LIVE ON

[CGLO 1944]
Melfa

There were five lay founders of this church in 1944 — Rosa Harris, Johnie Lofland, Elmer Ames, Grace Ames, and Mary Lofland — and for the latter two, who were sisters, the church was named. Jesse Handshaw was the preacher who was instrumental in founding the church. The new congregation met at first in private homes in the Melfa area, but soon raised a small frame building beside the highway on the northern edge of town.

In 1975 the congregation dedicated a major new addition to their original building. Shortly thereafter an automobile swerved off Route 13 into the building, destroying the new entrance.

Although this has never been a large congregation, it has remained strong across the years. There are at present about 25 regular worshipers. Jesse Handshaw, bishop of the church, visits it regularly for worship services throughout the year.

[Sources: 109, 123, 176]

Location: see MELFA

*GRACE METHODIST EPISCOPAL CHURCH

[ME 1884-1941]
Franklin City

The now-abandoned town of Franklin City grew up almost overnight around the first railroad tracks to touch the Virginia Shore, and the Methodists participated in the building boom. The Wilmington Conference of the northern church began construction of a new church there in 1884. The simple frame structure was two years in the building and cost $1200. Pews, shutters, and carpeting were not added until 1891. The church stood near the waterfront depot, and was known as Grace Church.

By 1895 the town was booming and the Methodists had outgrown their building, so a new lot was secured a few blocks north for a new and better church.

(photo 1941, as fire destroyed the building)

In 1895 the old building was moved to this site and a new sanctuary attached to it. The new building cost $3000 when completed. A parsonage was purchased nearby in 1902. The downtown waterfront section of the village was hit by a disastrous fire in 1896, which the church escaped only by moving.

Throughout its history Grace Church shared its pastors with other churches in Maryland. Much of its life was spent on the Stockton Circuit. Even after The Methodist Church created the Eastern Shore District in 1939, the Franklin City church maintained its Maryland connections. It was the only white Methodist church on the Shore at that time that was not a part of the Virginia Conference.

In 1941 sparks from a passing train ignited wood stored beneath the building, and the church went up in flames. Franklin City was by then a dwindling community, and Grace and Greenbackville Methodist (former M.P.) voted to merge. The decision to merge was unanimous in both churches, and merger was effected on June 8, 1941. The new congregation took the name Union Methodist Church, and money received from the fire insurance of Grace was used on the Greenbackville building, which the combined congregation has used ever since.

The town itself succumbed finally in 1962 after the disastrous Ash Wednesday storm. Many buildings and houses remain abandoned and decaying, and only the Methodist church of this once bustling community still lives on.

[Sources: 36, 112, 116, 117]

Location: see GREENBACKVILLE

GRACE UNITED METHODIST CHURCH

("Powelton Mission," "Wachapreague")
[ME 1879, M 1939, UMC 1968]
Locust Mount

This church was founded from Burton's and was first listed as a mission of that church in 1882, when George W. Young was pastor. The first church building was an abandoned schoolhouse that stood south of Wachapreague near Trower, purchased in 1879.

The town of Wachapreague did not exist when this church was founded. Locust Mount was the largest community in the area, a prosperous white settlement, and most of the blacks lived near the church in Trower. Shortly after this church was established, the whites of Locust Mount began to move to new homes in Wachapreague (Powelton), and the blacks began to move into Locust Mount behind them. It was not long before the Methodists of this congregation were debating whether or not to relocate in Locust Mount. In 1897 a lot was purchased there and the congregation began the construction of a new building. It was not until 1910 that the new church was ready for use.

The move from Trower to Locust Mount was accomplished in 1912, and it created a division in the congregation. The pastor at that time was Sister J. H. B. Hubbard, one of the first female pastors on record on the Shore. When the main body of the congregation, under her leadership, occupied the new building and dismantled the old, members living near Trower withdrew and formed Herbert Baptist Church, erected in 1912 on the old site. The Methodists in Locust Mount had less than $37 in hand when they moved into their new building, and yet over the next several years they raised over $2500 to finish and improve it. Once in the new building, the congregation took the name Grace Church.

Grace has had many ups and downs in this century. A smallpox epidemic hit the membership in 1914, yet four years later there were sixty conversions during a revival. W. H. Turner was the first pastor to occupy a new parsonage completed in 1922, yet he soon found himself shouldered with responsibility for Mt. Hope Church in Keller when strife weakened that congregation. Unemployment and poverty hampered the membership during the early 1930's, yet by 1935, the same year that Burton's was described as dead, Grace was reported to be active. The parsonage burned in the winter of 1959 and was quickly replaced, and yet five years later the congregation was strong enough to improve the church building and to add on two new rooms.

Grace has never been a large church and it has always shared its pastors with Burton's, from which it was founded. There are today 74 members, and the pastor of the Wachapreague Charge lives nearby in the new parsonage at Locust Mount.

[Sources: 113, 123, 176]

Location: see WACHAPREAGUE

GRACE UNITED METHODIST CHURCH

("Parksley")
[MP 1892, M 1939, UMC 1968]
Parksley

a - first building (photo prior to 1909)

In 1892 the Lee Mont Methodist Protestant Church established a mission in the new railroad town of Parksley and erected a small frame building on Wilson Avenue. Two blocks away stood another Methodist church, Parksley Methodist Episcopal, then only six years old.

The Parksley Mission quickly outdistanced both Lee Mont M.P. and Parksley M.E. to become the largest congregation in the vicinity and, within a few years, the largest M.P. congregation on the Eastern Shore of Virginia. In 1900 it was removed from Lee Mont and attached to Hunting Creek to become the new Parksley Charge. A parsonage was erected opposite the church in 1909, and the two churches remained together until 1917, when Parksley became a station and Hunting Creek was joined to Lee Mont.

On October 39, 1909, the church building was destroyed by fire, and in replacing it the congregation changed the name from "Parksley" to "Grace."

b - second building (dismantled 1975)

The second building was built with brick and cost $17,000. It was dedicated on June 4, 1911, by W. B. Judefind, the popular pastor who had served the church from 1900 to 1906 and who was the grandfather of Mrs. Spiro Agnew, wife of the Republican Vice-President. The new church contained a pipe organ, at that time the only one on the Shore, half of which was paid for by Andrew Carnegie.

Grace remained a station until 1938, when Calvary (Hunting Creek) rejoined it after Lee Mont burned. Grace was the largest Methodist Protestant congregation to enter The Methodist Church on the Eastern Shore of Virginia in 1939, and the two churches formed the only M.P. circuit that was not subsequently changed by the united denomination.

In October 1955 a large educational annex costing $87,000 was dedicated. Just as the debt on this building was liquidated in 1958, the parsonage burned and was replaced by the present one on the same site in 1959. In 1966 the pipe organ was rebuilt for $13,000, ten times the original cost of the instrument.

The second building, which was showing serious signs of deterioration, was dismantled in 1975, leaving the educational unit of 1955 intact, and the third sanctuary erected in its place. This building, also of brick, preserved the stained glass windows of the building of 1911.

Grace today has almost 500 members. Not all churches on the Shore keep strict membership records, but of those that do Grace is the fourth largest, after

Union Baptist in Chincoteague, Exmore Baptist, and Market Street Methodist in Onancock.

[Sources: 109, 114, 123, 145, 176]

Location: see PARKSLEY

*GRAHAM'S CHAPEL METHODIST EPISCOPAL CHURCH

[ME 1886-1898]
New Church

This church was founded in 1886, the year of the northern Methodist resurgence on the Eastern Shore. It alone of the several new churches established in that year was not visited by Bishop Mallalieu during his trip to the Shore.

The lot on which the church stands was secured in 1886, the congregation first listed by the denomination in 1888, and the building erected in 1890. The first pastor was W. K. Galloway, but the church was named for James E. Graham (1853-1905), pastor when the building was erected. The Wilmington Conference aided the local congregation financially in erecting the building.

Graham's Chapel was always a small congregation, its circuit affiliations often shifting. At various times throughout its short history it shared its pastors with the northern Methodist churches in Hallwood, Pittsville, and Modest Town. In 1897 it was joined to two churches in Northampton County, and the circuit named New Church & Exmore. That is the last year that denominational records list the church.

In 1905 Jacob White purchased the abandoned building, renovated it, and opened a store in it. It was used as such for many years and is still standing today on its original site.

In the local tradition of the village, this was sometimes known as "Red Eye Church," presumably from a single bright red window that was once over the front door. Older residents also recall that this congregation, like the northern Methodist congregation at Franklin City, were "shouting Methodists," who could be heard at worship from a distance of half a mile or more.

[Sources: 36, 117, 123]

Location: see NEW CHURCH

*GRANT MEMORIAL METHODIST PROTESTANT CHURCH

[MP 1893-1938]

Tasley

Grant Memorial, fifth and last church to be founded from Lee Mont M.P., was erected in 1893 and apparently named for one of its first trustees and early pillars, John D. Grant. The exact site of its first location has been lost, but it was on the Bayside Road near its intersection with the road to south Chesconnessex.

Grant Memorial fell heir to old Reese Chapel M.P., which stood about two miles north and which closed in the 1880's. When Reese Chapel was sold in 1895 the proceeds ($10) were "re-invested in other church property, known as Grant Memorial Methodist Protestant Church, situate [sic] near Deep Creek Mill." Even this bequest did not alleviate the congregation's financial problems; at an all-day meeting in the church in 1897 over $200 was raised to defray the debt on the church building.

In 1900 the old Accomac Circuit of the Methodist Protestants was divided, and Grant and Lee Mont became a circuit together. In this same year, the church bought a lot in the village of Tasley. Ten years later the church building was moved to this lot and reopened; cornerstone ceremonies were held in 1911. Though often known after this date as Tasley M.P., the church was still officially Grant Memorial.

In the mid-1930's a severe windstorm seriously damaged the church building, and it was condemned by the local authorities. Rather than repair the building,

1912

the denomination declared the church closed in 1938, the same year in which the other church on the circuit, Lee Mont, burned and was closed. Most of the members transferred to Drummondtown Methodist, some to Greenbush, and the building was subsequently dismantled.

[Sources: 105, 109, 110, 114, 123, 176]

Location: see TASLEY

GREATER MT. SINAI GOSPEL TABERNACLE CHURCH OF CHRIST DELIVERANCE

[Mt. Sinai Holy Church of America Inc., 1942]
Fairview

This church was founded by Estelle Dillard Smith, a member of the Mt. Sinai congregation in Cheapside. Smith was still a teenager when in 1942, after a remarkable conversion, she walked the nine miles from Cheapside to Fairview and began holding services in the home of an aunt. Within a short time the services had overflowed into a second Fairview home, and the Mt. Sinai Holy Church of America Inc. had set the young woman apart to pastor its second congregation on the Eastern Shore.

In 1943 the budding congregation purchased the abandoned church property of St. Paul's African Methodist Episcopal Church in Fairview. This building, which was itself the third building of Lower Northampton Baptist Church erected in 1869 and moved to Fairview in 1920, had seen no use for more than a decade, and was neglected and dilapidated. Nevertheless the enthusiastic congregation set about outfitting it for worship, and it was soon in use by the third group to use it in its long history.

The founder has been the only pastor this church has ever known, and over the years of her long pastorate the church has become one of the largest and most successful churches on the Shore. One sign of the prosperity of the church is the building itself, which has across the years been changed almost beyond recognition. Renovations and improvements have been almost constant, always under Elder Smith's direction. Today the church is more than twice as large as it was in 1943, and contains offices, a sacristy, and a baptistry. Of the original building, only the shell and the pews remain. The latest addition, which added two stories to the front of the building, was completed in 1975. The church building now seats several hundred people, and an average Sunday's attendance is about 200.

In 1948 Smith founded her second church, Mt. Zion in Bayside, which since 1970 has been in effect merged with the Fairview congregation for want of a building. She also founded Mt. Sinai Church of Christ Deliverance in Norfolk. A third church to be founded from this one was Bethlehem Temple Mission, almost across the street from this congregation, founded in 1955 by May Ella Harmon, a former member of Mt. Sinai.

Perhaps in reflection of its dynamic pastor, Mt. Sinai has had across the years an unusually high proportion of women in positions of leadership and authority. Among the many community-oriented projects in which the congregation has been involved is the use of its building by an extension of Norfolk State College in the past several years.

Mrs. Smith, who now lives in Cape Charles, has a number of degrees, earned and honorary, to her credit and for her work at Mt. Sinai was once given the key to the City of Cape Charles. She was ordained a bishop by the Mt. Sinai Holy Church in America in 1975.

[Sources: 109, 124, 176]

Location: see BAYVIEW

1975

GREENBACKVILLE

see: **Calvary Baptist Church*
**Grace Methodist Episcopal Church*
Union United Methodist Church

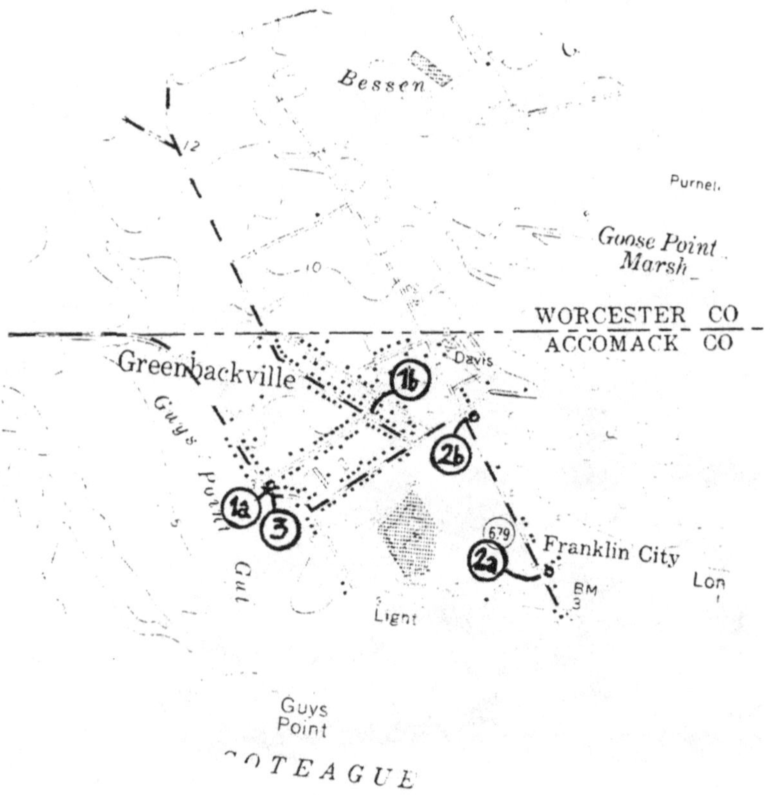

1a - Union Methodist: original site 1877-1895
1b - Union Methodist: since 1895
2a - Grace ME: original site 1884-1895
2b - Grace ME: site 1895-1941
3 - Calvary Baptist: site 1902-1911

GREENBUSH

see: **Amiss Chapel Methodist Episcopal Church South*
Greenbush United Methodist Church

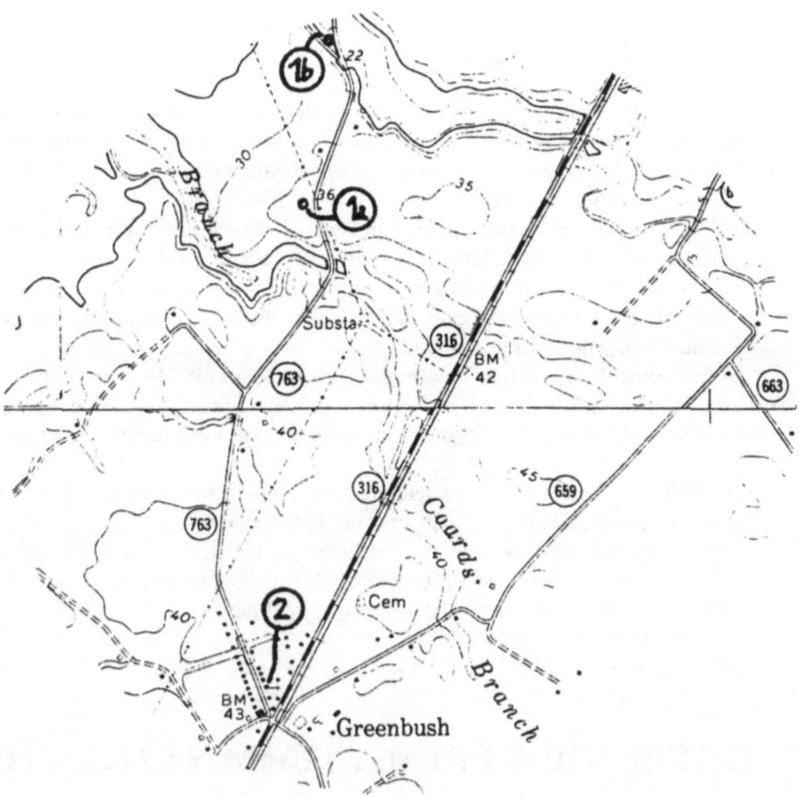

1a - Amiss Chapel ME: original site 1886-1912
1b - Amiss Chapel ME: building moved to this site 1912-c1970
2 - Greenbush Methodist

GREENBUSH UNITED METHODIST CHURCH

[MP 1908, M 1939, UMC 1968]
Greenbush

This church began in a series of bush arbor meetings in and around Greenbush in 1908. By the spring of 1911 as many as 45 persons were regular worshipers, and the fledgling congregation was given the use of Sam Melson's new store in the village until a building could be erected.

In 1911 the foundations for a new church were laid on a site east of the railroad, but construction ceased when the congregation decided that this site was unsatisfactory. Lloyd F. Hurst sold the present site to the congregation for $150 in 1911, and construction again commenced. In 1912 the Maryland Annual Conference reported that "Greenbush is nearly completed."

At first joined to Lee Mont to form the Accomac Circuit, Greenbush in 1917 was attached to Grant Memorial to become the Greenbush-Tasley Charge. Hallwood was added in 1933. The circuit pastor in that year received a salary of $1200.

In 1930 the frame building was elevated and a basement room added beneath it. The church has remained essentially unaltered since that time.

After some shifting charge boundaries following Unification in 1939, Greenbush was attached to Onley in 1946, and that arrangement still prevails. There are at present about 75 members. The pastor lives in Onley.

(Sources: 105, 114, 116, 123, 176)

Location: see GREENBUSH

*GREENVIEW PRESBYTERIAN CHURCH

[Pres 1919-1926]
Wachapreague

Greenview was the last Presbyterian congregation to be founded on the Virginia Shore, and the shortest lived. It was founded and abandoned within the short span of eight years.

The church was an outgrowth of the Powelton congregation, founded with the help of a home missionary from the Presbytery. It stood in an area south of Wachapreague that was at that time well-populated and prosperous. The congregation was organized in 1919. There were 43 members within the year, and the pastor was E. C. Clyde of Powelton and Naomi Makemie churches.

Almost as soon as the church was founded its members began to move away, many of them to Wachapreague. By 1924 membership had risen to 55, but the very next year it dropped to less than half, only twenty communicants. In 1926 a commission of the Presbytery assigned to investigate conditions at the failing church dissolved the congregation and transferred its members and property to Powelton.

The building, a simple frame structure, was shortly thereafter purchased and moved about a quarter of a mile west where its new owner intended to use it in building a new home. The house was never erected, and the building stood abandoned for another decade. In 1936 it was purchased again and moved away or used for lumber; its fate since that date has not been determined.

As late as the 1970's many maps of Accomack County still indicated the presence of this building on its second site, even after the little settlement in which it stood had long since disappeared.

[Sources: 119, 120, 176]

Location: see WACHAPREAGUE

*GROTONS WESLEYAN CHURCH

[IAHC 1916, PH 1922, W 1968-1970]

Grotons

It was at Grotons that William Vickers first appeared on the Eastern Shore of Virginia scene. Pitching his tent in a field, Vickers began there in 1916 the kind of spectacular meetings that were to make him a familiar figure, and to the Methodists notorious, up and down the Shore.

By 1917 there was a Holiness congregation in Grotons strong enough to purchase a lot and erect a church, a simple frame structure appropriate to the Holiness way of life. By 1925 there were 45 members. By 1932 the ladies of the church had organized a foreign missions society.

It was from this base in Grotons that Vickers extended the new faith to Saxis, Chincoteague, and, most successfully, to Bloxom. By 1930, Bloxom could boast a camp meeting, a parsonage, and a congregation large enough to rival the Grotons congregation in size. During the Depression years the Grotons area, which was more rural than Bloxom, lost population, and in 1938 the Bloxom congregation overtook and surpassed the Grotons church in size. Grotons was never again to regain its position of primacy. It had 32 members in 1938; seven years later membership had fallen below twenty, and it was never to climb above that figure again.

In September 1945 the church building was severely damaged by a storm; and the membership quickly raised $1200 to repair it.

After the successful pastorate of P. F. Bean (1941-48), whose wife was also an ordained minister, Grotons had a series of pastors who served only a short time, and two years during which there was no pastor at all. After 1965 membership dropped to ten, an all-time low, and the congregation barely survived to see the Pilgrim Holiness Church become the Wesleyan Church in 1968. The church was last listed by the denomination in 1970, when there were still ten persons listed as members, but virtually no activity at the church.

The church building still stands where Vickers himself preached. The sign next to the door reads not Wesleyan but "Pilgrim Holiness Church," mute testimony to the manner in which this important congregation dropped gradually and quietly from the pages of history.

[Sources: 121, 123, 176]

Location: see SANFORD

GUILFORD

see: *Guilford United Methodist Church*
**Muddy Creek Quaker Meetinghouse*
St. Thomas United Methodist Church

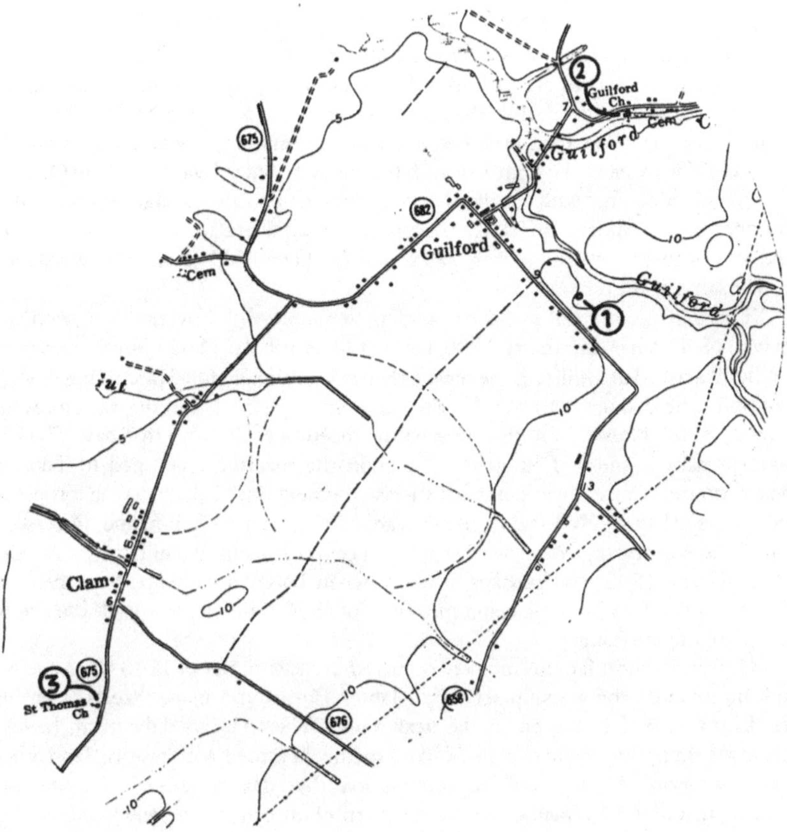

1 - Muddy Creek Meetinghouse (approximate site)
2 - Guildford Methodist: all buildings since 1799
3 - St. Thomas Methodist

GUILFORD UNITED METHODIST CHURCH

[ME 1795, ME-S 1860, M 1939, UMC 1968] Guilford

The stained glass window over the front door at Guilford Church claims that the congregation was established in 1785. That date cannot be substantiated, but Guilford is one of the oldest Methodist congregations on the Shore. By 1795 William Colbert, the circuit preacher, was meeting regular preaching appointments in the Guilford area in the homes of such people as Thomas Evans, William Onions, and Argol Bloxom. And Guilford can claim, as few other eighteenth-century churches on the Shore can, to have occupied the same site since its inception. The land was deeded to the church in 1799, and Guilford Methodists have worshiped on that same spot ever since.

The first mention of a church building at Guilford is in connection with the revival of Thomas Smith in 1800-1801. On April 1, 1801, Smith recorded: "When I arrived at Guilford, the meetinghouse was already filled [according to local tradition it held about 150 people], and hundreds were seated in the yard for want of room in the house." Smith convened the meeting at 10 a.m. that day, Thomas Ware preached, and at four in the afternoon the meeting adjourned to Thomas Evans' house, where it went on until sunrise the next day. "Such crying for mercy and shouts of joy surely Virginia never heard before," wrote Smith, and 44 persons joined the society that day. Similar scenes occurred again at Guilford in August 1801, March 1802, and perhaps in 1805, when Lorenzo Dow preached there on his way to the Pungoteague camp meeting. In 1836 Guilford was itself the site of a sizable camp meeting.

Guilford's most famous moment occurred in the summer of 1846 when a noisy mob interrupted the worship service of James Hargis and made threats upon his life if he returned to his pulpit the next week. When Hargis did return, he was accompanied by fifteen or twenty Guilford members armed with pistols "and other deadly weapons," who received communion that day so armed. Despite this disruption, Guilford remained in the northern church until the wholesale exodus of the Atlantic Circuit to the southern church in 1860. With the other southern churches on the Shore it was ordered closed by the Union army briefly in 1864.

Soon after the Civil War, a series of revivals brought new prosperity to the congregation, and in one single night in 1869, $700 was raised for a new building. The new building was dedicated on the same site in 1873, the original building having been moved aside to become Guilford School. In 1917 the third building was dedicated on the same site, the building of 1873 having been made into a moviehouse. By then Guilford had given birth to St. Thomas Church in 1891 and Bloxom in 1897, and the three churches had been fixed into one charge.

In the last month of 1948 the third Guilford building burned, and in 1950 the congregation dedicated the present structure, the fourth church to occupy the venerable site. The congregation that worships there today numbers about 180 members.

[Sources: 15, 16, 39, 70, 100, 103, 105, 107, 111, 116, 176]

Location: see GUILFORD

HALL'S CHAPEL CHURCH OF CHRIST

("Messongo Baptist")
[ABA 1886, Independent 1972]
Messongo

Hall's Chapel was organized in 1886 by five persons who had previously held prayer meetings in the Methodist church in Sanford. The church was known as Messongo Baptist Church until 1887, when it was renamed Hall's Chapel after Henry A. Hall, one of the founding members who donated the land on which the church was built.

From its earliest years Hall's Chapel shared its pastors with Shiloh Baptist, and after the 1920's usually with Hallwood Baptist. It never grew to great size; its maximum membership of 75 was reached in the mid-1950's.

By 1967 membership at Hall's Chapel had declined to 48. There followed a period of dormancy during which the church had no pastor. In 1969 it was listed by the Accomack Baptist Association on a charge with Hallwood, but after that year the church was in effect closed. Services resumed at the church in the spring of 1971, but in the fall of 1972 the congregation severed its ties with the Southern Baptist Convention and became Hall's Chapel Church of Christ, advertising itself as non-denominational. This congregation still continues, though quite small, under local pastors. There is no parsonage for the church.

The building still in use is the one erected in 1886. It was remodelled in 1920 at a cost of $4000 and was extensively renovated in 1954. The congregation also makes use of a small church hall next door to the church.

[Sources: 69, 122, 176]

Location: see SANFORD

HALLWOOD

see: *Faith Baptist Mission*
Hallwood Baptist Church
**Hallwood Methodist Episcopal Church*
Hallwood United Methodist Church

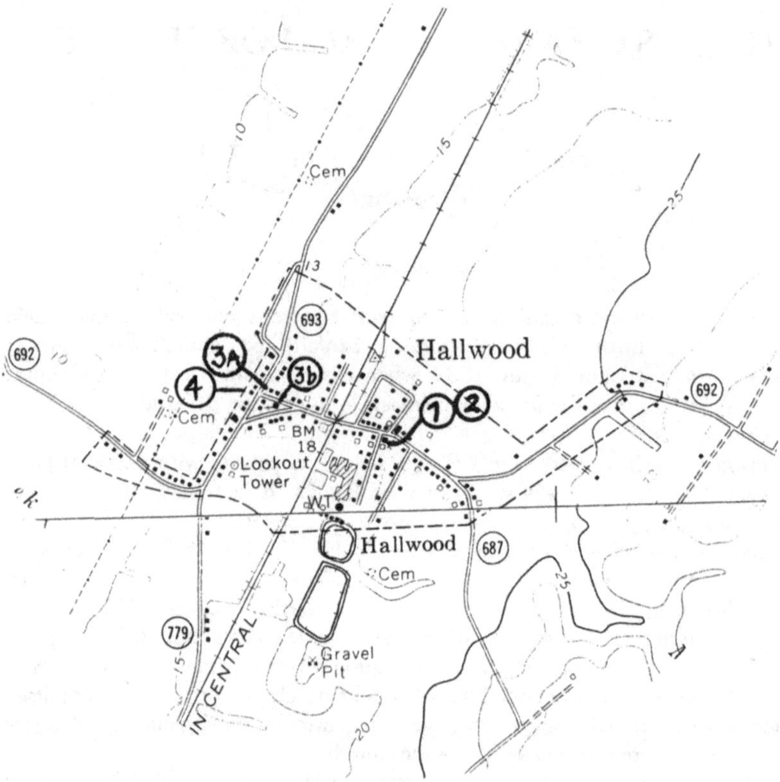

1 - Hallwood ME: site 1886-1901
2 - Hallwood Baptist
3a - Hallwood UMC: original site 1903-1919
3b - Hallwood UMC: site since 1919
4 - Faith Baptist Mission: occupied this building 1978

HALLWOOD BAPTIST CHURCH

[ABA 1901]
Hallwood

Twenty persons, most of them from Bethel Baptist Church, constituted this church in 1901. The following year the new congregation bought the building of Hallwood Methodist Episcopal Church, which was erected in 1886 and abandoned in 1901. The new owners made extensive additions and improvements to the building, for which they paid $400.

Hallwood shared its pastors with Bethel until 1914, at which time it began a period of frequent field realignments that characterized much of its history. By 1922 it was on a field with Hall's Chapel, Shiloh, and Saxis; Makemie Park joined the field after 1932. After 1940 the field consisted principally of Hallwood and Hall's Chapel, although Shiloh rejoined the field in 1948. In 1970 the church became a station, and it has remained one ever since.

The maximum membership of this church was reached in 1955, when there were 189 members.

Early in 1978 the church was hit by a schism, and a number of members withdrew with the former pastor to form Faith Baptist Mission. The membership of the church prior to this schism was about 170.

[Sources: 69, 122, 123, 176]

Location: see HALLWOOD

*HALLWOOD METHODIST EPISCOPAL CHURCH

[ME 1886-1901]
Hallwood

This is one of several churches founded during the northern Methodist resurgence of 1886. The land was purchased and the building erected in that year, and the church was officially dedicated by Bishop Willard Mallalieu that November.

The Wilmington Conference first listed a Hallwood Charge in 1887, when this church and Pittsville together mustered only nine members. Their local pastor, J. A. Connelley, faced ''bitter prejudice by our enemies in that vicinity,'' and was upon occasion assaulted with eggs by local residents.

Hallwood always remained a small and struggling church, its charge affiliations often shifting. In the thirteen years of its existence it was without a regular pastor three years. Only one pastor, E. F. Staats, the first appointee, was a conference member and more than just a local pastor.

In 1898 the supply pastor, J. S. Bozman, breathed some vitality into the little church, and in the following year a successful camp meeting was held. The vitality was short-lived, however. The year 1900 is the last in which a Hallwood appointment is listed, and there was no pastor assigned in that year. A 1901 missions collection from Hallwood, listed under the Parksley church, is the last mention of this congregation in denominational records.

In 1902 the building was purchased by the new Baptist congregation in Hallwood. Although substantially changed, it is still in use today.

[Sources: 109, 117, 123]

Location: see HALLWOOD

HALLWOOD UNITED METHODIST CHURCH

[MP 1903, M 1939, UMC 1968]
Hallwood

After Hallwood Methodist Episcopal Church closed and was purchased by the Baptists, the Methodist Protestants of the Conquest Circuit determined not to relinquish the village to the Baptists. And so in 1903, under the leadership of the Reverend A. A. Harryman, the second Methodist church in that village was erected just down the street from the first, on land purchased from James Hall for $1. The Maryland Conference first noted its presence in 1904, remarking that "at this last point we have not had a church heretofore."

Although founded from Conquest Chapel M.P., Hallwood quickly eclipsed that church in size. In 1906 the circuit divided, and these two churches became the Conquest Circuit. In 1911 they erected a parsonage together in the village near the newer church. In 1927 Conquest Chapel had declined to such an extent that the name of the circuit was changed to Hallwood.

In 1919 the church was moved to its present location and rebuilt, but not before a windstorm had blown it off its incomplete new foundations. The building was extensively altered at this time. To the original structure was added a steeple and a side room down the entire length of the building. Colored glass windows and plastered walls gave way to elaborate stained glass windows and metal walls and ceilings. Much of the work of rebuilding was done by local people, who worshiped with the Conquest Chapel congregation before the building was ready for use. The completed church was dedicated in 1920, and on the day the cornerstone was laid nearly $10,000 had been subscribed to the cost.

The 1930's were an especially hard period on both churches of this circuit. Conquest Chapel closed altogether early in the decade, and thereafter the Hallwood church was joined to the church in Greenbush, an arrangement which required a great deal of travel for the pastor. The Hallwood parsonage was sold in 1933 to liquidate the remaining debt on the building. Local members who had no money to contribute to the church during this decade would frequently sell trees and have them cut into boards in order to support the church.

In 1943 Hallwood was joined to the former southern Methodist churches of the Pocomoke Charge, and since that time the pastor has lived in Sanford. A large addition of classrooms and kitchen was added in 1966. The present membership is just under 100.

[Sources: 114, 123, 164]

Location: see HALLWOOD

HARBORTON

see: *Evergreen United Methodist Church*
**Harborton Baptist Church*
Harborton United Methodist Church
Mt. Olive Baptist Church
**Seatick Chapel*

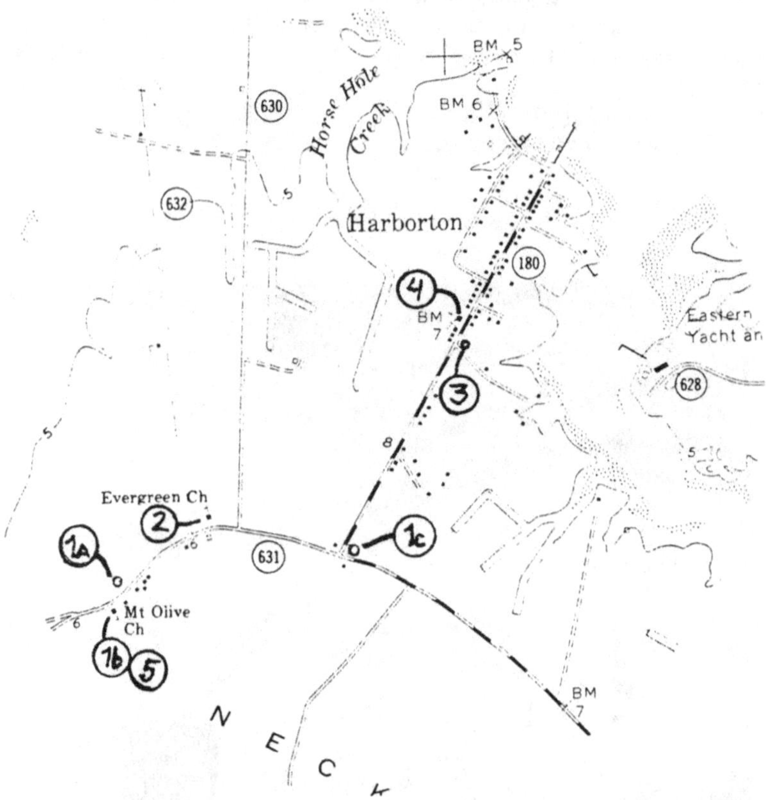

1a - Seatick Chapel: original site (approximate) 1848?-c1878
1b - Seatick Chapel: site (approximate) c1878-1887
1c - Seatick Chapel: site 1878-1907
2 - Evergreen UMC
3 - Harborton Baptist: site 1894-1944
4 - Harborton UMC
5 - Mt. Olive Baptist

*HARBORTON BAPTIST CHURCH

[ABA 1894-1932]
Harborton

(photo 1934)

Harborton Baptist Church was founded from Hollies, whose pastor, J. Manning Dunaway, first held services in the local schoolhouse in 1894. The Baptists of the new village secured a site in that year, laid the cornerstone of the new building on July 4, and dedicated the completed building on October 7, 1894. The new church seated 300 persons, cost $3500, and was said to be the finest frame church building on the Eastern Shore of Virginia at that time.

The congregation itself was not organized until some months later, on April 12, 1896, when 28 members withdrew from Hollies for that purpose. Dunaway served as the pastor until 1898, and there was a brief succession of pastors who served only this church. After 1909, Harborton shared its pastors with Hollies and Baker Memorial. C. P. Scott of Hollies was the last regular pastor. Beginning in 1921 the church was served by local supplies, and after 1928 services were only occasional.

Harborton Baptist and Harborton Methodist each had preaching on alternate Sundays, so there were religious services in the town each week at one church or the other. Hollies proposed merger to the declining congregation in 1925, but it was not effected. In 1929 the church claimed 42 members and an active Sunday school, but in 1930 it ceased to report to the Association. Two years later the Association dropped the church from its records.

The land on which the church was erected never belonged to the Baptist denomination and reverted to the original owners. The building and its furnishings were sold, and in 1944 the building was dismantled.

[Sources: 40, 69, 112, 123, 150]

Location: see HARBORTON

HARBORTON UNITED METHODIST CHURCH

[ME-S 1893, M 1939, UMC 1968]
Harborton

In 1893, only seven years after it had itself split from the Pungoteague church, Evergreen Church divided, and Harborton Methodist Episcopal Church, South, was born. Less than a mile away the Methodists began construction of their second new building in Hack's Neck. Lumber and cypress shingles arrived by schooner from North Carolina at Harborton's then-busy wharves. The building, which cost $2300, was dedicated in 1894. James Cannon, Jr., president of the Blackstone Female Institute and later a bishop, preached the dedicatory sermon.

The District Conference met at Harborton church shortly after the building was erected, and the church was said to be the largest southern Methodist building between Salisbury and Cape Charles at that time.

Like the Baptist church down the street, erected in the same year, Harborton Methodist Church prospered in the early years of its life with the town in which it was situated. With the fading of Harborton as a port, however, the church gradually dwindled in size with the town. The class meeting, a remnant of early Methodism, was still extant at this church in the second decade of the twentieth century.

Harborton today boasts about 140 members. As always throughout its history, it shares its pastor with Pungoteague and Evergreen, and the parsonage is in

Pungoteague. Except for some interior improvements, there have been no major changes to the building, the exterior of which looks basically as it did in 1894.

[Sources: 40, 109, 110, 111, 116]

Location: see HARBORTON

*HARMONY METHODIST EPISCOPAL CHURCH

("Barrett's")
[ME 1894-1898]
Jamesville

This church was founded by Melson's M.E. at Read's Wharf, with whom it always shared its pastors. The church lot in Jamesville was purchased for $1 in 1894, and construction of the building began in that year. The church was not "ready for dedication" until 1896, but services were held in it as early as 1895.

Harmony was an exceedingly short-lived congregation. One year after the building was completed, in 1897, Harmony and Melson's were joined on a circuit with Graham's Chapel in New Church, forty miles away. And the next year is the last time either of the two churches was listed in the records of the Wilmington Conference.

The deed to the land contained a reversion clause, so several years after the church was closed the owners claimed the building, moved it down the road towards James Wharf, and used it as a barn. After many years of service it has since disappeared.

In some records this church is known as Barrett's Church, after the local preacher Thomas S. Barrett, a native of Exmore who was supplying it when it was founded.

[Sources: 117, 124, 176]

Location: see JAMESVILLE

*HARMONY METHODIST PROTESTANT CHURCH

(see Lee Mont Methodist Protestant Church)

HERBERT BAPTIST CHURCH

[ESBA 1912]
Wachapreague

This church stands on the original site of Grace Methodist, and was founded by schism from it.

In 1912 the black Methodist congregation in Wachapreague, following a movement of blacks from Trower to Locust Mount, closed their old Trower church, dismantled it, and moved into a new building in Locust Mount. A number of members who lived in Trower, determined to maintain a church in their community, withdrew from the congregation and founded this church. By the end of the year a building had been erected on the old site, and to further complete the division the new congregation joined the Baptist association.

Since it was not altogether certain that the new congregation could obtain free title to the old church lot, the congregation sought the aid of E. T. Powell of the Presbyterian church in Wachapreague. Powell obtained the lot for them, and in gratitude the congregation named their church Herbert Baptist Church, for Herbert S. Powell (1898-1977), Powell's young son. The land was not officially deeded to the congregation until 1924, after E. T. Powell's death.

The building erected in 1912 has been often renovated, and enlarged at least twice. The first addition moved the back wall and extended the length of the sanctuary, almost doubling the size of the building.

Seven pastors have served the church since its formation, the first of whom was Thomas Turlington. The present pastor also serves Antioch Baptist Church in Treherneville. This black congregation maintained a cordial relation with Herbert S. Powell, for whom the church was named, that extended across the years until Powell's death in 1977.

[Sources: 26, 113, 123, 176]

Location: see WACHAPREAGUE

*HOG ISLAND METHODIST EPISCOPAL CHURCH
[ME 1795-1840?]
Hog Island

While it is doubtful that the first Hog Island society ever actually bore the name given here, it is given this separate listing because it was entirely separate from the second Hog Island congregation, known as Pullen's Chapel, founded in 1883.

Just when Methodism first found its way to Hog Island is not known, but there was a society of nineteen members there in 1795 when Colbert was circuit preacher, and it is apparent that it antedated Colbert's pastorate. It was from Hog Island that Colbert and Rowen set out in a boat for Philadelphia in September 1795, on that journey when they were forced ashore and first lodged with David Watt in Wattsville.

Stephen Fletcher of Hog Island was on the mainland during Thomas Smith's revival of 1800-1801, and he brought Smith home with him to the island, where yet another revival occurred. Although only 25 people were in the society after this revival, the effects of the revival are said to have changed the entire town. "An entire change of living came about among the people...even the ruder element was gradually brought under the influence of the gospel."

The Hog Island society was apparently seldom visited by the circuit preachers after Thomas Smith's pastorate, but strong local leaders arose, and one of them, Isma Fletcher, became an exhorter. The circuit held a camp meeting on the island in 1821.

By 1835 the society had dwindled to three persons, two of whom were Isma Fletcher and his wife. Within a few years all were dead, and the society disappeared.

It is unlikely that a church building was ever erected on the island, and apparently there was no further Methodist activity there until Thomas Pullen arrived in 1883.

[Sources: 15, 100, 101]

Location: Unknown

*HOLINESS CHRISTIAN CHURCH

("Full Gospel Mission")
[PH 1951-52, Holiness Christian Church (Reading, Pa.) 1953-1977]
Chesconnessex

William Vickers pitched his tent in this neighborhood in the 1930's, but it was not until 1951 that a Holiness congregation was formed in Chesconnessex. J. Milford Sullivan, pastor of the Bloxom congregation, began the work with two tent meetings.

There were nine charter members of this congregation, which called itself Full Gospel Mission, when in 1952 it purchased a lot and erected a building in south Chesconnessex. That was the last year the congregation was officially affiliated with the Pilgrim Holiness Church, for when it became obvious that the small group would not be able to support a full-time minister, Kenneth Prier, one of the original members, assumed the pastorate.

The congregation subsequently affiliated with another Holiness denomination, the Holiness Christian Church with headquarters in Reading, Pennsylvania. Many of the churches of this denomination were later merged with the Pilgrim Holiness Church. Those that were not, like the Chesconnessex congregation, continued to practice the ordinance of footwashing, the chief practical difference between the two denominations.

Prier served as pastor until shortly before his death in 1976. In that year the fifteen members of the congregation invited Mrs. Lindy Hinman, an Assembly of God pastor, to assume the pastorate. Hinman's own mission congregation was merged briefly with this church, but within a few months services had ceased to be held in the building. By late 1977 Aulden Corbin was the only surviving trustee. The building was sold in December of that year and the proceeds given to Bloxom Wesleyan Church, to which some of the members of this church transferred. [Sources: 109, 121, 123, 176]

Location: see CHESCONNESSEX

*HOLINESS TABERNACLE

[IAHC 1917, PH 1922-1930?]
Chincoteague

Chincoteague was the third Virginia community to be evangelized by William Vickers, who pitched his traveling tent there in 1917. The tabernacle that was erected there soon afterwards was the second Holiness church on the island.

It was a tabernacle and not a church that Vickers and his people erected on land purchased from Daniel and Ruth Watson, an open-sided structure with earthen floor, like many camp meeting structures. For a number of years Baptists and Methodists from the older churches on the island were among the many curious crowds who flocked to hear Vickers preach, but the work never took root here and was abandoned after little more than a decade.

In 1937 the new Church of God congregation occupied the abandoned tabernacle and used it for eleven years. Finally in 1948 services were discontinued there for a second time. The old tabernacle was remodeled into a dwelling, and a new Church of God was erected next door. The tabernacle still stands today on the corner of Poplar Street and Deep Hole Road, still in use as a dwelling and so changed in appearance that no one would guess its religious origins.

[Sources: 121, 123, 176]

Location: see CHINCOTEAGUE

HOLLIES BAPTIST CHURCH

(''Pungoteague'')
[ABA 1790]
Keller

Historic Hollies Baptist Church was founded by Elijah Baker in 1790, with the assistance of George Layfield. The church was originally known as Pungoteague Baptist Church, and not until 1918 was the name officially changed to Hollies, which is apparently a corruption of Hawley's, the name of an early landowner in the area of the church.

The land on which this church is situated was deeded by Mary Fox in 1792 for the price of twenty shillings ''and in consideration of an earnest desire to promote and encourage any religeous Institution and particularly the building of a babtist meeting House.'' The first building was erected at about that same time, and it is still in use. Although much changed and enlarged, it is the third oldest church building on the Eastern Shore of Virginia, after St. George's and Hungars.

It was at Hollies in 1809 that the Accomack Baptist Association was formed, and this church was already one of the leading Baptist churches on the Shore at that time. By the 1830's the congregation was operating three other meetinghouses which were used for worship and other events: Zoar near Daugherty, Crossroads near Onley, and Boggs in Sluitkill Neck. At the division of the Association over the missions question in 1831 a rival anti-mission congregation took over the Boggs Meetinghouse, but it faded out within a few years. The congregation organized its first local missionary society in 1834, and did not suffer severely from the missions controversy.

Hollies was very prosperous in the mid-nineteenth century. The building was significantly altered and enlarged in 1849, when the congregation was more than half black. A Sunday school was founded in 1852 and has been continuous from that date, except for two years during the Civil War. In 1856 several members were dismissed to form Onancock Baptist Church. But this period of prosperity ended abruptly. The maximum membership was reached in 1867 when there were 216 members. In 1868 the black members withdrew to form their own church, and membership at Hollies dropped to 105. The church did not report to the Accomack Association in 1869 and 1870, and the lowest membership figure was recorded in 1874: thirty members.

After this low ebb, life at the church picked up again during the last quarter of the century. Hollies joined with Onancock and Drummondtown to build the first Baptist parsonage on the Shore in Onancock in 1876. In 1887 the church building was again enlarged and improved; the two wings of the building date from this year. In 1894 the church became the mother church of Harborton Baptist. A great revival in 1904 brought forty new members into the church, and the building had to be further enlarged and improved, which alterations were completed in 1906.

Hollies purchased its own parsonage in the town of Keller in 1914, and it has been a station ever since. A classroom building was built next door to the church in 1949. Membership in this century peaked at 199 in 1964; it is presently about 150. Though not especially large, Hollies is today as ever a vigorous church, and has worshiped continuously in its building on its plot of ground longer than any other Baptist church on the Eastern Shore of Virginia.

[Sources: 69, 70, 71, 122, 150]

Location: see KELLER

HOLMES PRESBYTERIAN CHURCH

[Pres 1846]
Bayview

In 1846 the Home Mission Board of the Hanover Presbytery sent two pastors, Joseph Stiles and Nathaniel Locke, to the Eastern Shore of Virginia to found a new congregation. Out of their efforts was born Holmes Presbyterian Church, erected in 1846, organized in 1847, and named for a substantial contributor from Philadelphia.

The early history of Holmes is almost entirely female. Of the nine charter members, three of whom came by transfer from Makemie Church in Accomac, seven were women. By 1854 the membership had grown to 24, and all of them were women. The women of Holmes relied on friendly menfolk of the area from time to time, as in 1857 when the Presbytery met at Holmes and visitors from across the Bay had to be chauffeured to the church. When a Sunday school was established, a male superintendent was recruited from a nearby Methodist congregation. It was not until 1867 that the first two men joined Holmes by profession of faith. Thereafter a gradual influx of male members brought about a greater balance between the sexes.

Holmes was without a regular pastor until 1859, when James Dunlap Thomas of Makemie assumed the pastorate. Thomas, however, left the area at the outbreak of hostilities in 1861, and Holmes was vacant throughout the Civil War period. William Gwynn Coe, the independent Methodist preacher, preached there from June 1864 to July 1865. After the war Holmes became a field to itself, and the latter part of the nineteenth century was a prosperous period.

In 1874 Annie P. Thompson organized a Myrtle Society ("myrtle" means "hope") whose purpose was "to do anything and everything that they could to help with the expenses of both church and manse." Around 1900 Mrs. A. S. Venable, wife of the pastor, organized a Missionary Society. The two groups were joined in 1920.

Three other churches were founded from Holmes: Belle Haven, by twenty members dismissed in 1879; the short-lived Second Presbyterian in 1884; and First Presbyterian in Cape Charles, eight of whose charter members were dismissed from Holmes in 1890.

In 1929 the congregation erected and dedicated a church house near the church building. The original building, built in 1846, is still in use and has not been substantially altered. It is the seventh oldest church building of any denomination on the Eastern Shore of Virginia.

In 1943 the Reverend John A. Wood began a ten-year pastorate at this church. Wood's daughter Catherine, who never lived on the Shore, married the renowned

Presbyterian minister Peter Marshall. His wife Leonora was a respected student and writer of Eastern Shore history and was the subject of her daughter's novel **Christy**, published in 1967.

Holmes has always been a prosperous and vigorous church. Membership increased steadily over its first century until 1946, when it peaked at 201. The present membership is 157, making Holmes the largest of the Presbyterian churches on the Virginia Shore.

[Sources: 119, 120, 175, 176]

Location: see BAYVIEW

HOLY TRINITY BAPTIST CHURCH

[ESBA 1905]
Boston

Holy Trinity was born in a schism from nearby Shiloh Baptist Church, although the exact cause of the dispute has long since been forgotten.

In 1905 eighty-five members of Shiloh withdrew from that church to form a new congregation. George and Eleanor Evans sold the land on which a church building was erected, almost within sight of Shiloh, and on July 8, 1905, the new church was dedicated.

At the same time a cemetery was purchased not far from the church. The congregation subsequently also erected a small building for use as a church hall.

John A. Collins was the first pastor of this church. Since him five others have served as pastors, among them W. W. Gilchrist, who lived in Newport News and journeyed regularly to the Shore to preach here and at Horntown Tabernacle Baptist Church. This church has never owned a parsonage.

Across the years the church has remained a small one, never growing to the size of Shiloh from whence it came. The original building of 1905, picturesquely set in its grove of trees and much improved over the years, is still in use.

[Sources: 26, 109, 123, 176]

Location: see BOSTON

HOLY TRINITY EPISCOPAL CHURCH

[PE 1878]
Onancock

The only Episcopal services in Onancock were, for many years, occasional ones conducted by the rectors of St. James in Accomac. In the summer of 1878 Thomas Taylor, an Episcopal layman, opened a Sunday school in a rented room in the town hall. His was not, however, a parish effort; most of his students were non-Episcopalians, and the school was known as "Mr. Taylor's Sunday School." By 1878, however, the Accomac rector was visiting Onancock as often as twice a month for services.

Once when there was no rector, the diocese sent a "missioner" to hold services, and Taylor entertained him and the vestry and several ladies of the faith at dinner. After dinner the visiting minister remarked, "You good folks should have a small chapel in which to worship," and Taylor seized the opportunity for which he had been waiting. "Miss Finney," he said turning to one of his guests, "if you will give the land, I will give the lumber." She replied, "Select your lot tomorrow from any land I own." Before the guests left the table there were pledges of land, lumber, windows, baptismal font, and financial contributions ranging up to $200.

Construction on the church began in 1883. It took three years to complete the building, and on March 26, 1886, the Reverend John McNabb held the first service in it. "Onward Christian Soldiers" was the first hymn sung there. The debt was liquidated and the building consecrated in 1894.

Within a short time Holy Trinity was a separate parish and a prosperous, if not particularly large, church. The first rectory on East Market Street was purchased before the turn of the century, but was subsequently sold when the present one next to the church was purchased during the pastorate of John Cornick (1907-15). In 1903 the congregation operated a Sunday school in the former Bascom's Chapel Methodist Episcopal Church, South, which had been given to them for that purpose by J. P. L. Hopkins, a prominent layman.

The first change in the structure of the church building came in 1918, when the rector himself removed the steeple that had become "hazardous" to those entering the church. Shortly thereafter an auditorium was added to the back of the church, the gift of Anne Wise Craft in 1923. A second addition, consisting of kitchen and nursery, was added in 1951, and the home adjacent to the church on the west purchased as a parish house in the 1960's.

Membership at Holy Trinity has fluctuated during this century. From a maximum of 88 communicants in 1922 it dwindled to only 43 in 1949. In the past two decades the church has more than doubled in size, and its present membership of over 180 is the largest in its history. In 1971 Holy Trinity surpassed in size Christ Church in Eastville to become the largest Episcopal church on the Eastern Shore of Virginia.

[Sources: 62, 66, 110, 118, 147]

Location: see ONANCOCK

East Nave Window, Holy Trinity Episcopal Church

HOPETON

see: *Mt. Olive Pentecostal Church of Christ Disciples*

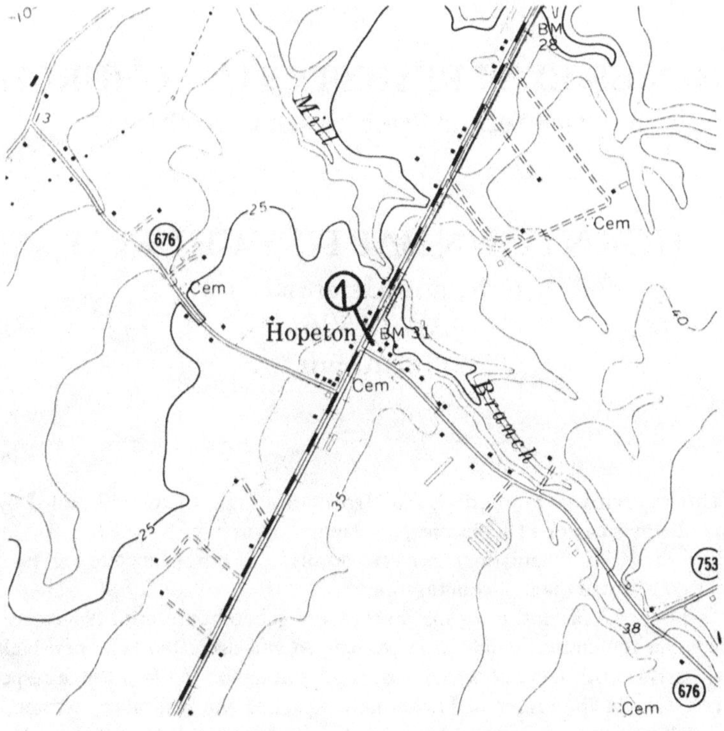

1 - Mt. Olive: site since 1976 (for previous locations, see ACCOMAC)

Location Unknown: Hopeton Baptist Mission (see Appendix I)

*HOPEWELL BAPTIST CHURCH

(see Cedar Grove Baptist Church)

*HOPEWELL PRESBYTERIAN CHURCH

(see Second Presbyterian Church)

HORNTOWN BAPTIST CHURCH

("Reamy Memorial")
[ABA 1896]
Horntown

This church was founded after a "great meeting" in the village led by A. Judson Reamy, pastor of Chincoteague Baptist Church in New Church. On the last day of 1896, twenty-four persons dismissed from Chincoteague for that purpose constituted the new congregation.

The Baptists of Horntown met in the local schoolhouse until November 28, 1897, when the church building was completed and dedicated. The new building cost almost $2000, most of which was paid by Solomon T. Johnson, a respected member. Dr. M. F. Fisher of Portsmouth preached the dedicatory sermon, and the church was named Reamy Memorial after its founder. It bore that name until 1904, when the name was changed to Horntown.

Horntown has always been a small church. Its maximum membership of 75 was attained in the early 1930's. It has always shared its pastor with Chincoteague Baptist, from whence it came, and between 1909 and 1965 with First Baptist in New Church as well. There has never been a parsonage for this church alone.

The congregation today numbers 34 and worships in the original building which is still substantially unchanged. A small building next door to the church is used as church and community hall.

[Sources: 36, 69, 110, 122]

Location: see HORNTOWN

HORNTOWN

see: *Deas Chapel United Methodist Church*
Horntown Baptist Church
Horntown United Methodist Church
Horntown Tabernacle Baptist Church

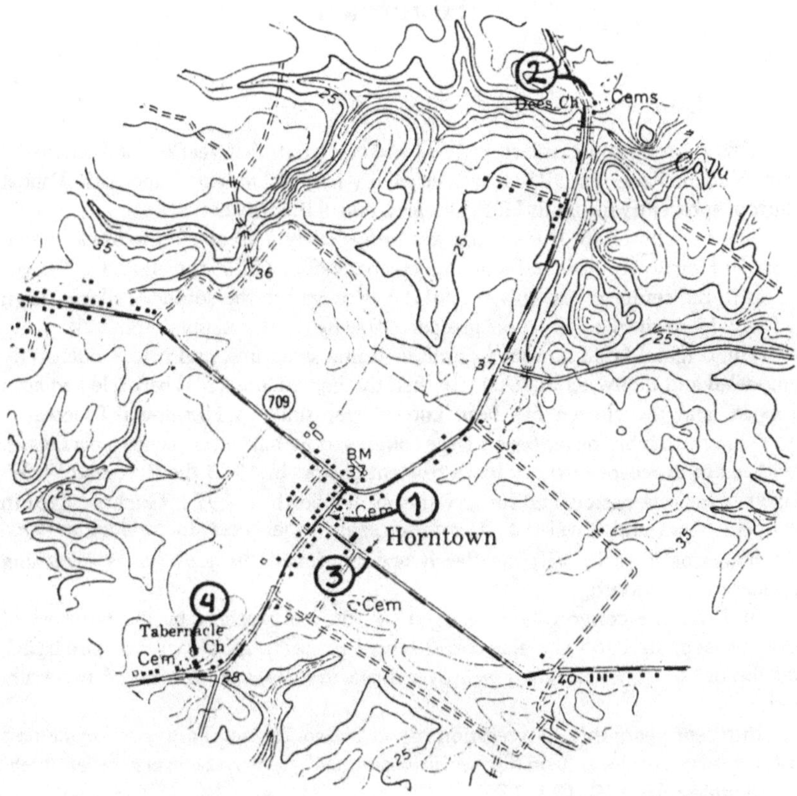

1 - Horntown Methodist
2 - Deas Chapel Methodist
3 - Horntown Baptist
4 - Tabernacle Baptist

HORNTOWN TABERNACLE BAPTIST CHURCH

("Douglas Tabernacle")
[ESBA 1892]
Horntown

This church was organized in 1892 and erected in that year on land purchased from William Parks for $25. It was originally named Douglas Tabernacle Baptist Church, apparently for Louis H. P. Douglas, one of the trustees.

The site chosen for this church was immediately adjacent to the black schoolhouse in Horntown. This old building, erected before 1835, served as a school for whites in the center of the village until it was moved to the southern edge of town in 1882. Here church and school prospered side by side for many years.

The original building was a primitive frame structure, and it was extensively remodeled and improved in 1901. By then the name Douglas Tabernacle had been dropped, and the church has been known ever since as Horntown Tabernacle.

This church has never been a large congregation, has never owned a parsonage, and has not in recent memory had a resident pastor. In 1943 the Reverend W. W. Gilchrist became pastor, and he served until his death in 1974. Gilchrist lived in Newport News and traveled to Horntown every other week to conduct services. His successor lived in Virginia Beach and continued the tradition of preaching services twice a month.

In 1962 the congregation enlarged the church property by the purchase of adjacent land. In 1965 the abandoned school property next door was purchased, and the old schoolhouse, then well over a century old, was dismantled two years later.

In recent years this congregation has dwindled in size. Today, as for the past half century or more, worship services are held here only every other week.

[Sources: 36, 109, 123, 176]

Location: see HORNTOWN

HORNTOWN UNITED METHODIST CHURCH

[ME 1806, ME-S 1860, M 1939, UMC 1968]
Horntown

Erected 1859; typical of the antebellum church buildings on the Eastern Shore

This is one of the oldest Methodist congregations on the Shore, but the exact date of its formation is unknown. Local tradition has it that the church was founded in 1800, and the congregation celebrated its 165th anniversary in 1965. The earliest date that can be substantiated, however, is 1806, when the Methodists of the Shore held a camp meeting nearby on Swan's Gut Creek. A second camp meeting was held near the village in 1807, and no doubt by then at the latest a society had been formed. Asbury found a friendly lodging among Methodists of the village when he visited in 1810 (modern editions of his journal incorrectly transcribe ''Hometown'' for ''Horntown''), as did Lorenzo Dow in 1813.

Chief among the early pillars of this church was Drummond Welbourn, postmaster, tavern-keeper, and local Methodist preacher. The bankrupt Welbourn hanged himself inside his uncompleted mansion in 1818, unaware that Francis Asbury had written of him in his journal: "Methodist preachers politicians — what a curse!"

For a full generation the Methodists of Horntown gathered in private homes and out-of-doors. A lot for a church building was obtained in 1824 but never used. The present site was purchased from William Cropper in 1827, and a small building erected on it soon afterwards. It was in this first building that a "great revival was held, conducted by Rev. [James] Brindle" in 1853. Eliza Cox organized the first Sunday school here in 1858. A year later the original building was dismantled and a larger one, the present structure, erected on the same site.

Like the rest of the Atlantic Circuit, Horntown seceded to the southern church in 1860, and was closed by the Union army for some weeks in 1864. Soon after the Civil War, in 1867, a revival broke out and the little congregation entered into a season of prosperity. The northern church attempted to form a congregation in the village in 1887, but without success.

Because the congregation remained small across the years, the Horntown building was not subjected to the kinds of changes that altered most of the other early church buildings up and down the Shore. The result is that of all the early Methodist buildings in the two counties, this one alone remains much as it was when it was erected before the Civil War. It is the seventh oldest Methodist structure on the Shore, and the only two substantial changes that have been made to it were the removal of the slave gallery in 1892 and the installation of a tin ceiling in 1914. The original box pews remain in a very simple interior, and a visitor to the church can still catch a glimpse of what Methodist churches were like during the middle of the last century.

Horntown remained a part of the Atlantic Circuit of the southern church until after unification in 1939. In 1945 it was attached to Chincoteague, but in the next year it was joined to Signpost and Greenbackville, where it has remained ever since. Of the surviving Methodist congregations on the Shore, only Cokesbury in Onancock is smaller. The present membership at Horntown is about 25.

[Sources: 3, 16, 101, 103, 111, 116, 123, 171, 176]

Location: see HORNTOWN

HUNGARS EPISCOPAL CHURCH

("Nuswattocks")
[CE 1646, PE 1819]
Bridgetown

Hungars is one of the most cherished historical spots on the Eastern Shore of Virginia, its building a source of pride not just to Episcopalians but to the entire Shore. The church has, however, had its ups and downs across the centuries, and for an entire generation at one point in its history its walls did not resound to the sounds of worship.

It was in 1646 or early in 1647 that the first Hungars was built. It stood in Church Neck west of Bridgetown near the estate "Pear Plain" and was early known as Nuswattocks Church. The name Hungars became firmly established in 1661, and the name of the parish became Hungars in 1691.

In 1680 the original Hungars building was dismantled and a second building erected on a new site in the village of Bridgetown, a mile to the east. This second building, like its predecessor a frame structure, was several years in the building, and it stood adjacent to the present church site. It may have been 1686 before it was completed. William Byrd of Westover worshiped in it in 1709 and noted in his diary the large size of the worshiping congregation.

It was on or about 1742 that the present brick church was constructed, about four years later than St. George's in Pungoteague, which is the only church building on the Eastern Shore of Virginia that is older. In 1752 Thomas Preeson gave the land on which the church stands in return for an assigned pew with his initials and the date. The church was open and active up until the time of the Revolution. One of the last rectors was Samuel McCroskey, whose sermon at Magothy Church did little to stem the Baptist tide in 1776.

With the disestablishment of the Church of England in 1784, old Hungars (then already almost a century and a half old) fell upon hard times and was closed. The building went unused and suffered considerable damage from neglect and vandalism. Leaden parts of the pipe organ that once stood in the building were used as sinkers for fishnets, and velvet hangings were cut into pieces and dispersed throughout the community. Johnson's Methodist was erected nearby in 1790, and its deed specifically provided that "friendly clergy of the Church of England (so-called)" could preach there, but Episcopalianism in this vicinity was dormant despite this provision. Methodism established itself strongly in the area, siphoning off many of the former Anglican gentry, and Hungars for all practical purposes died.

In 1819 Hungars was reopened after the church had stood vacant for more than thirty years. Repairs on the church building cost $1400, but they must have been minimal, for others were necessary continuously over the next several decades. There were repairs in 1828, repairs on the roof in 1837, and a complete remodeling of the interior in 1840. At that time the original center aisle was replaced by two side aisles, the box pews disposed of by lot and replaced with modern ones, and the high pulpit moved from the side door to the chancel (it has since disappeared altogether).

Despite all this work the building was determined to be unsound still in 1850. In March 1851 the congregation resolved "that the Old Hungars Church be taken down and a new one be erected on the same site using the materials in the old building, as far as might be considered sound and suitable." The following June the congregation reversed this decision and hired Thomas F. Stevenson of Snow Hill to repair the existing building. Under Stevenson's direction the church was shortened by several feet and a completely new front, with two doors instead of the one central one, erected. The side doors were replaced with windows, the barrel ceiling with a flat one. Stevenson was a master builder and the results were not only a sound building but one where the new brickwork could scarcely be distinguished from the old. Unfortunately Stevenson lost $100 on the project, despite the $1500 he collected.

When it was first determined that the building was unsound in 1850, the congregation worshiped in a nearby schoolhouse. Later, while Stevenson was reconstructing the building, they assembled in Johnson's Chapel. When the new Hungars was finished, the Episcopalians gave a stove to the Methodists "in consideration of their having kindly given to the Episcopal Congregation the use of their Chapel during the repairs."

Even after it was restored and reopened Hungars remained a small church. There were only 21 communicants in 1876. Growth in the twentieth century was slow but steady, and by 1975 there were 121 communicants. A parish house was erected on the church grounds in the 1960's. Although the Hungars Glebe of colonial times still stands in Church Neck, the rector now lives in Eastville, where he also serves Christ Church and Emmanuel in Cape Charles.

By date of formation (1646) Hungars is the oldest congregation on the Eastern Shore of Virginia, though it has been in continuous operation only since 1819.

[Sources: 62, 70, 90, 118]

Location: see BRIDGETOWN

HUNTING CREEK METHODIST PROTESTANT CHURCH

(see Calvary United Methodist Church)

*INDIANTOWN MISSION, METHODIST EPISCOPAL CHURCH

("Nassawadox Mission")
[ME 1839-1844]
Eastville

By the 1830's Methodism had spread to virtually every corner of the Shore with one glaring exception: Eastville. From as early as the 1790's Eastville had proven unreceptive to the Methodist faith. The circuit appointed a committee to investigate the possibility of building a church there in 1832 and again in 1834, but without success. In 1839 the denomination made a concerted effort to fill the gap with the establishment of the Indiantown Mission. James Hargis was the first pastor.

Exactly where most of the work of the mission was done is not known today; the name is that of a neck on the Seaside east of Eastville. But that its purpose was to place a Methodist church in the county seat is certain. At least two lots in the village were purchased during the time the mission was in operation. One, purchased from George Yerby in 1838, was returned the following year. The second, purchased from Sylvester Kelly for $1000, was located just north of the house

''Cessford.'' Neither lot was ever used, and the Methodist attempt to establish a church in the county seat failed.

The mission was conducted from 1839 to 1844 and was known both as Indiantown and as Nassawadox Mission. No pastor was assigned to the mission in 1845, and after that year the work was abandoned. Among those who served the appointment was Isaac R. Willett (1841-42), a native of Accomack County.

[Sources: 115, 124]
Location: Unknown

*IRONSIDE (or) OLD IRONSIDE BAPTIST CHURCH

(see Messongo Primitive Baptist Church)

Bethel United Methodist Church,
Jamesville

JAMESVILLE

see: *Bethel United Methodist Church*
**Harmony Methodist Episcopal Church*
**Mt. Zion African Methodist Episcopal Church*
St. Marys Baptist Church

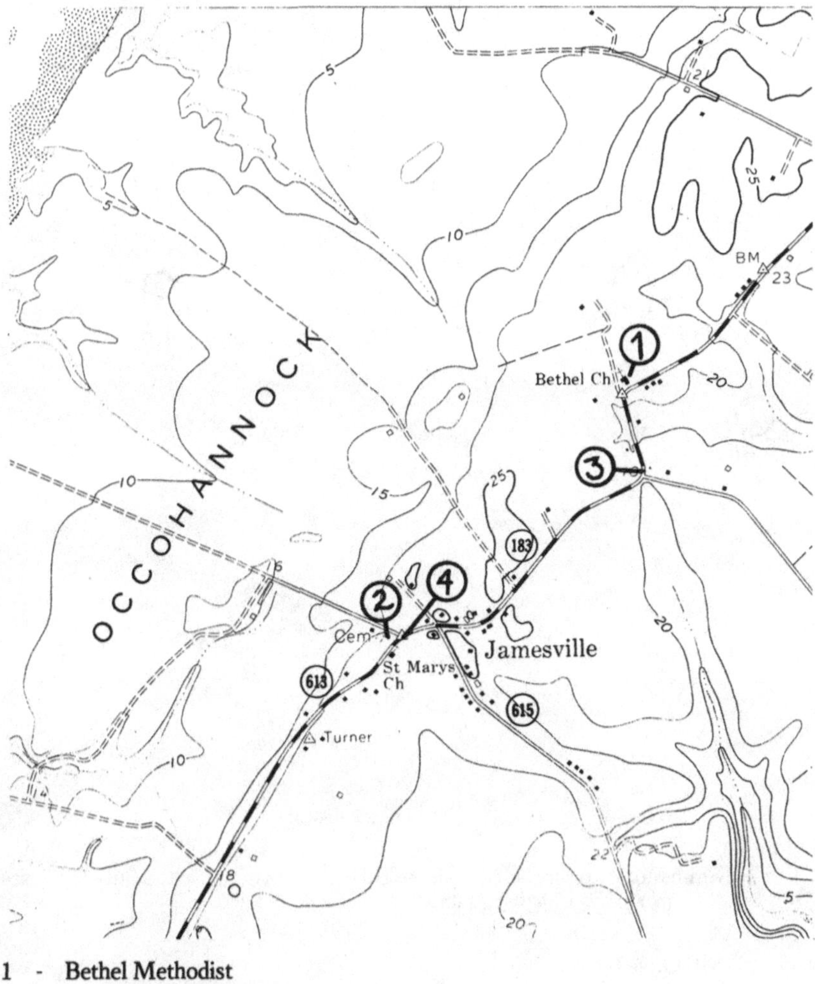

1 - Bethel Methodist
2 - Mt. Zion AME site
3 - Harmony ME: site 1894-c1910
4 - St. Marys Baptist

JENKINS BRIDGE

see: *Emmanuel Episcopal Church*
Mt. Olive Baptist Church
St. John's United Methodist Church

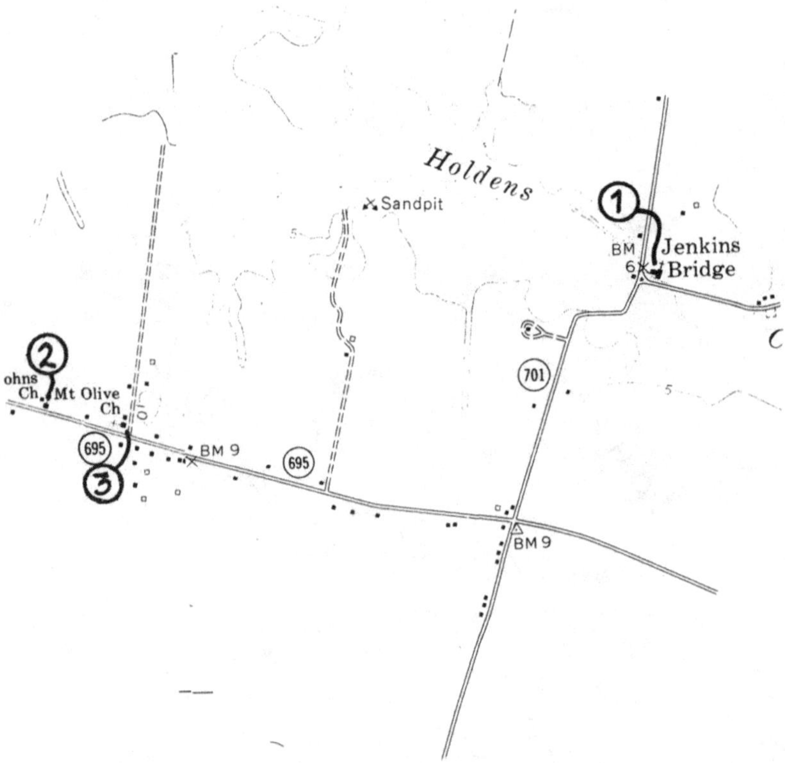

1 - Emmanuel Episcopal: site since 1887 (for original site 1860-1887 see TEMPERANCEVILLE)
2 - St. John's Methodist
3 - Mt. Olive Baptist

JERUSALEM BAPTIST CHURCH

[ESBA 1878]
Temperanceville

Jerusalem Baptist Church was organized by the Reverend James Cluff in 1878, and its original members are believed to have been at first members of First Baptist Church of Mappsville. Prior to the organization they had met for some time in private homes in the Temperanceville area. In 1878 a lot was purchased from Albert Matthews, and the first building erected.

Late in 1908, during the pastorate of Thomas T. Turlington, the third pastor, the church building was completely destroyed by fire. The present church building was occupied in 1910, but not before a number of the congregation, led by George H. T. Byrd, had withdrawn to organize Shiloh Baptist Church in 1909. .

Under H. B. Henderson, the sixth pastor, the congregation purchased a home which was renovated into a parsonage. Henderson was succeeded by Benjamin F. Burton, who led the congregation in the erection of a new parsonage (1955) and the addition of several rooms to the church building (1956). By the end of Burton's pastorate in 1970 the congregation numbered 200, and was one of the stronger churches in the black Association. Another addition to the building was dedicated in 1975, and in 1976 the church became the location of an Eastern Shore extension of Virginia Seminary of Lynchburg.

In all, eight pastors have served this church in its 100 years of existence. The building of 1910, much changed and enlarged, is still in use. The present membership is about 400.

[Sources: 109, 123, 155]

Location: see TEMPERANCEVILLE

JESTER'S CHAPEL METHODIST PROTESTANT CHURCH

(see Signpost United Methodist Church)

JOHNSON'S UNITED METHODIST CHURCH

("Johnson's Chapel")
[ME 1790, ME-S 1845, M 1939, UMC 1968]
Johnsontown

Old Johnson's Church 1857-1858

Five Methodist congregations on the Eastern Shore of Virginia are older than Johnson's (Downing's, Garrison's, Locustville, Drummondtown, and Cokesbury). But Johnson's is the oldest Methodist church in Northampton County, and has occupied its particular plot of ground longer than any other Methodist church on the Shore.

Asbury's first trip into Northampton occurred in October 1789, and on his return trip from the Cape he stopped at the home of Johannes Johnson south of Bridgetown. "We had an open time at Brother Johannes Johnson's," wrote the bishop. Richard Whatcoat was traveling with him, and according to Whatcoat's journal Asbury preached here, and his sermon was followed by exhortations from

Whatcoat and Joseph Everett, and a closing prayer by Jeremiah Cosden, the circuit preacher.

The next year Johnson and his wife Ansley, for a nominal sum, deeded a quarter-acre of land to the denomination "where there is now a Chapel...for the express purpose of building a preaching house on for the use of the Methodist preachers and friendly Clergy of the Church of England (so-called)." The deed is interesting for two reasons: the mention of a chapel already standing makes Johnson's Chapel the second Methodist congregation to erect a meetinghouse, after Garrison's; and the provision for friendly clergy of the Anglican Church bespeaks a fraternal relation with nearby Hungars. Hungars at this time was closed. Hungars Baptist (Red Bank) had been organized for seven years by this date, but not for another four years would it erect a meetinghouse.

From this early date Johnson's became, and remained, one of the strongest churches on the circuit, and one of the few accustomed to regular Sunday preaching. Thomas Smith's revival of 1800-1801 passed lightly over this congregation: "only a few conversions with now and then a quickening." Wrote Smith: "At Johnson's Chapel I labored hard, looked for help and power from on high but the word fell on unbroken ground. I returned to Brother Johnson's and to my chamber and wept because I saw no fruit of my labor." Even so the church prospered and grew. Among the local preachers who gave service there during the first part of the nineteenth century were Montcalm Oldham, George Westcott, Peter Williams, and Luther Nottingham.

In 1845 Johnson's became the first church on the Shore to secede to the Methodist Episcopal Church, South; the vote was 34 to seven. The church became a part of the southern Eastville Circuit in that year, and in 1847 it was the site of the circuit camp meeting, where fifty were converted. In 1851 the congregation received a gift of a stove from Hungars Church, "in consideration of their having kindly given to the Episcopal congregation the use of their Chapel during...repairs (of Hungars)."

The original Johnson's Chapel sat parallel to the road, the pulpit in the south end, the gallery across the north end. In 1857 this building was moved aside and construction on a new one commenced. The fate of the original building after that date is not known. The new one, erected from timber from the lands of Smith Nottingham, was dedicated in 1858 during the pastorate of Cyrus P. Doggett. It, too, had a gallery for the slaves and a vestibule beneath it. This building is still in use (fourth oldest Methodist building on the Shore), but it was extensively remodeled in 1911 when D. G. C. Butts was pastor. The gallery and vestibule were removed, stained glass installed throughout, and two steeples added.

The Woman's Missionary Society of this church, third oldest on the Shore, was organized in 1880. Eliza Scott, the first district secretary of missions work among the southern churches, was a member of Johnson's.

John C. Granberry, who served as pastor of this church in 1849, later became a bishop in the Methodist Episcopal Church, South.

In 1894 Johnson's was placed on a circuit with Franktown, an arrangement that still prevails. The membership of Johnson's is today slightly over 200, and the pastor lives in Franktown.

[Sources: 3, 15, 50, 70, 11, 116, 126]

Location: see TREHERNEVILLE

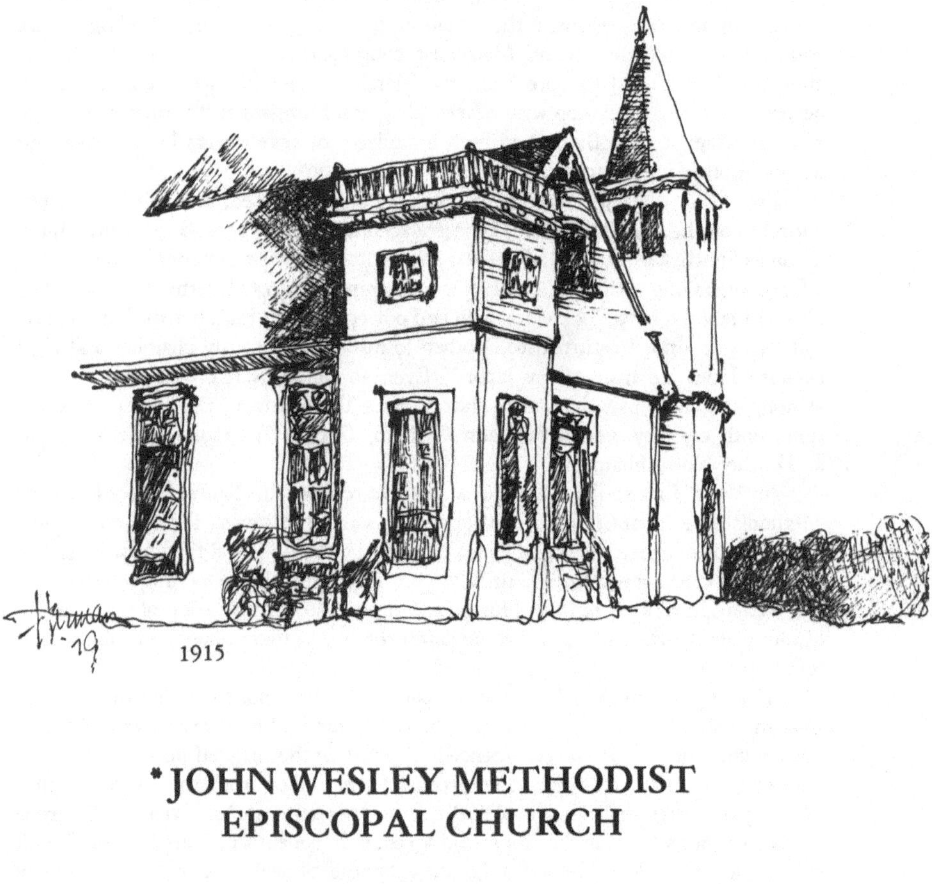

1915

*JOHN WESLEY METHODIST EPISCOPAL CHURCH

[ME 1889-1933]
Exmore

The black Methodists of Exmore faced a hard struggle for survival from the very first. ''At Exmore we have a Sunday school numbering 50 and upward,'' went their report to the Delaware Conference in 1889. ''By permission we held preaching services and Sunday school in a potato house from July to November, at which time the potatoes took their place and we had to close...'' At other times the infant congregation gathered in the home of Mrs. Comfort Brickhouse for worship. By 1894 there were nine members and fourteen probationers, and they purchased a lot and erected a church on the southern end of town at a cost of $1100. Although membership had increased to 54 by 1896, each year the church reported a ''critical financial condition.''

''Here we are in a territory already pre-empted by the Baptists and the African Methodists,'' reported the congregation to the Conference, but still it struggled on. In 1900 its status was changed from mission to charge, and it was joined to Snead's in Accomack County, but together the two churches were still not self-supporting. In 1903, when there were sixteen converts, the church was ''neatly painted, papered, carpeted, fenced in, and they have also purchased a bell.'' The building was again renovated in 1909.

In 1914 the church purchased a lot in Keller, and in two years it had given birth to Mt. Hope Church there. ''A church was badly needed here,'' reported the congregation, but the Keller church grew only at the expense of the mother church in Exmore. By 1919 the Exmore church was again a mission, although it managed to install electric lights in that year and rebuilt the church in 1921.

On October 11, 1924, while it was being served by the local preacher, J. R. Bowdoin, the Exmore church was destroyed by fire. The insurance had not been renewed, and since the congregation still owed $168 on the lot itself, the site was lost. The congregation began meeting in a rented hall, and in two years the membership grew from eight to 25. ''None but a few seem to have been very much interested in assuming the obligation of replacement,'' and the members began to drift away to other churches. The advent of the Depression dealt the final blow, and the church was last listed by the denomination in 1933.

Mt. Hope in Keller, the daughter church, survived the Depression and led in the establishment of a second Exmore church, Spence Memorial, in 1947. This, too, proved to be short-lived, and Methodist work among the blacks of both towns was over by 1968.

Today a service station occupies the site of the John Wesley Church.

[Sources: 110, 113, 124, 129]

Location: see EXMORE

KELLER

see: *Hollies Baptist Church*
Gospel Temple Baptist Church
Keller Church of Christ
Mears Memorial United Methodist Church
**Mt. Hope Methodist Church*
**Keller African Methodist Episcopal Mission*

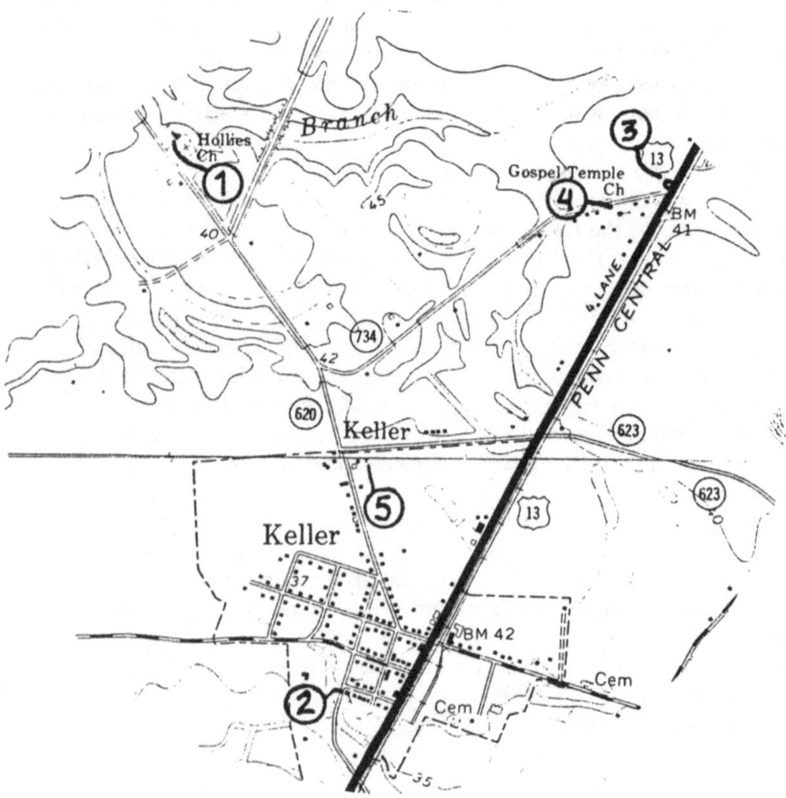

1 - Hollies Baptist
2 - Mears Memorial UMC
3 - Mt. Hope Methodist: site 1914-1967
4 - Gospel Temple Baptist
5 - Keller Church of Christ

Location Unknown: Keller AME Mission 1899-1903

*KELLER AFRICAN METHODIST EPISCOPAL MISSION

("Onley Mission")
[AME 1893-1903?]
Keller

At the turn of the century the African Methodist Episcopal Church attempted to establish a church on the railroad in the central part of the Shore. This work apparently began in 1893, when the Onley Mission was first listed with John R. West as pastor. West served the mission until 1898, when he was succeeded by Sam Poulson, who also served Mt. Olive A.M.E. Church in Hack's Neck.

Onley Mission drops from the records after 1898, but the following year the Keller Mission makes its first appearance, with S. P. Drummond as pastor. Drummond is said to have organized a Sunday school in Keller and purchased half an acre for the erection of a church building.

No church was ever built, and there is no mention of either mission after 1903. That these two missions were, as described here, essentially the same work is not certain. Since, however, they are not listed simultaneously, it seems likely that this short-lived A.M.E. work began in Onley, moved to Keller, and then disappeared from the scene altogether.

[Source: 7]

Location: Unknown

KELLER CHURCH OF CHRIST

("Accomack Church of Christ")
[Independent 1974]
Keller

This congregation, a mission of the Norfolk Church of Christ, was established in 1974 by Gregory Selby. Before the erection of the church building services were held in the Onancock armory.

The church building was erected in 1976 on land purchased from Preston Mears. When the Keller site was occupied, the congregation dropped its earlier name, Accomack Church of Christ.

This is one of several new fundamentalist churches that constitute the growing conservative fringe on the Eastern Shore. It is as yet a small congregation.

[Sources: 109, 123]

Location: see KELLER

*KIDD'S CHAPEL BAPTIST CHURCH

(see Baker Memorial Baptist Church)

KINGDOM HALL OF JEHOVAH'S WITNESSES, CHINCOTEAGUE CONGREGATION

[WBTS 1926]

Temperanceville

Ervin Thomas Liddell, the former Baptist minister turned independent evangelist, was inadvertently the cause of the founding of this congregation. Liddell, at one time pastor of Union Baptist Church on Chincoteague Island and later associated with Christ's Sanctified Holy Church there, conducted a series of evangelistic meetings at which he distributed materials printed by the Watchtower Bible & Tract Society, the parent corporation of Jehovah's Witnesses. Interested islanders answered an announcement in these materials and contacted the Society, and in September 1926 a man named VanAmberg arrived from New York and organized the new congregation.

The infant congregation was nurtured by members of the Cursin family, who arrived on the island shortly after VanAmberg's departure and lived for some time among the members. The first Witnesses on the island were for the most part from the Deep Hole community and frequently gathered there in private homes. Public meetings were at times held in a rented building downtown, but ultimately the Witnesses established their first Kingdom Hall in a small building in Deep Hole.

By 1955 the congregation had grown to 23 members. The following year a lot for a permanent Kingdom Hall was offered to them, not on the island but west of Makemie Park. Unable to build at that time, the congregation turned down the offer. When at last the old building in Deep Hole was abandoned, a new Kingdom Hall was opened in the second story of a rented store downtown, just north of the bridge.

In 1975 the Jehovah's Witnesses at last began construction of a permanent Kingdom Hall, located just north of Temperanceville. The congregation gathered temporarily in a rented building in Wattsville until the new structure was occupied late in 1975.

Although located now in Temperanceville, the congregation is still referred to as the Chincoteague congregation. The group is now larger than it has ever been before. The average attendance at meetings is about seventy, but it is not unusual for more than 100 people to gather in the new Kingdom Hall.

[Sources: 123, 176]

Location: see CHINCOTEAGUE, TEMPERANCEVILLE, WATTSVILLE

KINGDOM HALL OF JEHOVAH'S WITNESSES, EXMORE CONGREGATION

[WBTS 1920]
Exmore

A lone pioneer or "colporteur," his name long since forgotten, came preaching the Jehovah's Witness faith to the lower part of the Shore in 1920, and Tucker Mears, who lived near Cedar View Wharf, was the first to hear. Mears was soon converted to the new faith, and was instrumental in gathering a small congregation. The first public meeting was held in the Idle Hour Theatre in Belle Haven. The congregation later assembled on the second floor of a local drugstore, before outfitting a former hat shop as a Kingdom Hall in 1922.

In this area the Witnesses were spared much of the public disapproval that beset them in other parts of the country, but their growth, though steady, was slow. An impetus to growth and public approval occurred in 1937 when Nathan Knorr, a prominent Witness who later became its national president, visited the Shore and spoke in Redmen's Hall in Exmore.

The tiny hat shop served the congregation for more than twenty years. A church lot was obtained from Haywood and Claudette Ward in 1944, and three years later the present Kingdom Hall was completed there. This building was subsequently enlarged and improved several times, and the lot increased by the purchase of adjacent lands in 1956 and 1971.

By 1952, when hundreds of Witnesses from all over Delmarva gathered at Keller fairgrounds for a "circuit assembly," the Exmore congregation was already racially mixed. It has been ever since, one of the few congregations of any faith on the Shore where blacks and whites have worshiped together for decades.

Today this congregation serves an area stretching north from Cape Charles to Accomac. As many as 100 worshipers crowd into the small building for worship services, of whom fully eighty are active "publishers" of the Witnesses' message. Notable among the many pillars of this congregation over the years is Haywood Ward of Exmore, who served as a missionary to Ethiopia and today still serves the church in Baltimore.

[Sources: 110, 124, 176]

Location: see EXMORE

LEATHERBURY UNITED METHODIST CHURCH

[ME 1872, M 1939, UMC 1968]
Chesconnessex

This church bears the name of its founder, the Reverend Perry Leatherbury (18??-1897), a local preacher of the Cokesbury congregation in Onancock. Shortly after the Civil War, Leatherbury began holding meetings in the area of Chesconnessex, assisted by his daughter Edith, who played a portable organ and led the congregational singing. In 1872 a lot was purchased and a building erected. Two years later the Wilmington Conference first recorded the presence of the congregation and granted it $200 in aid.

Leatherbury was originally erected a short distance east of its present site. There it was rebuilt and enlarged in 1893. In 1913 the congregation moved the building to its present site, which was deeded to the church two years later. In 1942, a former schoolhouse across the street was purchased, moved, and annexed to the building. And in 1969 Bishop Paul Herrick visited the church to dedicate $12,000 worth of subsequent additions and improvements. The building is thus an amalgam of several separate structures, as can be seen by viewing it from the south.

Perry Leatherbury continued to serve this church until his death, and throughout the early history of the congregation it was attached to and associated with Cokesbury and the other northern Methodist churches founded from Cokesbury. In 1947 Leatherbury became a part of the Cashville Charge, and since then its pastor has lived in Cashville.

Although it sits in a rural area, Leatherbury has remained a strong and vigorous church. Its present membership is about 125.

[Sources: 110, 112, 116, 117, 123, 153, 176]

Location: see CHESCONNESSEX

LEE MONT

see: *Calvary United Methodist Church*
Faith Assembly of God
**Lee Mont Baptist Church*
**Lee Mont Methodist Protestant Church*

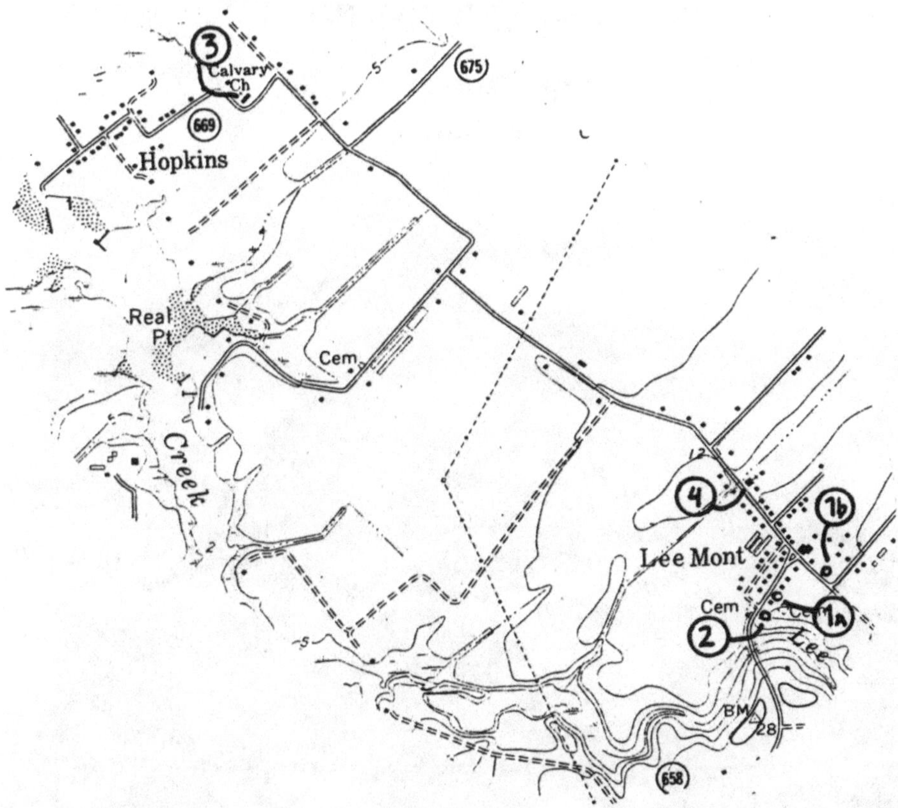

1a - Lee Mont MP: first site 1839-1898
1b - Lee Mont MP: second site 1898-1938
2 - Lee Mont Baptist: site 1878-1893 (approximate)
3 - Calvary UMC
4 - Faith Assembly of God

LEE MONT BAPTIST CHURCH

(see Parksley Baptist Church)

*LEE MONT METHODIST PROTESTANT CHURCH

[MP 1839-1938]
Lee Mont

(third building; photo c. 1915)

Lee Mont, while not the oldest Methodist Protestant church on the Shore, was certainly the central church of half of that denomination's work in Accomack County.

The first Lee Mont church was built in 1839, two years after the Northampton Circuit was created. It stood on half an acre east of the road leading south out of town, and was called "Fodder House," since it had been constructed out of an old barn.

This building was replaced by a new one on the same site in 1870. A third building was erected in 1898 at the corner of the road leading to Parksley. The congregation met in Lee Mont Baptist Church while this building was being erected. The second building was moved away and made into a store.

Lee Mont, known for much of its history as "Harmony" in denominational records, was the mother church of no fewer than five other congregations: Reese Chapel (1855), Conquest Chapel (1887), Hunting Creek (1888), Grace in Parksley (1892), and Grant Memorial (1893). It was indirectly the mother of Hallwood M.P., which was founded from Conquest Chapel in 1903. Except for Conquest Chapel and Hallwood, all these churches were at various times grouped together in circuits served by the same pastors. The final charge alignment was fixed in 1917, when Hunting Creek (Calvary) and Lee Mont were joined to form the Accomac Charge.

In 1915 the congregation raised the building and added a basement beneath it, and made other improvements on the building in 1921. However in 1938, as Unification approached, the building caught fire and burned to the ground, a total loss. Dr. A. E. Sexsmith, president of the Maryland Annual Conference, was making his annual visit to the Shore at the time and arrived just in time to see the building in flames. The church was never rebuilt. The denomination declared Lee Mont closed and the Accomac Circuit discontinued. Lee Mont had long since been eclipsed in size and importance by her daughter church, Grace in Parksley, and that church inherited its prestige and most of its members.

[Sources: 109, 114, 123, 145, 176]

Location: see LEE MONT

LEE'S BETHEL

(see Swain Memorial United Methodist Church)

LOCUST GROVE CHURCH OF GOD

(see Community Church of God)

LOCUSTVILLE

see: Locustville United Methodist Church

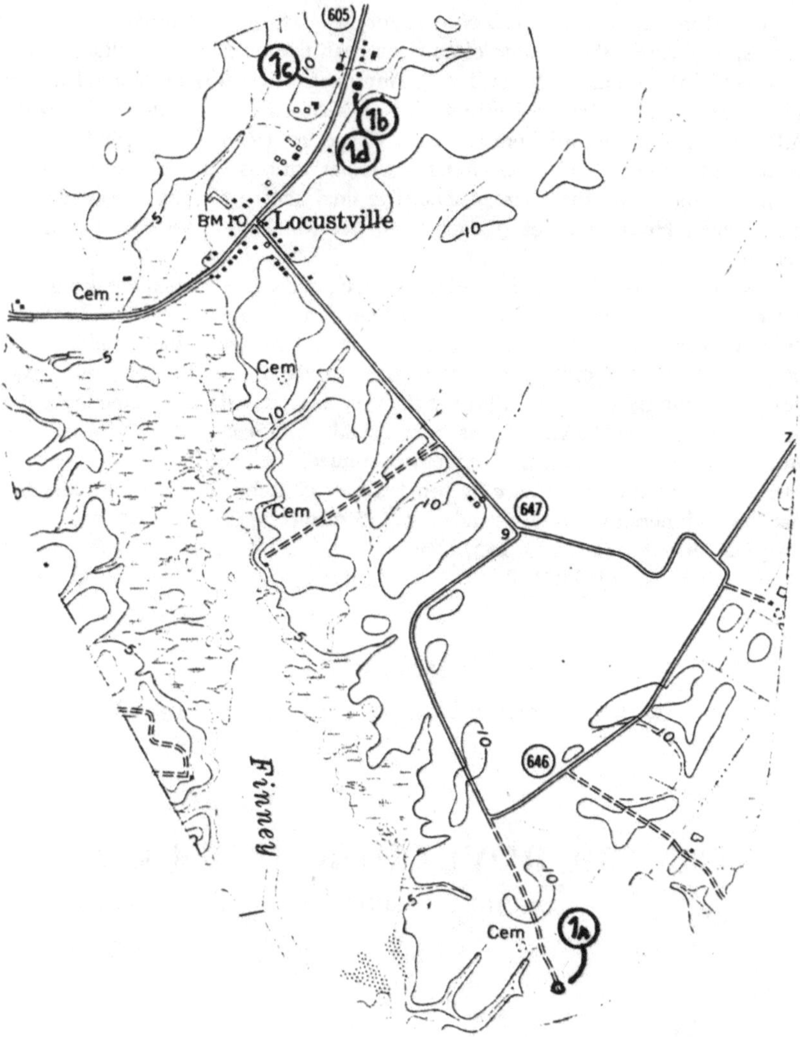

1a - Locustville Methodist: site of "Belle Vue," Paramore home and church site until 1816
1b - Locustville Methodist: site of Wesley 1816-1878
1c - Locustville Methodist: all buildings since 1878
1d - Locustville Methodist: building of 1878 moved to this site 1922

LOCUSTVILLE UNITED METHODIST CHURCH

("Paramore's," "Wesley," "Deep Creek," "Duncan Memorial") [ME 1784, ME-S 1860, M 1939, UMC 1968] Locustville

Locustville shares with Garrison's the distinction of being the second oldest Methodist congregation on the Eastern Shore of Virginia. There has been some sort of Methodist activity in this community since 1784. Only Downing's in Oak Hall can claim a longer history.

The Locustville church is descended from the society that first gathered in Belle Vue, the home of Colonel William Paramore of Locustville. Asbury visited Paramore in 1784 and described the Paramore family as "kind; the father, mother, son and niece have tender impressions." The bishop returned in 1787, 1789, and 1791, and by then Paramore was one of the leading Methodists on the Virginia Shore. In 1787 he was one of the trustees of Garrison's Chapel, and in that same year he freed his slaves, as Methodist practice required.

By 1800, when Thomas Smith's revival spread across Accomack County, as many as 500 persons were gathering for preaching at Paramore's home. The society flourished here and continued to meet at Belle Vue until 1816, the year of Paramore's death. At that time the meetings were moved to a schoolhouse in the village of Locustville, and shortly thereafter the congregation erected "Wesley," its first meetinghouse. Thomas Paramore, son of William, deeded the land to the church in 1822, and the deed called the building "the house called Deep Creek meeting house." The first person converted in the building is said to have been the Methodist preacher, Benjamin T. Ames.

Locustville seceded to the Methodist Episcopal Church, South, in 1860, and was closed by order of the Union army for a few weeks in 1864.

In 1878 the church purchased the present church lot from Thomas James and erected there a new building known as Duncan Memorial, for the Reverend James A. Duncan (1830-1877) of the Virginia Conference. The Wesley building stood abandoned across the street from it until sometime after 1915. In 1891 Onley Church was founded from Locustville.

In 1923 the congregation moved the second building aside, to the old Wesley site, and erected the present church building from plans suggested by the denomination. The older building was dismantled shortly thereafter. During the middle part of the twentieth century the congregation used the abandoned building of old Locustville Academy, next door to the old site, for social and community events.

As in so many other places on the Shore, this old congregation was in time eclipsed by its daughter church, Onley. In this century Locustville's charge affiliations have shifted several times. It is at present on the Melfa Charge, which was created in 1956. The present membership of Locustville is about eighty.

[Sources: 3, 15, 39, 70, 101, 110, 111, 116, 123, 176]

Location: see LOCUSTVILLE

LOWER NORTHAMPTON BAPTIST CHURCH

[ABA 1776]
Dalbys

Lower Northampton Baptist Church is, by date of organization (1778), the fourth oldest existing congregation on the Eastern Shore, after Hungars (1646), St. George's (1676), and Downing's (1772). Neither Hungars nor St. George's has, however, been continuously active since their formation, and activity at Downing's cannot be authenticated in the written record to earlier than 1783. Lower Northampton is, then, indeed historic. It is not only the oldest Baptist church on the Shore, but the oldest continuous congregation of any denomination whose existence can be authenticated by the written record.

After he arrived on the Shore on Easter Sunday 1776, the Baptist pioneer Elijah Baker labored for two years before he succeeded in organizing this church, and even then there were only five members in his congregation. Baker served as pastor until his death in 1798, and in that time he saw Lower Northampton grow into a vigorous and prosperous congregation.

The first building of this congregation stood by 1785, when Nathaniel Goffigon gave the land on which it stood. This location is not known today, for in 1798 after Baker's death, Goffigon exchanged it for another lot, the present one, and the second building was erected there soon afterwards.

As early as 1787 the Methodists were noting with disapproval that the region served by Lower Northampton was tainted with "Antinomianism," but this church remained relatively free of that thinking and prospered accordingly. By 1809, when the Accomack Baptist Association was founded, Lower Northampton had 219 members and was the largest Baptist church on the Shore. When the Association divided over the missions issue in 1831, Lower Northampton remained with the Association and led the other churches in number of new members gained in 1832 and 1834. There was a Domestic Missionary Society at the church as early as 1834. The first Sunday school was in operation by 1836, and the members were giving to foreign missions by 1848.

By 1869 Lower Northampton was in its third building, and from it in the last half of the century the congregation assisted in the formation of new congregations at Eastville (1877), Cheriton (1889), Cedar Grove (1898), and Oyster (1908). The formation of Cedar Grove proved almost fatal to the church, for Cedar Grove grew at the expense of Lower Northampton, many of whose members lived closer to the new church than to the old. Although only nineteen persons left Lower Northampton to form Cedar Grove in 1898, twenty years later Cedar Grove had surpassed Lower Northampton in membership, and the older church was declining in numbers.

The present building was erected in 1913, one of the earliest in a long line of brick churches erected up and down the Shore in the early part of the twentieth century. The earlier third building was moved aside, and is today part of the building of Greater Mt. Sinai Gospel Tabernacle in Fairview. Fire destroyed a considerable part of the interior of the new church in 1958 and again in 1974, but each time the damage was repaired in a short time. An educational building was erected behind the church in 1976.

By 1956 there were only 29 members at Lower Northampton, and they were without a pastor. The congregation, "believing that the interests of the Kingdom in Lower Northampton County would be served best by one Baptist church rather than two," invited the Cedar Grove congregation to take over its property and merge the two churches. The merger was effected on Easter Sunday 1956, and the daughter church became again a part of the parent congregation. With merger the membership of the church increased sharply to 175.

Since 1956 Lower Northampton has been a station church, and the parsonage is located in Townsend.

[Sources: 3, 52, 69, 70, 71, 122, 136, 139]

Location: see DALBYS

MACEDONIA AFRICAN METHODIST EPISCOPAL CHURCH

("Drummondtown")
[AME 1865]
Accomac

Macedonia is the oldest African Methodist Episcopal congregation on the Eastern Shore of Virginia and, after Union Baptist in Eastville and Friendship Methodist in Wattsville, the third oldest black church in the two counties. James H. A. Johnson founded the congregation on December 27, 1865, with eighteen charter members. His sermon text that day was from Psalm 62: "Trust in Him at all times, ye people, pour out your heart before Him; God is a refuge for us."

It is apparent that the new black congregation occupied the building of the white Drummondtown Methodist congregation, seized by the Union army in 1861 and subsequently abandoned by them. This building remained officially in the hands of the army until 1870, and it was presumably with permission from the occupying forces that the A.M.E. congregation met there.

In 1871 the white Methodists reclaimed their building, and the A.M.E. congregation under the Reverend Robert Davis was faced with the need for a building of their own. A lot on the southern edge of town was secured and on it was erected a church designed also "to be used as a School House for the tuition and education therein of the colored people." This building, although it has since been changed and improved many times, is still in use, and it shares with Bethel A.M.E. in Onancock, built at the same time, one distinctive feature indicating its original use as a schoolhouse; the sanctuary is on the second floor.

Although it was the earliest A.M.E. church, Drummondtown was very quickly eclipsed by the newer church founded in Onancock in 1868. By 1870, when the Drummondtown congregation was still in its borrowed building, there was a substantial church building in Onancock. The same pastor served both congregations, but the circuit was known not as "Drummondtown" but "Onancock." Robert Davis was the last pastor to serve both churches. In 1875 the Drummondtown Circuit was created, with J. W. Ruff as pastor. Five years later the new circuit consisted of three churches: Macedonia, St. Luke's in Daugherty, and Christian Union in Modest Town.

John H. Thomas was pastor in 1889 when the congregation erected a parsonage near the church and first became a station. The attempt to become independent was not entirely successful, and for the next decade the congregation had frequently to return to the fold of the circuit. However in 1899, during James Mackey's pastorate, the church became a self-supporting station and has remained so virtually ever since. The first two decades of the twentieth century were a time of growth and prosperity for the church. The debt on the parsonage was liquidated, the building renovated in 1912, and additional land adjacent to the church obtained for parking in 1919. One pastor, the Reverend George Williams, died while serving the church in 1905.

The members of this church were pioneers of public education for Negroes in this community. Robert Davis, the builder, taught school on this site during his pastorate here, and from the very first this location was both a religious and an educational site. It is not without significance that in 1932, when Accomack County erected its first consolidated Negro high school, it was built adjacent to this church.

Macedonia has remained a strong and vigorous church over the years. The building has received the constant care and attention of the people, and the most recent improvements occurred in 1976 when stained glass windows were installed throughout.

[Sources: 7, 123]

Location: see ACCOMAC

MACEDONIA BAPTIST CHURCH

[ESBA 1901]
Bloxom

This church was founded from First Baptist Church of Mappsville. By the turn of the century there were a number of members of First Baptist living near Bloxom who felt the "need of some place of worship near or in this...community." In 1901 a lot was purchased, and in 1903 First Baptist dismissed some of its members to establish Macedonia.

It is said that D. B. Savage, the first pastor, was not only the founder of the church but also the builder, the man chiefly responsible for the erection of the building itself. The original building is still in use, although there have been many changes and improvements made to it over the years. The church grounds were increased by the acquisition of adjoining property for a cemetery in 1927. In 1951 the congregation purchased an abandoned school building next door for use as a church hall.

It was under the sixth pastor, A. H. Brown, that this congregation first began to meet for worship every Sunday, in the early 1960's. Macedonia has never been a large church, and there is no parsonage.

[Sources: 123, 129]

Location: see BLOXOM

*MACEDONIA CHRISTIAN CHURCH OF THE USA

[Independent? 1915-1925?]
Eastville

This short-lived congregation enters the record in 1915, when it purchased the property of the Eastville Methodist Episcopal mission, abandoned since 1896, for $525.

Almost nothing is known of the life of this congregation. It was a black church, but the denomination of which it was a part, if it was part of a denomination, has not been determined; it may have been an independent congregation of local origin. It is not known how long the church functioned, and the date assigned here is purely conjectural.

By 1940 the building was a thing of the past, and Nellie Sykes was the sole surviving member. In that year the land was sold to Charles Toy. The site is now farmland, and the fate of the building which began as a Methodist church is not known.

[Source: 124]

Location: see EASTVILLE

MACHIPONGO

*see: *Macon Union Chapel*

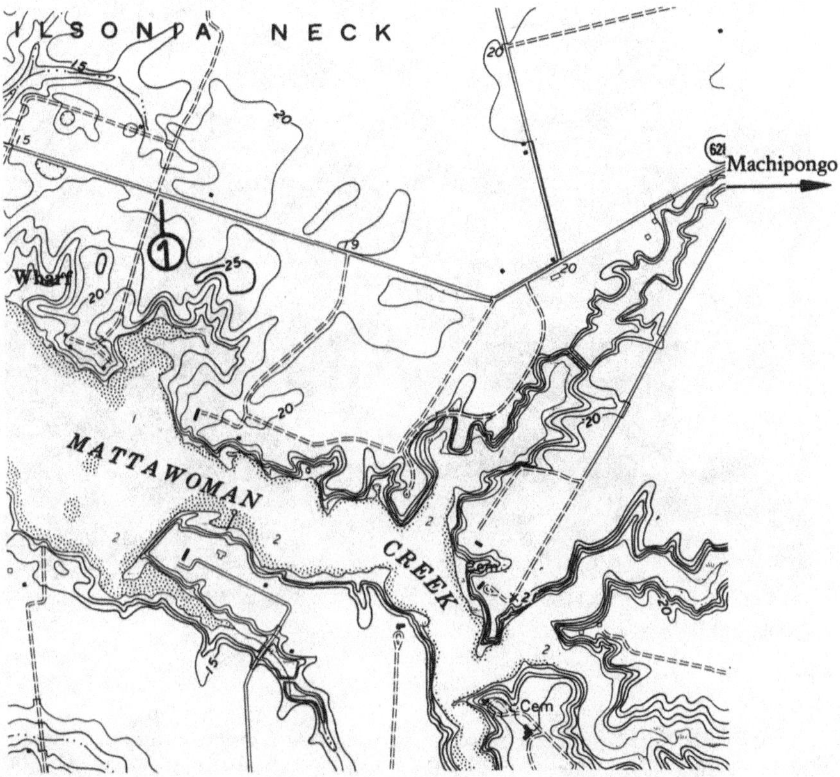

1 - Macon Union Chapel: site 1904-c1935

*MACON UNION CHAPEL

[Interdenominational 1904-1927?]
Wilsonia Neck

(photo 1913)

Wilsonia Neck, west of Machipongo, was at the turn of the century much more thickly settled than today. The most prominent citizens of the area were Mr. and Mrs. William Bullitt Fitzhugh, he at one time a member of the House of Delegates. In 1904 the Fitzhughs founded and built Macon Union Chapel, an interdenominational community church, to serve the people of the neck. Mrs. Fitzhugh was of the Macon family, and the chapel was named in her honor.

The building was virtually complete by the end of 1904, and speakers who had already led services there included local Baptist and Methodist preachers and Bishop A. M. Randolph of the Episcopal Church. The official dedication of the building on September 18, 1908, was "strictly a union affair." Dr. William E. Hatcher (Baptist), Rev. J. T. McBride (Presbyterian), and Rev. D. G. C. Butts (Methodist) all preached on that occasion.

The Fitzhughs remained the guiding force behind the chapel throughout the years of its existence, he as superintendent of the Sunday school, she as organist.

The chapel was widely attended not only by the people of Wilsonia Neck, but also by residents of Church Neck who came by boat across Hungars Creek. Local black residents also worshiped in the building alongside whites.

The only regular event at the chapel was the weekly Sunday school. At first local preachers of the different denominations took turns preaching there, usually on Sunday afternoons, but in its later years the chapel saw preaching services only two or three times a year. There was the usual round of church fairs and socials, lectures and concerts, some of the lecturers engaged by Fitzhugh from New York City. Christmas functions in particular seem to have been popular at the chapel; in 1905 as many as 500 people attended the Christmas festivities.

In time activity at the chapel, like the population of Wilsonia Neck, declined, and the building ceased to be used after the late 1920's. The little frame structure, complete with its stained glass windows, stood abandoned for about a decade. In the 1930's it was purchased by Charles Collins, dismantled, and the lumber used in the construction of a nearby home. For many years afterwards the only sign of the church was the old pump organ, which Collins left outdoors on the old site. It has since crumbled into dust, and when in recent years Collins' home burned, all traces of this unusual community church vanished.

[Sources: 108, 176]

Location: see MACHIPONGO

MAGOTHY BAY CHAPEL

(see Capeville United Methodist Church)

*MAGOTHY CHURCH

[CE 1691?-1784]

Dalbys

Historic Magothy Church was erected soon after 1691, when the Upper and Lower Parishes of Northampton County were reunited into one Hungars Parish. At his death two years earlier in 1689, Colonel John Stringer of Northampton bequeathed the new church 1000 pounds of tobacco for furnishings.

Magothy was apparently a substantial brick building, its walls as much as 28 inches thick. The only other brick church on the Shore at this time was the Assawoman Church at the other end of the Shore.

It was at Magothy in 1887 that the Baptist Elijah Baker began his work on the Shore, that Samuel McCroskey, the rector, preached against him, and that some members withdrew to form Lower Northampton Baptist Church. Shortly thereafter, in 1784, the Church of England ceased to be the state church in Virginia, and Magothy fell into disuse and abandonment.

In 1819 the Episcopal Church began to reestablish its work in Northampton, and an attempt was made to repair the ruined church. The attempt proved unsuccessful. The church was sold in 1826, and William Jarvis used the bricks in the erection of his home, "Piney Forest," just to the south.

Christ Church in Eastville is the successor to Magothy. In the year in which Magothy was sold Episcopal services were begun in the county seat, and two years later Christ Church was erected there. That congregation still owns a communion service given to Magothy Bay Church by John Custis in 1741, and a silver plate presented by Governor Nicholson about 1692.

[Sources: 62, 70]

Location: see DALBYS

MAKEMIE PARK

see: **Makemie Park Baptist Church*
St. John's Faith Church of God Live On
Smyrna Assembly of Yashua Disciples

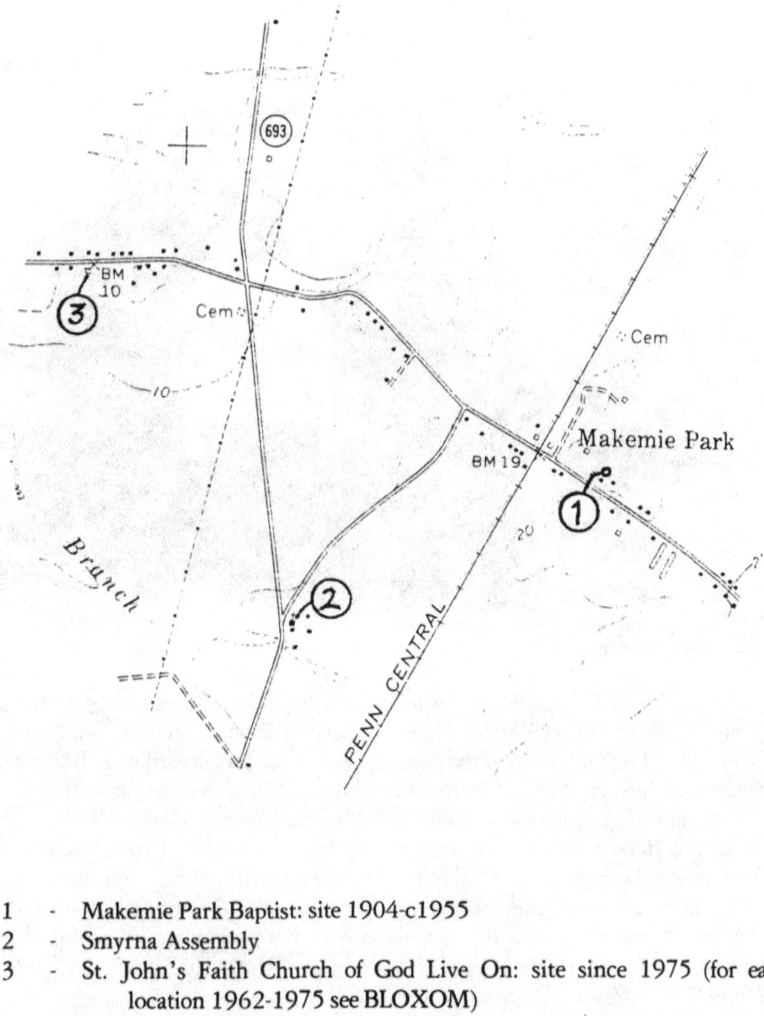

1 - Makemie Park Baptist: site 1904-c1955
2 - Smyrna Assembly
3 - St. John's Faith Church of God Live On: site since 1975 (for earlier location 1962-1975 see BLOXOM)

*MAKEMIE PARK BAPTIST CHURCH

(''Bloomtown'')
[ABA 1902-1937]
Makemie Park

Makemie Park Baptist Church steeple, only known view of the church

The village of Bloomtown grew up around the railroad west of Temperanceville, and in 1902 Walter Rhodes, pastor of Atlantic Baptist Church, established a mission there. The lot on which the church was erected was deeded in 1904, and in that year Bloomtown Baptist Church was admitted to the Accomack Association.

The name of the village was changed to Makemie Park in 1908, and with it the name of the Baptist church was changed to bear the name of the Presbyterian pioneer. Makemie Park Baptist Church remained a small congregation throughout its short history, its field alignments often changing. The last listing in the records of the Association are from 1932, when there were 34 members, preaching every other Sunday, a total yearly budget of $380, and a pastor shared with four other churches (Hall's Chapel, Hallwood, Saxis, and Shiloh).

In 1937 the Accomack Baptist Association reported that ''[Baker Memorial and] Makemie Park Churches have ceased to function. No services of any kind, either Sunday School or preaching are now held in these Churches. The members have withdrawn and gone to other churches...'' The church building stood on a side road that has now disappeared, north of the main road through the village.

It was a small clapboard building with a steeple. Benches, piano, and attendance board all remained in place for years while the building decayed around them. The church finally collapsed during a storm in the mid-1950's, and there is no evidence of its presence there today.

[Sources: 69, 105, 122, 123, 132. 176]

Location: see MAKEMIE PARK

MAKEMIE PRESBYTERIAN CHURCH

[Pres 1837]

Accomac

Francis Makemie had been dead for more than a century, and Presbyterianism virtually dormant on the Virginia Shore for more than a generation, when the East Hanover Presbytery sent the Reverend Leonidas L. Smith to reestablish the faith in Accomack in 1836. On August 13, 1837, the first permanent Presbyterian congregation on the Eastern Shore of Virginia was organized in Drummondtown by the Reverend John Daniel Matthews. There were two charter members.

The reestablishment of Presbyterianism on the Shore is said to have had a political context. Henry A. Wise moved back to Accomack County in 1830 and was in 1833 elected to Congress. Wise's wife was Anne Jennings Wise, and her father was a Presbyterian minister in Pennsylvania. Her father is said to have been the source of the suggestion to the Presbytery that a church be established in Drummondtown. If his motive were to make certain that his daughter had a church nearby to attend, it came to naught, for Anne Jennings Wise died in 1837.

The infant congregation erected their new building on Back Street on a lot purchased in 1840. One of the two charter members was William H. Beach, formerly of New York City. Through his efforts, the new building was furnished with furniture from Brick Church in that city. The congregation grew quite slowly. There were eight members in 1840. Three members were dismissed to aid in the formation of Holmes Presbyterian in Northampton County in 1846.

In 1861 the Union Army occupied Drummondtown, and the Presbyterian church was requisitioned for use as a stable for the soldiers' horses. The interior of the building, like that of the Methodist church just down the street, was ruined, but Dr. Edward J. Young, a local member, was able to rescue the pulpit and pulpit chairs. These he returned to the congregation when services were resumed after the war, and the congregation constructed simple benches out of rough-hewn dogwood to go with them.

The last quarter of the nineteenth century was the most prosperous in the life of this church. Pastors and people of Makemie led in the formation of two new congregations, Naomi Makemie in Onancock (1883) and Clarke in Daugherty (1894). The congregation numbered 116, its highest point, in 1900.

In 1895, during this prosperous period, the congregation redecorated the interior of the building, much to the displeasure of some members. Once again the pulpit furniture left the building, this time to the keeping of Miss Sarah Poulson, a local member, as a "peace offering." Matching light oak pulpit and pews were installed, typical of the period. They remained in use until 1925, when shortly before her death Sarah Poulson offered the original pulpit furniture to the congregation again on the condition that the interior of the church be restored to its original appearance. This restoration was accomplished with success, and the building, fifth oldest church building on the Eastern Shore of Virginia, looks today substantially as it did when it was first erected.

Makemie has declined steadily in membership in this century and is today, with only 24 members, the second smallest Presbyterian church on the Shore. Throughout much of its history it has shared its pastor with Naomi Makemie in Onancock, and it still does today.

[Sources: 43, 119, 120]

Location: see ACCOMAC

*MALLALIEU METHODIST EPISCOPAL CHURCH

(see Parksley Methodist Episcopal Church)

MAPPSVILLE

see: *First Baptist Church*
Mappsville Baptist Church

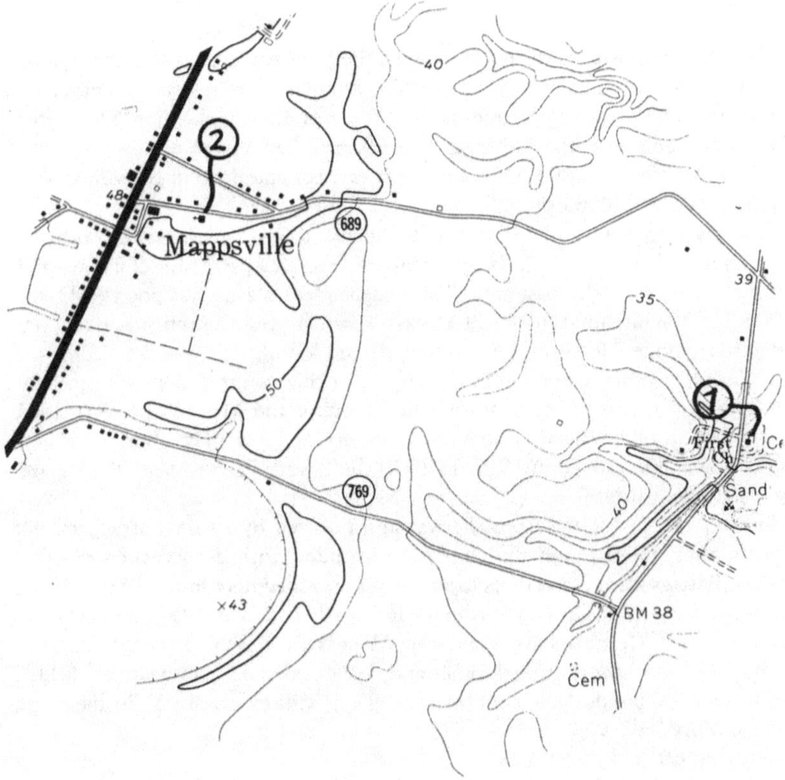

1 - First Baptist
2 - Mappsville Baptist

MAPPSVILLE BAPTIST CHURCH

[ABA 1888]
Mappsville

The white Baptists of Mappsville erected their church even before the congregation was officially established. Mappsville Baptist Church was organized on February 19, 1888, by which time the building was already standing. Dr. Alfred E. Dickinson, editor of the *Religious Herald*, preached at the dedication of the building on March 12, 1893. Oliver Baker, a layman and deacon, is credited with being the "founder" of the church.

From its inception until 1901, Mappsville was served by the pastors of Bethel Baptist Church. Early in 1902, the congregation erected a parsonage of its own and called E. S. Pierce to the pastorate. This independent status was short-lived, for by 1903 T. C. Whitehurst, pastor of Modest Town Baptist Church, was filling the pulpit at Mappsville. His successors continued to do so until 1935.

The most prosperous period in the history of this congregation was probably the first third of the twentieth century. The Reverend and Mrs. W. E. Warren led in the formation of a Woman's Missionary Society in 1911. The church building was enlarged and improved in 1927. In 1930 there were 78 members, the highest in the church's history.

From 1935 to 1939 Mappsville was again served by its own preachers, but the years after 1939 found the church again allied with a succession of other churches. Pastors from Drummondtown Baptist preached here from 1939 to 1946, and pastors from Modest Town from 1946 to 1951. Since 1951 the pastors of Atlantic Baptist Church have filled the Mappsville pulpit, although the two churches are independent of each other and do not officially constitute a "field."

The original building, erected before 1888, is still in use. In 1976 the membership at Mappsville was 36.

[Sources: 69, 110, 122, 123]

Location: see MAPPSVILLE

MARINER'S CHAPEL METHODIST EPISCOPAL CHURCH

(see Swain Memorial United Methodist Church)

MARKET STREET UNITED METHODIST CHURCH
[ME 1788, ICA 1861, ME-S 1866, M 1939, UMC 1968]
Onancock

a - prior to 1898 renovations

The largest Methodist church on the Eastern Shore of Virginia has had a long, involved, and well-documented history, dating from the day Francis Asbury first preached in Onancock in 1788. Much of the story is told, however, in the history of Cokesbury Church and Bascom's Chapel, to which this church fell heir. This sketch tells the story of the congregation beginning only at that relatively late date when the name and present site of Market Street Church were taken.

In 1882 the southern Methodists of Onancock abandoned Bascom's Chapel on King Street, site and name, and became Market Street Methodist Episcopal Church, South. The lot was purchased from Thomas Richardson and deeded after his death by his daughter, Georgie Quinby. The completed building was dedicated by Rev. W. W. Walker on November 9, 1884, and cost about $1800. The new church was a rectangular building topped by a central steeple, and the facade facing the street sported two spires and a front porch.

In 1898 work began on the renovation of this church, and the building was altered almost beyond recognition. The central steeple was removed and in its place

b - about 1910

c - following tornado damage 1977

arose two Romanesque towers of unequal size, flanking a beautiful new rose window of stained glass. The whole of the church was covered with brown shingles, and the interior balcony removed. Further interior renovations were made in 1915, and shortly thereafter an educational annex was added to the back of the building.

By now Market Street had long since outstripped Cokesbury as the larger Methodist church in Onancock, and it was one of the leading churches on the district. Up until 1915 it was joined with Andrew Chapel on a circuit, but in that year it became a station. It has remained a station ever since, except between 1947 and 1960, when Cokesbury was attached to it.

An extensive educational annex was added at the back of the church in 1950, and another in 1957. A pipe organ was installed in 1953 and a full-time professional minister of music hired in 1960.

By the beginning of the 1970's the congregation, cramped in their aging building, were laying plans to relocate in a new structure on the edge of town. In time, however, the church was able to secure more parking space at the old site and chose to renovate the building. Four small outside towers were added to reinforce the structure and provide elevators to the second-story sanctuary. At the same time the interior was remodeled and restored to its original Victorian appearance. These renovations, costing over $200,000, were dedicated by Bishop W. Kenneth Goodson on January 30, 1977.

A few weeks later, on April 5, 1977, a tornado swept through Onancock and struck the church. Though much of the steeple was destroyed and there was damage to the stained glass windows, the main part of the building, buttressed by its strong new towers. stood firm against the winds, which might otherwise have flattened it.

Market Street is today the largest United Methodist congregation on the Eastern Shore of Virginia and, after Baptist churches in Chincoteague and Exmore, the third largest congregation of any faith in the two counties. The membership is 530, and the church ministers as well to a number of regular attenders from other churches who reside at the nearby Hermitage.

[Sources: 109, 111, 116, 141, 168]

Location: see ONANCOCK

MARSHALL MEMORIAL METHODIST CHURCH

(see Signpost United Methodist Church)

*MARSHAPUNGO BAPTIST CHURCH

(''Fisher's Meetinghouse,'' ''Union Church'')
[ABA 1807-1815?]
Belle Haven

The brothers Caleb and Alfred Fisher were the leading forces behind the organization of this church, the seventh Baptist congregation on the Eastern Shore of Virginia and the first founded by someone other than Elijah Baker. There were 27 members when the church was constituted in 1807. Two years later the membership had grown to fifty.

It is apparent that the new Baptist congregation occupied a building erected by Christopher Satchell soon after the turn of the century. Satchell intended his chapel to be a ''union church'' for the use of all denominations, and it is known that Episcopal rectors occasionally preached there. In 1808 the Methodist preacher, Thomas A. Elliott, made an appointment to preach in the building, but he was not permitted to hold services there, probably because the newly-formed Baptist congregation was by then in possession of the chapel.

The records of the Accomack Baptist Association for the years 1809 through 1815 have not survived, and when the records resume in 1816 Marshapungo is no longer mentioned. The Baptist congregation faded out some time during that interim, and the Fisher brothers disappeared from the Eastern Shore scene.

In 1829 Satchell deeded the building, then known as Fisher's Meetinghouse, to the Baptists, who apparently made some attempt to repair it and restore worship in it. Even at this late date the builder reiterated his desire that the chapel be interdenominational, and stipulated that any person of any church could preach there ''provided their appointment do not interfere with the regular appointments of the baptist Ministry once in two weeks.'' If the Baptists wished to use the building more often than every two weeks, ''their extra meetings [were not to] interfere with the meeting of any other religious persons.''

The second Baptist occupation of the building, beginning in 1829, was apparently also short-lived. No new congregation there is mentioned in the records of the Association, but the building was restored, for in 1841 it became the site of the celebrated debate between pastors of the Methodist and Universalist churches of the area. The fate of the building after that year is not known.

Although the exact location of the building cannot be pinpointed today, it stood on the west side of Main Street in that part of Belle Haven that is in Northampton County.

[Sources: 69, 102, 124]

Location: see BELLE HAVEN

McMATH CHAPEL METHODIST EPISCOPAL CHURCH, SOUTH

(see Onley United Methodist Church)

MEARS MEMORIAL UNITED METHODIST CHURCH

[ME-S 1902?, M 1939, UMC 1968]

Keller

When the railroad came down the Shore, the venerable Oak Grove congregation gave birth to two new congregations at nearby points on the tracks: Keller and Melfa. The Keller church, though now the smaller, was the earlier.

As early as 1902 the circuit parsonage was located in the new town of Keller on the railroad, and it was not long after that that a "group of consecrated women" began operating a Sunday school in the village schoolhouse. From this lay endeavor the new Keller church evolved.

It was "under difficulties" that the new church was established, for the menfolk of the village were not particularly enthusiastic. Undeterred, the women of

Keller labored alone to establish the church. A lot for the building was secured in 1905, and three years later on July 4, 1908, the completed building was dedicated and named for B. Bowdoin Mears.

Mears Memorial did not grow to great size, and like the town in which it was situated dwindled as the years passed. For years it was shuttled back and forth between surrounding charges: founded from Oak Grove, it was on the Wachapreague Circuit by the 1930's, the Melfa Charge by the 1950's, and the Painter Charge by 1958.

In 1964 the church was made a station with a part-time minister, and so it remains today. Its present membership is about forty, and the average attendance at worship on Sundays is about fifteen.

[Sources: 109, 111, 116, 123]

Location: see KELLER

Melfa UMC

MELFA

see: **Christian Love Center*
Church of God of Melfa
Grace Mary Tabernacle of the Apostolic Faith Church of God Live On
Melfa United Methodist Church
Oak Grove United Methodist Church
St. Mark's Baptist Church

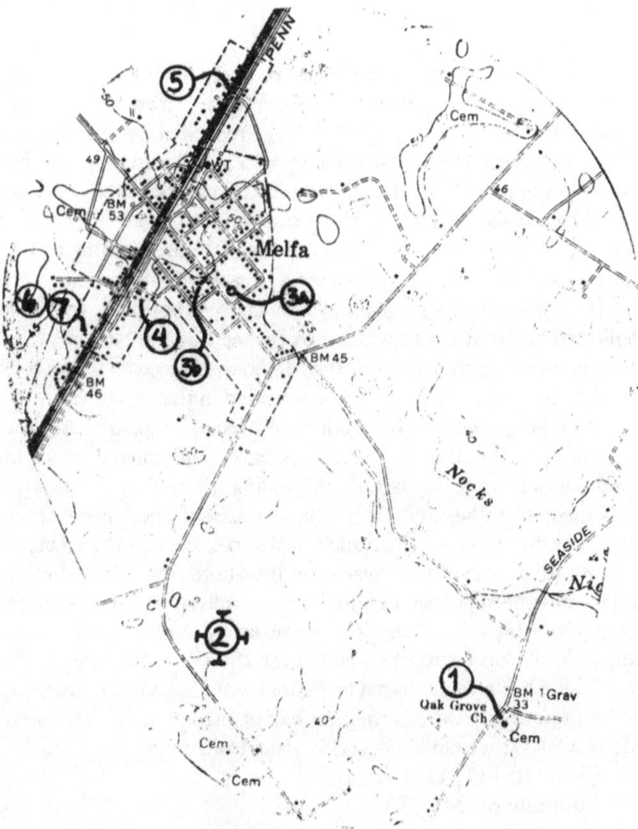

1 - Oak Grove Methodist: site since 1871 (for original site 1801-1870 see CHANCETOWN)
2 - Turlington Campmeeting Grounds: site 1871-1903
3a - Melfa Methodist: public school, site of original Sunday school 1911-12
3b - Melfa Methodist: site since 1912
4 - St. Mark's Baptist
5 - Grace Mary Tabernacle
6 - Christian Love Center: site 1971-76
7 - Church of God of Melfa

MELFA UNITED METHODIST CHURCH

[ME-S 1911, M 1939, UMC 1968]
Melfa

Melfa is one of the newer towns of the Eastern Shore. Even though the railroad came through this section in 1884, when the town received its supposedly Italian name from railroad workers, the village took shape quite slowly around the tracks. It was not until 1909 that the community schoolhouse was completed. It was in this building in 1911 that the Methodists first gathered for Sunday school.

The Sunday school in Melfa was an outgrowth of the venerable Oak Grove congregation to the east, and was under the direction of P. M. Hank, the pastor there. The Melfa Sunday school soon blossomed into regular worship services and a newly organized congregation. The church building was begun in 1912 and dedicated before the year was out by Bishop Eugene Hendrix. It was the last church to be founded on the Shore by the Methodist Episcopal Church, South, and is today the youngest white Methodist congregation in the two counties.

Not long after the Methodists of Melfa occupied their new building, the old community schoolhouse was closed, sold, and moved away in two pieces. The Methodists bought the part of the building where they had first gathered and moved it to their lot to be used for the Sunday school once more. It stood apart from the church until 1966, when an additional annex joined the two buildings.

As in so many other places on the Shore, the railroad caused a shift in population and the new town church soon outdistanced the older country church. By the 1930's Melfa had over 230 members, far more than Oak Grove. The membership at Melfa has been consistently over 200 since that time.

Melfa has always shared its pastors with Oak Grove, though charge boundaries shifted frequently during the first half of this century. The present Melfa Charge, Melfa, Oak Grove, and Locustville, dates from 1956.

[Sources: 111, 116, 123, 176]

Location: see MELFA

*MELSON'S METHODIST EPISCOPAL CHURCH

("Read's Wharf")

[ME-S 1886-1888, ME 1888-1898]

Morley's Wharf

The southern Methodists began construction of this church in 1886, but never completed it and put it up for sale. In 1888 it was purchased by the northern Methodist church for $150. The building was then completed, dedicated in 1888, and first listed as an appointment in 1890, when Julius A. Brewington was the pastor.

Melson's was named for Levin S. Melson of Bridgeville, Delaware, who "took great interest...and contributed largely to it." Perhaps without such financial help the church might never have existed, for it remained a very small and struggling church even with it. As late as 1893 there were only four members, and there were probably never more than seventeen. Nineteen conversions were reported in 1892, but much of that growth was siphoned off by the founding of nearby Harmony Church in 1894. Melson's operated a Sunday school in Birdsnest in 1892 and hoped to found a congregation in Exmore, but there was no lasting work in either of those communities.

By 1897 northern Methodist work in this area, Melson's and Harmony, was faltering, and the two churches were joined with Graham's Chapel in New Church, forty miles away, to form the New Church-Exmore Circuit. Melson's was last listed in 1898. The fate of the building after that date is not known, and even its location is not remembered today.

[Sources: 105, 109, 110, 117, 124]

Location: see WARDTOWN

*MESSONGO PRIMITIVE BAPTIST CHURCH

("Ironside")

[ABA 1779, Primitive Baptist 1831-1935?]

Poulson

Messongo was the second Baptist church on the Eastern Shore of Virginia, founded by Elijah Baker in 1779. The first building was erected soon afterwards, on the Bayside Road south of Messongo Creek, west of what is now Hallwood. In its earliest years the church prospered and grew, and in 1809 when the Accomack Baptist Association was formed it had 124 members.

Already by 1809 Thomas Waters, one of the foremost "anti-mission" Baptists on the Shore, was pastor at Messongo, and it was here that the anti-mission movement was most strongly felt. In 1824 the Association met at Messongo, and although the meeting was "forward-looking" and mission-minded the membership at Messongo under Waters had already declined by a third, to 81 persons.

The Accomack Baptist Association was meeting at this church in 1831 when it split into mission and anti-mission factions, and Thomas Waters and Thomas Delastatius of Messongo led the anti-mission defection. It was Waters who "assumed the authority to dissolve the Accomack Baptist Association" and announced that another meeting would be held in two days. When the delegates reconvened on that date, Messongo did not answer the roll call. The church never again communicated with the Association, which dropped it from its rolls in 1834.

Little is known of the life of this church after it was dropped from the Association until the turn of the century. It affixed the term "Primitive" or "Old-School" to its Baptist name and affiliated with the Salisbury Old-School Predestinarian Baptist Association. There was a gradual decline in membership over the years, presumably because the church's "high Calvinism" made it unconcerned to evangelize. According to one Baptist historian, the church was in 1894 "a church of good standing, but it has seen better days than the present," and one of its pastors had harmed the church by becoming a drunkard.

In 1864 Elder Thomas M. Poulson (1831-1913) became the pastor, and under him the congregation experienced its last great spurt of energy and activity. In 1905 land adjacent to the church was purchased, and shortly thereafter the old building was moved aside to it and a new one erected in its place. The 1905 deed to the new land calls the church "Messongo Predestinarian Baptist Church, whose principal articles of faith are the absolute predestination of all things, including the election of his people into eternal glory by Jesus Christ." Not only is this a succinct statement of the church's beliefs, but probably also the only theological affirmation recorded in the Accomack County deedbooks.

Although there were one regular and several part-time supply pastors after Poulson, the congregation declined steadily after his death in 1913. Messongo ceased to communicate with the Salisbury Association in 1914, and although services were held at the church after that date, they were on an increasingly sporadic basis. By the advent of the Depression there were only three remaining members, and the last services were believed to have been held there about 1935. Though opened occasionally for reunions after that date, the two church buildings stood abandoned by the side of the road and went gradually into ruin.

The older building stood parallel to the road and had a gallery across the north end which could be reached only by a back door (the main doors were on the sides). Both buildings were frame, and neither had a cornerstone.

By 1949 the older building had fallen completely into ruin. The newer structure stood intact, the Bible on the pulpit stand and everything in place, until the late 1950's, when members and families of the Primitive Baptist Church in Snow Hill, the nearest such congregation, removed what could be salvaged and saved. Windows and doors, stoves and benches were claimed by members and put to use in other places in the area, where they can still be pointed out. The Bible is now in the church at Snow Hill. The building itself, stripped of its contents, did not survive the 1950's.

Today the only tangible remains of this historic old church, except for its few scattered contents, is the small graveyard on the old site. Here the tombstone of Thomas Poulson rears its head above the others. The few remaining Primitive Baptists of upper Accomack County are members now of churches in Maryland.

[Sources: 47, 52, 69, 71, 105, 123, 176]

Location: see POULSON

METOMPKIN

see: **Metompkin Baptist Church (I)*
Metompkin Baptist Church (II)
**Middle Church (Church of England)*
Zion Baptist Church

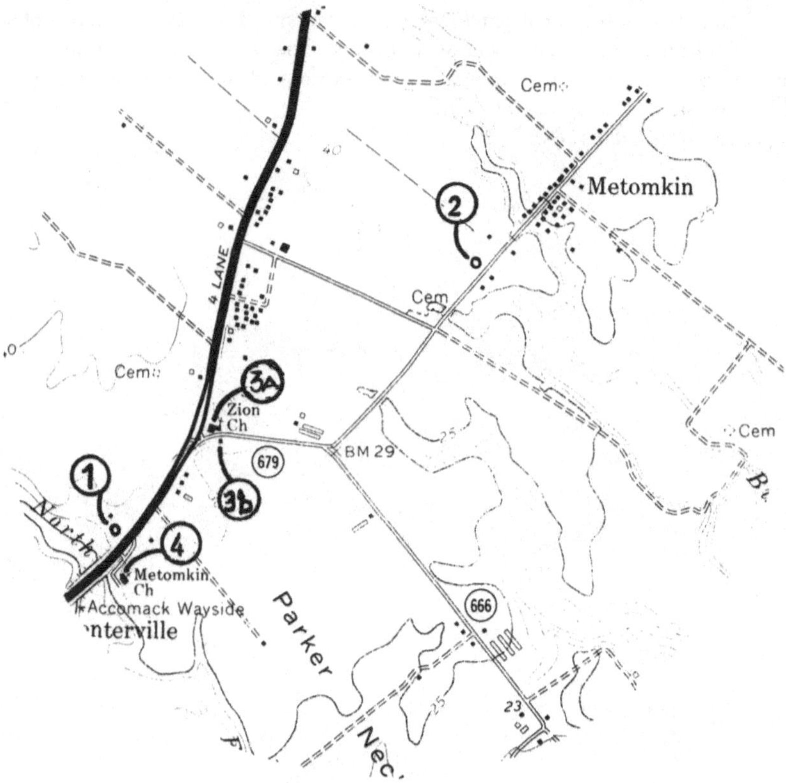

1 - Middle Church: original site 1728-1772 (for later site see RUE)
2 - Metompkin Baptist (I): approximate site 1790-1834
3a - Zion Baptist: buildings I and III
3b - Zion Baptist: building II
4 - Metompkin Baptist (II): site since 1877

*METOMPKIN BAPTIST CHURCH (I)

[ABA 1785-1834]
Metompkin

This church was organized by Elijah Baker in 1785. William and Elizabeth Warner provided a lot for it in 1790, and shortly thereafter the first building was erected there. This site is not now known, but it was on Seaside Road about a mile north of Zion Baptist Church.

In its early years Metompkin prospered and grew. By 1809 it had 105 members. In 1827 it licensed William Laws to preach, and two years later he founded the Baptist church in Modest Town. There was a campground near this church which was from time to time used by the Baptists of the Shore. However, sometime during the 1820's Elder Purnell Outten became the pastor at Metompkin; he was a staunch anti-mission Baptist, and it was during his pastorate that the missions controversy split the Association.

When the Baptists of the Eastern Shore divided over the missions question in 1831, Metompkin "wavered between the two camps." It did not answer the roll call of the reassembled missionary Association in that year and remained out of contact until 1833. In that year the Association invited itself to Metompkin for its annual meeting, only to find the anti-mission party in such predominance at the church that they were forced to meet in a nearby home. Yet Metompkin sent a messenger to the Association and reported the presence of two unlikely activities, a domestic missions society and a Sunday school.

This state of indecision was ended in 1834 when a tornado destroyed the church building. There was not sufficient interest to rebuild it. In 1835 the Baptists of Modest Town bought a lot nearby for a new church, and some years later Zion Baptist Church arose on this site and fell heir to the Baptists who remained in the area of Metompkin.

[Sources: 69, 70, 123]

Location: see METOMPKIN

METOMPKIN BAPTIST CHURCH (II)

("Colored Zion Mission")
[ESBA 1877]
Metompkin

The second Metompkin Baptist Church, a black congregation, was founded in 1877 by blacks from Zion Baptist Church, with the help of that white congregation. Abel J. Satchell assumed the pastorate of the Colored Zion Mission, as it was first called, and in 1877 the first building was erected half a mile south of Zion. The new congregation later assumed the name of the older Baptist church, destroyed by a tornado in 1834, that had once stood about a mile east.

Satchell served the church "dutifully" until his death in 1901, and under him the congregation grew rapidly. The church building was enlarged in 1900, shortly before Satchell's death, and Thomas Turlington, his handpicked successor, was pastor when the cornerstone was laid. Turlington served a 23-year pastorate and in 1914 oversaw the second major renovation and enlargement of the building.

In 1924 began the 23-year pastorate of the venerable J. C. Bond, a "prince of a preacher" who served until his death in 1947. During this long pastorate a parsonage was purchased, the membership increased threefold, and the building enlarged and improved yet two more times.

Bond's pastorate was followed by another long one, that of James M. Douglas (1948-1965). Under Douglas the church made the largest addition of all, a two-story annex costing $24,000, dedicated in 1951. A number of other improvements followed within the course of a few years, including a $4000 renovation of the sanctuary completed in the spring of 1957.

On December 17, 1957, the church building on which so much care and money had been lavished was completely destroyed by fire, and crowds gathered by the side of Route 13 to watch it go up in flames. The congregation worshiped in a nearby schoolhouse while, under Douglas leadership, the present contemporary building was erected. The new building, which cost $60,000, was occupied in 1959. The Turlington-Bond Memorial Annex was added to it during the pastorate of Leroy Mapp (1966-1974), Douglas' successor.

Metompkin is perhaps the prizewinner among all Eastern Shore churches for long pastorates. In the 100 years of its existence only six pastors have served, four of them for over twenty years each. The church today is a strong and vigorous one, a leader among the Shore's churches in community action.

[Sources: 26, 105, 123, 129]

Location: see METOMPKIN

METROPOLITAN MEMORIAL UNITED METHODIST CHURCH
(''Johnson's Metropolitan'')
[ME 1870, M 1939, UMC 1968]
Bayside

Metropolitan was founded in 1870. Who began the work of this church is not known, but the deed to the land refers to the church as ''Johnson's Metropolitan,'' and thus preserves perhaps the name of some lay or clerical pioneer. One early pastor was J. K. Adams, who from this base founded nearby Adams Church in 1878. Since that time the two churches have always shared the same pastors.

The original building of this congregation, which was improved by 1881, was replaced altogether by the present structure in 1889. The first circuit parsonage was erected nearby in ''Grape'' in 1898. The turn of the century was a prosperous period for the church, and by 1910 the congregation could boast a new organ, a church library, and a new $1900 parsonage across the street.

In December 1914 the congregation dedicated its renovated building, which cost $2700 and which could seat 700 persons. The Lee Mont Circuit was by this time the largest on the district and one of the largest in the Delaware Conference. As late as 1933, in the midst of the Depression, the church reported a vacation Bible school, an Epworth League, and continuing prosperity. By 1935 the lean years had caught up with this congregation. A breach with Adams had developed, and Metropolitan reported that it was ''considerably reduced.'' Not until 1943, when the pastor was reported to be ''shouting high,'' was the church restored to a degree of prosperity.

In 1975 Albert Gingrich became the first white pastor to serve this church, and during his pastorate the parsonage was replaced with a new one on the same site. With 194 members, this church is today second only to Adams in size among the black United Methodist congregations on the Shore.

[Sources: 113, 123, 176]

Location: see BAYSIDE

*MIDDLE CHURCH

[CE 1728-1784?]
Rue

In 1720 the inhabitants of central Accomack County petitioned the House of Burgesses for a church in their vicinity. At that time there was no church between Pungoteague and Assawoman, and Anglican services, when they were held at all in the central part of the county, were held in the courthouse.

It took several years to get the petition signed into law, but by 1728 the local vestry was meeting inside the new Middle Church. It was a frame building that stood west of Route 13 near ''Poorhouse Branch,'' near the present Accomack Wayside. Almost nothing is known of this first Middle Church. It was apparently not in use for long, for in 1772 the land on which it had stood was sold.

A second Middle Church was erected soon after 1773, the year in which Shadrach Bayly sold a second lot to the parish. This church stood about a mile north of the original site and on the opposite side of the road. Today Woodbury United Methodist Church sits almost squarely upon the site.

The second church, like the first, was short-lived, and little is known of it today. Presumably it ceased to function when the Church of England was disestablished in 1784. The fate of both buildings is unknown.

[Sources: 70, 90]

Location: see METOMPKIN, RUE

MIONA

see: **Pittsville Methodist Episcopal Church*
Pittsville United Methodist Church

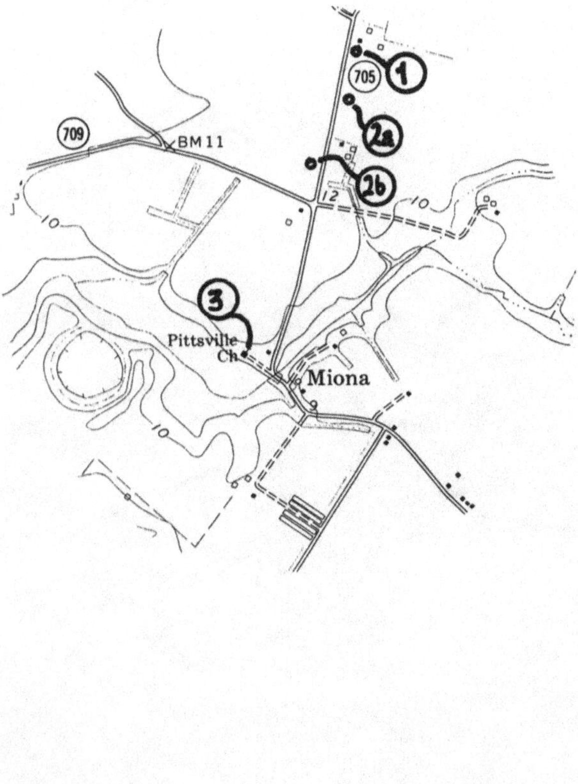

1 - Berea Methodist (New Church): original site (approximate) 1874-1885 (for location since 1885 see NEW CHURCH)
2a - Pittsville ME: original site 1886-c1901
2b - Pittsville ME: building moved to this site c1901-c1967
3 - Pittsville UMC

MODEST TOWN

see: **Christian Union African Methodist Episcopal Church*
**Ebenezer Methodist Episcopal Church*
Modest Town Baptist Church

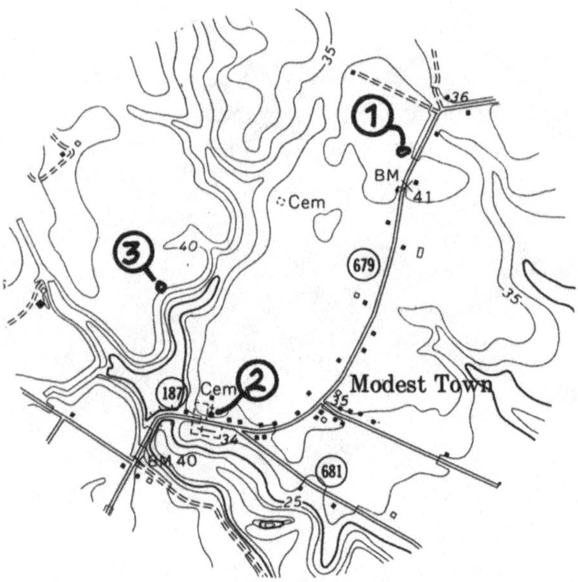

1 - Ebenezer ME: site 1827-1912
2 - Modest Town Baptist
3 - Christian Union AME: site 1866-c1900

MODEST TOWN BAPTIST CHURCH

[ABA 1829]
Modest Town

Modest Town Baptist Church was organized on July 19, 1829, by Levin Dix and Purnell Outten. The 22 charter members built their first house of worship on Seaside Road about half a mile south of Ebenezer M.E. Church, which had been erected two years earlier. Modest Town was admitted to the Accomack Baptist Association in 1831, the year that organization split over the missions issue. Its admission was "a bright spot in this turbulent meeting."

From the very start Modest Town was a vigorous church. In the two years between its organization and its admission into the Association its membership almost tripled. By 1834 the congregation had a Sunday school, a temperance society (one of the earliest on the Shore), and a domestic missions society. The Accomack Association often met on a campground near this church, and in addition to the church building the congregation also erected and used a "baptistry" building on a nearby millpond.

In 1838 there were only three Baptist Sunday schools on the Virginia Shore, and all of them were conducted by this congregation. The three schools met in regular rotation at Modest Town, at "Muddy Creek" near Bloxom, and at Zion. From the two other Sunday schools came ultimately two new Baptist churches, Zion and Bethel, both of which were founded from this church and both of which were organized in 1852 by 38 Modest Town members dismissed for that purpose.

The Civil War years were perhaps the most difficult in the church's history. After 1864 the Negro members withdrew to form their own churches, among them First Baptist Church of Mappsville. The following year the church found itself three years behind in paying the pastor's salary.

William Laws, the first pastor here, served no fewer than five pastorates during the first two decades of the church's history. Thereafter the church at various times shared pastors with "almost every church from Pungoteague to Chincoteague." In 1873, J. L. Lodge was called as the first full-time pastor at a salary of $700 per year. The church has been a station since that year, although the Modest Town preachers also filled the pulpit at Mappsville Baptist Church for short periods beginning in 1903 and 1946.

In 1876 the congregation began the mission work from which Atlantic Baptist Church was organized a year later.

The first building, erected in 1829, was replaced by a second in 1850. On August 6, 1922, the present structure, the third, was occupied on the old site. The second building stood behind it for a number of years and was used as a community hall. It was later sold and dismantled and the lumber used to build a store which still stands on Route 13 south of Mappsville. The interior of the new building was renovated in 1949 at a cost of $20,000.

At its centennial anniversary in 1929 this church had 241 members. The membership today is 173.

[Sources: 69, 122, 137, 176]

Location: see MODEST TOWN

MORRIS CHAPEL METHODIST EPISCOPAL CHURCH

(see Adams United Methodist Church)

MOUNT CALVARY BAPTIST CHURCH

(see New Mount Calvary Baptist Church)

*MOUNT HOPE METHODIST CHURCH

("New Mount Hope")
[ME 1914, M 1939-1967]
Keller

Mt. Hope was an outgrowth of the black Methodist church in Exmore, whose congregation purchased a Keller lot in 1914, started a Sunday school there in 1915, and in 1916 built a new church. The church stood on Route 13 north of Keller.

Under the pastorate of H. C. Snead this church prospered and grew so quickly that the original building had to be replaced by a larger one in 1920. There were 81 conversions in that year alone. However, with the appointment of a new pastor many members withdrew, and there was some effort made to take the church out of the Methodist Episcopal denomination. Strife continued until the appointment of J. O. Griffin as pastor in 1925.

Mt. Hope struggled for years to build a parsonage, and pastors came and went with great rapidity for want of one. Land for a parsonage was purchased as early as 1925, but when the Depression cast the church into severe economic straits a decade later the building had still not been erected. The years of the Depression were so difficult that the congregation suffered the sale of their church building in 1936, and not until 1941 were they able, with help from the Delaware Conference, to buy the church back.

The 1940's found Mt. Hope back on its feet financially, but still without a parsonage. The church divided in 1948 to create Spence Memorial Church in Exmore, and with that division Mt. Hope began its gradual decline. The parsonage was finally occupied in 1950, a quarter-century after first plans for it were laid, too late to save the church from extinction.

Across the next two decades the congregation dwindled in number to just a few. By 1964 the building stood abandoned and unused, and the Conference directed that it be sold. The building was sold and ultimately dismantled, and the few remaining members officially merged with Snead's in 1967. Shortly after the building was dismantled, Route 13 was widened to four lanes between Keller and Melfa, and the church site lies today beneath the southbound lane of that highway.

[Sources: 113, 123]

Location; see KELLER

MOUNT MESSIAS HOLINESS CHURCH OF GOD LIVE ON

[CGLO 1973] Treherneville

This is the newest of the Church of God Live On congregations on the Shore. Walter and Charlotte Trower began the work of the church with the purchase of a lot in Treherneville in 1973.

The completed church building was dedicated by Bishop Jesse Handshaw in the spring of 1976, and a week of special services followed the dedication. Charlotte Trower is pastor of this small congregation.

[Sources: 109, 124, 176]

Location: see TREHERNEVILLE

MOUNT NEBO BAPTIST CHURCH

[ESBA 1891]
Savageville

It was in 1891 that the black Baptists of Sluitkill Neck organized a church, paid $12 to Joseph Savage for a half-acre plot of ground, and promptly erected a new church. The little country church was named Mt. Nebo, and Thomas Turlington was called as its first pastor.

In 1898 the King Solomon Lodge No. 301 of the Society of Good Samaritans erected a building next door to the church. In 1960 the church purchased this building, long since abandoned, and used it as a church hall.

Mt. Nebo was erected in a rural area that has always been sparsely populated, and it never grew to be a large church. There has never been a parsonage for the church, and its ministers have often lived in other communities.

The original building of 1891 is still in use, having received many improvements and additions over the years. Mt. Nebo is today a small church. Its recent pastors have lived as far away as New Church.

[Sources: 26, 109, 123]

Location: see SAVAGEVILLE

*MOUNT OLIVE AFRICAN METHODIST EPISCOPAL CHURCH

(see Mount Olive Baptist Church)

MOUNT OLIVE BAPTIST CHURCH

[AME 1897-1919?, ESBA 1926]
Hack's Neck

Mt. Olive was an African Methodist Episcopal church when it was founded in 1897. In that year the lot was purchased and the building erected and the pastor, Samuel Poulson, shared with the new Onley Mission. The family of Frank Sample, a local pillar of the congregation, is said to have been the founders of the church.

Like the churches with which it shared its pastors, Mt. Olive proved to be a short-lived congregation, and apparently ceased to function after about fifteen years. In 1919 the building, which had been mortgaged by the congregation, was sold, and A.M.E. activity ceased there.

In 1926 the congregation was reorganized as a Baptist church. The building was repurchased, outfitted for worship again, and the congregation became a part of the black Baptist association. The Reverend Fred Gunter was called as pastor.

There have been only three Baptist pastors of this congregation. Gunter served for thirty years, until 1956. After a period in which there was no pastor, his son, Joseph Gunter, assumed the pastorate and served until 1963. The present pastor has served since 1964.

Mt. Olive is today a small congregation. The cornerstone of the building has two dates, 1897 and 1926, the dates of the two separate denominations that have worshiped here.

[Sources: 7, 26, 123]

Location: see HARBORTON

MOUNT OLIVE BAPTIST CHURCH

("Mount Holly")
[ESBA 1887]
Jenkins Bridge

John and Meshach Gaskins sold the land on which the black Baptists of the Jenkins Bridge area established their church in 1887. When they entered the deed in the books at the courthouse, the church's name was written as Mt. Holly. Except for that one deed, this church has always been known as Mt. Olive.

The original building, erected soon after 1887 during the pastorate of James Cluff, the first pastor, is still used by this congregation. The site chosen for the church was only a short distance east of St. John's, the black Methodist church established a decade earlier. The two churches very early established a tradition of cordial relations, and in 1903 purchased a plot of ground for joint use as a cemetery.

The earliest years of the twentieth century were probably the most prosperous in Mt. Olive's history. The congregation tripled the size of the church property by the purchase of additional land adjacent to the church in 1901. Three years later the congregation gave the school board a 25-year lease on some of its property; shortly thereafter a school for black children was erected just west of the church, and it continued in operation for a number of years.

Mt. Olive has never been a large church. Since there is no parsonage, its pastors have often lived outside the neighborhood.

[Sources: 109, 123, 176]

Location: see JENKINS BRIDGE

*MOUNT OLIVE CHURCH OF CHRIST DISCIPLES

[CCD 1944-1964]

Exmore

Sister Isabelle Finney of Cape Charles was the founder of this, the third Church of Christ Disciples on the Eastern Shore of Virginia. The new church was erected in 1944 on land purchased from R. T. Gladstone and given the name Mt. Olive.

Mt. Olive never grew to great size or strength, and experienced long periods of inactivity throughout its existence. The church would cease to function, only to be revived again by Sister Finney.

The church was vacant once again when, shortly after 1960, it burned to the ground. Since the Weirwood church of this sect had ceased to function, the building of that congregation was moved from Weirwood to Exmore, and Mt. Olive was again reopened. This final venture, too, ended after a short while. The church closed again, and in 1964 the property was sold.

The church stood at the end of Virginia Street in Exmore east of the railroad tracks, about a block away from Spence Methodist. The abandoned building went quickly to ruin and ultimately collapsed.

[Sources: 124, 176]

Location: see EXMORE

MOUNT OLIVE HOLINESS CHURCH

[Independent 1940]
Whitesville

This is one of the two churches founded by Elder Joseph Turner in 1940. In that year Turner erected a new frame building in Atlantic for his St. Joseph Church there, but in Whitesville he gathered his congregation in the abandoned building of Mt. Zion Baptist Church. Later that year the building was purchased from John and Ressie White for $190.

Like St. Joseph Church in Atlantic, Mt. Olive is Pentecostal in doctrine. Turner served both churches until his death, and since that time Mt. Olive, the smaller of the two, has maintained a cordial relationship with its sister church in Atlantic.

[Sources: 123, 176]

Location: see PARKSLEY

MOUNT OLIVE PENTECOSTAL CHURCH OF CHRIST DISCIPLES

[CCD 1937-1943, 1961-1965, 1976]
Hopeton

This church represents only a small portion of the life's work of Arthur R. Boggs, bishop in the Church of Christ Disciples. It has had an on-again, off-again existence as Boggs' work has carried him at times off the Shore and into other forms of ministry.

As a young man Boggs established the first Mt. Olive in the town of Accomac in 1937, the second church of that sect on the Shore. This church continued in operation until 1943, and after it was abandoned the building ultimately fell into ruin. Boggs later reopened the church near his home in Accomac in the 1960's, and for some time carried on the work in Parksley.

It was for additional church work in further fields that Boggs abandoned his work in Accomack County a second time. For about a decade he ministered in several capacities, chiefly youth work and evangelism, off the Shore, supporting himself in secular employment throughout this time.

In 1976 Boggs established the third Mt. Olive in a rented store building in Hopeton. His small congregation there still meets regularly, a maximum of about thirty worshipers, the latest work of this pastor of some forty years.

[Sources: 109, 176]

Location: see ACCOMAC, HOPETON

MOUNT SINAI BAPTIST CHURCH

[ESBA 1876]
New Church

Mt. Sinai is one of the oldest black churches in Accomack County. Yet the church sits so close to Maryland (the state boundary runs only a few yards behind the building) that it has seldom been listed or considered with Virginia churches. A recent history of Worcester County, Maryland, listed the church among the congregations of that county.

Major Hall and James Hall of Newtown, Maryland, sold the land on which this church stands in 1876, and the building was erected in that year. The deed states that the lot, for which the congregation paid $5, was "near the line of the county." The congregation was already, by 1876, affiliated with the Eastern Shore Baptist Association.

There have been many additions and improvements to the church building over the years, the most important of which was the major rebuilding of 1910. The structure now bears little resemblance to its original design.

On modern roads it is impossible to reach this church without crossing into Maryland. As might be expected, the congregation includes many Marylanders among its ranks.

[Sources: 123, 176]

Location: see NEW CHURCH

MOUNT SINAI CHURCH OF GOD

[Independent 1973]
Eastville

Cordelia Custis founded this congregation in 1973 when she began holding services in a small frame building on her own property in Stumptown, south of Eastville.

By 1978 the congregation numbered twelve persons. Though small in numbers, the membership was high in enthusiasm and undertook in that year the construction of a larger and more substantial church building adjacent to the first.

The congregation is Pentecostal in doctrine. Mrs. Custis, the founder, is still the pastor. Elizabeth West has served as her assistant from the beginning.

[Source: 176]

Location: see EASTVILLE

MOUNT SINAI GOSPEL TABERNACLE

(see Greater Mount Sinai Gospel Tabernacle)

MOUNT SINAI HOLY CHURCH

[Mt. Sinai Holy Church of America Inc. 1941]
Cheapside

Mt. Sinai Holy Church in Cheapside, the original congregation of this denomination on the Eastern Shore of Virginia, was founded by Lily Pertilder, a missionary and evangelist sent from the church in Philadelphia in the early 1940's. Pertilder's congregation, which at first consisted of only five members, held worship services in a building in Cheapside provided by the Morris Funeral Home.

It was while she was a member of this congregation that Estelle Dillard Smith founded the Fairview church, which was ultimately set apart as a separate unit under her pastorate.

The Cheapside church purchased a lot for a building from Benjamin Mears in 1941. It was not until 1945, by which time the Fairview congregation was already established in its building, that the church building in Cheapside was occupied.

Pertilder served the church until her death in 1971, when she was succeeded by Gladys Dillard Weeks, sister of Estelle Smith of Fairview. The Cheapside congregation, a small group of about a dozen, still worships regularly in their original building.

[Sources: 124, 176]

Location: see CHEAPSIDE

*MOUNT ZION AFRICAN METHODIST EPISCOPAL CHURCH

(''Occohannock Neck,'' ''Zions'')
[AME 1870-1914?]
Jamesville

Mt. Zion made its appearance in 1870, when it was one of four churches on the Pungoteague Circuit. In that year Herman and Cecelia Haupt sold a lot to ''Zions Church'' on the condition that worship there be ''orderly or in proper manner'' and that the neighborhood not be disturbed by the congregation. Presumably the church building was erected shortly thereafter.

The church was no sooner formed than it was hit by a disastrous schism. In 1871 Jasper Savage led a large number of persons out of the church and organized Ebenezer Baptist Church in Wardtown. This division seriously weakened Mt. Zion, which never grew to great size or importance. The church dwindled and closed sometime between 1906 and 1914, still on the Pungoteague Circuit.

The building stood for a great many years after the congregation abandoned it. It was dismantled about 1945, the intention being at that time that it would be rebuilt and the congregation revived. The church lot is today overgrown with trees and brush at the corner of the main neck road and the road to Battle Point. It is still used as a burial ground.

[Sources: 7, 26, 124, 176]

Location: see JAMESVILLE

MOUNT ZION AFRICAN METHODIST EPISCOPAL CHURCH

[AME 1895]
Treherneville

Frank Warren Overton, pastor of the Bridgetown Circuit, is credited with having begun the A.M.E. mission in Treherneville, but at his death in 1900 the congregation there was not sufficiently strong to have purchased a lot. Jesse and Sally Fuller sold the land on which the church was built in 1904, and in 1905 the completed building was dedicated.

Albert Roberts Montague was the first pastor of the completed church. This church with the other Mt. Zion in Jamesville formed the Jamesville Circuit, and the two churches purchased a parsonage in 1906. The Treherneville congregation ultimately proved to be the stronger, and its strength dates from early in the years of the church. By 1908 it could boast both a Christian Endeavor Society and a local chapter of the woman's missionary society.

In 1912 the congregation mortgaged its property in order to purchase more land from the Fullers and increase the size of the church lot. Three years later Antioch Baptist Church, which had assembled for years in the fraternal lodge near Mt. Zion, erected their new church building just down the street.

The building erected in 1905 was substantially rebuilt in 1961. The congregation today shares its pastor with Ebenezer in Capeville.

[Sources: 7, 109, 124]

Location: see TREHERNEVILLE

*MOUNT ZION BAPTIST CHURCH

[ESBA? 1920-1930?]
Whitesville

Short-lived Mt. Zion, a black church, was established in 1920. In that year two lots in Whitesville were purchased, and the infant congregation erected a simple frame building.

The anticipated growth did not materialize, and by 1924 the congregation had mortgaged the building to help pay its debts. Just when the church closed is not known, but it is probable that it did not survive the decade.

By 1936 the building had been deserted for years, and the church had completely defaulted. John and Ressie White purchased the property for $155, intending to convert it into a home. Instead it was sold four years later to the congregation of Mt. Olive Holiness Church, which has worshiped there ever since.

[Sources: 123, 176]

Location: see PARKSLEY

MOUNT ZION HOLY CHURCH

[Mt. Sinai Holy Church of America Inc. 1948]
Bayside

This congregation, the third of its denomination on the Shore, was the second to be organized by Estelle Dillard Smith. In 1948 Smith, anxious to extend her work to Accomack County, secured the use of the abandoned Wise Chapel and gathered a new congregation there.

The building used by Smith was already almost a century old. It had been erected in 1855 as Reese Chapel Methodist Protestant Church. In 1950 it was so badly damaged by a fire that county authorities declared it condemned. The new congregation thereupon erected a newer and larger building next door.

In 1970 the road through Bayside was widened and improved, affecting both church buildings. The older frame structure was demolished altogether, and the front steps of the new building were taken. Once again the congregation was forbidden to use the building, and worship there ceased.

The Mt. Zion congregation is not officially discontinued, for most of its members immediately assumed an active relationship with Mt. Sinai in Fairview, where two "carloads" of people from Accomack attend regularly. Both pastor and people consider the church still intact and plan to resume services in Accomack as soon as a suitable building is available.

[Sources: 123, 176]

Location: see BAYSIDE

MOUNT ZION UNITED METHODIST CHURCH

("New Mt. Zion")
[ME 1879, M 1939, UMC 1968]
Withams

Just when this church was founded is not certain, but it was probably in 1879. Before that year the Horntown Circuit consisted of three churches, Friendship, Deas Chapel, and St. John's, but in 1879 a fourth was added. In 1890 the Horntown Circuit was divided, and the Oak Hall Charge, consisting of this church and St. John's in Grotons, was created. By that year, this building was standing.

The first church building of Mt. Zion was "reseated" in 1894 and closed five years later during a smallpox epidemic. In 1904 the first building was replaced by the present structure. The fate of that first building is not known today. The charge was first called Withams in 1913.

The community hall next to the church was obtained in 1946. Mt. Zion is today the largest church on the Withams Charge, and the pastor lives near the church in Withams.

[Sources: 113, 116, 123]

Location: see WITHAMS

*MUDDY CREEK MEETINGHOUSE

[Society of Friends 1679-1736]
Guilford

When Quaker John Boweter visited the members of his sect on the Eastern Shore of Virginia in 1678, he found them all meeting in private homes, except in the Franktown area where there was already a meetinghouse. His visit became the impetus for the erection of a second Quaker meetinghouse on the Shore, and in 1679 William and Dorothy Jarman sold an acre of land near Guilford for that purpose. This second Quaker meetinghouse on the Virginia Eastern Shore was apparently erected soon afterward.

The first mention of the meetinghouse itself is from 1683, by which time there was also an adjacent cemetery. Since the law of that time required all Protestant dissenters to publish the times and places of their worship, the congregation at Muddy Creek prepared an affidavit to that effect in 1692: "Wee the people comonly caled quaker doe hereby Informe all persons conserned that we doe constantly meet on the first day of the weeke called Sunday at our meeting house built for that use neare Gilford in this County and on the fifth day of the week called thursday either at the house of Sara Coe widow or at the house of George Johnson deceased and our monthly and quarterlie meteings at the house of the said Geo Johnson."

Shortly before 1694 the first meetinghouse burned, and the congregation selected the home of Thomas Fowkes in Onancock as their place of assembly while a new building was being erected. The second meetinghouse stood upon the site of the first by 1697. In 1704 the congregation received a bequest of ten shillings from the will of William Cutting.

Within the next generation the Quaker community in northern Accomack dwindled. A visiting Friend held a meeting at Muddy Creek in 1728, the first there in a long time, and recorded that the Quakers of this region were at that time "insensible people that seemed very ignorant of any good." The last account of any regular meetings in the meetinghouse is from 1729. The building is not mentioned in Quaker records after 1736.

The last corporate act of Quaker worship on the Virginia Shore was a wedding at what is now Captain's Cove in upper Accomack in 1753. By then the Muddy Creek Meetinghouse stood vacant or had even disappeared. It stood south of Guilford toward Hopeton near Guilford Creek.

[Sources: 70, 83]

Location: see GUILFORD

*NANDUA CHURCH

[CE 1652-1667]
Cedar View Wharf

This short-lived Anglican church was built soon after 1652, when a new parish called Occohannock was created on the Shore. It stood near Cedar View Wharf in Accomack County, its site now indicated only by some large sycamore trees.

At Nandua Church, as at other churches up and down the Shore during the colonial period, the local citizenry had to undergo the punishments meted out by the court for various crimes and offenses. One was Joan Pettyjohn, who in 1653 had to stand "att the Church dore (during the tyme the psalme is singeinge) with a gagge in her mouth." Less fortunate was Genefra Jones, who in the same year was "towed over the Creek at Nandue." In 1663, Miriam Cornelius was punished for slander and had to make "acknowledgment in open Court and the next Saboth at Occohannock Church and the Sunday after at Nandue Church." Mary White received a similar sentence not long afterwards, requiring her to appear "once in open Court and once at either Church in this County."

The last reference to this church is from 1664, when John Major acquitted himself of the charge that he was not attending worship here by proving that he worshiped at Occohannock Church. By 1667, both Nandua and Occohannock had been discontinued.

[Sources: 70, 90]

Location: see BOSTON

NAOMI MAKEMIE PRESBYTERIAN CHURCH

("Onancock")
[Pres 1883]
Onancock

It was in the town of Onancock that the early Presbyterian pioneer, Francis Makemie, found his wife, settled down, and was licensed to preach. However, Presbyterianism faded from the town with the death of Makemie in 1708, and a permanent congregation was not established until almost two centuries later.

The pastors of Makemie Presbyterian in Accomac, among them John G. Anderson, preached from time to time in nearby Onancock prior to 1883, but it was Anderson who led in the formation of this congregation. Onancock Presbyterian Church was organized on July 15, 1883. The abandoned building of Bascom's Chapel Methodist Episcopal Church, South, on King Street was purchased in that year. There were twelve charter members, eleven of whom came from Makemie Church, and one of whom, Shepherd Horsey, was black.

The congregation began construction of a new building on Market Street in 1894 on land purchased from Upshur B. Quinby. The old building was sold, and the new building dedicated on November 29, 1896. Pastor at that time was Byron Clarke, also of Makemie and Clarke's Chapel, which was built by and named for him. The Norfolk Presbytery met with this church for the first time in 1897, when the building was still new.

In 1912 the congregation changed the name of the church to Naomi Makemie, in memory of Naomi Anderson Makemie of Onancock, wife of Francis Makemie. The church shared its pastor with Makemie in Accomac up until the 1920's, after which its field alignments shifted frequently among Belle Haven, Powelton, and Clarke.

The Onancock congregation remained a small one throughout the first half of the twentieth century, and only began to grow larger in the 1950's. In 1956 the congregation dedicated a $40,000 education annex and played host again to the Norfolk Presbytery. The church was again joined to Makemie in Accomac during this decade, an arrangement that still prevails. Maximum membership of 134 communicants was attained in 1960. The membership at the present is about one hundred.

[Sources: 105, 110, 119, 120, 123, 176]

Location: see ONANCOCK

NASSAWADOX

see: *Bethel Baptist Church*
Calvary Assembly of God
Faith Tabernacle Holiness Church of God Live On
Franktown United Methodist Church
**Nassawadox Methodist Episcopal Church, South*
**Nassawadox Meetinghouse*
New Allen Memorial African Methodist Episcopal Church

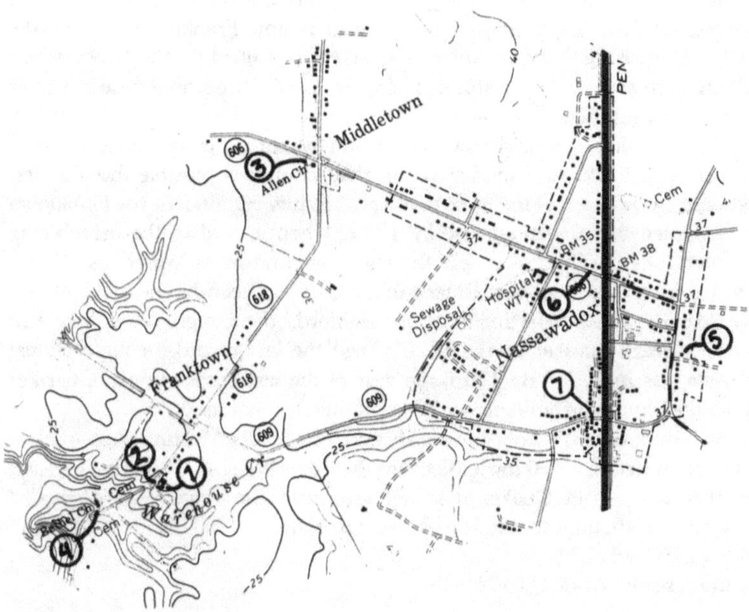

1 - Quaker Meetinghouse: site 1660-c1750
2 - Franktown UMC: site since 1843
3 - New Allen AME
4 - Bethel Baptist
5 - Nassawadox ME
6 - Calvary Assembly of God
7 - Faith Tabernacle

Location Unknown: Franktown Methodist [Floyd's Meetinghouse] prior to 1843

*NASSAWADOX MEETINGHOUSE

[Society of Friends 1660?-1729]
Franktown

It was perhaps as early as 1660, the year in which the Virginia colony passed a law to rid itself of the Quaker nuisance, that the Friends on the Eastern Shore of Virginia erected their first meetinghouse in what is now Franktown. Despite the anti-Quaker laws, a significant number of Quakers remained on the Shore, where they became increasingly respectable and prosperous. This meetinghouse was their first and principal seat of activity.

The Nassawadox Meetinghouse was definitely standing by 1689, for it is mentioned in a will recorded in Eastville in that year. It is possible that the first meetinghouse stood north of the present village, but it is certain that the Franktown site was occupied by a meetinghouse by 1717, when a deed to the neighboring property mentions it. The creek near the site, now known as Warehouse Creek, was often known as Meetinghouse Branch in the early eighteenth century.

Like Muddy Creek Meetinghouse in Guilford, the congregation here had dwindled to a small number by the 1720's, and the last recorded congregational meeting here was in 1729. By 1753, the year of the last corporate act of Quaker worship on the Shore, the building was still standing, but not used.

In 1843 the Methodists of this area abandoned Floyd's Meetinghouse in Hare Valley and relocated in Franktown. The site they purchased from Lewis D. Heath includes that of the old Quaker meetinghouse, and the Franktown Methodist Church of today is thought to stand on or near that spot.

[Sources: 70, 83, 124]

Location: see FRANKTOWN

*NASSAWADOX METHODIST EPISCOPAL CHURCH, SOUTH

[ME-S 1908-1928]
Nassawadox

The church was founded from Franktown Church when D. G. C. Butts was pastor. Members of that church living in Nassawadox, chief among them Pitts Westcott, first organized a Sunday school in their village. It met on the second story of the James storehouse. Later, in 1908, this congregation purchased a lot in town east of Seaside Road and erected there a little chapel, "a very creditable building," said Butts.

The Nassawadox Church never grew to great size or importance. By 1919 it was a struggling congregation and was removed from the Franktown-Johnsons Circuit and joined to Broadwater and Bethel. Here it lived out the remainder of its days.

By 1924 the church property was mortgaged for $1000, and the Woman's Missionary Society had disbanded. In 1928 the property was sold in two pieces, and all records of the church cease.

The building is still standing. It has been substantially altered and is today used as a dwelling.

[Sources: 8, 50, 111, 124, 176]

Location: see NASSAWADOX

*NASSAWADOX METHODIST EPISCOPAL MISSION

(see Indiantown Mission)

NEW ALLEN MEMORIAL AFRICAN METHODIST EPISCOPAL CHURCH

(''Allen Memorial,'' ''Franktown'')
[AME 1870]
Franktown

The African Methodist Episcopal church in Franktown is undoubtedly the work of John Henry Offer, second A.M.E. pastor on the Virginia Shore. The congregation was in existence in 1870, when Offer left the Shore and when it first became a part of the newly-created Pungoteague Circuit. The following year the congregation paid $40 to James Savage for a lot on which to erect a church, and the church building was probably erected soon afterward.

The church quickly grew into one of the larger A.M.E. congregations on the Shore. By 1893 it had purchased land for a parsonage of its own. A second parsonage site was secured in 1912, and the old site became a cemetery, across the street from the church. It was probably early in the twentieth century that the name of the church was changed to Allen Memorial, to honor Richard Allen (1760-1831), founder and first bishop of the African Methodist Episcopal Church.

The 1920's found the growing congregation in need of a new building, so in 1924 the abandoned building of Wardtown Baptist Church was purchased, moved several miles to this site, and restored for worship. The congregation used the older building for several years while work on the new structure proceeded apace next door. It was not until 1929 that the first service was held in the new structure. Further renovations on the building in 1940 resulted in the change of name to ''New Allen,'' and the building was renovated again in 1973.

New Allen is one of the stronger A.M.E. churches on the Shore today. The pastor lives in the parsonage near the church and serves this church alone.

[Sources: 7, 124, 176]

Location: see NASSAWADOX

NEW CHURCH

see: *Berea United Methodist Church*
**Bible Church*
Chincoteague Baptist Church
First Baptist Church
Gospel Tabernacle
**Graham's Chapel Methodist Episcopal Church*
Mt. Sinai Baptist Church
**New Church [Church of England]*
St. Mark's United Methodist Church

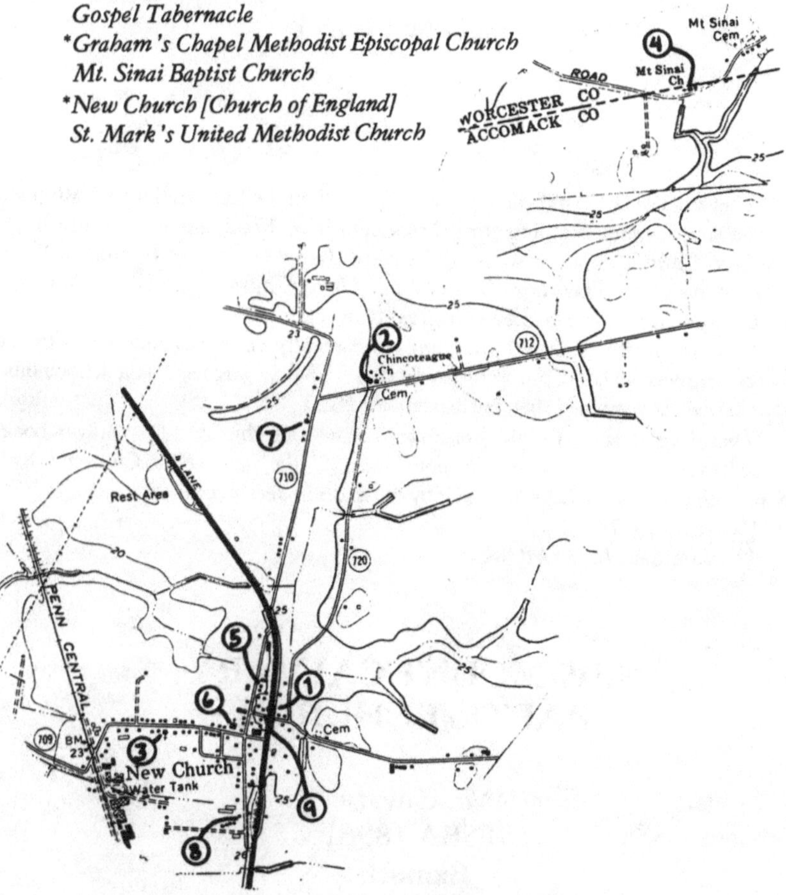

1 - New Church [Church of England]: approximate site
2 - Chincoteague Baptist: site since 1809-10
3 - Berea UMC: site since 1885 [for original site 1874-1885 see MIONA]
4 - Mt. Sinai Baptist
5 - Graham's Chapel ME
6 - First Baptist
7 - St. Mark's UMC
8 - Gospel Tabernacle
9 - Bible Church

Location Unknown: Chincoteague Baptist Church site before 1809-10

*NEW CHURCH

("Pocomoke Church," "Upper Church")
[CE 1762?-1784?]
New Church

This was the last Anglican church established on the Eastern Shore of Virginia. It was a simple frame building erected sometime after 1762, and it stood in what is now New Church at about where the present Route 13 crosses Horntown Road. It was often called "Pocomoke Church" or "Upper Church," and the little village that grew up around it was often known as "Churchtown."

Little is known of this church, and it apparently ceased to function with the disestablishment of the Church of England in 1784. It was used as a schoolhouse for a number of years and then burned around 1820.

There are today only two remnants of this old church: (1) a prayer book, rescued from the fire and still preserved, and (2) the name New Church, which became affixed to the village around it by the mid-nineteenth century.

[Sources: 36, 70, 90]

Location: see NEW CHURCH

NEW MOUNT CALVARY BAPTIST CHURCH

("Mt. Calvary")
[ESBA 1896]
Exmore

Four persons — Deacons George Lecator and George Shields, and Mr. and Mrs. George Annis — organized this church in 1896. Charles J. Henry of Snow Hill, Maryland, was called as the first pastor.

It took a year to complete the church building, and by the time it was dedicated in September 1897 Henry had been replaced as pastor by A. B. Lee. The new building was quite primitive; it had walls of wooden rails, seats of rough lumber, and a simple pulpit. It remained like this for a generation, although the cornerstone date of 1907 may indicate a time when some improvements were made.

In 1923 the building was almost completely rebuilt and enlarged. Plastered walls, church pews, and stained glass windows replaced the more primitive furnishings. The pastor at that time was A. D. Weaver, who was also serving Mt. Zion near Painter. Since the completion of these renovations the church has been known as New Mount Calvary.

This church, handsomely situated in a grove of trees on Bacon Hill north of Exmore, does not own a parsonage. It is today, as it has always been, a fairly small congregation.

[Sources: 26, 124]

Location: see EXMORE

NEW MOUNT ZION BAPTIST CHURCH

(''Mt. Zion'')
[ESBA 1881]
Painter

Thirty people, most of them from Shiloh Baptist, constituted this church in 1881. The first services were held under a bush bower until a building, only ten feet square, was erected. The Reverend Jasper Savage of Ebenezer in Wardtown conducted the first baptisms, but the new congregation was without a regular pastor for several years until Levi Duncan assumed the pastorate.

It was early in the 23-year pastorate of William Dixon, the second pastor, that a larger house of worship was erected on the same site, and subsequent years brought a series of pastors under whom the church was continually enlarged and improved. The building was remodelled under Isaac Arnold in 1913, who also oversaw the purchase of adjacent land for a cemetery. Two rooms were added under A. D. Weaver, whose long pastorate began in 1921.

In 1944, while Weaver was at the end of his pastorate and in failing health, a storm destroyed the church building. The congregation met in a nearby schoolhouse until a new structure was erected. Weaver was unable to see the project through to completion, and the building was dedicated in 1947 under Dennis Haughton, the sixth pastor. At its completion, the church took the name ''New Mount Zion.''

The seventeen years of Haughton's ministry were prosperous ones. In addition to the completion of the new building, a heating system was installed, many interior improvements made, and two members of the church ordained as ministers. Haughton was the first resident pastor, and the parsonage also dates from his pastorate.

In 1964 the congregation purchased an abandoned school building and put it to use as a parish hall.

Today New Mount Zion is a strong and flourishing congregation, one of the larger black churches on the Shore.

[Sources: 123, 129]

Location: see PAINTER

NEW TESTAMENT CONGREGATION

[Independent 1949]
Deep Creek

This church is a direct outgrowth of the congregation of the same name in Tangier, founded in 1946 by James Richardson. At that time there were many people living in the Deep Creek area on the mainland who were originally from Tangier or related to people there. A number of them traveled regularly to the island to worship with the new church until in 1949 Richardson established the second New Testament Congregation for their convenience.

Like the Tangier church, the Deep Creek congregation met principally in homes for some years. In 1953 a lot was purchased and the present building erected.

This congregation is identical to that in Tangier in belief and practice. It was to this area that Richardson first moved when he left the island in 1961 before leaving the Shore altogether. The heavy missions orientation is shared with the Tangier church, with whom this congregation has a frequent and regular contact.

As in Tangier, there is no professional clergy, and the congregation practices the priesthood of all believers.

[Sources: 123, 176]

Location: see CHESCONNESSEX

NEW TESTAMENT CONGREGATION

[Independent 1946]
Tangier

This congregation was founded in 1946 by James C. Richardson, who was until that time pastor of Swain Memorial Methodist Church in Tangier. Toward the end of his pastorate there, Richardson became convinced of the necessity of a deeper life and commitment than he was practicing as a Methodist, and around him gathered a nucleus of people with similar convictions. In 1946, when the Conference sent a new pastor to the island, Richardson elected to remain in Tangier, surrendered his credentials as a Methodist, and founded this church.

Although it was not much of a threat to the strength of Methodism on the island (fewer than twenty persons withdrew from Swain Memorial to the new church), the schism rocked the community. Tangier had always been exclusively Methodist, and many an island home and family were split by religious controversy and hard feeling. Richardson and his congregation occupied a rented storehouse on Main Street north of the Methodist church. Despite their intention not to become a rival church they did, in fact, become so within a relatively short time.

The name chosen by the new church was the New Testament Congregation, and it indicates the intention of its members to re-create the purity, simplicity, and devotion of the church of the first century. Immersion baptism was adopted, and many who had not received it were immersed. Communion was celebrated weekly, worshipers leaving their offerings at the communion table rather than passing a collection plate. And the "priesthood of all believers" became a cardinal tenet of the church, Richardson steadfastly refusing to become the professional clergyman and insisting that all members are ministers.

It was, in one sense, a latter-day Holiness church, although much of the language of that old movement was gone. Instead of a "second blessing" or a "sanctification" experience, the members sought a "deeper life," which they expressed by a more rigorous stewardship and commitment. St. Paul's statement, "I die daily" (I Cor. 15:31), was a constantly-recurring affirmation. The emotionalism of the old Holiness movement was also absent, and the new congregation was not significantly noisier at worship than the Methodists down the street.

By 1949, when a second New Testament Congregation was in operation in Deep Creek on the mainland, the new church was already strongly missions-minded. Half the yearly budget in that year went to missions. By 1962 the congregation had missionaries from Tangier at work in Pakistan, Nepal, Jamaica, Bahamas, and Nebraska, and was sponsoring island youth in colleges and Bible institutes in several places in this country.

In 1955 a lot on south Main Street was purchased, and in 1957 the congregation occupied its new building there. Membership at that time had grown to about 100. In 1958 a revival at the Methodist church under the Reverend Andrew Johnson dealt with the "deeper life" issue, and much of the old acrimony between the two churches was healed. Since that time the two congregations have existed peacefully and congenially side by side, each of them in its own distinctive way heir to the Wesleyan tradition of this unique island community.

[Sources: 123, 133, 176]

Location: see TANGIER

*OAK GROVE METHODIST EPISCOPAL CHURCH, SOUTH

[ME 1832, ME-S 1860-1864?]
Atlantic

By 1832 a Methodist society, born perhaps from the vigorous Downing's congregation, had sprung to life in the village of Atlantic. The village at that time was known as Accoman, not Atlantic, and the Methodist church there was always known as Oak Grove. In 1837 the Accomack Circuit held its Quarterly Conference on the "camp ground near Oak Grove," and the following year Oak Grove Chapel was erected on land given by Skinner Wallop.

Oak Grove became a part of the Atlantic Circuit when that circuit was created in 1858, and two years later joined its sister churches in seceding to the southern church. Like the rest of the circuit, it was closed for several weeks by the Union army in 1864. Thereafter this church fades from the records; there are no further mentions of it in the annals of Methodism.

In 1877 Baptists from Modest Town and Bethel began to hold services in the abandoned building, calling themselves Oak Grove Baptist Mission. The building was subsequently purchased by this group, and in it on July 1, 1877, Atlantic Baptist Church was organized. In 1888 the growing Baptist congregation substantially changed the building by adding twelve feet and a steeple to the front.

In 1919 the building was moved across the street to make way for the present brick building of Atlantic Baptist Church, which stands on the original site. The old building was used for church and community events for a number of years before it was abandoned and finally dismantled in 1964.

[Sources: 39, 103, 123, 132]

Location: see ATLANTIC

OAK GROVE UNITED METHODIST CHURCH

("Burton's Chapel")
[ME 1801, ME-S 1860, M 1939, UMC 1968]
Melfa

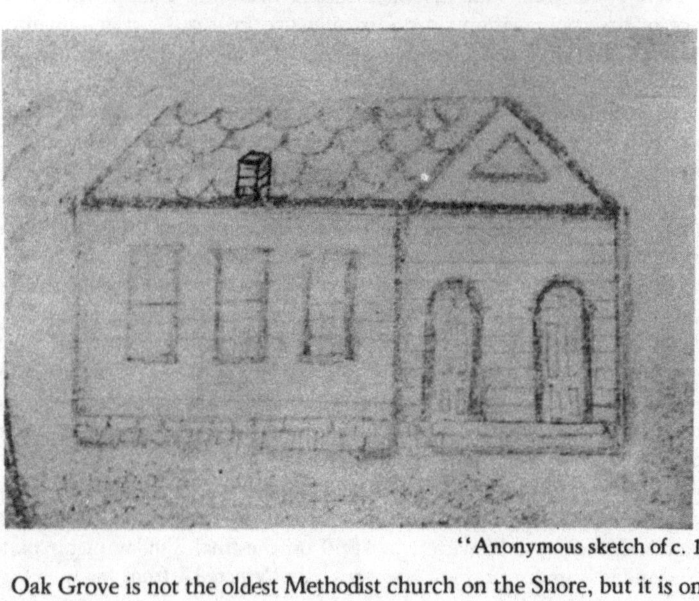

"Anonymous sketch of c. 1901"

Oak Grove is not the oldest Methodist church on the Shore, but it is one of the most venerable and perhaps the most famous. Thanks to a Sunday school said to be the oldest in the nation, it has been mentioned in more books and publications than any other Methodist church on the Eastern Shore of Virginia.

The home of Captain Thomas Burton near Chancetown was one of only four places visited by Francis Asbury in 1784, and on his earliest visits to the Shore the bishop almost always stayed with Burton, as in 1786, 1787, and 1788. Some rift must have developed between the two men, however, for after 1788 Burton's home dropped from Asbury's itinerary. When William Colbert was the circuit preacher in 1795 there was no Methodist activity in the vicinity of Burton's, and indeed the Captain himself had developed a reputation as a staunch Episcopalian and an anti-Methodist.

The church's continuous history must be dated from Thomas Smith's revival of 1800 and 1801. Burton was among those present at St. George's Episcopal Church in Pungoteague when the Reverend Cave Jones, alarmed at the spread of the Methodist revival in that community, preached the "funeral sermon of Methodism" on Christmas Day in 1800. Burton left the service unconvinced, ill at ease, and spent the next several days in distress. Finally summoning Thomas Smith, he plied him with questions, was satisfied that his antipathy towards the Methodists was ill-founded, and opened up his home to Smith for preaching services.

Smith preached at Burton's home on New Year's Day 1801, and immediately a revival began that lasted uninterrupted for thirteen days. When it was over, a new society was formed with Captain Thomas Burton's the first name on the membership list. Within a short time there were fifty whites and forty blacks in the congregation, and Burton's home, his barn, and the bower on his property could not hold them. Burton oversaw the erection of a chapel on his land and suggested the name "New Friendship" for it, but it became Burton's Chapel instead, at the insistence of the congregation. Burton's influence in it was paramount until his death in 1821, and his will deeded the meetinghouse to the congregation. His sons, Joshua and Garrison, stepped off the land and carried on in his stead.

In 1818 William Elliott of Bradford's Neck transferred to Burton's Chapel the afternoon Sunday school that he had been operating in his home since 1785, and the congregation gained what is said to be the oldest continuous Sunday school in America, and what is surely its main claim to fame and its only connection with the earliest days of Methodism on the Shore. Elliott oversaw the school until his death in 1836, when Joshua Burton became the superintendent.

In 1834 the original building was enlarged, and $50 was spent to make the room twenty feet longer and to extend the slave gallery. At its completion, Garrison Burton and his wife deeded the building to the Philadelphia Conference. Revivals continued and the congregation grew until in 1848 the old building was removed and a newer one erected in its place (the old building was used on a nearby farm until it burned about 1889). The new building contained fine pews and an organ, considered a popish scandal by some members.

In 1847 when James Brindle was pastor, Burton's Chapel put the question of the north-south division of the denomination to a vote and chose to remain in the Philadelphia Conference. However, in 1860 on the final Sunday of his pastorate there Alexander Wiggins of that conference was "ejected" from his pulpit by the members, and Major S. Colonna of the southern Virginia Conference was invited to replace him. During the Civil War the church was served almost entirely by local preachers, and like the other southern Methodist churches was closed by order of the Union army briefly in 1864.

On a Sunday afternoon in March 1870, the second church building burned, and the congregation decided to rebuild at a different site. They met in a barn until the present Oak Grove Church was dedicated in 1871. The old site and the old name were abandoned although the black members of the congregation, released to form their own church after the fire, took the old name and erected a building near the old site.

The new Oak Grove Church was a strong and vigorous congregation, considered one of the most up-to-date and progressive in the area. In the new building there was preaching every Sunday for the first time, and in 1878 the first Woman's Foreign Missionary Society on the Shore was founded here. Five other churches were born from this congregation: Burton's (1870), Wachapreague (1882), Smith's Chapel (1895), Mears Memorial (1908), and Melfa (1913).

Although the church was built on its present location to be in the center of a shifting population, the coming of the railroad a decade later shifted the population once again, and Oak Grove was ultimately eclipsed by its daughter church in nearby Melfa. Today the congregation shares its pastor with Melfa and Locustville. The present membership of the church is less than 100, and an average of about twelve persons still meet weekly for the ancient Sunday school.

[Sources: 3, 101, 102, 103, 104, 158, 176]

Location: see CHANCETOWN, MELFA

OAK HALL

see: Downing's United Methodist Church

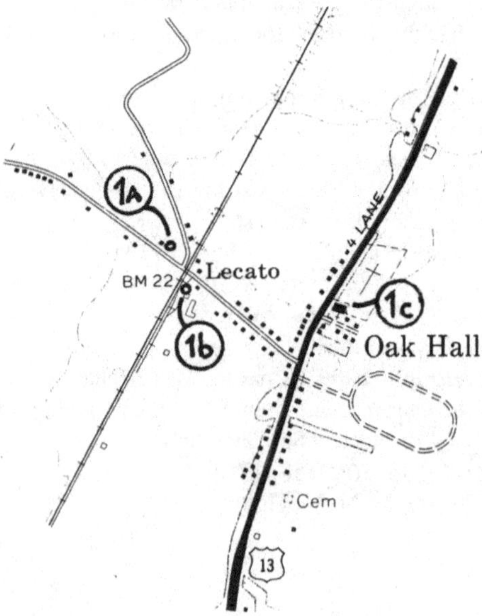

1a - Downing's Methodist: original site 1791-1854
1b - Downing's Methodist: second site 1854-1888
1c - Downing's Methodist: site since 1888

*OCCOHANNOCK CHURCH

[CE 1655-1663]
Belle Haven

Before the establishment of permanent county seats, the courts of the Eastern Shore counties met in a number of different communities, following the center of the expanding population. One such community was "Occohannock," near Belle Haven. Here Richard Kellam in 1655 gave the county permission to erect public buildings on his property at the head of Occohannock Creek.

One of the public buildings erected soon thereafter was Occohannock Church. With Nandua Church further north, it composed the new Occohannock Parish, and was the scene of several of the punishments inflicted upon local citizens for various offenses, criminal and ecclesiastical.

The court settled down at Occohannock for only a few years, and when the public interest was no longer served by county possession of the site, the location reverted to Kellam. The church dropped from the records altogether in 1663. The exact site of all this activity is not known today, but it was in the neighborhood of the estate, "Mount Pleasant," west of Belle Haven.

[Sources: 70, 90]

Location: see BELLE HAVEN

OCEAN VIEW UNITED METHODIST CHURCH

("Wachapreague")
[ME-S 1882, M 1939, UMC 1968]
Wachapreague

The southern Methodist church in Wachapreague was the second congregation to grow out of the interdenominational services held in Temperance Hall, south of the town, after 1875. Powelton Presbyterian Church was organized from this work in1880, and the Methodist congregation, an extension of Oak Grove Church, in 1882.

The first church building was erected on Main Street in Wachapreague on land purchased from George and Susan Fox. The building was used from 1882 until

1902, when the congregation built a second structure on a larger site a few blocks east. When the older building was abandoned, it was purchased by A. H. Gordon Mears, founder of the Wachapreague Hotel, and converted into an apartment building, which was later torn down to make room for a newer house now on the site.

The second building was dedicated in 1902 when J. Arthur Winn was pastor. A major church school annex had just been dedicated when on February 10, 1935, the building was completely destroyed by fire. The fire began during services on Sunday morning, but was contained at first in the rafters between the metal ceiling and the roof. Mrs. A. H. Gordon Mears, seeing the ceilings glow, was the first to suspect that the church was afire. The congregation was evacuated safely, and piano and pews were removed to across the street, only to be ignited and burned by sparks from the burning building. There was no fire department in the town at that time, and for a while flames threatened the entire village. The weather was, however, damp, and only this church was destroyed.

On August 25, 1935, the present brick structure was completed and dedicated. Dr. T. F. Carroll of Mt. Vernon Methodist Episcopal Church, South, in Danville preached the dedicatory sermon. When this building was occupied, the congregation took its present name, Ocean View.

Ocean View and Smith's Chapel in Quinby have shared the same pastors since their earliest years. The charge today is called Wachapreague-Quinby, and the parsonage is in Wachapreague. The present membership of this church is about 250.

[Sources: 101, 110, 111, 123, 176]

Location: see WACHAPREAGUE

ONANCOCK

see: **Bascom's Chapel Methodist Episcopal Church South*
Bethel African Methodist Episcopal Church
Cokesbury United Methodist Church
Glorious Church of Jesus Christ of the Apostolic Faith
Holy Trinity Episcopal Church
Market Street United Methodist Church
Naomi Makemie Presbyterian Church
Onancock Baptist Church
**Port Scarburgh Church (Church of England)*
Rock Church of the Eastern Shore
St. John's Baptist Church

1 - Port Scarburgh Church: approximate site
2a - Cokesbury Methodist: "Wesley," Seymour home, site of meetings 1788-1821
2b - Cokesbury Methodist: site since 1822
3 - Bascom's Chapel ME-South
4 - Onancock Baptist
5a - Market Street UMC: used Bascom's Chapel 1866-1882
5b - Market Street UMC: site since 1882
6a - Bethel AME: original site 1868-1908
6b - Bethel AME: site since 1908
7a - Naomi Makemie: used Bascom's Chapel 1883-1896
7b - Naomi Makemie: site since 1896
8 - St. John's Baptist
9 - Holy Trinity Episcopal
10 - St. Peter's Catholic: "Windward Hall" site 1942-1949 (see ONLEY)
11 - Glorious Apostolic Church
12 - Rock Church: site since 1978 (for original site 1976-1978 see ONLEY)

ONANCOCK

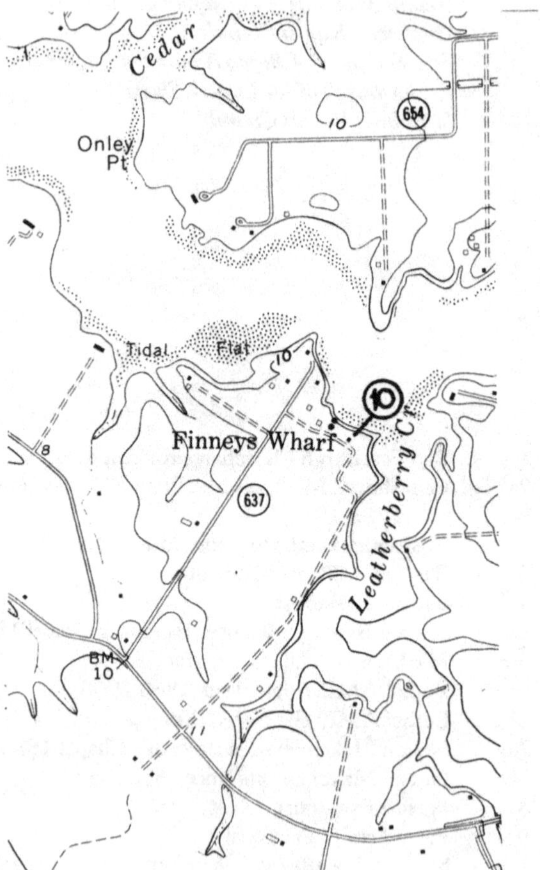
Cedar
Onley Pt
654
Tidal Flat
Finneys Wharf
637
Leatherberry Cr
BM 10

Onancock
North Branch
Onancock
Sewage Disposal
658
BM
North Br
Central Br
South Branch
BM 14
Cem
High Sch
BM 21
WT
Joynes
178
BM 32
Mt Holly Cem
Onancock
Fairlawn Cem
718
Radio Tower
Radio Tower
Onancock Cem
Titlow Cr
638
Titlow
BM 14
718
Joynes
2A
2b
3
7A
5A
6A
12
4
5b
7b
1
8
8
6b
11

ONANCOCK BAPTIST CHURCH

[ABA 1855]
Onancock

Onancock Baptist Church, like Drummondtown Baptist, was born in the mind of Anna C. Taylor, who at her death in 1850 left a trust of $2800 to build new churches in those two towns. Louis D. Drummond administered the estate and invested the money, and the church at Onancock was the first of the two to be built. In 1855 the new building was dedicated by Dr. Tiberias Gracchus Jones of Norfolk. It cost $2300 and had a gallery for black members. The church was constituted in 1856 by ten members, most of them from Hollies, and it was admitted into the Accomack Baptist Association in that same year.

Onancock's first pastor was Patrick Warren, Jr., a strong leader of marked southern persuasions. During his pastorate there, Union authorities singled out Onancock as the spot where "more mischief has been concocted in the way of blockade running and special disloyalty than in any other place of equal dimensions within this region." Warren was a good friend of William Gwynn Coe, pastor of the independent Methodist church in Onancock, and Coe preached an extended revival for him in the Baptist church in November and December of 1863. Warren served the church until 1868, died in 1871, and is buried in Onancock.

The first Baptist parsonage on the Shore was erected in Onancock by this church, Hollies, and Drummondtown in 1876. However, the Onancock congregation grew so rapidly during the last part of the nineteenth century that it erected a second parsonage of its own in 1890. In 1887 eleven members of this congregation withdrew to become charter members of Broadway Baptist Church in Cashville. A Woman's Missionary Society was formed in 1898, and in 1903 the congregation engaged its first full-time minister, James Long, for $750 a year. The church has been a station ever since.

In 1891 the old church building was moved back and turned around to become the Sunday school auditorium for a new and larger church building. The new building erected in front in that year cost $5677. In 1954 the church was given a piece of adjacent property, and a large educational annex was added to the back of the building.

Onancock Baptist Church is the fourth largest congregation of its denomination on the Eastern Shore of Virginia, after Union, Exmore, and Bethel. Its present membership is about 300.

[Sources: 39, 69, 99, 122, 142]

Location: see ONANCOCK

ONLEY

see: *Central Baptist Mission*
**Crossroads Baptist Meetinghouse*
**Faith Tabernacle Assembly of God*
Onley Baptist Church
Onley United Methodist Church
St. Peter's Roman Catholic Church

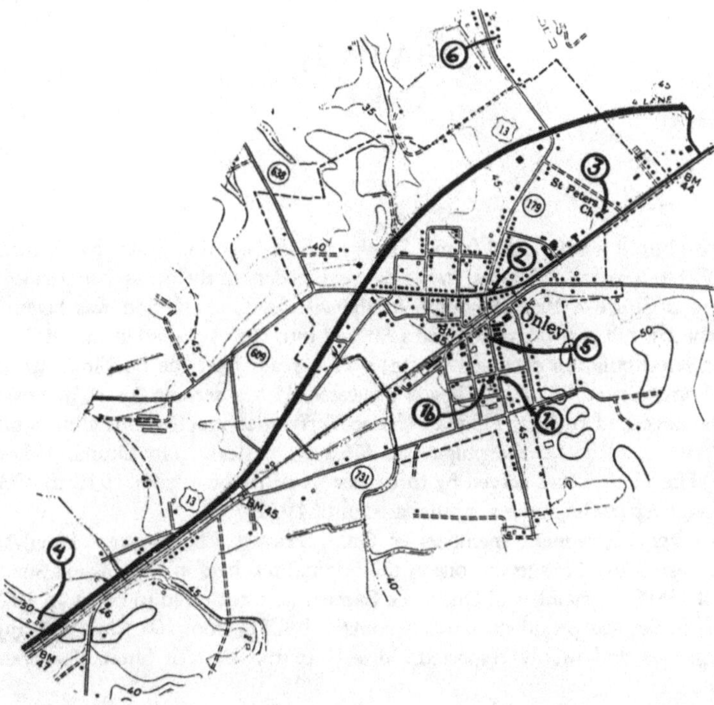

1a - Onley UMC: site since 1891
1b - Onley UMC: original building moved to this site 1913-1923
2 - Onley Baptist
3 - St. Peter's Catholic: site since 1949 (for original site 1942-1949 see ONANCOCK)
4 - Central Baptist: site since 1976 [for original site 1976-1976 see TASLEY]
5 - Rock Church: site 1976-1978 [for location since 1978 see ONANCOCK]
6 - Faith Tabernacle: worshiped in this building 1976-1977

Location unknown: Crossroads Baptist Meetinghouse sites
Keller-Onley AME Mission site 1893-1898 [see KELLER]

*ONLEY AFRICAN METHODIST EPISCOPAL MISSION

(see Keller African Methodist Episcopal Mission)

ONLEY BAPTIST CHURCH

[ABA 1905]
Onley

This church was founded from a Sunday school begun in Onley by Onancock Baptist Church in 1905. By the end of the year leaders of the group had decided to erect and organize a Baptist church in the village. Construction was begun in 1906, the church was organized and admitted into the Association in 1907, and the completed building occupied in 1909. Five years later the building was paid for, and on August 12, 1914, it was dedicated with a sermon by A. J. Fristoe.

The Reverend B. Lacy Hoge of Onancock Baptist supplied this church until 1908, then until 1912 the pulpit was filled by pastors from Drummondtown Baptist. The church was served by three pastors of its own from 1912 to 1931, even though a parsonage was not purchased until 1922.

Two very prominent members of Onley Baptist Church were Lloyd and Sadie Savage. Lloyd Savage was one of the original teachers in the mission Sunday school of 1905. A member of Onancock Baptist, he transferred to Onley in 1922. His wife, Sadie, was president of the Accomack WCTU from 1911 to 1939. Both were vigorous and highly respected "dries" in the Eastern Shore temperance movement.

In 1931, Onley joined Broadway Baptist in Cashville, and the two have shared their pastors ever since. In 1956 the congregation completed a large educational addition to the church building. The church today has over 180 members.

[Sources: 41, 69, 122]

Location: see ONLEY

ONLEY UNITED METHODIST CHURCH

("McMath Chapel")
[ME-S 1891, M 1939, UMC 1968]
Onley

(first building; photo prior to 1913)

The Onley Church was founded by Locustville in 1891. The building was dedicated on March 22, 1891, and the deed for the church lot refers to the church as McMath Methodist Episcopal Church, South.

The church, like the town in which it was built, grew quickly, soon outdistancing more rural Locustville. A Woman's Foreign Missionary Society was organized here in 1894, and the first parsonage was in use by 1898. The congregation had the building painted in 1899, and a new parsonage, the present one, was occupied in 1901.

In 1913 the old church was moved aside and construction of a new one begun on the same site. Former governor A. J. Montague spoke at the laying of the cornerstone on October 21, 1913, and the building was dedicated when P. M. Hank was the pastor. The original building burned in 1923.

Onley is today a church of over 230 members, and it has shared its pastors with the church in Greenbush since 1946.

[Sources: 50, 109, 110, 111, 123]

Location: see ONLEY

OYSTER

see: **Oyster Baptist Mission*
**Salem Methodist Episcopal Church, South*
Travis Chapel United Methodist Church

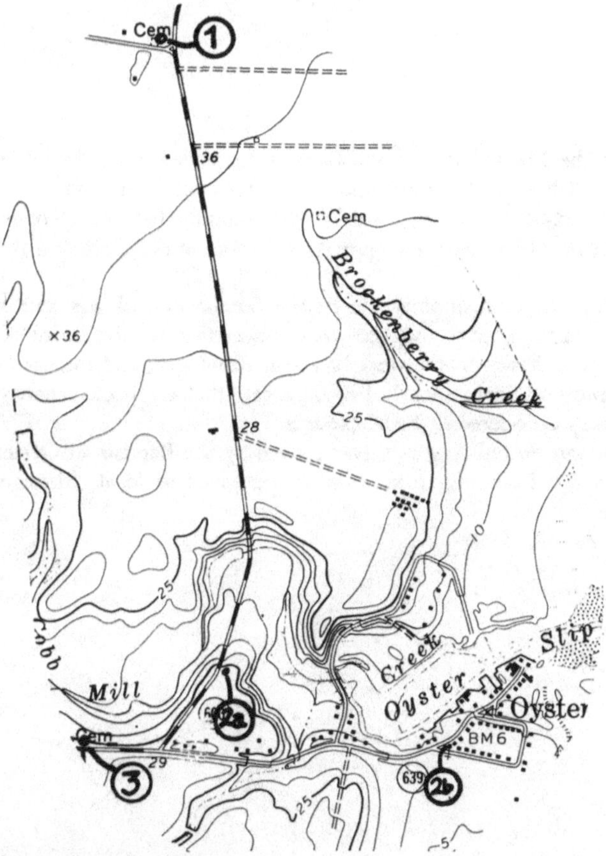

1 - Salem Methodist: site 1828-1911
2a - Travis Chapel Methodist: original site 1908-1925
2b - Travis Chapel Methodist: site since 1925
3 - African Baptist: original site 1869-1892 [for site since 1892 see CHERITON]

*OYSTER BAPTIST MISSION

[ABA 1908-1909]
Oyster

Both the Methodists and the Baptists descended upon the village of Oyster in the year 1908. In that same year in which Travis Chapel was established there by Salem Methodist Church, Lower Northampton Baptist Church opened a mission Sunday school there, with the apparent intention of establishing a Baptist church in Oyster.

During the first summer the Baptist Sunday school was successful. Lower Northampton reported to the Accomack Association an enrollment of 87 persons. Within a year, however, the work had been abandoned, and the minutes of Lower Northampton on September 4, 1909, indicate that the books, money, and organ in use there were offered to the Methodists.

Although no building was ever erected by the Baptists in Oyster, there was lumber on hand waiting to be used. It was given to local citizens who used it elsewhere.

[Sources: 69, 139]

PAINTER·

see: **Ames Chapel Methodist Episcopal Church*
Garrison's United Methodist Church
New Mt. Zion Baptist Church
**Painter Methodist Episcopal Church, South*
Snead's United Methodist Church
**Teaching the Way Center*

1a - Garrison's Methodist: original site 1784-1927
1b - Garrison's Methodist: site since 1927
2 - Ames Chapel Methodist: probable site
3 - New Mt. Zion Baptist
4 - Snead's Methodist
5 - Painter ME-South
6 - Teaching the Way Center

Old Painter Methodist Church

PAINTER

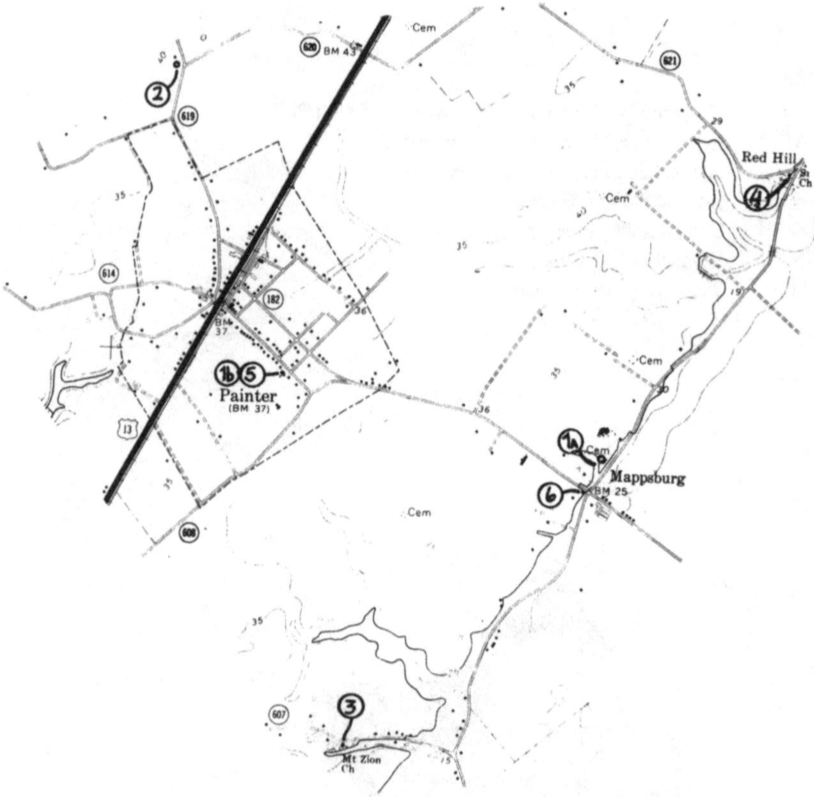
Cem
620 BM 43
621
2
619
35
Red Hill
Ch
4
Cem
614
35
182
BM 37
36
19
Cem
1b 5
Painter
(BM 37)
13
36
1a
Cem
Mappsburg
6
BM 25
608
Cem
35
3
607
Mt Zion Ch
15

*PAINTER METHODIST EPISCOPAL CHURCH, SOUTH

[ME-S 1905-1927]
Painter

For some years after the coming of the railroad the Garrison's congregation was wracked by controversy over whether or not to relocate near the railroad. Finally, in 1905 an amicable decision was reached, and part of the congregation withdrew to establish Painter Methodist Episcopal Church, South. A lot next to the schoolhouse in Painter was purchased in 1905, and the building erected in 1906. The new church was dedicated in February 1907 by the Reverend H. E. Johnson of Suffolk.

Painter and Garrison's remained on good terms and were served by the same pastors. The effect of the railroad on the shift in population was, however, permanent, and gradually the older church in Mappsburg began to decline. In 1927 the two congregations decided to merge and were reunited. The Garrison's building was moved to Painter and the buildings joined at the back.

The Painter building is today the church school section of the structure and sits parallel to the road. The reunited congregation took the old name, Garrison's.

[Sources: 109, 123, 176]

Location: see PAINTER

PARAMORE'S METHODIST EPISCOPAL CHURCH

(see Locustville United Methodist Church)

PARKSLEY

see: *Adams United Methodist Church*
**Christian Science Society of Parksley*
Disciples Church of New York
Grace United Methodist Church
Mt. Olive Holiness Church
**Mt. Zion Baptist Church*
Parksley Baptist Church
**Parksley Methodist Episcopal Church*

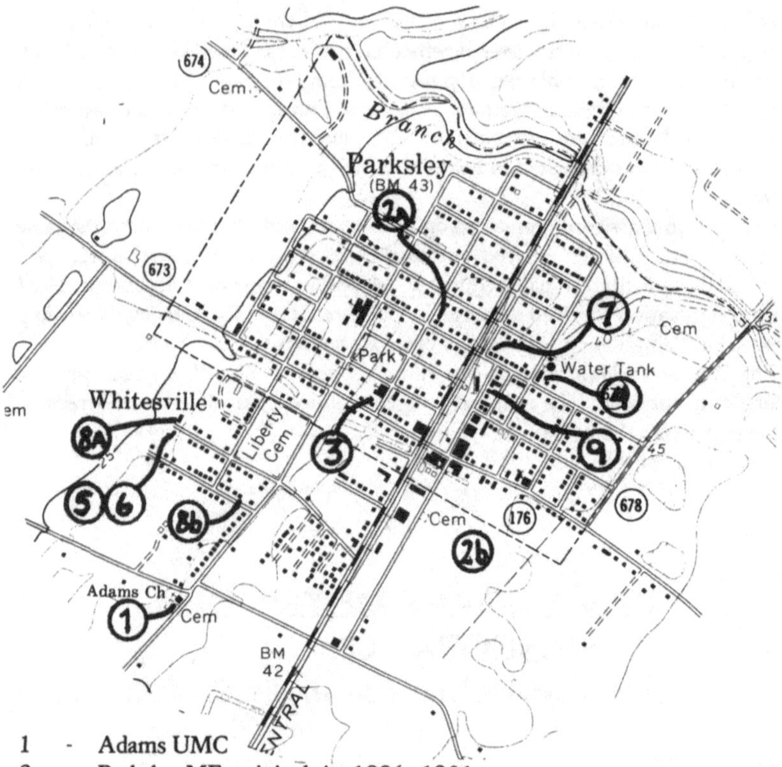

1 - Adams UMC
2a - Parksley ME: original site 1886-c1901
2b - Parksley ME: building moved to this site c1901-c1930
3 - Grace UMC
4 - Parksley Baptist
5 - Mt. Zion Baptist
6 - Mt. Olive Holiness
7 - Christian Science Society
8a - Disciples Church: this building used for residences
8b - Disciples Church: this building used for worship
9 - Baptist Bible Church: original site 1975-1976 [for present location see ACCOMAC]

PARKSLEY BAPTIST CHURCH

("Lee Mont")
[ABA 1878]
Parksley

This church was founded from Bethel Baptist Church, and established in Lee Mont in 1878, before the railroad came or the town of Parksley existed. The church building was erected and dedicated in 1878, and the congregation admitted into the Accomack Association in 1880.

In 1893 the Baptists of Lee Mont voted to remove to the growing new village of Parksley, even though there was no building there to house them. Services were held over the storehouse of D. H. Johnson until 1896, when a fire swept away books, chairs, and organ. Parksley Methodist Episcopal Church then offered the Baptists the use of their sanctuary, and the Baptists assembled there until a new building could be erected.

There were 25 members of the church when the cornerstone was laid in 1897. The building was dedicated two years later. An educational unit was added in 1954. The old Lee Mont building burned early in the twentieth century.

In its earliest years, the Lee Mont congregation shared its pastor with Bethel and Shiloh. Throughout much of the early part of this century, Parksley was on a field with Zion Baptist Church. The church became a station in 1956 and has been such ever since, although its pastor also supplied the pulpit of Shiloh between 1961 and 1965. There are today about 180 members, and the parsonage is in Parksley.

[Sources: 69, 122, 123, 176]

Location: see PARKSLEY

*PARKSLEY METHODIST EPISCOPAL CHURCH

("Mallalieu")
[ME 1886-1901]
Parksley

The northern Methodist church in Parksley was founded in 1886,the year of the resurgence of the Methodist Episcopal Church on the Eastern Shore of Virginia. It was dedicated in November of that year by Bishop Willard F. Mallalieu. Although it is said to have been named in his honor, the church is always referred to in denominational records as Parksley.

The church stood on Wilson Avenue on land purchased in 1886 for $200, behind the present district parsonage of the United Methodist Church. It was a simple frame building, the first church building within the town limits. After 1888, when the northern Methodists ceased to participate in the Turlington Campmeetings, camp meetings were held almost yearly near this church.

In 1891 the congregation remodeled and improved their building. There were 132 members on the Parksley Circuit at that point (Parksley, Crowsontown, and Ebenezer), the highest ever. By 1900 Parksley had been eclipsed in size by Crowsontown, which became a station appointment in that year. The Parksley Charge is last listed in the records of 1901, and apparently after that year the church was closed.

The church building was ultimately sold and moved to downtown Parksley, where it became a granary. It burned about 1940, and today its final site lies buried under the asphalt of the Colonial Store parking lot. The parsonage still stands on Wilson Avenue, next door to where the church stood.

[Sources: 110, 117, 123, 176]

Location: see PARKSLEY

PENTECOSTAL HOUSE OF PRAYER

[CCD 1956, Independent 1973]
Birdsnest

The Pentecostal House of Prayer was founded, built, and paid for through the efforts of Sister Madeline Beckett, who was at that time a member of the Philadelphia Church of Christ Disciples in Cape Charles. The church was established in 1956. Elder Southey Satchell of the Weirwood congregation preached here until his death, and thereafter Sister Beckett assumed the pastorate in her own right.

In the second decade of the church's existence, Sister Beckett was forced by ill health to leave her work in the hands of others, and her return to the scene four years later found the church virtually defunct. She again assumed the active pastorate and the work of building up the church again. Since that time the principal activity has been not regular worship services but a school for small children which she conducts on Sundays. The founder and her church have been, in recent years, independent of all denominational affiliations.

[Sources: 124, 176]

Location: see BIRDSNEST

PHILADELPHIA CHURCH OF CHRIST DISCIPLES

[CCD 1929]
Cape Charles

This is the first church of this sect (officially known as the Jerusalem General Assembly of Firstborn Church of Christ Disciples) on the Eastern Shore of Virginia, and it is esteemed as the mother church by the other congregations of the sect. Not only that, it is the first Pentecostal congregation of any sort, black or white, on the Eastern Shore of Virginia.

This church began in 1929 when Sister Kellam came to Cape Charles from Norfolk and gathered the first Church of Christ Disciples in worship services in private homes around the town. The new little congregation was a ''full gospel'' church; it stressed the gifts of the Spirit as taught by Paul, including speaking in tongues and divine healing. Sister Kellam soon moved on to found other congregations, but strong local leadership arose in the person of James Davis, later bishop, who saw the Cape Charles congregation through its earliest years.

In 1937 the congregation purchased the old colored school property on Washington Street in Cape Charles and converted the schoolhouse there into its first house of worship. The present block building was erected more than a decade later. The older building, which was Cape Charles' first schoolhouse, stood behind the newer building until 1976, when it was dismantled.

Other congregations in Exmore and Weirwood were founded from this one in the 1940's, but by the 1950's the mother church had itself begun to decline. Following the pastorate of H. L. Washington, now of Portsmouth, and the death of Bishop Davis, there was a period of more than a decade during which the church was without leadership and its activity dormant.

James E. Davis, Jr., the present pastor, began his pastorate in 1969 when there were fewer than half a dozen members, and under him the vitality of the church was restored. Davis, now bishop like his father before him, has about thirty members under his care. Other tongues-speaking congregations have since found their way to Cape Charles, but this is the original one there, and there today, as almost half a century ago, the gifts of the Spirit are still earnestly sought and practiced.

[Sources: 124, 176]

Location: see CAPE CHARLES

*PITTSVILLE METHODIST EPISCOPAL CHURCH

[ME 1886-1897]
Miona

Pittsville was the northernmost of the new churches dedicated by Bishop Mallalieu during his 1886 visit to the Eastern Shore. It was erected in that year in Miona, west of New Church, and first listed as an appointment, with Graham's Chapel in New Church, in 1888.

The northern Methodist church in Miona had a struggling history. The building was dedicated in 1890 by Rev. G. W. Bowman, yet two years later the Conference reported that the church had already "been closed for some time." There was a total of ten members in 1892. In 1893 the congregation added new seats, and four years later erected a fence around the property, but thereafter the church drops abruptly from the records. It is said that the church was discontinued "due to dissension among the members." A parsonage lot was sold for the church in 1900, but by then the church itself was closed, and it remained closed.

A short time later the building was purchased, moved across the street, and converted into a store. A number of merchants operated businesses there and lived above on the second story. The Miona post office was established in this building in 1901, and in 1910 the southern Methodists held an oyster supper inside the old church to benefit the new Pittsville Methodist Episcopal Church, South.

By the 1950's the building was vacant and unused. At the request of the owner it was burned in a training exercise by the New Church Volunteer Fire Department in the late 1960's.

[Sources: 105, 109, 110, 117, 123, 176]

Location: see MIONA

PITTSVILLE UNITED METHODIST CHURCH

[ME-S 1910, 1939, UMC 1968]
Miona

It was in 1903, six years after the closing of the first Pittsville Church, that the southern church organized a Sunday school in Miona and began talk of building a church. "It is to be hoped that talk will not be all," commented the county paper, "for [a church] is badly needed in this neighborhood."

Seven years later Pittsville Church was erected on land provided by Thomas Martin. On November 22, 1910, the congregation held an oyster supper to benefit the recently-completed church, but the event was not held in the new building. Instead the community dined in "the corner store at Miona," which was the original Pittsville M.E. building.

The present Pittsville church is substantially as it was in 1910. The original clear windows were replaced with colored glass during the pastorate of Robert Bryan in the early 1950's. The little church made the local news in 1964 when some unknown persons stole the Bible out of the pulpit and tried to sell it.

Pittsville was originally on the Pocomoke Circuit with Pocomoke, Sanford, and Saxis churches. After Unification it was attached to Berea, Wattsville, and Atlantic, former M.P. churches. It has been on a charge with Berea ever since, and is today part of the Atlantic-New Church Charge. There are about sixty members.

[Sources: 105, 110, 116, 123, 176]

Location: see MIONA

POCOMOKE UNITED METHODIST CHURCH

("Andrews Chapel")
[ME 1855, ME-S 1860, M 1939, UMC 1968]
Grotons

It is said that the first Methodist activity in this neighborhood was a camp meeting conducted by Joshua Thomas at nearby Flag Pond. While it is not unlikely that the venerable "Parson of the Islands" did labor in this area, the Pocomoke congregation did not emerge until after his death, and then it was from the region of Oak Hall, where residents of this area formed a class at old Downing's Chapel.

By the 1850's one of the classes at Downing's was beginning to take on the characteristics of a congregation. In the summer of 1855 a Sunday school was begun in this region. In 1858 William Andrews gave a plot of land, and a church building was erected. In October of that year a new congregation was organized. It was known at first as Andrews Chapel, but the name Pocomoke, which was the name of the general area in which the church stands, soon became standard. No sooner was the church founded than it found itself in the new Atlantic Circuit. In 1860 it seceded to the southern church, and in 1864, like the rest of the circuit, was closed briefly by the Union army.

In the 1880's Pocomoke was a very prosperous and vigorous congregation. Thirty-four new members joined at once after a revival in 1882, more than the present total membership, and three years later the congregation could boast a "singing school," a new organ, and a flourishing Sunday school. Sanford Church was founded in 1883, the result of a second Sunday school established by this congregation.

The building now in use is the original building erected in 1858, but it has been extensively changed. Renovations in 1902 included the removal of the slaves' gallery, the installation of stained glass windows, and the addition of two steeples. Bishop John C. Granberry preached when the renovated structure was reopened, but not before one member, Charles Fedderman, agreed to stand for the $600 remaining in debt on the building. The building was again remodeled and improved in 1962.

Pocomoke was originally served by pastors from Downing's, from which it was formed, but it ultimately became attached to the churches at Sanford and Saxis, to which Hallwood was added in 1943. In recent years the church has been much reduced in numbers, and it was for some years served by local and retired pastors.

[Sources: 39, 103, 105, 109, 110, 116, 176]

Location: see SANFORD

*PORT SCARBURGH CHURCH

[CE 1692?-1708?]
Onancock

Onancock was known as Port Scarburgh when, about 1680, the county court was moved briefly to that town. As often happened during the 1600's, religious services followed close upon the heels of the court, and soon there arose in Onancock a church with one of the shortest and most intriguing histories of any on the Shore.

The church definitely stood by 1692, for in May of that year the court ordered that a road be cleared to it from the region of what is now Daugherty. In October of the same year a proclamation by the governor was read "att the Church at Anancock."

But the lengthiest and most interesting mention of this church in any record is from 1708: "Whereas this Court was Informed that Sum Ill disposed person did put horse or horses into the Church at Onancock Town and fed them, the Court therefore Ordered that the Sherriff or any well Disposed person or persons doe Inquire to find out the person or persons that hath put the said horses into the said Church."

Who put the horses into the church, and why? Was the church still being used at the time? Whatever happened to this church? These and other questions will forever remain unanswered, for there are no further records of this church anywhere to be found. Its subsequent fate after 1708 is unknown.

The church is said to have stood near the Town Square in Onancock, but that is a modern conjecture. Even the name of the church, if it had one, is not known, and that assigned above was invented for the purposes of this sketch.

[Sources: 70, 90]

Location: see ONANCOCK

POULSON

see: **Messongo Primitive Baptist Church*
Shiloh Baptist Church

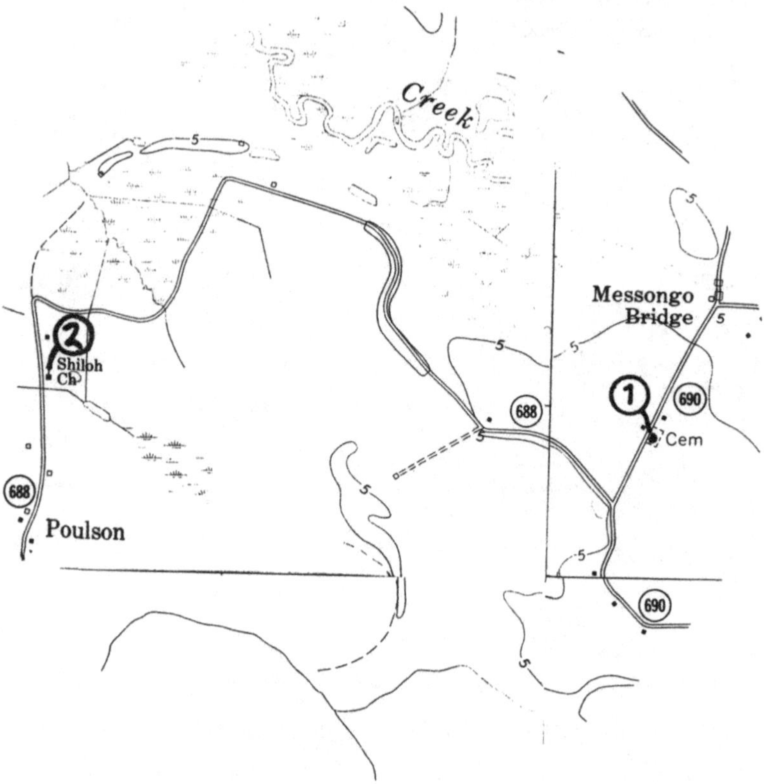

1 - Messongo Baptist: site 1779-1955?
2 - Shiloh Baptist

POWELTON PRESBYTERIAN CHURCH

[Pres 1879]
Wachapreague

The first religious services in the Wachapreague area were held not in the town itself but a mile south of town in a building known as Temperance Hall, erected in 1875. By 1879 an interdenominational Sunday school was in operation in this building, and Methodist and Presbyterian preachers alternated in the pulpit there in a setting long remembered for the disorderliness and unruliness of those who attended.

In 1879 the East Hanover Presbytery sent the Reverend John G. Anderson to this neighborhood to establish a church. Anderson, who later served Makemie in Accomac and founded Naomi Makemie in Onancock, succeeded in organizing a congregation of five members on July 4, 1880. However, none of the members were elders, or "presbyters," and Anderson's official capacity remained that of "evangelist" until 1884, when elders were elected and he was formally called by them to the pastorate.

Wachapreague at that time was known as Powelton, after the family of Powells who were developing the area. J. T. Powell, seeing numbers of children on the street in the village on a Sunday afternoon, concluded that Temperance Hall was too distant from the village and offered a site in town and $500 to the first denomination that would erect a church there. The new Presbyterian congregation accepted the offer, abandoned Temperance Hall, and erected and dedicated a church building in 1881. Shortly thereafter the Methodists also abandoned Temperance Hall and erected a church just down the street, in 1882.

Powelton shared its pastors with Makemie in Accomac in its early years. In 1919 another church, nearby Greenview Presbyterian, joined the field. When Greenview closed in 1926, Powelton was attached to Naomi Makemie in Onancock. In the 1940's it was rejoined to Makemie and Clarke. Since 1948 it has shared its pastors with Belle Haven, where the pastor lives.

Powelton has never been a large congregation. Its highest recorded membership, 99 communicants, was attained in 1960. Membership at the present is fifty.

The original building is still in use, substantially unchanged. An addition to the rear of the building was made in the 1920's and another in the 1960's. The stained glass windows, while apparently not original, are quite early, dating probably from before the turn of the century.

[Sources: 119, 120, 176]
Location: see WACHAPREAGUE

*PRESBYTERIAN MEETINGHOUSE

[Pres 1765-1791]
Accomac

The first Presbyterian church erected on the Eastern Shore of Virginia was built, not in the time of Francis Makemie, but in 1765 during one of those waves of evangelistic fervor that swept the East during the Great Awakening. This phase of the revival was Presbyterian, and the Reverend Samuel Davies of Delaware figured prominently in it. There is no record that Davies himself labored on the Virginia Shore, but during his revival Presbyterianism made a comeback on the Virginia Shore, and a building was erected in Drummondtown.

The building stood on what is still referred to as the "Meetinghouse Lot," south of Front Street on the corner of the Rural Hill estate. It was the first church building in Drummondtown. At that time St. James stood a mile south of town toward Onley.

Neither the church nor the congregation lasted long. By 1790 all Presbyterian activity had ceased there, and the trustees were empowered by the Assembly to sell the land and its buildings. The property was sold and the money applied to Margaret Academy and Washington Academy in Maryland. The building subsequently disappeared.

The last act of this congregation occurred in the next year. Apparently there remained a few who wished to carry on, for they petitioned for permission to meet in the courthouse. The ruling went against them: "It is the opinion of the court that they have no right to give liberty to any Profession to Occupy the Courthouse as a place of Worship." Despite this ruling, it is known that both Episcopalian and Methodist services were held in the courthouse during this period.

With the failure of this congregation, Presbyterianism remained dormant on the Shore until the establishment of Makemie Church in 1837.

[Source: 70]

Location: see ACCOMAC

*PULLEN'S CHAPEL METHODIST EPISCOPAL CHURCH, SOUTH

[ME-S 1883, M 1939-1940]
Hog Island

It was in 1883, almost fifty years after the first Hog Island Methodist society faded away, that the Reverend Thomas G. Pullen of Capeville came to Hog Island to reestablish the faith there. In 1884 Samuel and Nancy Kelly donated land for the church, but the little building already stood upon it, and it was already known for its founding pastor. Pullen's Chapel had a marked effect upon the village of Broadwater, and became the center of the life of the island. Twenty years later, in 1904, the lighthouse keeper, Charles Sterling, commented that the 250 islanders were all "intensely religious...orthodox to a painful degree."

By 1919 Pullen's Chapel was much reduced in numbers, for Hog Island, like Cobb's Island to the south, was washing away. Already a great many islanders had moved to the mainland, settling chiefly around Willis Wharf. Pullen's Chapel was by now such a burden on the Capeville Circuit that it was set apart and named Broadwater Mission in this year.

By 1931 there were only forty members left in the once-prosperous little church, and six years later the island was almost completely evacuated. The congregation was discontinued by The Methodist Church in 1940. Later that year the building itself was floated to the village of Oyster and attached to the main building of Travis Chapel. It is still in use today as a church school annex.

[Sources: 97, 101, 111, 116, 124, 176]

PUNGOTEAGUE

see: Pungoteague United Methodist Church
St. George's Episcopal Church
St. Paul's African Methodist Episcopal Church

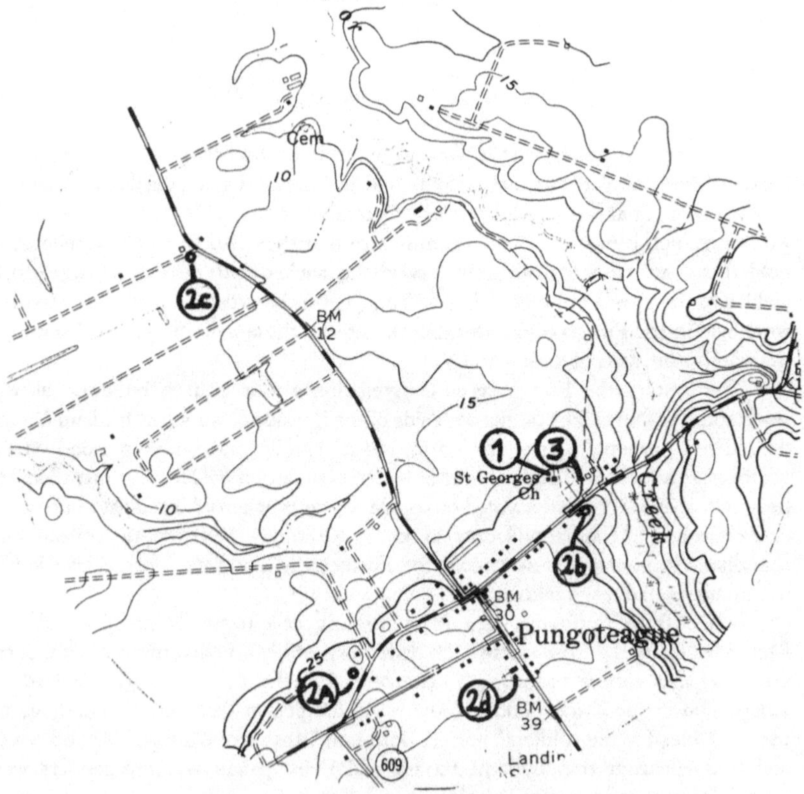

1 - St. George's Episcopal
2a - Pungoteague Methodist: first site 1812?-1847?
2b - Pungoteague Methodist: second site 1847?-1868
2c - Pungoteague Methodist: third site 1868-1888 [approximate]
2d - Pungoteague Methodist: site since 1888
3 - St. Paul's AME

Location unknown: Pungoteague camp meeting grounds of 1805 and 1806

PUNGOTEAGUE UNITED METHODIST CHURCH

[ME 1800, ME-S 1847, M 1939, UMC 1968]
Pungoteague

It was in Pungoteague that Thomas Smith held the first camp meeting on the Eastern Shore of Virginia and encountered the opposition of the Episcopalians of St. George's. That was in 1800, but by December of that year the Methodists were gathering such crowds in the old community that they had to rent a warehouse to hold them, and the revival there "awed the wicked into reverence, and people yielded to the power of grace." In 1805 and 1806 the great general camp meetings were held in the Pungoteague area, but the sites of these meetings, as well as that of the warehouse, are not known today.

The first of the Pungoteague congregation's four church buildings already stood south of the village on the west side of the Bayside Road when William Groton deeded the property to the church in 1812. The second building stood on the northern edge of the village opposite St. George's Church by 1847, at just about the time that the congregation voted to secede to the southern Methodist church, the first church in Accomack County to do so. Although there was no violence surrounding Pungoteague's secession, the northern Methodists charged that voting irregularities had taken place.

In 1860 in Pungoteague a mass meeting of citizens Methodist and non-Methodist formed a "committee" to drive northern Methodist ministers out of the area "by any means necessary." The next year the Federal army occupied the village and requisitioned both Methodist and Episcopalian church buildings for use as stables for the soldiers' horses. Both buildings were damaged beyond repair, and it is apparent that both Methodist and Episcopalian worship services were suspended in the village until after the war.

The third Methodist building in Pungoteague was erected in 1868, when the Methodists reclaimed the village. It stood west of the village towards Hack's Neck, south of the main road at "Reads Gate." Its location here indicates that the neck to the west of the village was increasing in population, and in fact the congregation established Seatick Chapel there prior to the Civil War. In 1885 the congregation divided, and half of the congregation moved the Reads Gate building further west and became Evergreen Church. The other part of the congregation erected the present Pungoteague building in the village, and dedicated it in 1888.

Pungoteague boasted an Epworth League in 1900, one of the earliest on record for the Shore. The Woman's Missionary Society was formed there in 1897.

In 1944 the present steeple was erected after the taller original was destroyed by a hurricane. The unusual front porch was added to the church during the 1920's.

Pungoteague now shares its pastor with Evergreen and Harborton, both of which ultimately derive from this congregation. The parsonage is in Pungoteague, and the present charge boundary was fixed in 1911. The church has 130 members.

[Sources: 15, 40, 61, 70, 101, 109, 110, 116, 123, 176]

Location: see PUNGOTEAGUE

Photo c. 1910

QUINBY

see: *Quinby Wesleyan Church*
Smith's Chapel United Methodist Church

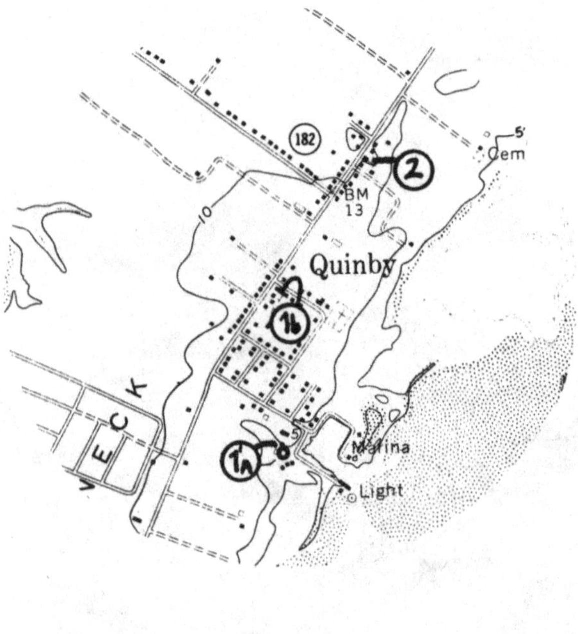

1a - Smith's Chapel: original site 1897-1922
1b - Smith's Chapel: site since 1922
2 - Quinby Wesleyan

QUINBY WESLEYAN CHURCH

[PH 1925?, W 1968]
Quinby

Quinby is yet another community evangelized by the tireless William Vickers of the Pilgrim Holiness Church. By at least as early as 1925 Vickers and his revival tent were an annual occurrence in the village. By 1931 the pastor of Smith's Chapel Methodist Church there was reporting to his superiors that few menfolk attended his services because they were drawn away to the Holiness meetings.

Although Vickers did not organize a congregation in Quinby, a small group were gathering for cottage meetings during the 1920's. When possible, members of the group traveled to Wachapreague for Sunday services.

The Quinby congregation functioned thus, without a building or formal organization, for almost a quarter century. In 1944, Mary Garrett, pastor of the Cape Charles church, organized Quinby and the Exmore congregation together, and the Quinby group was listed officially for the first time. "Brother Vickers has faithfully sown the good seed of the Gospel in this section of our District for some years," reported the district superintendent, "and now we are seeing some fruit."

Sister Garrett continued as pastor until 1947, by which time Quinby had erected its own building and was a separate congregation of fifteen members. The pastors, Milford Sullivan and Lida Brasure, conducted a revival in the newly-opened building in 1947. Although membership remained small, the congregation established itself on a firm footing under the pastorate of W. R. Sellers (1950-1957), during which time the debt on the building was liquidated.

The church's most prosperous period was the pastorate of Louetta Holden (1957-1967). She was the first to occupy the parsonage, completed in 1962, and under her the highest recorded membership — twenty — was reached in 1961. Holden, was, however, the only resident pastor; her successors came from as far away as Delmar, and membership dropped sharply under them.

Today the congregation still meets weekly under local pastors. The membership in 1975 was seven.

[Sources: 121, 123, 176]

Location: see QUINBY

*READ'S WHARF METHODIST EPISCOPAL CHURCH

(see Melson's Methodist Episcopal Church)

REAMY MEMORIAL BAPTIST CHURCH

(see Horntown Baptist Church)

RED BANK BAPTIST CHURCH

("Hungars Baptist")
[ABA 1783]
Marionville

This was the third Baptist church founded on the Virginia Shore, and it is the second oldest still in existence. Elijah Baker organized the church in 1783 and continued as pastor until 1789, when he was succeeded by John Elliott. For more than half a century Red Bank's pastors were most often shared with Lower Northampton.

Red Bank was originally located near Bridgetown, hence its early name "Hungars." The building was already standing in 1794, when Joab Bell gave the land on which it stood for the "use of the baptist preachers...to preach there forever and fcr no other use whatever." Somewhere around 1831, however, the congregation relocated in Marionville, and took the name Red Bank. The older site was abandoned and is today forgotten.

It was in the new church building in Marionville that the Accomack Baptist Association, still in the throes of schism, convened in 1832. Red Bank was one of the few Baptist congregations on the Shore not disturbed by the anti-missions controversy. In fact, the year 1832 saw a great revival at the church, and 51 new members were received by baptism.

The present church site was purchased from George Bell and John H. Powell in 1857 and a new building, the third, was occupied by 1858. In this building the Reverend William Thomas led a "precious" and powerful revival in 1872. Thomas died later that year and was buried near the church; when later the church building was enlarged, the congregation was careful to make certain that the new pulpit was constructed directly above his grave.

The present church building, second on this site and the congregation's fourth, was erected in 1899. The Reverend William Hatcher of Richmond preached on August 28, 1900, when the building was dedicated. An annex was added to the building in 1906, and in 1961 a separate church hall was constructed.

Red Bank joined with Lower Northampton to establish Eastville Baptist Church in 1877 and with Wardtown to establish Exmore Baptist Church in 1907. From its ranks have come three ministers and the missionary, Frances Carter Jones, daughter of the Reverend E. Pendleton Jones, who died in service in Nigeria in 1937.

From its very earliest years Red Bank has been a vigorous and prosperous church. Its first recorded membership, in 1809, was 125. Its maximum membership, in the mid-1950's, was almost double that amount. The church today boasts some 230 members.

[Sources: 52, 69, 70, 71, 109, 122, 124, 130]

Location: see WEIRWOOD

RED HILL METHODIST EPISCOPAL CHURCH

(see Snead's United Methodist Church)

*REESE CHAPEL METHODIST PROTESTANT CHURCH

[MP 1855-1885?]

Bayside

Methodist Protestantism had a number of prominent ministers named Reese when this congregation was established — Daniel, John, Levi, and Eli Yeates — and it is likely that the new church was named for one or all of them. The first of five churches to be founded from Lee Mont M.P., Reese Chapel was erected on land deeded by William Horsey in 1855. It stood about half a mile south of Ayres Chapel on the opposite side of the road.

Reese Chapel was a small church throughout its brief history, as the size of the building itself attested. It was an exceedingly small structure, with room for only two windows on either side of the sanctuary. There was a steeple and at one time a balcony.

Reese Chapel shared its pastors with the Methodist Protestant church in Lee Mont. William G. Coe of the independent Convention of Accomack preached here twice in 1862, at the invitation of the pastor.

The church was still listed as open in a directory of Accomack County published in 1881, sharing its pastor with Lee Mont, but it closed sometime shortly thereafter. In 1888, Hunting Creek (Calvary) M.P. was founded, and the county paper noted that "the church [Calvary] is to be named Reese Chapel, and is to take the place and to perpetuate the memory of the old one of that name located near Wiseville." Calvary M.P. never became known as Reese Chapel, but it apparently did effectively end the life of that earlier church.

In 1895 the building and lot were sold for $10 and the money invested in Grant Memorial M.P. Church. Ten years later a black Baptist congregation purchased the building and renamed it Wise Chapel. When years later it fell abandoned a second time, it was occupied by Estelle Dillard Smith and her congregation, in 1948, who renamed it Mt. Zion Holy Church. The building was damaged by a fire in 1950, and abandoned a third and final time. It stood, gradually decaying and considered haunted by neighborhood children, until it was demolished in a widening of the Bayside Road in 1970.

[Sources: 99, 110, 123, 176]

Location: see BAYSIDE

RIVERVIEW UNITED METHODIST CHURCH

[ME 1898, M 1939, UMC 1968]
Chesconnessex

Riverview was the last church founded from Cokesbury in the northern Methodist territory of the Bayside north of Onancock. In 1898 the Methodist Episcopal circuit purchased a schoolhouse in Chesconnessex and started a Sunday school there. The congregation grew gradually from that beginning.

The church site was purchased for $1 in 1902, but it was not until 1910 that the church building was erected. The Reverend Louis E. Barrett preached at the dedication of the building on June 19, 1910, and the crowd that attended paid the $750 that remained owing on the new building. The cornerstone was laid the following month by the Chesapeake Lodge No. 158 AF&AM.

Founded late in a rural area already heavily churched, Riverview never grew to great size. It has always shared its pastors with other churches, and in 1947 was made a part of the Cashville Charge. With 51 members, it is one of the smallest Methodist churches on the Shore.

[Sources: 109, 116, 117, 123]

Location: see CHESCONNESSEX

ROCK CHURCH OF THE EASTERN SHORE

[Independent 1976]
Onancock

This church is an outgrowth of the successful Rock Church in Virginia Beach, founded by the Reverend John Gimenez. Gimenez preached the first services of this new congregation on March 12, 1976.

The congregation first gathered in the old Eastern Shore Produce Exchange building in Onley, formerly owned by the Roman Catholic Church. In 1978 the congregation moved to a rented storebuilding on North Street in Onancock.

This is a Charismatic congregation. As yet small in numbers, it sponsors a Sunday afternoon broadcast on radio station WESR in Tasley.

[Source: 109]

Location: see ONANCOCK, ONLEY

Riverview UMC

RUE

see: **Middle Church [Church of England]*
Woodbury United Methodist Church

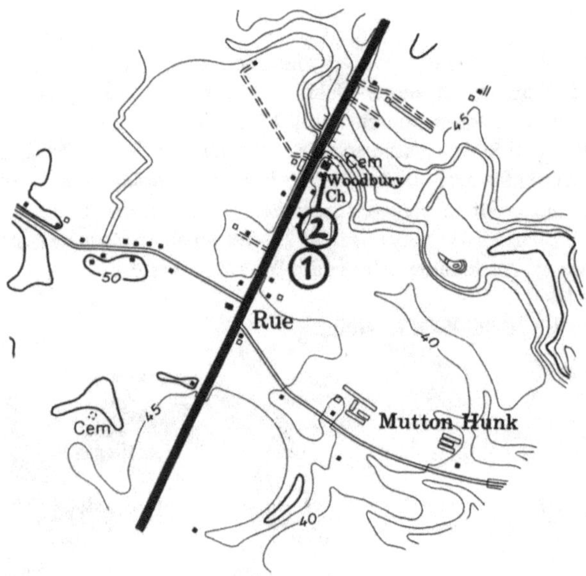

1 - Middle Church: second site c 1773-c1784 [for original site see ME-TOMPKIN]
2 - Woodbury UMC

*ST. ANDREW'S EPISCOPAL MISSION

[PE 1921-1925]
Cheriton

James R. McAllister, the pastor of Emmanuel Episcopal Church in Cape Charles, is credited with having begun this mission, but the congregation was officially organized on October 23, 1921, by M. Colgate Daughtrey, his successor. The mission congregation met in the first building of Cheriton Baptist Church, abandoned exactly one year before, and paid $11 a month in rent.

St. Andrew's had a struggling and short-lived existence. The ladies' guild was apparently the pillar of the church. They were the ones responsible for the "musical entertainment" given at the local high school in behalf of the church in the fall of 1922. Even so, the following year found the mission with only eleven members, twelve Sunday school pupils, a total yearly budget of $302, and "three months rent of the church building still due."

The Diocese of Southern Virginia listed St. Andrew's as a separate congregation only from 1922 to 1924. The only record of the church from 1925 is its payment of $8 to the work of the Diocese. Thereafter the church drops completely from the records.

The old Baptist church in which the congregation gathered still stands, and is now occupied by the First Lutheran Mission.

[Sources: 108, 118, 125]

Location: see CHERITON

ST. ANDREW'S ROMAN CATHOLIC CHURCH

[RC 1949]
Chincoteague

This church began in the efforts of local priests to minister to the Catholic residents of Chincoteague Naval Air Station, nearby on the mainland. As early as 1949 Father Bennet MacNulty of St. Peter's Church in Onley was celebrating Mass there on Sunday mornings in a building that had served as a movie theatre on Saturday nights. Later, priests from Holy Name of Jesus Church in Pocomoke City carried on the work.

In the 1950's, with the closing of the Station, the gathering-place was moved from the mainland to Chincoteague Island. Here Mass was celebrated in, among other places, a movie theatre and the American Legion Hall.

In 1964 the former Methodist Protestant church building was purchased from Christ's Sanctified Holy Church, who owned it at that time, and St. Andrew's was established. The congregation at that time was a mission of the Pocomoke City church. Father Emmett Michaels, a retired Navy chaplain living in Nelsonia, served the church frequently from that time to the present.

In 1975 the Catholic churches on the Virginia Shore were transferred from the Wilmington to the Richmond Diocese, and St. Andrew's was attached to St. Peter's Church in Onley. There are today about forty regular members, but during the summer tourist season on the island as many as 850 or 900 people attend Mass at St. Andrew's, making it at least during this season of the year one of the largest churches on the Virginia Shore.

[Sources: 110, 123, 176]

Location: see CHINCOTEAGUE

ST. CHARLES BORROMEO ROMAN CATHOLIC CHURCH

[RC 1889]
Cape Charles

In 1886 Bishop Curtis, new to the Roman Catholic Diocese of Wilmington, stood with a friend on the shore at Cape Charles and watched workers construct a pier. Struck with the need for a Catholic church in this new and promising town, the bishop turned to his friend, a bank clerk from Baltimore, and lightly suggested that he enter the priesthood in order to build the church in Cape Charles. A few days later the bishop repeated his appeal, this time more seriously: "Go to the Peninsula south of Delaware, live there among the people, make your own tracks through the woods and gather what stray Catholics you may find."

His young banker friend was named Edward Mickle. Mickle accepted the challenge, began immediately to study for the priesthood, was ordained in Rome in 1889, and later that year arrived in Cape Charles to begin his work.

Cape Charles did not at first warmly receive the Eastern Shore's first Catholic priest. "Few spoke to him, and the children were at times disrespectful." Mickle was undaunted. He himself built, almost singlehandedly, the brick church on Randolph Avenue. In his optimism, he made it large enough to seat 400 persons. He lived in the sacristy until the rectory was erected next door, also by his own hand, in 1893.

The parish consisted at first of a few German railroad workers and their families. By 1896 there had been forty conversions to the faith in Cape Charles. Two years later a parochial school, the School of the Holy Family, was opened on Tazewell Avenue behind the church. Staffed by the Sisters of St. Francis, it opened at first with four teachers and only four students. Though in a few years the students numbered 100, fully 85 of them were Protestant.

Mickle's parish at first included a large portion of the Eastern Shore of Maryland as well as all of Accomack and Northampton. There he erected churches at Easton (1889), Snow Hill (1891), Salisbury (1892), and Westover (1907). After 1910 the parish was divided, and only Accomack and Northampton Counties fell to Mickle's care.

The story of Roman Catholicism on the Eastern Shore of Virginia is almost the story of Father Mickle himself until 1930. Intent upon serving his entire parish, Mickle conducted several "missions" up and down the peninsula. "I hired a hall for a night — it was only a one-night stand — got a boy with a big cowbell, and paid him twenty-five cents to walk down main street, ring the bell, stop when he saw people and yell 'Catholic priest in town! Will be at such-a-hall at 7:30!' " When the curious arrived, they found the priest in cassock and surplice standing at the head of rows of empty chairs. Few came, fewer stayed, but to those who listened Mickle gently explained Catholic doctrines and fielded questions from the audience. Such missions were conducted at Chincoteague, Assateague (in a fish factory), Tangier, and even "midstream in Chesapeake Bay" aboard a steamer.

Intent as well upon promoting good relations with the overwhelmingly Protestant town in which he lived, Mickle brought forceful Catholic speakers to St. Charles to interpret Catholicism. One such mission was held in 1905, when "large crowds of every denomination" crowded into the church to hear the Very Reverend W. J. Guinon's ten sermons on the Catholic faith, and listened "spell-bound to the most eloquent speaker who has ever been on the Shore." "The object of the Mission," reported the *Eastern Shore Herald* of Eastville, "is to promote a better understanding and a spirit of charity among people of all denominations, in which worthy cause Father Mickle has labored so successfully for many years."

In 1915 Mickle was made Vicar-General of the Diocese. So popular was he with both Protestant and Catholic townspeople that the 25th anniversary of his ordination, in 1914, was a community-wide celebration. Citizens chipped in to buy him a car and built him a garage to house it. An even greater occasion occurred on September 29, 1927, when St. Charles was crowded with hundreds of people, including 32 visiting priests, for the investiture of Mickle as Domestic Prelate and the conferring of the title of Monsignor.

Mickle died in 1930. There were at that time about 300 Roman Catholics on the Eastern Shore of Virginia, only a fraction of whom lived near St. Charles. There were three priests at the church during the next ten years, and the school was closed in 1935. After World War II and the founding of St. Peter's Church in Onley, the parish was again divided. The years after the war, during the pastorate of Henry A. Miller (1941-1951), Mickle's fourth successor, were prosperous ones during which the church experienced its maximum membership.

The parish now includes all of Northampton County, and now numbers about 160 persons. It is a racially mixed congregation, and many worshipers travel regularly from the opposite end of the county to Mass. The church building of 1889 is still in use, substantially unchanged. The rectory next to it is also still used, the school behind it abandoned and in recent years rented to the Town of Cape Charles. Between the church and the rectory lies the grave of Edward Mickle (1857-1930), who chose to be buried in his beloved Cape Charles.

[Sources: 86, 108, 176]

Location: see CAPE CHARLES

ST. GEORGE'S EPISCOPAL CHURCH

("Pungoteague")
[CE 1676, PE 1785]
Pungoteague

St. George's is, quite simply, the Virginia Eastern Shore's oldest church. Other churches, Hungars among them, were founded before it was established. But St. George's has occupied its plot of ground since 1676, and its building has been in almost continuous use since 1738, and no other church in the two counties can equal either record.

The first church here stood partially completed in 1676, and the local citizens complained to the authorities that the vestry was planning to erect a new church at Assawoman while neglecting to complete this one at Pungoteague. The vestry noted their complaints, and Pungoteague Church, as it was then called, was completed in 1678. It was probably an insubstantial frame structure, for in 1738 it was replaced with the brick church still standing there today.

The years have not been kind to this venerable building, and in 1738 it was much larger and more beautiful than it is now. It was constructed in the shape of a Latin cross with a circular apse, and because of its shape the locals dubbed it the "Ace of Clubs" church. It had a gambrel roof and a circular arch over the front door, as can be seen from a drawing made in 1819 by James Wallis Eastburn, the young poet who was pastor in that year.

It was not long after 1763 that the name Pungoteague was dropped for St. George's, after the name of the parish. At the disestablishment of the Church of England, the vestry of St. George's incorporated, and this church remained open and functioning without a break. It was at St. George's that the only recorded anti-Methodist reaction occurred among the Episcopalians of the Shore, during the 1800 revival of Thomas Smith.

St. George's was 123 years old, a vital and functioning church, when the Union army occupied the village of Pungoteague in 1861. As in Oak Hall and Drummondtown, church buildings in the vicinity were seized for use by the army, and St. George's was put to use as a stable for horses. Over the next several years floors, galleries, and all interior woodwork were removed, and probably burned for firewood. One wing of the building was damaged when bricks were removed to build a cookhouse for the soldiers. In short, the army seized an elegant building in 1861, complete with molded columns, hand-carved woodwork, box pews, and mahogany pulpit, and left behind an empty brick shell with no interior furnishings and several gaping holes in the side. The building was in complete ruin, and within a few years cattle were grazing in the grass-covered brick aisles of the open-air interior.

The building remained in this ruined condition, Episcopal services discontinued in the village, until about 1880. By that time, neglect had even further ruined the structure. The nave walls were beyond repair and were torn down completely, the bricks used to seal up the holes left in the walls of the transept. The result was the plain rectangular building of today, which is only a portion of the original church. A steeple was added later, and the interior of the building carefully restored to a colonial style in 1966.

Since restoration in 1880, St. George's has been in continuous service. Still owned by this congregation is communion silver inscribed "This belongs to the Parish of Accomack" and dated 1734-5. A parish hall just south of the church was dedicated in 1962.

Throughout most of its history the congregation at St. George's has been quite small. There were only thirteen communicant members in 1929, and as late as 1940 only 21. The church has almost doubled in size in the past two decades and is now larger than at any other time in its modern history. In 1975 there were 81 communicant members.

[Sources: 21, 70, 90, 101, 118]

Location: see PUNGOTEAGUE

ST. JAMES EPISCOPAL CHURCH

("New Church")
[CE 1767, PE 1785]
Accomac

The town of Accomac did not exist in 1763 when it was decided to build a new church for Accomack Parish. So the new church was built southwest of the present village on the road to Onley still known as Church Road. It was a brick structure very much like Hungars Church, and it was completed in 1767.

Disestablishment of the Church of England was no setback for this church, which remained open and operating. In 1799 a solemn mock funeral was held there to honor George Washington, complete with coffin, pallbearers, and a funeral liturgy. By 1819 the church was known as St. James Church.

When the Town of Drummond was founded a mile away in 1786, the Episcopal church was left out in the country. The Methodists erected a church in Drummondtown in the 1790's and the Presbyterians in 1837. By then the number of communicants at St. James was dwindling, and the congregation voted to remove to the village.

In 1838 a lot was purchased in Drummondtown, the church building was torn down, and the bricks hauled by horsecart to Drummondtown to be used in erecting a second building there. The completed church, though smaller than the original, was a handsome building in Greek revival style, its walls twenty inches thick. A bell for the belfry, dated 1816, is of Spanish origin.

The original interior of the church was plain and unadorned, but in the 1850's or 1860's the church received its greatest treasure from the hand of Jean G. Potts. Potts was a traveling artist who was commissioned to paint the interior, and throughout the little building he executed an exceptionally fine example of illusionistic painting. On the wall behind the altar he painted columns and a hallway that suggest at first glance that the room is much larger than it is. Ceilings and side walls he painted with columns and designs suggesting plaster moldings. Potts' *trompe l'oeil* painting was typical of the period. He himself lived in the area for years and painted many other local buildings, but only his work at St. James survives. It was restored in 1929, and in 1969 the church was designated a Virginia and National Historic Landmark because of it.

St. James escaped serious destruction during the Civil War, unlike the two other churches in the village. One story thanks Miss Kitty Bayly, who interceded with her northern friends to persuade the Union army to remove the Negro troops who were for a short time quartered there. Another story gives credit to General Henry L. Lockwood, commander of the occupying forces, who was himself an Episcopalian and who saw to it that the church was not used by his soldiers except as a church. St. James remained open throughout the period of the Civil War and Reconstruction.

In 1884 the congregation purchased a rectory in the village on Back Street, a brick house of early nineteenth-century vintage that is worthy of architectural note in its own right. In the front yard of the rectory sat a small one-room frame building that had been both a doctor's office and a telegraph office. During the 1930's this "parish house" became the special project of Louisa Hope Parramore, a black member of the congregation who expended her energies and money to rescue and restore the building. It has since been used as a Sunday school room, and in 1935 and 1936 the congregation held worship services there.

The church building is one of the most famous and beloved buildings on the Virginia Shore, and it has not been substantially altered across the years. The small sacristy annex at the back of the church is not original, but is very old. The church narrowly escaped destruction in 1913, when a fire broke out around an overheated stove, and only the "prompt action of the citizens of the town" saved it. A separate parish house was erected behind the church in the 1970's.

The membership at St. James was never large in the early part of this century, and began to grow only in the 1950's. The church is now larger than it has ever been in modern times, and in 1975 had over eighty communicant members. The rector serves this church and St. George's in Pungoteague, and lives in the rectory on Back Street.

[Sources: 43, 66, 70, 94, 110, 118, 176]

Location: see ACCOMAC, TASLEY

ST. JOHN'S BAPTIST CHURCH

[ESBA 1884]
Onancock

St. John's was founded in 1884 by the Reverend Tom Byrd. The congregation purchased the lot on which the church stands in 1884, and in 1885 the present building was erected, the congregation organized, and the church admitted into the Eastern Shore Baptist Association.

Until 1908, St. John's was the only church situated in the black settlement of Onancock. In that year, however, Bethel A.M.E. was moved from its earlier location to its present site on Boundry Street, just down from this church.

The small Baptist congregation prospered enough to remodel its building in 1929, but the years of the Depression were especially hard on the congregation. In 1934 the church building was actually sold at public auction, but the congregation managed to retain it and survive.

Ten pastors have served this church since its formation, most of whom, since there is no parsonage, have had to supplement their incomes with other professions. It has always been a small congregation.

[Sources: 26, 105, 110, 123]

Location: see ONANCOCK

ST. JOHN'S FAITH CHURCH OF GOD LIVE ON

[CGLO 1962]
Makemie Park

John Crippen, founder and only pastor of this church, was a protege of ''Papa'' Joseph Turner of Atlantic when he began his preaching career in the mid-1950's. After 1962, Crippen confined his preaching to a small frame building near Bloxom, which he named St. John's and where he preached under the auspices of Bishop Jesse Handshaw.

Crippen occupied the Bloxom building for thirteen years. In 1975 he purchased an abandoned structure near Makemie Park, restored it at his own expense, and moved his services to it. This building was originally erected in 1948 as a garage, and had seen brief service in the interim as the church of a black "Jesus Only" preacher named Elder Brown. Jesse Handshaw dedicated the restored building when Crippen moved his services to it early in 1976.

Today about fifteen persons constitute Crippen's regular membership. The building is owned and maintained personally by the pastor. Like the other congregations under Handshaw, this church is Pentecostal in doctrine.

[Sources: 123, 176]

Location: see BLOXOM, MAKEMIE PARK

ST. JOHN'S UNITED METHODIST CHURCH

[ME 1915, M 1939, UMC 1968]
Atlantic

In the thirteenth year of his pastorate at Friendship in Wattsville, the Reverend J. S. Coulbourne led that congregation in the establishment of a new church in Atlantic. A lot was purchased in 1915, and the church building erected in 1918. It was dedicated in 1921, and the pews came from nearby Atlantic Baptist Church, which had just abandoned its older building.

In 1928 the county erected a new colored school in Atlantic, and St. John's purchased the old school building for use as a community hall. Some years later an addition was added to the front of the church building, and in 1975 an educational wing was built.

Shortly after it was founded, St. John's was removed from the Horntown Circuit and placed on the Oak Hall Circuit with Mt. Zion and St. John's in Messongo. The result is something that exists in only one other place in Virginia Methodism, a charge containing two churches with the same name.

St. John's has today about 100 members. The pastor lives in Withams.

[Sources: 113, 123, 132, 176]

Location: see ATLANTIC

ST. JOHN'S UNITED METHODIST CHURCH

[ME 1876, M 1939, UMC 1968]
Messongo

St. John's was founded by the Horntown Circuit in 1876, the third church on the circuit, after Friendship and Deas Chapel. In 1890 it became part of the Oak Hall Circuit with Mt. Zion in Withams. The pastor in that year was W. H. Hayman, who lived in Oak Hall, and there were 87 members in the two churches.

Like Mt. Zion, St. John's was "reseated" in 1894 and closed during a smallpox epidemic in 1899. When the Reverend John Wesley Waters arrived on the scene in 1900 he found twelve couples, all stalwart members, living together without benefit of clergy, a situation which he promptly rectified. It was during his pastorate that a parsonage was erected in Withams, and in 1904 St. John's was closed for a second time by the outbreak of smallpox among the membership.

By 1917 the church was feeling the effect of the migrations of its constituency to the North. Although the membership began to decline, the building was improved in 1920, and the church survived the Depression in relatively good shape.

In 1941 the church burned to the ground, the victim of a forest fire that raged around it. By the end of the same year the present structure, which cost $2500, was erected.

St. John's has always shared its pastors with Mt. Zion since that church was founded in 1879. The charge was first called Withams in 1913.

[Sources: 113, 123]

Location: see JENKINS BRIDGE

ST. JOSEPH AFRICAN METHODIST EPISCOPAL CHURCH

[AME 1870]
Belle Haven

This church first appears on the record in 1870, when it was one of the four churches grouped into the new Pungoteague Circuit of the A.M.E. Church.

Thomas M. Cole was the pastor in that year, and he also served the congregations in Pungoteague, Franktown, and Jamesville. Later when Pungoteague was removed from the circuit, the Belle Haven church became part of the Franktown Circuit. Among the pastors who served this church was the important John Henry Offer (1877-1879).

It seems likely that during its earliest years this congregation did not have a building of its own but worshiped in the Negro schoolhouse that, by 1886 at least, stood on the old site of the Universalist church north of Belle Haven.

In 1891 the circuit was again divided, and the Belle Haven Circuit, consisting of St. Joseph and Mt. Zion in Jamesville, came into being. William J. White was appointed pastor, and it is he who began the long process of erecting a church. Two pastors later in 1897, under the Reverend John R. West, the present church building was completed.

Belle Haven's infrequent appearance on the records of the A.M.E. Church suggests that it was not a large or important congregation in its early years. However, by 1907 it was sufficiently strong to cause the Methodist Episcopal congregation in Exmore to lament that "here we are in a territory already pre-empted by the Baptists and the African Methodists." It is apparent that the name St. Joseph was not in use at that time, but was chosen later in the century.

It was not until 1920 that the lot on which the church is situated was purchased from John and Fannie Hyslop. The congregation mortgaged the property in 1925 in order to make improvements on it, only to lose their building with the advent of the Depression. On August 26, 1933, the building and lot were sold at public auction, and only with much hard work and dedication were the people able to reclaim it.

The congregation, restored to more prosperous times, rebuilt their building in 1947 during the pastorate of R. A. Ward. The church today shares its pastor with St. Paul's in Pungoteague.

[Sources: 7, 105, 113, 123]

Location: see BELLE HAVEN

ST. JOSEPH HOLINESS CHURCH

[Independent 1940]
Atlantic

Joseph Turner, often known locally as "Papa Joe" Turner, was the pastor and chief figure in the organization and erection of this church. The church first enters the record in 1940, when it paid $900 for a plot of ground on the south side of the Wishart's Point road in Atlantic and erected a building there.

Despite its name, St. Joseph is not Holiness but Pentecostal in doctrine. Turner was one of the main pioneers of Pentecostal faith among the blacks of the Eastern Shore. Among those who were his proteges were Jesse Handshaw, John Crippen, and his own son, M. C. Turner.

The original building was used by the congregation until 1963, when a larger church was erected across the street from it. The older church still stands and has subsequently been used as a dwelling. The small congregation has maintained a working relationship across the years with Mt. Olive Holiness Church in Whitesville, which Turner founded simultaneously with this church. Turner served as pastor of both churches until his death. Since that time Alton Brown has assumed the pastorate here.

[Sources: 110, 123, 176]

Location: see ATLANTIC

ST. LUKE'S AFRICAN METHODIST EPISCOPAL CHURCH

[AME 1872, ME 1882, AME 1892]
Daugherty

St. Luke's, according to its cornerstone, was founded in 1872. The land on which it sits was deeded to the A.M.E. denomination in that year.

It seems, however, that in its earliest years of existence this church was on such a tenuous footing that it barely clung to existence, and that activity here was on-again, off-again. The first appearance of the church in any denominational record dates from 1882, when the church was under the care of the Delaware Conference of the Methodist Episcopal Church, not the African Methodist Episcopal Church.

In that year the Reverend George W. Snead of Burton's Church was the pastor. "The mission at Custis Neck is doing well," he reported, noting that the church had an active Sunday school and a "snug" new building.

There are no further records of activity here, perhaps because the church languished, until 1892, when the church appears for the first time on the records of the A.M.E. Church. The 1890's seem to have brought the first real life to the church. During this decade the church had a pastor of its own, and in 1897 the building was enlarged and improved.

In this century St. Luke's has been remodeled no fewer than three times, in 1911, 1941, and 1970, when a brick veneer was added to the frame building. A large annex was added to the building in 1978. In recent years the church has done a strong work in local community development. The church has been a station since the 1890's, and the pastor lives nearby in Daugherty.

[Sources: 7, 105, 109, 110, 113, 123, 129, 176]

Location: see DAUGHERTY

ST. MARK'S BAPTIST CHURCH

("Harmon Mission," "Sanford's Grove")
[ESBA 1934]
Melfa

St. Mark's is one of those churches that would probably never have been established were it not for the womenfolk. The determination to see a Baptist church erected in Melfa was first voiced by a weekly prayer band of women who met with Jane Allens in 1934. By 1936 this dedicated little band, who "walked, prayed, and did whatever they could to get a house to worship in," had raised $100 to buy a church lot. The lot was purchased from Mary Jane Knox, and the building begun.

The little congregation was beset with difficulties. For want of a building, the ladies taught their Sunday school in a tent which was so small that only the children could get inside and the teacher had to stand in the door. When a larger tent was obtained, it was promptly wrecked by a storm. When the building was nearing completion it, too, was leveled by a storm.

Undaunted, the group outfitted their new building for worship in 1936 and applied for membership in the Baptist association. Their first application was rejected, but by the end of the year Sanford's Grove Baptist Church was the newest member of the black association. It was named for S. E. Sanford, the first pastor.

The original church building, a frame structure built from donated lumber, was used for ten years. In 1946 the present building was erected in front of the first, which was subsequently sold and converted into a dwelling. When the present structure was completed, the congregation took the name St. Mark's.

St. Mark's has never been a large congregation. There is no parsonage, and its pastors have always supplemented their incomes by work at other occupations.

[Sources: 26, 123, 129, 176]

Location: see MELFA

ST. MARK'S UNITED METHODIST CHURCH

[ME 1896, M 1939, UMC 1968]
New Church

"At New Church, in Virginia, we have a Sunday School of over 30 scholars," reports the Delaware Conference of the Methodist Episcopal Church in 1896. "This is a growing town on the NYP&N Railroad, and ought to be looked after."

From this beginning came St. Mark's Church. The Sunday school work continued off and on until 1912, when the Reverend A. A. McDowell conducted a revival in the village and the Sunday school blossomed into a congregation. The report from the next year was that "New Church is a mission with a good Sunday school. The work is too small to give Ministerial support. If it were attached to some other work it can possibly be developed." Beginning in 1913, the new congregation was joined to the Horntown Circuit.

The plain frame building was completed in 1916. An addition was added to the front of the building in the 1970's.

Today as at the beginning St. Mark's is a small church. Its membership is 66, making it the smallest of the three churches on the Horntown Circuit.

[Sources: 113, 116, 123, 176]

Location: see NEW CHURCH

ST. MARY'S BAPTIST CHURCH

[ESBA 1913]
Jamesville

Tiny St. Mary's Baptist Church was founded by the Reverend George Burton, who thereupon served as its pastor for 34 years. The church began as a Sunday school organized by Burton in the Jamesville area in 1913. For years his little band met together ''sometimes in the heat, sometimes in the cold'' without a house of worship.

In 1920 the congregation purchased a lot, and in 1923 dedicated the church building. The church was officially constituted and entered the Baptist association that same year.

In the more than half a century that this church has been functioning, it has had only two pastors. Burton served until 1948, when ill health forced him to retire. He was succeeded in that same year by Morris H. Baines, who served until his death in 1978.

The tiny building erected in 1923 is still in use, substantially unaltered. The membership, like the building, has always been quite small.

[Sources: 26, 109, 124]

Location: see JAMESVILLE

*ST. MICHAEL'S EPISCOPAL CHURCH

[PE 1848-1868, 1906-1940]
Belle Haven

There have been two attempts to establish an Episcopal congregation in Belle Haven. Each time the church was named St. Michael's, and each time it proved impermanent.

The first St. Michael's was consecrated in 1849, and was a mission of St. George's in Pungoteague. It stood on the south corner of Main Street and the road to Rue's Wharf, but after a few years it was discovered that the land on which it had been erected did not in fact belong to the denomination. In 1868 the church was closed and the building moved to a new location, where it did service as a warehouse (in which cotton was "ginned"), a store, and the village post office. It stood adjacent to the bank until the early years of this century.

The second St. Michael's was founded from the opposite direction, from Emmanuel in Cape Charles, and first made its appearance in 1906. The congregation consisted of only eight families with $600 in hand with which to build a church.

Problems beset the congregation from the start. A lot for the church was obtained, not in Belle Haven but just over the county line in Exmore, but was lost in a dispute over the title to the property. A second lot on Main Street in Belle Haven (the deed for which contained the provision that it was "never to be conveyed to anyone of African blood or descent") was purchased in 1906. Contracts were let, but building was delayed. The year 1915 found the church small, neglected, and still without a building. "A little chapel could easily be built," read the report for that year. "We would be contented with a Service once a month."

In 1918 the treasurer of the congregation reported to the Diocese that the church guild was the mainstay of this church. "Our little Mission here has had many ups and downs. Notwithstanding we never have a service, nor a clergyman to come near us, nevertheless...we are still working, and want the Diocese to know that we are alive and are faithful..."

There were 23 communicants when, at last in 1920, the chapel was erected. Once in its long-awaited building, the congregation declined rapidly. In 1925 the church was still an "unorganized mission." By 1928, when membership was only eighteen, the rector lived across the Bay in Princess Anne County. The Depression sealed the fate of the church, and although the Diocese listed it as late as the 1940's, by then St. Michael's was virtually extinct. One of the last acts there was the annual visit of the bishop for confirmations in 1936, but at St. Michael's there was no one to be confirmed.

The building was to have been given to the Boy Scouts of Exmore in the middle 1940's, but when an attempt was made to move it, it collapsed into an utter ruin. Thereafter local families burned the lumber of Episcopalianism's second Belle Haven church as firewood.

[Sources: 66, 70, 105, 108, 109, 118, 123, 124, 176]

Location: see BELLE HAVEN

*ST. PAUL'S AFRICAN METHODIST EPISCOPAL CHURCH

[AME 1914-1943]
Fairview

The community of Fairview, below Cheriton, was one of the last places on the Shore to be evangelized by the African Methodist Episcopal Church. And like most of the later A.M.E. congregations on the Shore, the church established there was short-lived and faced a struggling existence.

St. Paul's first enters the record in 1914, when the congregation there had already erected a building on the land of Major Weeks. In that year Weeks donated the small church lot to the congregation, but three years later the congregation bought it outright anyway for $150.

In 1920 the original building was replaced by a new one, for in that year the congregation paid over $700 for the frame building recently vacated by Lower Northampton Baptist Church. This building, erected in 1869, was moved to Fairview and refitted for worship by the St. Paul's congregation.

Even so, the congregation remained small and struggling, and dwindled over the next decade. It is doubtful that regular worship services were held in the building after 1930. In 1933 the church had so declined that the church property was put up for public auction. Over the next decade A.M.E. activity in Fairview was virtually nonexistent, and the building neglected.

In 1943, Mt. Sinai Gospel Tabernacle purchased the property, and the building was restored. By then there were only a handful of members of St. Paul's left, and they transferred to Ebenezer in Capeville and St. Stephen's in Cape Charles. Years later when a second A.M.E. church, Cole's Chapel, was established in Fairview, they found a flourishing Mt. Sinai on the old property, and built elsewhere.

[Sources: 124, 139, 176]

Location: see BAYVIEW

ST. PAUL'S AFRICAN METHODIST EPISCOPAL CHURCH

("Pungoteague")
[AME 1870]
Pungoteague

John Henry Offer organized this congregation sometime between 1866 and 1870. The church first appears on the record in 1870, when it was separated from the original Eastville Circuit and made a part of the new Pungoteague Circuit. In 1880 it became a part of the Savageville Circuit, and there it remained until well into the twentieth century.

The black Methodists of Pungoteague chose as their gathering place a spot just north of old St. George's Episcopal Church, only a few yards away from the place where John Holden was lynched in 1866. The first church was built soon after 1870, even though the land was not deeded until 1883. The present building dates from 1886 and was erected during the pastorate of James A. Haynes. Haynes died four years later while serving as presiding elder in Richmond, and is buried at this church.

St. Paul's has always been a small church and seldom appears in local or A.M.E. records. Like most black churches on the Shore, it has often been rebuilt or improved. The most recent addition dates from the 1970's.

[Sources: 7, 39, 123]

Location: see PUNGOTEAGUE

ST. PAUL'S METHODIST PROTESTANT CHURCH

(see Signpost United Methodist Church)

ST. PETER'S ROMAN CATHOLIC CHURCH

[RC 1942]
Onley

This church was founded by Father Bennet McNulty of Philadelphia, who moved to the Shore, purchased and restored the estate Windward Hall at Finney's Wharf, and on Palm Sunday 1942 said the first Mass there for three worshipers. Within a short time Windward Hall had become the gathering place for a vital and growing Catholic congregation, the first on the Virginia Shore since the establishment of St. Charles in Cape Charles in 1889. During warmer months Mass was said on the porch of Windward Hall, and worshipers sat outdoors in a lovely rural setting on the edge of Onancock Creek.

In 1944 a lot was obtained in Onley, and in 1949 St. Peter's Church was erected and dedicated there. By virtue of its central location on what was then the main highway, this church quickly surpassed the Cape Charles congregation in size.

Father McNulty served the church until shortly before his retirement in 1965, after which priests were supplied from the Wilmington Diocese. Prior to the erection of the present church and during Father McNulty's pastorate, Windward Hall served as both rectory and parish house. The congregation purchased a rectory in Onley in 1965 and used the old Eastern Shore Produce Exchange building in Onley for a parish house from 1966 to 1975.

St. Peter's has from the beginning had a successful and congenial ministry to the many Latin American migrant laborers who pass through the Shore each summer. In 1975 the parish instituted a Mass in Spanish during the summer months to serve these migrant Catholics.

In 1975 St. Peter's was transferred from the Wilmington to the Richmond Diocese, and St. Andrew's Mission in Chincoteague was attached to it. The pastor of both churches lives in the Onley rectory. St. Peter's has today about 240 regular members. A major addition to the church building was begun in 1978.

[Sources: 123, 176]

Location: see ONANCOCK, ONLEY

ST. STEPHEN'S AFRICAN METHODIST EPISCOPAL CHURCH

[ME 1889, AME 1896] Cape Charles

"We have bought a church at Cape Charles, Northampton County, Virginia, for $600," reported the presiding elder to the Delaware Conference in 1889, "and we have organized a church and Sunday school." Such was the beginning of the present St. Stephen's Church, the third Methodist congregation in the new town of Cape Charles. M. V. Waters was the pastor of the new mission.

The building purchased by Cape Charles' black Methodists was the original building of Bethany Methodist Episcopal Church, whose white congregation dedicated it in 1887 and abandoned it for a larger building in 1889. It stood on the south corner of Monroe Avenue and Plum Street opposite the school grounds. The next year the white Methodists dedicated their new building on the corner of Peach and Randolph.

The church was at this time not African Methodist Episcopal, but Methodist Episcopal, a part of the Delaware Conference. Apparently it remained so for some years, although there is little mention of it in the records of that Conference. It is possible, but not certain, that Methodist Episcopal activity in the building ceased altogether after a few years.

In 1896 the African Methodist Episcopal Church first listed a "Cape Charles Mission" and sent a pastor to the church. The congregation took on new life under William J. Beckett, the first A.M.E. pastor. The building was repaired, a cornerstone set in place in 1897, and the name St. Stephen's adopted for the first time.

In 1912 the building was moved to its present site on the north side of Jefferson Street, and the original site was used for a dwelling. On its present site the building has been added to and improved several times over the years. The parsonage next door dates from 1920.

St. Stephen's has never been a large congregation. Its present membership is about 65, and recent pastors, who have not used the parsonage next door, have served this church and Cole's Chapel in Fairview.

The St. Stephen's building is the first and oldest church building erected in the town of Cape Charles. It is said that the first public school sessions were held here on the old site. When the building was moved the 1897 cornerstone was left behind, and it now rests in the museum of the Eastern Shore of Virginia Historical Society at Kerr Place in Onancock.

[Sources: 46, 113, 117, 124, 176]

Location: see CAPE CHARLES

ST. THOMAS UNITED METHODIST CHURCH

[ME-S 1893, M 1939, UMC 1968] Clam

"We have raised several hundred dollars towards building a church in Back Creek Neck, where we have much opposition from the Methodist Episcopal Church. We are now having the lumber sawed." So wrote J. W. Nicholson, pastor of the Accomack Circuit of the southern church in 1893. The church to be built was St. Thomas Church, south of Guilford on the Bayside. The area was one of the few remaining areas on the Shore where the northern church was predominant. Crowsontown M.E. Church, founded only nine years earlier, was only a mile away.

St. Thomas was erected on land given by Thorogood Mason in 1893. The building was dedicated on May 29, 1895. W. C. Vaden preached the dedicatory sermon. Founded in a rural area, it has never been a large church, but it has been consistently strong and vital throughout its history. It has always shared its pastors with the church at Guilford, from which it was founded.

The building erected in 1893 is still in use, although subsequent additions and changes have made it today almost twice its original size. The present membership at St. Thomas is about 150.

[Sources: 105, 111, 116, 123]

Location: see GUILFORD

*SALEM METHODIST EPISCOPAL CHURCH

(see Goodwill Methodist Episcopal Church)

*SALEM METHODIST EPISCOPAL CHURCH, SOUTH

[ME 1828, ME-S 1852-1911]
Chesapeake

Salem stood on Seaside Road in Northampton County at its junction with the crossroad to Chesapeake. It is not known exactly when the church was founded, but it was probably around 1828, when William Nottingham sold a lot for a church building for $5.

This little church gained nationwide headlines in 1846 during the division of the Methodist Episcopal denomination into northern and southern camps. In the spring of that year, the congregation voted, ten to six, to remain a part of the northern church, but several members contested the decision. In May the congregation submitted the issue to the Commonwealth's Attorney in Eastville, who ruled in favor of the southern minority and forbade the appearance of northern ministers at Salem.

In July 1846 the northern minister, Valentine Gray, arrived for his preaching appointment at Salem, but was bodily ejected from the building by an angry mob of southern sympathizers, most of whom were not Methodists. Gray was refused redress by the Commonwealth's Attorney, and described the incident to the *Christian Advocate and Journal* in New York, which gave the event considerable publicity, much to the indignation of its northern constituency.

Salem remained steadfastly northern despite community feeling and court resolutions, and apparently received no minister, northern or southern, for several years. In 1852, the Reverend William Lee Dalby, a native of the neighborhood and a member of the congregation, joined the Virginia Conference of the southern church and preached at Salem, and thereafter the church became a part of the southern church. Even though there was a northern minority in touch with the Accomack Circuit as late as 1859, the church remained southern throughout the Civil War and was closed along with other southern churches by the Union army in 1864. William Coe preached here once in 1864 and once in 1865.

In 1869 the original church building burned, and a new one, erected principally by two members, was dedicated on the same site in 1870. In 1878 a parsonage was erected in what is now Cheriton.

The Cheriton church was begun by Salem as a Sunday school in 1886 and erected in 1887. In 1893 the Sunnyside Circuit was formed, consisting of Salem, Capeville, and Cheriton (Sunnyside). In 1908, Salem became the mother church of Travis Chapel in Oyster and shortly thereafter fell into decline.

The church closed finally in 1911. The building was sold and dismantled, the lumber used in the construction of a barn on the adjoining farm on the crossroads. Most of the members transferred to Travis Chapel. Today only a few gravestones in the woods by the side of the road mark the site of this historic old church.

[Sources: 39, 55, 59, 99, 107, 111, 124, 128]

Location: see OYSTER

SANFORD

see: **Grotons Wesleyan Church*
Hall's Chapel Church of Christ
Pocomoke United Methodist Church
Sanford United Methodist Church

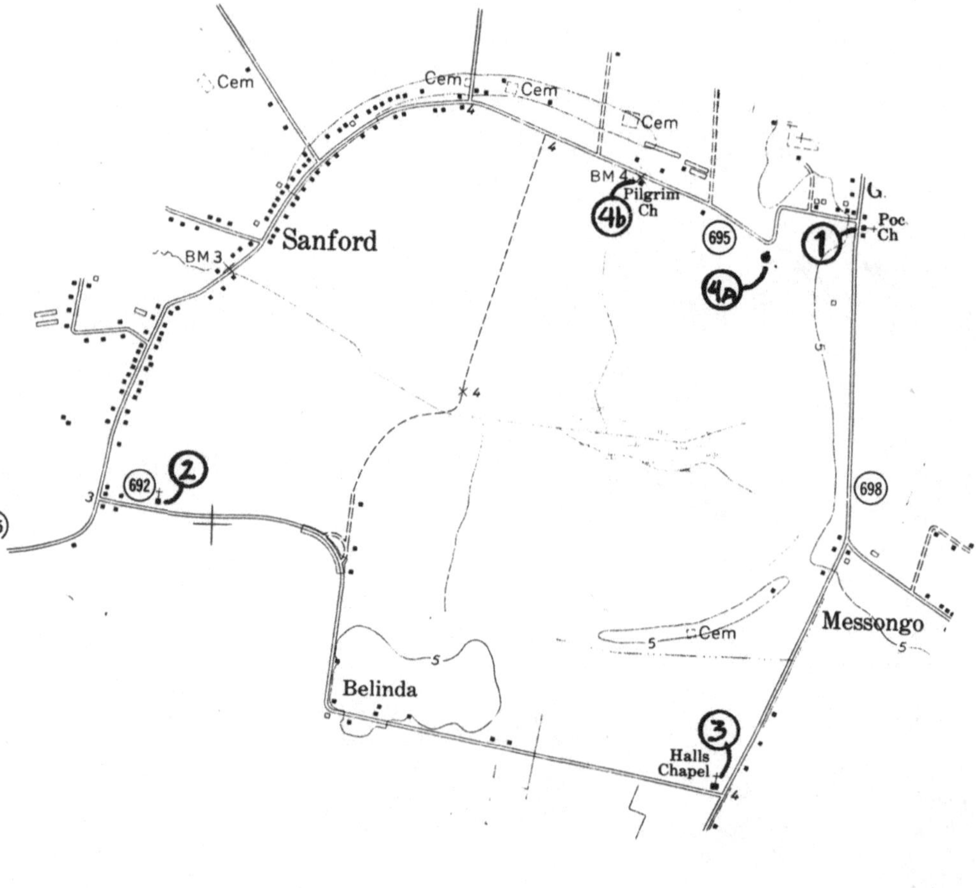

1 - Pocomoke UMC
2 - Sanford UMC
3 - Hall's Chapel
4a - Grotons Wesleyan: site of first tent meeting by William Vickers 1916
4b - Grotons Wesleyan: site of church building

SANFORD UNITED METHODIST CHURCH

[ME-S 1883, M 1939, UMC 1968]
Sanford

Both northern and southern Methodist denominations rushed to build a church in the region of the growing town of Sanford in 1883, but the southern church won. Sanford Methodist Episcopal Church, South, was founded by Pocomoke Church and erected in that year. It apparently stems from a Sunday school operated in the new village for a short time previously.

Like so many other churches on the Shore erected at the end of the nineteenth century, Sanford was built to serve a shifting population, and it quickly outdistanced its mother church in size and importance. By 1905 Sanford, Saxis, and Pocomoke, though still officially the Pocomoke Charge, built a new parsonage, and the site chosen was Sanford. Pittsville was added to the charge in 1910, but was dropped after Unification. Hallwood was added to the charge in 1943, and the four churches have been together ever since, still called Pocomoke Charge.

Sanford is today more than three times as large as its mother church. The building has been added to but not substantially altered since it was erected, although the stained glass windows are more recent.

[Sources: 109, 110, 111, 123, 176]

Location: see SANFORD

SANFORD'S GROVE BAPTIST CHURCH

(see St. Mark's Baptist Church)

SAVAGEVILLE

see: *Gaskin's Chapel African Methodist Episcopal Church*
Mt. Nebo Baptist Church
**Savageville Baptist Meetinghouse*

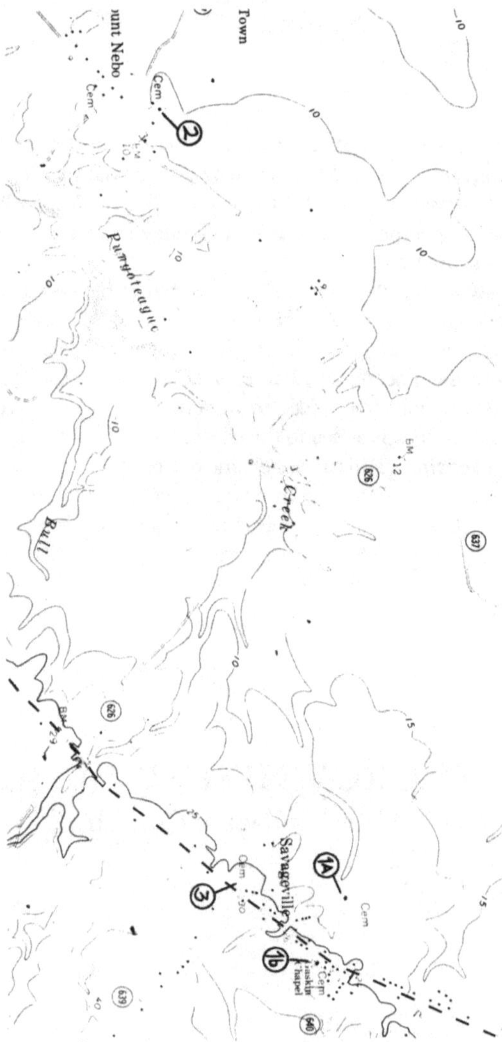

1a - Gaskin's Chapel AME: original site 1873-1951
1b - Gaskin's Chapel AME: site since 1951
2 - Mt. Nebo Baptist
3 - Savageville Baptist Meetinghouse: site 1903-1914?

*SAVAGEVILLE BAPTIST MEETINGHOUSE

[ABA 1903-1914?]
Savageville

Onancock Baptist Church erected this chapel in 1903 at a cost of $1000. That was the same year the Onancock Baptists engaged their first full-time minister, James Long, who undoubtedly preached at the new Savageville meetinghouse. Spencer Finney Rogers, the prominent layman, was, however, known as the most frequent speaker here.

The Baptist effort in Savageville was short-lived and never grew to great size. Five years after the church was built the Savageville Sunday school was still known as the "mission" school. The last known Baptist activity in the area is from 1910, when Savageville could boast one of the 29 Baptist Woman's Missionary Union societies on the Shore.

The building was apparently used for less than a decade. It was sold and moved away well before World War I; its fate after that time is not known.

[Sources: 69, 123, 142, 176]

Location: see SAVAGEVILLE

SAXIS

see: **Saxis Baptist Church*
Saxis United Methodist Church
Saxis Wesleyan Church

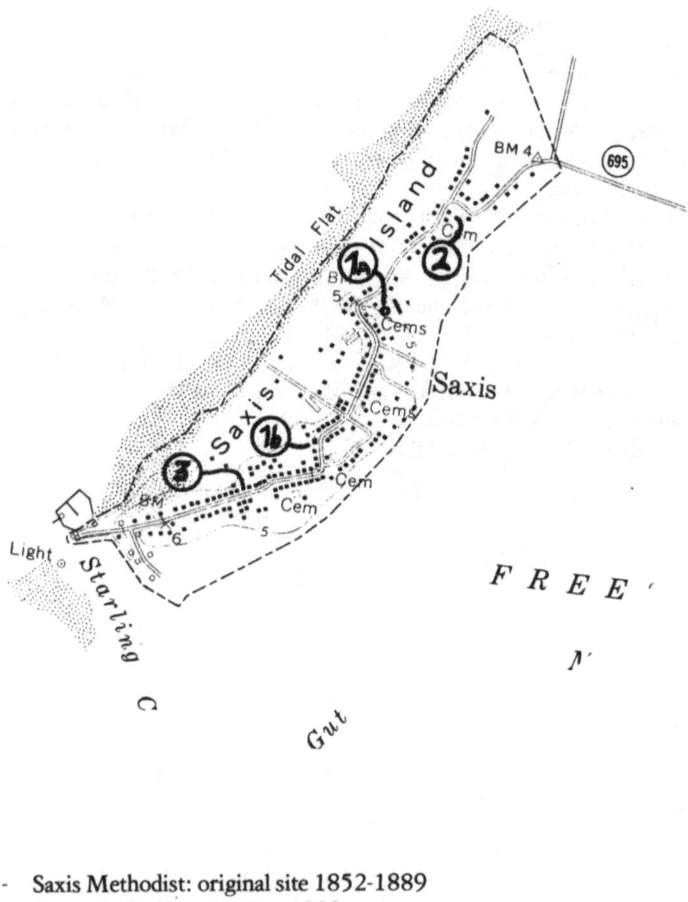

1a - Saxis Methodist: original site 1852-1889
1b - Saxis Methodist: site since 1889
2 - Saxis Baptist: site 1895-c1940
3 - Saxis Wesleyan

*SAXIS BAPTIST CHURCH

[ABA 1895-1939]
Saxis

Saxis Baptist Church, the second congregation in that town, was erected soon after 1895. In that year James and Nellie Hall sold the new congregation a lot on the northern end of the island for $7.50. The church was organized and admitted into the Accomack Baptist Association in 1897.

Throughout its history Saxis Baptist remained a small church. No parsonage was erected, and the congregation always shared its pastors with other churches. In 1932 the pastor of this church also served four others: Hallwood, Hall's Chapel, Shiloh, and Makemie Park.

By the advent of the 1930's the membership had declined to only fifteen. During the next decade membership dwindled from even that low figure, and 1938 was the last year in which the church made a report to the Accomack Baptist Association.

The building, a small frame structure, was dismantled shortly after the church closed and sold for lumber. Today a dwelling occupies the site.

[Sources: 69, 122, 123, 176]

Location: see SAXIS

SAXIS UNITED METHODIST CHURCH

("Conner's Chapel")
[ME 1851, ME-S 1860, M 1939, UMC 1968]
Saxis

During the first half of the nineteenth century Saxis, or Sykes' Island as it was then known, was a distant and inaccessible place, one of the few areas of the Shore which Methodism had not reached. In August 1851 the Methodists [illegible]red a camp meeting on the island, and the village congregation was born in tha[illegible] [illegible]eavor. By November 1851 there was a flourishing Sunday school, "the first...and only school of any kind on the Island." In 1852, George Crockett gave a quarter-acre lot, and on it was erected a church named Conner's Chapel. It is thought that the church was named for Frederick Conner, a prominent class leader at Downing's who may have been influential in founding the Saxis congregation.

The Methodists held three successive camp meetings on three successive summers in Saxis. In 1857 E. W. Stickney, a retired minister from New England, was hired as a third preacher on the circuit, and his appointment indicates that the island society was still isolated. Stickney's field of labor embraced "Saxes Island... and other places below the mouth of Pocomoke River on the bay side, where there are no regular preaching appointments at present filled by the travelling preachers on this Circuit." It is not known how long Stickney labored in this area. In 1858 the Saxis society became a part of the Atlantic Circuit. In 1860 it seceded to the southern church and in 1864 was temporarily closed by the Union army.

In 1875 the congregation bought a new lot from Avra Ellis in contemplation of building a bigger and better house of worship, but for reasons not now clear the new building was not erected for several years. It was probably completed in 1889, for in that year the congregation sold the old building to the county school board, who used it for many years as a schoolhouse. The new building, which is still in use, was formally dedicated in 1891. Once in it, the congregation dropped the name Conner's Chapel, and has been known as Saxis ever since.

Methodism remained the predominant faith of the community despite the founding of a Baptist church on the island in 1897 and a Pilgrim Holiness church in 1914. Saxis was by then a part of the Pocomoke Charge of the southern church, which included Pocomoke, Sanford, and, after 1910, Pittsville. It is the largest church on the charge.

The present membership of this church is about 180. The pastor lives in Sanford. The old Methodist "class meeting," a remnant of Asbury's day, was not abandoned at this church until well into the 1940's.

[Sources: 39, 103, 105, 110, 111, 116, 123, 176]

Location: see SAXIS

SAXIS WESLEYAN CHURCH

[IAHC 1918, PH 1922, W 1968]
Saxis

It did not take long for the Holiness work of William Vickers to move from Grotons to nearby Saxis. By 1918 Vickers was holding a four-week tent meeting in the island community, and from this work grew a small congregation that assembled at first in a private home. In that same year a lot was purchased, and through voluntary contributions and hard labor the Holiness people of Saxis erected the island's third church.

Saxis shared its pastors, Vickers among them, with the strong churches at Grotons and Bloxom, but the Saxis congregation, unlike the others, did not grow and prosper at first. Slowly but surely over the first twenty years membership declined. By 1945 the Sunday school had been discontinued. By 1954 there were only five members, there had been three years during which the church had no pastor, and the congregation was all but discontinued.

In 1955 the Reverend Bill Miller assumed the pastorate, a revival was held "at which there were many conversions and experiences of Holiness," and the congregation took on new life. J. D. Abbott, the district superintendent, reorganized the congregation on May 23, 1955. There were thirteen members, more than any year since 1937. The years that followed were among the most prosperous ever for the congregation, which purchased additional land adjacent to the church (1958 and 1972), bought an organ (1965), and improved the building several times. In 1960 the congregation reported eighteen members, the highest any time before or since. Miller served three pastorates in all (1955-1958, 1963-1965, and 1971 to the present).

Although Saxis recorded its lowest membership (six) in 1972, recent years have generally found it a healthy congregation. Its present membership is fifteen, and the average Sunday morning attendance at worship is twice that.

[Sources: 105, 121, 123]

Location: see SAXIS

*SEATICK CHAPEL

(Meetinghouse of Pungoteague Methodist Episcopal Church, South) [ME-S 1848?-1870?] Hack's Neck

This building was built privately "for religious purposes" by William T. "Billy June" Guy. It stood originally just west of the present Evergreen Church in Hack's Neck, perhaps on land which the Methodist congregation in Pungoteague purchased as early as 1848. Local residents dubbed it "Seatick Chapel" in honor of the ticks that abounded in the surrounding woods.

This Methodist outpost in Hack's Neck was used for many general community purposes, and it is apparent that Methodist activity in it ceased after about 1870. Temperance meetings were held in the building during the 1870's, and about 1878 it became a community schoolhouse. At this time it was moved across the road from its original location. Though it was a one-room schoolhouse, a curtain drawn across the middle of the room separated the male from the female students.

In 1887 the building was divided, and part of it was moved northward to the corner of the Harborton road, where it was made into a larger schoolhouse. The

Order of the Good Templars at one time occupied the second story here. The building continued in use as a school until 1907, after which it was moved a second time and converted into a residence on a nearby farm.

Methodism's second outpost in Hack's Neck proved more permanent. Evergreen Church was founded near the original site of this early chapel in 1885.

[Sources: 40, 123]

Location: see HARBORTON

*SECOND PRESBYTERIAN CHURCH

("Hopewell")
[Pres 1884-1891?]
Cedar Grove

R. D. Stimson, pastor of Holmes Presbyterian Church, led in the formation of this congregation and served as its pastor throughout its brief history. The church was known as Second Presbyterian Church, and also as Hopewell Presbyterian, after the name current at that time for the area just south of Cedar Grove.

Francis and Susan Parsons gave the lot on which the church was built in 1884, and it is not unlikely that the church building was already standing by that time. Parsons was himself a trustee of the congregation, as was also Thomas H. Dixon, a Methodist who served as the Sunday school superintendent.

The congregation had a brief history, although exactly when it was discontinued is not known. There is no record of any pastor other than Stimson, and he served Holmes until 1891. Apparently his successors did not continue to conduct services at the church, and it became in a short time a schoolhouse known as Hopewell School.

In 1898 when Cedar Grove Baptist Church was formed from Lower Northampton, the infant congregation used the old Presbyterian building until their own could be erected. The building was ultimately moved across the street, where it still stands today as a dwelling.

[Sources: 69, 124, 176]

Location: see CEDAR GROVE

SEYMOUR'S METHODIST EPISCOPAL CHURCH

(see Cokesbury United Methodist Church)

SHILOH BAPTIST CHURCH

[ESBA 1909]
Atlantic

The years have not preserved the exact causes of disagreement that resulted in the separation of this congregation from Jerusalem Baptist Church. Even so, in 1909 a number of Jerusalem's members, led by Deacon George H. T. Byrd, withdrew from that church and began gathering for services in private homes. Later that year they were organized as a separate congregation in Byrd's home in Temperanceville, and Byrd became the first pastor.

In 1912 the congregation purchased the present church site in Atlantic, and renovated for worship an old house that stood on it. This was replaced by the first church building, erected and dedicated in 1914.

In 1944 a severe storm completely destroyed the building, leveling it to the foundation and strewing the lumber across the road and surrounding field. All that survived was a single lamp, the pastor's chair, and the pulpit Bible, none of which was at all damaged. The piano too, like the church, was flattened into a pile of lumber, but Pastor A. H. Brown rescued it, took it home, and restored it for many more years' use.

The congregation erected the present building on a pay-as-you-go basis. Although it cost $5000, only $300 was owed when the new building was dedicated in May 1946. A further addition was added in 1974.

In all, five pastors have served this church, one of them, A. H. Brown, for 35 years, more than all the others combined. The congregation has never been a large one, and today numbers a little less than fifty.

[Sources: 123, 129, 176]

Location: see ATLANTIC

SHILOH BAPTIST CHURCH

[ESBA 1875]
Boston

Shiloh is the oldest black Baptist church in Accomack County, third oldest black Baptist church on the entire Eastern Shore of Virginia, and the oldest of the three churches on the peninsula named Shiloh. It was organized in 1875 by the Reverend T. W. Nettiles. Most of its members came from Hollies. Although at first its membership was quite small, the church grew into a strong one with the passing of the years.

The first church building was erected at about the time of the formation of the congregation. The present building is apparently the second structure and dates from 1904. The cornerstone with this date has been obscured by the addition of two front steeples, for Shiloh, like many other black churches on the Shore, has been renovated and improved many times.

Three other congregations were founded from Shiloh during its early years in three quite different ways. In 1881 a friendly division of the church occurred, and thirty members were dismissed to found Mt. Zion Baptist Church near Painter. In 1905 a not-so-friendly division occurred, and 85 members withdrew to establish Holy Trinity Baptist Church, only a few hundred yards away. Even later Shiloh contributed a great many members to Ebenezer Baptist Church in Wardtown, when a number of her people moved from this neighborhood to that one.

In the early years of this century it was not uncommon for camp meetings to be held on the church grounds. In 1908 the camp meeting gained local notoriety when one man attending it was shot and killed as he attempted to rob another. A brighter moment in the church's history occurred five years later on May 7, 1913, when Booker T. Washington spoke from the pulpit here.

Across the years Shiloh has maintained its position as one of the stronger black churches on the Shore, although it has not always managed to have full-time pastors.

[Sources: 26, 105, 110, 123]

Location: see BOSTON

SHILOH BAPTIST CHURCH

[ABA 1888]
Poulson

Shiloh Baptist Church, like Broadway in Cashville, is a monument to the labors of H. N. Quisenberry, employed by the Accomack Baptist Association in 1883 to serve the Baptists in rural areas not reached by churches. Twenty-six persons constituted the church at its formation in 1888.

Shiloh was built in the rural area south of Messongo Primitive Baptist Church and never grew to great size or importance. A Baptist historian writing in 1931 said of this church: "The opportunity for growth in this church is not great. It is largely circumscribed. Still it is serving a good purpose as it is the only church of any denomination in the immediate community." By that year, Shiloh was sharing its pastor with three other churches, Hall's Chapel, Hallwood, and Saxis.

The church declined steadily during the 1930's. Saxis Baptist closed in 1939,

first building

and Shiloh left the Hallwood-Hall's Chapel field and was supplied by local preachers after 1940. There was no report to the association in 1944, and in 1946 that body recorded that the church had ceased to function. By the next year, however, a new spurt of energy on the part of the congregation restored activity at the church. Repairs were made to the building, a Sunday school resumed, and ''efforts...made to get preaching services.'' Thereafter the small congregation struggled on. By 1958 when the church was seventy years old it had exactly the same number of members it had at its formation: 26.

Shiloh resumed its place on the field with Hallwood and Hall's Chapel in 1948 and continued there until 1960, when again, much reduced in size, it bounced back and forth between Hallwood, Parksley, and having no pastor at all. Much of the remaining strength of the church was sapped in 1973 when the building burned to the ground. Arson was suspected, and it was assumed by many that fire had finally erased Shiloh Baptist Church from the scene.

Even after the disastrous fire, the indomitable little congregation managed to keep going. From the ruins of the building arose a second structure, completed by 1975, and the congregation held services in Bethel Baptist Church until the new building was occupied in 1976. In 1977 Carlton Northam was ordained to the ministry here and called to the pastorate. With only ten members, Shiloh is today the smallest Southern Baptist congregation on the Shore, but it still holds its ground.

[Sources: 69, 122, 176]

Location: see POULSON

SHORTER CHAPEL AFRICAN METHODIST EPISCOPAL CHURCH

[AME 1870]
Bridgetown

This church was organized by John Henry Offer, the second A.M.E. pastor on the Shore, sometime before 1870. In that year Offer left the Shore, and the Bridgetown church was transferred from the Eastville to the Pungoteague Circuit under the Reverend Thomas M. Cole.

It is apparent that the Bridgetown congregation first gathered in a school building which was already there when the church was founded. The present building was erected in 1886. By 1890, when Israel L. Butt was completing a three-year pastorate, there was a parsonage as well, and both parsonage and church building had been recently improved.

In 1896, during the pastorate of Peter Sheppard, the school property in the village was purchased by the church, and the building was rebuilt. It seems likely that the school building was moved to the church site and added to the back of the church building at that time. Twelve years later the entire structure was rebuilt again. The cornerstone installed at that time reads: "Shorter Chapel A.M.E. Church, 1886 - rebuilt 1908 by Rev. L. P. Hering BD DD, Rt. Rev. A. L. Gaines BD PhD." It is apparent that the name Shorter Chapel, for Bishop J. A. Shorter of the A.M.E. Church, dates from this period.

The building was rebuilt yet again in 1928, and across the years has continued to receive the care and attention of the congregation. In the early years of this church there were a number of A.M.E. camp meetings held in and around Bridgetown, and Camp Meeting Day is still an annual event at Shorter Chapel.

[Sources: 7, 109, 124]

Location: see BRIDGETOWN

SIGNPOST

see: Signpost United Methodist Church

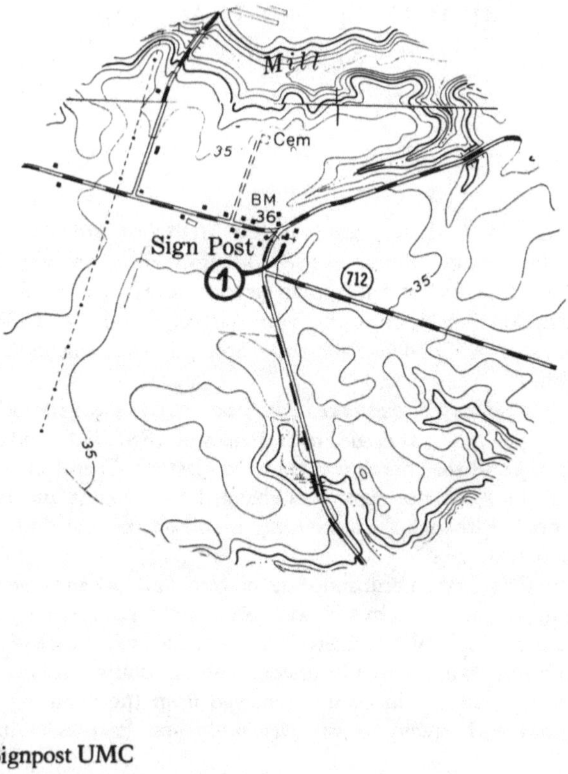

1 - Signpost UMC

SIGNPOST UNITED METHODIST CHURCH

(''St. Paul's,'' ''Jester's Chapel,'' ''Marshall Memorial'')
[MP 1887, M 1939, UMC 1968]
Signpost

The Reverend B. F. Jester, pastor of the Methodist Protestant church in Greenbackville, founded this church in 1887. It began with a revival in the nearby home of George T. Marshall, at which seven persons were converted. R. B. Sinnickson gave the land for the church in that year, and on March 11, 1888, the new church was dedicated. A. D. Melvin and James Straughn were among those present for the dedication.

In less than a century of existence, this little church has gone through four changes of name. The land was deeded to St. Paul's in 1887, but upon completion of the building in 1888 the church was known as Jester's Chapel in honor of the founding pastor. In 1924 the name was changed to Signpost and in 1947 to Marshall Memorial. Although the latter name is still official, the church is almost always referred to as Signpost.

In 1902 the congregation dismantled the original building and erected a newer and larger one in its place. This in turn was substantially rebuilt in 1924 at a cost of $8000. An annex of several rooms has since been added to the back of it.

This church has always shared its pastors with the church in Greenbackville. Unlike many other churches in villages removed from the main highways, this church has slowly and steadily grown over the years. Its present membership is 84.

[Sources: 36, 105, 114, 116, 123, 176]

Location: see SIGNPOST

SIMPKINS

see: *Church of God and True Holiness*

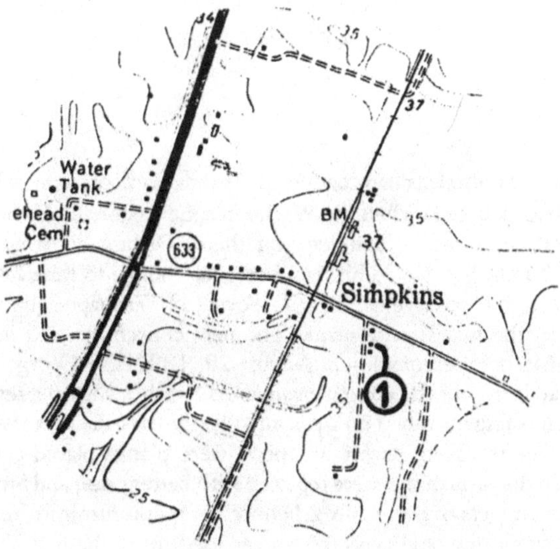

1 - Church of God and True Holiness

SMITH'S CHAPEL UNITED METHODIST CHURCH

(''Upshur's'')
[ME-S 1885, M 1939, UMC 1968]
Quinby

The southern Methodists had conducted a Sunday school in the schoolhouse at Quinby for at least a decade when the Wachapreague pastor, G. E. Booker Smith, resolved to establish a second congregation there. During his tireless efforts to build the new church, Smith sold his own horse and buggy to raise funds, and had thereafter to borrow a carriage from E. T. Powell of Wachapreague to travel the distance between the two appointments. The new church, erected in 1896, was dedicated with Masonic ceremonies on August 28, 1897. Dr. George H. Ray gave the dedicatory address, but the church was named Smith's Chapel after its founder.

The church originally stood on the south side of the village at the head of the harbor and was quite rustic. Its original pews were planks placed across wooden boxes. Gradually the furnishings were replaced with better ones, and Smith's Chapel fell heir to some artifacts of now-vanished churches: pulpit furniture and Bible from the Cobb's Island church, and pews (no longer used) from the first Wachapreague Methodist church, abandoned in 1902.

Because of complications to the title of the land, and because the church no longer sat in the center of the village, the congregation moved the building to its present site in 1922. Since that time the building has been considerably enlarged upon and improved, most recently with the addition of a fellowship hall and kitchen in 1964. The old Cobb's Island pulpit is not presently in use, having been replaced by a more recent one handcarved by a local member.

The present charge boundary linking Smith's Chapel to Ocean View in Wachapreague dates from 1956. Membership of the church at the present is about 170.

[Sources: 109, 110, 111, 123, 176]

Location: see QUINBY

SMYRNA ASSEMBLY OF YAJSHUA DISCIPLES

("Smyrna Church of Christ")
[Independent 1944]
Makemie Park

William Artis was the person primarily responsible for the founding of this congregation and one of the two persons who donated the land on which the church was erected. When established in 1944, the congregation was known as Smyrna Church of Christ.

Artis served as pastor until his death, and thereafter his work was carried on by his wife, Mary. Following a vision received on a cold winter morning in the early 1960's, "Sister Mary" became a "Barefoot Prophetess." Shortly thereafter the name of the church and its theological position underwent a marked change. Adopting a strong Old Testament orientation, the congregation became the Smyrna Assembly of Yajshua Disciples. Two indications of its emphasis upon the Old Testament are its use of the word Yajshua to refer to God and its custom of worshiping on Saturdays.

Although not its pastor, Sister Mary is still the principal figure among the people of this congregation, many of whom live in a cluster near the church and some of whom wear a distinctive dress. This congregation is theologically similar but not related to the Disciples Church in Whitesville. Because it worships on Saturdays, it is sometimes referred to locally as "adventist."

[Sources: 123, 176]

Location: see MAKEMIE PARK

SNEAD'S UNITED METHODIST CHURCH

("Red Hill")
[ME 1881, M 1939, UMC 1968]
Ames Ridge

This church was founded in 1881 when R. J. Waters, pastor of Burton's, began a "very large Sabbath School on the border of Northampton County." The present site was purchased in 1882 for $25, and by 1884 the first church building was almost complete. The church was apparently named for George E. Snead, the pastor who died in 1885.

In the early part of the twentieth century Snead's found itself allied with the newer churches in Exmore and Keller, with whom it shared its pastors. After John Wesley Church in Exmore closed in 1933, Snead's and Mt. Hope in Keller continued together as a circuit. Snead's suffered heavily during the Depression, and like its sister church in Keller suffered the sale of its building at public auction in 1936.

In the more prosperous 1940's the new Exmore church, Spence Memorial, again joined the circuit, and Snead's by then was the most prosperous church on the circuit. The other two churches dwindled over the years, and by 1964 the report stated that Snead's "carries the burden of the charge." In 1967 when Mt. Hope in Keller was officially closed, the congregation merged with Snead's, which assumed control of the property and the membership.

Snead's has never been a large church, although today it is the largest church on the Wachapreague Charge, to which it was subsequently joined. The present church building is the second, and was erected in 1919.

[Sources: 105, 113, 116, 123]

Location: see PAINTER

*SPENCE MEMORIAL METHODIST CHURCH

("Spence Chapel")
[M 1947-1967]
Exmore

There had been no black Methodist church in Exmore for two decades when, in 1947, plans were laid for a new congregation there to be attached to Mt. Hope in Keller. Oliver Spence, the superintendent of the Salisbury District of the Delaware Conference, led in the formation of the new church, and conducted worship services in the home of Charles Reid while the church was being erected.

The new church was dedicated on September 10, 1948, and cost $10,000. It was named Spence Memorial, for the founder, although W. H. Milburn was its first pastor.

At first Spence and Mt. Hope formed a charge called Keller-Exmore, first listed in 1948. But in a reverse of what had happened with the founding of Mt. Hope, Spence grew and the Keller church declined. Spence was made a station in 1954. Two years later the two churches could together claim only 54 members.

In 1957 the congregation paid off the debt on the church building, but by then it was obvious that the envisioned growth would not occur. Membership gradually dwindled, and the church was closed shortly before the merger of the Methodist Church with the Evangelical United Brethren in 1968.

The building stood unused and abandoned until it was struck by fire in 1974. Thereafter it caved in and ultimately disappeared from the scene. It stood on the east side of Virginia Street, where today there is no trace of it to be seen.

[Sources: 113, 124, 129]

Location: see EXMORE

SUNNYSIDE METHODIST EPISCOPAL CHURCH, SOUTH

(see Cheriton United Methodist Church)

SWAIN MEMORIAL UNITED METHODIST CHURCH

[ME 1805, M 1939, UMC 1968]
Tangier

The Methodist church on Tangier is as unique as the island itself, a church whose history is fully documented, a church whose influence upon its community has not been diminished by time and progress, a church in which can be seen as in microcosm much of the history of Methodism in America.

The early years of the Methodist society on the island are wrapped up in the personal history of Joshua Thomas, the "Parson of the Islands." Converted at Annemessex in 1805, Joshua Thomas and Thomas Crockett held the first prayer meeting on the island in the home of Crockett. Two were converted, and a revival, the first of many, swept the island, bringing in new converts. The little society met in private homes always under local leadership, principally Thomas'. Contact with the mainland churches and the regular circuit preachers seems always principally to have centered around the annual Tangier camp meeting, begun by William Seymour and William Lee of Onancock and held each year from 1808 to 1857, except during the War of 1812.

In 1825, the year Joshua Thomas moved to Deal Island, the Tangier society was officially organized into a church with only sixteen members. For another ten years the congregation met in private homes, until in 1835 the first building, Lee's Bethel, was erected on land provided by Henry Crockett (the present site).

From that date the history of the congregation is the story of successive revivals, each necessitating a new building for a growing congregation. This happened in 1840, when revival so increased the size of the congregation that the original Lee's Bethel (which was only eighteen feet square) had to be replaced by a second building, which was 22 feet by 26 feet. This in turn was enlarged in 1860. Ten years later an entirely new building, Mariner's Chapel, was built next door on the present site of the educational building at a cost of $2400. In 1890 the congregation had to spend another $1000 to enlarge even this building.

The Tangier camp meeting declined after the schism of 1844, but the Tangier congregation found a firmer footing as it declined. In 1845, under circuit preachers James Hargis and Valentine Smith, the church was regularly supplied with preaching from the mainland for the first time. Two islanders, John Crockett and Zachariah Crockett, were licensed to exhort in 1849, and in 1856, one year before the last camp meeting, Lewis Crockett and Catherine Sturgis began a Sunday school. The Civil War disrupted the supply of regular preachers from the mainland from 1861 to 1867. In 1883 the church was made a station. There were 147 members at the time and the new pastor, Charles S. Baker, received a yearly salary of $650.

In 1896 another revival added fifty members to the church in one night, and Mariner's Chapel was, like its predecessors, too small. A new church was completed in 1899, much larger and finer than any of the others. In 1900 it was named Swain Memorial after the beloved young pastor, C. P. Swain, who built it and died shortly after his removal from the island.

Beginning about 1904 and lasting until 1928, the church operated a second church on the northern ridge of the island known as Canaan. No church building was erected here. The congregation met in the schoolhouse until Canaan was abandoned in 1928.

In 1946 James Richardson, former pastor, founded a second congregation on the island, and the congregation was plunged into a long and difficult schism. In 1958 the Reverend Andrew Johnson, at one time a candidate for Vice-President of the United States, preached a revival at the Methodist church, and at that time many of the old wounds between the Methodists and Richardson's New Testament Congregation were healed. Relations between the two congregations are congenial today.

In 1963 Swain Memorial dedicated an educational building at a cost of $30,000. It stands on the former site of Mariner's Chapel. All the other church buildings have stood where the main church now stands and have disappeared.

This is one of the few congregations in the country that still retains the "class meeting," an ancient Methodist institution that has withered away virtually everywhere else in this country. Originally a mid-week sharing group of a few persons, the Tangier "class meeting" is now a Sunday morning assembly of as many as 100 or more persons. All ages attend the assembly, and as in early Methodism, personal testimonies, singing, and public prayer are still the mainstays. The "class meeting" is still led by laypersons and is in addition to a full Sunday school program conducted by the church.

With over 450 members, Swain Memorial is the third largest United Methodist congregation on the Shore today. Though still isolated, it may well be the best example in Virginia Methodism of a church that is still the center of the life of its community and the only one whose parsonage is the finest house in town.

[Sources: 67, 70, 103, 116, 117, 123, 133, 140, 176]

Location: see TANGIER

TABERNACLE BAPTIST CHURCH

(see Horntown Tabernacle Baptist Church)

TANGIER

see: *New Testament Congregation*
Swain Memorial United Methodist Church

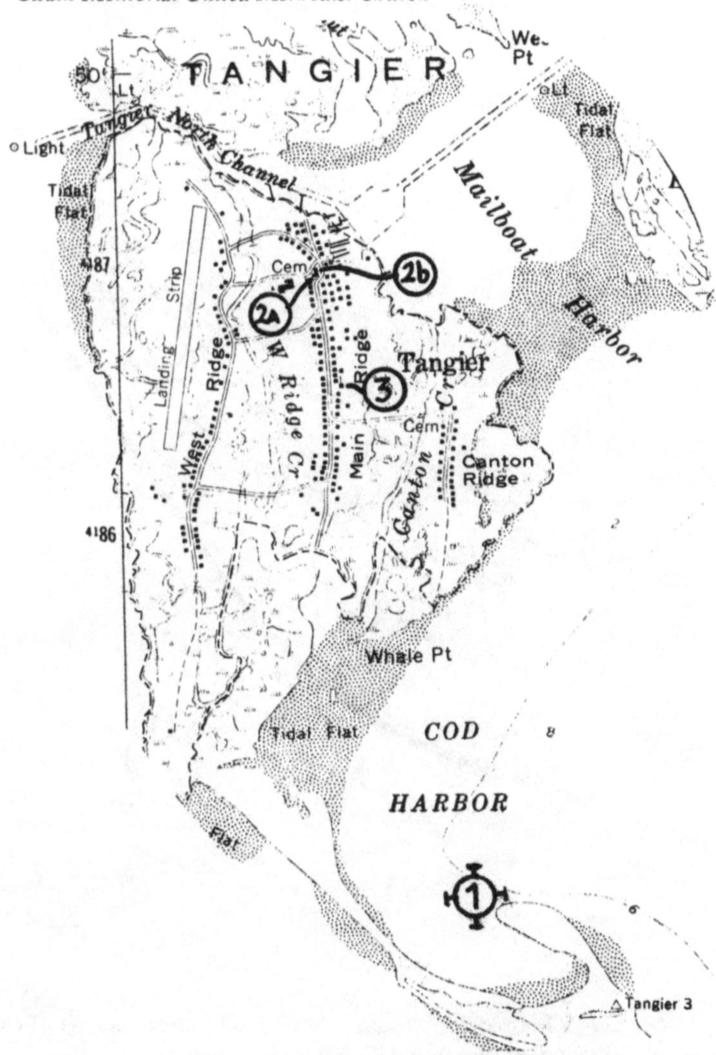

1 - Tangier camp meeting grounds: site 1808-1856 [approximate site; land now under water]
2a - Swain Memorial Methodist: site 1835-1870, since 1899
2b - Swain Memorial Methodist: site 1870-1899; educational building site since 1963
3 - New Testament Congregation

TASLEY

see: **Grant Memorial Methodist Protestant Church*
**Tasley Methodist Church*

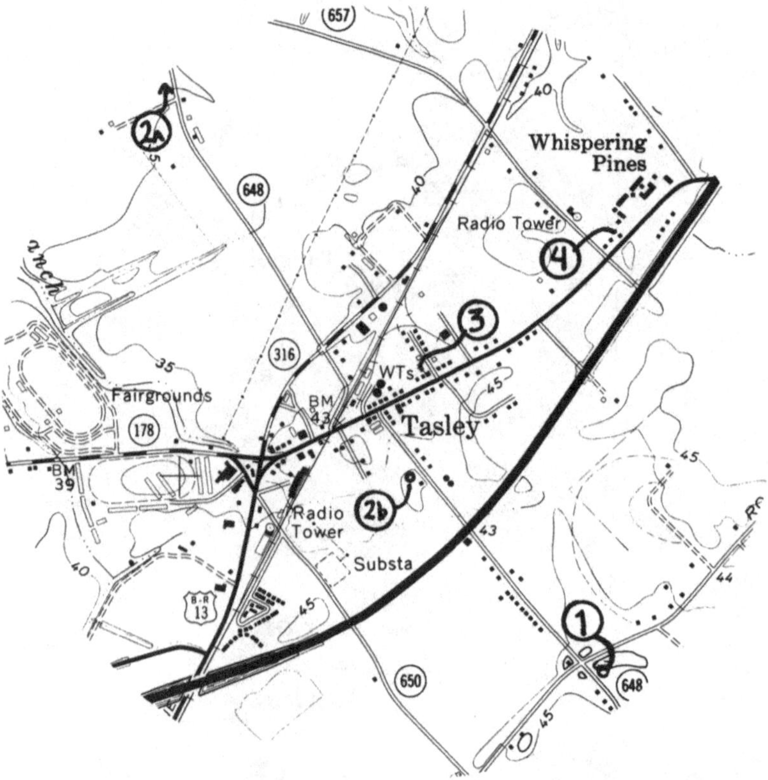

1 - St. James Episcopal (Accomac): original site (approximate) 1767-1838 [for present site see ACCOMAC]
2a - Grant Memorial MP: original site 1893-1910 [approximate; northwest about 2 miles on this road]
2b - Grant Memorial MP: site 1910-1938
3 - Tasley methodist
4 - Central Baptist Mission (Onley): original site 1975-1976 [for present site see ONLEY]

*TASLEY METHODIST CHURCH

[M 1948-1968]
Tasley

Tasley Methodist Church was the successor to old Grant Memorial M.P. Church, which closed in the village of Tasley in 1938. Ten years later J. Lee Marker, pastor of Drummondtown and Woodbury, led in the formation of a second church in the village. A new site was secured, a simple frame building erected, and on November 21, 1948, services began.

Tasley remained on the Accomac Charge but never grew to be a large or important church. By 1966 the membership had dwindled to 68, and Sunday morning attendance to nineteen. By 1968 the average attendance was only nine, the lowest on the District.

In 1968 the Tasley Church was declared closed. The congregation merged with Drummondtown once again, and that church assumed the care and control of the church property. Since 1968 the building has stood vacant and unused.

[Sources: 109, 116, 176]

Location: see TASLEY

*TAYLOR MEMORIAL BAPTIST CHURCH

("Taylor Chapel")
[ABA 1913-1937]
Birdsnest

This church was founded from Red Bank Baptist for the convenience of members living south of Marionville. In 1913 John and Bettie Downing sold a lot near Sheps End for the erection of the church, and the local citizenry built Taylor Chapel on it shortly thereafter.

Taylor Chapel remained a local endeavor for ten years, not a separate congregation. Sunday school was held regularly in the building, and worship services whenever preachers could be found, but no new church was organized there.

In 1923 J. A. Willoughby of Atlantic Baptist Church accepted an invitation to preach a revival at the church, and the event provided the stimulus for the formal organization of the congregation. After a week of revival, 55 persons presented themselves for baptism. A new church was constituted and admitted into the Association as Taylor Memorial Baptist Church.

Taylor Memorial was the last church ever founded on the Shore by the Accomack Baptist Association, and it led a short, struggling existence because the region was already fully churched. Red Bank Baptist stood less than two miles away. In 1931 the history of the Association asked: "Now the serious questions confronting this Association are: Are we not over-churched? and How can we remedy that situation?" By the 1930's the church was in serious decline. In 1931 it was supplied by the pastor at Exmore. In 1934 the youth group was still functioning, but in 1937 the church was only formally reporting to the Association. The last listing is from that year, when no membership statistics are given.

In the early 1940's the Downings offered the use of the building to Community Church of God, whose nearby chapel was smaller. It was used by the congregation until the mid-1950's, when they occupied a newer structure in Birdsnest. The twice-abandoned building still stands just off Seaside Road south of Sheps End.

[Sources: 72, 105, 110, 122, 124, 176]

Location: see BIRDSNEST

*TEACHING THE WAY CENTER

[Independent 1976]
Mappsburg

Frank Huffman, a Mappsburg grocer and former Baptist, was affiliated with the Christian Love Center when early in 1976 he received a vision to establish this center. Immediately he sold his stock and opened the Teaching the Way Center in his storehouse.

Several Charismatic preachers and speakers conducted services or classes at the Center for the next several months, among them Otis T. Burns, former pastor of Lower Northampton Baptist Church. Those who attended at the Center numbered on the average from ten to twenty and were racially mixed.

By the end of the year Huffman abandoned the project, sold the building, and moved out of the neighborhood, leaving Rock Church of the Eastern Shore the only Charismatic congregation in the two counties.

[Sources: 109, 176]

Location: see PAINTER

TEMPERANCEVILLE

see: **Conquest Chapel Methodist Protestant Church*
Jerusalem Baptist Church
Kingdom Hall of Jehovah's Witnesses, Chincoteague Congregation
Temperanceville United Methodist Church

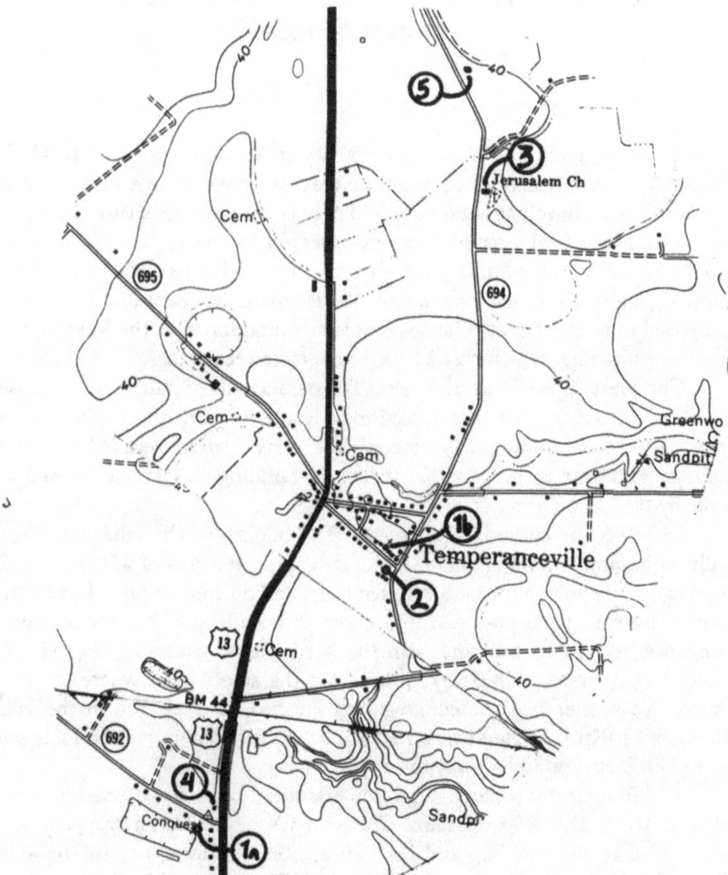

Map shortened

1a - Temperanceville Methodist: original site 1858-1886
1b - Temperanceville Methodist: site since 1886
2 - Emmanuel Episcopal [Jenkins Bridge]: original site 1860-1887 [for site since 1887 see JENKINS BRIDGE]
3 - Jerusalem Baptist
4 - Conquest Chapel MP
5 - Kingdom Hall

TEMPERANCEVILLE UNITED METHODIST CHURCH

("Conquest Chapel") [ME 1845, ME-S 1860, M 1939, UMC 1968] Temperanceville

The first record of Methodist activity in this area is from 1845, when the Accomack Circuit appointed a committee "to make the necessary arrangements for building a church at Mesongos." There is no evidence that a church was built, but during the next decade a society emerged in the region of Temperanceville. By 1855 there was a Sunday school with thirty scholars. Then in 1858 a second building committee was appointed "to estimate the probable cost of a Church proposed to be erected on Wallops Road at its junction with the Mesongers' Road." The new building, which cost $1500, was erected that year.

Conquest Chapel, as the new Temperanceville Church was known, stood south of the village at the intersection of Route 13 with the Hallwood Road. Two years after the building was erected, the congregation seceded to the southern church, and four years after that their new building was ordered closed for a brief time by the Union army.

In 1886 the congregation moved the building to the village of Temperanceville, enlarging and rebuilding it at the same time at a cost of $1000. The Reverend J. Wright Norris was the pastor at that time, and during the period when the church was being rebuilt he preached in a grove at the old site. No sooner had the congregation moved its building than the Methodist Protestants opened a Conquest Chapel of their own, in 1887, just across the street from where the church had stood. No sooner had the congregation finished their church in the village than the Episcopalians, located just across the street, tore down their building and moved it, in 1887, several miles away to Jenkins Bridge.

The first circuit parsonage for the Atlantic Circuit was erected in Temperanceville in 1874. By 1895 the name Conquest Chapel had been dropped. A basement was added to the building and later an additional annex, but the building is still the original one erected in 1858, one of the oldest Methodist structures on the Shore.

Temperanceville has always shared its pastors with Downing's. The present Oak Hall Charge (Temperanceville, Downing's, and Assawoman) dates from the 1950's. The church today has over 150 members.

In 1976 the church received a bequest of $80,000 from the estate of a late resident of Hallwood. The total budget for the church in that year was slightly over $9000.

(Sources: 39, 103, 109, 111, 116, 123]

Location: see TEMPERANCEVILLE

*TEMPLE OHEL ROOVEN

[Orthodox Jewish 1900?-1945]
Cape Charles

The only Jewish congregation on the Eastern Shore of Virginia was founded by William Brown, a Russian immigrant who arrived in Cape Charles in 1894. Within a few years Brown was instrumental in aiding his three brothers, Benjamin, Max, and Morton, to settle as well in Cape Charles, and the four men and their families banded together to continue the customs and observances of Orthodox Judaism that they had known in the old country.

For a number of years the congregation met only in private homes. Benjamin Brown was the most frequent leader of the services, although Hyman Kellam of Cheriton often assisted him. In 1925 the services were moved to the Times Building in Cape Charles, the second floor of which was outfitted for the use of the congregation. In 1933 J. W. Shapiro, a rabbi from Norfolk, arrived in Cape Charles to lead the group, but the congregation proved too small to support a rabbi and he remained on the Shore only a brief while.

The establishment of what is now Cape Charles Air Force Base nearby in 1940 brought to the area a number of Jewish servicemen, and during the war the congregation frequently included them in their religious holidays and observances. By 1945, however, as the original elders began to pass away and their families to move away, the group was disbanded.

The congregation was never large in number. It was of the Orthodox branch of Judaism, that branch which is the least Americanized and most faithfully adheres to the ancient traditions of the Jewish faith. Officially known as Temple Ohel Rooven, the "Tent of Reuben," it is the only Jewish congregation ever to have gathered on the peninsula south of Maryland.

[Sources: 105, 109, 176]

Location: see CAPE CHARLES

*"THE TOWNE" CHURCH

(''Lower Church'')
[CE 1634-1677]
"The Towne" near Cheriton

This is the earliest known church building on the Eastern Shore of Virginia. Just when it was erected or what it looked like is not known, but it was definitely in existence in 1634, for in that year the records reveal that it was in need of repair.

This church was part of that considerable early settlement known simply as ''the Towne,'' perhaps the first community on the Virginia Shore. This settlement was abandoned altogether in 1677, when the new community of Eastville became the site of the county court. Later the estate ''Townfields'' occupied the site, on the north side of King's Creek.

This church appears several times in the early records of the court, usually in connection with punishments meted out to local inhabitants. In May 1634, Daniel Cugley was convicted of a misdemeanor and sentenced to ''daubinge the Church as sone as the roof is repaired.'' In September of that same year Joan Butler was sentenced to be ''drawne over the Kinges Creek at the starne of a boate or canno.'' This is believed to have happened in front of the church. The next year one Henry Charleton said of the rector, William Cotton, that ''if he had had Mr. Cotton without the Church yeard, he would have kicked him over the Pallyzados calling of him a black cotted Raskoll,'' which suggests that the church and ''Towne'' stood within a wooden stockade. For his threat Charleton not only had to ask the rector's forgiveness, but also to build a pair of stocks and sit in them during the worship service for three Sundays in a row.

The Shore's second church, at Fishing Point to the south, was erected around 1641, and it is likely that this first Towne church was allowed to go to decay. Even so there is evidence that this or a second building on the same site still stood in 1663, when the Court ordered the ''Gentlemen of the Vestry to meet at the towne Church.''

After 1677 church and Towne were abandoned altogether, and this first known church on Virginia's Eastern Shore is known today only through antique court records.

[Source: 70]

Location: see CHERRYSTONE

TOWNSEND

see: **Townsend Methodist Episcopal Church, South*

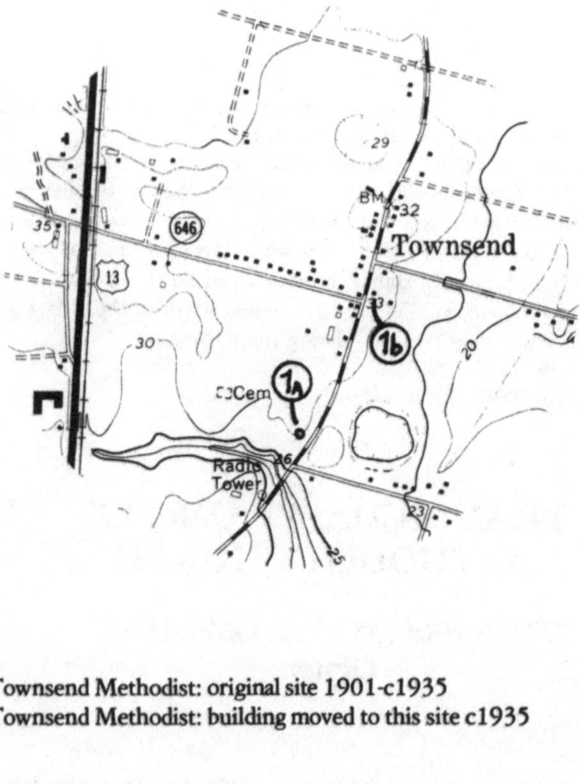

1a - Townsend Methodist: original site 1901-c1935

1b - Townsend Methodist: building moved to this site c1935

*TOWNSEND METHODIST EPISCOPAL CHURCH, SOUTH

[ME-S 1901-1930?]
Townsend

The Townsend Mission was an outgrowth of Capeville Church and was built on land purchased for $1 from John Parsons in 1901.

Townsend always shared its pastors with Capeville, and never became a large congregation. The Capeville Church itself was less than two miles away. Nonetheless the church stayed open and operating until the advent of the 1930's. It was then closed, its membership merged with Capeville, and the building sold.

The church building still stands. It was moved north on Seaside Road and is used today as a storage barn. The church site was south of the village and west of Seaside Road. A few graves in the woods now mark that site.

[Sources: 124, 176]

Location: see TOWNSEND

TRAVIS CHAPEL UNITED METHODIST CHURCH

[ME-S 1908, M 1939, UMC 1968]
Oyster

Travis Chapel was founded from Salem, and only three years after it was erected that older church closed its doors for good. The records of the Woman's Missionary Society of Salem end in 1912, and the society at Travis Chapel picks up where it left off in the following year.

The church originally stood on Seaside Road about a mile below the site of old Salem, on land purchased from William and Sarah Travis in 1908. The church building, said to have been erected chiefly through the efforts of Lucius Cobb, a faithful layman, was not dedicated until two years later. On September 21, 1910, more than 200 people were present for the dedication of the building. D. G. C. Butts preached on that occasion and the congregation raised the $500 needed to pay the remaining debt on the new building.

In the summer of 1925 the church was moved to its present site in the village of Oyster. In 1940 the abandoned building of Pullen's Chapel on Hog Island was floated to Oyster and attached to Travis Chapel, during the pastorate of Carl Sanders. Pullen's Chapel has been used as a church school annex ever since and is the oldest part of the building, having been erected in 1884. At the present time it bears little or no resemblance to its original appearance on Hog Island.

No fewer than three other denominations attempted without success to establish a rival congregation in Oyster: the Baptists, in an endeavor abandoned in 1909; the Pilgrim Holiness Church, between 1948 and 1950; and the Assemblies of God, between 1951 and 1958. No permanent establishment was made in either case, and Travis Chapel remains the only church of the village of Oyster.

Travis Chapel has always shared its pastors with Cheriton, another church founded from Salem. It is today a strong church of over 150 members.

[Sources: 50, 108, 124, 176]

Location: see OYSTER

Townsend Methodist Episcopal
Church, South

TREHERNEVILLE

see: *Antioch Baptist Church*
Johnson's United Methodist Church
Mt. Messias Holiness Church of God Live On
Mt. Zion African Methodist Episcopal Church

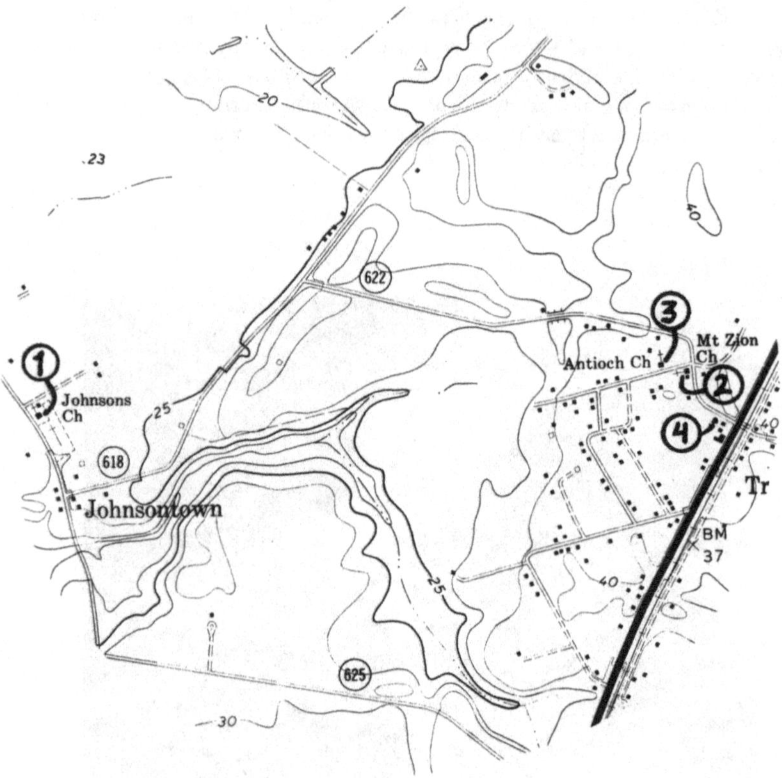

1 - Johnson's Methodist
2 - Mt. Zion AME
3 - Antioch Baptist
4 - Mt. Messias Holiness

*TRINITY METHODIST EPISCOPAL CHURCH

[ME 1846?, ICA 1861, ME 1866]
Hadlock

(photo c. 1900)

This church was founded by the pro-northern minority of Franktown Methodist Church. When that church voted to withdraw to the southern Virginia Conference in 1846, the vote was contested on the grounds that many inactive members had helped to sway the decision. A significant minority withdrew from Franktown and founded this church.

It is apparent that the congregation was supplied by pastors from the northern Philadelphia Conference as early as 1846, but where they assembled is not known. The church building was erected "in the suberbs of Hadlock Town" on land provided by Albert and Letetia Ward in 1851.

Trinity was the southernmost northern church on the Shore, and found itself in a hostile, pro-southern community as the Civil War approached. It was here that an angry crowd prevented the circuit preacher George Cummins from conducting services in 1860. Trinity became a part of the independent Convention of Accomack, but perhaps not until a year or two after the Convention was formed. William Coe preached here only six times, from October 1863 to February 1864. After the Convention itself divided in 1864, Coe preached in the neighborhood, but not in the chapel itself, which for some unknown reason stood vacant. His last sermon in the area was in a schoolhouse near Willis Wharf in October 1864. Trinity was listed as one of the independent churches closed by the Federal army bans in that year, but there is no evidence that Coe was still preaching there.

Trinity returned to the northern fold after 1866, but it was not again the site of regular services. The building stood abandoned for a number of years thereafter. In 1884 the railroad passed within a few feet of the building, and the deed to the property contained provisions to regulate train traffic and noise during hours of worship, a needless provision, since the church had not been used for years.

Broadwater Methodist Episcopal Church, South, was erected nearby in 1892, and the few remaining Trinity members affiliated with that congregation. Local tradition has it that the cornerstone of that new church had the name of both churches on it, but that when it was being put into place it fell out of the wagon with "Broadwater" rather than "Trinity" facing outward, and the "Trinity" inscription was obscured by the building and lost.

The church building, which stood only about fifty feet east of the railroad at the Hadlock crossing, was a simple frame structure almost square in shape. The building was still standing, although just barely, in 1911. It was dismantled shortly after that date.

[Sources: 39, 99, 102, 108, 111, 124, 176]

Location: see EXMORE

TRINITY UNITED METHODIST CHURCH

("Cape Charles Chapel," "Centenary")
[ME-S 1887, M 1939, UMC 1968]
Cape Charles

In the race to stake a claim to the bustling new town of Cape Charles, the southern Methodists quickly fell behind their northern rivals. The Methodist Episcopal Church, South, purchased a lot for a church building as early as 1885, but by the time George Rives, pastor of the Capeville Circuit, organized the new southern congregation in Cape Charles, Bethany Methodist Episcopal Church already stood on the corner of Monroe and Plum.

The new southern church was named Centenary, and it stood on the north side of Tazewell Avenue. It was dedicated on May 20, 1888, by the Reverend W. V. Tudor, and is still standing today, long since renovated into a dwelling.

Like their northern rivals, the southern Methodists of Cape Charles quickly outgrew their first building and began construction of another, but once again they fell behind. It was not until 1893, three years after Bethany's new building was completed, that Centenary began construction of its new brick building on the south side of Tazewell. Even then construction, plagued by financial difficulties, dragged on behind schedule. It was not until Captain and Mrs. James Boggs, faithful members of the congregation, finally mortgaged their farm to obtain money for the church that the building was completed. It was dedicated in 1895, when Samuel Eason was pastor. Eason died shortly thereafter, and there was a move to rename the church Eason Memorial in his honor, but it bore no fruit.

Once in its new building the congregation at Centenary grew slowly but surely. There were 58 members in 1900, 89 in 1910, and 290 in 1920, by which time the church had at last outdistanced Bethany and become the largest church in town. There were 366 members in 1925, when a large educational annex was added to the building. Another annex, costing over $40,000, was dedicated in 1954.

Centenary shared its pastors with the Capeville Circuit until 1896, when it became a station. It has been a station ever since.

In 1939 when the northern and southern Methodist denominations merged, Centenary and its old rival, Bethany, voted unanimously to merge, the only two congregations on the Shore to do so at that time. The combined congregation took the name Trinity and occupied the old Centenary building. With 668 members, Trinity was in 1940 the largest Methodist church on the Eastern Shore. About two-thirds of that number came from Centenary.

In more recent decades the church, like the town in which it sits, has declined in numbers. Today with about 350 members it is the sixth largest Methodist congregation on the Shore. Fewer than a quarter of its members attend worship on an average Sunday morning.

[Sources: 111, 116, 117, 124, 128]

Location: see CAPE CHARLES

UNION BAPTIST CHURCH

[ABA 1841]
Chincoteague

The first religious services on Chincoteague Island were conducted in a schoolhouse on the eastern side of the island by the Methodist Protestant preacher, Avra Melvin. Islanders of all faiths, Baptists and Methodists in particular, attended, and from this early interdenominational endeavor were born two churches, Union Baptist in 1841 and Bethel Methodist Protestant in 1853. When sixteen members constituted the island's first congregation in 1841, they called themselves Union Baptist Church, in honor of the ''union'' worship services that had occurred up until that time.

Union's first building, the first church ever erected on the island, was built on Church Street at Chicken City Road. It was a small building that seated fewer than 100 people. Like other churches of its time it had a gallery for black members, but in this case the stairs to the gallery were outside the building, so that the black members never entered the main floor of the church.

During its earliest years the church was very small and faced many struggles. The first pastor was William Wilkerson (1842-1852), but he was often off the island completing his theological studies. When Elder William Laws of Modest Town visited the island in 1847, his sermon was the first in the church in two years. The new congregation was at such a low ebb at this point that it seriously debated whether or not to merge with Chincoteague Baptist Church in New Church, but William P. Thornton, an islander, was appointed to take "general oversight of the church" and thus began his long career as the congregation's chief pillar. In 1854 Thornton became the first full-time pastor. He lived on the southern end of the island and worked as a laborer during the week, but for 21 years he poured his energies into the church, usually without financial remuneration, and relinquished the task only when feeble health required it.

In 1860 Union held a church trial to examine some of its members who had skated on the Sabbath, shot a gun at a target for sport, and failed to attend worship. The first mention of a Sunday school is from 1865, but apparently the present church school is not continuous from that date. The church was still small in the 1870's. A Methodist Episcopal congregation was founded on the island in 1869, and when a prominent Baptist deacon left the fold to join that church, it initiated a severe controversy over whether communion should be open. As late as 1874 there were only 130 members at Union, and in 1875 the Sunday school had only sixteen scholars. Union also lost members to two other Baptist churches, Christ's Union and Beulah, when they were founded on the island in 1876 and 1879 respectively.

In 1875 William Thornton's long pastorate ended, and an upswing in activity began under two non-island pastors, William Williamson (1875-1883) and S. U. Grimsley (1883-1887, 1894-1897). During Grimsley's second pastorate in 1896 the church building was destroyed by fire, shortly after it had been repaired at a cost of $800. On the day of the fire the members contributed more than $1000 to build a new church. A lot on Church Street was purchased, and the present building erected on it. It was dedicated free of debt in 1898.

In its new building the church took on new life. In 1906 a $5000 addition was added during the pastorate of E. T. Liddell, who published his sermons and dedicated the book to his members. There were twelve pastors from 1900 to 1925, one of whom was Oscar Whaley Sawyer, who served from 1916 to 1920. In his first year at Union, the congregation extended to women members the right to vote in all matters. Prior to that time they could vote only on the calling of a pastor.

In 1925 Sawyer returned for a second pastorate which proved to be the longest in the church's history, 32 years, ending in 1957. There have been only three pastors since 1925, and the history of the church since that year is largely the story of constant growth in numbers and new additions to the church property. In 1929 a $5400 pipe organ was installed, and in 1932 (when the church was the second largest Baptist church on the Shore, after Bethel in Bloxom) a large addition containing classrooms, chapel, and kitchen. In 1940 the interior was extensively remodeled, and the wooden exterior covered with a stone facade. In 1945 an adjacent home was purchased and its land used for parking lot, an action which occurred again in 1947 and 1956. In 1950 a second educational unit costing $24,000 was added, and a third costing $66,000 in 1966. The church began broadcasting its Sunday morning worship services on WESR radio in Tasley in 1957.

Today Union is the largest congregation on the Eastern Shore of Virginia, all faiths considered. It has over 1000 members, considerably more people than live in the town of Parksley. Its church property, valued at more than half a million dollars, covers a large portion of an entire city block and includes the old parsonage next to the church on Church Street. Its membership is not now as large as it once was; in 1959 it was 1244. But thanks to the struggles and perseverance of the people of this church, Chincoteague, the largest community on the Eastern Shore of Virginia, is predominantly Baptist, an irony on the heavily Methodist peninsula.

[Sources: 70, 105, 123, 143, 144, 148, 152, 176]

Location: see CHINCOTEAGUE

UNION BAPTIST CHURCH

[ESBA 1863]
Eastville

Union Baptist Church in Eastville is without question the oldest Negro church on the Eastern Shore of Virginia. It is said that even before the Civil War the blacks of the Eastville area were holding prayer meetings from house to house and talking of organizing their own church. The organization was effected in a private home in Townfields in 1863, nearer Cheriton than Eastville, but Samuel and Matilda Bibbens gave the present lot north of Eastville, and there on July 2, 1865, the first completely black church on the Virginia Shore was dedicated.

The new congregation called a Northampton native, Caleb Burrows, to be its pastor, and although he served only one year the new church grew quickly, and black Baptist work radiated outward from Eastville. African Baptist in Cheriton was founded from this church in 1869 and First Baptist in Capeville in 1877. African and Union joined to establish Cherrystone Baptist in 1879, and in that vicinity the black Baptist association, at first called Cherrystone, was organized five years later. The three churches erected a parsonage in 1880.

The Baptists of Union were intimately involved in schooling for the newly freed Negroes of the Shore. Eugenia Davis Burrows, wife of the first pastor, taught local children in the church building, the first public education for Negroes in that neighborhood. The third pastor, Isaac Lee (1885-1910), was the first chairman of the board of trustees of Tidewater Institute, a high school for blacks which the Eastern Shore Baptist Association established in Chesapeake, south of Eastville, in 1910.

Isaac Lee had a 25-year pastorate ending in 1910, and by then the congregation was in its third building. In the 27 years following his resignation there were only three pastors, one of whom, Charles H. Morton, served 22 years. During the Depression, Tidewater Institute closed, its services assumed by the county, but Union itself entered the 1940's strong and without debt. The 1940's were prosperous years for the congregation, and many improvements were made on the building during that decade.

On November 30, 1947, the church was completely destroyed by fire. The congregation worshiped at first in the basement of Bethel A.M.E. Church in Eastville, later with the people of Antioch Baptist Church in Treherneville while their new building was being erected. The present brick structure was dedicated in 1950, and in that year W. Tycer Nelson, a professor at Maryland State College in Princess Anne, was called as pastor. The new building cost $40,000.

Union is today a strong church of over 200 members, one of the leading black churches of the Shore. The present pastor is the ninth in the church's history, and he lives in the new parsonage adjacent to the church. Like nearby Bethel A.M.E., Union can claim to have hosted the state-level assembly of its denomination. The 24th annual session of the Baptist General Association of Virginia was held here in 1922.

[Sources: 26, 124, 135, 166, 176]

Location: see EASTVILLE

UNION UNITED METHODIST CHURCH

("Greenbackville M.P.")
[MP 1877, M 1939, UMC 1968]
Greenbackville

This first church in the far northeastern corner of Accomack County was built by the Methodist Protestants in 1877. The church was a simple frame building that stood on the south side of Church Street, at the opposite end of that street from the present building.

In 1895 this building was abandoned for the present structure on Stockton Avenue. In the same year the Methodist Episcopal church in Franklin City moved to its new location, only a few blocks away. In 1902 the village correspondent to the county papers wrote, "We have two churches at Greenbackville and Franklin City...both self-supporting and working so harmoniously together that it is hard for a newcomer to tell which church the members belong to." When the second M.P. building was finished, Calvary Baptist Church purchased the original building and used it from 1902 to 1911. The building was later dismantled and the lumber used in building a barrel factory in the village.

Greenbackville was a strong and vital church, and the report for 1913 records "remarkable outpourings of the Holy Spirit." The church shared its pastor with Signpost and the church in nearby Portersville, Maryland. At Unification in 1939, Portersville remained on the charge, the only Maryland church in the Virginia Conference. The Methodist Protestant congregation and charge in this neighborhood was often known as Franklin City until 1928, when the name Greenbackville became fixed.

In 1941 nearby Grace in Franklin City burned to the ground, and on June 8 of that year the former M.E. and the former M.P. congregations voted unanimously to merge. The new congregation took the name Union Methodist Church, occupied the M.P. building, and applied all insurance money from the fire to that structure. At the time of merger, the Greenbackville congregation was the smaller of the two.

The Portersville, Maryland, church was dropped from the charge with the merger in 1941, and the present Greenbackville Charge (Union, Signpost, and Horntown) was created in 1946.

A large church school annex was added to the back of the church in the 1950's, and a new parsonage erected next door in the 1960's. The present membership is 219.

[Sources: 36, 109, 112, 114, 116, 170]

Location: see GREENBACKVILLE

WACHAPREAGUE

see: *Grace United Methodist Church*
**Greenview Presbyterian Church*
Herbert Baptist Church
Ocean View United Methodist Church
Powelton Presbyterian Church
**Wachapreague Pilgrim Holiness Church*

1 - "Temperance Hall," site of first religious services in Wachapreague
2 - Powelton Presbyterian
3a - Ocean View Methodist: original site 1882-1902
3b - Ocean View Methodist: site since 1902
4a - Grace Methodist: original site 1879-1911
4b - Grace Methodist: site since 1911
5 - Herbert Baptist
6 - Wachapreague Pilgrim Holiness
7a - Greenview Presbyterian: original site 1919-1926
7b - Greenview Presbyterian: site 1926-1936

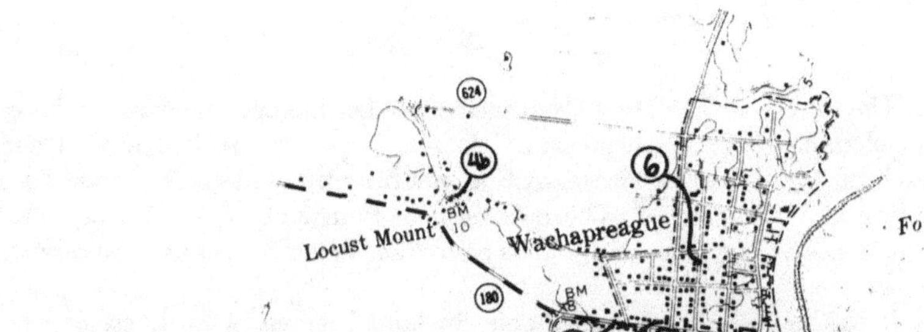
624
4b
6
Locust Mount
BM
10
Wachapreague
Fo
180
BM
3a
3b
605
10
2
Wachapreag
1
10
Cem
Light
4a
5
Herbert
Ch
Cem
Light
Haul
Over
6
10
6
7b
Piggen
Cem
622
BM
Old Trower
7a
x6

*WACHAPREAGUE PILGRIM HOLINESS CHURCH

[IAHUC 1907, IAHC 1913, PH 1922-1935]
Wachapreague

The Reverend Cole Hope "was used of the Lord to open up works in his early days of ministry at Wachapreague." It was Hope who invited three Holiness preachers, Mr. and Mrs. Harvey Adams and Miss Etta Gibson, to conduct a tent meeting in Wachapreague. The meeting bore fruit, and by 1907 a new church stood on Lee Street. Cole Hope was its pastor, and Levin Badger its most prominent layman.

It was in this church that Annie Bradford Pearson of Birdsnest first heard Holiness preaching in 1909 and returned home to start the group that ultimately became Community Church of God. The preachers she heard here were T. Lewis Adams and Etta Gibson, traveling evangelists.

By the early 1920's both Cole Hope and Levin Badger had moved to Shelltown, Maryland, and the Wachapreague church suffered in their absence. William Vickers arrived on the scene a few years later to find the church "practically gone down." Although Vickers spent more of his effort on the nearby village of Quinby than on Wachapreague, he nonetheless joined with the Reverend Merrick Lowry in reviving the earlier church, organizing it officially for the first time and bringing it under the regular ministry of the Pilgrim Holiness Church. This was accomplished in 1927, when there were eleven members. The following year, when Merrick was pastor, the membership increased to eighteen.

The attempted revival was not long-lived. By 1930 the denomination described the church as "small in membership and not self-supporting," and there were no regular services. The church remained dormant until 1934, when the team pastors, Etta Clough and Etta Mitchell, again revived it. "God is blessing their efforts, and we are expecting to be able to reorganize there in the near future," reported the district superintendent in that year, but the reorganization was never effected. Although the two pastors reported 27 members in 1934, there were none to report in 1935, and after that year the church is no longer mentioned in the records of the Pilgrim Holiness Church.

In 1935 Levin Badger sold the property for $200. The building was subsequently converted into a dwelling and is still used as such today.

[Sources: 121, 123, 176]

Location: see WACHAPREAGUE

*WARD'S CHAPEL AFRICAN METHODIST EPISCOPAL CHURCH

("Poulson Neck Mission")
[AME 1898-1959]
Chesconnessex

The Reverend Spencer J. Drummond, a native of Accomack County, led in the attempt to establish an A.M.E. church in Poulson Neck north of Onancock. He was pastor of the mission established there in 1898. It was at first a struggling work, as was evidenced three years later in 1901 when the mission was attached to Mt. Zion in Jamesville, more than twenty miles away in the next county. For the next four years Drummond served both these distant churches.

It was Oscar Theodore Day, pastor of Bethel Church in Onancock, who brought the work to fruition. Under his leadership a lot was obtained and a small frame building erected on it in 1905. Israel LaFayette Butt, presiding elder of the Norfolk District, dedicated the building on December 31, 1905. It was christened Ward's Chapel, after Bishop T. M. D. Ward of the A.M.E. Church, or perhaps after John Ward, one of the original trustees.

Ward's Chapel remained an active church for half a century, although it never grew to great size. As the years passed the membership dwindled, and the church finally closed its doors in 1959. Most of the remaining members transferred to Bethel in Onancock.

The building was used for storage for a number of years after that, and then stood abandoned. In recent years it has caved in altogether, and at present is nothing more than a pile of lumber in the woods beside the road, the steeple alone still intact and lying on its side. Ironically the official highway maps of Accomack County still indicate the presence of a church at this site, almost two decades after the African Methodists abandoned the hope of maintaining a congregation in this neighborhood.

[Sources: 7, 123, 176]

Location: see CHESCONNESSEX

WARDTOWN

see: *Ebenezer Baptist Church*
**Melson's Methodist Episcopal Church*
**Wardtown Baptist Church*

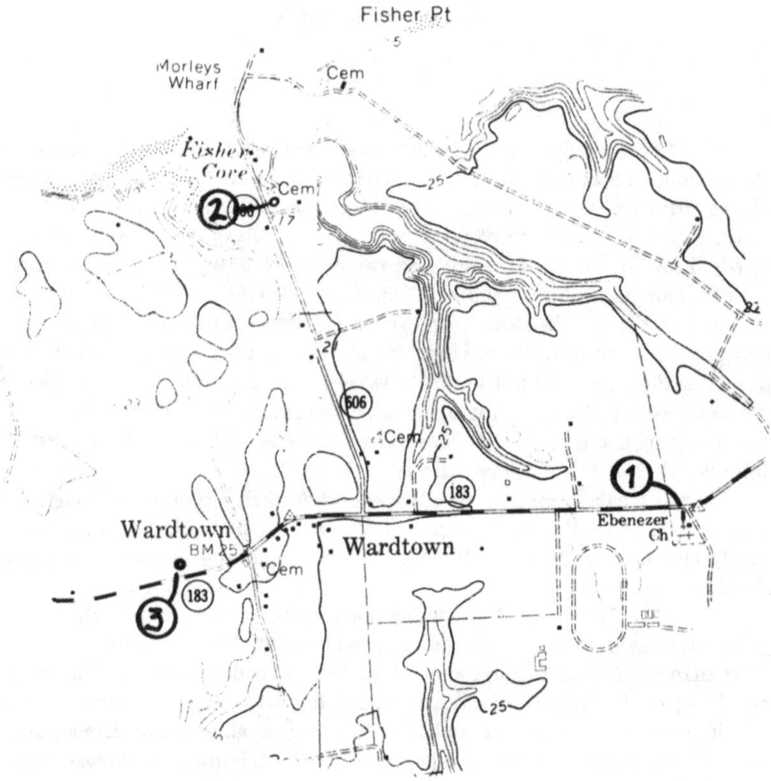

1 - Ebenezer Baptist
2 - Melson's ME: probable site
3 - Wardtown Baptist: original site 1896-1924

*WARDTOWN BAPTIST CHURCH

[ABA 1894-1917]
Wardtown

The railroad brought rapid growth and prosperity to the area around Exmore and Belle Haven, an area in which at that time there was no white Baptist church. This church was founded to stake a Baptist claim to that wide swath of the Shore that stretched from Red Bank in Marionville north to Hollies in Keller.

On October 4, 1894, the Baptists of the area held a fair at nearby Read's (Morley's) Wharf to benefit the proposed new church. That evening no less a person than the Reverend Thomas Dixon of New York, at that time one of the most famous preachers in America, lectured on behalf of the church. The following summer land was obtained and a building erected. In 1896 the congregation was admitted into the Accomack Baptist Association.

In 1907 Wardtown dismissed some of its members to help establish Exmore Baptist Church, a congregation which pastors John and Will Guy had begun with the Red Bank pastor. This action ultimately proved detrimental to Wardtown. Exmore Baptist, in the heart of the new growing town on the railroad, grew quickly and prospered. Wardtown Baptist, on a rural road west of town, declined.

Ten years later, in September 1917, the congregation voted to disband, and most of its members subsequently joined Exmore Baptist Church. In 1921 the property was sold, and the money applied to the building fund of the Exmore church.

In time the simple frame building was purchased by the members of Allen Memorial A.M.E. Church in Franktown, moved to that site, and refitted for worship. The building, substantially changed and improved over the years, is still used by that congregation today.

[Sources: 69, 109, 110, 124, 176]

Location: see WARDTOWN

WATTSVILLE

see: *Friendship United Methodist Church*
Wattsville United Methodist Church

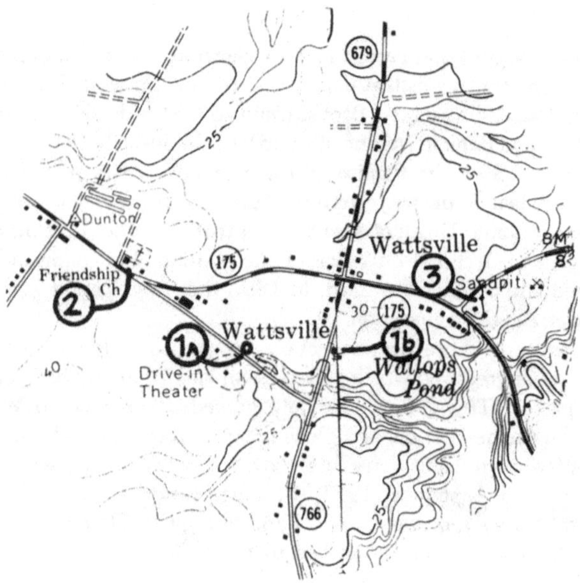

1a - Wattsville Methodist: original site 1840?-1919
1b - Wattsville Methodist: site since 1919
2 - Friendship Methodist
3 - Kingdom Hall of Jehovah's Witnesses: this building used by the Temperanceville (Chincoteague) congregation 1974-1975 (for site since 1976 since TEMPERANCEVILLE)

WATTSVILLE UNITED METHODIST CHURCH

("Friendship")
[ME 1795, MP 1832, M 1939, UMC 1968]
Wattsville

On September 30, 1795, two strangers knocked on the door of Captain David Watts' house on the mainland opposite Chincoteague Island. Their vessel, on its way from Northampton to Philadelphia, had been forced ashore by contrary winds, and this was the first door they had come to in hopes of getting a horse to continue on. Their names were Joseph Rowen and William Colbert, and they were the two circuit preachers trying to get to the Annual Conference in Philadelphia.

From this rather accidental beginning, the home of David Watts grew into a regular preaching point for the Methodists and ultimately into a Methodist congregation. Watts, who appears to have received everyone kindly, was visited after that by Colbert, Thomas Smith, and by Asbury himself in 1802. The revival came with the visits of Thomas Smith, and "heavenly fire ran from heart to heart when services were held at Brother David Watts'!"'

Watts was an influential figure in Eastern Shore Methodism during the first half of the nineteenth century. He was licensed to exhort in 1806 and to preach in 1811. By 1827, however, he had fallen under the sway of Avra Melvin of Newtown and was one of the Methodist "Reformers" who met at that place in that year. As the Reformers withdrew into the new Methodist Protestant Church, Watts withdrew with them, and resigned from the Methodist Episcopal Church in 1832, carrying his congregation with him. Wattsville thus became the earliest Methodist Protestant congregation on the Virginia Shore. In early records of that denomination it is known as Friendship, perhaps the legacy of Watts himself, and from it radiated much of the work of that denomination in upper Accomack County.

Watts gave the land on which the meetinghouse stood in 1840, and it is not unlikely that the building was not erected until about that time. He deeded the property for the "Protestant Methodist and other religious denominations to worship in," and it is said the Methodist Protestants did indeed share the building at first with others, probably with Methodist Episcopals. Shortly after 1840, however, all Methodist activity at Wattsville had become Methodist Protestant.

From the Wattsville congregation came for certain five other churches — Chincoteague (1853), Berea (1874), Greenbackville (1877), Signpost (1887), and Atlantic (1893) — and probably a sixth as well, Friendship in Wattsville (1865). By then the mother congregation had itself grown so large that a new building was needed, so the old one was demolished and a larger one erected in its place in 1895. In 1917, during the pastorate of E. W. Simms, a third building was projected. A new site, the present one, was procured from Elijah Hastings, and the present building dedicated on August 10, 1919. The second building was subsequently dismantled, its lumber used in erecting a black church down the county that has not been identified.

In recent years this congregation has declined greatly in numbers. Pastors were shared with daughter churches, especially Atlantic and Berea, until 1970. In that year the church was made a station with a part-time minister. Today the membership at this venerable old church is only sixty.

[Sources: 3, 15, 100, 105, 109, 110, 114, 116, 123, 163, 176]

Location: see WATTSVILLE

WAYMAN'S CHAPEL AFRICAN METHODIST EPISCOPAL CHURCH

(see Bethel African Methodist Episcopal Church [Eastville])

WEIRWOOD

see: *Red Bank Baptist Church*
**Weirwood African Methodist Episcopal Church*
**Weirwood Happy Mission Church of Christ Disciples*

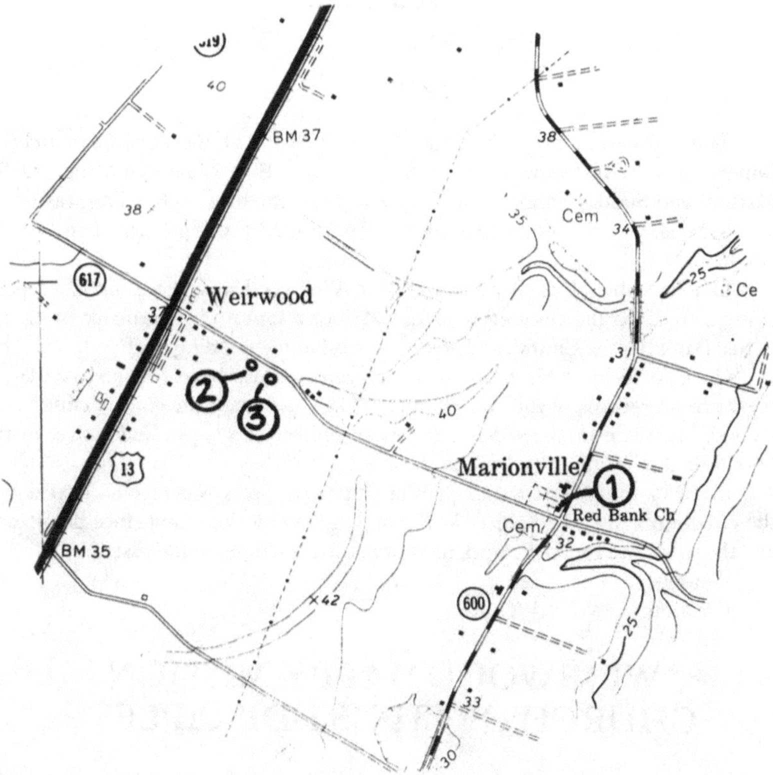

1 - Red Bank Baptist: site since 1857
2 - Weirwood AME: site (approximate)
3 - Weirwood Happy Mission: site 1945-1961 (approximate)

Location unknown: Red Bank Baptist site(s) prior to 1857

*WEIRWOOD AFRICAN METHODIST EPISCOPAL CHURCH

("Sea Side Mission")
[AME 1889-1920?]
Weirwood

This work was begun by Israel L. Butt, pastor of the A.M.E. churches in Jamesville and Bridgetown. On July 21, 1889, Butt organized "the Sea Side Mission and Sunday School" near Birdsnest. Apparently no building was erected at that time, but the work continued to be served by the pastors of the A.M.E. circuit.

In 1902 when J. C. Wyatt was pastor, Weirwood was first listed as a separate church. In 1906 the congregation paid $50 for a lot on the south side of the road to Red Bank Baptist Church and erected a small frame building on it.

Once in its new building the congregation must have declined rapidly, for there are no records of the church after 1906. Just when the church closed is not known, but since local residents do not remember it as open and active, it must have been discontinued by 1920 at the latest.

In 1945 the Weirwood Church of Christ Disciples was erected next door to the old church site. The old A.M.E. building had by then long since disappeared, and the short-lived A.M.E. work in Weirwood was a thing of the past.

[Sources: 7, 124, 176]

Location: see WEIRWOOD

*WEIRWOOD HAPPY MISSION CHURCH OF CHRIST DISCIPLES

("Happy Mission Number One")
[CCD 1945-1960]
Weirwood

This was the fourth congregation of the Firstborn Church of Christ Disciples on the Shore. It was established in 1945, when Willie and Jessie Wilson gave the land, which was immediately east of the site once occupied by the African Methodist Episcopal church in Weirwood. The land was cleared by the congregation and a simple frame building erected. James E. Davis, Jr., later bishop of the Cape

Charles congregation, participated in the ground-breaking ceremonies as a young boy.

Elder Southey Satchell was the pastor of this church, and he served continuously in this capacity until his death. When no one from the congregation arose to take his place, worship at the site ceased. The last year in which there is any record of activity at the church is 1960.

Shortly after the church closed, the building of Mt. Olive Church of Christ Disciples in Exmore burned, and this building was moved from Weirwood to Exmore to replace it. When later the Exmore congregation also ceased to function the building was allowed to go to ruin and ultimately disappeared.

The Weirwood church stood south of the crossroads to Marionville not far from the main highway. The site is still owned by the church.

[Sources: 124, 176]

Location: see WEIRWOOD

WESLEY METHODIST EPISCOPAL CHURCH

(see Locustville United Methodist Church)

*WISE CHAPEL BAPTIST CHURCH

[ESBA? 1905-1925?]

Bayside

This church was named for Spencer F. Wise, its founder and only pastor. In 1905 he and several trustees purchased the abandoned Reese Chapel and gathered there a new congregation. For the rest of his life Wise was the center of this church, a man beloved and respected by both whites and blacks of the area.

The new congregation had hopes of erecting a newer and better building on the lot they purchased in 1905, but the new building was never erected. The congregation remained a small one, and continued to use the formerly Methodist building as long as it functioned.

Wise died in the mid-1920's, and thereafter the congregation disbanded and the church was closed. It is known that some of the members went to St. John's Baptist Church in Onancock at that time.

The building remained vacant for another twenty years, until Estelle Dillard Smith established Mt. Zion Holy Church there in 1948. It was dismantled during a widening of the road through Bayside in 1970.

[Sources: 123, 176]

Location: see BAYSIDE

WITHAMS

see: *Church of God*
Mt. Zion United Methodist Church

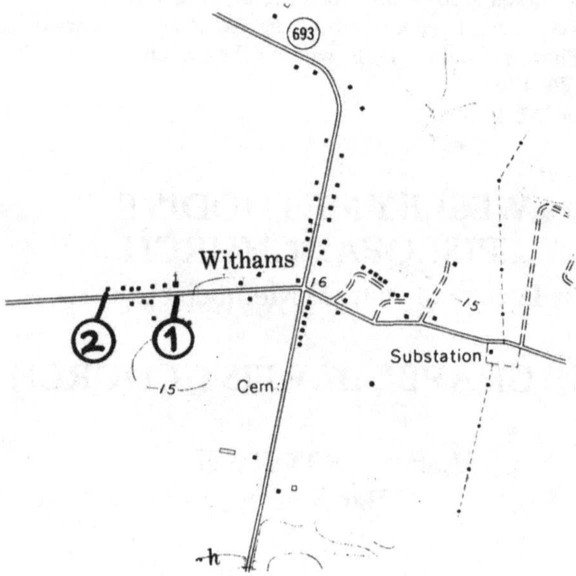

1 - Mt. Zion UMC
2 - Church of God

WOODBURY UNITED METHODIST CHURCH

[ME-S 1882, M 1939, UMC 1968]
Rue

(first building, photo c. 1915)

Woodbury Methodist Episcopal Church South was founded from Drummondtown and erected in 1882 on land which William Baker sold for $1. The church was built almost upon the exact site of the second Middle Church of the Church of England.

Although a rural church, Woodbury flourished and grew. The congregation purchased more land from William Baker in 1916, and still more in 1918 for a cemetery. By the 1920's the original frame building was outgrown, and plans were laid for the construction of a larger church.

In 1925 the congregation began construction of the present brick sanctuary. It was formally opened on July 18, 1926, and cost $16,000. Shortly after its completion the original building, which stood immediately north of it, was sold to two members who dismantled it and used the lumber elsewhere.

Woodbury has always shared its pastors with Drummondtown. It has never been a large congregation, and its present membership is 73.

[Sources: 109, 116, 123, 176]

Location: see RUE

ZION BAPTIST CHURCH

[ABA 1838]
Metompkin

Zion Baptist Church sits near the now-forgotten site of old Metompkin Baptist. In 1835, two years after Metompkin was destroyed by a tornado, the trustees of Modest Town Baptist Church purchased the site where Zion now stands for a meetinghouse for the "regular Baptists," apparently determined that there should be a Baptist church in this part of the county.

Thus Zion, like Bethel near Bloxom, began as a Sunday school operated by the vigorous Modest Town congregation. The Sunday school was in operation at Zion as early as 1838, but it is not certain that it was held continually from that date.

By 1852 the work here had grown, and Zion was organized into a separate congregation. There were in that year fifteen white and three black members. A revival under the Reverend William Fisher followed, and 52 members were added. When the church joined the Accomack Baptist Association in 1853 there were 74 members. By 1871 there were 108 members, and Zion was the second largest church in the Association.

The first church building, erected soon after the organization of the church in 1852, stood on the site of the present brick building. In 1871 a second building was erected across the road on land given by Edward Parks. This second structure still stands and is used as a social hall, but it was replaced by the present church building, on the original site, in 1917. Dr. Beasley, a prominent preacher of Lexington, spoke at the dedication of this building in August 1917. A large educational annex was added in 1961.

Two other congregations have been formed from Zion: Drummondtown in 1870, and the second Metompkin Baptist Church, originally known as the Colored Zion Mission, in 1877. The Woman's Missionary Society of this church was founded in 1890.

The early part of the twentieth century found Zion sharing its pastor with Parksley Baptist Church, but the two churches separated, and Zion became a station under the Reverend Ralph W. Mapp in 1956. Zion is today a vigorous church of almost 300 members. In addition to its own church school, which has been in operation every year except one (1963) since at least 1852, Zion also began in 1959 a mission Sunday school at nearby Accomack County Nursing Home. This mission now serves about 35 people.

[Sources: 69, 70, 109, 123]

Location: see METOMPKIN

*ZOAR BAPTIST CHAPEL

[ABA 1833-1851?]
Daugherty

This was one of three meetinghouses erected for various activities, including worship services, by Hollies (Pungoteague) Baptist Church in the first half of the nineteenth century. This building stood by 1833 and was erected by Joseph Gunter of Hollies. Zoar was built as "an additional place for holding meetings." Among those who preached here was William Laws, founder of Modest Town Baptist Church.

Joseph Gunter, the builder, died in 1840 and deeded to trustees of the congregation the half-acre "where the Baptist meeting house called Zoar now stands on seaside road." For at least a decade after his death the building was still in use, for William Fisher preached there in 1851.

There is no record of the building after 1851. Although its exact location cannot be determined today, it was east of Seaside Road south of Daugherty, a little below St. Luke's A.M.E. Church.

[Sources: 70, 150

Location: see DAUGHERTY

APPENDIX I:
Other Congregations on the Eastern Shore of Virginia

The following congregations, missions, and Sunday schools are known to have functioned briefly on the Eastern Shore. None of them issued into a permanent church, and there is not sufficient historical data available to do more than list them.

METHODIST EPISCOPAL SOCIETY in Parker's Neck
[mentioned once in the records of 1836]

CONVENTION OF ACCOMACK CONGREGATION in "the vicinity of Ayres Chapel"
[functioned 1864]

HOPETON BAPTIST MISSION
[conducted by Zion Baptist Church 1891]

BAPTIST SUNDAY SCHOOL MISSION, Wishart's Point
[conducted by Atlantic Baptist Church in the 1890's]

EPISCOPALIAN MISSION, Wishart's Point
[conducted by Accomack Parish, 1906]

BAPTIST SUNDAY SCHOOL MISSION, Savage's Neck
[operated for some time by Eastville Baptist Church, closed 1911]

CHURCH OF GOD, Tasley
[exact denominational affiliation unknown; functioned briefly ending in 1917]

PILGRIM HOLINESS MISSION, Oyster
[conducted by Rev. Mary Garrett of Cape Charles, 1948-1950]

"ONENESS" CHURCH, Makemie Park
[functioned early 1950's under "Elder" Brown]

SEVENTH-DAY ADVENTIST CONGREGATION, Cape Charles
[worshiped briefly in Emmanuel Episcopal Church, early 1960's]

NEW LIFE CHURCH OF GOD IN CHRIST, Cape Charles
[independent Pentecostal congregation of Rev. J. Brown, closed after building burned 1975]

MISSIONARY BAPTIST MISSION, Chincoteague
[independent white congregation, met in a private home on Daisey Street, 1977]

APPENDIX II: Recent Independent Congregations and Missions

The following congregations, missions, and Sunday schools are of very recent origin. All are independent of denominational affiliations, and none of them meets in a building originally designed as a church. Their separate histories have not been traced.

CHRIST CHURCH OF UNIVERSAL LOVE INC., Cheriton (1977)
[J. E. Byrd, Bishop and Founder; William Davis, Pastor. Independent black congregation meeting in a rented building at Cheriton Station]

CHURCH OF GOD MISSION, Pungoteague (1976)
[independent black congregation]

FIRST BORN CHURCH OF OUR LORD JESUS CHRIST, Exmore (1977)
[Bishop A. G. Reid, Pastor. Meets in a building on Route 13 south of Exmore. Independent black congregation]

FULL GOSPEL MISSION, Cape Charles (1976)
[Rev. Randy E. Lewis, Pastor. A white Charismatic mission meeting in a storefront building on Pine Street]

PEARLY GATES BAPTIST CHURCH, Exmore (1976)
[independent black congregation meeting in a former storehouse on Occohannock Street]

That other congregations of this sort have existed across the years on the Shore seems almost certain, but they have left no trace.

APPENDIX III:
The Oldest Church Buildings on the Eastern Shore of Virginia
(extant church buildings 100 years old or older)

1738 - St. George's Episcopal Church, Pungoteague
1742 - Hungars Episcopal Church, Bridgetown
1792 - Hollies Baptist Church, Keller
1828 - Christ Episcopal Church, Eastville
1838 - St. James Episcopal Church, Accomac
1840 - Makemie Presbyterian Church, Accomac
1846 - Holmes Presbyterian Church, Bayview
1854 - Downing's United Methodist Church, Oak Hall
Cokesbury United Methodist Church, Onancock
1855 - Garrison's United Methodist Church, Painter
Onancock Baptist Church (rear portion)
1857 - Johnson's United Methodist Church, Johnsontown
1858 - Chincoteague Baptist Church, New Church
Pocomoke United Methodist Church, Grotons
Temperanceville United Methodist Church, Temperanceville
1859 - Horntown United Methodist Church, Horntown
1860 - Emmanuel Episcopal Church, Jenkins Bridge (dismantled and reconstructed 1887)
1868 - Bethel African Methodist Episcopal Church, Onancock
Evergreen United Methodist Church, Hack's Neck
Friendship United Methodist Church, Wattsville
Greater Mt. Sinai Gospel Tabernacle, Fairview (central portion)
1870 - Drummondtown Baptist Church, Accomac (Bayly Memorial Hall, building I)
Shorter Chapel African Methodist Episcopal Church, Bridgetown
1871 - Craddockville United Methodist Church, Craddockville
Macedonia African Methodist Episcopal Church, Accomac
Oak Grove United Methodist Church, Melfa
Zion Baptist Church, Metompkin (building II)
1872 - Leatherbury United Methodist Church, Chesconnessex (original portion)
St. Luke's African Methodist Episcopal Church, Daugherty
1876 - Christ's Union Baptist Church, Chincoteague (abandoned)
Mt. Sinai Baptist Church, New Church (original portion)
1877 - Andrew Chapel United Methodist Church, Cashville
Deas Chapel United Methodist Church, Horntown

NOTES

The notes that follow refer only to Book One. An explanation of the system of notation used in Book Two precedes that portion of the work.

Two types of sources used extensively throughout the compilation of this material do not appear in the following notes:

(1) denominational records - annual conference journals, minutes of associations, dioceses, presbyteries, etc., and annual statistical reports and tables;

(2) legal county records, specifically marriage records, registers of wills, and especially deedbooks of Accomack and Northampton Counties.

Since the information obtained from these sources often does not lend itself to specific citations, reference is made to them only in the Bibliography which follows these notes.

NOTES TO INTRODUCTION:
"The Surprising Work of God"

1. Jonathan Edwards, *A Faithful Narrative of the Surprising Work of God in the Conversion of Many Hundred Souls in Northampton* in *Select Works of Jonathan Edwards* (London: The Banner of Truth Trust, 1965), vol. I,

2. John Wesley, *The Journal of the Rev. John Wesley* (London: J. M. Dent & Co., [nd]), vol. I, p. 158.

NOTES TO CHAPTER ONE
"The Setting"

1. Blanche Sydnor White, *History of the Baptists on the Eastern Shore of Virginia 1776-1959* (Baltimore: J. H. Furst Co., 1959) pp. 1-6.

2. Ralph T. Whitelaw, *Virginia's Eastern Shore* (Richmond: Virginia Historical Society, 1951), p. 1393.

3. *Ibid.*, pp. 122, 171, 173, 606, 650-651, 905, 1390.

4. *Ibid.*, pp. 1394, 1396.

5. Susie M. Ames, *Studies of the Virginia Eastern Shore in the Seventeenth Century* (Richmond: Dietz Press, 1940), p. 211.

6. Jennings C. Wise, *Ye Kingdome of Accawmacke, or the Eastern Shore of Virginia in the Seventeenth Century* (Richmond: Bell Book & Stationery Co., 1911), p. 258. Whitelaw, pp. 650-651, 154.

7. Whitelaw, pp. 122, 408, 650. Wise, p. 257.

8. Wise, pp. 256, 258-263, 268-272. Whitelaw, p. 1399. Mrs. P. W. Hiden, "Three Rectors of Hungars Parish and Their Wife," *The William and Mary Quarterly* (XIX, January 1939), pp. 34-41.

9. Wise, pp. 155-158. Ames, pp. 231-232, 236-238.

10. Kenneth L. Carroll, "Quakerism on the Eastern Shore of Virginia," *The Virginia Magazine of History and Biography* (LXXIV No. 2, April 1966), pp. 177-180, 187-188. Ames, p. 237.

11. Boyd S. Schlenther, *The Life and Writings of Francis Makemie* (Philadelphia: Presbyterian Historical Society, 1971), pp. 13-25.

12. Whitelaw, p. 1404.

13. Sydney E. Ahlstrom, *A Religious History of the American People* (New Haven: Yale University Press, 1972), p. 220.

14. Whitelaw, pp. 390-393, 705-706.

15. Whitelaw, pp. 142, 425-431, 326-327, 614, 958, 1128, 1130, 1189, 1327, 1393, 1396-1397.

16. Ames, pp. 230-231.

17. Wise, p. 253. A. F. Upshur & Ralph T. Whitelaw, "Library of the Reverend Thomas Teackle," *The William and Mary College Quarterly* (XIII No. 3, July 1943), pp. 298-308.

18. Whitelaw, pp. 1397-1398.

19. Whitelaw, pp. 874, 1398.

20. Wesley M. Gewehr, *The Great Awakening in Virginia 1740-1790* (Durham: Duke University Press, 1930), pp. 32-33.

21. Nora Miller Turman, *The Eastern Shore of Virginia 1603-1964* (Onancock: The Eastern Shore News Inc., 1964), p. 138.

22. Gewehr, pp. 33-34. Henry Boehm, *Reminiscences, Historical and Biographical* (New York: Carlton & Porter, 1865), p. 68.

23. White, pp. 4-5. Turman, pp. 131-132.

24. Lewis Peyton Little, *Imprisoned Preachers and Religious Liberty in Virginia* (Lynchburg: J. P. Bell Co., 1938), pp. 470-475.

25. White, pp. 5-6, 8-9.

26. Whitelaw, p. 1400.

27. Robert B. Semple, *A History of the Rise and Progress of the Baptists in Virginia* (Richmond: Pitt & Dickinson Pubs., 1894), p. 372.

NOTES TO CHAPTER TWO: "Riders from the North"

1. Boehm, *Reminiscences,* pp. 66-68.

2. Freeborn Garrettson, *The Experiences and Travels of Mr. Freeborn Garrettson, Minister of the Methodist Episcopal Church in North America* (Philadelphia: Jos. Crukshank, 1792), pp. 101-102.

3. Garrettson, p. 224. Francis Asbury, *The Journal and Letters of Francis Asbury,* Elmer T. Clark, ed. (Nashville: Abingdon Press, 1958), I, p. 292.

4. Asbury, I, p. 393. John Lednum, *A History of the Rise of Methodism in America* (Philadelphia: Published by the author, 1862), II, p. 341. Nelson Waite Rightmyer, *The Anglican Church in Delaware* (Philadelphia: Church Historical Society, 1947), pp. 65-66.

5. Asbury, I, pp. xvii, 91n, 471. Lednum, II, p. 341.

6. Asbury, I, p. 448.

7. Asbury, I, pp. 469-471.

8. Whitelaw, pp. 592, 869.

9. Asbury, I, p. 471.

10. Asbury, I, pp. 471-472.

11. Thomas Coke, "The Journal of Thomas Coke, Bishop of the Methodist Episcopal Church," *Arminian Magazine* [Philadelphia] (I, 1789), p. 287.

12. J. W. A. Elliott, *Unwritten History of the Eastern Shore* (unpublished 1886). Wessie Nock Eason, *Methodism on the Eastern Shore of Virginia* (unpublished 1909), p. 1.

13. Asbury, I, pp. 524, 552-553.

14. Eason, p. 3.

15. Joseph Everett, "An Account of the Most Remarkable Occurrences of the Life of Joseph Everett," *Arminian Magazine* [Philadelphia] (II, 1790), pp. 608-609.

16. Asbury, I, pp. 552, 581-582. Whitelaw, p. 1023.

17. Asbury, I, p. 612. Whitelaw, p. 353.

18. Asbury, I, p. 771.

19. William Warren Sweet, *Religion on the American Frontier 1783-1840: The Methodists* (New York: Cooper Square Publishers, 1964), p. 83.

20. Eason, pp. 24-25.

21. William Colbert, *A Journal of the Travels of William Colbert* (unpublished [nd]).

22. Garrettson, p. 144. White, p. 11.

23. White, p. 103.

24. White, p. 10.

25. Ahlstrom, p. 373.

26. White, p. 10.

27. Asbury, I, pp. 581, 612.

28. Asbury, I, p. 552. Emory Stevens Bucke, "American Methodism and the Love Feast," *Methodist History* I No. 4 (July 1963), pp. 10-11.

29. Asbury, I, p. 696. Halford E. Luccock & Paul Hutchinson, *The Story of Methodism* (New York: Abingdon Press, 1926), pp. 165-168.

30. Asbury, I, p. 655.

31. Asbury, II, p. 194.

NOTES TO CHAPTER THREE: "The Great Revival"

1. David Dailey, *Experience and Ministerial Labors of Rev. Thomas Smith* (New York: Lane & Tippet, 1848), pp. 57-58.

2. Dailey, pp. 56, 59-62, 68.

3. Dailey, pp. 68-70, 84-85.

4. Dailey, p. 70.

5. Dailey, pp. 64-65.

6. Dailey, pp. 72-78. Eason, pp. 6-9.

7. Dailey, p. 78.

8. Eason, pp. 11-12.

9. Eason, p. 6. Local tradition maintains that the Horntown church was founded in 1800, and that congregation celebrated its 150th anniversary in 1950. The earliest mention in written records is 1806.

10. Dailey, pp. 17-18. Turman, p. 156.

11. Boehm, pp. 71-73.

12. Asbury, II, p. 335.

13. Boehm, pp. 134-135.

14. Boehm, pp. 128, 133.

15. Donald E. Byrne, Jr., *No Foot of Land: Folklore of American Methodist Itinerants* (Metuchen, N.J.: Scarecrow Press, 1975), p. 286. Lorenzo Dow, *Exemplified Experience, or Lorenzo's Journal* (New York: Sheldon, Lamport & Blakeman, 1854), pp. 110-111.

16. Byrne, p. 241. Hulbert Footner, *Rivers of the Eastern Shore* (New York: Holt, Rinehart & Winston, 1944), pp. 78-79.

17. Dow, p. 110.

18. Dow, p. 111.

19. Boehm, p. 133.

20. Adam Wallace, *The Parson of the Islands* (Philadelphia: Published by the author, 1861), pp. 76-77.

21. Asbury, II, p. 500.

22. Boehm, pp. 152-153.

23. Boehm, p. 154. Eason, pp. 16-17. Joshua Thomas also described this incident to his biographer, but erred in dating it. See Wallace, pp. 78-79.

24. Boehm, p. 153.

25. Asbury, III, p. 370.

26. Wallace, pp. 84-85, 87-91.

27. S. J. Morris, ''Early History of Tangier Island and of Its Methodist Church,'' *Richmond Christian Advocate,* July 31, 1941, p. 14.

28. Wallace, pp. 98, 108.

29. Wallace, p. 153.

30. Wallace, p. 143ff.

NOTES TO CHAPTER FOUR: "The Early Fathers"

1. Wallace, p. 333.

2. Colbert, p. 49.

3. Colbert, p. 46.

4. Colbert, p. 26.

5. *Journal of the Quarterly Conference of the Accomack Circuit,* January 19, 1807, and *passim.*

6. Asbury, II, p. 634.

7. Whitelaw, pp. 1366-1367.

8. *Journal,* February 11, 1806; March 23, 1811.

9. Eason, pp. 14-16.

10. C. W. Baines, "The First American Sunday School," *Historical Bulletin No. 1* (Newport News: Virginia State Sunday School Association, 1910), *passim.* This article is based upon the researches of Wessie Nock Eason from the now-vanished original documents.

11. For further consideration of the question of priority of the two Sunday schools, see William Warren Sweet, *Virginia Methodism: A History* (Richmond: Whittet & Shepperson, 1955), pp. 307-308, and Melvin Lee Steadman Jr., "Thomas Crenshaw and the 'First' Sunday School," *Heritage* (I, No. 2, Autumn 1973), pp. 10-12.

12. Eason, p. 21.

13. J. W. A. Elliott, *A Narrative of My Business Life and Early Boyhood and Childhood* [unpublished 1887].

14. Elliott, *Unwritten History,* p. 11.

15. Lednum, II, p. 341.

16. Asbury, II, pp. 634-635.

17. Lednum, II, p. 341.

18. Wallace, pp. 100, 187. J. Shenton Lodge, *An Authentic History of Onancock Methodist Episcopal Church South* [unpublished 1935], p. 12. Victoria Pruitt, *A Brief History of Union Baptist Church from Its Constitution in 1841 to January 1, 1884* (unpublished 1932), p. 5.

19. *Journal,* January 8, 1808.

20. *Journal,* November 15, 1805; February 11, 1806; June 1, 1807; August 31, 1810.

21. *Journal,* December 29, 1804.

22. *Journal,* October 27, 1806. Also James Murray, *History of Pocomoke City, Formerly Newtown, From Its Origin to the Present Time* (Baltimore: Curry, Clay & Co., 1883), p. 199.

23. George Carey, *A Faraway Time and Place: Lore of the Eastern Shore* (Washington: Robert B. Luce Inc., 1971), pp. 53-55.

24. Whitelaw, p. 976. Wallace, pp. 72, 100.

25. *Journal,* February 28, 1817.

26. Wallace, pp. 113-115. This story is not borne out by existing records of local Methodism of the period.

27. Whitelaw, p. 976. Wallace, pp. 30, 121-122, 222-225, 276.

28. Wallace, pp. 215, 261-262. Whitelaw, p. 977.

29. L. W. George, *This Is Tangier Island and Its Church* (Martinsville, Va.: The Radio Fellowship, 1965), p. 15.

30. Wallace, pp. 350-352.

31. Wallace, p. 352. Carey, p. 53. *Eastern Shore News* (Onancock, Virginia), March 29, 1898.

32. Robert H. Burgess, *This Was Chesapeake Bay* (Cambridge, Md.: Cornell Maritime Press Inc., 1963), p. 36.

33. Wallace, p. 408.

NOTES TO CHAPTER FIVE:
"The Second Generation"

1. Whitelaw, pp. 870, 940. Eason, pp. 11, 20. Lodge, p. 2. Morris, p. 15.

2. Sunie Gibb Otwell, *History of the Methodist Episcopal Church and Sunday School of Horntown, Virginia* (unpublished 1934). Eason, p. 20.

3. *Richmond Christian Advocate,* June 25, 1931, p. 13.

4. *Journal,* May 30, 1806; March 14, 1812; September 10, 1814; September 4, 1830; June 6, 1835.

5. *Journal,* February 21, 1834; June 7, 1845.

6. *Journal,* February 26, 1831; June 30, 1832; February 21, 1834; February 28, 1835; June 6, 1835; August 22, 1835.

7. Eason, pp. 20-21.

8. Lodge, p. 11.

9. Whitelaw, p. 940.

10. *Journal,* June 14, 1805; August 20, 1831; February 13, 1836; February 19, 1842.

11. Wallace, pp. 205, 207.

12. Barton H. Wise, *The Life of Henry A. Wise of Virginia 1806-1876* (New York: Macmillan & Co., 1899), p. 123.

13. Wessie Nock Eason, *History of Burton's Church 1801-1901* (unpublished 1901).

14. Mrs. J. L. McCutcheon, *Modest Town Baptist Church 1829-1929: A Century of Church Life* (Parksley: Covington Print, 1929), pp. 5-8.

15. *Journal,* March 20, 1818; December 13, 1823; February 13, 1836. Whitelaw, pp. 915-916.

16. Robert W. Todd, *Methodism of the Peninsula* (Philadelphia: Methodist Episcopal Book Rooms, 1886), p. 47.

17. *Journal,* August 22, 1835. Elliott, *Unwritten History.*

18. F. E. Marine, *Sketch of Rev. John Hersey, Minister of the Gospel of the M.E. Church* (Baltimore: Hoffman & Co., 1879), pp. 21, 162-163. George, p. 20.

19. *Journal,* February 5, 1841.

20. White, pp. 24, 35-36. *Journal,* February 28, 1835; February 5, 1841; June 1, 1844; September 14, 1844; February 15, 1845.

21. Morris, p. 15. Otwell, *loc. cit.*

22. *Journal,* June 22, 1833.

23. Williamson, pp. 64, 66, 68.

24. Frances Lankford Taylor, *History of the Episcopal Church on the Eastern Shore of Virginia 1608-1924* (Cape Charles: Church School Institute of the Eastern Shore of Virginia, 1924), p. 19.

25. Whitelaw, p. 106.

26. L. Floyd Nock III, *Drummondtown, A One-Horse Town: Accomac Court House, Virginia* (Verona, Va.: McClure Press, 1976), pp. 162-163.

27. Whitelaw, pp. 1237, 1327.

28. Jemmie R. & Frances Fletcher, *History of Makemie Presbyterian Church at Accomac* (unpublished [nd]). Leonora W. Wood, *The Beginning of Organized Presbyterianism in Northampton County, Virginia, and the Founding of Holmes Church* [unpublished 1946]. Also records of the church on microfilm at Union Theological Seminary, Richmond, Virginia.

29. Elliott, *Unwritten History* (in *Peninsula Enterprise,* March 20, 1886). Ahlstrom, p. 482.

30. James E. Mears, "The Eastern Shore of Virginia in the Nineteenth and Twentieth Centuries," in Charles B. Clark (ed.), *The Eastern Shore of Maryland and Virginia* (New York: Lewis Historical Pub. Co., 1950), p. 574. See Also William Gwynn Coe, *Sermonbook* [unpublished].

31. White, p. 12. Williamson, p. 17.

32. Everett, p. 609. Asbury, I, p. 696.

33. Williamson, pp. 18-19.

34. White, pp. 21-22, 25, 29, 36, 27.

35. Sweet, *Virginia Methodism,* pp. 128-134, 179.

36. Emory Stevens Bucke (ed.), *The History of American Methodism* (New York: Abingdon Press, 1964), I, pp. 662-663.

37. Murray, pp. 226-227. Eason, p. 5.

38. Edward J. Drinkhouse, *History of Methodist Reform and Methodist Protestant Church* (Baltimore: Board of Publication of the Methodist Protestant Church, 1899), II, p. 119.

39. Murray, p. 223.

40. *Journal,* November 24, 1832.

41. *Peninsula Enterprise,* August 3, 1940.

42. *Journal,* November 24, 1832; August 22, 1835; February 28, 1846.

43. *Journal,* September 1, 1828; August 25, 1837; November 18, 1837. Eason, *History of Burton's Church, loc. cit.* Morris, *loc. cit.*

44. Marine, p. 163.

45. Whitelaw, pp. 944-945.

46. Henry A. Wise, *Seven Decades of the Union* (Philadelphia: Lippincott & Co., 1872), pp. 93-97.

47. Henry A. Wise, *Over on the Eastern Shore* (Onancock: Eastern Shore News, 1962), p. 74.

NOTES TO CHAPTER SIX:
"The Time of Troubles"

1. Bucke, II, p. 12.

2. Asbury, I, p. 582.

3. Whitelaw, p. 869.

4. Baines, p. 5. Eason, p. 11.

5. Eason, p. 10.

6. *Journal,* October 6-7[?], 1804; June 14-15, 1805; September 6, 1805; February 11, 1806; June 4-5, 1814; August 31-September 1, 1816; March 11, 1820; June 29, 1822; July 5, 1823; November 26, 1836.

7. Bucke, II, pp. 12-17, 27.

8. Sweet, *Virginia Methodism*, pp. 212-226.

9. Turman, p. 173.

10. Bucke, II, pp. 159-161.

11. *Richmond Christian Advocate*, August 24, 1848.

12. *Christian Advocate and Journal*, November 11, 1846.

13. *Journal*, February 28, 1846; September 5, 1846; November 21, 1846.

14. *Christian Advocate and Journal*, December 17, 1845.

15. *Richmond Christian Advocate*, September 2, 1847.

16. John Nelson Norwood, *The Schism in the Methodist Episcopal Church, 1844* (Alfred, N.Y.: Alfred University, 1923), p. 133.

17. *Christian Advocate and Journal*, October 21, 1846.

18. *Christian Advocate and Journal*, January 6, 1847. *Richmond Christian Advocate*, April 15, 1847.

19. George, p. 20.

20. *Richmond Christian Advocate*, April 22, 1847.

21. *Christian Advocate and Journal*, May 19, 1847; October 6, 1847.

22. *Richmond Christian Advocate*, September 9, 1847; September 16, 1847; September 30, 1847.

23. *Christian Advocate and Journal*, June 21, 1848. *Richmond Christian Advocate*, August 24, 1848.

24. Elliott, *Unwritten History. Journal*, February 18, 1848.

25. Elliott, *Unwritten History.*

26. *Richmond Christian Advocate*, June 3, 1847.

27. Whitelaw, p. 44.

28. Bucke, II, p. 161.

29. *Richmond Christian Advocate,* September 2, 1847; September 16, 1847.

30. Arthur L. Stevenson, *Native Methodist Preachers of the Eastern Shore of Virginia* (Brevard, N.C.: Transylvania Times, 1970), p. 12.

31. James E. Mears, *Hack's Neck and Its People, Past and Present* (Chicago: Published privately by the author, 1937), p. 55. Mamie Belote Bell, *A History of Johnson's Church* ([np], 1950), pp. 8-9. *Richmond Christian Advocate,* August 31, 1848.

32. George, p. 15. *Journal,* September 6, 1845.

33. *Journal,* May 24, 1851; May 30, 1857; May 16, 1859.

34. *Journal,* June 3, 1854; August 26, 1854. Andrew Manship, *Thirteen Years' Experience in the Itinerancy* (Philadelphia: Higgins & Perkinpine, 1856), pp. 377-378. Only a note in the unpublished papers of Wessie Nock Eason identifies the first convert in Garrison's Chapel as Georgie Richardson Quinby.

35. White, pp. 82, 100, 104-105.

36. Whitelaw, p. 1401. Nora Miller Turman, *The Episcopal Church in Accomack County from the Year 1652* (Onancock: Eastern Shore News, 1954), p. 21. Nora Miller Turman, *Eastern Shore Heritage: Our Buildings* (Onancock: Eastern Shore Printers, 1974), p. 30.

37. Todd, p. 179.

38. *Journal,* February 4, 1843; September 14, 1844.

39. Todd, pp. 187, 193.

40. Todd, pp. 73-78, 81.

41. Andrew Manship, *History of Gospel Tents and Experience* (Philadelphia: Published privately by the author, 1884), pp. 126-127.

42. Bucke, II, pp. 209-210.

43. Eason, *History of Burton's Church 1801-1901.*

44. Todd, p. 143.

45. Todd, pp. 143-149.

NOTES TO CHAPTER SEVEN: "Brothers at War"

1. *Journal,* July 28, 1860.

2. *Journal,* January 19, 1861.

3. Lodge, pp. 8-9.

4. *Journal,* May 25, 1861. *Richmond Christian Advocate,* June 25, 1931.

5. J. E. Armstrong, ''Biographical Sketch of Dr. Coe,'' *Baltimore Episcopal Methodist,* May 5, 1877. Henry Slicer Coe, *William Gwynn Coe: An Account by His Son* (unpublished [nd]). Lodge, p. 4. Lodge, and James E. Mears following him, incorrectly identifies the Ebenezer Chapel of the Convention as the Modest Town church of that same name. More recent examination of the circuit records proves that the Ebenezer referred to was the short-lived church in Sluitkill Neck.

6. Mears, ''Nineteenth and Twentieth Centuries,'' pp. 603-605. Whitelaw, p. 44.

7. Stevenson, pp. 11, 13.

8. Susie M. Ames, ''Federal Policy Toward the Eastern Shore of Virginia,'' *The Virginia Magazine of History and Biography* (LXIX No. 4, October 1961) pp. 442-446.

9. Nock, pp. 26-27, 177. Whitelaw, p. 1010. Another story of the rescue of St. James' Church attributes it to Lockwood, who as an Episcopalian ordered that the church was not to be used for anything other than its original purpose. See Nock, p. 169.

10. James E. Mears, *The Virginia Eastern Shore in the War of Secession and in the Reconstruction Period* [unpublished 1957], pp. 411-414.

11. Ames, ''Federal Policy,'' p. 456.

12. Turman, pp. 189-190. Henry Slicer Coe, *William Gwynn Coe.*

13. Mears, *War of Secession and Reconstruction Period,* pp. 308-309.

14. William Gwynn Coe, *Sermonbook* [unpublished], *passim.*

15. Coe, *Sermonbook.* Henry S. Coe, *William Gwynn Coe.*

16. Lodge, p. 4. *Journal,* August 2, 1862.

17. Bucke, II, pp. 248, 251.

18. Todd, p. 79. Mears, *War of Secession and Reconstruction Period,* pp. 265-266.

19. Mears, "Nineteenth and Twentieth Centuries," p. 609. Mears, *War of Secession and Reconstruction Period,* p. 307.

20. Mears, *War of Secession and Reconstruction Period,* pp. 292-294, 302, 307.

21. Mears, *War of Secession and Reconstruction Period,* pp. 363, 457. Lodge, p. 4.

22. William Gwynn Coe, *Journal* (unpublished). Lodge, p. 5.

23. Nannie Watson, *History of Cokesbury Methodist Church* (unpublished 1969). Todd, pp. 79-80.

24. Mears, *War of Secession and Reconstruction Period,* pp. 308-310.

25. Coe, *Journal.*

26. Coe, *Journal.* Henry S. Coe, *William Gwynn Coe.*

27. Coe, *Sermonbook.*

28. Coe, *Journal.* Mears, "Nineteenth and Twentieth Centuries," p. 572.

29. Coe, *Journal.*

30. Mears, "Nineteenth and Twentieth Centuries," pp. 569-570.

31. Lodge, p. 12.

32. Mears, "Nineteenth and Twentieth Centuries," p. 570.

33. Mears, *War of Secession and Reconstruction Period,* pp. 35R-36R.

34. Lodge, p. 12. Armstrong, "Biographical Sketch of Dr. Coe."

35. Lodge, p. 12.

36. Lodge, p. 4.

37. Williamson, p. 41.

NOTES TO CHAPTER EIGHT: "The Great Division"

1. Israel L. Butt, *History of African Methodism in Virginia* (Hampton: Hampton Institute Press, 1908), pp. 234-235.

2. Coe, *Sermonbook.*

3. Butt, p. 235.

4. James M. Douglas, ''Religious Progress of Negro Citizens on the Eastern Shore of Virginia,'' *Peninsula Enterprise,* September 21, 1961; October 26, 1961. *History of Union Baptist Church* (unpublished 1967), p. 1.

5. Williamson, p. 42. White, p. 41.

6. Mears, *War of Secession and Reconstruction Period,* pp. 13-17R, 20R, 34-35R.

7. Mears, *War of Secession and Reconstruction Period,* p. 22R.

8. Williamson, p. 42.

9. Dwight W. Culver, *Negro Separation in The Methodist Church* (New Haven: Yale University Press, 1953), pp. 52-53. J. Beverly F. Shaw, *The Negro in the History of Methodism* (Nashville: Parthenon Press, 1954), pp. 32-34, 61-69.

10. Patricia Savage *et al.,* ''Historical Sketch of the Eastern Shore Virginia-Maryland Baptist Association,'' in *Historical Souvenir Booklet,* published by the Association [np], 1970, p. 47.

11. Butt, p. 44. Douglas, August 17, 1961.

12. Butt, p. 95.

13. Eason, *History of Burton's Church 1801-1901.*

14. Charles S. Burke, "Organization of the African Baptist Church," in a 78th Anniversary Souvenir Booklet published by the church [np], 1947. Douglas, September 21, 1961. *History of Union Baptist Church*, p. 2. *Eastern Shore News*, June 23, 1977.

15. Williamson, p. 48. Douglas, August 23, 1961; August 31, 1961; September 28, 1961; October 12, 1961; October 19, 1961. *American Baptist Yearbook 1886*, p. 97. The name of the Association at that time was Cherrystone.

16. Williamson, pp. 54, 60.

17. Whitelaw, p. 46.

18. Williamson, p. 41. White, pp. 46, 81, 87, 89, 101.

19. Historical materials of the Norfolk Presbytery, Presbyterian Church in the U.S., Synod of Virginia, on microfilm in the library at Union Theological Seminary, Richmond, Virginia. Whitelaw, p. 706.

20. Kelly B. Conklin, "A History of Christ United Methodist Church, Chincoteague, Virginia" [unpublished 1975].

21. Except where otherwise indicated, this sketch of the Turlington Campmeeting is derived from Fairy Mapp White, *Turlington Camp Meetings* (unpublished 1957).

22. *Peninsula Enterprise*, August 15, 1885.

23. James Cannon Jr., *Bishop Cannon's Own Story: Life As I Have Seen It* (Durham: Duke University Press, 1955), pp. 20-21.

24. Kirk Mariner, *Nothing Ever Happened in Arcadia* (Richmond: Cooper-Trent Printers, 1968), pp. 27-28.

NOTES TO CHAPTER NINE:
"New Horizons"

1. Mears, "Nineteenth and Twentieth Centuries," pp. 589-590.

2. Turman, pp. 200-202, 216.

3. Ellen Parsons, *Cape Charles Then and Now* (Cape Charles: [np], 1961), pamphlet published by the Cape Charles Chamber of Commerce.

4. *Directory of Cape Charles Circuit, M.E. Church, South* (Cape Charles: [np], 1900), p. 3.

5. Douglas, August 10, 1961. White, p. 84. M. D. Ashbury, *Handbook and History of Emmanuel Church, Cape Charles, Virginia* ([np], 1933), p. 1. *A Brief History of the First Presbyterian Church of Cape Charles* (unpublished 1939).

6. E. M. Flick, "Father Mickle of Cape Charles," *The Catholic Virginian*, May-June 1932.

7. Raymond Allen Cook, *Fire From the Flint: The Amazing Careers of Thomas Dixon* (Winston-Salem, N.C.: John F. Blair, 1968), pp. 88ff, 108ff, 162ff. Parsons, *loc. cit.*

8. Mariner, pp. 39-42. *Peninsula Enterprise*, October 5, 1895.

9. *Peninsula Enterprise*, November 16, 1886.

10. *Peninsula Enterprise*, July 2, 1887; July 16, 1887.

11. Butt, p. 164.

12. Nell Scott, "History of Grace Church," *Eastern Shore News*, November 23, 1967. *Peninsula Enterprise*, April 1, 1893; October 7, 1893; February 18, 1888; April 30, 1910.

13. Butt, pp. 24, 174, 198.

14. White, pp. 101-102.

15. Turman, *Episcopal Church in Accomack County*, pp. 9, 21. Ashbury, p. 1. Sarah Ann Steele, *A History of Holy Trinity Episcopal Church* (Onancock: [np], 1961), p. 1.

16. *Richmond Christian Advocate*, June 25, 1931.

17. Eason, pp. 11-12. Mears, *Hack's Neck and Its People*, p. 55.

18. S. E. Emrich and W. Carlisle Redden, *A Brief History of Cheriton United Methodist Church 1886-1970* (Portsmouth: Printcraft Press, 1970), pp. 1-2. *Richmond Christian Advocate*, June 25, 1931.

19. *Richmond Christian Advocate*, June 25, 1931. *Mears,* Hack's Neck and Its People, *p. 56.*

19. *Richmond Christian Advocate,* June 25, 1931. Mears, *Hack's Neck and Its People,* p. 56.

20. Amine Kellam, "The Cobb's Island Story," *Virginia Cavalcade* XXIII No. 4 (Spring 1974), p. 26. James Wharton, "Virginia's Drowned Village," *Virginia Cavalcade* VII No. 3 (Winter 1957), pp. 8-11.

21. *Richmond Christian Advocate,* June 25, 1931.

22. White, pp. 90-91.

23. White, pp. 47-48.

24. Nannie Dunton Savage, *Methodist Women and Missions of the Eastern Shore of Virginia* ([np], 1955), pp. 13-14, 16, 20, 23, 25, 28, 31, 42, 64-65ff, 68.

25. Savage, p. 97. Butt, p. 240.

26. White, pp. 49-50, 52-55.

27. Savage, p. 212. Addie S. Watson, "History of The Women of the Church of Clark" [unpublished 1949]. "History of Woman's Auxiliary of Naomi Makemie Church" (unpublished [nd]).

28. Savage, pp. 141, 148, 201-207. White, pp. 48-49, 53. *Eastern Shore Herald,* June 3, 1919; June 10, 1910; July 1, 1910.

29. Charles Kay, "History of Chincoteague Baptist Church" (unpublished 1961). Mary Nottingham Sturgis, *An Appreciation: Frances Carter Jones* (Nassawadox: Printed privately by the author, 1950). Savage, pp. vi-vii.

30. White, pp. 51, 54. Savage, pp. 210-211.

31. White, p. 47.

32. James E. Mears and Willye E. Evans, *The Temperance Movement on Virginia's Eastern Shore* (Onancock: Eastern Shore News, 1966), pp. 11, 14-17. *Peninsula Enterprise,* December 15, 1881; February 16, 1882.

33. Mears and Evans, pp. 14-16, 19-28, 30, 55-57.

34. Cook, p. 89.

35. Mears and Evans, pp. 33-35, 72, 106.

36. F. M. White, *Turlington Camp Meetings,* p. 26. Mears and Evans, pp. 48-50, 53, 106-107. Biographical sketches of other prominent temperance leaders on the Shore are found in Mears and Evans, pp. 52-80.

37. Mears and Evans, p. 49.

38. Ronald E. Shibley, *G. Walter Mapp: Politics and Prohibition in Virginia, 1873-1941* (University of Virginia Master's Thesis, unpublished [nd]), pp. 2, 7-8, 17-18, 36n, 45, 60.

39. Mears and Evans, pp. 50-58. Shibley, pp. 3, 22, 25-26.

40. Virginius Dabney, *Dry Messiah: The Life of Bishop Cannon* (New York: Alfred A. Knopf, 1949), pp 100-101.

41. *Richmond Virginian,* February 24, 1916. *Peninsula Enterprise,* November 4, 1916.

42. Dabney, p. 112.

43. Sweet, *Virginia Methodism,* p. 348. Mears, ''Nineteenth and Twentieth Centuries,'' p. 566.

44. Mears and Evans, p. 50.

NOTES TO CHAPTER TEN:
"A Not-So-Plain and Simple People"

1. *Peninsula Enterprise,* July 22, 1893; October 12, 1895; March 7, 1896.

2. *Peninsula Enterprise,* February 7, 1885.

3. Henry A. Wise, *Yesteryears on the Eastern Shore* (Onancock: Eastern Shore News Inc., 1968), pp. 27-28.

4. John Leland Peters, *Christian Perfection and American Methodism* (New York: Abingdon Press, 1956), pp. 32ff.

5. Boehm, p. 153.

6. Ahlstrom, pp. 816-818.

7. *Peninsula Enterprise,* March 1, 1884.

8. *Peninsula Enterprise,* September 20, 1884. ''A Brief Statement of History, Christ Methodist Church, Chincoteague, Virginia'' [unpublished (nd)].

9. Joseph B. Lynch and Sarah E. Collins, *The Doctrines and Discipline of Christ's Sanctified Holy Church* (Salisbury: Advertise Job Printing, 1893), pp. 3-5.

10. Reginald V. Truitt and Millard G. Les Callette, *Worcester County: Maryland's Arcadia* (Baltimore: Waverly Press, 1977), p. 416. *Peninsula Enterprise,* June 18, 1892; October 29, 1892; August 19, 1893.

11. Lynch, pp. 15, 20.

12. *Peninsula Enterprise,* November 10, 1894.

13. Lynch, p. 9.

14. *Peninsula Enterprise,* January 12, 1895; March 23, 1895.

15. Lynch, p. 29.

16. *Peninsula Enterprise,* September 29, 1894; October 6, 1894.

17. *Peninsula Enterprise,* September 8, 1894.

18. Lynch, p. 5. *Peninsula Enterprise,* April 23, 1892; September 8, 1894.

19. *Peninsula Emterprise,* September 29, 1894.

20. *Peninsula Enterprise,* October 27, 1894.

21. *Peninsula Enterprise,* November 10, 1894; November 17, 1894.

22. *Peninsula Enterprise,* December 1, 1894.

23. *Peninsula Enterprise,* December 1, 1894; December 22, 1894; May 4, 1895; July 6, 1895; October 26, 1895; April 17, 1897. *Eastern Shore News,* April 4, 1943.

24. *Peninsula Enterprise,* June 13, 1896; October 3, 1896; March 13, 1897; April 17, 1897.

25. *Peninsula Enterprise,* May 22, 1897.

26. *Peninsula Enterprise,* June 20, 1903; July 18, 1903.

27. Ahlstrom, p. 507. *Peninsula Enterprise,* September 28, 1894; November 10, 1894; December 8, 1894. *Eastern Shore News,* November 25, 1969.

28. *Religious Bodies: 1936* (Washington: Government Printing Office, 1941), vol. II, part I, p. 439.

29. Charles Edwin Jones, *Perfectionist Persuasion: The Holiness Movement and American Methodism, 1867-1936* (Metuchen, N.J.: Scarecrow Press, 1974), pp. 121-125.

30. *Richmond Christian Advocate,* June 25, 1931.

31. *Eastern Shore Herald,* July 8, 1922; September 16, 1923.

32. Turman, pp. 227-228, 236.

33. Mears, "Nineteenth and Twentieth Centuries," p. 599. Turman, pp. 230, 232-233, 236-237.

34. Nell Scott, "History of Grace Church," *Eastern Shore News,* November 23, 1967. Clarence Moore, *Lower Northampton Baptist Church History* ([np], 1976), p. 35. Herbert P. Hall, "History of the Atlantic Methodist Church [unpublished 1966]. Emrich and Redden, p. 3. Conklin, "A History of Christ United Methodist Church, Chincoteague, Virginia" [unpublished 1975]. White, pp. 81, 86, 88, 106. "A Brief History of First Presbyterian Church, Cape Charles" [unpublished 1939]. *Richmond Christian Advocate,* June 25, 1931. *Eastern Shore News,* October 7, 1936.

35. Nora Miller Turman, "Trompe l'oeil in Accomac: St. James Episcopal Church," *Virginia Cavalcade* XXIII No. 4 (Spring 1974), p. 9. Asbury, p. 6.

36. *Peninsula Enterprise,* November 3, 1923.

37. J. A. Willoughby, *Natural and Supernatural Curiosities* ([np], printed privately by the author, 1954), p. 60.

38. White, pp. 73-74.

39. *Eastern Shore Herald,* June 20, 1917; March 13, 1920. *Eastern Shore News,* April 11, 1925; April 9, 1927. *Peninsula Enterprise,* June 5, 1926.

40. *Eastern Shore Herald,* May 3, 1919.

41. *Accomack News,* December 31, 1920.

42. *Peninsula Enterprise,* May 18, 1945.

NOTES TO CHAPTER ELEVEN: "Full Circle"

1. Robert T. Handy, "The American Religious Depression, 1925-1935," *Church History* XXIX No. 1 (March 1960), pp. 3-16.

2. Turman, pp. 237-238.

3. Douglas, December 7, 1961.

4. Douglas, January 11, 1962.

5. Ahlstrom, p. 925. *Eastern Shore News,* October 10, 1963.

6. Sweet, *Virginia Methodism,* p. 400.

7. James E. Mears, "The Shore Line," *Eastern Shore News,* June 16, 1966.

8. *Eastern Shore News,* March 29, 1973.

9. Ahlstrom, p. 820ff. Vinson Synan, *The Holiness-Pentecostal Movement in the United States* (Grand Rapids, Mich.: Wm. B. Eerdmans Pub. Co., 1971), pp. 145-146, 219-221.

10. Arthur Huff Fauset, *Black Gods of the Metropolis: Negro Religious Cults of the Urban North* (Philadelphia: University of Pennsylvania Press, 1944) p. 16.

11. "Trouble in Tangier," *Newsweek* XXX No. 74 (October 13, 1947), pp. 74-75.

12. George, p. 35.

13. William C. Jason Jr., "The Delaware Annual Conference of The Methodist Church, 1864-1965," *Methodist History* IV No. 4 (July 1966), pp. 36-37.

14. Maury Enright, *Atlantic Baptist Church: The First Hundred Years 1877-1977* (Denton, Md.: [np], 1977), p. 34.

NOTES TO: "GOING FORWARD AN AUTOBIOGRAPHICAL POSTSCRIPT

1. Dailey, p. 77. Boehm, p. 152.

2. Wallace, p. 88.

3. Wallace, p. 233-234.

4. Cannon, pp. 20-21.

5. Samuel S. Hill Jr., *Southern Churches in Crisis* (New York: Holt Rinehart & Winston, 1966), p. 112ff. I am heavily indebted to Hill's perceptive work throughout these paragraphs, although Hill was writing about the South in general, and not about the Eastern Shore in particular.

BIBLIOGRAPHY

I. Books

(1) Ahlstrom, Sydney E. *A Religious History of the American People.* New Haven: Yale University Press, 1972.

(2) Ames, Susie M. *Studies of the Virginia Eastern Shore in the Seventeenth Century.* Richmond: Dietz Press, 1940.

(3) Asbury, Francis. *The Journal and Letters of Francis Asbury* (Elmer T. Clark, ed.). Nashville: Abingdon Press, 1958.

(4) Boehm, Henry. *Reminiscences, Historical and Biographical.* New York: Carlton & Porter, 1865.

(5) Bucke, Emory Stevens (ed.). *The History of American Methodism.* New York: Abingdon Press, 1964.

(6) Burgess, Robert H. *This Was Chesapeake Bay.* Cambridge, Md.: Cornell Maritime Press, 1963.

(7) Butt, Israel Lafayette. *History of African Methodism in Virginia.* Hampton: Hampton Institute Press, 1908.

(8) Butts, Daniel Gregory Claiborne. *From Saddle to City by Buggy, Boat and Railway, [np], [nd].*

(9) Byrne, Donald E. *No Foot of Land: Folklore of American Methodist Itinerants.* Metuchen, N.J.: Scarecrow Press, 1975.

(10) Cannon, James Jr. *Bishop Cannon's Own Story: Life As I Have Lived It.* Durham: Duke University Press, 1955.

(11) Carey, George. *A Faraway Time and Place: Lore of the Eastern Shore.* Washington: Robert B. Luce Inc., 1971.

(12) Cook, Raymond Allen. *Fire From the Flint: The Amazing Careers of Thomas Dixon.* Winston-Salem, N.C.: John F. Blaire Publishers, 1968.

(13) Culver, Dwight W. *Negro Separation in The Methodist Church.* New Haven: Yale University Press, 1953.

(14) Dabney, Virginius. *Dry Messiah: The Life of Bishop Cannon.* New York: Alfred A. Knopf, 1949.

(15) Dailey, David. *Experience and Ministerial Labors of Rev. Thomas Smith.* New York: Lane & Tippet, 1848.

(16) Dow, Lorenzo. *Exemplified Experience, or Lorenzo's Journal.* New York: Sheldon, Lamport & Blakeman, 1854.

(17) Drinkwater, Edward J. *History of Methodist Reform and Methodist Protestant Church.* Baltimore: Board of Publication of the Methodist Protestant Church, 1899.

(18) Edwards, Jonathan. *A Faithful Narrative of the Surprising Work of God in the Conversion of Many Hundred Souls in Northampton* in *Select Works of Jonathan Edwards.* London: The Banner of Truth Press, Vol. 1, 1965.

(19) Fauset, Arthur Huff. *Black Gods of the Metropolis: Negro Religious Cults of the Urban North.* Philadelphia: University of Pennsylvania Press, 1944.

(20) Footner, Hulbert. *Rivers of the Eastern Shore.* New York: Holt, Rinehart & Winston, 1944.

(21) Forman, H. Chandlee. *The Virginia Eastern Shore and Its British Origins.* Easton, Md.: Eastern Shore Publishers Associates, 1975.

(22) Garrettson, Freeborn. *The Experience and Travels of Mr. Freeborn Garrettson, Minister of the Methodist Episcopal Church in North America.* Philadelphia: Jos. Crukshank, 1792.

(23) Gewehr, Wesley M. *The Great Awakening in Virginia 1740-1790.* Durham: Duke University Press, 1930.

(24) Hallman, E. C. *The Garden of Methodism.* Produced by the Peninsula Conference of The Methodist Church. [np], [nd].

(25) Hill, Samuel S. Jr. *Southern Churches in Crisis.* New York: Holt, Rinehart & Winston, 1966.

(26) *Historical Souvenir Booklet.* Published by The Eastern Shore Virginia-Maryland Baptist Association and Its Allied Bodies. [np], 1970.

(27) Jones, Charles Edwin. *Perfectionist Persuasion: The Holiness Movement and American Methodism.* Methuchen, N.J.: Scarecrow Press, 1974.

(28) Lafferty, John J. *Sketches and Portraits of the Virginia Conference, Methodist Episcopal Church, South.* Richmond: Christian Advocate Office, 1890.

(29) Lednum, John. *A History of the Rise of Methodism in America.* Philadelphia: Published privately by the author, 1862.

(30) Little, Lewis Peyton. *Imprisoned Preachers and Religious Liberty in Virginia.* Lynchburg: J. P. Bell Co., 1938.

(31) Luccock, Halford E. and Paul Hutchinson. *The Story of Methodism.* New York: Abingdon Press, 1926.

(32) Lynch, Joseph B. and Sarah E. Collins. *The Doctrines and Discipline of Christ's Sanctified Holy Church.* Salisbury, Md.: Advertise Job Printing, 1893.

(33) Manship, Andrew. *History of Gospel Tents and Experiences.* Philadelphia: Published privately by the author, 1884.

(34) Manship, Andrew. *Thirteen Years Experience in the Itinerancy.* Philadelphia: Published privately by the author, 1855.

(35) Marine, F. E. *Sketch of Rev. John Hersey, Minister of the Gospel of the M.E. Church.* Baltimore: Hoffman & Co., 1879.

(36) Mariner, Kirk. *Nothing Ever Happened in Arcadia.* Richmond: Cooper-Trent Printers, 1968.

(37) Mead, Frank S. *Handbook of Denominations in the United States.* Nashville: Abingdon Press, 1975.

(38) Meade, Bishop William. *Old Churches, Ministers, and Families of Virginia.* Philadelphia: Lippincott, 1857.

(39) Mears, James E. "The Eastern Shore of Virginia in the Nineteenth and Twentieth Centuries," in Charles B. Clark (ed.), *The Eastern Shore of Maryland and Virginia.* New York: Lewis Historical Publishing Co., 1950.

(40) Mears, James E. *Hack's Neck and Its People, Past and Present.* Chicago: Published privately by the author, 1937.

(41) Mears, James E. and Willye E. Evans, *The Temperance Movement on Virginia's Eastern Shore.* Onancock: Eastern Shore News, 1966.

(42) Murray, James. *History of Pocomoke City, Formerly Newtown, from Its Origins to the Present Time.* Baltimore: Curry, Clay & Co., 1883.

(43) Nock, L. Floyd III. *Drummondtown, A One-Horse Town: Accomac Court House, Virginia.* Verona, Va.: McClure Press, 1976.

(44) Norwood, John Nelson. *The Schism in the Methodist Episcopal Church 1844.* Alfred, N.Y.: Alfred University Press, 1923.

(45) Peters, John Leland. *Christian Perfection and American Methodism.* New York: Abingdon Press, 1956.

(46) Parsons, Ellen. *Cape Charles Then and Now.* Cape Charles: Cape Charles Chamber of Commerce, 1961.

(47) Pittman, R. H. *Biographical History of Primitive or Old School Baptist Ministers of the United States.* Anderson, Ind.: Herald Publishing Co., 1909.

(48) *Religious Bodies: 1936.* Washington: Government Printing Office, 1941.

(49) Rightmyer, Nelson Waite. *The Anglican Church in Delaware.* Philadelphia: Church Historical Society, 1947.

(50) Savage, Nannie Dunton. *Methodist Women and Missions of the Eastern Shore of Virginia.* [np], 1955.

(51) Schlenter, Boyd S. *The Life and Writings of Francis Makemie.* Philadelphia: Presbyterian Historical Society, 1971.

(52) Semple, Robert B. *A History of the Rise and Progress of the Baptists in Virginia.* Richmond: Pitt & Dickinson, Publishers, 1894.

(53) Shaw, J. Beverley F. *The Negro in the History of Methodism.* Nashville: Parthenon Press, 1954.

(54) Shibley, Ronald E. *G. Walter Mapp: Politics and Prohibition in Virginia, 1873-1941.* Charlottesville, Va.: University of Virginia [unpublished Master's Thesis], [nd].

(55) Stevenson, Arthur Lynwood. *Native Methodist Preachers of the Eastern Shore of Virginia.* Brevard, N.C.: Transylvania Times, 1970.

(56) Stevenson, Arthur Lynwood. *Natives of the Eastern Shore of Virginia in the Methodist Ministry.* Brevard, N.C.: Transylvania Times, 1972.

(57) Sturgis, Mary Nottingham. *An Appreciation: Frances Carter Jones.* Nassawadox: Printed privately by the author, 1950 [pamphlet].

(58) Sweet, William Warren. *Religion on the American Frontier 1783-1840: The Methodists.* New York: Cooper Square Publishers, 1964.

(59) Sweet, William Warren. *Virginia Methodism: A History.* Richmond: Whittet & Shepperson, 1955.

(60) Synan, Vinson. *The Holiness-Pentecostal Movement in the United States.* Grand Rapids, Mich.: Wm. B. Eerdmans Pub. Co., 1971.

(61) Todd, Robert W. *Methodism of the Peninsula.* Philadelphia: Methodist Episcopal Book Rooms, 1886.

(62) Taylor, Frances Lankford. *History of the Episcopal Church on the Eastern Shore of Virginia 1608-1624.* Cape Charles: Church School Institute of the Eastern Shore of Virginia, 1924.

(63) Truitt, Reginald V. and Millard G. Les Callette. *Worcester County, Maryland's Arcadia.* Baltimore: Waverly Press, 1977.

(64) Turman, Nora Miller. *Eastern Shore Heritage: Our Buildings.* Onancock: Eastern Shore Printers, 1974.

(65) Turman, Nora Miller. *The Eastern Shore of Virginia 1603-1964.* Onancock: Eastern Shore News Inc., 1964.

(66) Turman, Nora Miller. *The Episcopal Church in Accomack County from the Year 1652.* Onancock: Eastern Shore News, 1954.

(67) Wallace, Adam. *The Parson of the Islands.* Philadelphia: Published by the author, 1861.

(68) Wesley, John. *The Journal of the Rev. John Wesley.* London: J. B. Dent & Co., Vol. I. [nd].

(69) White, Blanche Sydnor. *History of the Baptists on the Eastern Shore of Virginia 1776-1959.* Baltimore: J. H. Furst Co., 1959.

(70) Whitelaw, Ralph T. *Virginia's Eastern Shore.* Richmond: Virginia Historical Society, 1951.

(71) Williamson, Robert. *A Brief History of the Origin and Progress of the Baptists on the Eastern Shore of Virginia.* Baltimore: J. F. Weishampel, 1878.

(72) Willoughby, Julian A. *Natural and Supernatural Curiosities.* Printed privately by the author [np], 1954.

(73) Wise, Barton Haxall. *The Life of Henry A. Wise of Virginia 1806-1876.* New York: Macmillan & Co., 1899.

(74) Wise, Henry A. [I]. *Seven Decades of the Union.* Philadelphia: Lippincott & Co., 1872.

(75) Wise, Henry A. [II]. *Over on the Eastern Shore.* Onancock: Eastern Shore News Inc., 1962.

(76) Wise, Henry A. [II]. *Yesteryears on the Eastern Shore.* Onancock: Eastern Shore News Inc., 1968.

(77) Wise, Jennings C. *Ye Kingdome of Accawmacke, or The Eastern Shore of Virginia in the Seventeenth Century.* Richmond: Bell Book & Stationery Co., 1911.

II. Periodicals

(78) Ames, Susie M. ''Federal Policy Toward the Eastern Shore of Virginia.'' *The Virginia Magazine of History and Biography,* LXIX (October 1965).

(79) Armstrong, J. E. ''Biographical Sketch of Dr. Coe.'' *Baltimore Episcopal Methodist,* May 5, 1877.

(80) Baines, C. W. ''The First American Sunday School.'' *Historical Bulletin No. 1* (Newport News, Va.: Virginia State Sunday School Association) 1910.

(81) Brydon, G. MacLaren. ''A List of Clergy of the Protestant Episcopal Church Ordained After the American Revolution, who served in Virginia between 1785-1814.'' *The William and Mary College Quarterly* XIX No. 4 (October 1939).

(82) Bucke, Emory Stevens. ''American Methodism and the Love Feast.'' *Methodist History, I* (July 1963).

(83) Carroll, Kenneth L. ''Quakerism on the Eastern Shore of Virginia.'' *The Virginia Magazine of History and Biography* LXXIV (April 1966).

(84) Coke, Thomas. ''The Journal of Thomas Coke, Bishop of the Methodist Episcopal Church.'' *Arminian Magazine* (Philadelphia) I (1789).

(85) Everett, Joseph. ''An Account of the Most Remarkable Occurrences of the Life of Joseph Everett, in a Letter to Bishop Asbury.'' *Arminian Magazine* (Philadelphia) II (1790).

(86) Flick, E. M. ''Father Mickle of Cape Charles.'' *The Catholic Virginian,* May-June 1932.

(87) Handy, Robert T. ''The American Religious Depression 1925-1935.'' *Church History,* XXIX (March 1960).

(88) Hiden, Mrs. P. W. "Three Rectors of Hungars Parish and Their Wife." *The William and Mary College Quarterly,* XIX (January 1939, July 1939).

(89) Jason, William C. Jr. "The Delaware Annual Conference of The Methodist Church, 1864-1965." *Methodist History,* IV (July 1966).

(90) Mason, George Carrington. "The Colonial Churches of the Eastern Shore of Virginia." *The William and Mary College Quarterly,* XX No. 4 (October 1940), XXI No. 3 (July 1941).

(91) Kellam, Amine Cosby. "The Cobb's Island Story." *Virginia Cavalcade,* XXIII (Spring 1974).

(92) Steadman, Melvin L. Jr. "Thomas Crenshaw and the 'First' Sunday School." *Virginia United Methodist Heritage,* I (Autumn 1973).

(93) ______________, "Trouble in Tangier." *Newsweek,* XXX No. 74 (October 13, 1947).

(94) Turman, Nora Miller. "Trompe l'oeil in Accomac: St. James' Episcopal Church." *Virginia Cavalcade,* XXIII (Spring 1974).

(95) Upshur, A. F. and Ralph T. Whitelaw, "Library of the Reverend Thomas Teackle." *The William and Mary College Quarterly,* XIII (July 1943).

(96) Warren, Maude Radford. "The Island of Chincoteague." *Harper's Monthly Magazine,* CXXVII No. 761 (October 1913).

(97) Wharton, James. "Virginia's Drowned Village." *Virginia Cavalcade,* VII (Winter 1957).

III. Unpublished Records and Manuscripts

(98) Coe, Henry Slicer. *William Gwynn Coe: An Account by His Son.* Original in the possession of Rev. Melvin L. Steadman Jr., Virginia Beach, Virginia.

(99) Coe, William Gwynn. *Sermonbook* and *Journal.* Originals in the possession of Rev. Melvin L. Steadman Jr., Virginia Beach, Virginia.

(100) Colbert, William. *A Journal of the Travels of William Colbert.* Typed copy in the World Methodist Building, Lake Junaluska, North Carolina.

(101) Eason, Wessie Nock. *Methodism on the Eastern Shore of Virginia.* An unfinished work of 1909. Also a notebook from which it was taken containing additional material. Originals in the possession of Miss Virginia B. Benson, Fairfax, Virginia.

(102) Elliott, John Wesley Andros. *Unwritten History of the Eastern Shore,* and other folios of materials. Originals in the possession of Miss Virginia B. Benson, Fairfax, Virginia.

(103) *Journal of the Quarterly Conference of the Accomack Circuit 1804-1868* and *Accomack Circuit Marriage and Baptismal Records 1853-1889.* Original records in the possession of Cokesbury United Methodist Church, Onancock, Virginia.

(104) Mears, James E. *The Virginia Eastern Shore in the War of Secession and in the Reconstruction Period.* [Unpublished 1957]. Copy in the Eastern Shore Public Library, Accomac, Virginia.

(105) Mears, John Neely. *Miscellaneous Papers 1908-1968.* Scrapbooks of material in the Eastern Shore of Virginia Historical Society, Kerr Place, Onancock, Virginia.

(106) White, Fairy Mapp. *Turlington Camp Meetings.* [Unpublished 1957]. Copy in the Eastern Shore Public Library, Accomac, Virginia.

IV. Newspapers

(107) *Christian Advocate and Journal,* New York

(108) *Eastern Shore Herald,* Eastville, Virginia

(109) *Eastern Shore News,* Onancock, Virginia

(110) *Peninsula Enterprise,* Accomac, Virginia

(111) *Richmond Christian Advocate,* Richmond, Virginia

(112) *Virginia Methodist Advocate,* Richmond, Virginia

V. Denominational Records

Methodist

(113) Delaware Annual Conference, Methodist Episcopal Church, The Methodist Church

(114) Maryland Annual Conference, Methodist Protestant Church

(115) Philadelphia Annual Conference, Methodist Episcopal Church

(116) Virginia Annual Conference, Methodist Episcopal Church South, The Methodist Church, United Methodist Church

(117) Wilmington Annual Conference, Methodist Episcopal Church

Episcopalian

(118) Diocese of Southern Virginia

Presbyterian

(119) East Hanover Presbytery, Norfolk Presbytery

(120) Also microfilmed records of the local churches at Union Theological Seminary, Richmond, Virginia

Pilgrim Holiness/Wesleyan

(121) Delmarva District, Eastern District

Baptist

(122) Accomack Baptist Association

VI. Legal Records

(123) Accomack County, Court Record Books: Deeds, Wills

(124) Northampton County, Court Record Books: Deeds, Wills

VII. Local Church Histories, Printed or Published

(125) Ashbury, M. D. *Handbook and History of Emmanuel Church, Cape Charles, Virginia.* (np), 1933.

(126) Bell, Mamie Belote. *A History of Johnson's Church.* (np), 1950.

(127) *Brief History of Bethel Baptist Church* (Bloxom). (np), (nd).

(128) *Directory of Cape Charles Circuit, Methodist Episcopal Church South.* Cape Charles: (np), 1900.

(129) Douglas, James M. "Religious Progress of Negro Citizens on the Eastern Shore of Virginia," *Peninsula Enterprise.* A series of articles on the history of local churches, August 10, 1961 - January 11, 1962.

(130) Dunton, Irma. "History of Red Bank Baptist Church," *Peninsula Enterprise,* October 13, 1939.

(131) Emrich, Stanley E. and W. Carlisle Redden. *A Brief History of Cheriton United Methodist Church 1886-1970.* Portsmouth, Va.: Printcraft Press, 1970.

(132) Enright, Maury. *Atlantic Baptist Church: The First One Hundred Years 1877-1977.* Denton, Md.: (np), 1977.

(133) George, L. W. *This Is Tangier Island and Its Church.* Martinsville, Va.: Radio Fellowship, 1955.

(134) Gladstone, Frances. *Epworth Methodist Church.* (np), 1963.

(135) *History of Union Baptist Church* (Eastville). (np), (nd).

(136) *Lower Northampton Baptist Church.* (np), (nd).

(136) McCutcheon, Mrs. J. L. *Modest Town Baptist Church 1829-1929: A Century of Church Life.* Parksley: Covington Print, 1929.

(138) McKenney, Anne T. Roberts and Louis Earl McKinney. *Eastville Baptist Church 1877-1977.* (np), 1977.

(139) Moore, Clarence. *Lower Northampton Baptist Church History.* (np), 1976.

(140) Morris, S. J. "Early History of Tangier Island and of Its Methodist Church." *Virginia Methodist Advocate,* July 31, 1941.

(141) Nock, Ann Bryant. *History of Market Street Methodist Church.* (np), 1964.

(142) Parker, L. A. and Lloyd A. Parker Jr. *The Onancock Baptist Church 1855-1955.* Onancock: The Eastern Shore News, 1955.

(143) Pruitt, Victoria. *A Brief History of Union Baptist Church* (Chincoteague) *from Its Constitution in 1841 to January 1, 1884.* (np), 1932.

(144) Sawyer, O. W. and Melvina Clear Shepherd. *Brief History of Union Baptist Church, Chincoteague, Virginia, from Its Constitution August 1841 to 1966.* (np), 1967.

(145) Scott, Nell. "History of Grace Church (Parksley)." *Eastern Shore News,* November 23, 1967.

(146) *Seventy-Eighth Anniversary of the African Baptist Church, Cheriton, Virginia.* (np), 1947.

(147) Steele, Sarah Ann. *A History of Holy Trinity Episcopal Church.* Onancock: [np], 1961.

(148) Thornton, W. L. *Brief History of Union Baptist Church* [Chincoteague] *from Its Constitution in August 1841 to 1941.* [np], 1941.

(149) Turner, Burleigh B. Sr. "History of Bethel Methodist Church, Jamesville, Virginia." *Peninsula Enterprise,* July 31, 1952.

(150) Tyndall, Arlene and Willi Behnken. *175 Years of God's Grace: Hollies Baptist Church 1790-1965.* (np), 1965.

VII. Local Church Histories, Unpublished

(151) Blevins, Reuben W. Jr. *Berea Church in Historical Perspective.* Unpublished 1960.

(152) Bowden, Reida. *Those Who Walk with Him.* Unpublished McMaster Essay, 1955. [Local churches of Chincoteague].

(153) *A Brief History of Leatherbury United Methodist Church.* Unpublished 1969.

(154) *A Brief Statement of History, Christ Methodist Church, Chincoteague, Virginia.* Unpublished 1957?

(155) Bruce, Edward L. *Historical Sketch of Jerusalem Baptist Church.* Unpublished 1976.

(156) Conklin, Kelly B. *A History of Christ United Methodist Church, Chincoteague, Virginia.* Unpublished McMaster Essay, 1975.

(157) Crowson, Elmer T. *The Crowsontown Methodist Episcopal Church.* Unpublished 1971.

(158) Eason, Wessie Nock. *History of Burton's Church 1801-1901.* Unpublished 1901.

(159) Emurian, S. K. *A Brief History of First Presbyterian Church of Cape Charles.* Unpublished [nd].

(160) Finney, Leon H. *History of Gaskin's Chapel AME Church.* Unpublished 1977.

(161) Fletcher, Jemmie R. and Frances. *History of Makemie Presbyterian Church at Accomac.* Unpublished [nd].

(162) Fosque, Annie L. *History of Powelton Presbyterian Church.* Unpublished 1929.

(163) Hall, Herbert P. *History of the Atlantic Methodist Church.* Unpublished 1966.

(164) Hall, Nancy C. *History of the Hallwood Methodist Church.* Unpublished 1976.

(165) *The History of the African Baptist Church.* Unpublished 1963.

(166) *History of the Union Baptist Church* [Eastville]. Unpublished 1967.

(167) Kay, Charles. *History of Chincoteague Baptist Church.* Unpublished 1961.

(168) Lodge, J. Shenton. *An Authentic History of Onancock Methodist Episcopal Church South.* Unpublished 1935.

(169) Matthews, Delema. *The History of Bethel AME Church, Onancock, Virginia.* Unpublished 1977.

(170) McKeawn, John R. *History of Union Methodist Church.* Unpublished 1957.

(171) Otwell, Sunie Gibb. *History of the Methodist Episcopal Church and Sunday School of Horntown, Virginia.* Unpublished 1934.

(172) Ward, Eva LeCato. *Historical Sketch of the Belle Haven Presbyterian Church.* Unpublished 1943.

(173) Watson, Addie S. *History of Clark Church* and *History of the Women of the Church of Clark.* Unpublished 1949.

(174) Watson, Nannie. *History of Cokesbury United Methodist Church.* Unpublished 1969.

(175) Wood, Leonora W. *The Beginning of Organized Presbyterianism in Northampton County, Virginia, and the Founding of Holmes Church.* Unpublished 1946.

VIII. Interviews and Correspondence

[176] A great many persons contributed information, resources, reminiscences, photographs, or otherwise helped in the preparation of this work. Among those to whom the author is particularly indebted are:

Mrs. Bessie Ames, Whitesville
Mr. Fulton Ayres, Parksley
Mr. B. Miles Barnes, Onancock
Mrs. Joyce Beasley, Melfa
Mrs. Madeline Beckett, Cape Charles
Miss Virginia B. Benson, Fairfax
Rev. Marcus H. Bloodworth, Accomac
Bishop A. R. Boggs, Parksley
Dr. Edward Bruce, Temperanceville
Rev. Robert F. Bryan, Mechanicsville
Mr. Carl H. Bundick, Painter
Mr. Ken Butler, Cape Charles
Mrs. Margaret Cannon, Falls Church
Mrs. Carrie Carter, Onancock
Mrs. Herbert Charnock, Machipongo
Mrs. Stella Collins, Chincoteague
Mr. Kelly B. Conklin, Chincoteague
Rev. John Crippen, Withams
Dr. E. T. Crowson, Rock Hill, S.C.
Mrs. Audelle Davis, Davis Wharf
Bishop James E. Davis, Jr., Cape Charles
Rev. Paul Dieter, Denton, Md.
Mrs. Thelma Douthat, Greenbush
Mrs. Wesley Elliott, Painter
Dr. Stanley E. Emrich, Atlantic
Mr. W. Maurice Enright, Wattsville

*Ms. Virginia Evans, Cape Charles
Mr. & Mrs. Leon H. Finney, Melfa
Mrs. Carrie Forrest, Cape Charles
Mrs. Jan Fraumann, Marietta, Ga.
Mrs. Florenz Gallagher, Onancock
Rev. Albert Gingrich, Bedford
Mrs. Vilies Godwin, Sanford
Mrs. Nancy C. Hall, Hallwood
*Mrs. Corrine Harmon, Cape Charles
*Mr. Jack Harmon, Cape Charles
Mrs. Dorothy Nebel Harr, Messongo
Mr. George Temple Jarvis, Machipongo
Mr. W. Robert Keeney, Accomac
Mrs. Amine C. Kellam, Belle Haven
Mrs. Lily Lathbury, Quinby
Mrs. Hattie Lewis, Mappsville
Mrs. Spencer Lewis, Temperanceville
Mr. Steven R. Long, Wallops Island
Dr. James B. Lynch, Silver Spring, Md.
Rev. Charles F. Mapp, Cheriton
Mr. & Mrs. G. Walter Mapp, Accomac
Mrs. John Matthews, Onancock
Mrs. Preston Mears, Onley
Mrs. Frances Meredith, Richmond
Mrs. Jean Mihalyka, Cherrystone
Rev. W. J. Milliner, Bloxom
Rev. Clarence P. Moore, Townsend
Mr. Clarence P. Nelson, Modest Town
Mr. Kenneth J. Nock, Melfa
Mr. L. Floyd Nock III, Onancock
Mrs. Beulah Parks, New Church
Rev. John Parrish, Exmore
*Miss Ellen Parsons, Capeville
Miss Pearl Pearson, Birdsnest
Rev. T. Burton Pierce, Fairfax
*Mr. Herbert S. Powell, Wachapreague
Mrs. Lillian Mears Rew, Hallwood
Mrs. Burleigh Riley, Cape Charles
Rev. William Rucker, Eastville
Miss Nell Scott, Parksley
Bishop Estelle D. Smith, Cape Charles
Mrs. Pearl Brown Sine, Baltimore, Md.
Rev. Melvin L. Steadman, Jr., Virginia Beach
Mr. E. Graham Stewart, Jamesville
Mrs. Marceline Stratton, Philadelphia, Pa.

*Rev. Brantley B. Thornes, Bloxom
Rev. Walter Trower, Cape Charles
Mrs. Nora Miller Turman, Parksley
*Mr. Burleigh B. Turner, Sr., Jamesville
Mr. Scott Walker, Jr., McLean
Rev. Thomas B. Walsh, Cape Charles
Miss Nannie Watson, Onancock
Mrs. Nicki West, Chincoteague
Mr. Otho Wilkerson, Miona
Rev. C. Robert Wines, Cheriton
Mrs. Leonora W. Wood, Purcellville
Mr. L. W. Wyatt, Jr., Exmore
Mr. & Mrs. J. Morris Young, Exmore
Mrs. Miriam Young, Bloxom

* deceased

INDEX

A

Abbott, Clarence J., 219, 334.
Abbott, J. D., 587.
Accomac, 10, 14, 83, 194, 196, 204, 206, 212, 219, 223, 224, 244, 254, 262, 274, 336, 354-357, 425, 427, 449, 457-468, 496, 504, 543, 544, 562-563, 640. See also Drummondtown.
Accomac Circuit, 400, 406, 453, 605.
Accomack Baptist Association, 261, 263, 278, 295, 300, 321, 331, 355, 359, 375, 411, 418, 424, 456, 466, 474, 480, 483, 489, 524, 526, 530, 535, 552, 585, 590, 606, 627, 636; founded 85; divided by missions controversy 86-87; during 1840-1850 105; during Civil War 122, 131; loss of black members 137, 144; after Civil War 145; growth 1886-1900 162; missions 167, 169, 170-172; growth 1900-1923 205, 206; during Depression 212-213; since 1940 216.
Accomack Church of Christ, 447.
Accomack Circuit, 23, 34, 69, 73, 78, 82, 90, 102, 107, 111, 115, 116, 117, 119, 134, 167, 303, 353, 363, 514, 577, 578, 608.
Accomack County, great revival in 31, 35-41; Methodist secessions to southern church 102; Unionist stance in 1860-1861 103, 116; racial troubles during Reconstruction 138; vote on relocation of court house 154; population decline 211.
Accomack County Fair, 147, 179.
Accomack County Nursing Home, 637.
Accomack News, 180, 207.
Accomack Parish, 3, 5, 10, 254, 562, 638.
Accomack Wayside, 486.
Accoman, 514.
Adams, Harvey, 198, 624.
Adams, J. K., 142, 245, 485.
Adams, T. Lewis, 198, 624.
Adams United Methodist Church, 142, 212, 229, 245, 297, 485, 534.
African Baptist Church, 142, 217, 246, 310, 311, 316, 340, 362, 377, 529, 619.
African Methodist Episcopal Church, 135; founded 139; growth 1866-1883 140; Annual Conference in Eastville 140, 144; growth 1886-1900 162; missions 169.
African Methodist Episcopal Zion Church, 139.
Agnew, Mrs. Spiro, 398.
Aikens, James, 42, 88.
Allen, Beulah Nock, 170, 322.
Allen Memorial A.M.E. Church, 140, 203, 505, 508, 627. See also New Allen Memorial A.M.E. Church.
Allen, Richard, 508.
Allen, Walter, 170.
Allens, Jane, 569.
Alpha and Omega Church, 227, 247, 298, 299.
altar call, 42, 231-232, 236.
American Baptist Publication Society, 86.
American Revolution, xxii, 5, 10, 13, 15, 28.
Ames, Benjamin T., 119, 121, 125, 126, 129, 131, 132, 455.
Ames Chapel, 72, 73, 90, 248, 344, 531-532.
Ames, Elmer, 394.
Ames, Grace, 394.
Ames, Jesse, 248.
Ames, Richard, 142, 248, 294.
Ames Ridge, 27, 35, 72, 127, 129, 132, 133, 136, 248, 597.
Ames, Thomas, 35, 248.
Ames, Warner, 249.
Amiss Chapel, 164, 165, 248, 249, 357, 405.
Amiss, Joseph H., 164, 249.
Anderson, John G., 504, 543.
Andrew Chapel United Methodist Church, 132, 167, 250, 263, 290, 293, 304, 363, 473, 640.
Andrew, James O., 98, 250.
Andrews Chapel, 539.
Andrews, Edward G., 190-191.
Andrews, William, 539.
Annemessex Circuit, 24, 25, 31, 41-42, 45-47, 76, 232.
Annis, George, 333, 510.
Annis, Mary, 333.
Antinomianism, 24, 25, 85-87, 456.
Antioch Baptist Church, 251, 420, 299, 614, 620.
Anti-Saloon League, 178, 179-180, 182.
Arminianism, 86-87.
Arnold, Isaac, 511.
Artis, Mary, 227, 597.
Artis, William, 597.
Asbury, Francis, 18-28, 30, 31, 32, 38, 40, 41, 43, 46, 47, 53, 54, 55, 57, 59, 60, 62, 71, 73, 77-78, 86, 95, 109, 235, 237, 303, 338, 352, 355, 356, 386, 433, 434, 442, 455, 471, 516, 586, 629.

Ashby, James, 96.
Ashby, Sally, 79.
Assateague Baptist Chapel, 252, 318-320.
Assateague Island, 252, 559.
Assawoman, 159, 253, 486, 561.
Assawoman Episcopal Church, 3, 9, 10, 15, 83, 105, 159, 253, 254, 366, 463.
Assawoman United Methodist Church, 165, 253, 255, 353, 608.
Assemblies of God, 220, 613.
Atkins, I. T., 280.
Atkinson, John, 366.
Atlantic, 82, 83, 90, 141, 145, 161, 176, 201, 206, 215, 224, 254, 256, 257, 258, 332, 352, 385, 393, 495, 514, 565, 568, 589.
Atlantic Baptist Church, 145, 203, 256, 257, 278, 295, 466, 470, 489, 514, 565, 605, 638.
Atlantic Circuit, 105, 111, 115, 121, 132, 255, 353, 364, 410, 434, 514, 539, 586, 608.
Atlantic District, 121.
Atlantic-New Church Charge, 258, 272, 539.
Atlantic United Methodist Church, 161, 203, 215, 256, 257, 258, 272, 539, 629, 630.
Ayres Chapel, 104, 119, 126, 127, 129, 131, 132, 133, 145, 146, 160, 201, 212, 259, 266, 339, 347, 388, 553, 638.
Ayres Chapel Charge, 259-260.
Ayres, Dick, 112.
Ayres, Francis, 259.
Ayres, J. F. F., 260.
Ayres, Levin, 259.
Ayres, Thomas, 117.
Azusa Street Revival, 218-219.

B

Back Creek Neck, 577.
Bacon Hill, 511.
Bacon's Rebellion, 5.
Badger, Levin, 198, 199, 201, 624.
Bagwell, Christiana Newson, 61.
Bagwell, Isaiah, 61, 97.
Bagwell, Thomas, 97.
Bagwell, William, 97.
Baha'i Group of Northampton, 227, 260.
Baha'u'llah, 260.
Bailey, Thomas H., 101-102. 356.
Baines, Morris H., 571.
Baker, Charles S., 601.
Baker, Elijah, 1-2, 10, 12-16, 25, 27, 60, 64, 135, 227, 261, 277, 303, 321, 355, 381-382, 423, 456, 474, 479, 483, 552.
Baker, Leonard, 2.
Baker Memorial Baptist Church, 261, 308, 336, 355, 418, 466.
Baker, Oliver, 470.
Baker, Robert, 379.
Baker, William, 635, 636.
Baltimore (Md.), 22, 119, 122, 154, 156, 194, 211, 449.
Baltimore Annual Conference, 117-118, 133, 135.
Baltimore Christian Advocate, 115.
Baptist Bible Church, 223, 244, 262, 534.
Baptist Church of Christ of Pungoteague, 250, 263, 290, 304.
Baptist General Association of Virginia, 620.
Baptist Young People's Union, 205.
Baptists, strength in 1790's 28; polity 29; theology 29. See also Accomack Baptist Association, Eastern Shore of Virginia-Maryland Baptist Association.
Baptizing Point, 381.
Barber, Franklin, 227, 247.
Barbon, Thomas, 76.
"Barefoot Prophetess," 227, 597.
Barnes, Powhatan, 224, 392.
Barratt's Chapel, 18, 22.
Barrett, Louis E., 174, 554.
Barrett, Thomas S., 419.
Barrett's Methodist Episcopal Church, 264, 419.
Bascom, Henry, 264.
Bascom's Chapel, 102, 122, 133, 264-265, 427, 471, 504, 521, 522-523.
baseball, 77, 185.
Bates, W. G., 303.
Batson, Thomas, 14.
Battle Point, 499.
Bayley, Katy, 88.
Bayly, Kitty, 121, 563.
Bayly, Shadrach, 485.
Bayside (White Rabbit), 104, 220, 259, 260, 266, 402, 485, 500-501, 553-554, 633.
Bayview, 129, 216, 246, 267, 283, 340, 403, 425-426, 573, 640.
Beach, William H., 468.
Bean, P. F., 289, 408.
Beckett, Madeline, 225, 536.
Beckett, William J., 161, 576.
Bell, George, 552.
Bell, Joab, 552.
Bell, Mrs. G. V., 173.

Belle Haven, 3, 24, 27, 74, 84-85, 105, 127, 129, 131, 132, 140, 145, 151, 164, 170, 176, 178, 202, 206, 212, 226, 268, 269, 270, 271, 344, 365, 449, 474, 519, 543, 566-567, 571-572, 627.
Belle Haven Circuit, 567.
Belle Haven-Craddockville Charge, 344.
Belle Haven Presbyterian Church, 145, 268, 269, 270, 425, 504, 543.
Belle Haven Station, 333.
Belle Haven United Methodist Church, 164, 268, 269, 270, 344.
Belle Haven Universalist Church, 268, 269, 270, 271, 567.
Belle Vue, 454-455.
Bennett, Henry R., 180.
Berea United Methodist Church, 145, 158, 161, 215, 258, 272, 487, 509, 539, 629, 630.
Berkeley, William, 5.
Bethany Methodist Episcopal Church, 155, 173, 178, 180, 205, 215, 273-274, 298, 299, 576, 616, 617.
Bethany Methodist Protestant Church (Pocomoke City, Md.), 89.
Bethel A.M.E. Church [Eastville], 136, 139, 140, 158, 169, 212, 274-275, 358, 362, 620.
Bethel A.M.E. Church [Onancock], 140, 141, 276, 389, 458, 521, 522-523, 564, 625, 640.
Bethel Baptist Church [Bloxom], 83, 105, 216, 257, 277-278, 287, 413, 470, 489, 514, 524, 535, 591, 619, 636.
Bethel Baptist Church [Franktown], 144, 217, 279, 505.
Bethel Methodist Protestant Church, 104, 146, 212, 280-281, 318-320, 325, 326, 330, 558, 617, 629.
Bethel United Methodist Church, 27, 61, 102, 104, 132, 282, 368, 388, 439, 507.
Bethlehem Temple Mission, 267, 283, 402.
Beulah Baptist Church, 145, 284-285, 318-320, 618.
Bevans, Addie W., 173.
Bibbins, Matilda, 137, 619.
Bibbins, Samuel, 137, 619.
Bible Church, 222, 285, 509.
Big Woods, 142.
Billings, C. M., 300.
Birdsnest, 198, 219, 286, 341, 479, 536, 605-606, 624, 632.
Bishop Mallalieu's Tent, 159.
Black, D. J., 377.
Black Jews, 333.
Black, William, 10, 11.
Blackstone Female Institute, 151, 418.
Bloomtown, 466.
Bloomtown Baptist Church, 466.
Bloxom, 83, 105, 162, 200-201, 211, 224, 277-278, 287, 288, 289, 290, 323, 366, 378, 459, 489, 564-565, 619, 636.
Bloxom, Argoll, 54, 410.
Bloxom Camp Meeting, 200-201, 287, 288, 289, 290.
Bloxom Circuit, 338.
Bloxom, David W., 288.
Bloxom, Scarburgh, 27, 61.
Bloxom United Methodist Church, 165, 287, 288.
Bloxom Wesleyan Church, 207, 259, 287, 288, 289-290, 323, 374, 407, 422, 586.
Bloxom's Bridge, 277.
Boatwright, F. W., 355.
Boehm, Henry, 42-43, 45, 46, 47.
Boggs, Arthur R., 225, 496.
Boggs Chapel, 90, 102, 250, 263, 290.
Boggs, Francis, 250.
Boggs, James, 250, 263, 617.
Boggs Meetinghouse, 250, 263, 290, 293, 304, 345, 424.
Bolton, Francis, 2, 5, 11.
Bond, J. C., 484.
Boone, M. T., 378.
Boston (Va.), 142, 291, 362, 426, 503, 589-590.
Bowden, Aaron T., 193, 329.
Bowden, Parker, 195.
Bowdoin, Flora Himel, 323.
Bowdoin, J. R., 445.
Bowen, Jethro, 19.
Bowen, Littleton P., 380.
Boweter, John, 502.
Bowling, L. R., 301.
Bowman, G. W., 538.
Bowser, J. W., 390.
Boxiron (Md.), 190.
Boyce, Paul, 220, 374.
Bozman, J. S., 364, 414.
Bradford, Thomas, 61.
Bradford's Neck, 23, 56, 516.
Brasure, Lida, 551.
Brewington, Julius A., 479.
Brick Presbyterian Church (New York, N.Y.), 468.
Brickhouse, Comfort, 445.
Brickhouse, Thomas, 104.
Bridgetown, 25, 140, 176, 292, 362, 435-437, 442, 552, 592, 632, 640.
Bridgetown Circuit, 499.
Brindle, James, 69, 101, 388, 434, 516.

Brittingham, Esther, 272.
Brittingham, John, 272.
Broaddus, Andrew Jr., 359.
Broadwater, 368, 545.
Broadwater Chapel, 164, 165, 293, 367-368, 507, 616. See also Epworth United Methodist Church.
Broadwater Mission, 368, 545.
Broadway Baptist Church, 293, 304, 363, 524, 526, 590.
Brotherhood Society, 274.
Brown, A. H., 259, 589.
Brown, Alton, 568.
Brown, Benjamin, 609.
Brown, Elder, 565, 638.
Brown, Max, 609.
Brown, Morton, 609.
Brown, William 156, 209.
Bryan, Robert F., 222, 539.
Buckingham County, 279.
Buckland, Richard, 4.
Bundick, William T., 176-177, 178, 179.
Bunting, John W., 284.
Bunting, Susan, 284.
Burns, Otis T., 606.
Burrows, Caleb, 362, 619.
Burrows, Eugenia Davis, 142, 619.
Burton, Benjamin F., 441.
Burton, Garrison, 49, 60, 516.
Burton, George, 571.
Burton, Joshua, 60, 97, 516.
Burton, Mary E., 194.
Burton, Thomas, 21, 22, 25, 38-40, 49, 59-60, 71, 96, 141, 232, 294, 516.
Burton, Woolsey, 194.
Burton's Chapel, 21, 24, 37, 40, 53, 56, 59, 60, 71, 76, 79, 82, 90, 96, 101-102, 105, 111, 115, 132, 141, 294, 308, 515-516. See also Oak Grove United Methodist Church.
Burton's United Methodist Church, 142, 204, 212, 294, 308, 396, 517, 569, 597.
Butler, B. F., 125.
Butler, Joan, 610.
Butt, Israel Lafayette, 592, 625, 632.
Butts, D. G. C., 443, 462, 507, 612.
Byrd, George H. T., 441, 589.
Byrd, J. E., 639.
Byrd, Tom, 279, 564.
Byrd, William (of Westover), 9, 10, 11, 436.

C

Calcasieu County (La.), 197.
Caldwell, James, 335.
Callahan, Griffin, 26, 54, 96.
Calvary Assembly of God, 295, 375, 505.
Calvary Baptist Church, 295, 404, 621.
Calvary Bible Church, 223, 296, 298, 299.
Calvary United Methodist Church, 161, 245, 297, 397, 398, 451, 453, 554.
Calvin, John, 29.
Cambridge (Md.), 19, 209, 214n.
camp meetings, 37, 42-49, 65, 66, 76, 79-80, 87, 91-92, 101, 104, 105, 107, 147-152, 200, 232, 233-234, 338, 339, 341, 385, 389, 410, 421, 433, 443, 483, 489, 536, 539, 548, 585, 586, 590, 592.
Camp Occohannock, 215, 344.
Camp Wise, 122.
Campbell; G. C., 377.
Canaan Ridge, 601.
Cane Ridge (Ky.), 42.
Cannon, James Jr., 150-151, 180, 182, 184, 234, 418.
Cape Charles (peninsula), 10, 24, 28, 195, 442.
Cape Charles (town), 153, 154, 155-158, 160, 161, 162, 164, 173, 176, 177, 178, 180, 201, 203, 204, 205, 208, 215, 217, 218, 220, 221, 223, 224, 227, 247, 273-274, 296, 298-299, 300, 301, 325, 335, 339, 340, 361, 362, 365, 376-377, 380-381, 393, 403, 418, 425, 437, 449, 536, 557, 558-560, 572, 573, 575, 576, 609, 616-617, 632-633, 638, 639.
Cape Charles Air Force Base, 380, 609.
Cape Charles Baptist Church, 155, 162, 169, 298, 299, 300, 312, 359.
Cape Charles Chapel, 164, 303, 314, 616.
Cape Charles Mission, 576.
Cape Charles Wesleyan Church, 207, 208-209, 298, 299, 301, 373, 551.
Capeville, 28, 40, 84, 137, 140, 142, 169, 170, 246, 271, 302, 303, 361-362, 499, 545, 573, 619.
Capeville Circuit, 155, 164, 545, 616, 617.
Capeville United Methodist Church, 28, 72, 99-100, 121, 132, 165, 167, 302, 303, 314, 578, 612.
Captain's Cove, 7, 502.
Car, R. A., 283.
Carleton, Henry, 4, 610.
Carlisle, Joseph, 78.
Carnegie, Andrew, 398.
Carrick, J. L., 205.
Carrington, W. B., 246.
Carroll, J. W., 249.
Carroll, T. F., 520.

Cashville, 90, 102, 174, 250, 263, 290, 293, 304, 363, 450, 524, 526, 590, 640.
Cashville Charge, 250, 450, 554.
Castles, Mrs. J. W., 178.
Cedar Grove, 145, 162, 305, 306, 588.
Cedar Grove Baptist Church, 216, 305, 306, 457, 588.
Cedar Island, 249.
Cedar View Wharf, 3, 449, 503.
Centenary Methodist Episcopal Church South, 155, 203, 215, 274, 307, 365, 380, 616, 617.
Central Baptist Mission, 223, 307, 525, 604.
Central Jurisdiction, 214-215, 216, 228.
Cessford, 438.
Chambers, John, 46-47.
Chancetown, 261, 294, 308, 516.
Chandler, J. W., 372.
Chandler, William, 194.
Chandler, William P., 41-44, 47, 338.
Charismatic movement, 220-221, 373, 555, 606.
Chase, Rev., 84, 271.
Cheapside, 220, 309, 362, 402, 498.
Cheriton, 3, 142, 154, 164, 203, 215, 217, 246, 267, 310-311, 312, 313, 312, 316, 333, 340, 365, 380, 381, 392, 557, 573, 578, 609, 610, 619, 639.
Cheriton Baptist Church, 203, 206, 300, 310, 311, 312, 313, 380, 457, 557.
Cheriton Charge, 314.
Cheriton United Methodist Church, 164, 165, 168, 203, 303, 310, 311, 312, 313-314, 578, 613.
Cherrystone, 315, 315, 610.
Cherrystone Baptist Association, 316, 619.
Cherrystone Baptist Church, 142, 246, 315, 316, 619.
Cherrystone Creek, 135, 136.
Cherrystone Wharf, 139, 144, 315, 316.
Chesapeake, 72, 142, 578-579, 620.
Chesconessex, 146, 159, 162, 201, 204, 206, 207, 317, 375, 400, 422, 450, 512, 554, 625, 640.
Chinchtown, 151.
Chincoteague, 76, 104, 105, 119, 137, 140, 144, 145, 146, 152, 159, 160, 163, 172, 176, 178, 185, 187, 190, 191, 192, 193, 195, 196, 197, 198, 199, 200, 203, 204, 207, 211, 212, 217, 219, 226, 252, 280-281, 284-285, 318, 320, 321, 325-326, 329-330, 331-332, 334, 383-384, 385, 390-391, 407, 423, 448, 449, 557-558, 559, 575, 617-619, 629, 638, 640.
Chincoteague Baptist Church, 15, 86, 158, 170, 205, 295, 321-322, 372, 379, 430, 489, 509, 618, 640.
Chincoteague Naval Air Station, 258, 557.
Christ Church of Universal Love Inc., 310, 311, 639.
Christ Episcopal Church [Bloxom], 162, 211, 287, 288, 289, 323, 366.
Christ Episcopal Church [Eastville], 83, 324-325, 358, 428, 437, 464, 640.
Christ Lutheran Church (Norfolk), 380.
Christ United Methodist Church, 146, 159, 160, 172, 203, 204, 211, 280, 281, 318-320, 325-326, 391, 434, 618.
Christian Advocate and Journal, 100-101, 578.
Christian Endeavor Society, 499.
Christian Love Center, 221, 327, 335, 373, 477, 606.
Christian Methodist Episcopal Church, 139.
Christian Science Society of Parksley, 226, 327-328, 534.
Christian Union A.M.E. Church, 136, 138, 139, 328, 378, 458, 488.
Christ's Sanctified Holy Church, 190-198, 207-208, 281, 318-320, 329-330, 391, 448, 558.
Christ's Sanctified Holy Church Colored, 197-198, 330.
Christ's Union Baptist Church, 144, 318-320, 331-332, 618, 640.
Christy, 426.
Church Neck, 10, 435, 437, 463.
Church of England, xxiii, 2-7, 9-12, 15-16, 217, 227; Methodist societies formed within xxii; infiltrated by Puritanism 4-5; disestablished 15; becomes Episcopal Church 15.
Church of God (Anderson, Indiana), 188, 198, 341.
Church of God (Cleveland, Tennessee), 219, 334, 335.
Church of God [Tasley], 638.
Church of God [Withams], 332, 634.
Church of God and Saints of Christ, 332-333, 370-371.
Church of God and True Holiness, 333, 595.
Church of God Live On, 225.
Church of God Mission, 639.
Church of God of Chincoteague, 219, 318-320, 334, 423.
Church of God of Melfa, 219, 327, 335, 477.
Church of Our Lord Jesus Christ of the Apostolic Faith, 335.

Church of the Lord Jesus Christ of the Apostolic Faith, 220, 298, 299, 335.
Church Road, 562.
Churchtown, 510.
civil rights movement, 228.
Clam, 577.
Clarke, Byron, 336, 504.
Clarke Presbyterian Church, 162, 169, 261, 3365, 349, 468, 504, 543.
Clarke's Chapel, 336.
class meeting, 30-31, 186, 190, 205, 221, 418, 586, 601.
Clement, Charles, 295, 372, 379.
Clough, Etta, 301, 374, 624.
Cluff, James, 441, 493.
Clyde, E. C., 407.
Coard, William H., 249.
Coard's Branch Church, 249, 337.
Cobb, Lucius, 612.
Cobb, Nathan, 337.
Cobb, Sally, 337.
Cobb, William, 293.
Cobb's Island, 84, 157, 163-164, 165, 271, 337-338, 545.
Cobb's Island Mission, 163-164, 165, 303, 337-338, 596.
Cockburn, George, 49-51.
Coe, Henry Slicer, 122, 123.
Coe, Sara, 6, 502.
Coe, Timothy, 254.
Coe, William Gwynn, 117-119, 122-133, 136, 191, 248, 259, 264, 270, 271, 339, 356, 363, 388, 425, 524, 553, 578, 616.
Coffey, Ella Rue, 168, 169, 178, 288.
Coke, Thomas, 22, 23, 24, 37, 53, 355.
Cokesbury United Methodist Church, 71, 78, 82, 102, 105, 106, 117, 119, 126, 131, 133, 145, 146, 152, 160, 174, 215, 259, 264, 265, 338-340, 347, 388, 434, 442, 450, 471, 473, 521, 522-523, 554, 640.
Colbert, William, 26-28, 41, 54, 61, 248, 270, 282, 303, 410, 421, 516, 629.
Colclazer, Henry, 115, 116.
Cole, Thomas M., 567, 592.
Coles Chapel A.M.E. Church, 216, 267, 310, 311, 340, 573, 576.
Coles, Eli H. B., 340.
Collins, Charles, 463.
Collins, John, 194.
Collins, John A., 426.
Collins, Sarah, 190, 191, 192, 194, 329.
Colonna, Major S., 97, 111, 516.
Colored Methodist Episcopal Church, 139.
Colored Zion Mission, 484, 637.
Community Chapel, 341.
Community Church of God, 198, 286, 341, 606, 624.
Concord Wharf, 27, 282.
Connelley, J. A., 159-160, 413.
Conner, Frederick, 97, 586.
Conner's Chapel, 105, 132, 342, 585-586.
Conquest Chapel [Methodist Episcopal, South], 104, 105, 132, 161, 342, 366, 608. See also Temperanceville United Methodist Church.
Conquest Chapel [Methodist Protestant], 161, 212, 342, 414, 415, 453, 607, 608.
Conquest Circuit, 342, 414.
Convention of Accomack, 117, 118, 126, 127, 130-132, 133, 162, 191, 259, 264, 339, 356, 363, 388, 615-616, 638; formed 117; divided 126; closed by Union army 130-132; dissolved 133.
Cook P. W., 377.
Cooke, John E., 389.
Copes, Thomas, 264.
Copes, William, 259.
Corbett, C. L., 306, 372.
Corbin, Aulden, 422.
Corbin, William H., 246.
Corbitt, C. L., 295.
Cornelius, Miriam, 503.
Cornick, John, 427.
Cosden, Jeremiah, 26, 443.
Cotton, William, 4, 5, 610.
Coulbourne, J. S., 385, 565.
Cox, Eliza, 434.
Craddockville, 176, 178, 212, 215, 343-344, 640.
Craddockville United Methodist Church, 72, 102, 104, 132, 144, 270, 343-344, 640.
Craft, Anne Wise, 427.
Crawley, Charles B., 270.
Crenshaw, Thomas, 57-58.
Crippen, John, 224, 564-565, 568.
Crippen, Laurinetta, 332.
Crockett, George, 585.
Crockett, Henry, 600.
Crockett, John, 48, 65, 601.
Crockett, Lewis, 601.
Crockett, Thomas, 49, 600.
Crockett, Zachariah, 601.
Cropper, William, 434.
Crosdale, John, 366.
Crossroads, 345.
Crossroads Meetinghouse, 345, 424, 525.
Crowdy, William S., 332-333.
Crowson, Sally Dennis Rew, 347.
Crowsontown, 158-159, 346-347.
Crowsontown Methodist Episcopal Church, 159, 160, 212, 259, 339, 346-347, 536. 577.
Crozer Theological Seminary, 373.

Cugley, Daniel, 610.
Cummins, George, 111-113, 615.
Custis, Cordelia, 497.
Custis, John IV, 6, 464.
Custis Neck, 569.
Cutlet, George P., 127, 388.
Cutting, William, 502.

D

Dalby, Hezekiah, 104.
Dalby, William Lee, 55, 105, 578.
Dalbys, 348, 377, 381-382, 456-457, 463-464.
dancing, 61, 173, 185, 186.
Daugherty, 140, 162, 169, 261, 294, 336, 349, 424, 458, 468, 540, 568-569, 637, 640.
Daugherty, James, 336.
Daughtrey, M. Colgate, 365, 557.
Davenport, W. H., 376.
Davies, Samuel, 544.
Davis, Andrew D., 159, 176, 255, 347.
Davis, James, 219, 537.
Davis, James Jr., 219, 537, 632-633.
Davis, Noah, 86.
Davis, Robert, 274, 458.
Davis, Sam, 258.
Davis, W. H., 275.
Davis, William, 639.
Day, Oscar Theodore, 625.
Deal Island (Md.), 64, 68, 69, 70, 90, 233, 600.
Deas Chapel United Methodist Church, 140, 211, 212, 215, 350, 384, 385, 431, 501, 566, 640.
Deas, R. M. H., 350.
Deep Creek, 222, 512, 513.
Deep Creek Meetinghouse, 455.
Deep Creek Methodist Episcopal Church South, 350.
Deep Creek Mill, 161, 400.
Deep Hole, 448.
Delastatius, Thomas, 480.
Delaware, xxii, xxiii, 14-15, 18-20, 41, 44, 117, 121.
Delaware Annual Conference, 107, 139, 140, 141, 142, 145, 155, 158, 160-161, 169, 173, 211, 212, 214, 228, 245, 360, 383, 385, 444, 485, 491, 568, 570, 576, 598.
Delmar (Md.), 551.
Dennis, Levin, 107.
Depression, 208, 210-214, 216, 246, 275, 294, 333, 347, 378, 379, 385, 407, 445, 480, 485, 490, 564, 566, 567, 572, 598, 620.
Dickerson, John F., 333.
Dickinson, Alfred E., 293, 359, 470.
Diocese of Southern Virginia, 557, 572.
Disciples Church of New York, 227, 351, 534, 597.
Discipline, 117.
dissenters, 4-8.
Dix, Levin, 489.
Dixon, Solomon, 107.
Dixon, T. S., 201, 209, 259.
Dixon, Thomas, 62.
Dixon, Thomas Jr., 157-158, 177, 337, 338, 627.
Dixon, Thomas H., 588.
Dixon, W. H., 376.
Dixon, William, 511.
Doctrines and Discipline of Christ's Sanctified Holy Church, 191, 192, 193.
Dodd, Dr., 85, 271.
Doggett, Cyrus P., 443.
Dolbow, A. J., 196.
Domestic Missionary Society, 456.
Dormas, Tabitha, 62.
Doughty, Francis, 5.
Douglas, George, 254.
Douglas, James M., 393, 484.
Douglas, Louis H. P., 432.
Douglas Tabernacle Baptist Church, 351, 432.
Dow, Lorenzo, 42-45, 47, 53, 65, 339, 344, 352, 356, 386, 410, 433.
Downes, Mrs. A. S., 300.
Downing, Bettie, 605, 606.
Downing, John, 605, 606.
Downing, Samuel, 54.
Downing, William, 20-21, 23, 24, 54, 55, 62, 71, 96, 352.
Downing's United Methodist Church, 2n, 21, 22, 23, 25, 30, 31, 40, 41, 46, 53, 82, 104, 105, 106, 121, 122, 132, 137, 255, 339, 352-353, 385, 386, 388, 389, 442, 455, 456, 514, 539, 540, 586, 608, 640.
Downing's Wharf, 74.
dress and jewelry, 60-61, 80, 149-150, 200.
Drummond, Esther, 355.
Drummond, John, 355.
Drummond, Louis D., 354, 524.
Drummond, S. P., 447.
Drummond, Spencer J., 625.
Drummond, Stephen, 54.
Drummondtown, xxiii, 10, 14, 22, 25, 31, 36, 41, 46, 54, 73, 83-84, 91, 96, 99, 101, 105, 112, 116, 119, 121, 122, 123, 125, 129, 132, 133, 136, 139, 140, 145, 154, 164, 174, 178, 203, 467, 468, 544, 561, 562. See also Accomac.

Drummondtown A.M.E. Church, 457.
Drummondtown Baptist Church, 145, 169, 180, 203, 244, 261, 354, 355, 424, 470, 524, 526, 637, 640.
Drummondtown Circuit, 164, 249, 458.
Drummondtown United Methodist Church, 102, 105, 121, 176, 181, 203, 244, 249, 401, 442, 458, 562, 605, 635, 636.
Dukes, H. D., 301.
Dunaway, James Manning, 312, 417, 418.
Dunaway, T. S., 261, 355.
Duncan, James A., 455.
Duncan, Levi, 511.
Duncan Memorial Methodist Episcopal Church South, 455.
Dutton, W. C., 176.

E

Early, John, 99-100.
Eason, Samuel, 617.
Eason, Wessie Nock, 23, 58.
East, E. L., 174.
East Hanover Presbytery, 269, 467, 543.
Eastburn, James Wallis, 9, 561.
Easter, George, 365.
Easter, Mrs. Hamilton, 337.
Easterling, E. A., 389.
Eastern Shore Community College, 254.
Eastern Shore District, 147, 169, 214-215, 228, 249, 344, 395.
Eastern Shore Herald, 560.
Eastern Shore Ministerial Association, 206.
Eastern Shore of Virginia-Maryland Baptist Association, 139, 162, 393, 497, 564, 569, 571, 620; formed 139; growth 1886-1900 162.
Eastern Shore of Virginia Produce Exchange, 180, 555, 575.
Easton (Md.), 559.
Eastville, 27, 35, 40, 78, 83-84, 99-100, 104, 121, 129, 136, 137, 139, 140, 142, 144, 145, 154, 160, 161, 169, 174, 206, 211, 212, 217, 246, 260, 271, 274-275, 316, 324-325, 358-361, 377, 385, 428, 437, 438, 457, 460, 464, 497, 506, 560, 578, 610, 619-620, 640.
Eastville Baptist Church, 145, 169, 300, 312, 358, 359, 457, 553, 638.
Eastville Circuit, 102-104, 121, 132, 136, 137, 274, 303, 362, 383, 443, 574, 592.
Eastville Mission Methodist Episcopal Church, 160, 358, 360, 460.
Eastville Presbyterian Church, 206, 211, 358, 361.
Eastville Station, 160, 358, 360.
Eaton, Nathaniel, 5.
Ebenezer A.M.E. Church, 140, 169, 309, 361-362, 377, 499, 573.
Ebenezer Baptist Church, 162, 362-363, 377, 499, 511, 590, 626.
Ebenezer Methodist Episcopal Church [Cashville], 102, 119, 250, 304, 363.
Ebenezer Methodist Episcopal Church [Modest Town], 72, 132, 133, 145, 159, 160, 363, 364-365, 400, 488, 489, 536.
Edmunds, John W., 357.
Edwards, Jonathan, xxi, xxii, xxiii, 12, 40, 42, 232, 237.
Edwards, Robert, 224, 393.
Elizabeth City (N.C.), 195.
Elliott, John, 29, 552.
Elliott, John Wesley Andros, 59, 174-175, 185.
Elliott, Thomas, 1, 2, 13.
Elliott, Thomas Andros, 57-59, 474.
Elliott, William, 23, 24, 39, 55-59, 60, 71, 82, 95, 516.
Ellis, Avra, 586.
Elzey, C. C., 289.
Elzey, William L., 179, 180.
Emmanuel Episcopal Church [Cape Charles], 155, 162, 204, 298, 299, 325, 365, 380, 437, 557, 572, 638.
Emmanuel Episcopal Church [Jenkins Bridge], 105, 162, 254, 323, 366, 440, 607, 608, 640.
Emmerson, Arthur, 11.
Episcopalians, organized 15; oppose Methodism 37-38; resurgence in 1819 83; during 1840-1860 105; during Civil War 122; after Civil War 145; in New Church 158; growth 1886-1900 162; since 1940 217.
Epworth League, 205, 245, 350, 385, 485, 548.
Epworth United Methodist Church, 165, 180, 215, 293, 367-368, 370-371.
Essex County, 5.
Estes, Sallie Smith, 170.
Evangelical United Brethren Church, 227, 599.
Evans, Eleanor, 426.
Evans, George, 426.
Evans, Thomas, 27, 36, 40.
Evans, Virginia, 247.
Everett, Joseph, 24, 25, 27, 60, 86, 237, 303, 443.
Evergreen United Methodist Church, 164, 174, 176, 369, 416, 418, 548, 549, 587, 588, 640.
exhorting, 53-54, 107.

Exmore, 154, 159, 160, 161, 165, 179, 180, 201, 212, 215, 216, 219, 221, 226, 260, 295, 327, 332-333, 367-368, 370-374, 419, 444-445, 449, 479, 490, 491, 494-495, 510-511, 537, 567, 572, 598-599, 616, 627, 633, 639.
Exmore Baptist Church, 166, 206, 216, 221, 278, 370-371, 372-373, 399, 473, 524, 553, 606, 627.
Exmore Wesleyan Church, 295, 301, 370-371, 373-374, 557.

F

Fair Oaks Circuit, 294.
Fairview, 206, 220, 267, 283, 402-403, 457, 498, 501, 573, 576, 640.
Faith Assembly of God, 220, 374, 375, 451.
Faith Baptist Mission, 375, 412, 413.
Faith Tabernacle Assembly of God, 375, 525.
Faith Tabernacle Holiness Church of God Live On, 376, 505.
Fedderman, Charles, 540.
Female Benevolent Society, 167.
Ferebee, J. B., 206.
Finney, Isabelle, 225, 494-495.
Finney, William B., 102, 356.
Finney, William R., 61.
Finney's Wharf, 575.
First Baptist Church [Cape Charles], 155, 162, 217, 298, 299, 362, 376-377.
First Baptist Church [Capeville], 142, 217, 246, 348, 361, 377, 619.
First Baptist Church [Mappsville], 142-143, 378, 441, 459, 469, 489.
First Baptist Church [New Church], 158, 205, 206, 322, 379, 430, 509.
First Born Church of Our Lord Jesus Christ, 639.
First Lutheran Mission, 217, 310, 311, 365, 380, 557.
First Presbyterian Church, 155, 162, 204, 298, 299, 361, 380-381, 425.
Firstborn Church of Christ Disciples, 225.
Fisher, Alfred, 474.
Fisher, Caleb, 474.
Fisher, M. F., 430.
Fisher, William, 636, 647.
Fisher's Meetinghouse, 474.
Fishing Point, 381.
Fishing Point Church, 3, 4, 348, 381-382, 610.
Fitzhugh, William Bullitt, 206, 462, 463.
Flag Pond, 539.
Fletcher, Eleanor, 366.
Fletcher, Isma, 40, 421.
Fletcher, James, 366.
Fletcher, James H., 336.
Fletcher Memorial Hall, 336.
Fletcher, Spencer, 366.
Fletcher, Stephen, 40, 421.
Flournoy, W. C., 361.
Floyd, Benjamin, 27, 71, 72, 383.
Floyd, Matthew, 72, 383.
Floyd's Meetinghouse, 27, 34-35, 40, 72, 382-383, 505, 506.
Fodder House, 452.
footwashing, 333, 334, 422.
Ford, L. Leon, 279.
Foreign Missionary Society, 150.
Fornsberger, Robert, 296.
Fort Monroe, 125, 138.
Fosque, Elizabeth, 129, 131, 264.
Fowkes, Thomas, 502.
Fox, George, 6, 519.
Fox, Mary, 423.
Fox, Susan, 519.
Franklin City, 152-153, 160, 190, 203, 326, 329, 394-395, 400, 404, 620, 621.
Franktown, 6, 72, 140, 144, 279, 382-383, 444, 502, 505, 508, 567, 627.
Franktown A.M.E. Church, 508.
Franktown Circuit, 567.
Franktown United Methodist Church, 27, 102, 132, 165, 211, 443, 505, 506, 507, 615.
Franktown-Johnson's Charge, 507.
Freedmen's Bureau, 132, 138.
Freewill Methodist Episcopal Church, 140, 185, 211, 212, 318-320, 383-384, 385.
French, George H., 132, 138.
Friendship Methodist Protestant Church, 385, 629.
Friendship United Methodist Church, 137, 140, 141, 215, 350, 384, 385-386, 457, 501, 565, 566, 628, 629, 640.
Fristoe, A. J., 526.
Fruitlands, 383.
Full Gospel Mission, 298, 299, 422, 639.
Fuller, Jesse, 499.
Fuller, Sally, 499.
fundamentalism, 218, 221-223.

G

Gaines, A. L., 592.
Galloway, W. K., 399.
gambling, 180.
Garrett, Mary, 208, 301, 373, 551, 638.
Garrettson Chapel, 386.
Garrettson, Freeborn, 19, 22, 23, 24, 28, 355.

Garris, Elder, 333.
Garrison, James, 117, 131.
Garrison, Jonathan, 21, 22, 71, 386, 388.
Garrison, Joshua, 116, 388.
Garrison's United Methodist Church, 21, 22, 24, 25, 26, 27, 30, 40, 41, 53, 54, 73, 101-102, 105, 109-110, 111-112, 117, 119, 122, 123, 127, 129, 131, 133, 165, 204, 211, 282, 386-389, 442, 443, 455, 531, 532, 533, 640.
Gaskin, John, 389.
Gaskin's Chapel, 140, 389, 582.
Gaskins, John, 493.
Gaskins, Meshach, 493.
Gerge Sisters, 205.
Gibb, William, 14.
Gibson, Etta, 624.
Gilchrist, W. W., 426, 432.
Gimenez, John, 555.
Gingrich, Albert, 229, 245, 485.
Girdletree (Md.), 207.
Girls' Auxiliary, 261.
Gladstone, R. T., 494.
Glorious Church of Jesus Christ of the Apostolic Faith, 390, 521, 522-523.
Gloucester (Va.), 1, 2, 13.
Goffigon, John Henry, 377.
Goffigon, Nathaniel, 456.
Goggin, Julian, 220, 295.
Good Templars, 174, 175, 178, 588.
Good Templar News, 176.
Goodson, W. Kenneth, 303, 473.
Goodwill Methodist Episcopal Church, 159, 160, 188-191, 195-196, 211, 318-320, 326, 329, 330, 390-391.
Goodwill School, 391.
Gospel Mission House of Prayer, 310, 311, 392.
Gospel Tabernacle, 224, 392, 509.
Gospel Tabernacle of the Apostolic Faith of God Live On, 224, 298, 299, 393.
Gospel Temple Baptist Church, 217, 224, 393, 446.
Gospel Trumpet, 341.
Grace Mary Tabernacle of the Apostolic Faith Church of God Live On, 224, 393, 394, 477.
Grace Methodist Episcopal Church [Franklin City], 160, 215, 394-395, 400, 404, 621.
Grace United Methodist Church [Locust Mount], 142, 169, 173, 215, 294, 396, 420, 622-623.
Grace United Methodist Church [Parksley], 161, 168, 185, 203, 215, 297, 397-399, 453, 534.
Graham, James E., 399.
Graham's Chapel, 158, 159, 160, 399-400, 419, 479, 509, 538.
Granberry, John C., 443, 540.
Grant, John D., 400.
Grant Memorial Methodist Protestant Church, 161, 204, 212, 400-401, 406, 453, 554, 604, 605.
Grape, 485.
Gray, Charlotte, 192, 197.
Gray, Valentine, 100-101, 578.
Great Awakening, xxii, xxiii, 12, 42, 232, 544.
Greater Mt. Sinai Gospel Tabernacle, 220, 267, 283, 402-403, 457, 498, 501, 640.
Green Run Life Saving Station, 192.
Greenbackville, 7, 152, 176, 207, 230-231, 295-296, 395, 404, 620-621.
Greenbackville Charge, 215n, 621.
Greenbackville Methodist Protestant Church, 152, 173, 215, 272, 280, 295, 395, 434, 592, 620, 621, 629. See also Union United Methodist Church.
Greenbush, 164, 249, 405-406.
Greenbush-Tasley Charge, 406.
Greenbush United Methodist Church, 206, 401, 405, 406, 415, 528.
Greenview Presbyterian Church, 206, 211, 406-407, 543, 622-623.
Greta, 201.
Grice, C. A., 152, 347.
Griffin, J. O., 490.
Griffith, D. W., 158.
Grimsley, S. U., 618.
Groton, William, 548.
Grotons, 7, 8, 104, 199, 407-408, 501, 539-540, 586, 640.
Grotons Wesleyan Church, 207, 289, 407-408, 580-586.
Guilford, 6, 27, 35-36, 40, 54, 61, 100-101, 164, 176, 409-411, 502, 506, 577.
Guilford Creek, 502.
Guilford School, 410.
Guilford United Methodist Church, 35, 132, 164, 288, 409-411, 577.
Guinon, W. J., 560.
Gunter, Benjamin T., 180, 181.
Gunter, Edward, 259.
Gunter, Fred, 493.
Gunter, Joseph, 493, 637.
Guy, John W., 176, 177, 372, 627.
Guy, Will, 372, 627.
Guy, William T., 587.

H

Hack's Neck, 104, 162, 164, 176, 206, 369, 418, 492-493, 548, 587-588, 640.
Hadlock, 27, 34, 102, 119, 132, 145, 383, 615-616.
Half Moon Island, 259.
Hall, Henry A., 411.
Hall, James, 414, 497, 585.
Hall, Major, 497.
Hall, Nellie, 585.
Hall's Chapel, 162, 222, 411, 413, 466, 580, 585, 590, 591.
Hallwood, 152, 154, 159, 161, 201, 342, 364, 375, 412-415, 479, 608.
Hallwood Baptist Church, 206, 278, 375, 411, 412-413, 414, 466, 585, 590, 591.
Hallwood Circuit, 160, 342, 413, 414.
Hallwood Methodist Episcopal Church, 159, 160, 169, 364, 400, 412-413, 414.
Hallwood United Methodist Church, 161, 212, 342, 406, 412, 414-415, 453, 540, 581.
Hampton, 307.
Handshaw, Jesse, 224-225, 376, 393, 394, 491, 564-565, 568.
Hank, P. M., 206, 478, 528.
Hanover Presbytery, 425.
Happy Mission Number One, 632.
Harborton, 164, 176, 205, 212, 369, 416-419, 493, 587, 588.
Harborton Baptist Church, 162, 212, 261, 416-418, 424.
Harborton United Methodist Church, 164, 221, 369, 416, 418-419, 549.
Hardesty, William, 31, 32.
Harding, Maude, 169, 336.
Hare Valley, 27, 383, 506.
Hargis, James, 69, 100-101, 410, 437, 601.
Harmon, Fannie, 170-171.
Harmon, May Ella, 283, 402.
Harmon Mission, 569.
Harmony Methodist Episcopal Church, 159, 160, 264, 419, 439, 479.
Harmony Methodist Protestant Church, 419, 453.
Harris, Rosa, 394.
Harryman, A. A., 414.
Harvard, 5.
Hastings, Elijah, 630.
Hastings, Newton, 322.
Hatcher, William E., 306, 462, 552.
Haughton, Dennis, 511-512.
Haupt, Cecelia, 498.
Haupt, Herman, 498.
Hayes, Lucille, 168.
Hayman, W. H., 566.
Haynes, James A., 574.
Headlight, 157.
Heath, Lewis D., 506.
Henderson, H. B., 441.
Hendrix, Eugene, 478.
Henry, Charles J., 510.
Herbert Baptist Church, 251, 396, 420, 622-623.
Hering, L. P., 592.
Hermitage, 215, 276, 473.
Herrick, Paul, 450.
Herron, James, 270.
Hersey, John, 78, 80-81, 91, 119.
Hill, A. J., 391.
Hinman, Lindy, 375, 422.
Hoffman, Etta Gibson, 198.
Hog Island, 14, 27-28, 41, 49, 72, 164, 165, 368, 421, 545-546, 613.
Hog Island M. E. Church, 421.
Hoge, B. Lacy, 526.
Holden, John, 137, 574.
Holden, Louetta, 551.
Holden's Creek, 366.
Holiness Christian Church, 317, 375, 422.
Holiness Christian Church (Reading, Pa.), 422.
Holiness movement, 186-202, 207-209; female pastors 173; origins 186-188; relation to pentecostalism 218-219; relation to fundmentalism 221, 223.
Holiness Tabernacle, 200, 212, 219, 318-320, 334, 423.
Hollies Baptist Church, 15, 86, 142, 144, 167, 169, 250, 261, 263, 324, 345, 355, 417, 418, 423-424, 446, 524, 589, 627, 637, 640.
Hollywood Baptist Church, 155, 376.
Holmes Presbyterian Church, 84, 129, 131, 145, 169, 267, 269, 313, 361, 380, 425-426, 468, 588, 640.
Holston Annual Conference, 124.
Holy Name of Jesus Catholic Church (Pocomoke City, Md.), 281, 557, 558.
Holy Trinity Baptist Church, 291, 426, 590.
Holy Trinity Episcopal Church, 162, 265, 325, 427-428, 521, 522-523.
Home Mission Board [Presbyterian], 425.
Hope, Cole, 198, 199, 201, 624.
Hope, James M., 300.
Hopeton, 162, 225, 429, 496, 502.
Hopeton Baptist Mission, 162, 429, 638.
Hopewell Baptist Church, 306, 430.

Hopewell Presbyterian Church, 430, 588.
Hopewell School, 305, 588.
Hopkins, 161, 245, 297, 451.
Hopkins, J. P. L., 265, 427.
Horntown, 40, 54-55, 71, 72, 75, 82, 140, 154, 159, 162, 211, 215, 350, 364, 385, 430-434, 640.
Horntown Baptist Church, 162, 295, 322, 379, 430-431.
Horntown Circuit, 140, 385, 501, 565, 566, 570.
Horntown Tabernacle Baptist Church, 162, 426, 431, 432.
Horntown United Methodist Church, 105, 132, 144, 215, 215, 431, 433-434, 621, 640.
Horsey, Shepherd, 504.
Horsey, William, 553.
Hosier, "Black Harry," 22.
Hubbard, Mrs. J. H. B., 173, 396.
Hudston, Calvin, 301.
Huffman, Frank, 606.
Hughes, W. J. L., 350.
Humphreys, Joshua, 112, 117, 119.
Hundley, John W., 257, 293.
Hundley, William T., 359.
Hungars Baptist Church, 552.
Hungars Episcopal Church, 3, 9, 10, 15, 35, 83, 292, 324, 325, 424, 435-437, 443, 456, 561, 562, 640.
Hungars Glebe, 10, 437.
Hungars Parish, 3, 10, 11, 365, 435, 463.
Hunting Creek M.P. Church, 297, 397, 437, 453, 554.
Hunt's Point, 381.
Hurricane Hazel, 339.
Hurst, Harriet, 249.
Hurst, James, 249.
Hurst, Jesse, 249.
Hurst, Lloyd, 406.
Huske, Myron S., 336.
Hyslop, Fannie, 567.
Hyslop, John, 567.

I

ice-skating, 61, 618.
Independent Order of Temperance, 174.
Indiantown Mission, 104, 358, 437-438, 507.
instrumental music, 61, 76, 516.
interdenominational cooperation, 205-206.
International Apostolic Holiness Church, 243.
International Apostolic Holiness Union and Churches, 198, 243.
International Brotherhood of Yahshuas Disciples for the Finishing Work Inc., 227, 351.
Ironshire (Md.),
Ironside Baptist Church, 438, 479.

J

James, Hezekiah, 282.
James, Sarah, 282.
James, Thomas, 455.
James Wharf, 419.
Jamestown (Va.), xxiii, 4, 5, 6, 102.
Jamestown Exposition, 69.
Jamesville, 61, 140, 159, 260, 282, 368, 388, 419, 439, 498-499, 567, 571, 625, 632.
Jamesville Circuit, 499.
Jarman, Dorothy, 502.
Jarman, William, 502.
Jarrett, Devereux, 12.
Jarvis, William 464.
Jehovah's Witnesses, 226, 318-320, 370-371, 448-449, 607.
Jenkins Bridge, 105, 162, 254, 323, 366, 440, 493-494, 566, 607, 608, 640.
Jerusalem Baptist Church, 144, 217, 332, 441, 589, 607.
Jerusalem General Assembly of Firstborn Church of Christ Disciples, 537.
Jester, B. F., 594.
Jester's Chapel, 161, 441, 594.
"Jesus Only," 220, 335, 565.
Jews, 156-157, 609.
Jimmerson, George, 275.
John Wesley M. E. Church, 160-161, 212, 370-371, 444-445, 490, 567, 598.
Johns, John W., 192.
Johnson, Andrew, 222, 514, 601.
Johnson, Ansley, 443.
Johnson, D. H., 535.
Johnson, George, 6, 502.
Johnson, H. Clay, 368.
Johnson, H. E., 533.
Johnson, Isaac, 107.
Johnson, James H. A., 135, 136, 137, 139, 142, 144, 274, 276, 328, 361-362, 457.
Johnson, Johannes, 25, 442, 443.
Johnson, Joshua, 277.
Johnson, S. C., 220, 335.
Johnson, Shadrack, 54.
Johnson, Solomon T., 430.
Johnson's Metropolitan M. E. Church, 485.
Johnson's United Methodist Church, 25, 27, 35, 40, 53, 54, 99, 104, 105, 132, 167, 170, 198, 341, 383, 386, 436, 442-444, 614, 640.

Johnsontown, 176, 442-444, 640.
Jones, Cave, 37, 38, 516.
Jones, E. Pendleton, 553.
Jones, Edward, 222, 285.
Jones, Frances Carter, 171, 553.
Jones, Genefra, 4, 503.
Jones, George P., 190, 191.
Jones, Sam, 178.
Jones, Tiberias Gracchus, 524.
Judefind, W. B., 398.
Judkins, W. E., 255.

K

Kearney, Belle, 178.
Keith, George, 7.
Kellam, Erastus, 344.
Kellam, Hyman, 609.
Kellam, James, 46-47.
Kellam, Richard, 519.
Kellam, Sister, 219, 537.
Keller, 27, 154, 165, 206, 215, 217, 224, 248, 393, 396, 423-424, 444, 445, 446-447, 490-491, 598, 627, 640.
Keller A. M. E. Mission, 162, 446, 447, 525.
Keller Church of Christ, 223, 390, 446, 447.
Keller-Exmore Charge, 598.
Keller Fairgrounds, 186, 226, 449.
Kelly, Nancy, 545.
Kelly, Samuel, 545.
Kelly, Sylvester, 437.
Kemp, E. E., 79.
Kenney, J. L., 146, 325.
Kernodle, Clara, 327.
Kerr, John S., 75, 338.
Kerr Place, 338, 576.
Key, Francis Scott, 51.
Kidd, H. S., 261, 355.
Kidd's Chapel, 261, 355, 448.
King, Martin Luther Jr., 373.
King Solomon Lodge, 492.
Kingdom Hall of Jehovah's Witnesses [Chincoteague], 318-320, 448-449, 607, 628.
Kingdom Hall of Jehovah's Witnesses [Exmore], 371-372, 449.
King's Creek, 3, 610.
Knorr, Nathan, 226, 449.
Knox, Mary Jane, 569.
Ku Klux Klan, 158.

L

Ladies Aid Society, 168, 336.
Ladies Sewing Society, 167.
Langford, J. W., 383.
Laws, John, 69, 364.
Laws, John Jr., 364.
Laws, Mary Welbourn, 364-365.
Laws, William, 77, 483, 489, 618, 637.
Lawson, R. C., 335.
Layfield, George, 27, 28, 67, 68, 423.
Leatherbury, Edith, 146, 171, 176, 450.
Leatherbury, Perry, 146, 450.
Leatherbury United Methodist Church, 146, 160, 201, 250, 259, 317, 339, 450, 640.
LeCato, George W., 174.
LeCato, William, 59-60.
Lecator, George, 510.
Lee, A. B., 246, 510.
Lee, Isaac, 620.
Lee Mont, 89, 90, 104, 137, 145, 161, 220, 297, 374, 375, 451-453, 535.
Lee Mont Baptist Church, 145, 162, 451, 452, 453, 535.
Lee Mont Circuit, 245, 485.
Lee Mont M. P. Church, 89-90, 104, 161, 212, 297, 342, 397, 398, 400, 401, 406, 451, 452-453, 553-554.
Lee, William, 49, 55, 65, 338-339, 600.
Lee's Bethel, 72, 453, 600, 601.
"Lemonade Lucy", 168.
Lewes (Del.), xxii, 12.
Lewis, Jefferson, 78-80.
Lewis, Randy E., 639.
Liddell, Ervin Thomas, 187, 196-197, 448, 618.
Lightbourne, Victor, 202.
Lincoln, Abraham, 111.
local option, 174.
Locke, Nathaniel, 425.
Lockwood, Henry H., 121, 124-125, 563.
Locust Grove Church of God, 341, 453.
Locust Mount, 26, 169, 173, 174, 294, 396, 420.
Locust Mount Circuit, 294.
Locustville, 11, 21, 40, 71, 119, 132, 174, 176, 261, 345, 454-456.
Locustville Academy, 455.
Locustville United Methodist Church, 165, 204, 216, 249, 282, 442, 454-456, 478, 517, 527, 528.
Lodge, J. L., 489.
Lofland, Johnie, 394.
Lofland, Mary, 394.
Long, Handy, 107.
Long, James, 524, 583.
Long, John, 62.
Long, Littleton, 62.
love feast, 30-31, 82.
Lower Church, 610.

Lower Northampton Baptist Church, 2, 14, 15, 28, 86, 144, 167, 169, 203, 205, 295, 300, 306, 312, 313, 348, 359, 381, 402, 456-457, 464, 530, 552, 553, 573, 588, 606.
Lower Parish, 3, 463.
Lowry, Merrick, 201, 624.
Loyal Temperance League, 178.
Luker, Susan, 26.
Lumsden, G. L., 84-85, 271.
Lunenburg County, 2, 12.
Lutherans, 217, 380.
Lynch, Joseph B., 188-196, 198, 208, 329, 391.
lynching, 137, 574.
Lyon, John, 5, 16.
Lyon, Richard, 96.

M

Macedonia A. M. E. Church, 136, 139, 244, 274, 276, 356, 457, 458, 640.
Macedonia Baptist Church, 287, 378, 459.
Macedonia Christian Church, 358, 360, 460.
Machipongo, 260, 296, 461-463.
Mackey, James, 458.
Macon Union Chapel, 206, 211, 461-463.
Madron, A. R., 262.
Magothy Bay Chapel, 303, 463.
Magothy Church, 1-2, 3, 9, 10, 15, 83, 86, 324, 348, 382, 436, 463, 464.
Major, John, 4, 503.
Makemie, Francis, 7-8, 84, 250, 467, 504, 544.
Makemie, Naomi Anderson, 7, 250, 504.
Makemie Park, 224, 225, 227, 351, 448, 465-467, 564-565, 597, 638.
Makemie Park Baptist Church, 204-205, 212, 257, 295, 413, 465-467, 585.
Makemie Presbyterian Church, 84, 121, 145, 244, 336, 425, 467-468, 304, 543, 544, 562, 640.
Mallalieu M. E. Church, 468, 535.
Mallalieu, Willard F., 158-159, 164, 347, 364, 399, 413, 535, 538.
Manship, Andrew, 110.
Mapp Act, 183.
Mapp, Charles F., 246.
Mapp, G. Walter, 180-184.
Mapp, Leroy, 484.
Mapp, Ralph W., 637.
Mappsburg, 21, 204, 221, 386-388, 532, 533, 606.
Mappsville, 144, 162, 176, 378, 441, 469-470, 489, 490.
Mappsville Baptist Church, 162, 169, 257, 278, 469-470, 489.
Mardela Springs (Md.), 201.
Margaret Academy, 544.
Mariner's Chapel, 470, 601.
Marionville, 176, 552-553, 605, 627, 631, 633.
Marker, J. Lee, 605.
Market Street United Methodist Church, 167, 215, 264, 340, 399, 471-473, 521, 522-523.
Marshall, Catherine, 425-426.
Marshall, George T., 594.
Marshall Memorial Methodist Church, 473, 594.
Marshall, Peter, 426.
Marshapungo Baptist Church, 85, 268, 271, 474.
Martin, J. A., 377.
Martin, Thomas, 539.
Martindale, Thomas E., 186.
Maryland Annual Conference, 173, 406, 414, 453.
Maryland State College, 620.
Mason, George W., 126, 174, 339, 389.
Mason, Thorogood, 577.
Massey, James A., 74, 75, 111-113, 115, 117.
Mather, Cotton, 8.
Mather, Increase, 9.
Matthews, Albert, 441.
Matthews, John Daniel, 467.
McAllister, J. R., 206, 557.
McBride, J. T., 462.
McCarter, J. M., 146, 325.
McCroskey, Samuel, 1-2, 5, 436, 464.
McCune, Charles, 333.
McCune, Margaret, 333.
McDowell, A. A., 570.
McKendree, William, 53, 352.
McKenney, Louis E., 359.
McMath Chapel, 164, 475, 527.
McNabb, John, 427.
McNulty, Bennet, 557, 575.
Mears, A. H. Gordon, 180, 520.
Mears, B. Bowdoin, 476.
Mears, Benjamin, 498.
Mears Memorial United Methodist Church, 165, 215, 216, 446, 475-476, 517.
Mears, Mrs. Benjamin, 275.
Mears, Preston, 447.
Mears, Tucker, 449.
Mears, William, 344.
Mears, Winifred, 201, 289.
Mearsville, 201.
Meetinghouse Branch, 506.
Meetinghouse Lot, 544.

Melfa, 23, 147, 154, 165, 217, 219, 221, 224, 234, 327, 335, 393, 394, 475-476, 477-478, 491, 595-517, 569-570, 640.
Melfa Charge, 456, 476, 478.
Melfa United Methodist Church, 165, 206, 475, 477, 478, 517.
Melson, Levin S., 479.
Melson, Sam, 400.
Melson's M. E. Church, 159, 160, 164, 165, 419, 479, 626.
Melvin, A. D., 594.
Melvin, Avra, 62, 88-89, 280, 617, 629.
Melvin, James, 54.
Melvin, William, 54, 62, 97.
Melvin's Chapel, 62.
Merrill, George, 107.
Merrill, William, 115.
Messongo, 140, 162, 222, 565, 566, 608.
Messongo Baptist Church, 411.
Messongo Presdestinarian Baptist Church, 480.
Messongo Primitive Baptist Church, 15, 86-87, 212, 479-481, 542, 590.
"Methodist" [boat], 67, 68, 69.
Methodist Church, The, formed by unification 214; membership 1949 215; membership decline 216; merged 227.
Methodist Episcopal Church, formed 1784 xxii, 22-23; during Revolution 18; during 1790's 26, 28; polity and theology 29; conference connectional system 30; increasing institutionalization 72-73; attitude on moral issues 60-61, 74-77; slavery rules 77, 95, 98; growing prosperity 81; schism (M.P.) 87-90; division into northern and southern bodies 98-103; growth in 1850's 104; black members 107-110; forms black conferences 139; growth of black churches 140-141; after Civil War 145-146; camp meetings 152-153; resurgence late 1880's 158-160; during Depression 211-212; merged 214.
Methodist Episcopal Church, South, formed 98; black members 107-108; early growth 104; churches closed by Union army 130-132; inertia after Civil War 144-145; growth with railroad 163-166; forms mission societies 167-169; during Depression 211-212; merged 214.
Methodist Protestant Church, formation 87-90; during 1850's 104; black members 107; during Civil War 121, 131; after Civil War 145; growth before 1900 161-162; during Depression 210, 212; merged 214.
Metompkin, 82, 83, 482-484, 486, 636-637, 640.
Metompkin Baptist Church [I], 15, 86, 482, 483, 484, 636.
Metompkin Baptist Church [II], 144, 217, 378, 482, 484, 637.
Metropolitan Memorial United Methodist Church, 142, 209, 212, 229, 245, 266, 485.
Michael, Ralph, 375.
Michaels, Emmett, 558.
Mickle, Edward, 155-156, 206, 558-560.
Middle Church, 10, 15, 482, 486, 556, 636.
migrant labor, 575.
Milbourne, Mrs. C. A., 173.
Milburn, W. H., 598.
Milford Baptist Church, 295.
Miller, Bill, 587.
Miller, Henry A., 560.
Miona, 145, 158, 272, 487, 538, 539.
missionaries, 170-171, 221, 322, 513, 553.
Missionary Baptist Mission, 638.
Missionary Society [Presbyterian], 169, 269, 336, 425.
missions movement, 87, 90, 166-173.
Missouri Synod, 217, 380.
Mitchell, Betsy, 62.
Mitchell, Etta, 301, 374, 624.
Mitchell, Sally, 62.
Modest Town, 72, 77, 83, 132, 136, 138, 139, 145, 159, 160, 176, 323, 328, 363, 364-365, 378, 400, 458, 488-490.
Modest Town Baptist Church, 77, 82, 83, 85, 86, 144, 167, 169, 203, 257, 277, 278, 328, 378, 470, 483, 488-490, 514, 618, 636, 647.
Monds, R. S., 278.
Montague, A. J., 528.
Montague, Albert R., 499.
Montross (Va.), 195.
Moore, Lloyd, 121, 131, 132.
Moore, Paul, 257.
Moore's Woods, 151.
Moorman, Samuel T., 99, 102.
moral issues, attitudes on: baseball 77, 185; dancing 61, 173, 185, 186; dress and jewelry 60-61, 80, 149-150, 200; gambling 180; ice-skating 61, 618; instrumental music 61, 76; target shooting 61, 618; theatre 61, 173, 185, 186; tobacco 75, 77, 151, 173, 192; total abstinence 62, 75, 87, 192.

Morley's Wharf, 159, 164, 479, 627.
Mormons, 195, 196-197.
Morris Chapel, 245, 490.
Morton, Charles H., 620.
Mt. Calvary Baptist Church, 490.
Mt. Holly Baptist Church, 493.
Mt. Hope Methodist Church, 206, 212, 215, 396, 445, 446, 490-491, 598.
Mt. Messias Holiness Church of God Live On, 491, 614..
Mt. Nebo Baptist Church, 162, 492, 582.
Mt. Olive A. M. E. Church, 162, 206, 447, 492, 493.
Mt. Olive Baptist Church [Hack's Neck], 162, 206, 416, 492-493.
Mt. Olive Baptist Church [Jenkins Bridge], 162, 440, 493-494.
Mt. Olive Church of Christ Disciples, 219, 370-371, 494-495, 633.
Mt. Olive Holiness Church, 224, 495, 500, 534, 568.
Mt. Olive Pentecostal Church of Christ Disciples, 219, 225, 244, 429, 496.
Mt. Pleasant, 519.
Mt. Sinai Baptist Church, 144, 496-497, 509-640.
Mt. Sinai Church of Christ Deliverance (Norfolk), 402.
Mt. Sinai Church of God, 358, 497.
Mt. Sinai Gospel Tabernacle, 497, 573.
Mt. Sinai Holy Church, 309, 402, 498.
Mt. Sinai Holy Church of America Inc., 220, 225, 402-403.
Mt. Vernon M. E. Church South (Danville), 520.
Mt. Zion A.M.E. Church [Jamesville], 140, 362, 439, 498-499, 567, 625.
Mt. Zion A.M.E. Church [Treherneville], 162, 169, 362, 499, 614.
Mt. Zion Baptist Church [Painter], 144, 217, 511-512, 590.
Mt. Zion Baptist Church [Parksley], 211, 495, 500, 534.
Mt. Zion Holy Church, 220, 266, 402, 500-501, 554, 633.
Mt. Zion United Methodist Church, 140, 211, 332, 501, 565, 566, 634.
Muddy Creek, 277, 487, 502.
Muddy Creek Meetinghouse, 409, 502, 506.
Myrtle Society, 425.

N

Nandua Church, 3, 4, 291, 503, 519.
Naomi Makemie Presbyterian Church, 145, 169, 265, 269, 407, 468, 504, 521, 522-523, 543.
Nassawadox, 165, 203, 225, 279, 295, 375, 376, 383, 505-508.
Nassawadox Meetinghouse, 505, 506.
Nassawadox M. E. Church South, 165, 211, 383, 507.
Nassawadox Mission, 437-438, 505.
National Recorder, 116.
Neely, John, 174.
Negroes, 22, 28, 107-110, 134; form black churches 136ff; separate from white churches 144; education in Northampton County 142; at camp meetings 151; migrations to North 210-211; at unification 214-215; black preacher-centered churches 223-226.
Nelson, W. Tycer, 620.
Nelsonia, 558.
Netherton, Oliver E., 247.
Nettles, T. W., 377, 589.
New Allen Memorial A.M.E. Church, 505, 508. See also Allen Memorial A.M.E. Church.
New Church (village), 10, 15, 144, 145, 152, 154, 155, 158, 159, 160, 161, 170, 203, 205, 206, 215, 222, 224, 272, 285, 321-322, 366, 379, 392, 399-400, 419, 430, 479, 492, 496-497, 509-510, 538, 539, 570, 618, 640.
New Church [Anglican], 10, 15, 83, 509, 510.
New Church Baptist Field, 205, 222, 285.
New Church Charge, 258, 272.
New Church-Exmore Circuit, 160, 400, 479.
New Life Church of God in Christ, 298, 299, 638.
New Mt. Calvary Baptist Church, 370-371, 510-511. See also Mt. Calvary Baptist Church.
New Mt. Hope Church, 490.
New Mt. Zion Baptist Church, 144, 217, 511-512, 531, 532. See also Mt. Zion Baptist Church [Painter].
New Testament Congregation [Deep Creek], 222, 317, 512, 513.
New Testament Congregation [Tangier], 222, 512, 513-514, 601, 603.
New York City, 154, 157, 176, 211, 578, 627.
Newman, Bishop, 69.
Newport News, 390, 426, 432.
Newton, Christiana, 20, 60-61.
Newton, Mrs. J. W., 178.
Newtown (Md.), 20, 31, 43, 60, 62, 73, 82, 88-89, 107, 121, 497, 629. See also Pocomoke City.
Nicholson, Governor, 464.

Nicholson, J. W., 577.
Nock's Branch, 151.
Norfolk, 7, 23, 121, 127, 152, 196, 203, 218, 220, 380, 392, 402, 524, 537, 609.
Norfolk Church of Christ, 447.
Norfolk District [A.M.E.], 625.
Norfolk Presbytery, 269, 504.
Norfolk State College, 403.
Norris, J. Wright, 608.
North Carolina-Virginia Annual Conference, 228.
Northam, Carlton, 591.
Northampton (Mass.), xxi.
Northampton-Accomack Memorial Hospital, 203.
Northampton Baptist Association, 139.
Northampton Circuit, 73, 78, 85, 89, 99, 108, 271, 303, 452.
Northampton County, entrance of Methodism 24-25; absence of great revival 40; secessions to southern church 102, 103; secessionist stance 103, 116; racial attitudes after Civil War 138; vote on relocation of court house 154.
Northampton Public Library, 381.
Northern Neck, 195.
Nottingham, John E., 174, 180.
Nottingham, Luther, 104, 443.
Nottingham, Smith, 443.
Nottingham, William, 578.
Number One Mission House of Prayer, 392.
Nuswattocks Church, 435.

O

Oak Grove Baptist Mission, 514.
Oak Grove Chapel [Atlantic], 90, 132, 145, 256, 257, 352, 514.
Oak Grove United Methodist Church, 26, 39, 141, 149, 151, 164, 165, 167, 174, 178, 294, 308, 475, 476, 477, 478, 515-517, 519, 640. See also Burton's Chapel.
Oak Hall, 2n, 21, 23-24, 54, 71, 106, 121, 123, 339, 352-353, 455, 518, 539, 561, 566, 640.
Oak Hall Charge, 211, 255, 353, 501, 565, 566, 608.
Oakland Park, 201, 207, 373.
Oath of Allegiance, 122, 123, 125.
Occocomson Church, 254.
Occohannock Church, 3, 4, 268, 502, 519.
Occohannock Neck, 27, 166, 282, 362, 498.
Occohannock Parish, 503, 519.
Ocean View United Methodist Church, 215, 519-520, 596, 622-623.
Offer, John Henry, 136, 139-140, 274, 276, 362, 389, 508, 567, 574, 592.
O'Kelly, James, 87.
Old Plantation Creek, 1, 3, 4, 381.
Old-School Baptists, 480.
Oldham, Montcalm, 443.
Omar (Del.), 330.
Onancock, 3, 6, 7, 9, 25, 27, 35, 40, 49, 55, 61, 65, 71, 75, 78, 88, 97, 102, 105, 106, 109, 116, 117, 119, 122, 126, 127, 129, 131, 133, 134, 140, 141, 142, 145, 146, 160, 162, 167, 174, 176, 178, 180, 215, 220, 264-265, 269, 276, 279, 293, 325, 338-340, 366, 389, 390, 399, 424, 427-428, 434, 447, 450, 458, 468, 471-473, 502, 504, 521-524, 540-541, 543, 554, 555, 564, 575, 576, 600, 625, 633, 640.
Onancock A.M.E. Church, 276.
Onancock Baptist Church, 122, 127, 137, 157, 167, 176, 179, 293, 354, 355, 424, 521, 522-523, 524, 526, 583, 640.
Onancock Circuit, 126, 159, 339, 347, 458.
Onancock Council of Friends of Temperance, 174.
oneness doctrine, 220, 335, 638.
Onions, William, 27, 54, 410.
Onley, 154, 164, 173, 178, 179, 180, 183, 217, 221, 223, 293, 307, 323, 327, 345, 375, 406, 424, 447, 525-528, 555, 557, 558, 560, 562, 575.
Onley A.M.E. Mission, 447, 492, 525, 526.
Onley Baptist Church, 180, 206, 261, 293, 525, 526.
Onley United Methodist Church, 164-165, 203, 249, 406, 455-456, 525, 527, 528.
Orthodox Judaism, 156-157, 609.
Outen, E. T., 384.
Outten, Purnell, 483, 489.
Overton, Frank W., 499.
Oyster, 165, 201, 295, 301, 529, 530, 546, 578-579, 612-613, 638.
Oyster Baptist Mission, 457, 529, 530, 613.

P

Painter, 21, 27, 144, 154, 204, 248, 282, 386-389, 511-512, 531-533, 590, 598, 606, 640.
Painter-Bethel Charge, 388.
Painter Charge, 476.

Painter M.E. Church South, 165, 211, 388, 531, 532, 533.
Paramore, Thomas, 27, 282, 388, 455.
Paramore, William, 21, 22, 25, 27, 30, 37, 38, 40, 71, 95, 96, 237, 282, 388, 455.
Paramore's M. E. Church South, 533.
Parham, Charles E., 218.
Parker, B. T., 293.
Parker, Charity, Elizabeth, 389.
Parker, Fred, 390.
Parker, Mayme, 201, 389.
Parker's Landing, 347.
Parker's Neck, 638.
Parks, Charles, 61.
Parks, Edward, 636.
Parks, John, 47-48, 61.
Parks, William, 432.
Parksley, 142, 145, 152, 154, 159, 161, 168, 178, 180, 185, 196, 203, 205, 211, 215, 224, 226, 245, 262, 297, 323, 327-328, 351, 366, 397-399, 453, 495, 496, 500, 534-536, 619.
Parksley Baptist Church, 162, 323, 534, 535, 591, 637.
Parksley Charge, 397, 536.
Parksley M. E. Church, 159, 160, 347, 397, 414, 534, 535, 536-537.
Parramore, Louisa Hope, 563.
Parsons, Francis, 588.
Parson, John, 612.
Parsons, Susan, 588.
Payne, Daniel, 135, 136, 140, 144, 158, 274.
Pear Plain, 435.
Pearly Gates Baptist Church, 370-371, 639.
Pearson, Annie Bradford, 198, 208, 341, 624.
Pearson, Pearl, 341.
Peele, W. W., 314.
Peninsula Annual Conference, 214, 215, 228.
Pentecostal House of Prayer, 219, 286, 536.
Pentecostalism, 218-221, 224, 225.
perfection, doctrine of, 186-187, 247.
Perry (Ga.), 196.
Pertilder, Lily, 220, 498.
Petty, Henry, 300, 312, 354-355.
Pettyjohn, Joan, 4, 503.
Philadelphia Annual Conference, 26, 28, 30, 31, 53, 59, 68, 98, 99, 100, 102, 103, 108, 110, 111, 116, 117, 124, 125, 126, 130, 131, 145, 264, 339, 516, 615, 629.
Philadelphia Church of Christ Disciples, 219, 298, 299, 536, 537, 632-633.
Pierce, E. S., 470.
Pilgrim Holiness Church, 188, 198-202, 207-208, 243, 613.
Piney Forest, 464.
Pitt, Ezekiah, 61.
Pitt, R. H., 355, 379.
Pitt's Wharf, 119, 154, 158.
Pittsville, 272.
Pittsville M. E. Church, 159, 160, 165, 400, 413, 487, 538, 539.
Pittsville M. P. Church, 272, 487.
Pittsville United Methodist Church, 165, 258, 272, 487, 538, 539, 581, 586.
Poch, Martin C., 380.
Pocomoke Charge, 415, 539, 580, 586.
Pocomoke Church [Anglican], 510.
Pocomoke City (Md.), 20, 43, 226, 281, 327, 352, 366, 384, 557, 558. See also Newtown.
Pocomoke United Methodist Church, 104, 105, 132, 164, 352, 539-540, 580, 581, 586, 640.
Pollett, Frost, 107.
Pope Pius XI, 156.
Port Scarburgh Church, 521, 522-523, 540-541.
Portersville Methodist Church, 215, 621.
Portsmouth, 274, 430, 537.
Potts, Jean G., 563.
Poulson, 201, 479-481, 542, 590-591.
Poulson, James, 97.
Poulson Neck Mission, 625.
Poulson, Samuel, 447, 492.
Poulson, Sarah, 468.
Poulson, Thomas L., 124-125, 126, 131.
Poulson, Thomas M., 480, 481.
Powell, E. T., 420, 596.
Powell, Herbert S., 420.
Powell, J. T., 543.
Powell, James, 27.
Powell, John H., 552.
Powelton, 164, 396, 543. See also Wachapreague.
Powelton Mission, 396.
Powelton Presbyterian Church, 145, 169, 211, 269, 406, 407, 420, 504, 519, 543, 622-623.
preacher-centered church, 218, 223-226.
Preachers' Educational Society, 353.
predestination, doctrine of, 85-86, 481.
Preeson, Thomas, 436.
Presbyterian Meetinghouse, 244, 544.
Presbyterians, early revivals xxiii, 8, 12, 22; first presbytery 7; dormant on Eastern Shore after Makemie 8; re-established 84; during Civil War 122; after Civil War 145; growth to 1900 162; missions 169, 172; since 1940 217.

Prettyman, Levin, 69.
Prier, Kenneth, 422.
Primitive Baptists, 479-481.
Princess Anne (Md.), 620.
Princess Anne County, 572.
Prohibition, 179, 183-184, 212.
Prohibition Act of 1916, 183.
Prohibition Party, 174, 176, 222.
protracted meeting, 79, 110.
Pullen, Thomas G., 163-164, 337, 421, 545.
Pullen's Chapel, 164, 165, 368, 421, 545-546, 613.
Pungoteague, 9, 37, 42-47, 49, 65, 83, 104, 111, 121, 123, 137, 140, 154, 164, 248, 250, 254, 369, 419, 436, 486, 516, 547-549, 561-562, 567, 571, 574, 639, 640.
Pungoteague A.M.E. Church, 574.
Pungoteague Baptist Church, 423, 489. See also Hollies Baptist Church.
Pungoteague Camp Meeting, 41-47, 151, 187, 232, 338, 410, 547, 548.
Pungoteague Church, 561.
Pungoteague Circuit, 147, 498, 499, 508, 566, 567, 574, 592.
Pungoteague United Methodist Church, 72, 73, 102, 121, 122, 164, 167, 248, 344, 369, 418, 547, 548-549, 587.
Puritanism, 4-5.

Q

Quakers, 5-7, 383, 409, 502, 506.
Quart-a-Month Act, 183.
Quarterly Meeting, 25, 26, 27, 30, 31, 35, 36, 61, 62, 65, 73, 78, 79, 82, 89, 96, 97, 107, 108, 115, 116, 117, 123, 127, 131.
Queen Anne, 366.
Quigley, Thomas J., 84-85, 271.
Quinby, 56, 164, 185, 201, 338, 520, 550-551, 596, 624.
Quinby, Georgie Richardson, 105, 170, 471.
Quinby, Upshur B., 504.
Quinby Wesleyan Church, 207, 301, 373, 550-551.
Quisenberry, H. N., 293, 590.

R

railroad, 152-153, 154-158, 160, 163, 166, 174, 616.
Randolph, A. M., 365, 462.
Randolph, J. B., 376.
Randolph-Macon College, 104, 150.
Ray, George H., 596.
Ray, Rev., 148.
Read's Gate, 548.
Read's Wharf, 419, 479, 627.
Read's Wharf M.E. Church, 552.
Reams, J. W., 312.
Reamy, A. Judson, 430.
Reamy Memorial Baptist Church, 430, 552.
Rechabites, Independent Order of, 174.
Red Bank Baptist Church, 15, 29, 86, 167, 169, 171, 174, 180, 295, 300, 312, 359, 372, 443, 552-553, 605, 606, 627, 631, 632.
Red Eye Church, 400.
Red Hill M.E. Church, 553, 597.
Red Hills, 152.
Reese Chapel, 104, 142, 161, 220, 266, 297, 400, 453, 500, 553-554, 633.
Reese, Daniel, 553.
Reese, Eli Yeates, 553.
Reese, J. M., 188, 326, 391.
Reese, John, 553.
Reese, Levi, 553.
Reform movement, 88-89, 629.
Rehobeth (Md.), 7.
Reid, A. G., 639.
Reid, Charles, 598.
Reid, George E., 246.
Religious Herald, 293, 470.
revivals, 24, 31-32, 34-41, 65, 76, 79, 104, 105, 144, 202, 218, 231-236, 245, 246, 269, 275, 282, 301, 350, 372, 377, 383, 385, 410, 421, 424, 434, 443, 455, 516, 524, 540, 551, 552, 587, 600, 601, 605, 606, 629; introduction of revivalistic means, 42, 232.
Rew, William, 117, 363.
Rhodes, Walter, 322, 466.
Rice, Luther, 86.
Richardson, Daniel, 5.
Richardson, James C., 221-222, 512, 513, 601.
Richardson, Thomas, 117, 471.
Richmond Christian Advocate, 101, 103.
Richmond Diocese [Catholic], 558, 575.
Richmond Virginian, 182, 183.
Rigmaiden, C. E., 197.
Riverview United Methodist Church, 146, 159, 160, 201, 206, 250, 317, 339, 554.
Rives, George, 155, 164, 616.
Robinson, Ida., 220.
Robinson, William, 6.
Rock Church of the Eastern Shore, 221, 327, 521, 522-523, 555, 606.
Rodgers, William, 363.

Roe, Samuel, 20.
Rogers, E. E., 245.
Rogers, Spencer Finney, 179, 180, 583.
Roman Catholic Church, established on Shore 155-156; since 1940 217.
Rosebud Society, 205.
Rounds, James, 263.
Rowen, Joseph, 26, 27, 28, 54, 421, 629.
Royal, W. C., 205.
Rozier, John, 5.
Rue, 164, 486, 556, 635-636.
Rue, Bettie A., 168, 172, 178, 179, 180.
Rue, William James, 180.
Rue's Wharf, 180, 571.
Ruff, J. W., 458.
Rural Hill, 544.
Rush, Benjamin, 41.
Ryan, Howard, 295.

S

Sabbath-Keeping, 61, 74-75, 77, 133, 152, 173, 186, 221.
St. Andrew's Catholic Church, 217, 281, 318-320, 330, 557-558, 575.
St. Andrew's Episcopal Mission, 310, 311, 365, 557.
St. Charles Borromeo Catholic Church, 156, 203, 298, 299, 558-560, 575.
St. George's Episcopal Church, 3, 9, 10, 15, 37, 83, 121, 137, 145, 254, 324, 424, 436, 456, 516, 548, 561-562, 563, 571, 574, 640.
St. George's Parish, 10, 561.
St. James' Episcopal Church, 10, 15, 83, 121, 203, 204, 244, 427, 544, 562-563, 604, 640.
St. John's Baptist Church, 162, 212, 276, 279, 521, 522-523, 564, 633.
St. John's Faith Church of God Live On, 224, 287, 465, 564-565.
St. John's United Methodist Church [Atlantic], 141, 206, 215, 256, 385, 565.
St. John's United Methodist Church [Messongo], 140, 211, 440, 493, 501, 565, 566.
St. Joseph's A.M.E. Church, 140, 213, 268, 271, 566-567.
St. Joseph Holiness Church, 224, 256, 393, 495, 568.
St. Luke's A.M.E. Church, 140, 294, 349, 458, 568-569, 637, 640.
St. Mark's Baptist Church, 217, 477, 569-570.
St. Mark's United Methodist Church, 158, 160-161, 215, 385, 509, 570.
St. Mary's Baptist Church, 439, 571.
St. Michael's Episcopal Church, 105, 206, 212, 268, 365, 571-572.
St. Paul's A.M.E. Church [Fairview], 206, 220, 267, 402, 573.
St. Paul's A.M.E. Church [Pungoteague], 140, 547, 567, 574.
St. Paul's M.P. Church, 574, 594.
St. Peter's Catholic Church, 217, 521, 522-523, 525, 557, 558, 560, 575.
St. Stephen's A.M.E. Church, 160-161, 273, 298, 299, 340, 573, 576.
St. Stephen's Holiness Church (Norfolk), 392.
St. Thomas United Methodist Church, 164, 288, 409, 210, 577.
Salem M.E. Church [Chincoteague], 390, 391, 577.
Salem M.E. Church South, 72, 84, 99-100, 102, 104, 132, 164, 165, 170, 303, 313, 314, 529, 530, 578-579, 612, 613.
Salisbury, (Md.), 15, 31, 113, 124, 151, 182, 341, 418, 559, 598.
Salisbury Old-School Predestinarian Baptist Association, 480.
Sample, Frank, 492.
sanctification, 186-187, 189, 190, 191, 192, 198, 208, 218, 220.
Sanders, Carl, 313, 613.
Sanford, 408, 411, 415, 580-581.
Sanford, S.E., 569.
Sanford United Methodist Church, 164, 411, 539, 540, 580-581, 586.
Sanford's Grove Baptist Church, 569, 581.
Satchell, Abel J., 378, 484.
Satchell, Christopher, 474.
Satchell, Southey, 225, 536, 633.
Savage, D. B., 459.
Savage, James, 508.
Savage, Jasper, 362, 499, 511.
Savage, Joseph, 492.
Savage, Lloyd, 180, 526.
Savage, Sadie, 180, 183, 526.
Savage's Neck, 359, 638.
Savageville, 127, 140, 162, 389, 492, 582-583.
Savageville Baptist Meetinghouse, 582-583.
Savageville Circuit, 389, 574.
Sawyer, Oscar Whaley, 618.
Saxis, 105, 132, 174, 200, 205, 584-587.
Saxis Baptist Church, 162, 212, 413, 466, 584-585, 586, 590.
Saxis United Methodist Church, 132, 221, 539, 540, 581, 584, 585-586.
Saxis Wesleyan Church, 207, 407, 584, 586-587.

Scarburgh, George P., 99, 100.
School of the Holy Family, 559, 560.
Scott, C. P., 418.
Scott, Eliza, 167-168, 169, 170, 172, 359, 443.
Scott, Henrietta, 360.
Scott, Herod, 107.
Scott, John, 359.
Scott, Levi, 109.
Scott, Thomas, 360.
Scott, William L., 155.
Seaside Mission, 362.
Seatick Chapel, 104, 369, 416, 548, 587-588.
Second Great Awakening, 34ff, 42, 232.
Second Presbyterian Church, 145, 162, 305, 425, 588.
Selby, Gregory, 447.
Sellers, W. R., 551.
Seventh-Day Adventists, 365, 638.
Sexsmith, A. E., 453.
Seyda, Daniel, 335.
Seymour, William, 25, 47, 49, 55, 65, 71, 75, 338-339, 600.
Seymour, William D., 97, 339.
Seymour's M. E. Church, 588.
Shapiro, J. W., 609.
Sharpley, Evaline, 280.
Shelltown (Md.), 198, 624.
Shelton, H. M., 335.
Shepherd, Charles, 115.
Sheppard, Peter, 592.
Sheps End, 605, 606.
Shields, George, 510.
Shiloh Baptist Church [Atlantic], 256, 332, 441, 589.
Shiloh Baptist Church [Boston], 142, 144, 291, 362, 426, 511, 589-590.
Shiloh Baptist Church [Poulson], 278, 411, 413, 466, 535, 542, 585, 590-591.
Shorter Chapel, 140, 169, 292, 362, 592, 640.
Shorter, J. A., 592.
shouting Methodists, 30, 31, 35, 45, 48, 59, 66, 67, 79, 92, 339, 400, 485.
Signpost, 152, 161, 207, 593-594.
Signpost United Methodist Church, 434, 593-594, 621, 629.
Simms, E. W., 629.
Simpkins, 333, 595.
Simpkins, Conner, 388.
Simpkins, Coventon, 27, 388.
Simpkins, Moses, 224, 357.
Sinnickson, R. T., 594.
Sisters of St. Francis, 559.
Slater, Robyn, 260.
slavery, 77, 95-98, 109-110, 111, 235.
Sluitkill Neck, 119, 250, 263, 293, 363, 424, 492.
Smith, Estelle Dillard, 220, 402-403, 498, 500-501, 554, 633.
Smith, G. E. Booker, 164, 596.
Smith Island (Md.), 49, 79.
Smith, John, 377.
Smith, Jonathan, 40.
Smith, Kenneth Lee, 373.
Smith, Leonidas L., 467.
Smith, Mary W., 312.
Smith, Thomas, 34-41, 46, 59, 60, 151, 232, 237, 294, 356, 383, 410, 421, 443, 455, 516, 548, 561, 629.
Smith, Valentine, 69, 601.
Smith, Vaughn, 124.
Smith's Chapel, 164, 185, 201, 517, 520, 550, 551, 596.
Smyrna Assembly of Yajshua Disciples, 227, 351, 465, 597.
Smyrna Church of Christ, 597.
Snead, G. E., 142, 294, 569, 598.
Snead, H. C., 490.
Snead, Margaret, 276.
Snead's United Methodist Church, 142, 212, 294, 445, 491, 531, 532, 597-598.
Snow Hill (Md.), 22, 116, 436, 510, 559.
Snow Hill Primitive Baptist Church, 480, 481.
Society for the Propagation of the Gospel, 9, 11.
Society of Good Samaritans, 492.
Somerset County (Md.), 12, 19, 41, 42, 64, 65, 76.
Southern Baptist Convention, 169, 222-223, 375, 379, 411.
Spady, Alfred J., 246.
Sparks, Robert, 24.
Spence Chapel, 598.
Spence Memorial Methodist Church, 215, 216, 370-371, 445, 491, 495, 598-599.
Spence, Oliver, 598.
Spry, Christopher, 26, 388.
Staats, E. F., 414.
stained glass windows, 105, 200, 204, 322, 324, 339, 353, 357, 359, 366, 388, 414, 443, 458, 473, 511, 540, 543, 581.
Stengle, Adam, 326.
Sterling, Charles, 545.
Stevens, William, 7.
Stevenson, Thomas F., 436.
Stickney, E. W., 105, 586.
Stiles, Joseph, 425.
Stimson, R. D., 588.
Stockley's Gate, 178.
Stockton (Md.), 207, 384.

Stockton Circuit, 395.
Stone, W. H., 272.
Straughn, James H., 258, 594.
Stribling, Christopher, 381.
Stringer, John, 463.
Stumptown, 497.
Sturgis, Catherine, 601.
Sturgis, J. R., 338.
Suffolk, 393, 533.
Sullivan, J. Milford, 422, 551.
"Sunbeams", 169, 205.
Sunday, Billy, 205-206.
Sunday school, 56, 82-83, 87, 205, 515-517.
Sunnyside, 164, 313.
Sunnyside Circuit, 578.
Sunnyside M.E. Church South, 313, 578, 599.
Sussex County (Del.), 188, 191.
Swain, C. P., 601.
Swain Memorial United Methodist Church, 221-222, 513, 514, 600-602, 603.
Swain, Nathan, 34.
Swan's Gut Creek, 433.
Sykes Island, 105, 585.
Sykes, Nellie, 460.

T

Tabernacle Baptist Church, 602.
Tabler, T. F., 196.
Taft, John, 132.
Tailer, Samuel, 254.
Tangier, 45, 48-51, 53, 55, 61, 65, 66, 67, 68, 72, 80, 82, 90, 91-93, 101, 104, 123, 131, 133, 145, 147, 151, 160, 163, 174, 176, 178, 205, 212, 221-222, 339, 512, 513-514, 559, 600-602, 603.
Tangier Camp Meeting, 48-51, 91-93, 151, 339, 600, 601, 603.
Tasley, 161, 204, 307, 375, 400-401, 563, 604-605, 638.
Tasley Methodist Church, 216, 357, 604-605.
Taylor, Anna C., 354, 524.
Taylor Chapel, 605.
Taylor, Edward Wharton, 254.
Taylor, Jack B., 353.
Taylor, John S., 233.
Taylor, Leroy, 316.
Taylor Memorial Baptist Church, 212, 286, 341, 605-606.
Taylor, Stephen, 89.
Taylor, Thomas, 427.
Taylor, William, 254.
Taylor's Island (Md.), 198.
Teaching the Way Center, 221, 531, 532, 606.
Teackle, Thomas, 5, 6.
temperance movement, 75-76, 87, 168, 173-184, 192.
Temperanceville, 104, 105, 144, 161, 162, 168, 332, 342, 366, 441, 448, 449, 466, 589, 607-608, 640.
Temperanceville United Methodist Church, 255, 352, 353, 607-608, 640. See also Conquest Chapel.
Temple Ohel Rooven, 157, 298, 299, 609.
The Towne, 3, 4, 315, 381, 610.
theatre, attitudes toward, 61, 173, 185, 186.
Thomas, J. D., 312.
Thomas, J. H., 389, 458.
Thomas, James Dunlap, 425.
Thomas, John, 64-65, 69.
Thomas, Joshua, 45-51, 55, 61, 62-70, 71, 72, 91, 108, 151, 232-233, 234, 539, 600.
Thomas, Lotty, 68.
Thomas, Martha Hall, 65.
Thomas, Rachel Evans, 65.
Thomas, Stella, 221.
Thomas, William, 552.
Thomas, William Seymour, 55.
Thompson, Abraham, 54.
Thompson, Annie P., 425.
Thorntown, William P., 618.
Tidewater Institute, 142, 620.
Tiffany, Mrs. E. M. B., 355.
tobacco, attitudes toward, 75, 77, 151, 173, 192.
Tomkinson, T. L., 127.
Townfields, 137, 610, 619.
Townsend, 457, 611, 612.
Townsend, Bertie, 180.
Townsend M.E. Church South, 165, 212, 303, 611, 612.
Townsend, William, 180.
Toy, Charles, 460.
Tract Society, 90, 110.
Travis Chapel, 165, 314, 529, 530, 546, 578, 579, 612-613.
Travis, Sarah, 612.
Travis, William, 612.
Treherne, Leonard, 139, 251, 362.
Treherneville, 162, 169, 225, 251, 362, 376, 420, 444, 491, 499, 614, 620.
Trinity M.E. Church, 102, 105, 108, 111, 119, 129, 133, 145, 368, 370-371, 383, 615-616.
Trinity United Methodist Church, 215, 274, 298, 299, 307, 616-617.
Trower, 396, 420.
Trower, Charlotte, 376, 491.

Trower, Walter, 376, 491.
Tucker, Bishop, 323.
Tudor, W. V., 616.
Turlington Camp Meeting, 147-152, 200, 202, 234, 289, 536.
Turlington Campgrounds, 176, 177, 178, 183, 186, 477.
Turlington, James, 147.
Turlington, Thomas T., 420, 441, 484, 492.
Turner, J. W., 300.
Turner, Joseph "Papa", 224, 393, 495, 564, 568.
Turner, M. C., 224, 568.
Turner, W. H., 396.
Twyford, Charles, 20.
Tyler, George, 117, 126, 127, 129.
Tyler, John, 126.

U

Union Baptist Church [Chincoteague], 105, 137, 144, 146, 187, 196, 252, 278, 280, 284, 285, 318-320, 325, 326, 331, 399, 448, 473, 524, 617-619.
Union Baptist Church [Eastville], 137, 142, 217, 246, 316, 358, 377, 385, 457, 619-620.
Union Church, 474.
Union United Methodist Church, 215, 231, 395, 404, 620-621.
Unitarianism, 84.
Universalism, 84-85, 129, 474.
Upper Church, 254, 390, 391, 510.
Upper Parish, 463.
Upshur's Chapel, 596.

V

Vaden, W. C., 577.
Venable, A. S., 361, 380.
Venable, Mrs. A. S., 425.
Vickers, William, 198-202, 207, 208-209, 219, 289, 301, 373, 407, 408, 422, 423, 551, 580, 586, 624.
Vicks, Earl, 227, 351.
Vicks, Joseph, 227, 351.
Virginia Annual Conference, 99, 102, 104, 115, 134, 169, 172, 173, 212, 214, 215, 228, 250, 264, 274, 275, 337, 344, 353, 383, 395, 455, 516, 578, 615.
Virginia Baptist State Mission Board, 354.
Virginia Beach, 260, 432, 555.
Virginia School, The, 170.
Virginia Seminary [Lynchburg], 279, 441.
Vital Christianity, 341.

W

Wachapreague, 21, 142, 164, 170, 178, 180, 198, 201, 206, 207, 212, 215, 251, 261, 269, 396, 406-407, 420, 519-520, 543, 596, 622-624.
Wachapreague Circuit, 294, 337, 396, 476, 598.
Wachapreague Hotel, 520.
Wachapreague M.E. Church South, 517, 519, 543, 596.
Wachapreague Pilgrim Holiness Church, 341, 551, 622-623, 624.
Wachapreague-Quinby Charge, 520.
Walker, W. W., 471.
Wallace, Adam, 69, 108-110, 124, 126, 127, 131.
Wallop, George, 385.
Wallop, Skinner, 514.
Wallop's Island, 28.
Wallop's Station [N.A.S.A.], 258.
Walls, F. C., 201, 289.
War of 1812, 49-51, 600.
Ward, Albert, 615.
Ward, Claudette, 449.
Ward, Haywood, 449.
Ward, John, 625.
Ward, Letetia, 615.
Ward, R. A., 567.
Ward, Stephen, 107.
Ward, T. M. D., 625.
Ward's Chapel, 317, 625.
Wardtown, 157, 162, 362-363, 377, 479, 499, 511, 590, 626-627.
Wardtown Baptist Church, 162, 166, 372, 508, 553, 626, 627.
Ware, Thomas, 35, 36, 53, 410.
Warehouse Creek, 506.
Warner, Daniel, 341.
Warner, Elizabeth, 483.
Warner, William, 483.
Warren, Patrick, 122, 125, 126, 127, 524.
Warren, W. E., 470.
Warrington, Levi., 224, 392.
Washington Academy, 544.
Washington, Booker T., 246, 590.
Washington, George, 562.
Washington, H. L., 537.
Watchtower Bible and Tract Society, 226, 243, 448.
Waters, John Wesley, 566.
Waters, Levin, 107.
Waters, M. V., 576.
Waters, Mrs. C. R., 173.
Waters, R. J., 597.
Waters, Stephen, 107.
Waters, Thomas, 321, 480.
Watson, Daniel, 423.

Watson, Ruth, 423.
Watt, David, 28, 40, 55, 71, 88, 96, 214, 427, 629.
Watters, William, 23.
Wattsville, 28, 41, 46, 55, 71, 88, 90, 137, 140, 141, 151, 161, 215, 350, 385-386, 421, 448, 449, 457, 565, 628-630, 640.
Wattsville United Methodist Church, 28, 72, 104, 137, 145, 161, 215, 216, 258, 272, 280, 342, 385, 539, 628, 629-630.
Wayman, A. W., 140, 158, 274.
Wayman's Chapel, 136, 274, 630.
Weathers, C. C., 279.
Weaver, A. D., 511.
Weeks, Gladys Dillard, 498.
Weeks, Major, 573.
Weirwood, 162, 219, 495, 553, 641-633.
Weirwood A.M.E. Church, 162, 631, 632.
Weirwood Happy Mission, 219, 495, 536, 631, 632-633.
Welbourn, Drummond, 54-55, 71, 75, 364, 433-434.
Welbourn, Mary Henderson, 364, 365.
Wertenbaker, C. C., 167.
Wescott, George, 97, 443.
Wescott, T. T., 174.
Wesley, John, xxi, xxii, xxiii, 12, 18, 22, 29-30, 38, 75, 77, 87, 95, 135, 186, 187, 191, 198, 235, 237.
Wesley Chapel, 71, 454-455, 633.
Wesleyan Church, 243.
West, Elizabeth, 497.
West End United Methodist Church [Portsmouth], 274.
West, John R., 447, 567.
Westcott, Pitts, 507.
Westover (Md.), 559.
Whale, Margaret, 11.
Whatcoat, Richard, 25, 26, 53, 352, 355, 386, 442-443.
Wheatley, Baynard, 347.
Whispering Pines, 307.
White, Alward, 46.
White, Emery, 366.
White, Frank J., 125, 127, 129, 130, 131, 132.
White, Henry, 6.
White, Jacob, 400.
White, James, 23.
White, John, 495, 500.
White, Mary, 503.
White, Milton, 392.
White Rabbit, 266.
White, Ressie, 495, 500.
White, Thomas, 18.
White, William J., 567.
Whitefield, George, xxii, xxiii, 12.
Whitehurst, T. C., 470.
Whitesville, 142, 224, 227, 245, 297, 351, 495, 500, 568, 597.
Wiggins, Alexander, 111, 516.
Wilkerson, William, 321, 618.
Willard, Frances E., 178.
Willett, Isaac R., 438.
Williams, George, 458.
Williams, Mrs. J. W. M., 169.
Williams, Peter, 443.
Williams, Robert, 23, 352.
Williams, W. F., 276.
Williamson, William, 618.
Willis, Henry, 20.
Willis Wharf, 74, 164, 165, 168, 368, 545, 616.
Willoughby, Julian A., 204-205, 605.
Wills, D. P., 353.
Wilmer, Simon, 324.
Wilmington Annual Conference, 145, 152, 159, 173, 190, 203, 255, 326, 364, 394, 399, 413, 419, 450.
Wilmington Diocese [Catholic], 558, 560, 575.
Wilson, Jessie, 632.
Wilson, John A. B., 155, 273.
Wilson, Willie, 632.
Wilsonia Neck, 206, 462-463.
Wiltshire, George, 248.
Winder, A. F., 212, 294.
Windward Hall, 521, 522-523, 575.
Winn, J. Arthur, 520.
Wise, Anne Jennings, 84, 468.
Wise Chapel, 266, 500, 554, 633.
Wise, Henry A., 76, 84, 91-93, 468.
Wise, Spencer F., 633.
Wiseville, 554.
Wiseville Circuit, 212, 245.
Wishart's Point, 366, 568, 638.
Withams, 140, 173, 332, 352, 501, 565, 566, 634.
Withams Charge, 501.
Woman's Auxiliary [Presbyterian], 336.
Woman's Board of Foreign Missions, 172.
Woman's Christian Temperance Union, 178-179, 180, 183, 274, 526.
Woman's Foreign Missionary Society [Pilgrim Holiness], 289.
Woman's Guild [Episcopal], 365.
Woman's Missionary Union [Baptist], 169, 261, 300, 321, 470, 524, 583, 637.
women in leadership roles, 82, 84, 166-173, 178-180, 425, 475, 569, 618.
Women's Foreign Missionary Society [M.E. South], 105, 167-168, 288, 443, 507, 517, 528, 548, 612.

Woo, Peter Davis, 170.
Wood, John A., 425-426.
Wood, Leonora, 426.
Woodbury United Methodist Church, 164, 203, 357, 486, 556, 605, 635-636.
Worcester County (Md.), 19, 190, 207, 496.
Workman, James, 192, 193, 194.
World War I, 206.
Wyatt, J. C., 632.
Wyatt, L. W., 327.

Y

Yerby, George, 437.
YMCA, 361.
Young, Brigham, 195.
Young, Edward J., 121, 468.
Young, George W., 396.
Young People's Missionary Society, 169.

Z

Zion Baptist Church, 83, 105, 144, 162, 167, 169, 203, 261, 354, 482, 483, 484, 489, 535, 636-637, 638, 640.
Zions Church, 498.
Zoar Baptist Meetinghouse, 345, 349, 424, 637.

About the Author

(from the 1979 edition)

Two things keep Kirk Mariner from spending all his time writing the history of Virginia's Eastern Shore: sheer economic necessity, and a call to the ministry.

When he is not wandering the backroads or researching the past of his native Eastern Shore (which means most of the time), Mariner serves as pastor of the United Methodist Church in Centreville in suburban Fairfax County, Virginia. A native of New Church on the Shore, he studied for the ministry at Randolph-Macon College and Yale Divinity School, and received the Doctor of Ministry degree from Wesley Theological School in 1979.

Mariner's first venture into local history was a small book entitled *Nothing Ever Happened in Arcadia*, published in 1968. In addition to a number of other small articles of local history and chauvinism, his creative endeavors have thus far produced several hymntunes, a growing collection of serious church music for the congregation at Centreville, and some not so serious satirical church music as yet held under wraps.

The parsonage at Centreville has now been Mariner's home longer than any other place except the Eastern Shore, and there except for Saturday nights and an occasional pastoral emergency he lives a peaceful existence with his library, his stamp collection, and a grand piano upon which, after more than four years, he is still determined to learn to play "Pictures at an Exhibition."

About the Illustrator

(from the 1979 edition)

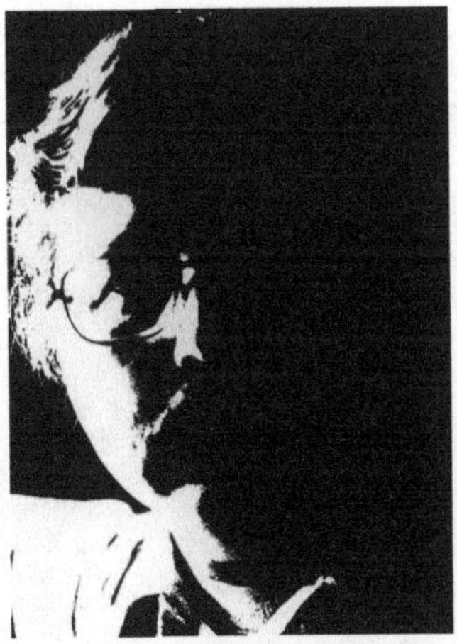

Ron Harman, Owner/Art Director of the Odyssey Collective Graphic Design Studio, both designed and illustrated this text. He provides graphic design and medical illustration services for businesses and physicians in the Washington, D.C. metropolitan area.

Ron graduated from the Art Institute of Pittsburgh (Pa.). Prior to receiving a B.S. degree in medical illustration from the Ohio State University College of Medicine, he served four years in the U.S. Marine Corps, including 19 months in Vietnam. He recently earned a Master of Fine Arts degree from the Catholic University of America. Since 1977, Ron has won several local, national and international awards for excellence in graphic design.

Ron and his wife Laurinda reside in Centreville, Virginia.